MANAGING PROJECTS WITH MICROSOFT® PROJECT 4.0

FOR WINDOWS™ AND MACINTOSH®

Managing Projects with Microsoft® Project 4.0

For Windows™ and Macintosh®

Gwen Lowery

VNR VAN NOSTRAND REINHOLD
New York

Library of Congress Catalog Card Number: 94–7815

ISBN 0–442–01768–5

Van Nostrand Reinhold is an International Thomson Publishing Company.
ITP logo is a trademark under license.

Printed in the United States of America.

Van Nostrand Reinhold
115 Fifth Avenue
New York, New York 10003

International Thomson Publishing
Berkshire House, 168-173
High Holborn
London, WC1V 7AA
England

Thomas Nelson Australia
102 Dodds Street
South Melbourne 3205
Victoria, Australia

Nelson Canada
1120 Birchmount Road
Scarborough, Ontario
M1K 5G4, Canada

ITP Germany
Königswinterer Str. 418
53227 Bonn
Germany

International Thomson Publishing Asia
38 Kim Tian Rd., #0105
Kim Tian Plaza
Singapore 0316

International Thomson Publishing Japan
Kyowa Building, 3F
2-2-1 Hirakawacho
Chiyada-Ku, Tokyo 102
Japan

16 15 14 13 12 11 10 9 8 7 6 5 4 3 2

Library of Congress Cataloging-in-Publication Data

Lowery, Gwen.
Managing Projects with Microsoft Project 4.0: For Windows and Macintosh / Gwen Lowery.
p. cm.
Includes index.
ISBN 0–442–01768–5
1. Microsoft Project for Windows. 2. Microsoft Project.
3. Industrial project management–Computer programs. I. Title.
HD69.P75L694 1994
658.4'04'02855369–dc20 94–7815
CIP

To Eric and Sam (the cat)

who put up with the creation of yet another edition of this book

Contents

Preface xi

Acknowledgments xiii

Part I Project Management and Microsoft Project 1

1 About Project Management 3
Why Plan? 4
How a Computer Helps You Plan and Manage a Project 5
Why Use Microsoft Project? 7

2 About Microsoft Project 11
Conventions Used in this Book 12
How Microsoft Project Keeps Track of Project Information 13
Microsoft Project Tables 15
Microsoft Project Filters 16
Microsoft Project Views 18
Microsoft Project Basics 44
Customizing Microsoft Project 49

Part II Planning A Project and Creating the Schedule 53

3 Setting Project Goals 55
Setting Clear Project Goals, Scope, and Assumptions 56
Using Microsoft Project 59

4 Breaking Your Project into Tasks and Milestones 65
What are Tasks and Milestones? 65
Listing Tasks and Milestones 69
Organizing Tasks and Milestones 70
Using Microsoft Project 73

5 Estimating Time to Perform Tasks 87
Determining Duration 89
Using Microsoft Project 90

6 Making Tasks Happen at the Right Time 97
Deciding Task Sequence 98
Determining Relationships Between Tasks 98
Indicating Overlap or Delay Between Tasks 99
Setting a Start or Finish Date for a Task 100
Using Microsoft Project 102

7 Assigning People, Equipment, and Costs to Tasks 117
Estimating Resource Needs 118
Estimating Costs 119
Using Microsoft Project 120

Part III Refining and Communicating the Plan 137

8 Evaluating the Schedule 139
Project Dates 140
Critical Tasks 140
Slack Time and Noncritical Tasks 143
Task Order, Relationships, and Constraints 143
Resources 144
Cost 144
Using Microsoft Project 144

9 Refining the Schedule and Freezing the Baseline 165
Refining the Schedule 165
Freezing the Schedule 167
Using Microsoft Project 167

10 Communicating the Plan 195
Different Reports for Different People 195
Using Microsoft Project 196

Part IV Tracking Progress and Managing the Project 233

11 Tracking Progress and Updating the Schedule 235
Collecting Project Data 236
Using Microsoft Project 238

12 Controlling the Project to Stay on Track 255
Evaluating Progress to Date 256
Analyzing Variance 256
Determining Corrective Action 258
Using Microsoft Project 259

13 Communicating Progress 277
Using Microsoft Project 278

Part V Multiple Projects, Sharing Information, and Using the Tools 299

14 Managing Multiple Projects 301
Using a Project Template 302
Using Subprojects 303
Linking Tasks Between Projects 309
Sharing Resources Among Projects 309
Viewing Multiple Projects 311

15 Sharing Information 317
Sharing Tools 319
Exchanging Information with a Spreadsheet or Database Application 320
Using Project Information in Microsoft Word 332

16 Using Microsoft Tools 335
Tables 336
Filters 344
Views 351
Customizing the Menus 356
Calendars 359
Sorting 364
Formatting the Gantt Chart 365
Formatting the Resource Graph 367
Customizing Toolbars 370
Custom Edit Forms 374
Macros 377

Index 379

Preface

In the four years since the first edition of this book was released, the need to respond quickly and accurately to business needs has only increased. As businesses run "leaner and meaner," how well you manage the multitude of projects that come your way impacts not only your success in your career but also how well your company continues to thrive in the tough economic times. The project management software available today is truly amazing; it does much of what was tedious about project management and does it very fast, giving you almost instant results so you can make educated decisions for the remainder of the project.

But as powerful as the software is, even more important to your success is a thorough understanding of the steps you, as project manager, must follow to make a project happen. You are in control of the planning, tracking, and managing of the project to get from where you are today to the goal—on time and on budget. This book is about managing projects—not just about using Microsoft Project but about how you get from here to there—successfully.

Part I briefly describes project management and Microsoft Project. In Parts II, III, and IV, each chapter covers one step in the project management process. Each chapter in these three parts contains two types of information: information about project management and information about Microsoft Project.

The general project management information is at the beginning of each chapter. Read this information, up to the "Using Microsoft Project" section, if you want to know about the project management theory behind the step covered in the chapter. If you just want information about using Microsoft Project, skip the introductory sections.

Because Microsoft Project is so flexible and allows you to do things in several ways, the "Using Microsoft Project" sections often include more than one method to accomplish a step so that you can pick the method that is best suited to your work style. For example, more than one method is presented for entering tasks and for entering resources.

Part V includes information specific to Microsoft Project. It covers topics that will make your life easier but are not strictly part of the project management process, such as how to work with multiple projects, how to share information with other people and use project information in other software packages, and procedures for using Microsoft Project tools.

Acknowledgments

Thanks to the following people: Lois Oien, Jim McKendry, and Jim Dunnigan for their patience in reviewing the book and for offering so many valuable suggestions; the development team of Brian MacDonald, Jeff Lill, John Clifford, Cory Reina, Glenn Slayden, and many others for creating such great software; Mark Consuegra, Rich Brown, and the rest of the program management team, and Jeff Camp for patiently (or at least pretending) answering all my questions about version 4 of the software; Bob Esposito and Jeanne Glasser of VNR for making sure the book happened; and Eric Hawley and Lisa Maynard for editing, design, and typesetting services.

PART I

PROJECT MANAGEMENT AND MICROSOFT PROJECT

How well you manage a project has a direct effect on the outcome of the project. There are several parts in the project management equation, two of which are the project management steps and the tools you have to support these steps. Part I introduces both the project management process and one tool to help you track and manage your project, Microsoft Project.

Chapter 1 discusses the benefits of project planning and of using a computer. You'll also learn about Microsoft Project and how it schedules your project.

Use Chapter 2 as a reference to Microsoft Project. The chapter includes:

- How Microsoft Project sees a project.
- Description of Microsoft Project tables, filters, and views, and how these three tools are used to give you the information you want about your project.
- Basics of working with Microsoft Project, including how to use menus, commands, and dialog boxes.
- Tables showing what you can change in Microsoft Project to match the way you work so that it gives you exactly the information you want, the way you want it, as efficiently and quickly as possible.

1

About Project Management

A *project* is a one-time set of activities that ends with a specific accomplishment. It originates when something out of the ordinary has to be accomplished. A project has the following characteristics:

- A set of non-routine tasks performed in a certain sequence leading to a goal.
- A distinct start and finish date.
- A limited set of resources that may be used on more than one project.

A project is not an ongoing process, such as preparing weekly payroll or manufacturing a product on an assembly line. These processes have no real completion date, which is a requirement of a project, nor are they in any way unique. Rather, they are part of the everyday business.

Project management is the defining, planning, scheduling, and controlling of the tasks that must be completed to reach your goal and the allocation of the resources to perform those tasks. *Defining* and *planning* are necessary so you know what you will do. *Scheduling* is important so you know when you will do it. And *controlling* is important because things never work out exactly as planned. To meet your goal, it's important that you be on top of changes. This means constantly tracking and rescheduling as the project progresses.

As a project manager, you are successful when you satisfy the requirements of your client or management, and meet your project goals on schedule and within your budget. Project management software simplifies and speeds up this process. It gives you easy access to important information so you can make decisions while there is still time to take corrective action. You use the software to model your project so you can plan your resource requirements and avoid conflicts.

WHY PLAN?

One of the most tedious and possibly time-consuming steps for the project manager is creating the initial plan before the project is even under way. But, it is also the most important step. A plan simulates the project and lists what you will do. It is a model of your project used to predict the future.

Creating your schedule involves three basic steps. First, you specify *what* you are going to do by defining the tasks that must be completed to reach your goals. Then you specify *when* by scheduling the tasks. Actually, the computer does the scheduling for you; you just give it information about the sequence of the tasks, how they are related to one another, and if any tasks must start or finish at a specific time. Then you specify *how* by assigning people, equipment, and costs to complete the tasks. The computer program creates the schedule based on the information you provide.

Of course, the steps are not independent. After seeing the first schedule, you will probably re-evaluate your task and resource lists to ensure you are creating the best schedule to fit the situation. And you can't do this alone. You will have a better schedule and more support for the project if you involve the project team in the planning process.

You can use a project plan and its schedule for many things. For example, it can help you:

- Communicate to others in your organization what you are going to do.
- Get support from project team members.
- Gain approval for the project or justify the need to management.
- Show a customer how you will deliver a product or service.
- Prove the need for additional staff and manage resource work loads.
- Determine cash flow needs.
- Keep a record of what happened on the project, to be compared to the original plan, and to be used as the basis of future schedules for similar projects.

You can also use a project schedule as the baseline against which you check the progress of your project.

So, you *plan* so you know what is to be done, when it will be done, who will do it, and how much it will cost. Having a plan helps everyone see who needs to do what and when they need to do it. It helps communication, makes everyone aware of deadlines, and reduces uncertainty. And by tracking the actual progress of the project and comparing it to your original schedule, you can see deviations from the plan, anticipate any problems, and correct any delays before they become severe. With a plan, there is a better chance of completing the project successfully!

HOW A COMPUTER HELPS YOU PLAN AND MANAGE A PROJECT

Whether you use project management software or not, it is up to you to define the project goals, plan the tasks and resources, and carry out and manage the project. But, the computer can help you immeasurably. It provides up-to-date information, and it gives you the ability to test ideas and see the results in the schedule and costs.

First, a computer-based project management system calculates the schedule for you. Imagine how time-consuming it would be to manually calculate the schedule dates for all the tasks. And imagine trying to create the optimal schedule; you could spend a very long time just doing calculations. The truth is, you wouldn't have time to do this.

When you use a computer and project management software, any change you make to a task is automatically incorporated as the computer recalculates the schedule for you, leaving you with more time to spend on planning and tracking your projects. The more complex the project, the more important it is to have the computer system.

There are several other benefits of using project management software:

- The schedule is created and revised quickly; you can easily analyze the schedule resources, and costs to evaluate alternative schedules and to find the best solution to scheduling problems.
- Because you have one scheduling tool, it can help centralize planning throughout an organization.

- Output is in a standard format, quick and easy to produce, accurate and consistent for all projects.
- Since the same information can be presented in detail or summarized, as appropriate, for each level of management, everyone has timely and valid information for making decisions.
- You have the information you need to track progress and control your schedule, resources, and costs.

When you are using a computer to schedule your project, you must enter:

- All the tasks that must be done to complete the project.
- The sequence in which the tasks must occur, and their dependencies on other tasks and dates.
- The resources used to perform the tasks and the cost of using each.
- Calendar information, such as working days and times.

Project management software calculates the schedule, completion date, total work, and cost to complete the project. You save this information as a baseline schedule so you can compare progress to this plan.

In the tracking stage, you enter progress on tasks, including:

- Actual start and finish dates.
- Percent complete of tasks in progress.
- Actual work.
- Actual costs.

Once you have entered this "actual" information, you can use the software to do the following:

- Compare the actual dates with the baseline schedule to spot delays.
- Check resource availability and reschedule as necessary.
- Compare work and costs with the baseline schedule to see if you are within budget.
- Look at alternatives to decide how best to keep the schedule on track.

Another advantage to tracking your project is that you create an accurate record of the project and the time it took to perform each task. This historical data can help you make estimates for future projects.

Remember that project management software is just a tool. It cannot help you determine the tasks and their relationships, but it can help you optimize the schedule and reduce time and costs. The software does all the schedule calculations quickly so you can experiment with options. By simulating the project, you can do "what-if" analyses to find the optimal balance of costs, resources, and time.

The Critical Path Method The critical path method (CPM) is the scheduling method used in virtually all project management software today, including Microsoft Project. CPM was developed by DuPont and Remington Rand in the 1950s to improve project scheduling techniques. It is a modeling process that defines all the project's critical tasks—those tasks that must be completed on time if the entire project is to be completed on time—and calculates the start and finish dates of tasks in the project.

With CPM, calculations of the schedule are based on the durations of the tasks and the relationships between the tasks. The schedule is calculated twice—first from the earliest start date forward, and then from the latest finish date backwards. The difference between the pairs of start and finish dates for each task is the float or slack time for the task. Slack time is the amount of time a task can be delayed without delaying the project completion date. The critical path is that sequence of tasks that represent the longest total time required to complete the project. A delay in any task on the critical path causes a delay in the completion of the project. Noncritical tasks—tasks not on the critical path—have slack time.

One advantage of this method is that you can experiment with accelerating the project by shortening various critical tasks, and then check the time, costs, and resources to see how they are affected by the change. By experimenting in this way, you can determine the optimal schedule for a project.

WHY USE MICROSOFT PROJECT?

Microsoft Project is a powerful tool that will help you control your projects and complete them successfully. It gives you flexible viewing of project information, a powerful scheduling tool, resource management capability, and quality reports.

When selecting project management software, there are certain features important to the project manager. The following list describes some of the features of Microsoft Project that will make your life easier. This list gives you only a glimpse into the power of Microsoft Project:

- Save the original schedule so you have something to compare to progress; Microsoft Project saves your original schedule separately from the current schedule so you can compare the two.
- Track progress on tasks by entering actual start and finish dates, actual durations, remaining durations, actual cost, and actual work.
- Allocate resource usage so resources are available when needed for tasks, but are not assigned to too many tasks simultaneously.
- Create calendars for each project and modify the calendar for each resource; Microsoft Project uses the calendars to schedule the tasks.
- Dynamically link information between projects or between a project and another application, such as Microsoft Graph or Microsoft Excel. When the information changes in one place, it changes everywhere.
- Change the presentation of information, from spreadsheet-like tables, to charts and graphs, showing task information or resource information according to your needs.
- Change the type of information presented about each task or resource so you get just the information you need at the time. For example, you can look at a list of tasks and their start and finish dates, and then change the information to see the tasks and their resources and costs.
- Enter tasks that occur regularly, such as weekly project status meetings, with one command.
- Filter the information shown to display only those tasks or resources that include certain information. For example, you can list only those tasks that use a particular resource.
- Change the order of the information, such as alphabetizing the list of resources.

Besides these, Microsoft Project includes other features designed to make the application's power more accessible and useful:

- Drop-down menus that list all the commands.
- Windows so you can change from one view of your data, such as a Gantt Chart, to another view, such as a spreadsheet presentation or a monthly calendar.

- Toolbars so you can quickly choose common commands and other actions; since the toolbars are completely customizable, you can control what every button does and how it looks to make Microsoft Project most convenient for you. If you want to know what a button is for, just hold your mouse pointer over it; a short description tells you what it does.
- Spelling checker so you can check the spelling in your project.
- Built-in Help system and cue cards to help you know what to do next.
- Quick-to-use reporting system to generate reports showing exactly the information you want, in the format you want.
- Special mouse capabilities so you can graphically change the schedule of a task, move tasks and resources, assign resources, outline tasks, and more.
- Macros so you can automate often-repeated procedures, such as printing a series of monthly reports or searching through notes.
- GanttChartWizard to help you make the Gantt Chart look just the way you want.
- PlanningWizard to give you helpful tips as you work.
- Templates to use as a starting point for a project.
- Workgroup features—electronically route the project to a group of people, send requests to resources for commitments to task assignments, add tasks to Microsoft Schedule+, and request task status by electronic mail.

You can easily share information with other Windows or Macintosh products, such as Microsoft Excel, Microsoft Word, or Lotus 1-2-3.

2

About Microsoft Project

Microsoft Project is easy to use, yet has the power and flexibility to do exactly what you need. For example, you can create a simple schedule quickly by entering all your tasks and then using one command to make each task start after the previous task finishes. Or you can create a detailed schedule, entering all the project information you have gathered—including tasks, resources, costs, and detailed work information for each resource—and use this schedule to track the progress of the project. Either way, Microsoft Project can give you exactly what you need.

As with every software product, understanding a few basics will make it easier for you to take advantage of the features in Microsoft Project. If you are a Windows or Macintosh user or have used another Microsoft product such as Microsoft Excel or Microsoft Word, you'll find that you already know the basics: the window has the same basic features, the commands are listed in the menus at the top of the window, and you choose commands and use dialog boxes in the same way. If you are unfamiliar with these concepts, they are covered briefly at the end of this chapter. For more information, see your Windows or Macintosh documentation.

CONVENTIONS USED IN THIS BOOK

Throughout the book, the following conventions are used when referring to Microsoft Project commands, key combinations, and the mouse:

- Commands are listed with the menu name first and then the command name. For example, to choose the Edit Copy command, you select the Edit menu, and then choose the Copy command.
- When you choose some commands, a second menu of commands appears to the left or right of the menu. In this book, a slash separates the submenu command from the menu and command names. For example, to choose the Edit Clear/Entire Task command, you select the Edit menu, choose the Clear command, and then choose the Entire Task command from the submenu.
- Key combinations indicate you need to press more than one key. They appear in two ways, depending on how you press the keys.

Key combination	Description
Plus sign between two keys—for example, Shift+Spacebar	Press and hold down the first key, press the second key, and then release both keys—for example, hold down Shift while you press the Spacebar.
Comma between two keys—for example, Alt, Spacebar	Press one key after the other—for example, press and release Alt, and then press and release Spacebar.

- Terms used for mouse actions are described in the following table.

Mouse term	Description
Point	Position the mouse pointer over the item.
Click	Point to an item and click the mouse button. If your mouse has more than one button, click the left button, unless told to use the right button.
Double-click	Click the mouse button twice rapidly.
Drag and drop	Position the mouse pointer at the starting point, press and hold down the mouse button, move the pointer to the new location, and then release the mouse button. Again, use the left button.

- Select means to highlight the tasks or resources you want a command to act on. For example, if you want to copy a group of tasks, you first select them and then choose the Edit Copy command.

To select	Keys	Mouse
One task or resource	Use arrow keys to move to the item	Click the item
Adjacent tasks or resources	Shift+arrow keys	Drag over the items
Non adjacent tasks or resources	Press F8 and select the first group; press Shift+F8 and move to the next group; repeat the steps until all groups are selected	Select the first group; hold down Ctrl in Windows or Command on the Macintosh to select the next group

HOW MICROSOFT PROJECT KEEPS TRACK OF PROJECT INFORMATION

Whether or not you use a computer, a project has two lists—a list of all your tasks and a list of all your resources. The two lists are connected by assigning the resources to the tasks.

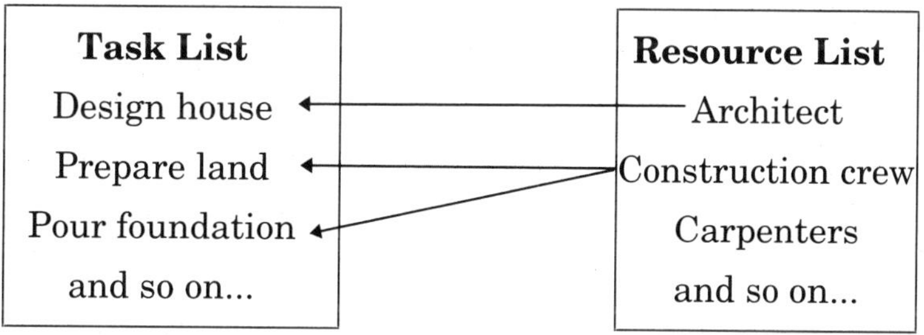

When you enter a task into Microsoft Project, over 100 fields are created to describe the task. Picture it as a big spreadsheet that includes the task ID, task name, duration, start date, finish date, cost information, and much other information.

ID	Name	Duration	Start	Finish	Milestone	Fixed	Cost	Work	and so on...
7	Build walls	1 week	6/1/94	6/5/94	No	No	$1000	80h	

The values in these fields are either entered by you or calculated by Microsoft Project. Some are used for scheduling the task, some for keeping track of progress on the task, some for keeping a record of the original schedule, and so on. There may not be values in all fields. For example, if you choose not to keep track of the cost on a project, you won't enter values in the fields for cost information.

When you enter a list of resources—called a resource pool—Microsoft Project creates over 30 fields for each resource, including resource ID, resource name, rate of pay, and so on. As with task fields, some resource fields are entered by you and some are calculated; there may not be values in every field.

You link the two lists together by assigning the resources to the tasks. Again, there are fields, called resource assignment fields, that contain this information. For example, there is a field for the amount of work a resource has to do on each task to which the resource is assigned.

Microsoft Project has three basic tools to look at the tasks, resources, and resource assignments.

- *Tables* specify which fields you see.
- *Filters* control which tasks or resources are displayed—all, or a subset of your choosing.
- *Views* display your project information in a variety of perspectives, such as a spreadsheet-like presentation, a chart presentation, a calendar, or a form. Some views show task information, some show resource information, and some show either task or resource information plus resource assignment information.

You change the table, filter, and view to see the fields and the tasks or resources you want, displayed in the format you want.

MICROSOFT PROJECT TABLES

Obviously, you are not going to use all 100+ task fields simultaneously—probably only a handful at any time, depending on what you want to accomplish. For example, if you are entering new tasks, you'll want one set of fields, such as task ID, task name, task duration, and resources assigned to the task; if you are entering progress information about a task, perhaps you'll want, besides the task ID and name, a field for the date when the task actually started and another showing the percentage of the work finished on the task. Microsoft Project supplies all these fields.

Tables are just a way to control which set of fields is displayed; you change the fields by applying a different table.

Microsoft Project comes with 18 tables. Each includes the appropriate fields to show a certain type of information. For example, initially, the Entry table is applied to two of the views that show task information. You use this table to enter basic task information; it includes fields you'll most likely use when entering new tasks, including the ID field, Task Name field, Duration field, Start and Finish date fields, Predecessors field (where you list the tasks that this task depends on), and the Resource Names field (where you list the resources you want to use on the task). If, instead, you want to see cost information for the task, you would apply the Cost table; to enter progress information for the tasks, you would apply the Tracking table.

If you have a different combination of fields that you want to use when entering tasks or tracking tasks—or for reporting information about tasks—you can create your own table showing just those fields you want.

You use the Table command on the View menu to apply a table and to change the fields in a table. The available tables are different depending on the active view: one list is available for task views and one list for resource views. Not all views use tables. If a view does not use a table, no tables are available to be applied to the view.

To see a list of all the tables in Microsoft Project, choose View Table/More Tables. Select the Task option to see the task tables; select the Resource option to see the resource tables.

TO APPLY A TABLE

1. From the View menu, choose Table.
2. Choose the table from the list.
   To apply those tables not included in the list, choose More Tables, select the name of the table in the Tables box, and then press Enter or click the Apply button.

You also use the More Tables command to change or create tables. When you change or create a table, you specify the fields in the table, the width of the columns, and the column titles. You can use any of the fields in Microsoft Project in a table. Microsoft Project also includes several "custom" text and number fields; use a custom field when Microsoft Project doesn't include a field you need, changing its title so you know what the field contains. For example, if you want to include an accounting code, you can use a custom field for this code.

The quickest way to change a column in the table you are currently using is to double-click the column title. A description of the column appears so you can change the type of information displayed, the column title, alignment, or width.

Because you can add tables to or remove tables from the menus, you can customize Microsoft Project so it is quick and easy to apply those tables you use most. For more information about creating and changing tables and customizing Microsoft Project, see Chapter 16, "Using Microsoft Project Tools."

MICROSOFT PROJECT FILTERS

Filters are just a way to control the tasks or resources displayed in a view. When you apply a filter, Microsoft Project displays only those tasks that fit the "criteria"—the requirements named in the filter. For example, you can apply a filter that shows only those tasks that are critical, or in progress, or over budget. A filter can contain a combination of requirements such that, for example, all critical tasks in progress are displayed.

All filters can also be applied as highlighting filters. When you apply a filter as a highlighting filter, all tasks or resources are displayed, but those that fit the criteria are highlighted to stand out from the rest of the tasks or resources.

Microsoft Project comes with 31 filters. Each includes certain requirements that the task or resource must meet to be displayed or highlighted. When you apply a filter, Microsoft Project compares the value in a field with the value you specify. For example, the Critical filter checks the Critical field to see if it contains a "Yes" or "No." If a task is critical, it contains "Yes" in the Critical field and is displayed or highlighted when you apply the filter. If the task is noncritical, it will not be displayed or highlighted when you apply the filter.

Some filters compare the values in two fields. For example, the Slipping Tasks filter compares the original finish date (the value in the Baseline Finish field) with the date a task is now scheduled to finish (the date in the Finish field). If the current finish date is later than the baseline finish date, the task is displayed or highlighted. The Slipping Tasks filter also checks that there is no date in the Actual Finish field—that is, that the task hasn't already finished. Filters that compare values in two fields or more are called calculated filters.

When you apply some filters, you must specify the value or values against which the filter is to compare. For example, if you apply the Date Range filter to display or highlight all tasks scheduled to start between two dates, Microsoft Project prompts you to specify the two dates each time you apply the filter. You don't have to recreate the filter each time you want to check for tasks expected to start during the next week or month. Filters that ask for values are called interactive filters.

If you want to look for a different set of tasks or resources, you can create your own filter. A filter can look for information in any of the task or resource fields. You can also create your own calculated filters and interactive filters.

You use the Filter box on the Formatting toolbar to apply a filter. You can also use the Tools Filtered For command to apply a filter, and to change or create filters. The list of filters is different depending on the active view: one list is available for task views and one list for resource views.

To see a list of all the filters in Microsoft Project, choose Tools Filtered For/More Filters. Select the Task option to see the task filters; select the Resource option to see the resource filters.

TO APPLY A FILTER

- From the Filter box on the Formatting toolbar, choose the filter you want to apply. You can also choose Tools Filtered For and select the filter you want to apply.
- To apply the filter as a highlighting filter, hold down Shift as you select the Filtered For command. The filter you select will then be applied as a highlighting filter.

You use the Tools Filtered For/More Filters command to change or create filters and to apply filters not in the Filtered For list. When you change or create a filter, you change the criteria in the filter so Microsoft Project looks for a different set of tasks or resources. Because you can add new filters or remove filters from the menus, you can customize Microsoft Project so it is quick and easy to apply those filters you use most often. For more information about creating filters and customizing Microsoft Project, see Chapter 16, "Using Microsoft Project Tools."

MICROSOFT PROJECT VIEWS

In Microsoft Project, you look at different aspects of your project information by using the different views. Some views show you tasks, some show resources; some are in a spreadsheet-like format, others show information as a chart. Each view gives you a different perspective. For example, you can look at a view showing the project tasks and how they relate to one another; or you can use a view to see when the resources are scheduled and whether any are overallocated. Each view shows you a subset of the task, resource, and resource allocation fields.

TO DISPLAY A VIEW

- From the View menu, choose the view you want to display.

Several views, such as the Task Sheet and Task Form, are not on the View menu; to display these views, or any view not on the View menu, choose View More Views, select the name of the view in the View box, and then press Enter or click the Apply button.

Microsoft Project comes with the following views:

Task views	**Resource views**
Calendar	Resource Allocation
Delay Gantt	Resource Form
Detail Gantt	Resource Graph
Gantt Chart	Resource Name Form
PERT Chart	Resource Sheet
Task Details Form	Resource Usage
Task Entry	
Task Form	
Task Name Form	
Task PERT	
Task Sheet	
Tracking Gantt	

There is also a view, called Module Editor, in which you can create and edit Microsoft Project macros that automate tasks you perform routinely. Use this view to edit a macro recorded in the project window or created in the Module Editor.

You also use the View More Views command to change or create views. When you change or create a view, you pick the basic style you want, and then pick a table and filter, if the view can use them. This allows you to create custom views that you can use, for example, to generate status reports in the same format, week after week. Once created, a custom view is always available; the next time you want to present information in that format, just display and print the view. For more about creating views, see Chapter 16, "Using Microsoft Project Tools."

Because you can add new views or remove views from the View menu or any menu, you can customize Microsoft Project so it is quick and easy to apply those views you use most often.

The next several pages contain information about each view in Microsoft Project. Use this information as a reference when you need help with using the view or changing the appearance of the view.

GANTT CHART

Use the Gantt Chart to enter tasks and to see your schedule graphically as the tasks are displayed over time. You can print the Gantt Chart so others can review the schedule.

The Gantt Chart shows a list of your tasks on the left side of the screen, and a bar chart on the right side of the screen. The bar chart shows graphically the duration and schedule information for each task. At the top of the bar chart is a timescale that can be changed to show the time periods you want (from minutes to years).

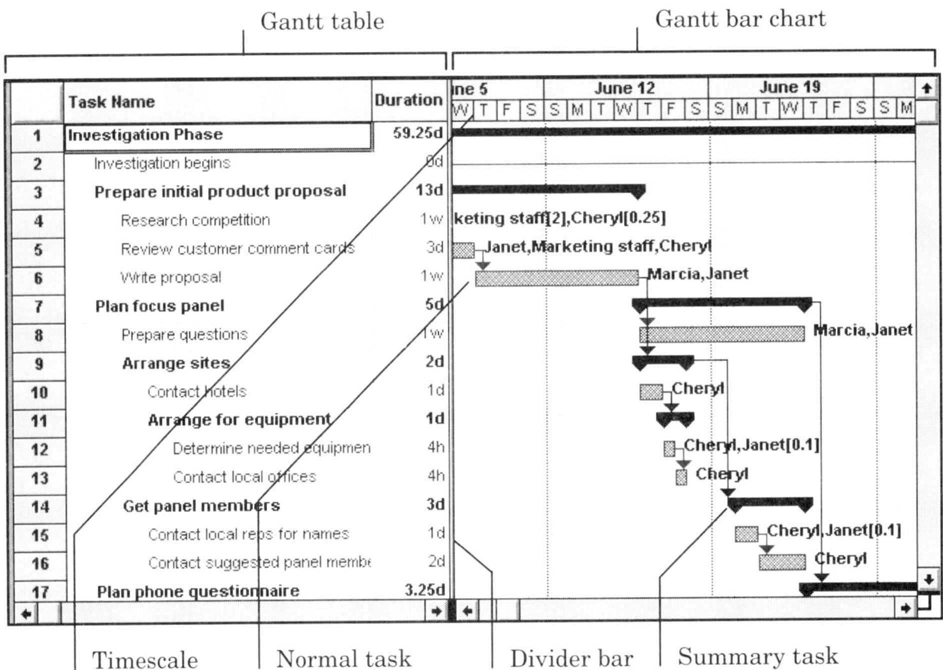

The pattern and color of the bars indicate the type of bar. For example, in the above illustration, gray bars are normal task bars; black bars with triangles at the ends are summary task bars. Summary tasks are used in outlines and span all tasks that they summarize.

The Gantt table has more columns than you can see at one time. Use the arrow keys or the scroll bar to scroll the table horizontally, or move the divider bar right or left.

To make the Gantt Chart look just the way you want and show exactly the information you want, first use the GanttChartWizard (click the

GanttChartWizard button on the Standard toolbar or choose Format GanttChartWizard) to change the look. If it doesn't give you what you want, try the various commands listed below.

- To control the look of a category of bars, including pattern, color, markers at the ends, which bars are shown, and whether text appears on the Gantt Chart, use the Format Bar Styles command. To display this dialog box, you can double-click the chart.
- To make one bar stand out, use the Format Bar command.
- To control the look of text for a category of tasks, use the Format Text Styles command; to make one task stand out, use the Format Font command.
- To control the look of gridlines, use the Format Gridlines command.
- To control the information in the view, you can: sort the list of tasks using the Tools Sort command; use filters to display or highlight certain tasks; use tables to change the type of information shown for each task.
- If you are using an outline, you can control its appearance using the Outline Options on the View tab in the Tools Options dialog box.
- To control the timescale, double-click the timescale or choose the Format Timescale command. You can show everything from hours over minutes to years, depending on the level of detail you want. You can also use the Zoom In and Zoom Out buttons on the Standard toolbar to change the timescale.

To move through the tasks and through time, use the scroll bars. Use the arrow keys to move through the tasks with the keyboard. To move through time with the keyboard in Windows, hold down Alt, and press an arrow key, the PgUp or PgDn key, or Home or End. On the Macintosh, hold down Option and press a navigation key.

Included with Microsoft Project are three variations on the Gantt Chart: the Delay Gantt, the Detail Gantt, and the Tracking Gantt. These views are based on the Gantt Chart, with additional bars and text on the chart. You format and move on these just as you do on the Gantt Chart. To display these views, choose View More Views. In the Views box, select the view. Choose the Apply button.

Gantt Chart History During World War I, Henry L. Gantt used a bar chart showing tasks plotted on a timescale to indicate start and finish dates. This chart was later called a Gantt Chart in his honor.

Delay Gantt

Use the Delay Gantt when a resource is assigned to too much work at one time and you want to move tasks around to get rid of the overallocation—this is called *leveling resources*. One way to level resources is to delay tasks so resources are not assigned to too many tasks at one time.

The Delay Gantt uses the Delay table, which shows the amount of time each task has been delayed and includes the Successors field so you can see which tasks will be affected if you delay a task. In addition to the bars on the Gantt Chart, the chart includes a bar showing the delay and another showing slack time.

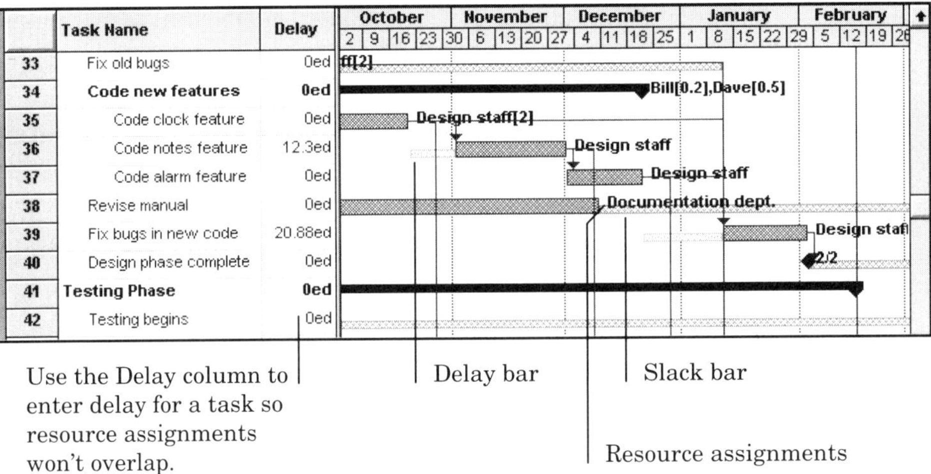

Detail Gantt

Use the Detail Gantt to check for slack time and slipping tasks. The Detail Gantt uses the Entry table, just like the Gantt Chart. In addition to the bars on the Gantt Chart, the chart includes a bar showing the slippage, and another showing slack time. The amount of slippage is displayed on the left end of each bar; the amount of slack is displayed on the right end.

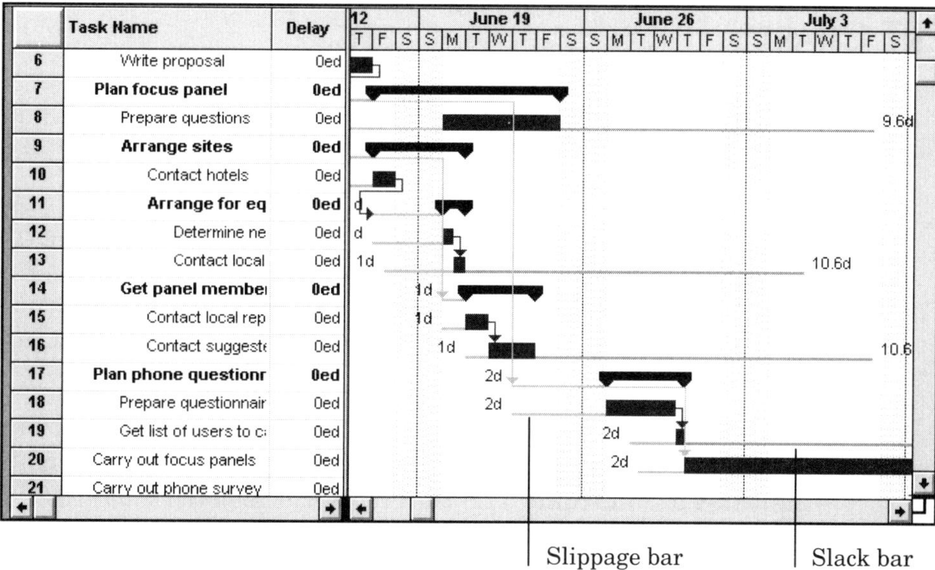

Tracking Gantt

Use the Tracking Gantt to compare your current schedule to the original schedule after the project is under way and you have entered information about progress on tasks. This view shows how each task was originally scheduled, how each is currently scheduled based on the latest information you entered about progress on tasks, and the percent complete for each task.

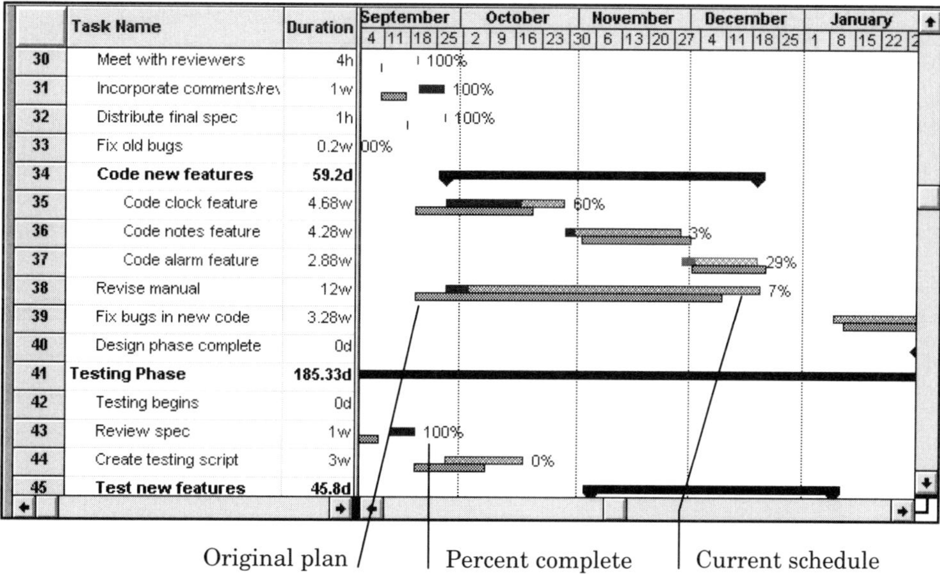

PERT CHART

Use the PERT Chart to see the dependencies between the tasks in your project. You also can enter new tasks on the PERT Chart, and you can create relationships between tasks.

The PERT Chart shows each task as a box or node, with lines between the nodes indicating that a relationship exists between the tasks. Each node initially contains the task name, ID number, duration, and start and finish dates; these fields can be changed to contain any five fields you want.

The borders on the nodes show the type of task. For example, in the following illustration, the double border on "Investigation begins" indicates a milestone. The thin border is a noncritical task. Although no critical tasks show in the art, they have a bold border and the critical path is bold. On a color monitor or printer, the critical tasks and milestones are red; the noncritical tasks and milestones are black. You change the colors and patterns using the Format Box Styles command.

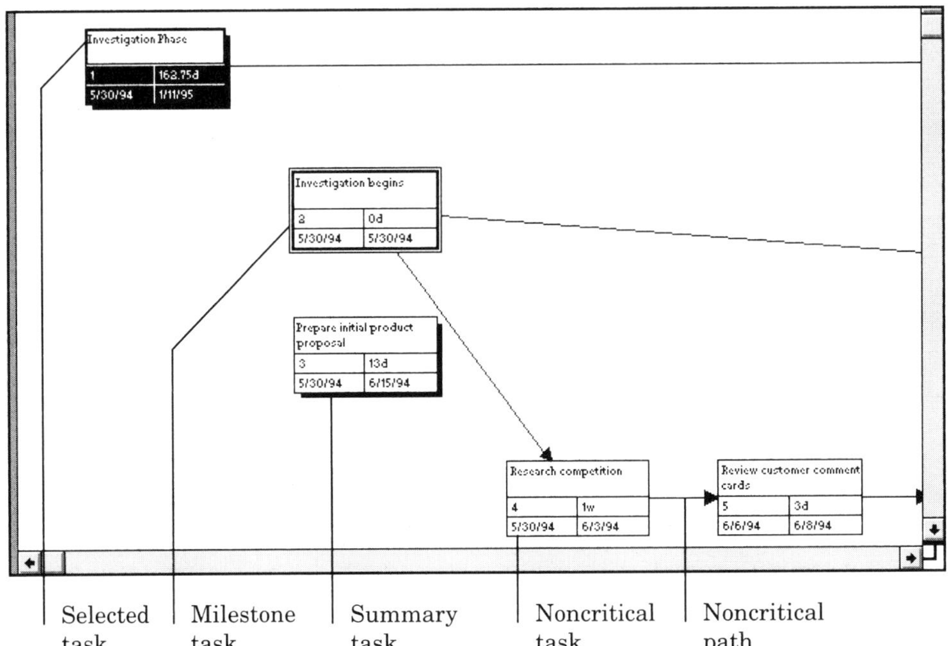

Using the mouse on the PERT Chart, you can create new nodes with or without a relationship to another task, and you can move single nodes or groups of nodes.

To create a new task node, drag the mouse diagonally on the screen. If you want to create a new node that is a successor to an existing node, drag from the inside to the outside of the existing node. The new task will have a finish-to-start relationship with the existing task, which means it will be scheduled to start after the original task finishes.

You can make the PERT Chart look just the way you want and show exactly the information you want.

- To control the fields included in each node and the node size, use the Format Box Styles command/Contents tab. To display this dialog box, you can double-click the PERT Chart outside the nodes.
- To control the style and color of the border for each type of node, use the Format Box Styles command/Borders tab. To display this dialog box, you can double-click a node border.
- To control the text, use the Format Text Styles command.
- To control the lines between the nodes and whether there are arrows on the lines, use the Format Layout command. To arrange the nodes, use the Format Layout Now command.
- To change between a detailed view of the PERT Chart (each node shows all fields selected in the Box Styles dialog box) and a big picture view (each node shows ID number only), choose Format Box Styles and select Smallest (ID Only) in the Size box on the Contents tab.

To move through the tasks, use the scroll bars, or use the arrow keys and the Home and End keys. To select a field in a node, click the field or press the Tab key.

To move a node, just drag the border of the node or select the node and press Ctrl+arrow key. To move a group of nodes, click the border of each node you want to move and then drag to the new position.

To check or change relationships on the PERT Chart, double-click the line between the nodes. In the Task Dependency dialog box, you can change the relationship type and enter, change, or remove lag time. You also use this dialog box to delete the relationship between two tasks.

CALENDAR VIEW

Use the Calendar view to create or review your schedule on a monthly calendar. Each task appears as a bar on the calendar, spanning the days on which it is scheduled. The text in the bar can include any fields you want.

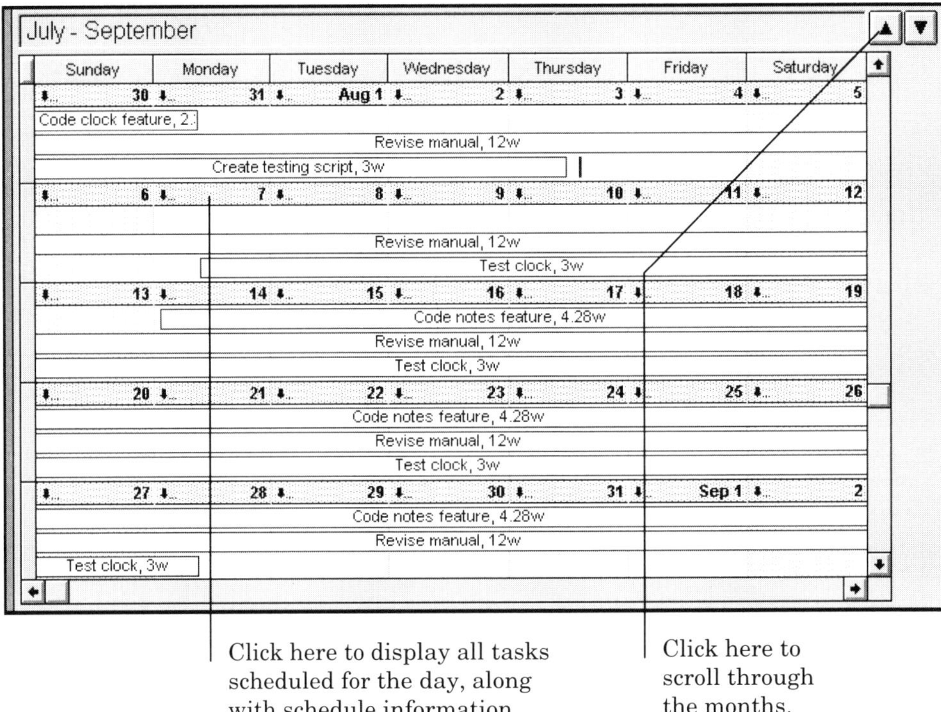

To display all the tasks that occur on a particular day, along with their durations and start and finish dates, double-click the top or bottom row of the date box. If the top or bottom row doesn't show, use the Date Boxes tab in the Format Timescale dialog box to change it.

To add or edit information about a task, double-click the task bar to display the Task Information dialog box.

To select a task, click the task bar; to select more than one task, hold down Ctrl and click the task bars you want to select.

To create a task, drag in any date box until the new task bar represents the duration you want. To link tasks in a finish-to-start relationship, point to the predecessor task bar and drag to the successor task bar. To move a task, point to the task border and drag the task to the new location.

You can make the Calendar look just the way you want and show exactly the information you want.

- To change the appearance of the calendar, including the formats for month and day titles, the patterns and colors for date boxes, and the format and placement of text in boxes, use the Format Timescale command. To display this dialog box, you can double-click the calendar (not on a task).
- To change the Calendar width, drag any vertical line between date boxes to the left to decrease the width or to the right to increase the width. To fit the Calendar in the project window, double-click a vertical line between date boxes. To adjust all week rows to the height required to fit the greatest number of task bars in any one week, double-click a horizontal line between weeks.
- To control the look of the bars, including the pattern, color, text, and whether it has a shadow, use the Format Bar Styles command.
- To control thc look of the text and gridlines, use the Format Text Styles and Format Gridlines commands.
- To control the order of the tasks or which tasks are displayed, you can sort the tasks using the Tools Sort command or filter the tasks using the filters available in the Filters box on the Formatting toolbar.

Since the number of tasks displayed on a day depends on the row height, you may want to limit the information in the view by applying a filter, such as the Using Resource filter. By doing this, you see all tasks assigned to the resource you specify when you apply the filter, but no other tasks.

When used in a combination view, the Calendar must be the top view. If the bottom view is a task view, it shows details about the tasks selected on the calendar; if it is a resource view, the view shows the resources assigned to the tasks selected on the Calendar, along with information about those resources.

Task Form

Use the Task Form for entering new tasks or assigning resources to a task. You also use the Task Form to review information about a task. For example, you can see the resources scheduled to work on the task and the start and finish date for each resource. Or, you can see cost or work information for each resource assigned to the task.

The Task Form is also the place you insert and edit objects from other applications, such as a chart from Microsoft Graph or part of a spreadsheet from Microsoft Excel.

The Task Form shows information about one task at a time. At the bottom are fields you can change to see different information related to the task. Initially, the Task Form shows the resources fields (resources assigned to the task) and the predecessors fields (tasks on which this task depends). These fields show information about the resource assignments that can't be viewed elsewhere. To change the fields, use the Format Details commands.

To display the Task Form, choose View More Views, select Task Form in the Views box, and choose the Apply button.

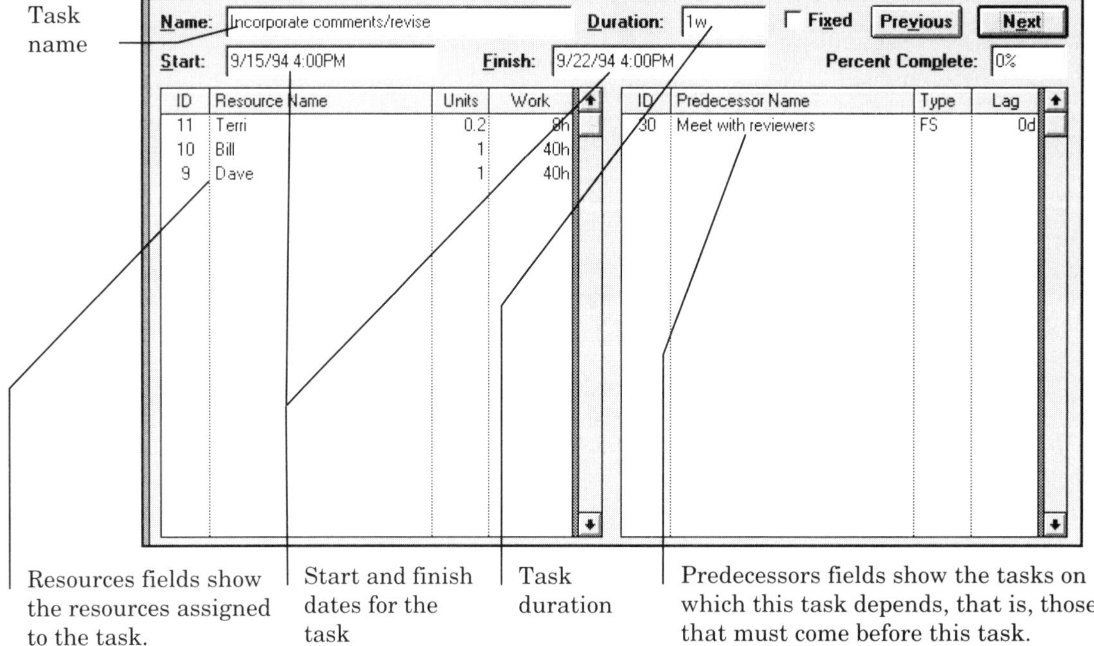

Use the entry bar at the top of the window to enter information in the form. The boxes and buttons in the form work just like in a dialog box.

When you enter information in the Task Form, the Previous and Next buttons change to OK and Cancel. When you finish entering information about the task, press Enter or click OK. If you want to cancel all information you have entered, press Esc or click Cancel. After you press Enter or Esc, or click OK or Cancel, the buttons change back to Previous and Next so you can go to another task.

You can change the information at the bottom of the Task Form depending on what you want to know about the resources assigned to the task on the form. This area can also be used to add or view a note about the task and to insert and edit an object from another application.

- To change the type of information at the bottom of the form, choose a Format Details command. For the resources assigned to the task, you can view the schedule, work, or cost. You can also view and assign predecessors and successors.
- To enter or edit a note or an object, use the Format Details/Notes or Format Details/Objects command.
- To control the order of the tasks or which tasks are displayed, you can sort the tasks using the Tools Sort command or filter the tasks using the filters available in the Filters box on thc Formatting toolbar.

To move around the form, click the place you want to type. With the keys, use Tab and Shift+Tab to move through the options; use the arrow keys to move through the fields at the bottom of the form. In Microsoft Project for Windows, you can press Alt+1 to move into the fields at the left or Alt+2 to move into the fields at the right.

Included with Microsoft Project are two variations on the Task Form: the Task Details Form and the Task Name Form. These views have different options at the top of the form, but the fields at the bottom of the form are identical. To display these views, choose View More Views, select the view in the Views box, and choose the Apply button.

The options on the top part of the Task Details Form are the same as many in the Task Information dialog box. If you find you need these options frequently, such as to change constraints, enter a WBS code, or use a subproject, consider creating a combination view with the Gantt Chart on top and the Task Details Form on the bottom.

Task Details Form

Use the Task Details Form when you want to enter constraints, actual start and finish dates, a subproject, priority, or WBS code. Most of these fields are also available in the Task Information dialog box.

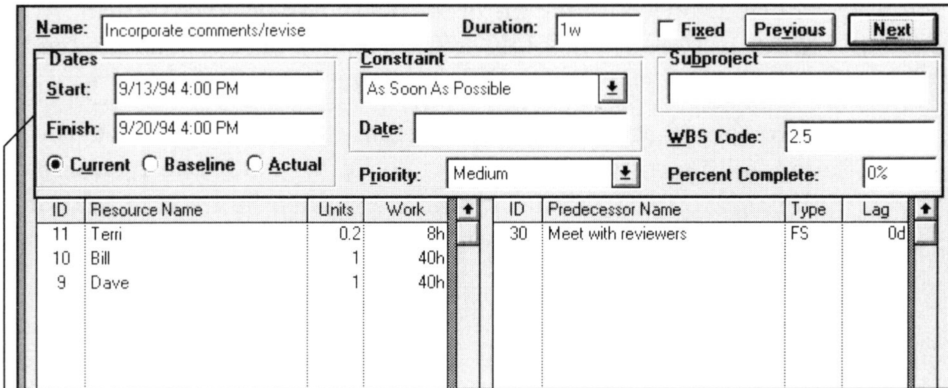

Additional options

Task Name Form

Use the Task Name Form when you want as much room as possible to view an object or to view predecessors or resource assignments. You control what appears below the Name box using the Format Details commands.

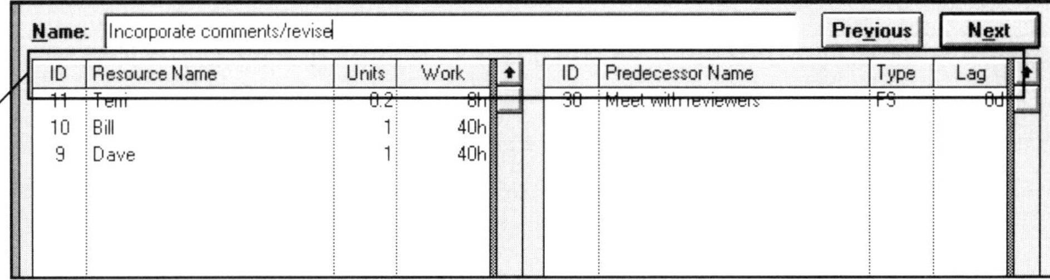

Change these fields with the Format Details commands.

TASK PERT CHART

Use the Task PERT Chart to quickly identify the immediate predecessors and successors to a task. This view is best used at the bottom of a combination view—two views in one window—to see the predecessors and successors of the task selected in the top view.

The Task PERT Chart shows one task at a time, with its immediate predecessors (tasks that it depends on) and successors (tasks that depend on it). Each task is in a box or node, with predecessors to the left, and successors to the right. The type of relationship between each pair of tasks is shown on the line between the tasks.

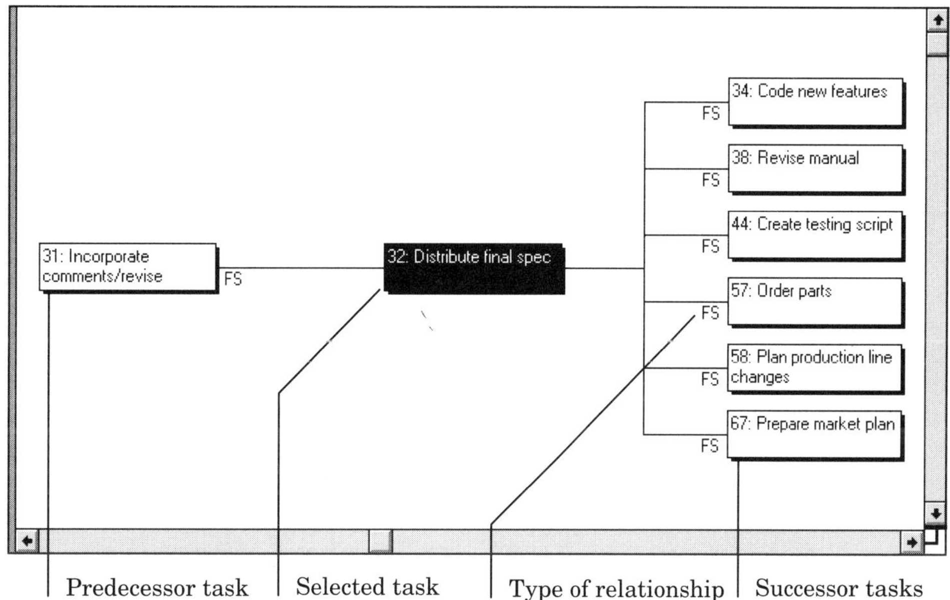

On the Task PERT, you can change the order of the tasks using the Tools Sort command, and you can apply a filter to the view. When you step through the tasks, you do so in the sort order or through the filtered tasks only.

Use the scroll bars or arrow keys to move through the tasks.

TASK SHEET

Use the Task Sheet to enter new tasks or as a convenient way to review the entire list of tasks. You also can use this view to brainstorm a list of new tasks or to create a project outline. Use it when creating reports to show only the fields you want by changing the table applied, or use it when exchanging data with another program, such as Microsoft Excel.

The Task Sheet lists task information in a spreadsheet-like format, with the information organized in rows and columns. The table applied to the Task Sheet controls the fields displayed.

To apply the Task Sheet, choose View More Views, select Task Sheet in the Views box, and then choose the Apply button.

The table applied controls the field names listed at the top of each column and the type of information shown for each task.

	Task Name	Duration	Start	Finish	Predecessors	Resource Nam
1	**Investigation Phase**	**63.25d**	**5/30/94 8:00AM**	**8/25/94 10:00AM**		
2	Investigation begins	0d	5/30/94 8:00AM	5/30/94 8:00AM		
3	**Prepare initial product propos**	**16d**	**5/31/94 8:00AM**	**6/21/94 5:00PM**		**Marcia[0.1]**
4	Research competition	1w	5/31/94 8:00AM	6/6/94 5:00PM	2	Marcia,Marketing
5	Review customer comment ca	3d	6/10/94 8:00AM	6/14/94 5:00PM	4	Janet,Marketing
6	Write proposal	1w	6/15/94 8:00AM	6/21/94 5:00PM	5	Marcia,Janet
7	**Plan focus panel**	**5d**	**6/22/94 8:00AM**	**6/28/94 5:00PM**		
8	Prepare questions	1w	6/22/94 8:00AM	6/28/94 5:00PM	6	Marcia,Janet
9	**Arrange sites**	**2d**	**6/22/94 8:00AM**	**6/23/94 5:00PM**	**6**	
10	Contact hotels	1d	6/22/94 8:00AM	6/22/94 5:00PM		Cheryl
11	**Arrange for equipment**	**1d**	**6/23/94 8:00AM**	**6/23/94 5:00PM**	**10**	
12	Determine needed equi	4h	6/23/94 8:00AM	6/23/94 12:00PM		Cheryl,Janet[0.1
13	Contact local offices	4h	6/23/94 1:00PM	6/23/94 5:00PM	12	Cheryl
14	**Get panel members**	**3d**	**6/24/94 8:00AM**	**6/28/94 5:00PM**	**9**	
15	Contact local reps for nam	1d	6/24/94 8:00AM	6/24/94 5:00PM		Cheryl,Janet[0.1
16	Contact suggested panel m	2d	6/27/94 8:00AM	6/28/94 5:00PM	15	Cheryl
17	**Plan phone questionnaire**	**3.25d**	**6/29/94 8:00AM**	**7/4/94 10:00AM**	**7**	
18	Prepare questionnaire	3d	6/29/94 8:00AM	7/1/94 5:00PM		Marcia,Marketing
19	Get list of users to call	2h	7/4/94 8:00AM	7/4/94 10:00AM	18	Cheryl
20	Carry out focus panels	4w	7/4/94 10:00AM	8/1/94 10:00AM	17	Marcia,Marketing
21	Carry out phone survey	1w	8/1/94 10:00AM	8/8/94 10:00AM	20	Research Inc

Summary tasks are bold.

You can make the Task Sheet look just the way you want and show exactly the information you want.

- To control the look of the text for a category of tasks, use the Format Text Styles command; to make one task stand out, use the Format Font command.
- To control the look of gridlines, use the Format Gridlines command.

- To control the order of the information in the view, you can sort the list of tasks using the Tools Sort command.
- To control which tasks are displayed or to highlight certain types of tasks, use the filters in the Filters box on the Formatting toolbar or create your own filter to show just what you want using the Tools Filtered For/More Filters command.
- To change the type of information displayed about each task, change the table, either by applying a new one using the View Table commands, by creating a new one, or by changing one of the columns in the table. To change one of the columns in the table you are using, just double-click the column title. To change the column width so it best fits the information in the column, double-click the border to the right of the column title.
- If you are using an outline, you can control its appearance using the Outline Options on the View tab in the Tools Options dialog box.

To move through the tasks, use the scroll bar. Use the arrow keys, Home, End, PgUp, and PgDn to move through the tasks with the keyboard.

When you double-click a task on the Task Sheet or any task view with a table, such as the Gantt Chart, one of the following happens.

- If the task is a summary task, which means it summarizes the tasks indented beneath it in an outline, double-clicking it collapses its subordinate tasks so they are hidden. If the tasks are already collapsed, double-clicking expands the subordinate tasks so they show again. For more information about outlining, see Chapter 4, “Breaking Your Project into Tasks and Milestones.”
- If that task is a subproject task, which means it represents the tasks in another project, double-clicking the task makes the subproject the active project and opens the subproject if it was closed. For more information about subprojects, see Chapter 14, “Managing Multiple Projects.”
- If the task is neither a summary task nor a subproject task, the Task Information dialog box is displayed when you double-click the task. Use this dialog box to enter additional information about the task you double-clicked, such as changing the constraint to control the date on which the task starts or finishes, or entering a subproject filename if you want to make the task a subproject task.

Resource Form

Use the Resource Form for entering new resources. You also use the Resource Form for reviewing resource assignment information. For example, you can see the list of tasks that the resource is scheduled to work on and the start and finish date for the resource for each task. Or you can see cost or work information for the resource for each task.

The Resource Form is also the place you insert and edit objects from other applications, such as a chart from Microsoft Graph or part of a spreadsheet from Microsoft Excel.

The Resource Form shows information about one resource at a time. At the bottom of the Resource Form are fields you can change to see different types of resource assignment information for the resource. Initially, the Resource Form shows the schedule fields. To change the fields, use the Format Details commands.

To display the Resource Form, choose View More Views, select Resource Form in the Views box, and choose the Apply button.

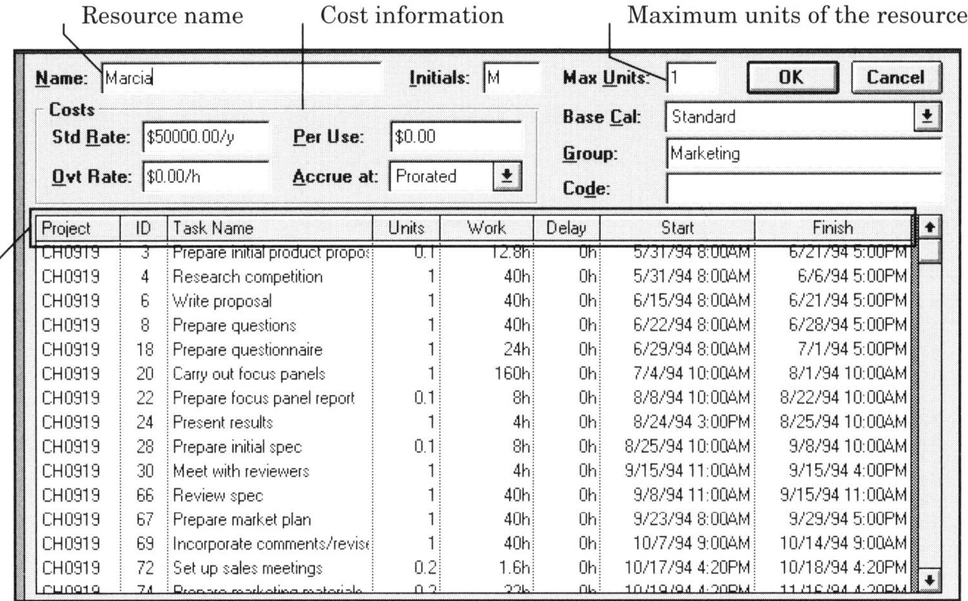

Project	ID	Task Name	Units	Work	Delay	Start	Finish
CH0919	3	Prepare initial product propos	0.1	12.8h	0h	5/31/94 8:00AM	6/21/94 5:00PM
CH0919	4	Research competition	1	40h	0h	5/31/94 8:00AM	6/6/94 5:00PM
CH0919	6	Write proposal	1	40h	0h	6/15/94 8:00AM	6/21/94 5:00PM
CH0919	8	Prepare questions	1	40h	0h	6/22/94 8:00AM	6/28/94 5:00PM
CH0919	18	Prepare questionnaire	1	24h	0h	6/29/94 8:00AM	7/1/94 5:00PM
CH0919	20	Carry out focus panels	1	160h	0h	7/4/94 10:00AM	8/1/94 10:00AM
CH0919	22	Prepare focus panel report	0.1	8h	0h	8/8/94 10:00AM	8/22/94 10:00AM
CH0919	24	Present results	1	4h	0h	8/24/94 3:00PM	8/25/94 10:00AM
CH0919	28	Prepare initial spec	0.1	8h	0h	8/25/94 10:00AM	9/8/94 10:00AM
CH0919	30	Meet with reviewers	1	4h	0h	9/15/94 11:00AM	9/15/94 4:00PM
CH0919	66	Review spec	1	40h	0h	9/8/94 11:00AM	9/15/94 11:00AM
CH0919	67	Prepare market plan	1	40h	0h	9/23/94 8:00AM	9/29/94 5:00PM
CH0919	69	Incorporate comments/revis	1	40h	0h	10/7/94 9:00AM	10/14/94 9:00AM
CH0919	72	Set up sales meetings	0.2	1.6h	0h	10/17/94 4:20PM	10/18/94 4:20PM

Schedule fields show the tasks the resource is assigned to and the start and finish date for the resource on each task. You can change these fields to show other information such as work or cost for the resource for each task.

Use the entry bar at the top of the window to enter information in the form. The boxes and buttons in the form work just like in a dialog box.

When you enter information in the Resource Form, the Previous and Next buttons change to OK and Cancel. When you have finished entering information about the resource, press Enter or click OK. If you want to cancel all information you have entered, press Esc or click Cancel. After you press Enter or Esc, or click OK or Cancel, the buttons change back to Previous and Next so you can go to another resource.

You can change the information at the bottom of the Resource Form depending on what you want to know about the tasks to which the resource is assigned. This area can also be used to add a note about the resource and to insert and edit an object from another application.

- To change the type of information at the bottom of the form, choose a Format Details command. You can view schedule, work, or cost information for each task to which the resource is assigned.
- To enter or edit a note or an object, use the Format Details/Notes or Format Details/Objects command.
- To control the order of the resources or which resources are displayed, you can sort the resources using the Tools Sort command or filter the resources using the filters available in the Filters box on the Formatting toolbar.

To move around the form, click the place you want to type. With the keys, use Tab and Shift+Tab to move through the options; use the arrow keys to move through the fields at the bottom of the form. In Microsoft Project for Windows, you can press Alt+1 to move into the fields at the bottom.

The Resource Information dialog box looks like the top half of the Resource Form and works the same way. You use it when you want to change a detail about a resource—or several resources at once—when the Resource Form is not displayed.

Included with Microsoft Project is also the Resource Name Form. Use the Resource Name Form when you want as much room as possible to view an object or to view tasks to which the resource is assigned. You control what appears below the Name box using the Format Details commands. To display this view, choose View More Views, select Resource Name Form in the Views box, and choose the Apply button.

RESOURCE GRAPH

Use this view to check for overallocated or underallocated resources or to check cumulative work or cost over time for the project as a whole, for a group of resources, or for any one resource.

The Resource Graph shows the peak demand, allocation, work, or cost for one resource, a group of resources, or both—period by period. It is a graphic representation of resource information over time. The graph shows the peak number of units of this resource allocated during the period on the timescale. For example, if the timescale shows weeks, and an allocation of five, it does not necessarily mean that five units are allocated on each day, but on at least one day.

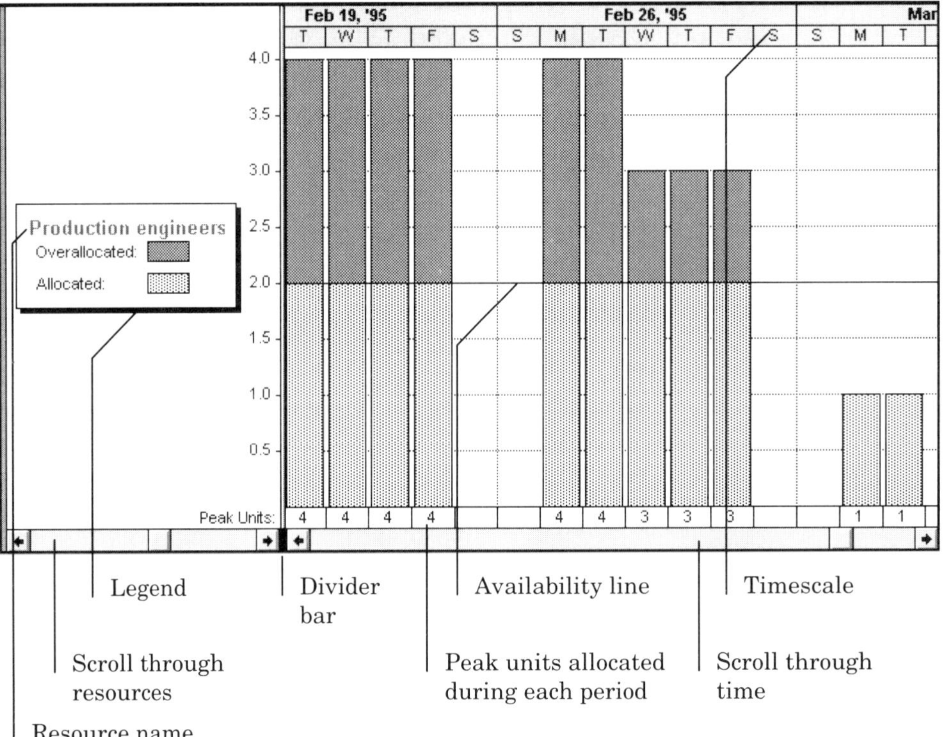

In the illustration, the availability line is at two, showing you have a maximum of two production engineers. The bars show that, during nine days, the resource is overallocated—you have more than two units assigned to tasks; during two days, the resource is working below capacity—you have assigned fewer than two units to tasks.

The legend to the left shows the resource name or group name and the color or pattern for the graphs. You can change the look of the graphs and the type of information displayed to get the information you want.

- To change the type of information displayed, choose a Format Details command: Peak Units, Work, Cumulative Work, Overallocation, Percent Allocation, Availability, Cost, or Cumulative Cost.
- To control the look of the graph, including which graphs show, graph type (bar, area, step, line, or step line), color, and pattern, use the Format Bar Styles command. To display this dialog box, you can double-click the graph.
- To control the look of the text and gridlines, use the Format Text Styles and Format Gridlines commands.
- To control the order of the resources or the resources that are displayed, you can sort the resources using the Tools Sort command or filter the resources by applying a filter.
- To control the timescale, double-click the timescale or choose the Format Timescale command. You can show everything from hours over minutes to years, depending on the level of detail you want. You can also use the Zoom In and Zoom Out buttons on the Standard toolbar to change the timescale.

If the Resource Graph is the only view, is at the top of a combination view, or is below a resource view, you can see information for one resource or a group. You can show up to two graphs for a resource group and two graphs for an individual resource, such as two graph showing overallocated resources and allocated resources for the group and two more showing overallocated and allocated for one resource, or you can show any combination of these graphs.

When the Resource Graph is below a task view, you always see information for one resource. You can show up to four graphs for tasks to which the resource is assigned: two for all tasks and two for selected tasks.

To move through the resources and through time, use the scroll bars. Use the arrow keys to move through the resources with the keyboard. To move through time with the keyboard in Windows, hold down Alt, and press an arrow key, the PgUp or PgDn key, or Home or End. On the Macintosh, hold down Option and press a navigation key.

RESOURCE SHEET

Use the Resource Sheet to enter new resources or as a convenient way to review the complete list of resources. Use it when creating reports to show just the fields you want by changing the table applied and use it when exchanging data with another program, such as Microsoft Excel.

The Resource Sheet lists resource information in a spreadsheet-like format, with the information organized in rows and columns. The table applied to the Resource Sheet controls the fields displayed.

Resources that are overallocated, such as Marcia and Production engineers, are shown in bold (or red on a color monitor or printer). You can change this using the Format Text Styles command.

The table applied controls the field names listed at the top of each column and the type of information shown about each resource.

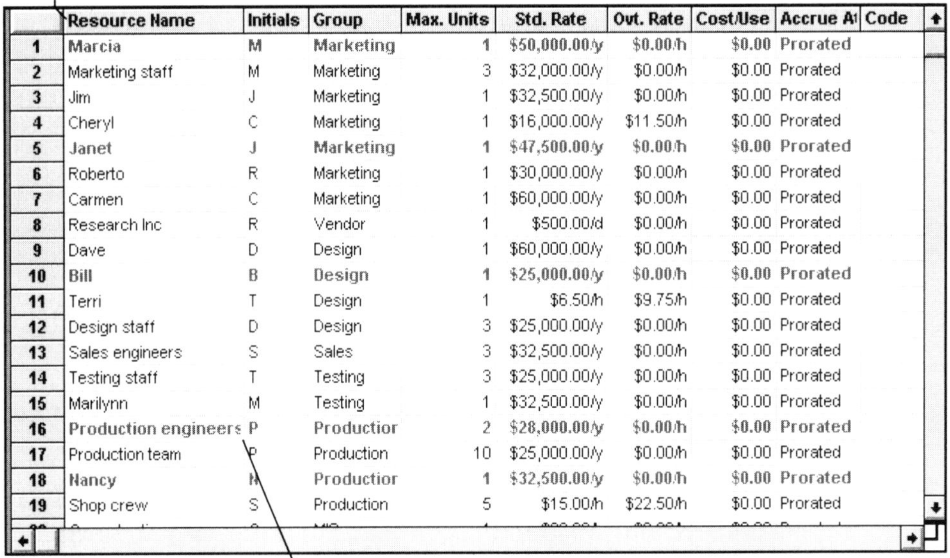

	Resource Name	Initials	Group	Max. Units	Std. Rate	Ovt. Rate	Cost/Use	Accrue At	Code
1	**Marcia**	**M**	**Marketing**	**1**	**$50,000.00/y**	**$0.00/h**	**$0.00**	**Prorated**	
2	Marketing staff	M	Marketing	3	$32,000.00/y	$0.00/h	$0.00	Prorated	
3	Jim	J	Marketing	1	$32,500.00/y	$0.00/h	$0.00	Prorated	
4	Cheryl	C	Marketing	1	$16,000.00/y	$11.50/h	$0.00	Prorated	
5	**Janet**	**J**	**Marketing**	**1**	**$47,500.00/y**	**$0.00/h**	**$0.00**	**Prorated**	
6	Roberto	R	Marketing	1	$30,000.00/y	$0.00/h	$0.00	Prorated	
7	Carmen	C	Marketing	1	$60,000.00/y	$0.00/h	$0.00	Prorated	
8	Research Inc	R	Vendor	1	$500.00/d	$0.00/h	$0.00	Prorated	
9	Dave	D	Design	1	$60,000.00/y	$0.00/h	$0.00	Prorated	
10	**Bill**	**B**	**Design**	**1**	**$25,000.00/y**	**$0.00/h**	**$0.00**	**Prorated**	
11	Terri	T	Design	1	$6.50/h	$9.75/h	$0.00	Prorated	
12	Design staff	D	Design	3	$25,000.00/y	$0.00/h	$0.00	Prorated	
13	Sales engineers	S	Sales	3	$32,500.00/y	$0.00/h	$0.00	Prorated	
14	Testing staff	T	Testing	3	$25,000.00/y	$0.00/h	$0.00	Prorated	
15	Marilynn	M	Testing	1	$32,500.00/y	$0.00/h	$0.00	Prorated	
16	**Production engineers**	**P**	**Production**	**2**	**$28,000.00/y**	**$0.00/h**	**$0.00**	**Prorated**	
17	Production team	P	Production	10	$25,000.00/y	$0.00/h	$0.00	Prorated	
18	**Nancy**	**N**	**Production**	**1**	**$32,500.00/y**	**$0.00/h**	**$0.00**	**Prorated**	
19	Shop crew	S	Production	5	$15.00/h	$22.50/h	$0.00	Prorated	

Bold text indicates a resource is assigned work beyond its capacity.

You can make the Resource Sheet look just the way you want and show exactly the information you want.

- To control the look of categories of text, such as overallocated resources, highlighted resources, and row and column titles, use the Format Text Styles command.
- To control the look of the gridlines, use the Format Gridlines command.
- To control the order of the information in the view, you can sort the list of resources using the Tools Sort command.
- To control which resources are displayed or to highlight certain types of resources, use the filters in the Filters box on the Formatting toolbar.
- To change the type of information displayed about each resource, change the table, either by applying a new one using the View Table commands, by creating a new one, or by changing one of the columns in the table. To change one of the columns in the table you are using, just double-click the column title. To change the column width so it best fits the information in the column, double-click the border to the right of the column title.

To move through the resources, use the scroll bar. Use the arrow keys, Home, End, PgUp, and PgDn to move through the resources with the keyboard.

When you double-click a resource name on the Resource Sheet or on any resource view with a table, such as the Resource Usage view, or in the legend of the Resource Graph, the Resource Information dialog box is displayed. Use this dialog box when you want to change details for the resource, such as cost information, the maximum units available, or the base calendar used for the resource.

Resource Usage View

Use the Resource Usage view to check the allocation, work, or cost of resources during each period. You also can enter resources on this view. If you have several projects that share resources, this view can show you resource use for all the projects.

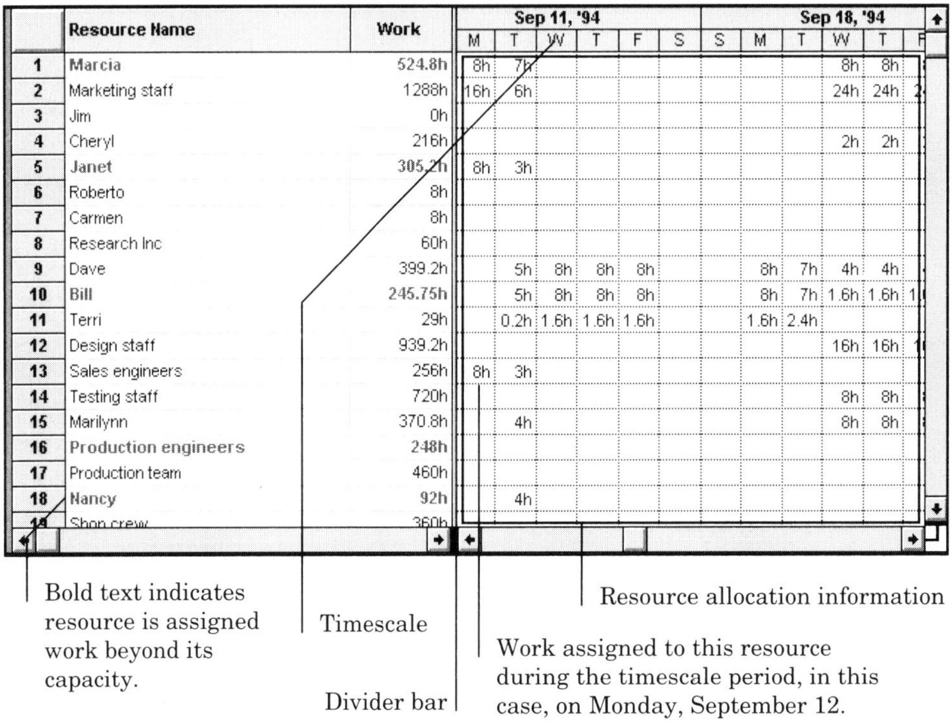

	Resource Name	Work	Sep 11, '94						Sep 18, '94					
			M	T	W	T	F	S	S	M	T	W	T	F
1	Marcia	524.8h	8h	7h								8h	8h	
2	Marketing staff	1288h	16h	6h								24h	24h	2
3	Jim	0h												
4	Cheryl	216h										2h	2h	
5	Janet	305.2h	8h	3h										
6	Roberto	8h												
7	Carmen	8h												
8	Research Inc	60h												
9	Dave	399.2h		5h	8h	8h	8h			8h	7h	4h	4h	
10	Bill	245.75h		5h	8h	8h	8h			8h	7h	1.6h	1.6h	1
11	Terri	29h		0.2h	1.6h	1.6h	1.6h			1.6h	2.4h			
12	Design staff	939.2h										16h	16h	1
13	Sales engineers	256h	8h	3h										
14	Testing staff	720h										8h	8h	
15	Marilynn	370.8h		4h								8h	8h	
16	Production engineers	248h												
17	Production team	460h												
18	Nancy	92h		4h										
19	Shop crew	360h												

Bold text indicates resource is assigned work beyond its capacity.

Timescale

Divider bar

Resource allocation information

Work assigned to this resource during the timescale period, in this case, on Monday, September 12.

The Resource Usage view shows a list of resources and information about resource use over time. The period covered by the boxes on the right can be changed so you can look at resource allocation for any time period, from minutes to years. You can show a variety of information on the Resource Usage view, such as the time each resource is scheduled to work for each period, the percentage allocation, or the cumulative cost or work for each resource. The information on the Resource Usage view can be copied and used in a spreadsheet application, such as Microsoft Excel, so you can analyze cost or other data.

Overallocated resources, such as Marcia in the previous illustration, are shown in bold (or red on a color monitor or printer). You can change this using the Format Text Styles command.

To show more or less of the table and chart, move the divider bar right or left.

You can change the look of the Resource Usage view and the type of information displayed depending on what you want to know about the resource or resources.

- To change the type of information displayed, choose a Format Details command: Peak Units, Work, Cumulative Work, Overallocation, Percent Allocation, Availability, Cost, or Cumulative Cost.
- To control the look of categories of text, such as overallocated resources, use the Format Text Styles command.
- To control the look of the gridlines, use the Format Gridlines command.
- To control the information in the view, you can: sort the list of resources using the Tools Sort command; filter the resources to display or highlight certain resources; change the type of information displayed about each resource using the View Table commands.
- To control the timescale, double-click the timescale or choose the Format Timescale command. You can show everything from hours over minutes to years, depending on the level of detail you want. You can also use the Zoom In and Zoom Out buttons on the Standard toolbar to change the timescale.

When the Resource Usage view is below a task view in a combination view, you can display information for all tasks or for the tasks selected in the top view. Use the Format Details/Selected Tasks Only command when you want to view limited information.

To move through the resources and through time, use the scroll bars. Use the arrow keys to move through the resources with the keyboard. To move through time with the keyboard in Windows, hold down Alt, and press an arrow key, the PgUp or PgDn key, or Home or End. On the Macintosh, hold down Option and press a navigation key.

Combination Views

Microsoft Project also comes with two combination views, the Task Entry view and the Resource Allocation view. A combination view has two views in the same window, one on top and one on the bottom. The bottom view shows information about the task or resource selected in the top view. You can combine any two views that are not already combination views to create your own combination views. In a combination view, commands or typing affect the active view. The active view bar along the left side of the view shows which view is active. The split bar between views can be dragged up or down to change the size of either view.

Task Entry View

The Task Entry view has the Gantt Chart on top and the Task Form on the bottom. Use this view when you want to enter a lot of task details as you enter new tasks on the Gantt Chart.

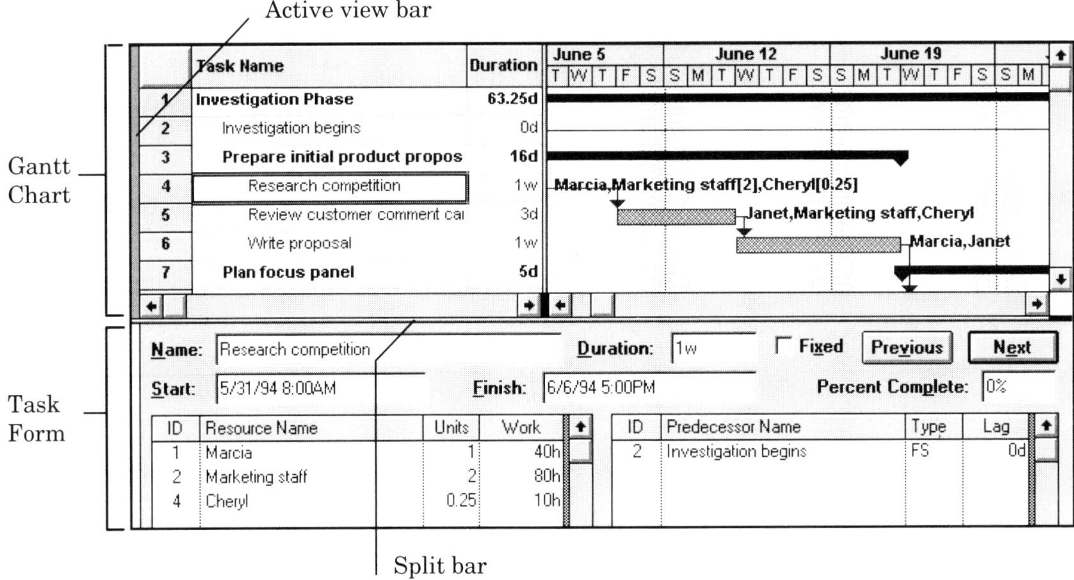

The Task Form shows details about the task selected on the Gantt Chart.

Resource Allocation View

The Resource Allocation view helps you level resources. When you select an overallocated resource on the Resource Usage view on top, the Delay Gantt on the bottom displays tasks causing the overallocation. In the Delay field, you can enter the amount of time to delay a task so a resource is no longer overallocated.

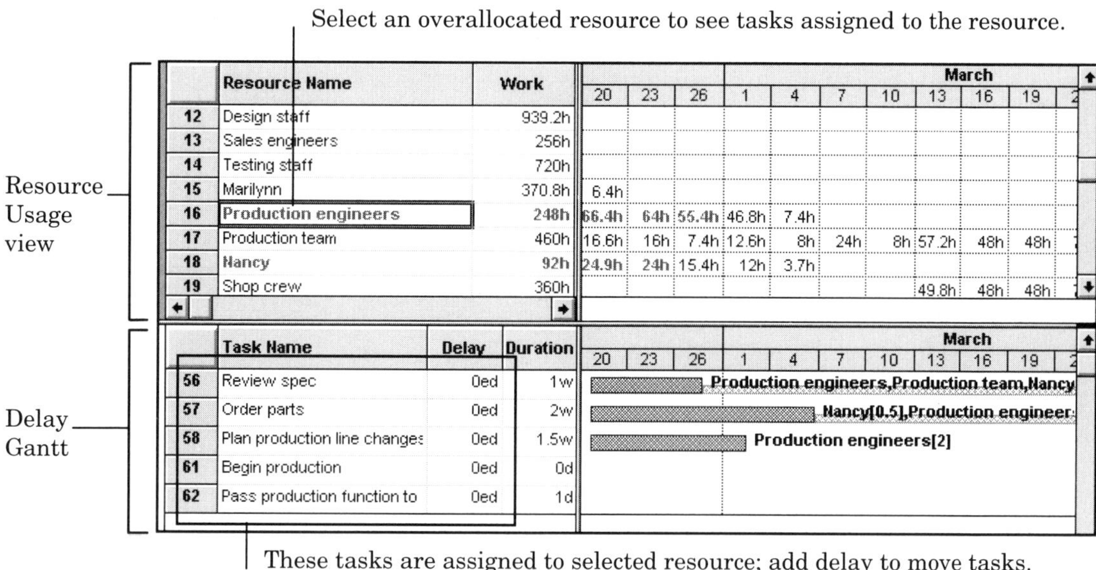

To	Do this
Switch between top and bottom views	Press F6 or click view you want.
Change one view in a combination view	Select view you want to replace, and choose another view.
Change single-pane view to combination view	Display view you want on top; hold down Shift and choose view for bottom.
Replace combination with single-pane view	Hold down Shift and choose view from View menu.
Split a single-pane view	Press Shift+F6, press arrow keys to move split bar, press Enter; with mouse, drag split box or double-click split box.
Close a pane in a combination view	Press Shift+F6, press Up or Down Arrow to close view, press Enter; with mouse, drag split bar or double-click split bar.

MICROSOFT PROJECT BASICS

This section will help you if you are unfamiliar with Windows or the Macintosh. It explains briefly the parts of a window, menus, commands, and how to use dialog boxes. It also explains the toolbars and how to use the entry bar, where you enter information into Microsoft Project.

The following illustration shows the parts of the window.

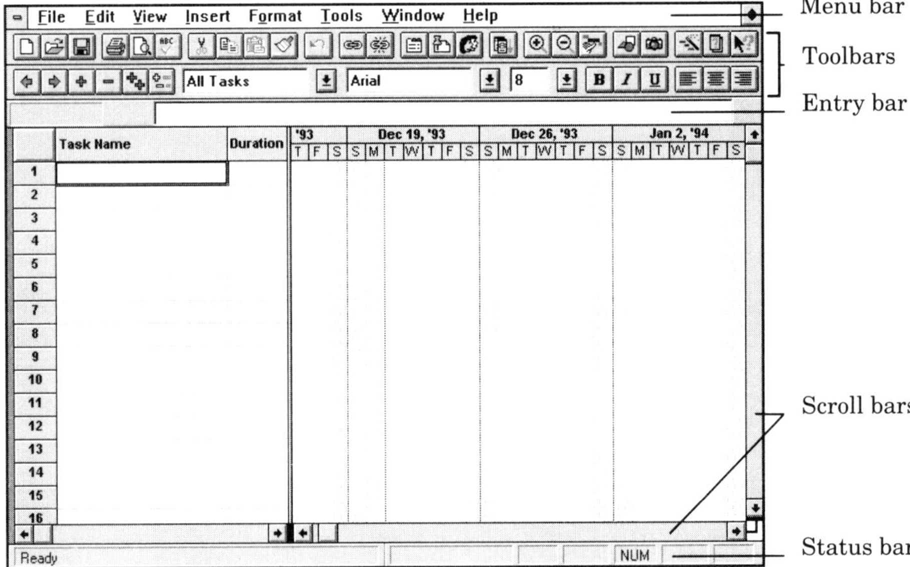

- *Menu bar* lists the menus.
- *Toolbars* contain buttons to carry out common actions.
- *Entry bar* is used to enter information into Microsoft Project.
- *Scroll bars* are used with the mouse to scroll through information.
- *Status bar* tells you about commands or what Microsoft Project is doing.

CHOOSING A COMMAND

The menu bar at the top of the screen contains the menus on which you'll find all the commands in Microsoft Project. To choose a command, first select the appropriate menu, and then choose the command from the menu.

When you choose some commands, additional commands appear on a submenu. You choose these commands in exactly the same way.

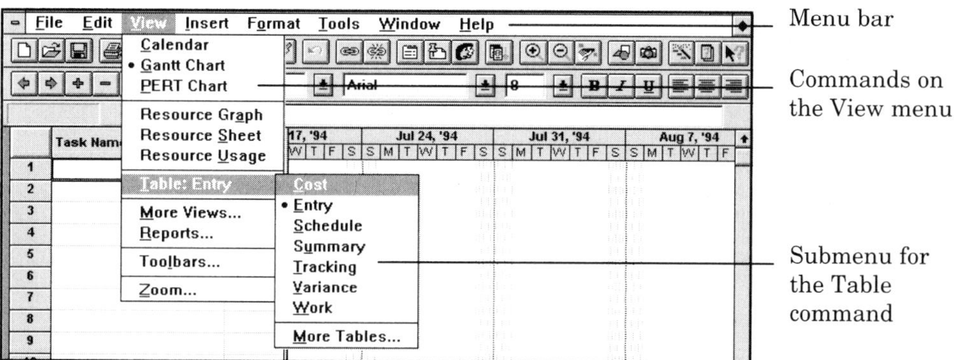

TO CHOOSE A COMMAND

- In Windows, click the menu name and then click the command name. For example, to choose File Open, click File and then click Open. You can also press Alt, and then the letter underlined in the menu name and command name. For example, press Alt+F+O to choose File Open.
- On the Macintosh, point to the menu name and then drag to the command name. For example, to choose File Open, point to the File menu, and then hold down the mouse button and drag to the Open command.

USING A DIALOG BOX

When you choose certain commands—those followed by an ellipsis (...)—Microsoft Project displays a dialog box in which you set other options for the command. In a dialog box, you either type or select information. If you can select information, there is either a box containing a list of items, or there is an arrow at the right end of the option.

To move around a dialog box using the mouse, click the option. To move from option to option with the keys, press Tab. In Windows, to move to a specific option, hold down Alt and press the underlined letter in the option name.

The following illustrations show the types of options; each illustration is followed with a brief description of using that type of option.

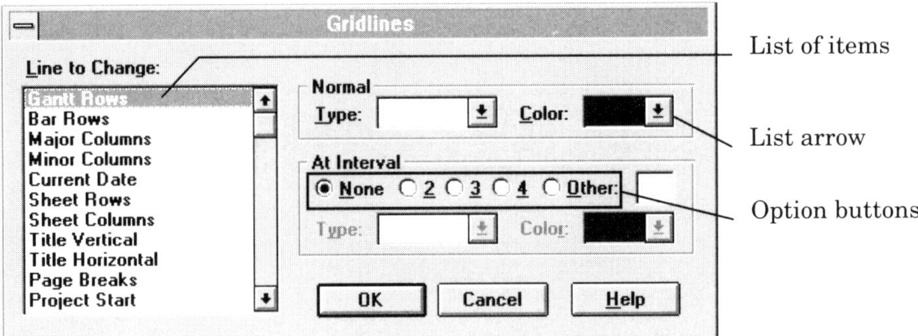

- In a *list of items*, you select an item. Press the Up or Down Arrow key to select the item you want, or click it with the mouse.
- A *list arrow* means there is a list of items from which you can select. Click the arrow to see the list. In Windows, you can also select the option and press Alt+Down Arrow to see the list. To select the item you want, click it with the mouse or press the Up or Down Arrow key and then press Enter.
- In a group of *option buttons*, you can select only one in a group. To select, click the option you want with the mouse or, in Windows, press Alt+underlined character.

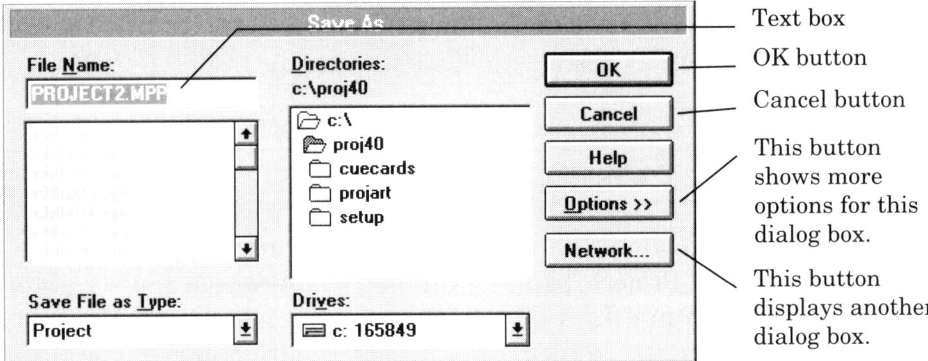

- In a *text box*, type the text you want.
- Click the *OK button* or the button with the bold border, or press Enter, when the settings are as you want them and you want to carry out the command.
- Click the *Cancel button* or press Esc to cancel the command. In some dialog boxes, this button changes to Close after you have done things that cannot be canceled, such as created a new table.

- When you choose a *button with* >>, such as the Options button in the above illustration, options are added to the dialog box.
- When you choose a *button with* ..., such as the Network button in the above illustration, another dialog box appears.

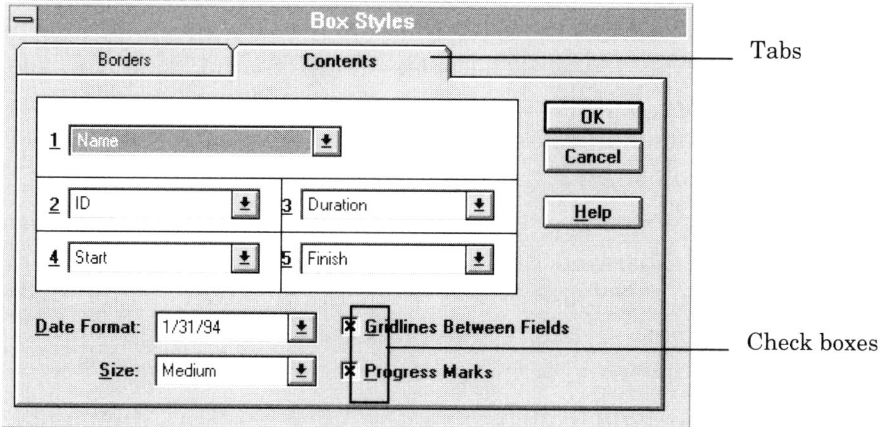

- *Tabs* are used in dialog boxes with many options to group similar options together, with the tabs indicating the type of options included there. To move between tabs, click the tab or press an arrow key.
- *Check boxes* are yes-or-no options. You can select more than one check box in a group of check boxes. To select or clear a check box, click the box or, in Windows, press Alt+underlined character. An X indicates the box is selected. Sometimes check boxes are gray, which means the items you have selected have a mixture of settings.

USING THE TOOLBAR

The buttons on the toolbars are used to choose commands quickly and carry out common actions. To use a button, just click it with the mouse.

Initially, two toolbars are displayed—the Standard toolbar and the Formatting toolbar.

Use the Standard toolbar to work with files, print and preview documents, edit tasks and resources, link tasks, assign resources, zoom in and out on the timescale, and get help.

Use the Formatting toolbar to work with outlines, apply a filter, and format text.

Standard toolbar

Formatting toolbar

To see what each button does, pause the mouse pointer over a button. A ToolTip tells what the button is for. If you want more information about a button, hold down the mouse button and read the toolbar button description in the status bar at the bottom of the screen. Drag away from the toolbar before releasing the mouse button so you won't carry out the toolbar button action.

In addition to these toolbars, Microsoft Project includes seven others: Drawing, Microsoft (to start other Microsoft applications), Microsoft Project 3.0 (for those of you who can't live without the toolbar from the last version), Resource Management, Tracking, Visual Basic, and WorkGroup.

To show or hide toolbars, use the View Toolbars command. This is also where you can customize the buttons and toolbars. Another way to show or hide a toolbar is to click any toolbar with the right mouse button, if your mouse has multiple buttons, or hold down the Ctrl button as you click if your mouse has only one button. On the context-sensitive menu that appears, click the toolbar you want to show or hide.

You can move a toolbar anywhere you want on the screen (just drag it with the mouse), change the buttons on the toolbars, or create your own buttons or toolbars. The look, order, and action of each button is completely customizable so you can match the toolbars to your needs. For information about customizing toolbars, see Chapter 16, "Using Microsoft Project Tools."

USING THE ENTRY BAR

The entry bar is used to enter information into Microsoft Project. Often, there is a list of choices from which you can select. You know if there is a list because the entry bar arrow appears when you select the field. Then you can choose from the list instead of typing. For example, you can choose a resource from the list in the entry bar.

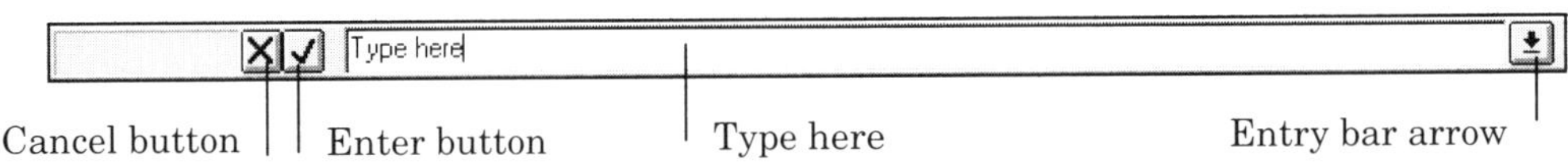

TO USE THE ENTRY BAR

1. Select the field or box where you want to enter information.
2. Type the information or select it from the entry bar list.

   If you can select information, the entry bar arrow appears at the right end of the entry bar.

   To see the list, click the arrow with the mouse. In Windows, you can press Alt+Down Arrow; on the Macintosh, you can press Option+Down Arrow. Then click the item with the mouse or press the Up or Down Arrow key to select the item you want.
3. To indicate you have finished with your entry, press Enter, or click the enter button.

   To cancel what you have done so far in the entry bar, press Esc, or click the cancel button.

CUSTOMIZING MICROSOFT PROJECT

There are many things about Microsoft Project you can change. The following table shows what you can customize and how you do it in Microsoft Project. For information and examples for creating all the elements, see Chapter 16, "Using Microsoft Project Tools."

What you can customize	Use this command
Create new views, change existing views	View More Views
Create new tables, change existing tables	View Table/More Tables
Create new filters, change existing filters	Tools Filtered For/More Filters
Create new reports, change existing reports	View Reports, Custom button
Create new calendars, change existing calendars	Tools Change Working Time
Create new macros, change existing macros	Tools Macros and Tools Record Macro
Create new dialog boxes, change existing ones	Tools Customize/Forms

What you can customize	Use this command
Change the buttons on the toolbars and the action assigned	Tools Customize/Toolbars
Change the menus	Tools Customize/Menu Bars
Use views, tables, filters, reports, toolbars, and so on from another project	View More Views, Organizer button (also in other dialog boxes)

There are also a number of preferences you can set. For example, you can change whether the entry bar, toolbars, and scroll bars are displayed or how Microsoft Project displays the date and time. The following tables show items you can change and the setting you change on the tabs in the Tools Options dialog box.

GENERAL SETTINGS

On the General tab in the Tools Options dialog box, you can change the following options.

You can change	Use this option
Whether you get advice from the PlanningWizard on using Microsoft Project, about errors, and about scheduling	General tab/PlanningWizard
Whether you get tips and the Welcome dialog box when you start Microsoft Project	General tab/Show Tips At Startup and Show Welcome Dialog On Startup
Whether you want to be asked if you want to add a new resource to the pool, or if you want Microsoft Project to add it automatically	General tab/Automatically Add New Resources
Standard and overtime rates for resources when you don't type a rate	General tab/Default Standard Rate and Default Overtime Rate
Whether, when you start Microsoft Project, the last file you were using is opened	General tab/Open Last File On Startup

CALENDAR SETTINGS

On the Calendar tab in the Tools Options dialog box, you can change the following options.

You can change	Use this option
Number of hours worked each day	Calendar tab/Hours Per Day
Number of hours worked each week	Calendar tab/Hours Per Week
Month in which the year starts, for fiscal years	Calendar tab/Fiscal Year Starts In
Day (Sunday or Monday) on which the week starts	Calendar tab/Week Starts On

SCHEDULE SETTINGS

On the Schedule tab in the Tools Options dialog box, you can change the following options.

You can change	Use this option
Whether you want the duration tracking fields to determine the resource work and cost tracking fields, or if you prefer to enter work values yourself	Schedule tab/Updating Task Status Updates Resource Status
Amount of slack time that makes a task critical	Schedule tab/Tasks Are Critical If Slack <= *x* Days
Messages that warn you about scheduling inconsistencies	Schedule tab/Show Scheduling Messages
Date on which new tasks start—the current date or the project start date	Schedule tab/New Tasks Start On
Whether tasks are automatically linked after adding or moving	Schedule tab/Autolink Inserted Or Moved Tasks
Units used (minutes, hours, days, or weeks) when you don't type a unit	Schedule tab/Show Duration In and Show Work In

VIEW SETTINGS

On the View tab in the Tools Options dialog box, you can change the following options.

You can change	Use this option
Whether you want to see the status bar, scroll bars, or entry bar	View tab/Status Bar, Scroll Bars, Entry Bar
Initial view displayed when you start Microsoft Project	View tab/Default View
Appearance of currency	View tab/Currency Symbol, Placement, Decimal Digits

PART II

PLANNING A PROJECT AND CREATING THE SCHEDULE

In Part II, you learn the basic steps for gathering project information and entering that information into Microsoft Project. These steps include:

- Setting your project goals.
- Listing the tasks.
- Estimating how long each task will take.
- Deciding the sequence of the tasks and the relationships between tasks.
- Assigning people, equipment, and costs for the tasks.

In following these steps, you and your planning team spend the majority of your time gathering and analyzing information. Then you just enter the information into Microsoft Project. Once all this information is entered, you'll see the power of Microsoft Project as it helps you analyze your project model.

Each chapter in Part II describes a discrete step. In reality, each step depends on the others. You may find it easier to do all your planning at once, and then enter all the information into the computer. Or you may want to do one step at a time as you go through each chapter.

3

Setting Project Goals

When planning a new project, setting the goals is the first and the most important step. This means deciding what you want to accomplish, when it has to be finished, and what your budget is. Setting goals ensures that everyone understands and agrees with the purpose of the project. Without goals, you have no way of measuring when the project is complete, and you have no way of knowing if others support your goals.

When you list your goals, be sure to include the scope of the project and the assumptions on which your goals and scope are based. Scope defines the area covered by the project and the limits of the project. Assumptions are what you expect will be true. For example:

Goal: Install New Phone System

Scope	Do:	Replace trunk lines Add lines
	Do not:	Rewire existing lines Replace existing phones
Assumptions	Existing phones will work with new system Existing wiring is OK	

If you later discover that some of the wiring has been eaten by squirrels, obviously your first assumption is no longer valid, and the scope of the project has now changed.

As the project manager, you must drive the goal setting and make sure the scope and assumptions are included. Depending on your organization, you'll probably want to work with project team leaders to further analyze and define the project, and to ensure your assumptions are valid and the goals and scope realistic. By including others in the planning, you increase their commitment to make the project successful, and end up with a more solid plan.

Once you have determined project goals, scope, and assumptions, you can enter some general information about the project into Microsoft Project. For example, you can record the project start date, project title, company name, project manager, and notes about the project, including the goals, scope, and assumptions.

This is also a good time to set up your calendar. The calendar tells Microsoft Project the working hours and days for the project, and is also the place you specify holidays and other days off that affect all the workers on the project.

SETTING CLEAR PROJECT GOALS, SCOPE, AND ASSUMPTIONS

When you set goals, make sure they state clearly what you are trying to accomplish or what the project is. There are several ways you can analyze your goals as you develop them. For example, try the following approaches.

- Think about what you want to achieve or where you want to be at the end of the project—what is the end product?
- State the goal in user or customer terms—what does this person want?
- Decide how you will know when you are finished.
- Look at where you are now and then contrast it with where you want to be.
- Analyze alternatives to your goals to decide if there is a more appropriate goal.
- Think of other ways to state the goal to be sure you are pinpointing exactly what the project is.

Once you have determined your goals, test the goals by answering the following questions.

- Are the goals measurable and specific in terms of time, cost, quality, quantity, and the end result?
- Are the goals realistic and achievable?
- Are the goals stated clearly so they are understandable and unambiguous to everyone working on the project?

If the answer to any of these questions is "no," restate the goals so the goals pass the tests.

SCOPE

By defining scope, you define the work that needs to be done and also what will not be done. Explicitly stating the scope helps others understand what the project is and what it isn't, and helps you and others focus as you complete the necessary steps to plan the project. Stating the scope also helps you as the project progresses because any changes in scope will be easy to identify and justify. Even if you are not sure of the scope, getting your best guess down on paper gives you a starting point, helping you identify when the scope has changed.

One way to define scope is to state what is and what is not part of the project. For example, you could decide that a new product will be manufactured by an outside contractor; that the scope of the project is to complete the design and final specifications only. If it is later decided to manufacture the product in house, it will be obvious that the scope has changed, and that the original budget, time, and schedule no longer match the scope.

Defining scope is especially important when working with outside contractors. If you do not accurately define scope, the work they do may be either inadequate or overdone, and can adversely affect your schedule and budget. If you just assumed a contractor understood the scope, you may be charged for work you considered part of the project, but the contractor considered extra. You can't expect others to do what you want unless you tell them clearly what it is.

ASSUMPTIONS

When you plan anything, you always make assumptions. Explicitly stating your assumptions now helps you later identify when things have changed, and helps you know how to get the project back on track. It is important to state assumptions clearly and concisely so everyone knows the premises on which your goals and the schedule are based.

Many of your assumptions may turn out to be inaccurate. What is more important than the eventual accuracy or inaccuracy of the assumptions is that you are conscious of the assumptions you make. By stating them clearly, you will better be able to tune into changes when they occur.

Suppose, for example, that you are assuming an outside contractor will be available to manufacture your new product. You state this up front, so everyone understands that your goals and scope hinge on this assumption being true. If the contractor is not available, your assumption becomes false, and your scope changes, requiring a change in the plan.

If incorrect assumptions could dramatically affect the schedule, be sure to put together a contingency plan and be ready to go with it. For example, if your outside contractor is not available to manufacture the new product, what will you do instead? If you plan for this contingency now, you'll know exactly what to do if it occurs, and you'll lose the least amount of time in the schedule.

It is crucial that all project team leaders review the assumptions and agree that your assumptions are sound. Assumptions let others understand how and why you came up with your schedule and budget.

How do you decide what assumptions you are making? Think about the following questions to help you get started listing your assumptions.

- What are you assuming will have been done before you start?
- What external factors, out of your control, are you expecting to go a certain way? The weather? Or materials that must come from an outside vendor? That inflation won't go through the roof, driving your costs over budget?
- What are you expecting to happen at the end? Do you consider, for example, that the project will be finished when you hand the manufacturing plans to the outside contractor to begin production? Or do you assume you will monitor the outside contractor?

When you have prepared your goals, scope, and assumptions, share them with others. You may end up repeating the goal-setting process several times until you have the agreement and support of both your management and the rest of the project team, but in the long run, taking the time to do this now will save time and ensure success later.

USING MICROSOFT PROJECT

In this first step, you enter general project information into Microsoft Project, such as the project start date, project name, description, company, and manager. You can also set the calendar so Microsoft Project won't schedule tasks when your company is closed for a holiday or resources are unavailable to do the work.

ENTERING GENERAL PROJECT INFORMATION

You enter general project information in the Summary Info dialog box. You can get to this dialog box in one of two ways. Any time you choose File New or click the New button on the Standard toolbar to start a new project, this dialog box is displayed automatically so you can enter information about the new project. This dialog box does not come up when you first start Microsoft Project, however, so when you start a new project from this point, choose File Summary Info so you can enter this information.

You don't want to skip this step because this is how you tell Microsoft Project the starting date for the new project.

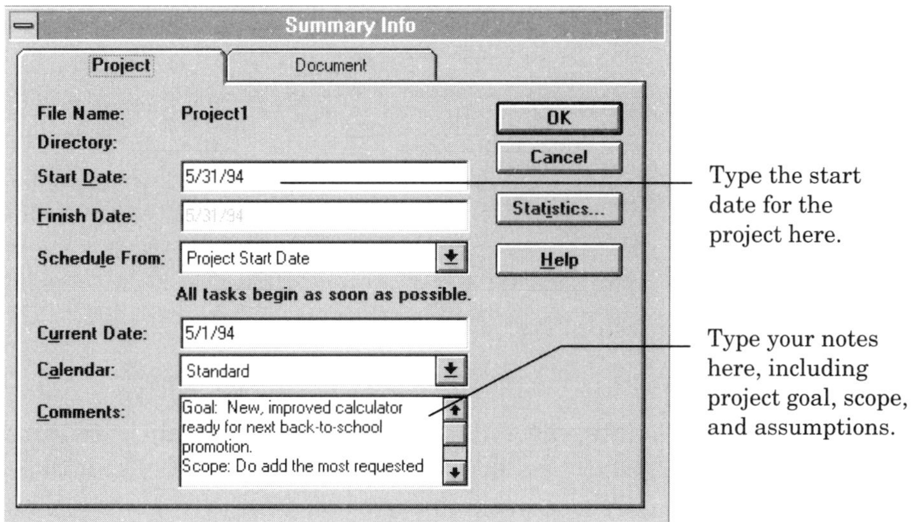

When you enter a project start date, Microsoft Project schedules your project forward from this date, scheduling each task to begin as soon as possible. If you enter a target project finish date in the Finish Date box, Microsoft Project schedules backwards from this finish date, with each task finishing as late as possible to make the finish date. If you want Microsoft Project to calculate the latest possible date that you can start and still make the schedule, select Project Finish Date in the Schedule From box and then type your target finish date in the Finish Date box. This does not create the ideal schedule, however, because if any task is late, the project end date will slip. It does give you useful information, though, if you want to know the latest possible start date for your project after you have entered all task information.

You cannot enter both a start date and finish date for a project. If you already know both, you don't need Microsoft Project!

To enter information about the document itself, such as the title of the project, the company, the manager, and so on, click the Document tab in the Summary Info dialog box.

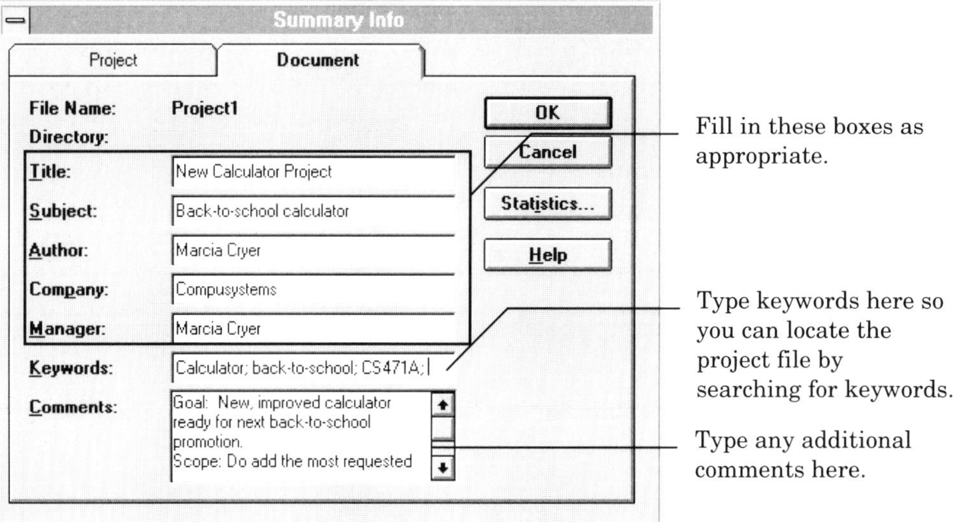

When you are finished, choose OK.

How important is the information in this dialog box?

- The start date you entered on the Project tab is required. To make sure your project reflects reality, you must enter that date.

- The Comments box is a convenient place to record the goal, scope, and assumptions so everyone can refer to them.
- On the Document tab, the information from Title to Manager is all optional. You decide if it is useful.
- Typing keywords in the Keywords box means you can use the File Find File command to locate a file based on keywords. Keywords could be the managers who are working on phases of the project; they could be accounting code numbers; they could be anything that would help you find a project. Again, this is optional. If you have one or two projects going at a time, you may never use this feature. If you have many projects and many people accessing these projects, keywords may help you and others find the project files without having to remember filenames.

SETTING THE CALENDAR

In Microsoft Project, calendars define the working and nonworking days and hours for the project. You set the calendars so Microsoft Project will schedule tasks and resources at the times you want them scheduled. Tasks are scheduled only on the working days and hours in the calendars.

Calendars in Microsoft Project look like a wall calendar with each month appearing individually. Microsoft Project has two kinds of calendars—base calendars and resource calendars. In the base calendar, you indicate the hours and days that are most standard for your company or for this project. It is your way to tell Microsoft Project the normal working hours for the project. For example, if you normally work Monday through Friday, 8 a.m. to 5 p.m., with an hour for lunch, you put this information in the base calendar. You also show holidays and other time away from work that apply to the project or the group of workers.

Resource calendars establish hours for individual resources. Each resource has a calendar; the information in each resource calendar, such as holidays, working days, and working hours, comes from the base calendar. You change the information in the resource calendar only if the resource does not work the same hours as those in the base calendar and to schedule vacation or other time away from work that is different from other resources. For more information about resource calendars, see Chapter 7, "Assigning People, Equipment, and Costs to Tasks."

When scheduling tasks that have resources assigned, Microsoft Project uses the working days and hours in the resource calendars for the resources assigned to the tasks. For tasks that do not have resources assigned, or for tasks that do not depend on the number of resources for their duration, the base calendar is used.

You may find it convenient to create more than one base calendar. For example, if you have groups of resources working similar hours and days—such as three shifts—you can create three base calendars, one for each shift. Each calendar would contain the most general information, such as working days and hours plus holidays, for one shift. By choosing the appropriate base calendar for each resource, the working days and hours in the resource calendar are correct and all you have to do is add vacation hours, or other changes specific to each resource. For more information about creating multiple base calendars, see Chapter 16, "Using Microsoft Project Tools."

You don't have to create any calendars. If you don't, Microsoft Project uses its default calendar, which has the following settings:

- Workdays: Monday–Friday
- Work hours: 8 a.m.–12 noon and 1 p.m.–5 p.m.
- No holidays

Use the default calendar as it is, or change it to fit your project. The default calendar is called Standard.

To change the Standard calendar, choose Tools Change Working Time. The Change Working Time dialog box shows the current working days and hours.

- To change working days, select in the calendar the day or days you want to change and select Working or Nonworking under Make Date(s).
- To change working hours for the selected days, type the hours in the From and To boxes under Working Time.

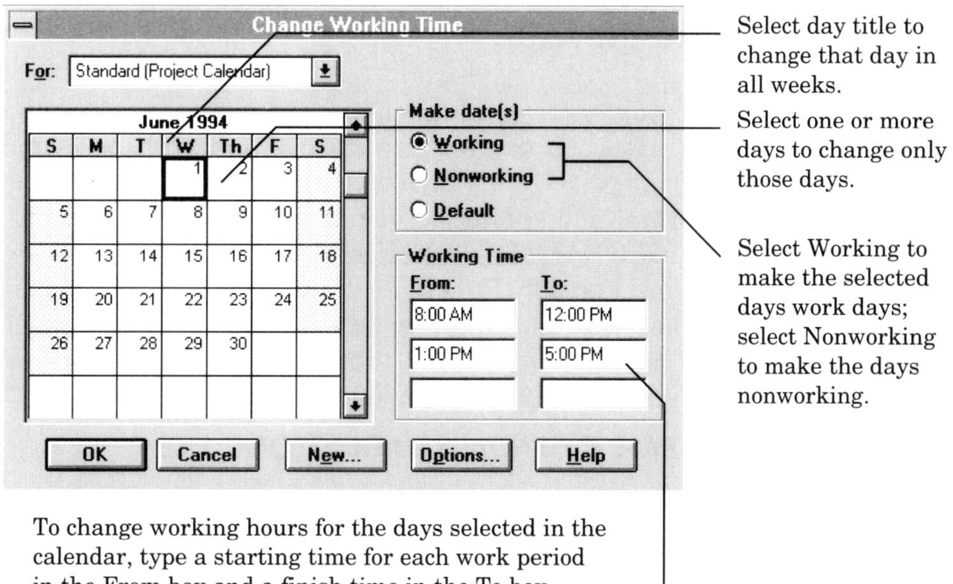

USING MULTIPLE BASE CALENDARS

In a project, you may have one base calendar, or you may have several. You can create as many base calendars as you need. For example, you can take a single base calendar and make variations of it to suit the schedules of different groups within the company. If you have three shifts working on a project, you can create three base calendars, one for each shift, and name each one appropriately, such as Day, Swing, and Graveyard. Or if one group of resources takes every other Friday off, create a base calendar just for that group. You specify the base calendar to use when you enter details about your resources.

If you plan to use multiple base calendars, first create one base calendar that is the most general—it should include the holidays and working days and hours that apply to most of the tasks and resources. You can create this calendar by editing the Standard calendar or by starting with a new calendar. Then copy this calendar, and change those parts that are different. For example, if you have three shifts, make the Day calendar first, and then copy the Day calendar, name it Swing, and change the working hours. The holidays and working days are carried over from the Day calendar.

For more information about creating calendars, see Chapter 16, "Using Microsoft Project Tools."

Saving Your Calendars

Each time you save, your calendars are automatically saved in the file with your project. If you want to use customized base calendars in other projects, or if you want a new calendar to become the default calendar for all future new projects, you can copy calendars into the global template: GLOBAL.MPT in Microsoft Project for Windows or Global Template in Microsoft Project for the Macintosh. The global template is the file that contains all the defaults used when you create a new project. It contains your views, tables, filters, calendars—everything you put there and want in a new project.

To Copy Base Calendars to the Global File

1. Choose View More Views.
2. Choose the Organizer button.
3. Select the Calendars tab.
4. On the project side, select the calendars you want to copy to the global template.
5. Choose the Copy button.
6. Choose Close.

By saving base calendars in the global template, you can make sure your new projects always start with the correct calendar. You can also use the Organizer to share calendars with others in your organization. If one group, such as personnel, has all the information on the working days and hours for your organization, they can create the base calendars and then make them available in a project file or global file on the network so everyone has access to the information. Everyone in the organization can use this file to ensure consistency within the organization.

Now that you know your goals for this project and have set up the calendars, the next step is to break the goals into the separate tasks needed to reach the goals.

4

Breaking Your Project into Tasks and Milestones

Okay. So, you have decided on your project goals. You stated the scope and assumptions. The next step is to break your project into the tasks that must be accomplished to meet these goals and to list the milestones that will help you track the project. Creating this list of tasks is a fundamental step in your plan because any task missing from the list won't be scheduled, making the plan invalid.

How do you determine what these tasks and milestones are? The best way is to have those who will do the work or manage the work take part in creating the list of tasks and milestones. Listing and organizing tasks and milestones requires the knowledge, skill, and experience of those responsible for and experienced in doing the work. Once you have your task list, you enter it into Microsoft Project.

But, just what is a task? And what is a milestone? And why do you need them in your project?

WHAT ARE TASKS AND MILESTONES?

Tasks are activities that must be finished to achieve the end result of the project. Milestones are checkpoints used to track your project. They represent the completion of a certain set of tasks or a certain portion of the project. For example, if your goal is to prepare a marketing plan, the tasks could include "Research competition" and "Perform cost analysis." A milestone might be "Research phase complete."

Since tasks and milestones provide the basis for the rest of your plan and for tracking the progress of your project, it is important that the task list be detailed and clear. You want tasks and milestones to be clearly worded and unambiguous so those using the plan know exactly what is expected as the result of each task.

TASKS

A task has an identifiable start and end; it usually requires people or equipment to complete it; and it is specific enough to permit both intermittent progress and the final result to be measured. For example, the task "Research competition" calls for one or more people to do the research. Progress on the task can be measured by comparing the number of competitors you plan to study with the number you have finished studying; you know when you are finished because you have studied all the competition.

Precise and Detailed Identify tasks as precisely as possible and in as much detail as necessary. Tasks should be detailed enough that the time to complete each one is short compared to the overall project. For example, if you plan to study six competitors in depth, you may want to break the "Research competition" task into six tasks, one for each competitor. This helps you make a more reliable estimate for the task duration (the time to complete the task) and the people and equipment needed to complete the task.

Significant Tasks must also be significant enough to be included in the plan. Insignificant or non-schedule related tasks only clutter your project task list. For example, in the "Research competition" task, the fact that you may go to the library to get financial information on competitors may be important in completing the task, but it is not significant enough to include as a separate task and does not affect how the tasks are scheduled.

Appropriate Level of Detail The level of detail in your list of tasks should be appropriate to the amount of planning and control you want. For example, if you are hiring an outside consultant to do a study, you are interested in when the consultant starts and when the study will be in your hands, but you aren't interested in the detailed tasks performed by the consultant. In your list of tasks, you would include one task for the study, showing the duration for the whole, rather than many tasks indicating each step in the study.

But if you are doing the study yourself, the separate steps in completing the study are crucial to you. Your list of tasks would include every step necessary to do the study.

Task Scope and Assumption Just as when you set your project goals, when you list your tasks and milestones you must be aware of the scope of the tasks and the assumptions on which the tasks and milestones are based. This helps you identify changes and measure progress.

Complete Be complete. Remember to include reports, reviews, and coordination activities in your list of tasks. And remember to include tasks for anticipated rework or modifications after a task has been completed, such as revising a manual or reworking and retesting a new product.

Naming Tasks Name a task using a verb and noun, such as "Build walls," "Install second floor phone outlets," or "Distribute design for review." Make the names as explicit as possible, and keep the style of the names consistent throughout. This consistency will help others understand each item in your schedule.

MILESTONES

A milestone is a task with a duration and cost of zero. Milestones help you measure the progress of your project and can increase motivation and productivity of those working on the tasks by providing interim goals. By placing your milestones appropriately, you keep track of the project schedule throughout its life, instead of being surprised when the project isn't on schedule at the end. Milestones help you catch scheduling problems early, enabling you to act to bring the project back on schedule.

Placement Usually you'll want to put a milestone at the start and end of a series of tasks so it stresses the importance of starting and completing the tasks by a certain time. For example, at the beginning of the Research phase, you could include the milestone "Research phase begins" and at the end, "Research phase complete."

Appropriate Level of Detail Since milestones serve as checkpoints to help you track the schedule throughout the project, include milestones only down to the level of detail you want to monitor. If it is not important to you when the Research phase starts, don't include the milestone.

Related to Tasks Be sure that milestones are related to tasks so you know when the milestone is achieved. For example, the milestone "Research phase complete" is directly related to the completion of the tasks preceding it. It will be obvious when you reach the milestone because the tasks in the Research phase will be complete. On the other hand, if you are writing the documentation for a new software product, the milestone "First testing release finished" won't tell you anything about the state of the documentation because it is not related to the writing tasks.

Events Outside Your Control Include milestones that represent events outside your control if they influence your schedule. For example, include a milestone showing when you must have a bank loan to be able to proceed with a building project. As you approach the milestone, you can check on the loan to assure it will be in your hands when it is needed. Or, include the milestone "First testing release finished" because, while it is not directly related to your writing tasks, you know that your milestone "First draft of manual finished" must follow the testing release by one month.

Identifying Milestones Milestones should be identified by the managers and workers who use them and must meet them. For example, if milestones are to help top management know how a project is progressing, these managers should take part in identifying milestones.

Naming Milestones Name a milestone in a way that it is clear when the milestone is reached. Use a noun and a verb, such as "Walls complete," "Funding request due," "Loans approved," or "Manuscript reviewed." Make the names as clear as possible. The style of the names should be consistent throughout. This consistency will help others understand each item in your schedule.

LISTING TASKS AND MILESTONES

To determine your list of tasks and milestones, you can use two basic methods:

- Top-down method—start with major project phases, and then complete the details for each phase.
- Bottom-up method—list all possible tasks, and then group the tasks into phases.

Use the method that best suits what you know about the project. For example, if you are planning a project that is new to you, such as creating a product using a new technology, you may not be able to use a bottom-up approach because you are not yet familiar with all the necessary tasks. Or you may use a combination of the two—a top-down approach to create the basic structure of the project, and then bottom-up to fill in that structure.

Whether you start with the major phases, or with the details, there are several ways you can generate your task list. For example, you can use brainstorming—a method in which members of a group spontaneously propose ideas and solutions—to identify major phases or detailed tasks. You can begin with the last milestone—the goal or purpose of the project—and work backward to the start of the project; or start with the present and work forward to the goal.

Whatever your approach, it is especially important that those involved in doing the work also participate in creating the task list. The schedule will be more accurate and the chances are increased that the project will be completed successfully and punctually. The team members understand the necessary tasks better than any single person can, and support for the project will be stronger because the team will have confidence in the list of tasks and the plan.

When you list your tasks, answer the following questions for each one:

- Does it have an identifiable start and finish?
- Is the scope of the task clear?
- Is it clear who or what organization is responsible for getting it done?
- Is it significant, is the level of detail appropriate, and does it clearly play a role in the schedule?

If the answer to any of these questions is "no," either break the task into more detailed tasks, or change the scope of the task. Or, if it is unimportant, do not include it.

TOP-DOWN METHOD

Using the top-down method, you identify the major phases first, and then identify the milestones and tasks within each phase. You continue breaking tasks into smaller and smaller units until you reach the level of detail you want.

One advantage of this approach is that you have a version of the plan, although not very detailed, as soon as you decide the major phases. Once you determine this top-level schedule, you can distribute the major phases to the appropriate managers and have them work with their teams to create the detailed schedules.

For example, suppose your project is to add a new calculator to your product line. The major phases might be Investigation, Design, Testing, Manufacturing, and Sales. The manager in charge of each phase can then work with the appropriate team members to create the individual task lists for each phase.

BOTTOM-UP METHOD

Using the bottom-up method, you list all the tasks and milestones, and then organize them into logical groupings or by work flow. For example, you could identify all tasks that would be performed by each department, such as all marketing department tasks to market a new product, all manufacturing tasks to manufacture a new product, and all procurement tasks to procure materials for a new product.

Since it may not be easy to know how the tasks from different departments are interrelated, this method works best to create the initial list of tasks for smaller projects that involve one department.

ORGANIZING TASKS AND MILESTONES

Organizing your tasks helps you make sure that the task list is complete and the flow of the tasks makes sense. There are a couple of tools you can use to organize the tasks. One is outlining; the other is a work breakdown structure.

OUTLINING

Using an outline makes the organization of the project obvious and helps you spot missing tasks or flaws in the logical flow of the tasks. It's a good way to organize your tasks and makes it easy to share the appropriate level of information with others.

You can create an outline using either the top-down or bottom-up method. Either way, the main outline headings are the main phases in your project. For example:

I Investigation Phase
II Design Phase
III Testing Phase
IV Manufacturing Phase
V Sales Phase

Under each main heading are the tasks that you must do to complete the phase. For example:

I Investigation Phase
 A) Prepare initial product proposal
 B) Set up focus panel
 C) Plan phone questionnaire
 D) Carry out focus panel
 E) and so on
II Design Phase
 A) Meet with marketing staff for report
 B) and so on
III Testing Phase

Under each task, you list the more detailed tasks that must be done to complete the task. For example:

I Investigation Phase
 A) Prepare initial product proposal
  1) Research competition
  2) Review customer comment cards
  3) and so on
 B) Set up focus panel

You continue filling in and indenting the more detailed tasks until you get to the level of detail you want.

When you want to share information about the project, you can share just the main phases or as much detail as required by the recipient of the information by showing as much of the outline as appropriate. For example, to top management, you might share the five main phases; to the marketing manager, you might share the five main phases, plus all the tasks in those phases in which the marketing staff is involved, such as the Investigation Phase and the Sales Phase.

WORK BREAKDOWN STRUCTURE

A work breakdown structure, or WBS, is a tree-type of structure that includes every task and every result. It looks like an organizational chart for your company but is task oriented instead of people oriented. Each level of the WBS depicts the project at a different level of detail; the higher the level on the WBS, the less detailed are the tasks. Usually, there are three to five levels, depending on the project.

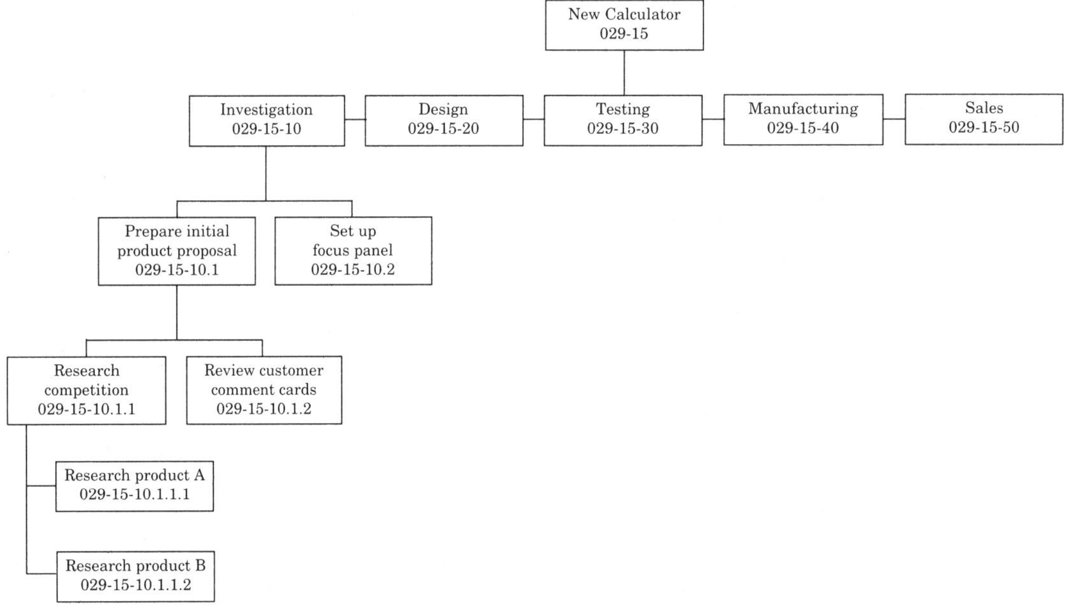

At the bottom or lowest level of a WBS is a *work package*; this is where the actual work is done and the resources are assigned. The characteristics of a work package are similar to those of a task. In the previous illustration, "Research product A" and "Research product B" are examples of work packages.

Each task is given a code number. This number shows the level of the task and where the task fits in the hierarchy. You can use these codes for sorting and filtering tasks to look at a limited part of the project information. For example, if a department code is part of the WBS code, you could filter the task list to display only those tasks that include a certain department code.

When you create a WBS, you start with the project goals and then divide and redivide tasks until you get to the level of detail you need. This assures that all required tasks are logically identified and grouped. In the previous illustration, the first divisions are by project phases, but they could be by work units (engineers, programmers, production line, and so on), financial cost codes, departments (marketing, accounting, lab, and so on), or major units of the product (if you are building a car, for example, the major units might be engine, transmission, body, suspension, and so on), depending on the organization of your project and company.

USING MICROSOFT PROJECT

Now that you have your list of tasks and milestones, you are ready to enter them into Microsoft Project. Of course, you can also brainstorm a list of tasks at the computer, entering them as they come to mind. If you do this, just be sure that you share this list with the rest of the team to get their input and to ensure the list is complete.

This section includes steps for entering tasks and milestones, organizing the tasks and milestones in either an outline or work breakdown structure, and then printing the list so you can check your work and share it with others.

Entering Tasks and Milestones

Entering tasks and milestones into Microsoft Project is easy. When you start Microsoft Project, you see a blank Gantt Chart. The first field is selected on the Gantt Chart, ready for you to type your first task.

You don't have to type a task number. Each task is numbered sequentially by Microsoft Project.

Entering a Task

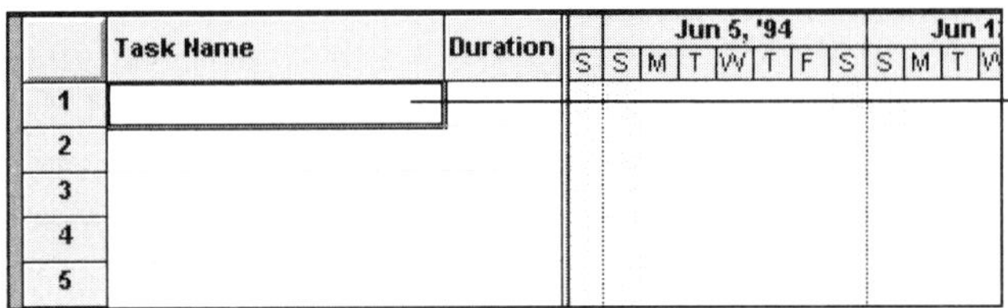

The first field is selected, ready for you to type a task name. Type the task name and press Enter.

After you press Enter, the next row is selected so you can type the next task.

Initially, all tasks are scheduled to occur simultaneously and have a duration of one day (1d).

Entering a Milestone

Entering a milestone is similar to entering a task, except you need to specify that it is a milestone by typing **0** (zero) in the Duration field.

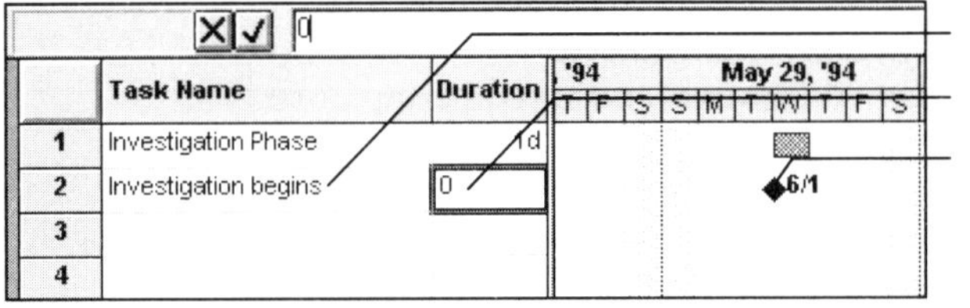

Type the milestone name.

In the Duration field, type **0**.

After you press Enter or click the enter button, the Gantt bar changes to a diamond to indicate a milestone.

You enter tasks and milestones on the Task Sheet in the same way.

Entering a Task on the PERT Chart

You can also enter tasks and milestones on the PERT Chart. Choose View PERT Chart. To create a task, drag diagonally with the mouse.

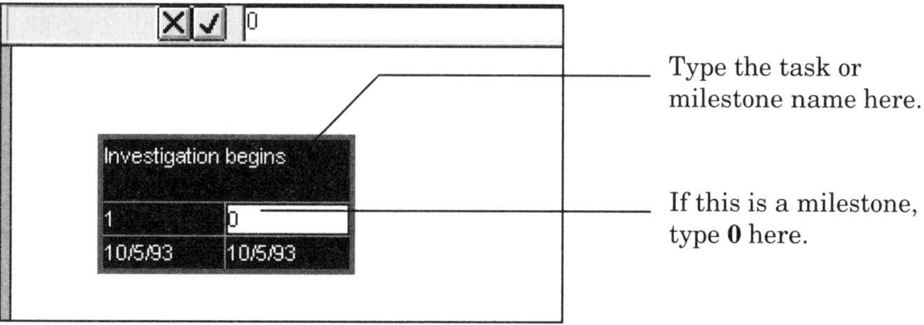

To enter another task, repeat the steps. To move tasks around so you can see all the tasks, either drag the node with the mouse or press Ctrl+direction key.

Tips for Entering Tasks

Saving Your Work Periodically as you work, you should save your project. To save, choose File Save. If PlanningWizards are on, the Save A Baseline? dialog box appears. Select the Save Without A Baseline option and choose OK. You'll save a baseline in Chapter 9, after your project is all set up. If this is the first time you've saved the project, the Save As dialog box appears, so you can name the project. Type the name and choose OK.

Changing Several Tasks to Milestones Simultaneously If you want to change several tasks to milestones, you can select all the tasks to be changed, and then click the Information button on the Standard toolbar or choose the Insert Task Information command. Type **0** in the Duration box. Choose OK.

Changing a Task with a Duration to a Milestone Although milestones usually have zero duration, in Microsoft Project you can make any task a milestone, even one with a duration other than zero. To do this, select all the tasks that will be milestones, and then click the Information button on the Standard toolbar or choose the Insert Task Information command. Select the Advanced tab and then select the Mark Task As Milestone check box. Choose OK.

Importing an Existing List of Tasks If you already have a list of tasks created in a spreadsheet or database program, such as Microsoft Excel, you can import this list into Microsoft Project. Microsoft Project can read files created in Microsoft Excel, Microsoft Access, dBase III and

IV, Lotus 1-2-3, and ASCII or other text file formats. For more information, see Chapter 15, "Sharing Information."

Changing the Default View The Gantt Chart is the default view displayed when you start Microsoft Project or open a project. If you prefer to use another view most of the time, such as the PERT Chart, you can change the default view. Choose Tools Options. On the View tab, select the view you want from the list in the Default View box. Choose OK.

Moving Tasks After you enter a list of tasks, you may need to move them around to organize them. Select the rows for the tasks you want to move and click the Cut button on the Standard toolbar or choose Edit Cut. Move to the new location, and click the Paste button or choose Edit Paste. Other ways to move or copy tasks include clicking the right mouse button in Windows, or Ctrl+click on the Macintosh, on a task to see the short cut menu, which includes Cut, Copy, and Paste, or using drag and drop to move the task. You can also use Microsoft Project's outlining feature to group the tasks and reorganize them.

Adding Cost Account Numbers If you have cost account numbers that you use for your tasks, you can add a column to the Gantt Chart or Task Sheet to enter these numbers. You use a custom field such as Text1 or Number1. Microsoft Project includes 10 custom text fields for tasks and 5 custom number fields for tasks. You can then sort and filter on this field to show the exact information you need. For more information about adding a column to a table, see Chapter 16, "Using Microsoft Project Tools."

Subprojects A subproject is a group of tasks that has its own project file, but is represented as a single task in another project. Use subprojects to keep the most detailed tasks in a project separate from the master project, or when you have similar sets of tasks that you perform in many projects. For more information, see Chapter 14, "Managing Multiple Projects."

Using a Project Template Use a project template when many of your projects have basically the same steps—such as construction jobs or similar types of publications done repeatedly. To create a template, open the project you want to use as a template or create a new project file. Choose the File Save As command, type a name for the file, and then, in the Save File As Type box, select Template. When you open this file, it is opened with all tasks in place, ready for you to name it and change the details. For more information, see Chapter 14, "Managing Multiple Projects."

PlanningWizard As you work, the PlanningWizard may appear and give you a tip about your work in Microsoft Project. For example, if you enter the same information three times, you may see a tip about using group entry. You can turn off these tips by choosing Tools Options. On the General tab, turn off all PlanningWizards by clearing the Advice From PlanningWizard check box, or turn on or off any of the three areas: using Microsoft Project, errors, or scheduling.

ORGANIZING TASKS AND MILESTONES

In Microsoft Project, you can organize your tasks using an outline or a work breakdown structure. When you create an outline, Microsoft Project also creates a WBS for you.

Outlining

Outlining is a powerful feature of Microsoft Project. You use outlining to:

- Enter and organize your tasks and milestones.
- Reorganize your task list by moving summary tasks (all their subordinate tasks move with them).
- Collapse and expand your task list to see different levels of detail.
- Present summary level information, including cost, work, and duration for the tasks.

In a Microsoft Project outline, tasks fall into two categories: summary tasks and subordinate tasks. A subordinate task or subtask is any indented or "demoted" task. A summary task:

- Has tasks indented beneath it.
- Summarizes cost, work, and duration of the indented tasks.

In Microsoft Project, an outline looks like this:

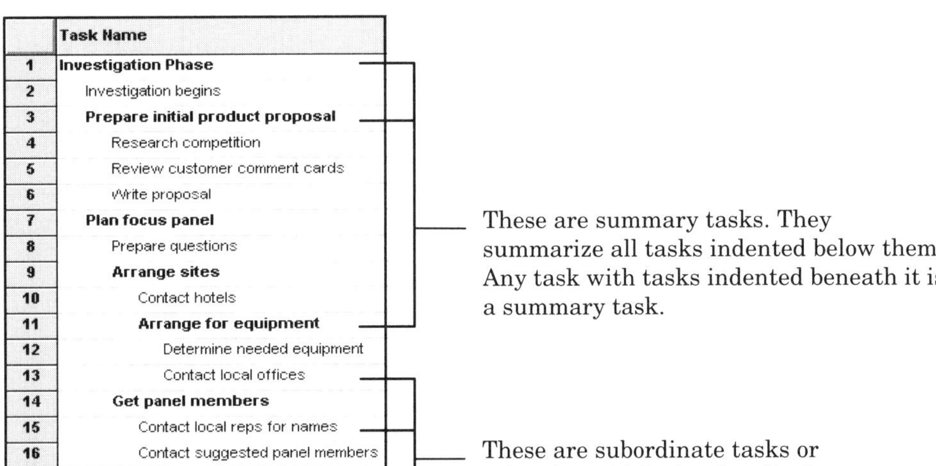

In the preceding illustration, tasks 2 through 21 are subordinate to task 1, "Investigation Phase." Several tasks—3, 7, 9, 11, and 17—are also summary tasks because they have tasks indented beneath them. In Microsoft Project, you can create up to 10 levels; a summary task can be at any level except 10.

You can create an outline using either the top-down method, in which you list the major phases first and then insert the more detailed tasks for each phase, or the bottom-up method, listing all the tasks first, and then grouping them into categories until you work your way to the major phases.

To create an outline, you just assign tasks or milestones to an outline level using the outline buttons at the left end of the Formatting toolbar, or the commands on the Tools Outlining submenu. You can also drag the task to the appropriate position in the outline. Microsoft Project indents, or "demotes," the task or milestone to show its outline level.

In Microsoft Project, you can outline on the Gantt Chart or Task Sheet.

Creating an Outline Using the Top-down Method The following illustrations show how to create an outline using the top-down method, listing major phases first, and then adding the details.

	Task Name	Duration
1	Investigation Phase	1d
2	Design Phase	1d
3	Testing Phase	1d
4	Manufacturing Phase	1d
5	Sales Phase	1d
6		

Type all the major phases in your project. These will all be summary tasks.

To insert tasks under a phase name, select the number of rows you want to insert, starting with the row below which you want to insert.

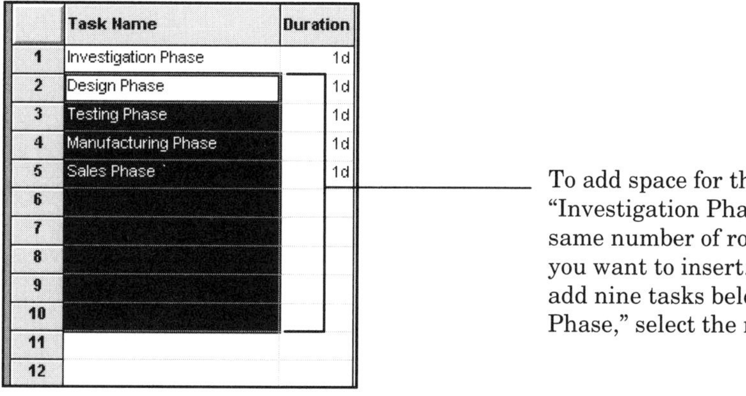

To add space for the tasks under "Investigation Phase," select the same number of rows as tasks that you want to insert. For example, to add nine tasks below "Investigation Phase," select the nine rows below it.

Choose Insert Insert Task or press Ins.

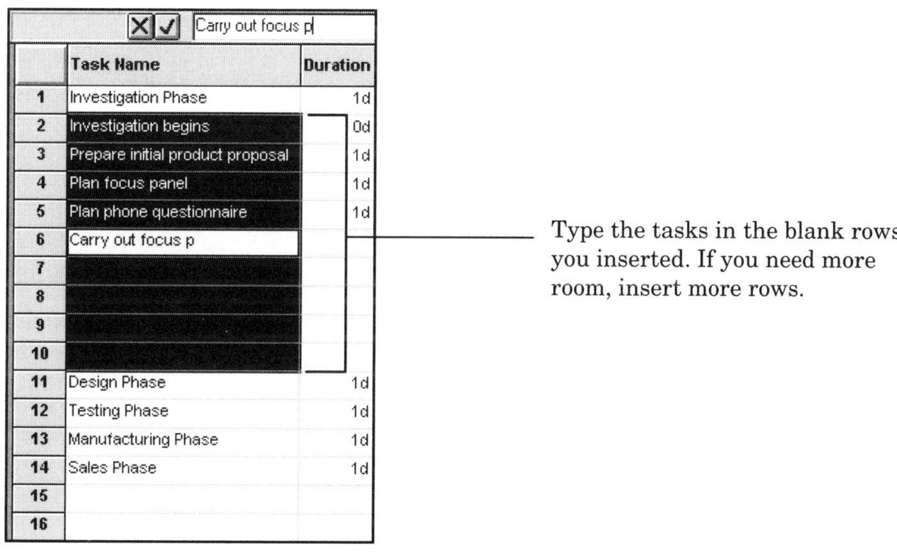

Type the tasks in the blank rows you inserted. If you need more room, insert more rows.

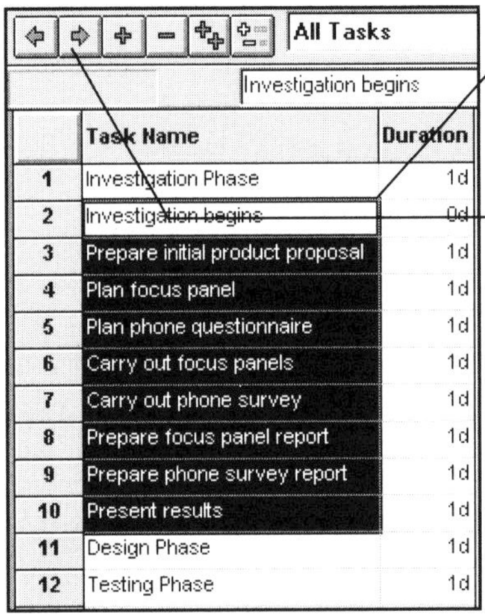

	Task Name	Duration
1	Investigation Phase	1d
2	Investigation begins	0d
3	Prepare initial product proposal	1d
4	Plan focus panel	1d
5	Plan phone questionnaire	1d
6	Carry out focus panels	1d
7	Carry out phone survey	1d
8	Prepare focus panel report	1d
9	Prepare phone survey report	1d
10	Present results	1d
11	Design Phase	1d
12	Testing Phase	1d

Select all the tasks you just typed so you can indent them under the summary task "Investigation Phase."

To indent the tasks, click the Indent button.

You can also demote tasks using the mouse. Point to the left end of the task name. When the pointer changes to a two-headed arrow pointing left and right, hold down the mouse button and drag the task to indent it or outdent it.

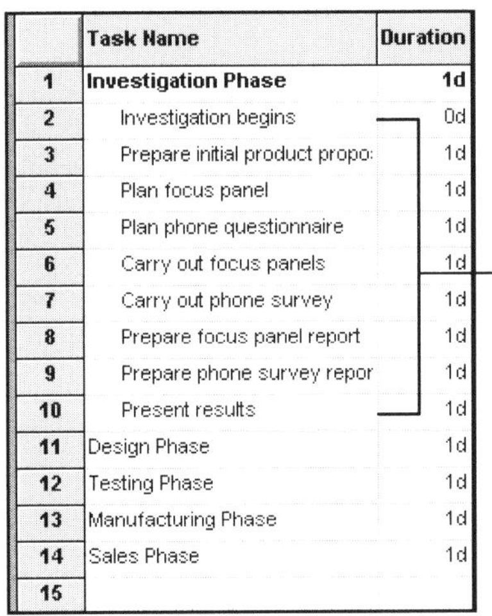

	Task Name	Duration
1	**Investigation Phase**	**1d**
2	Investigation begins	0d
3	Prepare initial product propo:	1d
4	Plan focus panel	1d
5	Plan phone questionnaire	1d
6	Carry out focus panels	1d
7	Carry out phone survey	1d
8	Prepare focus panel report	1d
9	Prepare phone survey repor	1d
10	Present results	1d
11	Design Phase	1d
12	Testing Phase	1d
13	Manufacturing Phase	1d
14	Sales Phase	1d
15		

The detailed tasks are now indented under their summary task, "Investigation Phase."

You can continue adding and indenting subordinate tasks where appropriate under each task.

If you do not see the indentation, choose Tools Options. On the View tab, select the Indent Name check box under Outline Options. To select or clear the check box, click the check box with the mouse.

Creating an Outline Using the Bottom-up Method If you have already listed all your tasks, you can create an outline by grouping them, adding the summary tasks, and then demoting the subordinate tasks. To insert space for summary tasks, follow the steps described in the top-down method for adding space for tasks and typing the tasks. Then, again as described in the top-down method, you select and demote the subordinate tasks.

Summary Task Durations The duration for a summary task is the total work time between the earliest start date and latest finish date of the subordinate tasks and is calculated using the project calendar.

Outline Buttons Don't Work? Since outline buttons work only when the Gantt Chart or Task Sheet is the active view, first confirm you are using one of these views. If you are using the Gantt Chart or Task Sheet and the outline buttons don't work, check the following:

- Choose Tools Options/View tab and make sure the Show Summary Tasks check box under Outline Options is selected.
- Choose Tools Sort/Sort By. If it is not sorted by ID, either select ID in the Sort By box or select the Keep Outline Structure check box to maintain the outline structure in the sorted project, and choose the Sort button.

Reorganizing Your Outline Once you have created your outline, it's easy to reorganize your project. When you move a summary task, all its subordinate tasks go with it. If you delete a summary task, all its subordinate tasks are deleted too.

Collapsing and Expanding Your Outline You can collapse an outline to show just the summary tasks and then expand all or part of the outline to see the level of detail you want. For example, the following illustration shows the outline collapsed to show just the highest level summary tasks, and then the "Investigation Phase" task expanded to show one level of subordinate tasks.

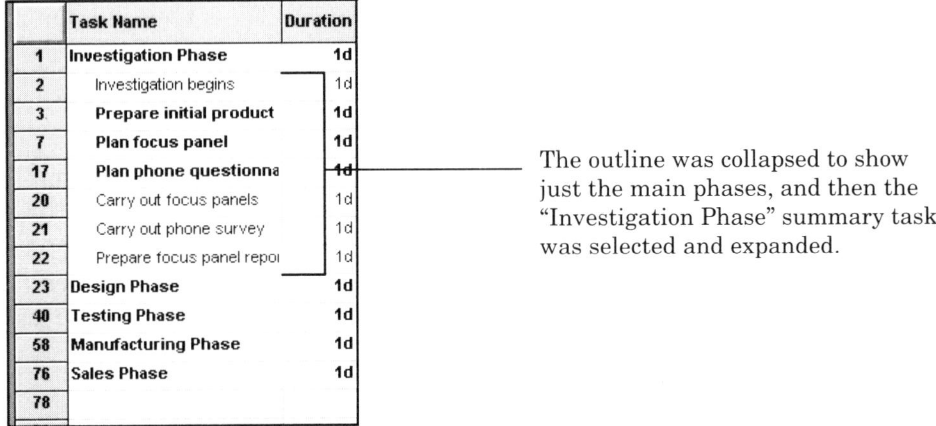

	Task Name	Duration
1	Investigation Phase	1d
2	Investigation begins	1d
3	Prepare initial product	1d
7	Plan focus panel	1d
17	Plan phone questionna	1d
20	Carry out focus panels	1d
21	Carry out phone survey	1d
22	Prepare focus panel repoı	1d
23	Design Phase	1d
40	Testing Phase	1d
58	Manufacturing Phase	1d
76	Sales Phase	1d
78		

The outline was collapsed to show just the main phases, and then the "Investigation Phase" summary task was selected and expanded.

When you collapse a summary task, its subordinate tasks are hidden. When you expand a summary task, the next level of subordinate tasks is displayed. You can collapse and expand parts of your outline to show exactly the information you want, in as much or as little detail as appropriate.

To collapse a summary task, select the task and click the Hide Subtasks button on the Formatting toolbar or choose Tools Outlining/Hide Subtasks.

To expand a summary task and show its subtasks, select the summary task and click the Show Subtasks button on the Formatting toolbar or choose Tools Outlining/Show Subtasks. To expand all summary tasks and show all subtasks, click the Show All Tasks button or choose Tools Outlining/Show All Tasks.

You can also double-click a summary task to switch between collapsed and expanded. Double-click an expanded summary task to collapse it; double-click a collapsed summary task to expand it.

Adding Numbers and Symbols to Your Outline You can add numbers to your outline as well as plus and minus symbols to indicate whether a task is a summary task.

	Task Name
1	**1 Investigation Phase**
2	1.1 Investigation begins
3	**1.2 Prepare initial product proposal**
4	1.2.1 Research competition
5	1.2.2 Review customer comment cards
6	1.2.3 Write proposal
7	**1.3 Plan focus panel**
8	1.3.1 Prepare questions
9	**1.3.2 Arrange sites**
10	1.3.2.1 Contact hotels
11	**1.3.2.2 Arrange for equipment**
12	1.3.2.2.1 Determine needed equipment
13	1.3.2.2.2 Contact local offices
14	**1.3.3 Get panel members**
15	1.3.3.1 Contact local reps for names
16	1.3.3.2 Contact suggested panel members
17	**1.4 Plan phone questionnaire**
18	1.4.1 Prepare questionnaire

The numbers show the position of the task within the outline. They are assigned by Microsoft Project.

The plus means the task is a summary task, with subtasks beneath it.

The minus means the task is not a summary task.

To add numbers on your outline, choose Tools Options, and then select the View tab. Under Outline Options, select the Show Outline Number check box. To add symbols on the outline, select the Show Outline Symbol check box. You can also click the Outline Symbols button on the Formatting toolbar to show symbols.

Work Breakdown Structure

If you want to enter your project in a work breakdown structure format, use Microsoft Project's outlining feature. Microsoft Project numbers each task and milestone for you when you create an outline, and collapses and expands the outline based on these numbers to allow you to see the various levels of detail.

You can view these outline numbers in the WBS Code box on the Advanced tab in the Task Information dialog box. The Task Details Form (choose View More Views and then Task Details Form) also includes the WBS Code box. If you have a WBS coding system you want to use in addition to Microsoft Project's outline numbers, you can replace the number in the WBS Code box. Microsoft Project still retains the outline number it assigned to the tasks, using these numbers to collapse and expand the outline.

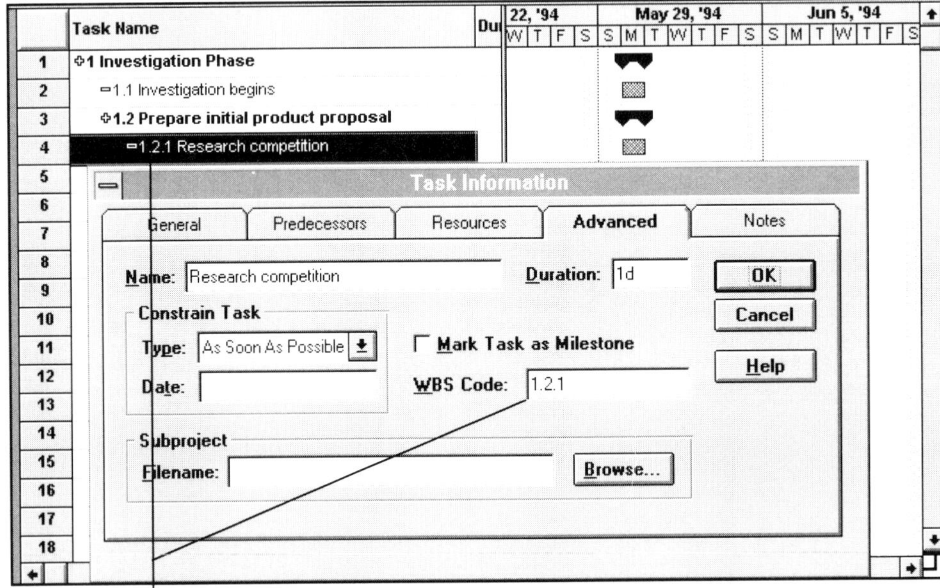

The number in the WBS Code box matches the number in the outline. To enter your own WBS code number, type it in the box.

You can also enter WBS codes for your tasks by adding the WBS field to the Task Sheet. Type the WBS code in the WBS field as you enter your tasks.

You do not have to create an outline to use a WBS coding system. However, if you want to be able to use the outlining features, such as collapsing and expanding the task list to see the levels of detail, the hierarchy in your WBS coding system should match the outline hierarchy. Despite the WBS number you enter, the tasks must be entered at the appropriate level in the outline. All tasks at the same level in the WBS should be entered at one level in the outline.

Use the WBS code to sort and filter tasks. For example, you can filter the task list to display only those tasks that have a WBS code for a certain department, or, if your coding system indicates processes, filter the tasks to see all tasks associated with one process.

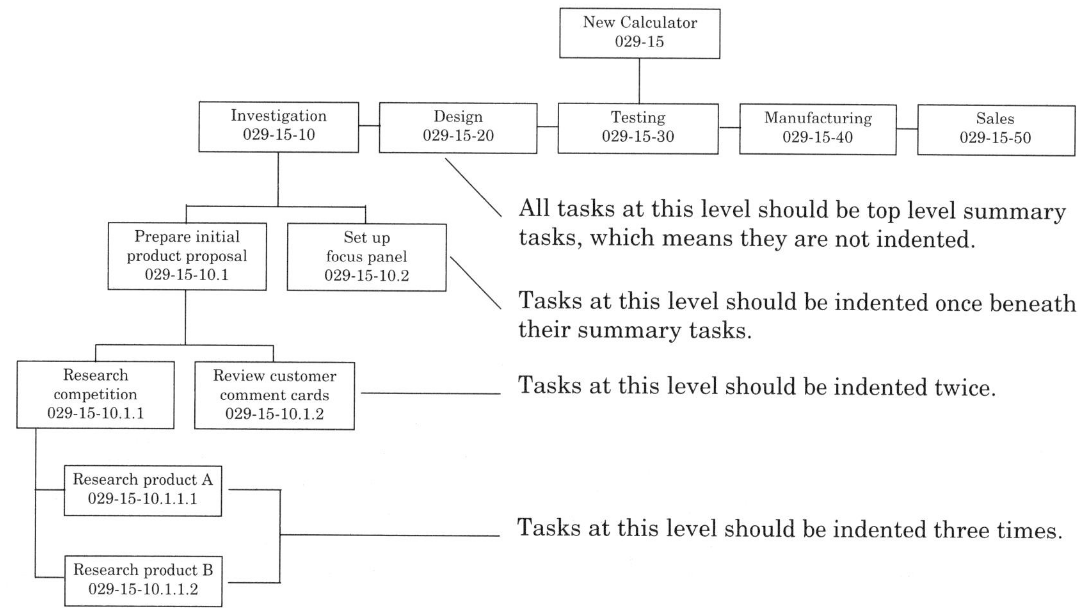

Saving Your List of Tasks

When using computer software, it is always smart to save your work frequently. You never know when a power failure will cause you to lose your work and cause you great frustration.

To Save Your Work

1. Click the Save button on the Standard toolbar or choose File Save.
2. The PlanningWizard will ask if you want to save a baseline for your project. Since you aren't to that point in your plans (you'll save a baseline in Chapter 9), select the Save Without A Baseline option and choose OK.
3. Type a name for the file and then choose OK.

Printing Your List of Tasks

To review the information you have entered into Microsoft Project, print the Task Sheet. If you have included WBS codes and want to check them, add the WBS field to the Task Sheet before you print it. For information about adding a column, see Chapter 16, "Using Microsoft Project Tools."

To Print the Task Sheet

1. Choose View More Views.
2. In the Views box, select Task Sheet.
3. Choose the Apply button or press Enter.
4. Click the Print button on the Standard toolbar, or choose File Print and then choose OK.

Before You Print In Microsoft Project for Windows, be sure the appropriate printer is selected in the File Print dialog box and that the options for the printer are what you want. In Microsoft Project for the Macintosh, be sure the appropriate printer is selected in the Chooser. For more information, see the chapter on printing in your systems manual. You may also want to check and change the settings in the File Page Setup dialog box. These settings control margins, text at the top and bottom of each page, and the style of the text. For more information, see Chapter 10, "Communicating the Plan."

Sharing the List of Tasks You can copy and share the printed Task Sheet with others on the team. Or, if your company uses Microsoft Mail, you can send the project in electronic mail. If Microsoft Mail is already on your computer when you install Microsoft Project, the Send command and the Add Routing Slip command are added to the File menu. Use the File Send command to send your project to any group of people; use File Add Routing Slip when you want to route the project sequentially and to track the status of the routing, although you can also choose to send to all at once.

The next step in the planning process is to estimate the duration for each task and enter the durations into Microsoft Project.

5

Estimating Time to Perform Tasks

To start molding your list of tasks into a working schedule, your next step is to determine how long each task will take. The more accurately you can estimate this task duration, the better your schedule will be. If your tasks are detailed and precise, estimating time to perform the tasks will be easier and the results more accurate.

Task duration is the time between the start of the task and the finish of the task. Since the schedule calculations and costs are based on these time estimates, they must be as accurate as possible. It takes time to analyze each task, but it saves time down the line because you'll have a better understanding of your schedule—which will help you analyze changes that may occur later.

Since the time estimates for tasks have a tremendous impact on your schedule and on how successfully you meet your end date, encourage those involved in estimating tasks to be realistic. Optimistic estimates can ensure failure because you cannot make the dates. Pessimistic estimates can mean that tasks finish more quickly than expected, causing problems for tasks that follow; supplies, equipment, and other resources may not be scheduled or available because they are not required by the plan until a future time. Pessimistic estimates can also mean not getting contracts because the final dates in your schedule are unacceptable.

While you do your best to come up with accurate estimates based on the information you have about each task, it is important for everyone, including management, to remember that these are estimates. There is a chance that any task will finish either early or late because you can't possibly foresee how each task will actually progress. This is one of the main reasons for including the assumptions you made when estimating durations.

Those who are knowledgeable about a task should estimate task duration. These are the same people who were involved in determining the tasks. For example, you can ask two or three people to estimate how long tasks will take, and then talk to those who will actually perform the tasks. If those who will do the work are uncomfortable about the estimates, meet with all those involved to reach a compromise. Using this method, you avoid an estimate that is either too optimistic because the worker is trying to give you what you want, or too conservative because the worker wants to look good by finishing early.

By having those who do the work involved in estimating the duration, you will have more accurate estimates, more support for the plan (they decided on it), a greater chance of success (they feel responsible to meet the schedule and live up to their own estimates), and higher morale (they feel in control of their work environment).

When you estimate durations, use these guidelines:

DO

- Consider each task independently of other tasks.
- Remember the scope of work described by the task and the assumptions made when the task was included in the task list.
- Consider the most likely experience level of those who will perform the task.
- Estimate time in the unit—minutes, hours, days, or weeks—appropriate to the task.
- Assume normal working conditions, so if you need to speed up the schedule, you have room to do so.
- Be as realistic as possible, which makes you and the schedule believable.

DON'T

- Don't consider resource availability when you estimate duration (Microsoft Project will help you take care of this later).
- Don't consider the target finish date for the project when figuring task estimates (after seeing the schedule, you can decide what to shorten if your schedule is too long).

- Don't schedule "tight" to force people to work harder (they generally won't and it hurts morale).
- Don't allow management to determine the time estimates (they can't estimate as accurately as those who do the work).
- Don't include extra time for a cushion (estimate as accurately as possible so your duration estimates will be trusted).

After you estimate the durations, you enter them into Microsoft Project and note any assumptions you made for each task duration. You also indicate one of two scheduling methods for each task: either the duration changes when you change the number of resources assigned, or the duration remains fixed at the original duration you entered.

DETERMINING DURATION

Pinning down the time to perform a task is tricky because you are trying to predict the future based on whatever assumptions about the task you can make today. But there are three ways that may help you and those who are estimating the durations make more accurate estimates. You can base your estimates on history, on your experience, or on the weighted average of three estimates—an optimistic time, pessimistic time, and most likely time.

ESTIMATING DURATIONS BASED ON HISTORY

The best way to make a good estimate is to look at how long similar tasks took on past projects. When you use historical data, note any differences between the new task and similar tasks in the past. Be sure to take these differences into account when you estimate the duration for the current task.

Keeping task history to use as a basis for future projects is a side benefit of tracking the progress of your projects. If you keep track of every task to the end of a project, you'll have an accurate record of actual task durations, as well as other historical data.

ESTIMATING DURATIONS BASED ON YOUR EXPERIENCE

In this method, you make an estimate based on how long the task would take you to do. If you are very experienced, you can assume it would take the average worker longer to do the task; if you are not experienced, you can assume the task would be done faster by an average worker. Those intimately familiar with the task are the best people to use this method.

ESTIMATING DURATIONS BASED ON THREE ESTIMATES

When you use this method, you estimate three durations—optimistic time, pessimistic time, and most likely time—for each task. The duration you use in the schedule is then calculated based on the formula used in the PERT scheduling method, as follows:

Duration = (O+4*L+P)/6

where O = optimistic time, which occurs 5% of the time

L = most likely time

P = pessimistic time, which occurs 5% of the time

This method can be time-consuming, but may help you estimate time for tasks when you have little or no previous experience.

The PERT Method The PERT scheduling method was created by Lockheed and the US Navy for projects where there was much uncertainty. This is not the scheduling method used by Microsoft Project, and is not related to the PERT Chart in Microsoft Project. But, using this equation can help you estimate durations in special cases.

USING MICROSOFT PROJECT

There are three pieces of information you enter for each task:

- Duration estimate
- Notes about the assumptions you made when estimating duration
- Scheduling method

ENTERING DURATIONS

When you type a duration in Microsoft Project, you type a number followed by the duration unit. You can type the duration in minutes, hours, days, or weeks or elapsed minutes, hours, days, or weeks. If you don't type a unit, Microsoft Project uses the default unit. Initially, this is days. To change the default unit, choose Tools Options. On the Schedule tab, change the unit in the Show Duration In box and choose OK.

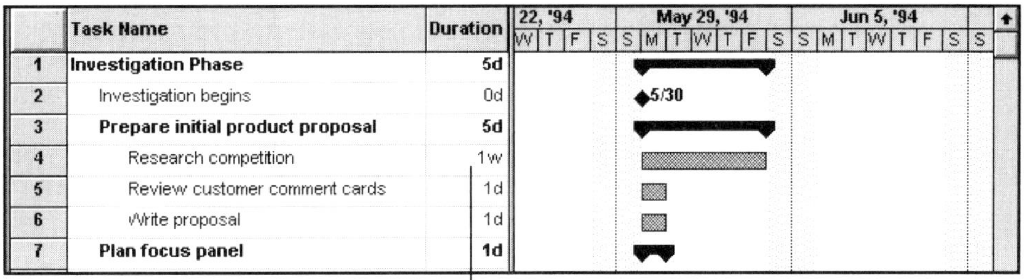

	Task Name	Duration
1	**Investigation Phase**	**5d**
2	Investigation begins	0d
3	**Prepare initial product proposal**	**5d**
4	Research competition	1w
5	Review customer comment cards	1d
6	Write proposal	1d
7	**Plan focus panel**	**1d**

Type the duration here and then press Enter or click the enter button.

If you want to show a duration unit other than the default units (initially days), type one of the following abbreviations after the duration estimate.

Unit	Abbreviation	Elapsed unit	Abbreviation
Minutes	m	Elapsed minutes	em
Hours	h	Elapsed hours	eh
Days	d	Elapsed days	ed
Weeks	w	Elapsed weeks	ew

Use elapsed time instead of working time when the passing of a certain amount of time is important. For example, use elapsed duration to reflect the number of continuous hours needed for concrete to cure until it is usable.

Elapsed duration is based on 24 hours a day rather than the working hours in a day. A duration of 1d may represent 8 working hours (the initial setting for the Hours Per Day option on the Calendar tab in the Tools Options dialog box), while a duration of 1ed represents 24 consecutive hours.

Using Microsoft Excel to Generate Duration Estimates If you decide to estimate durations based on the average of three estimates, you can set up a Microsoft Excel worksheet to do the calculations for you. The details of this procedure start on page 327 in Chapter 15, "Sharing Information."

NOTING TASK ASSUMPTIONS

It's a good idea to keep track of all assumptions made when estimating durations. In Microsoft Project, you can include notes for each task by choosing the Insert Task Notes command or clicking the Attach Note button on the Standard toolbar, and then typing the note in the Notes box. When you include assumptions with each task, they are always handy to refresh your memory about what you expected to happen when you estimated the duration, and to help you analyze why a task is taking more or less time than estimated.

Click the Attach Note button on the Standard toolbar or choose Insert Task Notes.

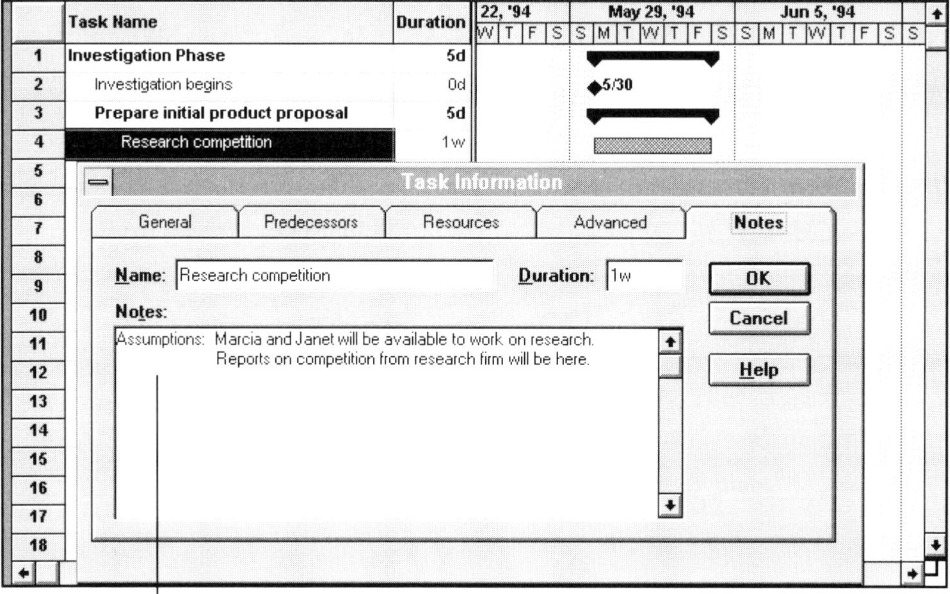

Type notes here for the selected task.

MICROSOFT PROJECT SCHEDULING METHODS

Microsoft Project offers two ways to schedule task duration. One method is called resource-driven scheduling: the duration is recalculated if you change the number of resource units or the amount of work for a group of resources assigned to the task. Use this method when you want duration to change with the number of resource units assigned to a task. Microsoft Project uses resource-driven scheduling unless you specify otherwise.

In the other method—fixed-duration scheduling—Microsoft Project does not change the duration regardless of how many resource units you enter. To schedule your project as realistically as possible, use the method best suited to each task.

Use resource-driven scheduling for tasks where adding resources will shorten the duration. For example:

- Three painters might be able to paint a building in one-third the time one painter can.
- A landscape crew of four might do twice the work of a crew of two in a day.
- If you double the size of the marketing staff, you expect the research on the competition to be finished in half the time.
- If you have three teams presenting a new product to clients instead of one team, you can reach all the clients in one-third the time.

Use fixed-duration scheduling for those tasks that will not be shorter, no matter how many resources are assigned. For example, assigning more resources won't speed up concrete curing nor help you drive faster from Seattle to Portland. Time for reviewing a marketing plan is also fixed, since regardless of the number of reviewers, they all have the same amount of time, such as one week.

If you are not assigning resources to tasks, you don't have to pick a scheduling method. Microsoft Project will use the durations you enter and will not recalculate them.

SPECIFYING THE SCHEDULING METHOD

To change the scheduling method for an individual task, use the Duration Type box on the Resources tab in the Task Information dialog box. The default scheduling method is resource driven. Specify a scheduling method only if the default method is not what you want for this task.

Select the task whose scheduling method you want to change. Click the Information button on the Standard toolbar or choose Insert Task Information. Click the Resources tab.

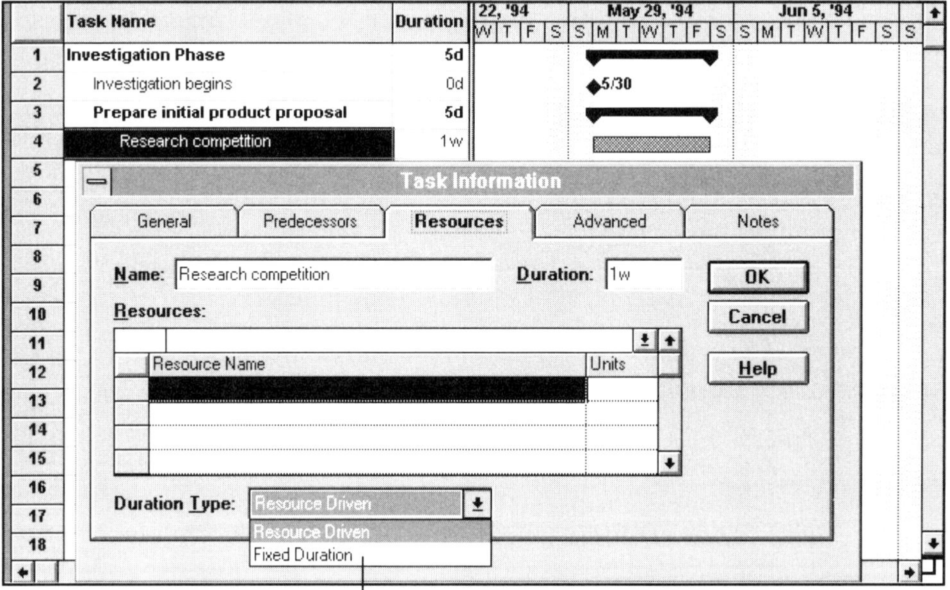

To use fixed-duration scheduling, select Fixed Duration in the Duration Type box.

You can also add the Fixed field to the Task Sheet. This field contains "Yes" if the task uses fixed-duration scheduling and "No" if the task uses resource-driven scheduling.

Changing the Scheduling Method for Several Tasks If many of your tasks have fixed durations, you can use the Resources tab in the Multiple Task Information dialog box to simultaneously change them all to fixed. To do this, select all tasks for which you want a fixed duration, and then click the Information button on the Standard toolbar or choose

Insert Task Information. Select the Resources tab. In the Duration Type box, select Fixed Duration, and then choose OK.

Changing the Default Scheduling Method If you want to use fixed-duration scheduling for most tasks, you can change the default method of scheduling using the Tools Options command. Choose Tools Options and select the Schedule tab. In the Default Duration Type box, select the default scheduling method you want, and then choose OK.

Changing the Hours per Day and Week Used for Calculations When Microsoft Project schedules tasks, it converts the durations you enter to hours, using the values in the Hours Per Day and Hours Per Week options on the Calendar tab in the Tools Options dialog box. Initially, these are set to 8 hours per day and 40 hours per week. If you work 12 hours per day, for example, change the Hours Per Day option to reflect this so Microsoft Project will schedule the appropriate amount of work each day.

VIEWING AND PRINTING THE SCHEDULE

Look at the Gantt Chart (choose View Gantt Chart). All tasks now include the estimated duration and the Gantt bars reflect those durations.

	Task Name	Duration	May 29, '94 / Jun 5, '94 / Jun 1
1	**Investigation Phase**	**20d**	
2	Investigation begins	0d	5/30
3	**Prepare initial product proposal**	**5d**	
4	Research competition	1w	
5	Review customer comment cards	3d	
6	Write proposal	1w	
7	**Plan focus panel**	**5d**	
8	Prepare questions	1w	
9	**Arrange sites**	**1d**	
10	Contact hotels	1d	
11	**Arrange for equipment**	**0.5d**	
12	Determine needed equipment	4h	
13	Contact local offices	4h	
14	**Get panel members**	**2d**	
15	Contact local reps for names	1d	
16	Contact suggested panel members	2d	
17	**Plan phone questionnaire**	**3d**	
18	Prepare questionnaire	3d	
19	Get list of users to call	2h	

Because the relationships between tasks have not yet been entered, all tasks are scheduled to start as soon as possible.

If you want to check your list of tasks and durations, and share this information with others, print the Task Sheet. If you have Microsoft Mail, you can also send the project through electronic mail.

TO PRINT THE TASK SHEET

1. Choose View More Views.
2. In the Views box, select Task Sheet.
3. Choose the Apply button or press Enter.
4. Click the Print button on the Standard toolbar, or choose File Print and then choose OK.

Use this printed information to help determine the order of the tasks and to analyze task relationships in the next chapter.

6

Making Tasks Happen at the Right Time

You have set your goals, listed the tasks, and estimated how long each task should take. But, all the tasks are still scheduled to start simultaneously. The next step in scheduling your project is to determine the sequence of tasks, how the tasks are related to one another, and if they are tied to certain dates or deadlines. Getting the work done at the right time is just as important as ensuring your task list is complete.

There are four pieces of information you can specify for each task so it will be scheduled at the right time. You can specify:

- Task sequence—which tasks must happen before or after each task
- Task relationship—how tasks are related to other tasks
- Lead or lag time—if you want an overlap or delay between two tasks
- Constraint—that a task must start or finish on, before, or after a certain date

Together, this information is referred to as *task dependencies*. When you have decided this information for each task, you enter it into Microsoft Project.

DECIDING TASK SEQUENCE

The first thing to do is decide the sequence of the tasks. To decide the sequence, answer the following questions for each task or group of tasks.

- Which tasks does this task depend on? For example, which tasks must finish before this task can start?
- Which tasks depend on this task? For example, which tasks cannot start until this task starts or finishes?

A task that another task depends on—for example, one that must be finished before another task can start—is called a *predecessor task*. A task that depends on another task—for example, one that cannot start until another task is finished—is called a *successor task*.

When deciding the predecessor tasks, list only those tasks that a task directly depends on. For example, because you must build walls before you can paint them, building walls is a predecessor to painting walls. But, although the building must be designed before the walls can be painted, the design task is not an immediate predecessor to painting. Designing the building is an immediate predecessor to, for example, starting construction. When you list predecessors, think only of those tasks that directly affect the task.

DETERMINING RELATIONSHIPS BETWEEN TASKS

Now that you know the sequence of the tasks, the next step is to decide how tasks are related. Tasks may not have to follow sequentially such that the predecessor finishes before the successor starts. Perhaps two tasks can be worked on simultaneously, either starting or finishing at the same time.

The following list shows the four ways that two tasks can be related. The illustration for each relationship type shows how the bars for that relationship look on the Gantt Chart.

Finish-to-start The start of the successor task depends on the finish of its predecessor. When one task must follow another task, use a finish-to-start relationship. For example, a marketing proposal cannot be reviewed until it is finished, so you would want a finish-to-start relationship between the two tasks—the "Prepare marketing proposal" task must finish before "Distribute proposal for review" can start.

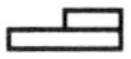

Finish-to-finish The finish of the successor task depends on the finish of its predecessor. Use a finish-to-finish relationship when you want two tasks to finish simultaneously. For example, if you are building a house and want the landscaping to be finished when the interior decorating is finished, you could use a finish-to-finish relationship between "Decorate interior" and "Landscape exterior."

Start-to-start The start of the successor task depends on the start of its predecessor. A start-to-start relationship is useful when tasks can start simultaneously. For example, you may want materials procurement to begin while the design drawings are finalized. Use a start-to-start relationship between "Prepare final drawings" and "Procure materials."

Start-to-finish The finish of the successor task depends on the start of its predecessor. A start-to-finish relationship is seldom used, but is included in the software so every possible relationship is available.

Use the relationship that most accurately reflects the way you will do the work. In many projects, tasks do not have to follow one another sequentially using finish-to-start relationships. Finish-to-start relationships may make the schedule longer than necessary and may not use time and resources as efficiently as possible. If two tasks can be worked on simultaneously, be sure to schedule them that way.

INDICATING OVERLAP OR DELAY BETWEEN TASKS

When analyzing task relationships, you might have noticed situations in which, although it was not appropriate to have the two tasks start or finish at the same time, the tasks could be worked on simultaneously. They could be overlapped. Or you might want two tasks to be staggered so there is a delay between the finish of a task and the start of its successor. To show overlap or delay between tasks, use lead or lag time.

Suppose you are conducting a market survey. You start compiling data before all results are in, but you cannot finish until after the completion of the market survey. The most appropriate relationship between the two tasks may be finish-to-start, but with lead time so the successor task "Compile survey results" starts before the predecessor "Conduct market survey" is finished. The Gantt bars would look like this:

Or perhaps, since you compile results as you go, the best relationship is finish-to-finish, with a one-day lag time between the finish of the predecessor "Conduct market survey," and the successor "Compile survey results" because you know it will take one day after the last survey day to finish compiling results. The Gantt bars would look like this:

Maybe you want to allow time for a mail survey to be returned before you compile results. Here, the most appropriate relationship might again be finish-to-start, but with a one-month lag between the end of the predecessor "Mail survey" and the beginning of the successor "Compile survey results." The Gantt bars would look like this:

Suppose you can start painting the walls after half the walls are built. These two tasks would have a finish-to-start relationship, but with a 50 percent overlap or lead time. The Gantt bars would look like this :

Or you might use lag time when you want to wait for the paint to dry before laying carpet. Again, the tasks would have a finish-to-start relationship, but with a one-day waiting period between the finish of "Paint walls" and the start of "Lay carpet." The Gantt bars would look like this:

Using lag and lead time can shorten the schedule and make it more efficient. Check your task list for tasks that can be overlapped to use time most efficiently. Again, think about how tasks actually will be done; if there are tasks that can start before their predecessors are finished, make the schedule reflect this.

SETTING A START OR FINISH DATE FOR A TASK

When you use project scheduling software, tasks are scheduled based on the task sequence and relationships you enter. Sometimes, though, you want a task to happen at a certain time. If you have a task that is tied to a certain start or finish date, you can specify that this date be used instead of the start or finish date calculated by the software.

When you tie a task to a certain date, you are placing a constraint on the task and restricting its start or finish date. This date is a *constraint date*; it may conflict with dates calculated for the task by the scheduling software, so use constraint dates carefully and not arbitrarily.

For example, if you specify that a task must start on a certain date, and its predecessors are scheduled to finish two weeks earlier, you may end up with two weeks of dead time; conversely, a must-start-on date may not allow enough time for predecessors to finish before the constraint date.

If starting or finishing a task on a certain date is necessary for a satisfactory outcome of the project, use the constraint, and adjust the scheduling of the predecessors so the schedule will work out; if it is unnecessary, delete the constraint.

The following list shows the types of constraints you can place on a task to control when it starts or finishes:

- **As soon as possible** A task is scheduled to start as soon as allowed by its predecessors. Unless you specify otherwise, all tasks are scheduled to start as soon as possible.
- **As late as possible** A task is scheduled to start as late as possible, but such that its successor tasks can be completed on time.
- **Must start on** You specify the date on which the task must start. Use this constraint only when a task absolutely must start on a certain date.
- **Must finish on** You specify the date on which the task must finish. Use this constraint only when a task absolutely must finish on a certain date.
- **Start no later than** You specify the date on or before which the task must start. Use this constraint when a task must start by a certain date, for example, if a clause in a contract states that you will pay a penalty if a task or project phase has not started by a certain time.
- **Finish no later than** You specify the date on or before which the task must finish. Use this constraint when a task must finish by a certain date, for example, if a clause in a contract states that you will pay a penalty if a task or project phase has not finished by a certain time.
- **Start no earlier than** You specify the date on or after which the task must start.
- **Finish no earlier than** You specify the date on or after which the task must finish.

Generally, you want tasks to start as soon as possible. This allows the most flexibility in your schedule. Use the other constraints only when starting or finishing a task by a specific time is important to the outcome of the project.

For example, use a constraint date in the following situations:

- Your contract states that you will be penalized for not starting or finishing by a certain date, or that you will receive a bonus for finishing early.
- You can decrease costs on a project. Suppose your contract states that grass must be established on a playing field by May 1. You can either sow seed in October of the previous year, or lay sod in April, which increases costs. You could use a Start No Later Than constraint on the "Sow grass seed" task to make sure the predecessor tasks are scheduled to allow you to sow seed in October.
- You want to make a go/no go decision on getting a new product to market. Suppose a new computer game must be finished by September to be available for the Christmas shopping season; if you are not ready by September, you want to wait until the next spring. Use a Finish No Later Than constraint on the "Second prototype completed" milestone so, if you make the milestone, you can decide to proceed with the product; if you miss the milestone, you can decide to delay the product.
- Your project depends on certain weather conditions. Suppose you are to build a new ski lift. Certain things you can do during the winter, but you want the actual building to occur during the summer. You might place a Start No Earlier Than constraint date of May 1 at the beginning of the building phase.

USING MICROSOFT PROJECT

Having decided the sequence, relationship, lead or lag time, and constraints—all the task "dependencies"—enter this information into Microsoft Project, which uses this information to calculate your schedule.

If most of your tasks have a finish-to-start relationship, you can quickly link them with one command. Then you can add lead or lag time between the tasks as appropriate, or add a constraint date if needed. If you have a more complex schedule, with a variety of relationships, and lead and lag time, enter the predecessors, relationships, and lead and lag time individually for each task.

LINKING SEVERAL TASKS WITH A FINISH-TO-START RELATIONSHIP

If all or most of your tasks have finish-to-start relationships with other tasks, Microsoft Project includes a quick way for you to "link" all the tasks. First, on the Gantt Chart or Task Sheet, select the tasks you want to link. Then click the Link Tasks button on the Standard toolbar or choose Edit Link Tasks.

When you select the tasks, the tasks do not have to be adjacent. You can select all tasks that logically follow one another in finish-to-start relationships, skipping those not appropriate.

In the first of the next two illustrations, the tasks chosen follow one another logically in a finish-to-start relationship. The tasks not selected do not have to follow in a finish-to-start relationship. Some can occur simultaneously with those selected, and some have a finish-to-start relationship with other tasks. You can make several passes until all tasks have the correct relationships.

Choose View Gantt Chart.

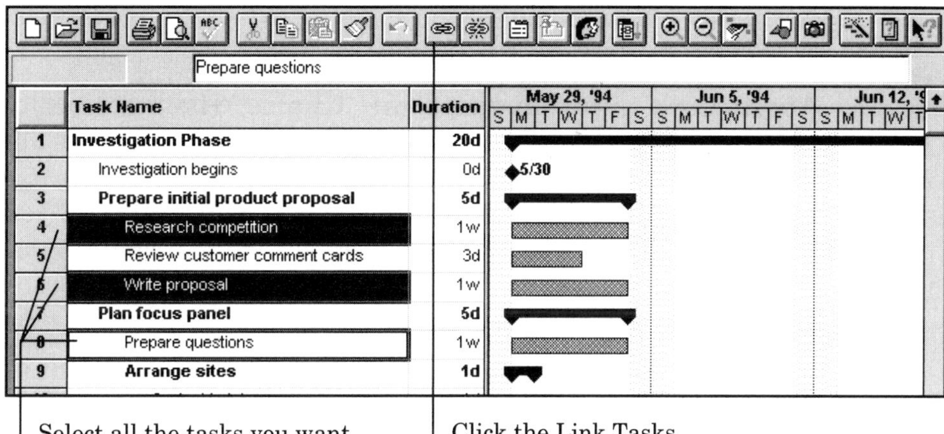

Select all the tasks you want to link with a finish-to-start relationship.

Click the Link Tasks button or choose Edit Link Tasks.

After linking the tasks, you see the bars representing the task durations spread out on the Gantt Chart.

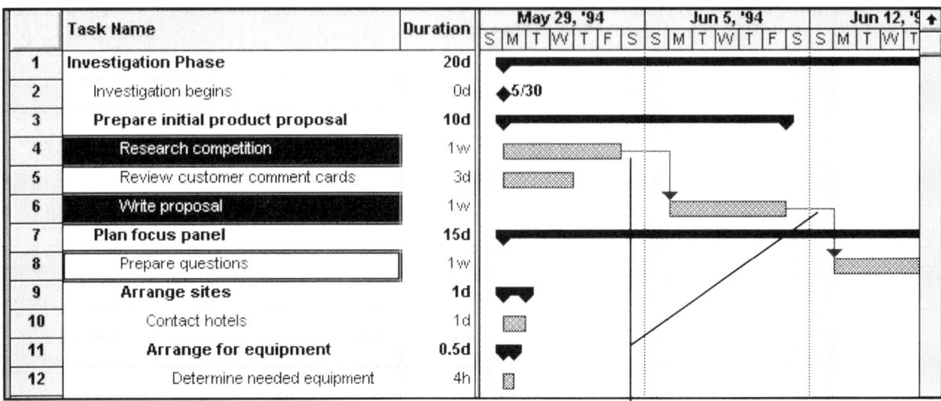

Lines show the links between the tasks. Double-click to change the relationship type or delete the link.

You can link tasks on the Task Sheet in exactly the same way.

Selecting Tasks To select adjacent tasks, either hold down Shift and press the Up or Down Arrow key, or drag the mouse over the tasks. To select nonadjacent tasks, press F8, select the first group of tasks, press Shift+F8, move to the next group of tasks, and repeat the sequence. With the mouse, hold down Ctrl in Windows or Command on the Macintosh as you select additional tasks.

About Link Lines on the Gantt Chart The link lines on the Gantt Chart connect tasks that are linked. Double-click a link line to see the Task Dependency dialog box, in which you can change the relationship type, add lead or lag time, or delete the link altogether. If you don't want to see link lines on the Gantt Chart, or want to change the look of the lines, choose Format Layout. Under Links, select the option you want, and then choose OK.

Removing Relationships Between Tasks If you want to remove all the relationships from a group of tasks, select the tasks to be unlinked. Then click the Unlink Tasks button on the Standard toolbar or choose the Edit Unlink Tasks command.

ENTERING A PREDECESSOR, RELATIONSHIP, AND LEAD OR LAG TIME

The Task Entry view is probably the easiest for entering predecessors, relationships, and lead or lag time because it has a separate box for each type of information. To display the Task Entry view, choose View More Views. In the Views box, select Task Entry, and then choose the Apply button or press Enter.

Entering a Predecessor

To enter a predecessor, you can either type the task number or click the predecessor task with the mouse.

First select the task for which you want to enter a predecessor.

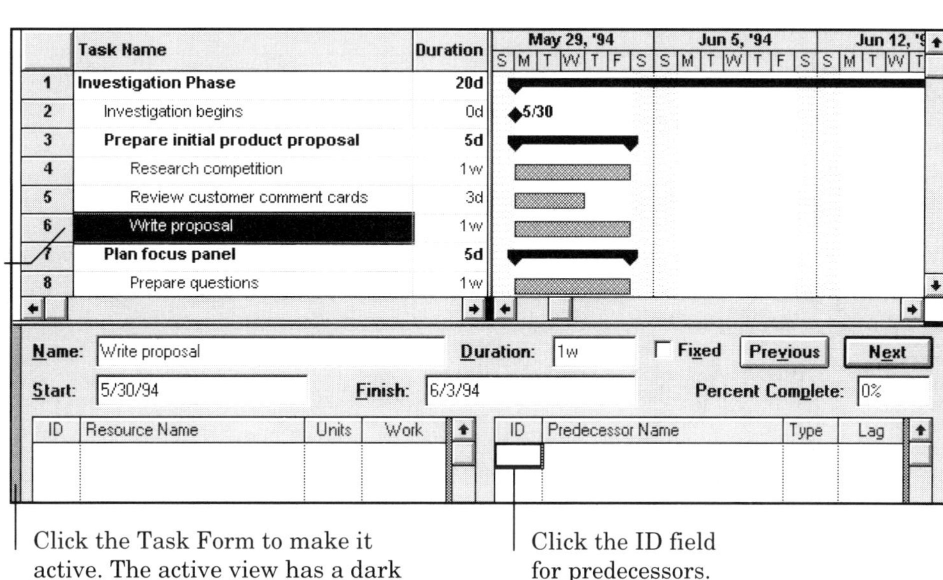

Click the Task Form to make it active. The active view has a dark or blue bar on the left.

Click the ID field for predecessors.

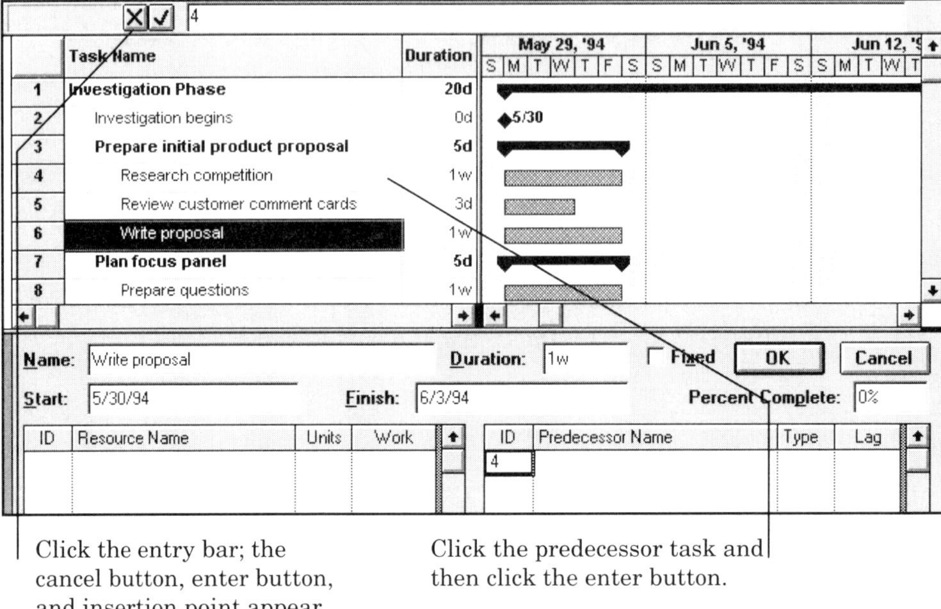

Click the entry bar; the cancel button, enter button, and insertion point appear.

Click the predecessor task and then click the enter button.

To enter a predecessor with the keys instead of the mouse, just type the ID number of the task that is a predecessor to the selected task and press Enter.

Entering a Relationship

Microsoft Project assigns a finish-to-start relationship automatically. If you want to change the relationship, move to the Type field on the Task Form, and then type or select the relationship. The relationship abbreviations correspond to the following relationship types:

Abbreviation	Relationship type
FF	Finish-to-finish
FS	Finish-to-start
SF	Start-to-finish
SS	Start-to-start

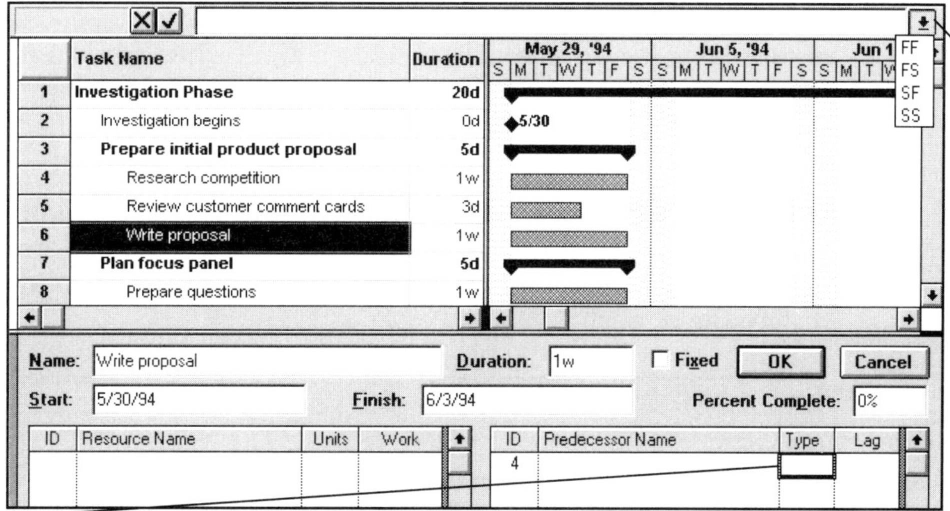

If the two tasks have a relationship type other than finish-to-start (FS), click the Type field or press the Right Arrow key.

To display the relationships in the entry bar, click the entry bar arrow. Select the relationship you want.

Press Enter or click the enter button.

Entering Lead or Lag Time

In Microsoft Project, you indicate lead or lag time as:

- Number of minutes, hours, days, or weeks
- Elapsed minutes, hours, days, or weeks
- Percentage of the duration of the predecessor task
- Elapsed percentage of the duration of the predecessor task

Lead time is shown by a minus sign; lag is shown by a plus sign. To enter the exact time, use the same abbreviations as for durations:

Unit	Abbreviation	Elapsed unit	Abbreviation
Minutes	m	Elapsed minutes	em
Hours	h	Elapsed hours	eh
Days	d	Elapsed days	ed
Weeks	w	Elapsed weeks	ew

To indicate a two-day lead time between two tasks, type **–2d**; to indicate a four-hour lag, type **4h**. Use elapsed time when you want consecutive 24-hour periods, such as to allow time for paint to dry. Type **2ed** to indicate a two-elapsed-day (48 hour) lag between two tasks.

To enter lead or lag as a percentage, type the percentage of the predecessor task by which the successor will be delayed or overlapped. Type **–25%** to show a 25% lead time between a task and its predecessor or type **50%** for a 50% lag time. To enter elapsed percentage, type an e before the %, such as **25e%**.

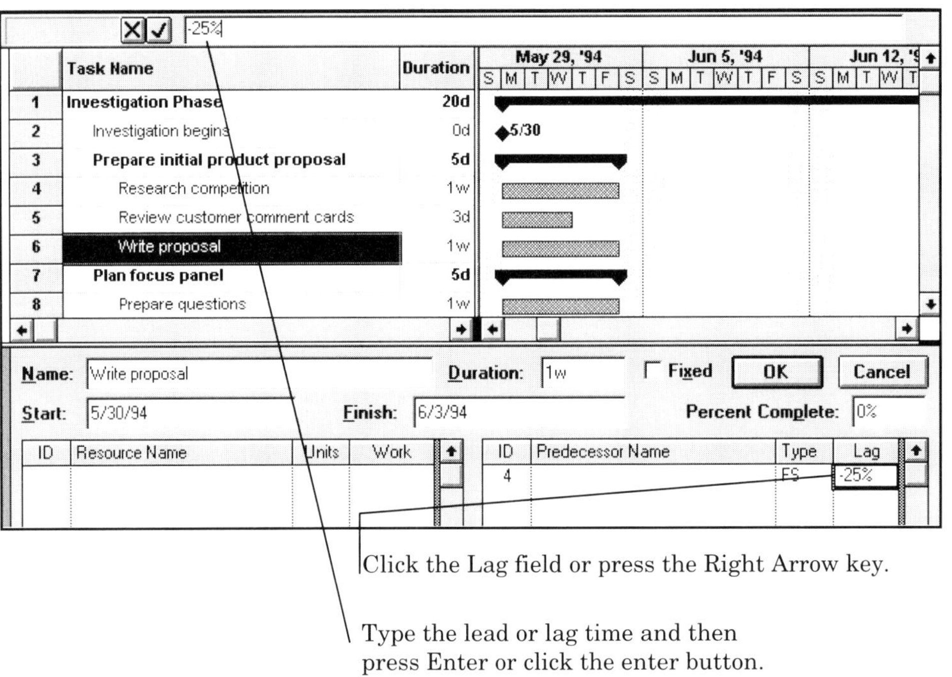

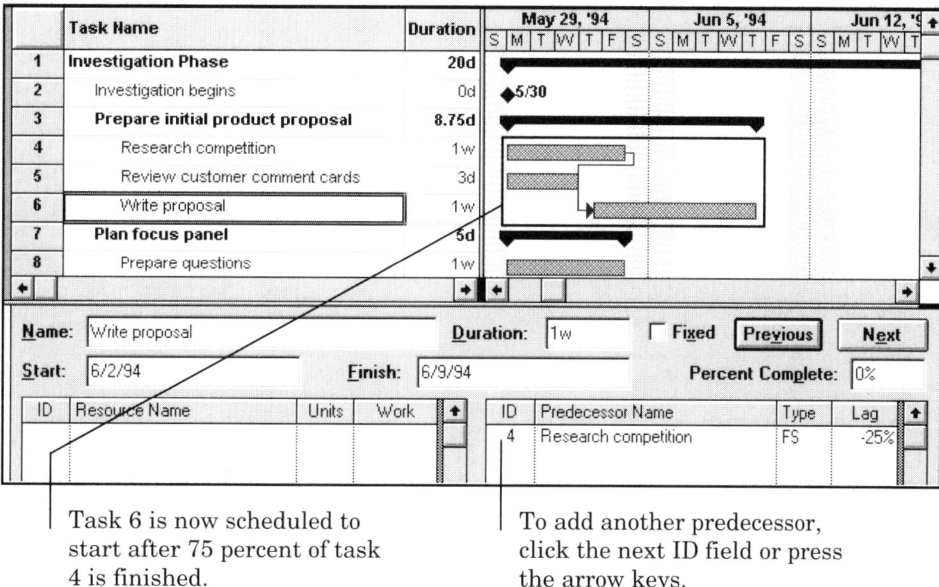

Task 6 is now scheduled to start after 75 percent of task 4 is finished.

To add another predecessor, click the next ID field or press the arrow keys.

Deleting a Relationship on the Task Form If you want to delete a relationship on the Task Form, select the Predecessor Name or ID field, and then choose Edit Delete Task or press the Del key.

Entering Successor Tasks If you want to enter successor tasks instead of predecessor tasks, you do so in exactly the same way. On the Task Form, choose Format Details/Resources & Successors to display the successors fields in place of the predecessors fields at the bottom of the Task Form. Or, to look at and enter predecessors and successors at the same time, choose Format Details/Predecessors & Successors. You do not have to enter both predecessors and successors for each task, however. Microsoft Project determines the successors based on the predecessors you enter, and vice versa.

Entering Dependencies on the Task Sheet

You can also enter the predecessor, relationship, and lead or lag time on the Task Sheet, in the Predecessors field. Again, to enter a predecessor, you can either type the task number or click the predecessor task with the mouse.

Choose View More Views. In the Views box, select Task Sheet, and then choose the Apply button or press Enter.

4

	Task Name	Duration	Start	Finish	Predecessors
1	**Investigation Phase**	**20d**	**5/30/94**	**6/24/94**	
2	Investigation begins	0d	5/30/94	5/30/94	
3	**Prepare initial product proposal**	**5d**	**5/30/94**	**6/3/94**	
4	Research competition	1w	5/30/94	6/3/94	
5	Review customer comment cards	3d	5/30/94	6/1/94	
6	Write proposal	1w	5/30/94	6/3/94	4
7	**Plan focus panel**	**5d**	**5/30/94**	**6/3/94**	
8	Prepare questions	1w	5/30/94	6/3/94	
9	**Arrange sites**	**1d**	**5/30/94**	**5/30/94**	
10	Contact hotels	1d	5/30/94	5/30/94	
11	**Arrange for equipment**	**0.5d**	**5/30/94**	**5/30/94**	
12	Determine needed equipment	4h	5/30/94	5/30/94	

Click the Predecessors field for the task.

Click the entry bar.

Click the predecessor task, and then the click the enter button.

To use the keys instead of the mouse, press the arrow keys to move to the Predecessors field, and then type the predecessor task ID number.

If the two tasks have a relationship other than finish-to-start (FS) or have lead or lag time, type the relationship abbreviation after the predecessor ID, followed by the lead or lag time.

4fs-25%

	Task Name	Duration	Start	Finish	Predecessors	Resource Names
1	**Investigation Phase**	**20d**	**5/30/94**	**6/24/94**		
2	Investigation begins	0d	5/30/94	5/30/94		
3	**Prepare initial product proposal**	**5d**	**5/30/94**	**6/3/94**		
4	Research competition	1w	5/30/94	6/3/94		
5	Review customer comment cards	3d	5/30/94	6/1/94		
6	Write proposal	1w	5/30/94	6/3/94	4fs-25%	
7	**Plan focus panel**	**5d**	**5/30/94**	**6/3/94**		
8	Prepare questions	1w	5/30/94	6/3/94		
9	**Arrange sites**	**1d**	**5/30/94**	**5/30/94**		
10	Contact hotels	1d	5/30/94	5/30/94		
11	**Arrange for equipment**	**0.5d**	**5/30/94**	**5/30/94**		

Type the relationship abbreviation after the predecessor ID, followed by the lead or lag time.

Use the following relationship abbreviations:

Relationship type	**Abbreviation**
Finish-to-finish	FF
Finish-to-start	FS
Start-to-finish	SF
Start-to-start	SS

You can enter as many predecessors as the task has, up to 100 for each task.

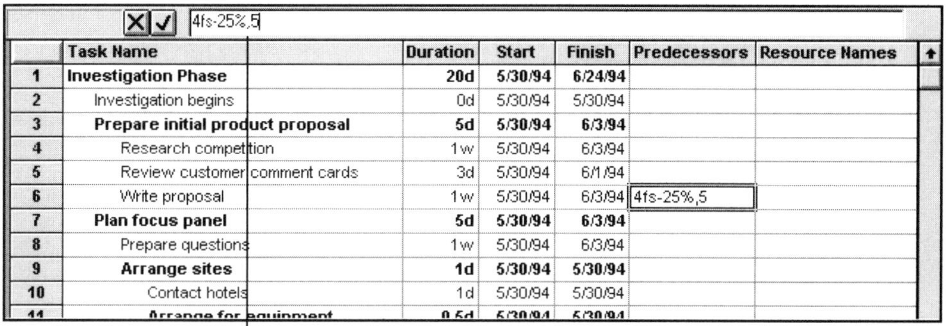

4fs-25%,5

	Task Name	Duration	Start	Finish	Predecessors	Resource Names
1	**Investigation Phase**	**20d**	**5/30/94**	**6/24/94**		
2	Investigation begins	0d	5/30/94	5/30/94		
3	**Prepare initial product proposal**	**5d**	**5/30/94**	**6/3/94**		
4	Research competition	1w	5/30/94	6/3/94		
5	Review customer comment cards	3d	5/30/94	6/1/94		
6	Write proposal	1w	5/30/94	6/3/94	4fs-25%,5	
7	**Plan focus panel**	**5d**	**5/30/94**	**6/3/94**		
8	Prepare questions	1w	5/30/94	6/3/94		
9	**Arrange sites**	**1d**	**5/30/94**	**5/30/94**		
10	Contact hotels	1d	5/30/94	5/30/94		
11	**Arrange for equipment**	**0.5d**	**5/30/94**	**5/30/94**		

Type a comma and the next predecessor. Type the relationship and lead or lag time only if necessary. Press Enter or click the enter button.

Using the List Separator The character used to separate entries in a list, such as the list of predecessors, is usually a comma or semi-colon, depending on the country for which your system is set. To identify the list separator character, choose Tools Options. On the Module General tab, check the character following List Separator.

Adding the Successors Column You can change the Task Sheet to show the Successors column instead of the Predecessors column. Or you can show both columns. For information about adding a column, see Chapter 16, "Using Microsoft Project Tools."

Deleting a Relationship on the Task Sheet On the Task Sheet, select the field containing the relationship you want to delete. Choose Edit Clear/Contents.

Specifying Task Dependencies on the PERT Chart

You can also set dependencies on the PERT Chart either after or while you enter the tasks. You must have a mouse to use this method.

Choose View PERT Chart.

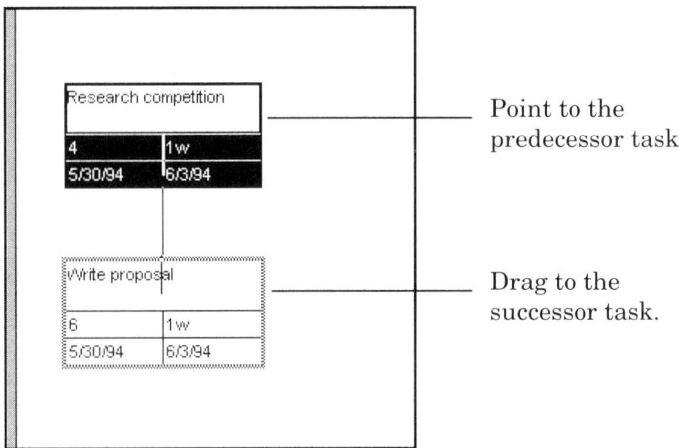

Microsoft Project applies a finish-to-start relationship between the two tasks, with no lead or lag time.

Adding a New Task To add a new task on the PERT Chart, with a finish-to-start relationship to its predecessor, point to the predecessor and drag outside the task node. The new node is formed when you release the mouse button. Type the task name and duration in the node.

Changing the Relationship If you want to change the relationship between two nodes or add lead or lag time, double-click the line between the nodes. In the Task Dependency dialog box, choose the type of relationship you want and type the lead or lag time in the Lag box.

Placing the Task Form Below the PERT Chart If you are using a full-screen PERT Chart, and want to create a combination view with the Task Form below it, double-click the split box at the bottom of the vertical scroll bar. The Task Form is automatically placed below.

If you are already using a combination view, press F6 to choose the bottom view or click the view, and then choose View More Views. In the Views box, select Task Form, and then choose the Apply button.

Deleting a Relationship You can also delete a relationship on the PERT Chart. Double-click the line between the nodes, and then choose the Delete button in the Task Dependency dialog box.

Entering a Constraint

Constraints other than As Soon As Possible must be used carefully as you do not want to introduce unnecessary scheduling restrictions.

Constraints may restrict your flexibility later when you are rescheduling tasks. If you do not indicate a constraint, Microsoft Project uses As Soon As Possible.

When you create a task by dragging on the Gantt Chart or Calendar, or move a bar on the Gantt Chart or Calendar, Microsoft Project imposes a constraint date on the task. Microsoft Project assumes that, since you started dragging on a certain date, you are indicating a start or finish date for the task. The constraint imposed is Start No Earlier Than or Finish No Earlier Than, depending on where you start and finish dragging. Microsoft Project imposes the same constraints when you type a start or finish date for a task.

Constraint dates may override the dates calculated by Microsoft Project for the task. For example, suppose the "Landscape exterior" task has a two-week duration, and you include a Must Finish On constraint date of May 25. When Microsoft Project calculates the schedule, the predecessor to "Landscape exterior" is scheduled to finish on May 18. Without the constraint date, Microsoft Project would schedule the "Landscape exterior" task to finish two weeks later, on June 1. Because of the constraint date, Microsoft Project is restricted to scheduling the task to finish on May 25, and indicates a problem.

If the PlanningWizard is turned on, the PlanningWizard will indicate the problem and give you options, from not setting the constraint to setting it and continuing. Choose the appropriate option, depending on your situation, and continue. If the PlanningWizard is not on, you'll see a message that the task is scheduled to finish after the late finish date of May 25. The message lets you know there is "negative slack" in your schedule; that is, there is not enough time to complete the predecessor task and the "Landscape exterior" task by the Must Finish On constraint date.

You can see that if the constraint date shows an important deadline in your project, the information Microsoft Project gives you is most useful. It lets you know that as the schedule is now, you will not make the dates. If the constraint date is not an important deadline, however, it places needless restrictions on your project.

When you have a group of tasks that must be finished by a certain date, enter a milestone at the end of the tasks, and use a Finish No Later Than constraint on the milestone. If the schedule slips and there is insufficient time to complete the predecessors to the milestone, Microsoft Project will display the PlanningWizard or the message that the scheduled finish is after the late finish date. When you see the message, you know that you have to take some action to correct the slippage and make the milestone date.

Changing the Constraint Type

Choose View Gantt Chart. Double-click the task, or select the task and click the Information button on the Standard toolbar or choose Insert Task Information. Select the Advanced tab. Under Constrain Task, select the constraint.

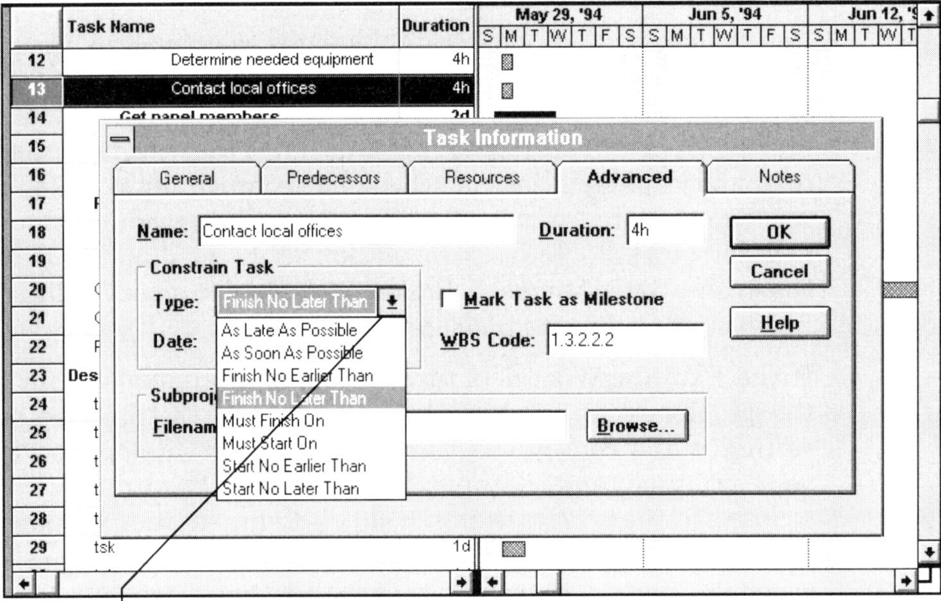

To see the list of constraints, click the Type arrow. To select a constraint, click the constraint or press the Up or Down Arrow key and press Enter.

Typing a Constraint Date

If you selected a constraint other than As Soon As Possible or As Late As Possible, you must enter a constraint date. If you do not type a constraint date for those constraints requiring a date, Microsoft Project uses the current date.

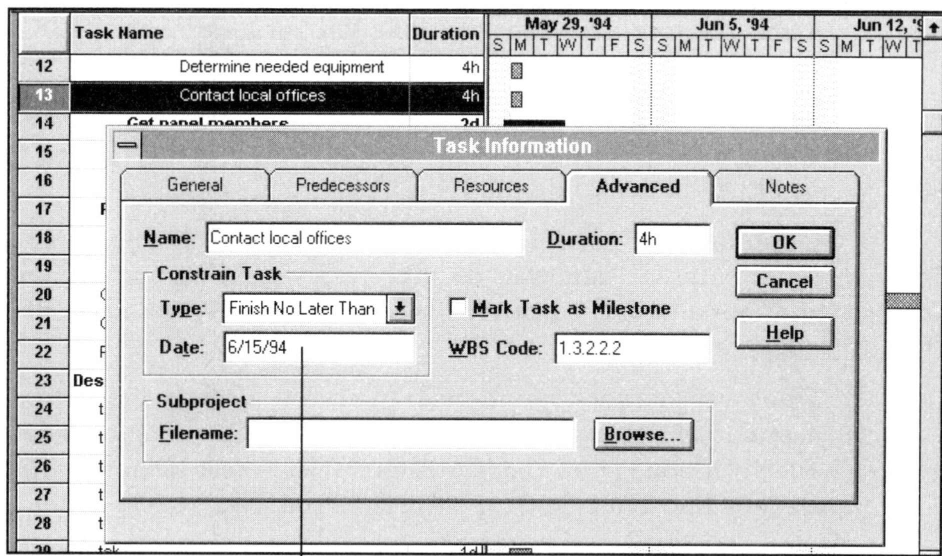

To move to the Date box, click the box or press Tab. Type the constraint date and time. Press Enter or click OK.

If you do not type a time, Microsoft Project adds the default time of 8:00 a.m. for a constraint on the start of a task and a time at the end of the day for a constraint on the finish of a task.

If you type a start or finish date for a task, Microsoft Project sets a Start No Earlier Than or Finish No Earlier Than constraint for that task, using the date you typed as the constraint date. If you move a task bar on the Gantt Chart or Calendar such that the start and finish dates change, Microsoft Project sets a Start No Earlier Than or Finish No Earlier Than constraint depending on where you start and finish dragging.

You can also enter constraints on the Task Sheet by applying the Constraint Dates table. This table includes columns for Constraint Type and Constraint Date. You can also add the Constraint Type and Constraint Date fields to the Entry table, or create a new table with just the columns you use when you enter new task information. For more information about changing or creating a table, see Chapter 16, "Using Microsoft Project Tools."

Date and Time Hints When you type a date in the current year, all you have to type is the month and day, such as 1/20 for January 20. Microsoft Project fills in the rest. If the date is in another year, you do have to type the year. When you type the month, you can type the full name (January), an abbreviation (Jan), or a number (1). To separate the day, month, and year, you can use any separator character—for example, a space, hyphen, slash, or comma.

If you want to enter the current date, type **today**; type **tomorrow** to enter the current date plus one.

If you are using the 12-hour clock, set to match the systems setting on your computer, and you do not specify a.m. or p.m., Microsoft Project assumes a.m. if the time you type is between 7:00 and 11:59 and p.m. for any other.

When you do not type a time, Microsoft Project uses 8:00 a.m. as the default time except on "finish" constraints. To change the default, choose Tools Options. On the Calendar tab, select Default Start Time or Default End Time, and type the time you want. Press Enter.

PRINTING THE SCHEDULE

To print a record of what you have entered so far and to share this information with others on the team, you can print the following views:

To see	**Print**
List of tasks, durations, predecessors, relationships, and lead or lag time	Task Sheet, with Entry table applied
List of tasks and constraints	Task Sheet with Constraint Dates table applied
List of tasks and durations, and their task bars shown over time	Gantt Chart
Task relationships	PERT Chart
Tasks on calendar	Calendar

TO PRINT YOUR SCHEDULE

1. Choose the view you want to print.
2. Click the Print button on the Standard toolbar, or choose File Print and then choose OK.

If you are using Microsoft Mail, you can use the File Send command to share the project electronically.

Next, you will enter the resources needed to complete the tasks.

7

Assigning People, Equipment, and Costs to Tasks

Now that you have entered the predecessors, relationships, lead and lag time, and constraints, you have a first pass of your schedule. But your project plan is still incomplete. You still need to plan the project resources—the people and equipment—that will do the work on the tasks, and determine the costs for these resources.

Of course, it is not mandatory that you assign resources or enter cost information if your current project does not require you to track resources and costs. However, the more tasks in the project and the longer the project, the more likely it is that you will want to track resources and costs, because this improves your ability to control the project.

Including resources in your plan accomplishes several things. It shows:

- Who will do the tasks
- When resources are needed during the project
- Whether resources are assigned to too many or too few tasks so you can plan future resource requirements

Be sure to plan your staff carefully. How well you plan the resources can make or break your project. If you plan well, your project has another plus going for it; if you do not plan well, do not have the appropriate staff available, or fail to assign the necessary resources to the tasks, you are almost guaranteeing failure.

Including cost information gives you a preliminary budget for your project, allowing you to estimate cash flow needs over the life of the project.

To complete this step, you need to estimate the type and quantity of resources needed for each task. If you want to track cost information, you also need to determine the cost for each resource.

In Microsoft Project, you can enter resources, costs for resources, and fixed costs for tasks. You also can control the days and times when each resource is available to work using the resource calendars.

ESTIMATING RESOURCE NEEDS

When you estimate the resources needed for a task, remember the duration and scope of the task. Ask yourself the following questions for each task as you assign the resources.

- What type of people are needed for the task? What level of skill must each person have? Can any skilled worker perform the task, or is there only one person able to do this task?
- How many resources do you need to finish the task in the time allotted? For example, if the task is "Frame walls" and the resource is "Carpenters," how many carpenters do you need to finish the task on time?
- What other resources do you need? What equipment or computer time, for example.

One way to analyze resource requirements for a task is to check similar tasks in past projects. Be sure to consider any differences between the two tasks and make the appropriate adjustments so your resource estimate is as accurate as possible. For example, if you are comparing two design tasks, and the current task is for a space 30 percent larger than the previous task, factor in this increase in scope as you estimate resource needs. Or if the experience level of the workers available to you now is considerably different from that available on a previous project, assign more or fewer resources as appropriate to compensate for the experience levels.

As always, have those who know the task best estimate resources. They can estimate most accurately.

As you estimate resource needs, you may find that breaking a task into smaller tasks improves your ability to predict the resources and work for the task. If so, repeat the steps to enter the new tasks, estimate duration, and add the appropriate relationships with other tasks so the new tasks fit into the schedule.

ESTIMATING COSTS

In many projects, the most important parameter is cost. Cost controls how quickly tasks are performed and how resources are used by allowing, or not allowing, additional expenses to accelerate the schedule—for example, by adding overtime work or hiring additional staff. Most of the costs for completing a project are directly associated with the execution of the tasks. The project budget is based on these task and resource costs. To develop a project budget, you assign a cost to each resource, and then calculate the cost for each task.

By planning your costs, you can:

- Check the anticipated cash flow, so you know how much money you will spend and when you will spend it.
- Experiment with juggling resources to cut costs. For example, can you substitute two less costly resources for one expensive resource and possibly decrease the cost to complete the task?
- Assign cost responsibility to a manager or department, whose responsibility is to see that the phases of a project can be costed, monitored, and kept on budget. This may be required on some contracts.
- Generate more accurate bid proposals. By setting up your schedule and including costs for resources, you have an estimate for the project cost and can bid accordingly. You can use this initial schedule to look for ways to cut costs to ensure your bid is as low as possible, yet reasonable and realistic.

For all resources you will be using in your project, you need to know:

- How much the resource costs per time period
- Whether there is a cost per use for the resource, such as a flat rate every time you use the main computer, in addition to the per-time-period rate

For all tasks in your project, you need to know any fixed cost instead of or in addition to resource costs.

USING MICROSOFT PROJECT

There are two basic approaches you can use when entering new resources into Microsoft Project. You can:

- Enter all the resources at one time and then assign them to tasks later.
- Enter new resources as you assign them to tasks.

All resource information is stored in a *resource pool.* Microsoft Project stores the resource pool with your project unless you choose to use a resource pool in another project. If the same resources work on multiple projects, use a shared resource pool to keep track of the resource use and requirements for all projects.

Of course, before you can share a resource pool, you must have one to share. If this is your first project in Microsoft Project, you obviously do not have a resource pool, so sharing is not an option. If this is not your first project, and you want to use the resource pool in another project, you can. For more information, see Chapter 14, "Managing Multiple Projects."

When you enter resources, you can also enter costs for each resource; from these individual resource costs, the task, resource, and project costs are calculated. You can also enter a fixed cost for the task. For example, you might enter a task cost when you are using a contractor to do a task for a set fee.

If you have salary information in a Microsoft Excel spreadsheet, you can link this information into Microsoft Project. As salary information changes over time, the rates in your project will be updated automatically with the new information from Microsoft Excel. For more information, see Chapter 15, "Sharing Information."

You use resource calendars to control when a resource is available to work. Each resource has its own calendar, in which you enter working information specific to the resource, such as vacation time or part-time hours. The initial working days and hours in each new resource calendar match the information in the base calendar.

HOW MICROSOFT PROJECT SCHEDULES RESOURCES

When you assign resources to a task, you enter a resource name and the number of units of that resource that will work on the task. Microsoft Project calculates the work load of each resource assigned to the task using this formula: work = duration * resource units

Work is the total work for all the units of a resource assigned to the task. For example, if duration is 40h for the "Prepare market plan" task, and you enter the following resources and units, the work is calculated by Microsoft Project as follows:

Resource you assign	Units you assign	Calculated work
Marcia	1	40h
Marketing staff	3	120h
Cheryl	0.25	10h

All resources are assigned to work for the duration of the task; each resource group will take the same amount of time (the full duration) to complete the task. Cheryl works on the task one-quarter of each day, while the other resources work full days on the task.

When you estimated duration for each task, you chose a scheduling method—either resource-driven or fixed-duration. If you now change the work or units, Microsoft Project recalculates duration if you are using resource-driven scheduling, but not if you are using fixed-duration.

Resource-driven Scheduling

If you change duration, work, or units for a task that uses resource-driven scheduling, Microsoft Project does the following:

If you change	Microsoft Project recalculates
Duration for the task	Work for each resource.
Work for a resource	Duration for the resource; if this resource is finishing last on the task, recalculates task duration.
Units	Duration for the resource; if this resource is finishing last on the task, recalculates task duration.

For example, if you change the work for Marcia to 50 hours, Marcia's duration is recalculated to 50 hours (50 hours divided by 1 unit); the duration for the task is also changed to 50 hours because Marcia's work on the task will take the longest. The work for the other two resources is not changed.

If you decrease to two the number of Marketing staff assigned to the task, the duration is recalculated by dividing the work (120 hours) by the units (2). The new duration for this resource is 60 hours. The duration for the task will also increase because the finish date for Marketing staff is the latest; their work on the task will take the longest—60 hours, as opposed to 50 hours for Marcia.

Resource	Units	Work	Resource duration
Marcia	1	50h	50h
Marketing staff	2	120h	60h
Cheryl	0.25	10h	40h

The duration for each resource does not appear anywhere in Microsoft Project. You can calculate it by dividing work by the number of resource units; you can also look at the scheduled start and finish dates for the resource on the Task Form by choosing Format Details/Resource Schedule.

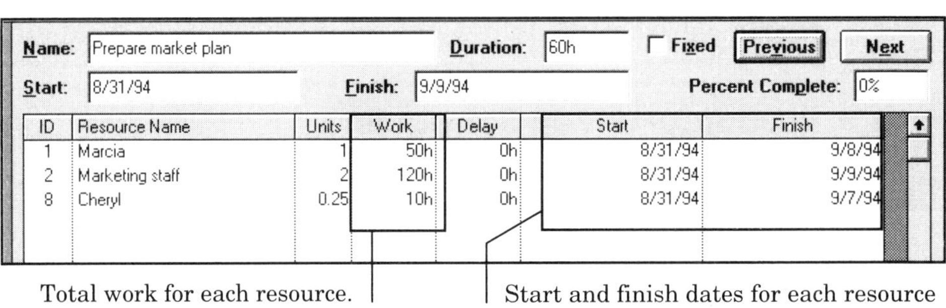

Total work for each resource. You can change the value that Microsoft Project calculates.

Start and finish dates for each resource group assigned to the task. Microsoft Project calculates these dates.

Whenever you assign more than one resource to a task, the resource with the latest finish date on the task is the one that controls the duration for the task. Changing the units or the work for a resource may not change the duration of the task. In the simplest case, if you add a resource unit, duration decreases; if you take away a resource unit, duration increases.

Fixed-duration Scheduling

When a task uses fixed-duration scheduling, Microsoft Project does the following:

If you change	Microsoft Project
Duration for the task	Recalculates work for each resource.
Work for a resource	Does not change duration for the task, but does change the scheduled start and finish date for the resource on the task; if this resource is now scheduled to finish after the task finish date, Microsoft Project tells you so, but does not change duration.
Units	Does not change duration for the task, but does recalculate the work for the resource by multiplying duration by units.

With fixed-duration scheduling, the task duration you enter does not change no matter how many resource units you assign to the task or what the work is.

Entering New Resources

If you have a list of new resources for the project, you may find it quickest to enter all resource information at one time using the Resource Sheet, and then assign the resources to the tasks by selecting the appropriate resource name from a list while using the Gantt Chart or Task Sheet. You can also enter new resources on the Resource Form, which shows one resource at a time.

When you enter new resources, you need to know the following:

- Resource name
- Maximum number of resource units available
- Base calendar for the resource, if you are using more than one in the project

Resources can be individuals (Tom, Mary, John) or groups (carpenters, machinists, engineers). Use resource groups if the members of a group are interchangeable on a job. If the workers are not interchangeable, list each resource individually.

If you are interested in tracking resource costs, you also need to know:

- Standard rate of pay per minute, hour, day, week, or year
- Overtime rate per minute, hour, day, week, or year, if applicable
- Per-use rate you pay each time you use the resource, if applicable
- When costs are accrued—at the time the task starts, when the resource finishes on the task, or prorated as the task progresses

When you enter costs, type a number, and then a slash (/) and the unit of time. For example, type 10/h for $10 per hour. If you don't type the slash and time unit, Microsoft Project assumes the rate is per hour. Use the following abbreviations for the time:

Rate of pay per	Abbreviation
Minute	m
Hour	h
Day	d
Week	w
Year	y

If you know a monthly rate, change it to weekly or yearly; Microsoft Project uses the abbreviation m for minutes, not months.

You can also enter a group and code for each resource, such as the department that employs the resource or an accounting code. Based on this group and code information, you can sort or filter resources to show all resources by department, or only resources that have a certain code.

Notes on the Currency Symbol The currency symbol depends on the country settings for your system. To check the currency settings, choose Tools Options. On the View tab, under View Options, the currency symbol, placement, and decimal digits are listed. If the currency symbol isn't what you want, type the correct symbol in the Symbol box. To change its placement, select one of the options in the Placement box. For software for English/USA, the currency symbol is a dollar sign.

Entering Resources on the Resource Sheet

The Resource Sheet looks like a spreadsheet, with rows and columns; all the resources are listed down the left side of the sheet. To see the Resource Sheet, choose View Resource Sheet.

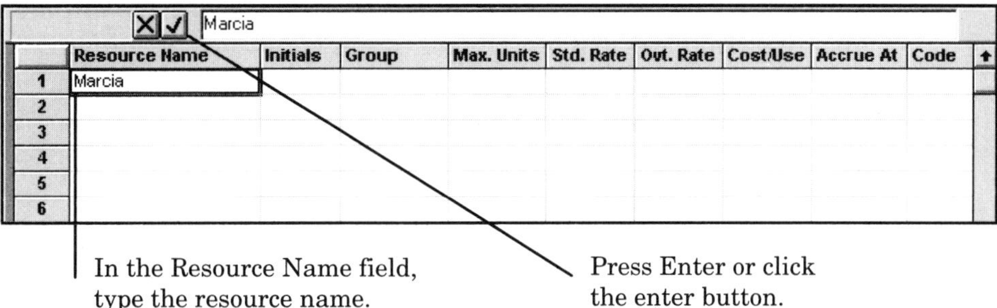

When you type a name on the Resource Sheet, information is entered into several fields, including Max. Units, Std. Rate, and Ovt. Rate. If you entered a resource group, change the number in the Max. Units field to reflect the actual number you have available of that resource. Then enter the correct rate information for the resource. Check the Accrue At field and change if needed.

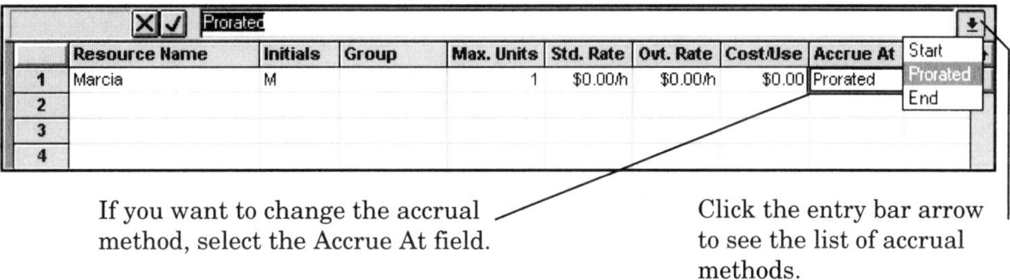

About the Accrual Methods There are three accrual methods. *Start* means that all costs for the resource accrue as soon as the resource starts work on the task. *Finish* means that all costs for the resource accrue when the resource finishes work on the task; costs are zero as long as the resource's work on the task is less than 100 percent complete. *Prorated* means that as the percent complete or work changes on the task, the costs change in proportion to the percent complete.

Changing Resource Information Simultaneously If several resources require the same information in a field, such as the standard rate or accrual method, or if you want to assign a code to several resources, you can simultaneously change that information for selected resources. Select all the resources you want to change and then click the Information button or choose Insert Resource Information. In the Multiple Resource Information dialog box, change the information that is common to all the selected resources and choose OK.

Entering the Same Information for Several Resources You can also use the Edit Fill Down command to enter the same information for several resources. Select the field with the information you want to copy, and then hold down Ctrl in Windows or Command on the Macintosh and select the fields in which you want the same information. The field containing the information must be on top. The fields into which you want to copy the information do not have to be adjacent. You can select the fields in rows 3, 5, 6, and 8, for example. After you select all the fields, choose Edit Fill Down.

Changing the Default Standard Rate or Overtime Rate If many of your resources have the same standard rate or overtime rate, you can set this rate so it is automatically entered when you enter a new resource. Initially, Microsoft Project enters rates of 0 (zero). Choose Tools Options and then select the General tab. To change the standard rate that is entered automatically, select Default Standard Rate and type the value you want; to change the overtime rate entered automatically, select Default Overtime Rate and type the value you want. Choose OK.

Entering a Skill Level for Resources or the Manager Responsible Microsoft Project includes "custom" fields you can use in any way you want. When you add a custom field to a table, you can name the column to indicate the information it will contain. There are five custom text fields you can add to a resource table—Text1 through Text5. If you want to note the skill level or the manager responsible for each resource, you can add one of the Text fields to the Entry table (or any table). Then, in the Title box in the Column Definition dialog box or in the Table Definition dialog box, you would type "Skill Level" or "Manager" for the title. You can sort and filter on the information in a custom field, just as on any field. Using sorting, for example, you could sort so all those with a skill level of 1 are together, and so on. Or filter so only resources reporting to a certain manager are displayed. For more information about changing or creating tables, see Chapter 16, "Using Microsoft Project Tools."

Entering Resources on the Resource Form

You can also enter new resources on the Resource Form, one resource at a time. To see the Resource Form, choose View More Views. In the Views box, select Resource Form and then choose the Apply button.

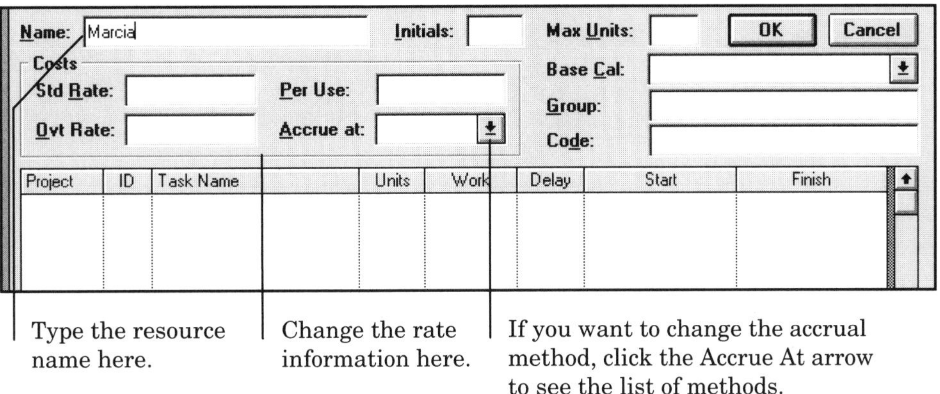

Type the resource name here.

Change the rate information here.

If you want to change the accrual method, click the Accrue At arrow to see the list of methods.

Press Enter or click OK when you finish changing information for this resource. Press Enter again or click the Next button to go to a blank form to enter the next resource.

ASSIGNING RESOURCES TO TASKS

You assign resources to tasks on any of the task views. When you assign a resource to a task, you do not have to type the resource name if it is already in the resource pool. In the Resource Assignment dialog box or in the entry bar list, Microsoft Project displays the list of resources in the resource pool. If you do type a resource name, Microsoft Project checks the resource pool for the name you typed; if the resource does not exist, you can add it to the resource pool and later enter additional information about it, such as the maximum units and cost information.

When you assign resources to tasks, you need to know certain information for each task.

- What resources do you want to assign to the task?
- How many units of each resource do you want to assign to the task? You can assign less than one unit if a resource will work part-time on a task.

- What is the amount of work (man-hours) each resource will do on the task, if it is less than the full duration of the task?
- How much time should pass before the resource's work begins if the resource should start work after the start of the task?

Assigning Resources on any Task View

The quickest way to assign a resource to a task is to use the Resource Assignment dialog box.

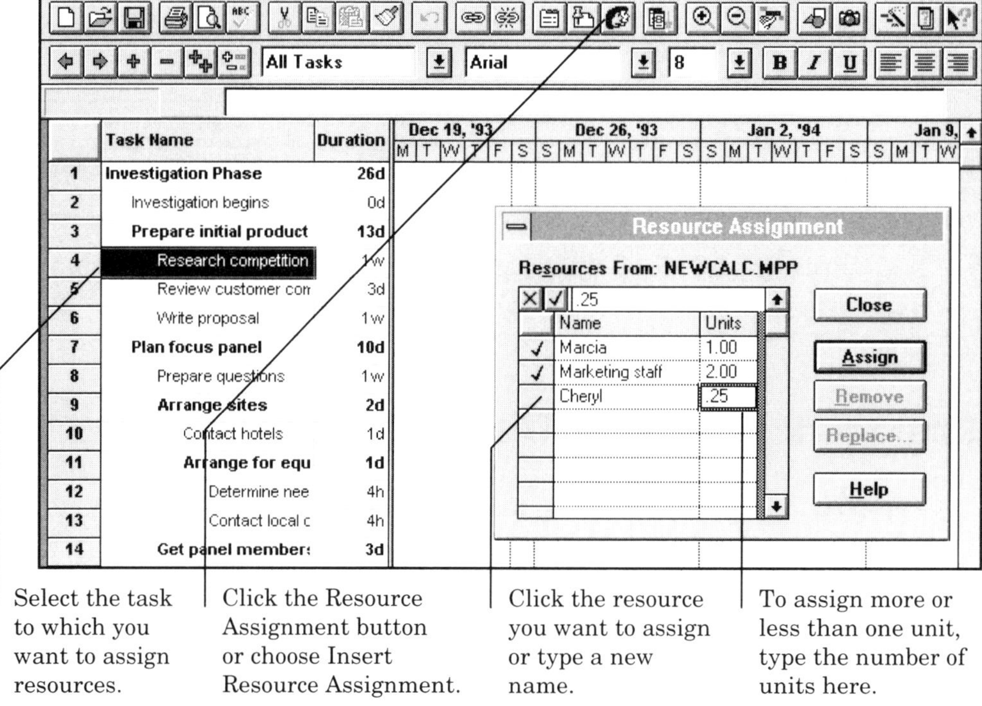

You can assign more than one resource by selecting all those you want assign. Hold down Shift to select a series of resources; hold down Ctrl in Windows or Command on the Macintosh to select nonadjacent resources.

When you are finished selecting resources, choose the Assign button.

Instead of clicking the Assign button, you can also drag the resources to the task. Select the resources you want to assign. Move the pointer to the left of the resource names. The pointer will change to one head if one resource is selected or two heads if more than one is selected. Drag to the task.

When resources are assigned to selected tasks, a check mark appears next to the resource name in the Resource Assignment dialog box.

Assigning Resources on the Gantt Chart or Task Sheet Another way to assign resources is to use the Resource Names field on the Gantt Chart (scroll right to see it) or Task Sheet. You can type names in this field or select names from the entry bar list. All resources in the resource pool are included in the entry bar list. Separate the resource names with a comma (or whatever the list separator character is if not a comma). To assign more or less than one unit, type the number in square brackets after the resource name; for example, type **Marketing staff [2]** to assign two marketing staff units. To assign less than one unit, type a fraction representing the time that the resource is assigned to the task. For example, type **Cheryl [.25]** to assign one-quarter of Cheryl's time.

If you want to change the amount of work the resource is assigned to on the task or, if the resource is not working for the entire duration of the task, use the resource schedule fields at the bottom of the Task Form, described next in this chapter.

Assigning Resources to Summary Tasks and Subproject Tasks When you assign a resource to a summary task or subproject task (a subproject task is the task in the master project that represents a subproject—for more information, see Chapter 14, "Managing Multiple Projects"), the resource is assigned to work for the full duration of the summary task or subproject. If the duration changes, the work for the resource assignment also changes.

Level Message As you assign resources to tasks, you may see a message in the status bar that a resource needs to be leveled. This means the resource is overallocated—that is, more than its maximum number of units are assigned to tasks. For example, if you have three marketing staff available, but have assigned five marketing staff to tasks on a certain day, you will see a message to level marketing staff. You can take care of this now or later, either by shifting tasks or resources yourself or by using Microsoft Project's leveling feature to move tasks around. Leveling resources is discussed in Chapter 9, "Refining the Schedule and Freezing the Baseline."

Assigning the Same Resources to Several Tasks If several tasks use the same resources, you can enter the resources for all tasks simultaneously. First, on the Gantt Chart or Task Sheet, select the tasks that use the same resources. Then click the Resource Assignment button on the Standard toolbar or choose Insert Resource Assignment. Select or type the resources to be assigned to all selected tasks. To assign other than one unit, type the units for each resource in the Units column.

Adding Cost Information for a New Resource If you type a new resource name in the Resource Assignment dialog box, it's easy to add cost or other details for the resource. Double-click the resource name you just typed. The Resource Information dialog box will appear, so you can enter cost and other resource details.

Changing or Delaying Work

You use the Task Form to check the amount of work for each resource assignment. When you assign resources to tasks, each resource is listed on its own line in the fields at the bottom of the Task Form. Work for each resource is calculated by multiplying the duration by the number of units of each resource assigned to the task.

On the Task Entry view, click the Task Form or press F6 to make the Task Form the active view.

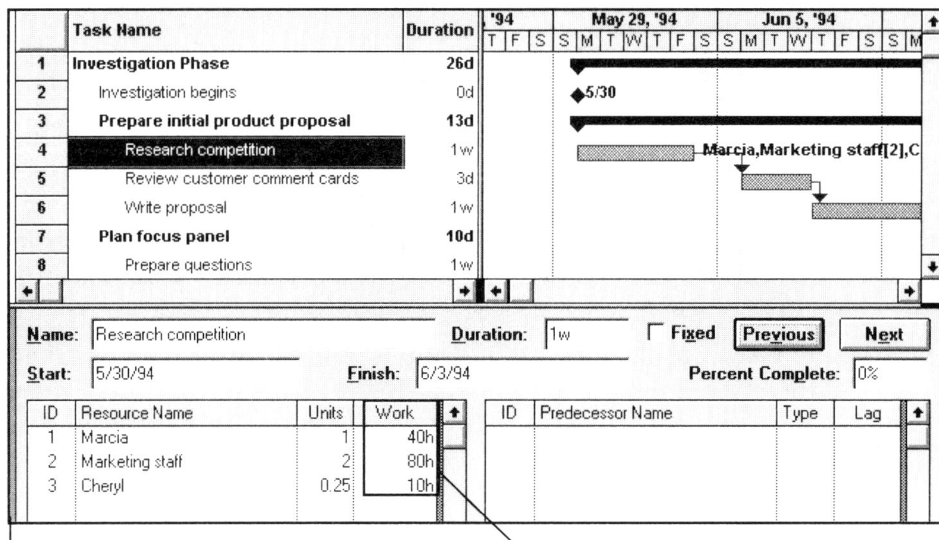

To activate the Task Form, press F6 or click the view. You can identify the active view by the bar on the left.

Review the work for each resource assigned to the task.

If the work is not what you want, change it. For example, if one of the resources will work for a few hours at the beginning of the task, and then not be involved for the remainder of the task, change the work amount for that resource.

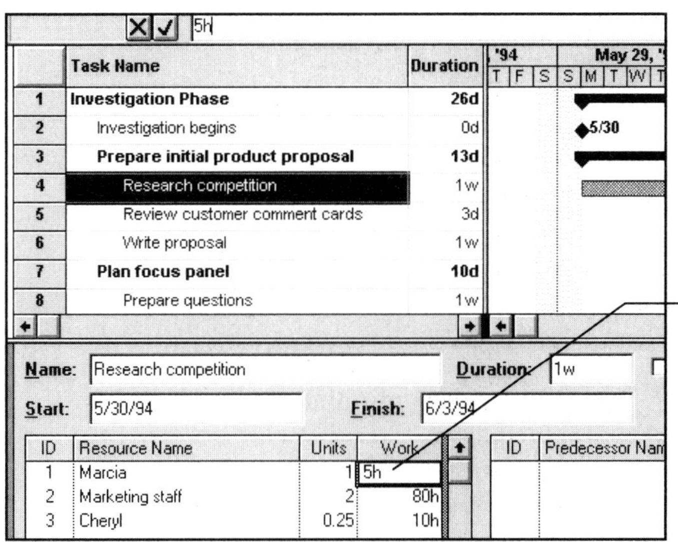

Click the Work field. Type the amount of work this resource is to do on the task. Use the duration abbreviations for minutes, hours, day, and weeks.

Press Enter or click the enter box.

If a resource is not assigned for the full duration of the task, you can also use the Task Form to control when the work occurs on the task. For example, a supervisor may work at the beginning of a task to help the team get started, and then again at the end of a task to review results. You control when these two periods of involvement occur using the Delay field for resources. The Delay field for resources is available on the Task Form by choosing Format Details/Resource Schedule or on the Resource Form by choosing Format Details/Schedule. The resource schedule fields summarize each resource's involvement on the task. In the Delay field, you enter how long the resource should wait before beginning work. When the delay is 0h, the resource begins work at the beginning of the task.

On the Task Form, choose Format Details/Resource Schedule.

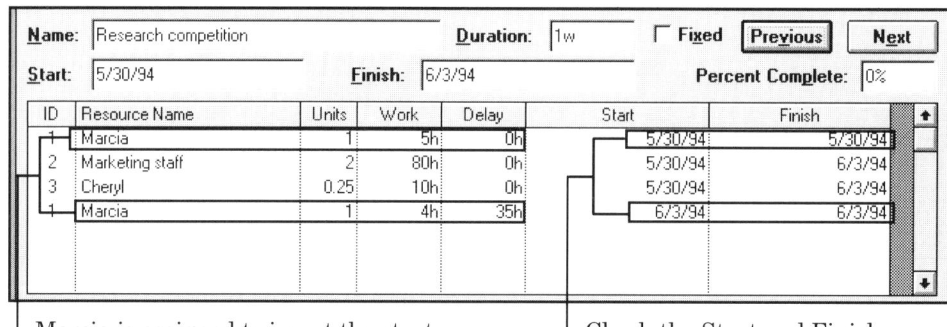

Marcia is assigned twice: at the start of the task (0h delay) and at the finish of the task (35h delay).

Check the Start and Finish fields to see when each assignment is scheduled.

Marcia is assigned to the task twice: once at the beginning for 5 hours and again at the end for 4 hours. The value in the Work field for each assignment shows how much work Marcia will do each time. The value in the Delay field for each assignment shows when the work will occur. The first assignment has a delay of 0h, so the work occurs at the beginning of the task. The second assignment has a delay of 35h, and so occurs at the end of the task.

By using the Work field and the Delay field, you can assign one resource to a task as many times as necessary and control when the work occurs to create as accurate a model of resource assignments as is appropriate for your project.

Assigning Resources on the Task Form You can also assign resources on the Task Form. Just select a Resource Name field at the bottom of the Task Form, and then select a resource name from the list in the entry bar or type a name. One unit is automatically assigned. If you want to change the number of units, move to the Units field and type the number of units you want to assign. To add another resource to the task, move down to the next Resource Name field and repeat the steps.

Controlling How New Resources are Added to the Resource Pool When you type a new resource name in the Resource Names field on the Gantt Chart or Task Sheet, or in the Resource Name field on the Task Form, you can control whether the resource name is added to the resource pool automatically, or if you are asked first. To control this option, use the Automatically Add New Resources check box on the General tab in the Tools Options dialog box. Initially, this check box is selected so you can add resources without the new resource being verified.

CHANGING A RESOURCE CALENDAR

Every resource has a resource calendar. This calendar is created by Microsoft Project and matches the settings in the base calendar you created in Chapter 3. If you are using more than one base calendar—for example, one for day shift, one for swing shift, and one for graveyard shift—you can specify the base calendar for the resource in the Resource Information dialog box.

The base calendar you choose controls the initial working days, working hours, and holidays for the resource. All settings in the base calendar are transferred to the resource calendar. You can change the settings to reflect the resource's actual working habits, adding to the resource calendar vacation time, part-time hours, or other exceptions to the base calendar.

For example, Jim works the swing shift, so his resource calendar has the settings from the Swing Shift base calendar. In his resource calendar, you add his vacation time. Jim will be scheduled to work the days and hours in the Swing Shift base calendar, but not scheduled to work during his vacation time.

When Microsoft Project schedules the resource, it uses the resource calendar settings to determine when the resource is available. Changes you make to the base calendar are also made in the resource calendar; if settings in the resource calendar conflict with those in the base calendar, the resource calendar settings are used.

If you are using fixed-duration scheduling for any tasks, the settings in the resource calendar are ignored when these tasks are scheduled.

Changing a Resource's Base Calendar

If you have created more than one base calendar in your project, such as Day, Swing, and Graveyard for three shifts, be sure the appropriate base calendar is used by each resource. If you create new resources using the Resource Form, you can indicate the base calendar in the Base Cal box. Otherwise, use the Resource Information dialog box to change the base calendar. To display the Resource Information dialog box, double-click the resource name or select the resource and click the Information button on the Standard toolbar or choose Insert Resource Information. Select the base calendar in the Base Cal box and choose OK.

When you display the resource calendar, as described in the next section, the base calendar used for each resource is displayed at the top of the resource calendar.

Changing Working Days or Hours for a Resource

You change a resource calendar to indicate when the working days or hours for this resource differ from its base calendar—for example, you would show vacation days or part-time hours in the resource calendar.

To change a resource calendar, choose Tools Change Working Time.

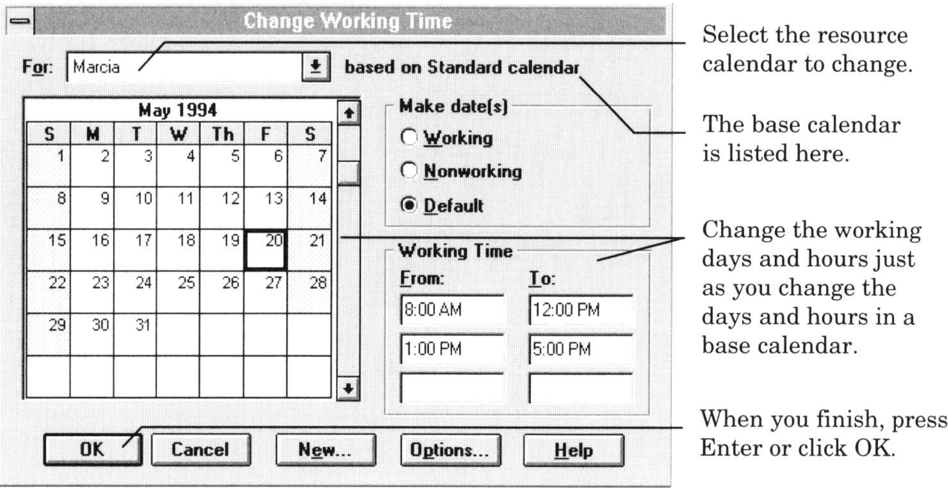

If you have changed the working days or hours in the resource calendar, you can use the Default option to change them back to the original setting in the base calendar or to match the other settings for that day in the resource calendar. For example, if you have changed the hours on Fridays for the resource calendar to half days and want to change them to match the base calendar, select the Friday title, and then select the Default option.

ENTERING A FIXED COST FOR A TASK

When you know exactly how much it will cost to perform a task or use a resource, or if there is a cost in addition to the cost of the resources, enter a fixed cost. A fixed cost is a specific amount that does not rely on how much time and man power is spent to complete a task. For example, enter a fixed cost when you have accepted a bid from an outside contractor or if you know a certain task always costs a certain amount. If you know the cost for supplies associated with a task and this cost does not vary depending on the work on the task, you could enter this amount as a fixed cost.

To enter a fixed cost for a task, you apply the Cost table to the Task Sheet. Then you type the fixed cost in the Fixed Cost field.

Choose View More Views. In the Views box, select Task Sheet, and then choose the Apply button. To display the Cost table, choose View Table/Cost.

1000

	Name	Fixed Cost	Total Cost	Baseline	Variance	Actual	Remainin
11	**Arrange for equipment**	**$0.00**	**$0.00**	**$0.00**	**$0.00**	**$0.00**	**$0.**
12	Determine needed equipment	$0.00	$0.00	$0.00	$0.00	$0.00	$0.
13	Contact local offices	$0.00	$0.00	$0.00	$0.00	$0.00	$0.
14	**Get panel members**	**$0.00**	**$0.00**	**$0.00**	**$0.00**	**$0.00**	**$0.**
15	Contact local reps for names	$0.00	$0.00	$0.00	$0.00	$0.00	$0.
16	Contact suggested panel members	$0.00	$0.00	$0.00	$0.00	$0.00	$0.
17	**Plan phone questionnaire**	**$0.00**	**$0.00**	**$0.00**	**$0.00**	**$0.00**	**$0.**
18	Prepare questionnaire	$0.00	$0.00	$0.00	$0.00	$0.00	$0.
19	Get list of users to call	$0.00	$0.00	$0.00	$0.00	$0.00	$0.
20	Carry out focus panels	$0.00	$0.00	$0.00	$0.00	$0.00	$0.
21	Carry out phone survey	1000	$0.00	$0.00	$0.00	$0.00	$0.
22	Prepare focus panel report	$0.00	$0.00	$0.00	$0.00	$0.00	$0.

First select the Fixed Cost field for the task to which you want to assign a fixed cost.

Type the cost and then press Enter or click the enter button.

You can also enter a fixed cost for a resource. For example, you may be using a contractor for part of a task and paying a fixed rate for that contractor, but also using your own resources. To enter a fixed rate for a contractor, you use the Task Form and display the cost fields by choosing Format Details/Resource Cost. Type **0** in the Units box for that resource assignment on the Task Form and then enter the cost of that resource in the Cost field on the Task Form.

PRINTING THE RESOURCES AND SCHEDULE

All the project information is now entered into Microsoft Project. To review this information and share it with others, there are several views you can print.

To see	Print
List of resources in resource pool, and information about each resource	Resource Sheet
List of tasks, including resources assigned to each task	Task Sheet
Summary of work and cost for each resource	Resource Sheet, with Summary table applied
Graphical view of tasks over time	Gantt Chart or Calendar

TO PRINT A VIEW

1. Choose the view you want to print.
2. Click the Print button on the Standard toolbar, or choose File Print and then choose OK.

As always, if you are using Microsoft Mail, you can use File Send to electronically mail the project to the team.

In Part III, you will review all the information you have entered to decide where to optimize the schedule.

PART III

REFINING AND COMMUNICATING THE PLAN

You now have an initial schedule for your project. But it's very likely that this schedule won't cut it. Maybe it takes too long—or costs too much. Or maybe you just want to optimize the schedule so that all resources are used as efficiently as possible, and so the project is finished as soon as possible at the lowest cost. Perhaps you get a bonus for finishing early, or need to move people or equipment to other projects.

So, how do you make the schedule fit your needs? The next steps in the process are:

- Evaluate the schedule using Microsoft Project's views, tables, and filters to check dates, critical tasks, slack time, task order, resources, and costs (Chapter 8).
- Refine the schedule by adding and reassigning resources, adding overtime work, breaking up tasks, reducing the scope of the project, changing task sequence and constraints, and changing durations until you have the best schedule for your needs on this project (Chapter 9).
- When you are comfortable with the schedule, save the baseline schedule (Chapter 9). You will use the baseline schedule when you are tracking the project in Part IV.
- Communicate the plan to the team and management (Chapter 10).

You repeat the first two steps until you resolve all areas of concern in the project plan.

8

Evaluating the Schedule

As you entered information about tasks, durations, relationships, and resources, Microsoft Project calculated the schedule. Now you need to look at this schedule and evaluate it to make sure it fits your needs.

The purpose of evaluating your schedule is to find errors, inconsistencies, and areas for improvement. For example, when you evaluate the schedule, you may find tasks that still start at the beginning of the project because you neglected to indicate their predecessors. You may find tasks or resources entered or ordered incorrectly, or resources assigned to the wrong tasks. This is your chance to review everything you have entered to make sure it reflects your intentions.

In addition to looking for mistakes made when entering the project information, check the schedule itself. Check that the project is finishing when you need it to finish and within budget, that the project meets the requirements of the client, customer, or management, and that resources are available as needed for all tasks. You may have to find ways to speed up the schedule, move tasks or resources around so resources are available as needed, lower costs to meet budget constraints, and so on.

This chapter explains how to check your schedule to decide which parts are okay and which parts need some help. Once you know which parts of the schedule you need to concentrate on, read the next chapter for ways to change and improve your schedule so it meets your needs.

When you evaluate the schedule, you look at six major areas:

- Project finish date and task dates
- Critical tasks and the critical path
- Slack time
- Task sequence, relationships, and constraints
- Resources
- Costs

Keep your assumptions in mind as you review each area. Note any assumptions that have changed so you can adjust the schedule appropriately. Make sure, too, that all the project objectives have been satisfied.

PROJECT DATES

The first date you want to check is the project finish date to see if it is acceptable. This shows you how much, if any, you need to shorten the critical path so the project finishes on time.

You also want to look over the task bars on the Gantt Chart or task nodes on the PERT Chart, just to check for anything that is out of place. For example, you may see a task linked to the wrong task, or to no task at all such that it starts at the beginning of the project instead of at the appropriate time.

CRITICAL TASKS

The tasks on the critical path determine the project finish date. The *critical path* is that sequence of tasks adding up to the longest total time required to complete the project. The duration of the project is the total duration of these critical tasks. To shorten the project duration, focus on the critical path. You can shorten the critical path by changing dependencies between tasks and by shortening critical tasks.

In the critical path method of scheduling, the critical path is determined by calculating the schedule twice. First, a forward pass is made from the start date of the project. This pass determines the earliest start and finish dates for each task. For example, if you have three tasks, each one day long and occurring on consecutive days, the forward pass might look like this:

Monday	Tuesday	Wednesday	Thursday	Friday
Task A	Task B	Task C		

The early start and finish dates are summarized in the following table:

	Early start	**Early finish**
Task A	Monday, 8 a.m.	Monday, 5 p.m.
Task B	Tuesday, 8 a.m.	Tuesday, 5 p.m.
Task C	Wednesday, 8 a.m.	Wednesday, 5 p.m.

Then a backward pass is made, calculated from a finish date you enter or from the date computed in the first pass. This pass determines the latest start and finish dates for each task. For example, if the latest finish date for Task C is Friday, the backward pass would look something like this:

Monday	Tuesday	Wednesday	Thursday	Friday
		Task A	Task B	Task C

The late start and finish dates are summarized in the following table:

	Late start	**Late finish**
Task A	Wednesday, 8 a.m.	Wednesday, 5 p.m.
Task B	Thursday, 8 a.m.	Thursday, 5 p.m.
Task C	Friday, 8 a.m.	Friday, 5 p.m.

The difference between the two sets of dates is the slack time. The three tasks in the example each have two days of slack time, from their early start date (for example, for Task A, Monday, 8 a.m.) to their late start date (for Task A, Wednesday, 8 a.m.).

The critical path is that path that has no slack time from project start to project finish. There may be more than one critical path through the project if different phases of the project are worked on simultaneously. For critical tasks, the early and late start dates are the same, as are the early and late finish dates.

Aside from identifying the critical path, the critical path method of scheduling tells you:

- Earliest and latest start and finish dates for all tasks. Use this information to move tasks around to level resources.
- Which tasks cannot slip if the project completion date is to be maintained. If a critical task does slip, you must adjust the remaining tasks on the critical path, maybe by working on critical tasks simultaneously or by adding resources to critical tasks, to meet the project end date.

The critical path is recalculated every time you change task data, so it is constantly changing. A critical task may become noncritical and a noncritical task critical as you move resources, change dependencies, and so on. For example, if you find a way to shorten a critical task, perhaps by adding resources to accomplish the task faster, this task may no longer be critical, but another task may become critical. The time you save on the first task might not be reflected fully in the end date of the project because of the changing critical path.

In the following illustration, Tasks B, C, and D are on the critical path. The finish date for Task D and the project is Friday, June 10, at 5 p.m.

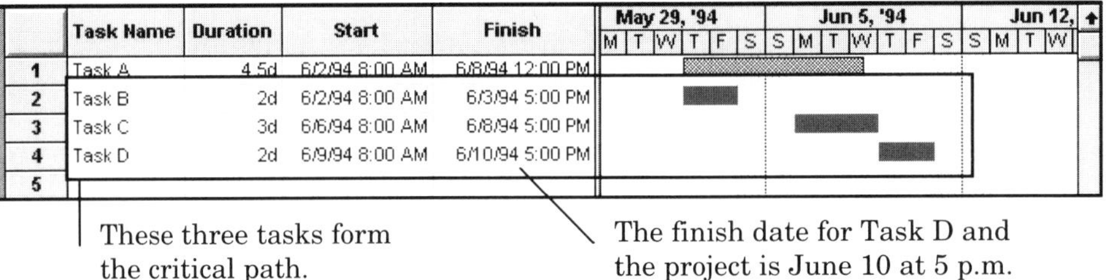

	Task Name	Duration	Start	Finish
1	Task A	4.5d	6/2/94 8:00 AM	6/8/94 12:00 PM
2	Task B	2d	6/2/94 8:00 AM	6/3/94 5:00 PM
3	Task C	3d	6/6/94 8:00 AM	6/8/94 5:00 PM
4	Task D	2d	6/9/94 8:00 AM	6/10/94 5:00 PM
5				

If you find a way to shorten Task C from 3 days to 1.5 days, saving 1.5 days, the finish date changes to Friday at noon, a savings of only half a day. Tasks B and C are no longer critical, but Task A is now critical.

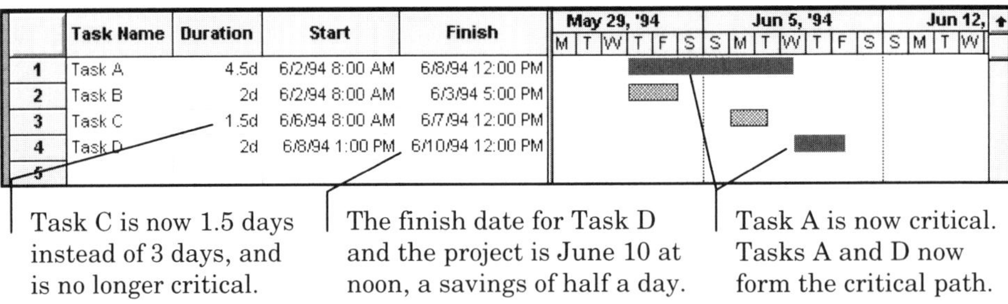

	Task Name	Duration	Start	Finish
1	Task A	4.5d	6/2/94 8:00 AM	6/8/94 12:00 PM
2	Task B	2d	6/2/94 8:00 AM	6/3/94 5:00 PM
3	Task C	1.5d	6/6/94 8:00 AM	6/7/94 12:00 PM
4	Task D	2d	6/8/94 1:00 PM	6/10/94 12:00 PM
5				

SLACK TIME AND NONCRITICAL TASKS

When the schedule is calculated, slack time is also calculated. *Slack* is how much time a task can be delayed without delaying the project end date. You can also look at slack time as the difference between the critical path duration and the duration of any other path. Noncritical tasks have slack time; critical tasks do not. Noncritical tasks can start and/or finish later than their scheduled dates, up to the available slack time, without affecting the project finish date.

There are two kinds of slack time: total slack and free slack.

- *Total slack time* is the amount of time a task can be delayed without delaying the end date of the project. It is the difference between the date a task is scheduled to start and the late start date for the task calculated by the backward pass. Total slack includes all the slack between this task and the end of the project. If you use all the total slack on one task, those tasks dependent on this task have no more slack and become critical.

  When the duration for a task is longer than the time allowed by the scheduled dates, total slack is negative instead of positive. Negative slack in your schedule tells you that, as currently scheduled, there is not enough time to complete those tasks with negative slack.
- *Free slack* is the amount of time a task can be delayed without delaying any other task.

Looking at the slack time for tasks helps you decide how to best use resources. Shift tasks with slack time to even out resource use.

TASK ORDER, RELATIONSHIPS, AND CONSTRAINTS

When you looked at the critical path, you identified those tasks whose durations you want to shorten. Now that you know which tasks you need to concentrate on, check the task dependencies—task sequence, relationships between tasks, and constraints. Be sure you have not imposed a sequence or relationship that is not absolutely necessary nor added unnecessary constraints. You may find that by changing the task sequence, overlapping tasks, or removing constraints, you can shorten project duration.

RESOURCES

Next, check that you have sufficient resources at the right times to do the work. Where there are overallocated resources—resources assigned to more tasks than the resource can do simultaneously—adjust the tasks and resources to resolve the problems.

Also look at how resources are used over the life of the project. You want to use resources evenly throughout the project, with as few peaks and valleys as possible. To achieve this, you may want to move tasks around within their slack time.

COST

Check the total project cost. If it is unacceptable, look at the individual task and resource costs to determine what you can do to lower costs. For example, can you use a less costly resource on a task? Or maybe request additional bids for a task to be performed by an outside contractor to lower the cost of the task?

USING MICROSOFT PROJECT

When you evaluate the schedule, use Microsoft Project views, tables, and filters to see exactly the information you need. You can check:

- Project finish date
- Critical path and all the tasks on the critical path
- Slack time and noncritical tasks
- Relationships and constraints
- How resources are assigned to tasks and used over time
- Project, task, and resource costs

The following table lists a few of the many ways to evaluate the schedule in Microsoft Project.

To see	Use
When the project is scheduled to finish	File Summary Info, Project tab or Statistics button
Critical path and tasks on the critical path	Gantt Chart; PERT Chart; Task Sheet with Critical filter applied
Slack time, to determine how you can shift tasks to use resources more efficiently	Task Sheet with Schedule table applied; Delay Gantt; Detail Gantt
Relationships between tasks, to decide if tasks can occur simultaneously to speed up the schedule or sequentially to use overallocated resources more efficiently	Gantt Chart over Task PERT Chart
Constraints, to verify all are necessary	Task Sheet with Constraint Dates table and Tasks With Fixed Dates filter applied
All resources, their cost and work, plus peak usage	Resource Sheet with Summary table applied
Level of resource use over the life of the project	Resource Usage view
When resources are scheduled to work on tasks	Resource Form with schedule fields displayed
Highs and lows in peak resource usage	Resource Graph
If project costs are within budget	File Summary Info, Statistics button, or Project Statistics button on Tracking toolbar
Resource cost over the life of the project	Resource Graph showing cumulative cost for all resources
Task costs, to decide what to cut	Task Sheet with Cost table applied, over Task Form with resource cost fields displayed

CHECKING THE PROJECT FINISH DATE AND PROJECT COSTS

Use the File Summary Info command or the Project Statistics button on the Tracking toolbar to check the project finish date and total costs. For example, in the calculator project, one of your goals is to have a new calculator ready for the back-to-school promotion. If this is scheduled to occur in August, finishing the project on April 3 will be okay unless, of course, you were hoping to finish nine months earlier.

To see project statistics, click the Project Statistics button on the Tracking toolbar, or choose File Summary Info and then the Statistics button.

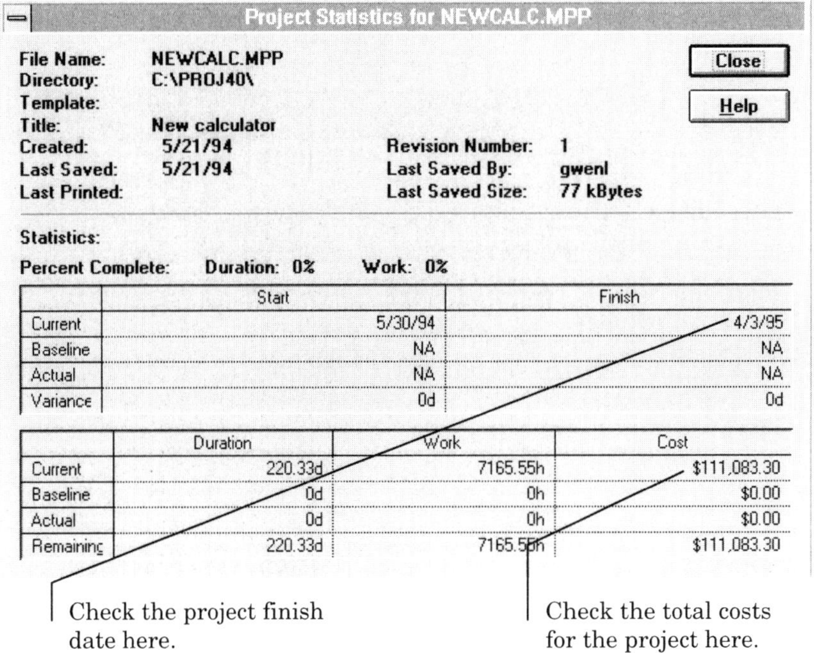

Project Statistics for NEWCALC.MPP

Close
Help

File Name: NEWCALC.MPP
Directory: C:\PROJ40\
Template:
Title: New calculator
Created: 5/21/94
Last Saved: 5/21/94
Last Printed:
Revision Number: 1
Last Saved By: gwenl
Last Saved Size: 77 kBytes

Statistics:
Percent Complete: Duration: 0% Work: 0%

	Start	Finish
Current	5/30/94	4/3/95
Baseline	NA	NA
Actual	NA	NA
Variance	0d	0d

	Duration	Work	Cost
Current	220.33d	7165.55h	$111,083.30
Baseline	0d	0h	$0.00
Actual	0d	0h	$0.00
Remaining	220.33d	7165.55h	$111,083.30

Check the project finish date here.

Check the total costs for the project here.

If the project finish date is too late, the next step is to look at the critical path and the tasks on the critical path to see how you can speed things up. If the costs are too high, you need to look at individual task and resource costs to find costs to reduce.

Displaying the Tracking Toolbar Microsoft Project comes with several toolbars. The Standard toolbar and Formatting toolbar are displayed when you first start Microsoft Project. To display the Tracking toolbar, choose View Toolbars, select Tracking, and then choose Show.

CHECKING CRITICAL TASKS

By identifying the critical tasks, you know which tasks to accelerate if you need to finish the project earlier than currently scheduled. In Microsoft Project, you can look at the critical path and critical tasks on the Gantt Chart or PERT Chart. You can also look at a list of critical tasks and milestones on the Task Sheet. In Microsoft Project, tasks with the Must Start On and Must Finish On constraints are always critical.

Changing the Amount of Time that Makes a Task Critical Initially, Microsoft Project considers any task with zero total slack time a critical task. But you can change this. For example, if you have a two-year project, you may want any task with slack of less than one week to be considered a critical task. To change the amount of time that makes a task critical, choose Tools Options. Select the Schedule tab. In the Tasks Are Critical If Slack <= *x* Days box, type the number of days of slack time a task can have and still be critical. For example, type **5** if you want tasks with one week of slack time to be critical. Choose OK.

Critical Path on the Gantt Chart

Initially, the Gantt Chart doesn't show the critical path. It is easy to make the critical tasks stand out, however, by using the GanttChartWizard to change their color. Click the GanttChartWizard button on the Standard toolbar or choose Format GanttChartWizard. On the second screen, select the Critical Path option. Continue through the Wizard screens, selecting any other options you want. When you are finished, your Gantt Chart will show critical tasks in red.

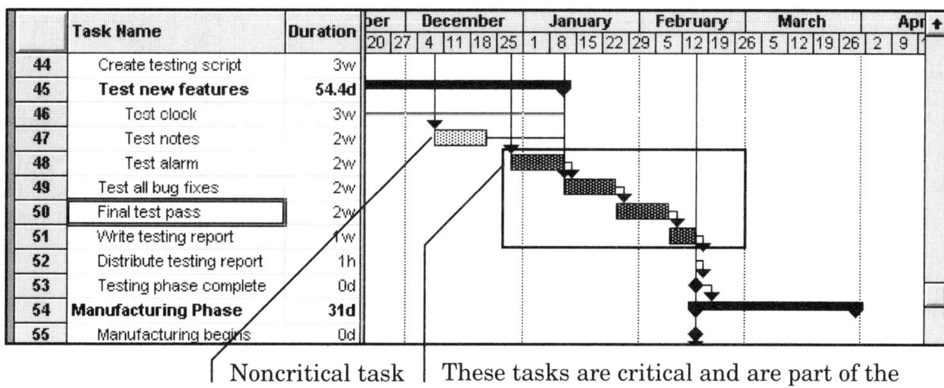

Noncritical task

These tasks are critical and are part of the critical path. This is one area where you can look for ways to accelerate the tasks.

Critical Path on the PERT Chart

On the PERT Chart, the node borders and the lines connecting the nodes identify the critical tasks and critical path.

By following the red or bold critical path through the PERT Chart, you'll see which tasks you need to concentrate on if you need to bring in the finish date.

The following illustration shows a zoomed out PERT Chart so you can better see the relationships among the various types of nodes.

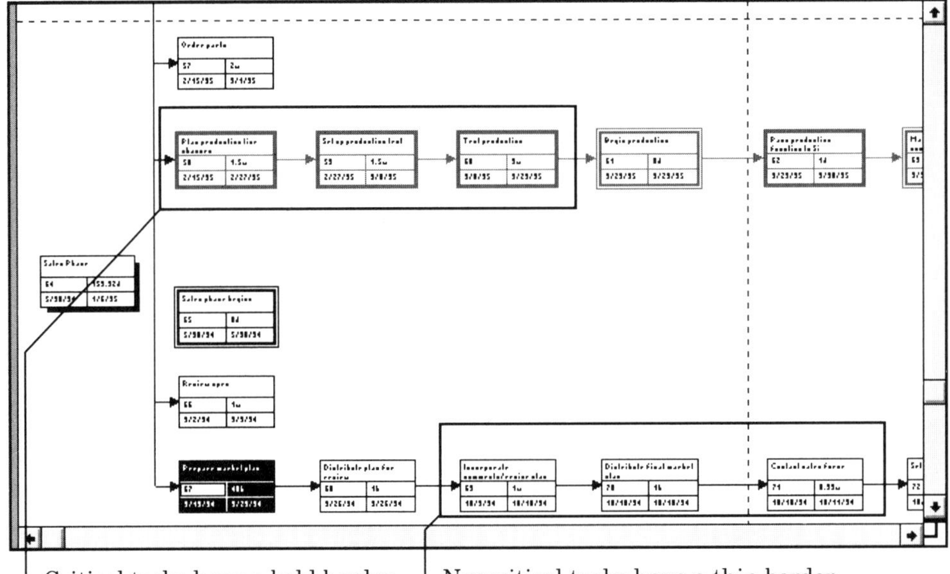

Critical tasks have a bold border and the critical path is bold.

Noncritical tasks have a thin border and the noncritical path is a thin line.

Critical Tasks on the Task Sheet

There are several ways to look at critical tasks on the Task Sheet. One way to pick out critical tasks from the rest of the tasks is to change the color or style of critical task names. To do this, choose Format Text Styles.

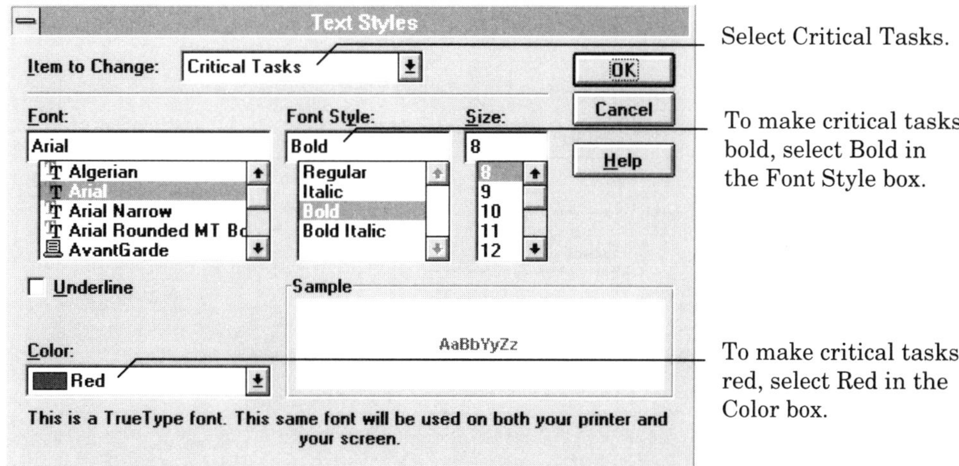

Select Critical Tasks.

To make critical tasks bold, select Bold in the Font Style box.

To make critical tasks red, select Red in the Color box.

If you want to see a list of critical tasks only, apply the Critical filter to the Task Sheet. When the Critical filter is applied, only those tasks and milestones that are critical are displayed in the view.

Apply the Critical filter by selecting Critical from the Filter box on the Formatting toolbar. Or choose Tools Filtered For/Critical.

	Task Name	Duration	Start	Finish	Predecessors	Resource Names
34	**Code new features**	**67.8d**	**9/19/94 8:00AM**	**12/21/94 3:24PM**	**32**	**Bill[0.2],Dave[0.5]**
36	Code notes feature	4.28w	11/2/94 8:00AM	12/1/94 11:12AM	35	Design staff
37	Code alarm feature	2.88w	12/1/94 11:12AM	12/21/94 3:24PM	36	Design staff
45	**Test new features**	**54.4d**	**10/27/94 11:12AM**	**1/11/95 3:24PM**		**Marilynn[0.25]**
48	Test alarm	2w	12/28/94 3:24PM	1/11/95 3:24PM	37FS+1w	Testing staff
49	Test all bug fixes	2w	1/11/95 3:24PM	1/25/95 3:24PM	33,46,47,48	Testing staff[2],Mari
50	Final test pass	2w	1/25/95 3:24PM	2/8/95 3:24PM	49	Testing staff[2],Mari
51	Write testing report	1w	2/8/95 3:24PM	2/15/95 3:24PM	50	Marilynn
52	Distribute testing report	1h	2/15/95 3:24PM	2/15/95 4:24PM	51	Terri
53	Testing phase complete	0d	2/15/95 4:24PM	2/15/95 4:24PM	52	
54	**Manufacturing Phase**	**31d**	**2/15/95 4:24PM**	**3/30/95 4:24PM**	**53**	
58	Plan production line chanç	1.5w	2/15/95 4:24PM	2/27/95 11:24AM	32	Production engineer
59	Set up production test	1.5w	2/27/95 11:24AM	3/8/95 4:24PM	58	Production team,Pro
60	Test production	3w	3/8/95 4:24PM	3/29/95 4:24PM	59	Production team[3],S
61	Begin production	0d	3/29/95 4:24PM	3/29/95 4:24PM	60	Production team[5],F
62	Pass production function	1d	3/29/95 4:24PM	3/30/95 4:24PM	61	Nancy,Production e

All the tasks now displayed on the Task Sheet are critical tasks. The list of ID numbers is no longer complete. For example, tasks 38 through 44 are missing, which means they are not critical tasks.

If you then sort the tasks by duration, the critical tasks will be in order from the longest to the shortest. This helps you see where to put your efforts in shortening tasks.

Choose Tools Sort/Sort By.

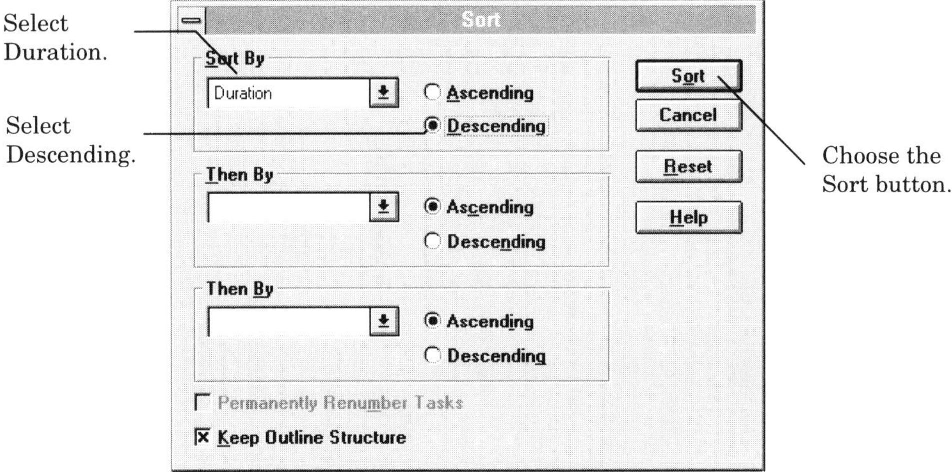

	Task Name	Duration	Start	Finish	Predecessors	Resource Names
45	**Test new features**	**54.4d**	**10/27/94 11:12AM**	**1/11/95 3:24PM**		**Marilynn[0.25]**
48	Test alarm	2w	12/28/94 3:24PM	1/11/95 3:24PM	37FS+1w	Testing staff
49	Test all bug fixes	2w	1/11/95 3:24PM	1/25/95 3:24PM	33,46,47,48	Testing staff[2],Mari
50	Final test pass	2w	1/25/95 3:24PM	2/8/95 3:24PM	49	Testing staff[2],Mari
51	Write testing report	1w	2/8/95 3:24PM	2/15/95 3:24PM	50	Marilynn
52	Distribute testing report	1h	2/15/95 3:24PM	2/15/95 4:24PM	51	Terri
53	Testing phase complete	0d	2/15/95 4:24PM	2/15/95 4:24PM	52	
34	**Code new features**	**67.8d**	**9/19/94 8:00AM**	**12/21/94 3:24PM**	**32**	**Bill[0.2],Dave[0.5]**
36	Code notes feature	4.28w	11/2/94 8:00AM	12/1/94 11:12AM	35	Design staff
37	Code alarm feature	2.88w	12/1/94 11:12AM	12/21/94 3:24PM	36	Design staff
54	**Manufacturing Phase**	**31d**	**2/15/95 4:24PM**	**3/30/95 4:24PM**	**53**	
60	Test production	3w	3/8/95 4:24PM	3/29/95 4:24PM	59	Production team[3],S
58	Plan production line chang	1.5w	2/15/95 4:24PM	2/27/95 11:24AM	32	Production engineer
59	Set up production test	1.5w	2/27/95 11:24AM	3/8/95 4:24PM	58	Production team,Pro
62	Pass production function	1d	3/29/95 4:24PM	3/30/95 4:24PM	61	Nancy,Production e
61	Begin production	0d	3/29/95 4:24PM	3/29/95 4:24PM	60	Production team[5],F
63	Manufacturing phase com	0d	3/30/95 4:24PM	3/30/95 4:24PM	62	

The longest critical task is now at the top of the list. The shortest is at the bottom.

To return to ID number order, Tools Sort/By ID.

To display all the tasks again, select All Tasks in the Filter box on the Formatting toolbar or choose Tools Filtered For/All Tasks.

If you want to see the status of all tasks in the project, add the Critical column to the table. If a task or milestone is critical, this field contains Yes; if the task or milestone is not critical, the field contains No.

Applying the Critical filter as a Highlighting Filter Another way to check critical tasks is to apply the Critical filter such that it highlights the critical tasks instead of displaying only the critical tasks. To do this, select the Tools menu. Hold down Shift and choose Filtered For. Choose Critical. All tasks are still displayed, but critical tasks will now be blue. You can change the color of the highlighted tasks using the Format Text Styles dialog box.

CHECKING SLACK TIME

Another way to analyze your schedule is to look at the amount of slack time the tasks have. By minimizing slack time, you make your schedule as efficient as it can be and use resources more effectively. You can look at slack time on the Task Sheet or Gantt Chart.

Microsoft Project tells you when a task has negative total slack, which means the task is scheduled to take longer than its predecessors and successors allow.

Negative slack appears as a negative number in the Total Slack column on the Task Sheet when you have the Schedule table applied.

Turning Off the Scheduling Message for Negative Slack When a task has negative slack, Microsoft Project tells you every time it recalculates the schedule, which, if Microsoft Project is calculating automatically, is every time you change something. If you don't want to deal with a scheduling problem now, and you don't want to keep getting the message, you can turn it off. If you are getting advice from the PlanningWizard, you can select the Don't Tell Me About This Again check box in the Wizard to turn off that message; to turn off the PlanningWizard altogether, choose Tool Options. On the General tab, clear the appropriate option under PlanningWizard. If the PlanningWizard is off, you'll still see a message from Microsoft Project warning you about the problem in the schedule. To turn off the error message, choose Tools Options. On the Schedule tab, clear the Show Scheduling Messages check box. Choose OK.

Turning Off Automatic Calculation If you turn off automatic calculation, Microsoft Project calculates the schedule only when you tell it to. To turn off automatic calculation, choose Tools Options. On the Calculation tab, select the Manual option, and choose OK. When you are ready to calculate the schedule, choose Tools Options/Calculate, select the Calculate Project button, and choose OK.

Slack Time on the Task Sheet

To see the free slack time and total slack time for each task, apply the Schedule table to the Task Sheet.

Choose View More Views. In the Views box, select Task Sheet, and then choose the Apply button. Choose View Table/Schedule.

	Task Name	Start	Finish	Late Start	Late Finish	Free Slack	Total Slack
21	Carry out phone	7/26/94 10:00AM	8/2/94 10:00AM	8/5/94 3:48PM	8/12/94 3:48PM	0d	8.6d
22	Prepare focus	8/2/94 10:00AM	8/16/94 10:00AM	8/12/94 3:48PM	8/26/94 3:48PM	0d	8.6d
23	Prepare phone	8/16/94 10:00AM	8/18/94 3:00PM	8/26/94 3:48PM	8/31/94 10:48AM	0d	8.6d
24	Present results	8/18/94 3:00PM	8/19/94 10:00AM	8/31/94 10:48AM	8/31/94 3:48PM	0d	8.6d
25	Investigation ph	8/19/94 10:00AM	8/19/94 10:00AM	8/31/94 3:48PM	8/31/94 3:48PM	8.6d	8.6d
26	**Design Phase**	**8/19/94 10:00AM**	**2/2/95 4:12PM**	**8/31/94 3:48PM**	**3/30/95 4:24PM**	**0d**	**8.6d**
27	Design begins	8/19/94 10:00AM	8/19/94 10:00AM	8/31/94 3:48PM	8/31/94 3:48PM	0d	8.6d
28	Prepare initial s	8/19/94 10:00AM	9/2/94 10:00AM	8/31/94 3:48PM	9/14/94 3:48PM	0d	8.6d
29	Distribute for re	9/2/94 10:00AM	9/2/94 11:00AM	9/14/94 3:48PM	9/14/94 4:48PM	0d	8.6d
30	Meet with revie	9/9/94 11:00AM	9/9/94 4:00PM	9/21/94 4:48PM	9/22/94 11:48AM	0d	8.6d
31	Incorporate com	9/9/94 4:00PM	9/16/94 4:00PM	9/22/94 11:48AM	9/29/94 11:48AM	0d	8.6d
32	Distribute final s	9/16/94 4:00PM	9/16/94 5:00PM	9/29/94 11:48AM	9/29/94 1:48PM	0d	8.6d
33	Fix old bugs	8/19/94 10:00AM	8/22/94 10:00AM	1/10/95 3:24PM	1/11/95 3:24PM	102.55d	102.55d
34	**Code new fea**	**9/19/94 8:00AM**	**12/21/94 3:24PM**	**9/29/94 1:48PM**	**12/21/94 3:24PM**	**0d**	**0d**
35	Code clock	9/19/94 8:00AM	10/20/94 11:12AM	9/29/94 1:48PM	11/1/94 5:00PM	0d	8.6d
36	Code notes	11/2/94 8:00AM	12/1/94 11:12AM	11/2/94 8:00AM	12/1/94 11:12AM	0d	0d
37	Code alarm	12/1/94 11:12AM	12/21/94 3:24PM	12/1/94 11:12AM	12/21/94 3:24PM	0d	0d
38	Revise manual	9/19/94 8:00AM	12/9/94 5:00PM	1/5/95 4:24PM	3/30/95 4:24PM	78.93d	78.93d
39	Fix bugs in new	1/11/95 1:00PM	2/2/95 4:12PM	3/8/95 1:12PM	3/30/95 4:24PM	0d	40.03d

Free slack and total slack; negative slack is indicated by a minus sign.

Zero total slack indicates a critical task.

Slack Time on the Gantt Chart

To see the slack time graphically for each task, display the Delay Gantt or the Detail Gantt. You can also use the GanttChartWizard or the Format Bar Styles command to add these bars to any Gantt Chart.

The following illustration shows slack on the Detail Gantt. Slack is shown with a narrow bar (teal on a color monitor); the amount of slack time is indicated at the right end of the bar. Slippage is also shown on this view, but since no baseline has been saved and no actual information entered, there is no slippage in the illustration. To display the Detail Gantt, choose View More Views. In the Views box, select Detail Gantt, and choose the Apply button.

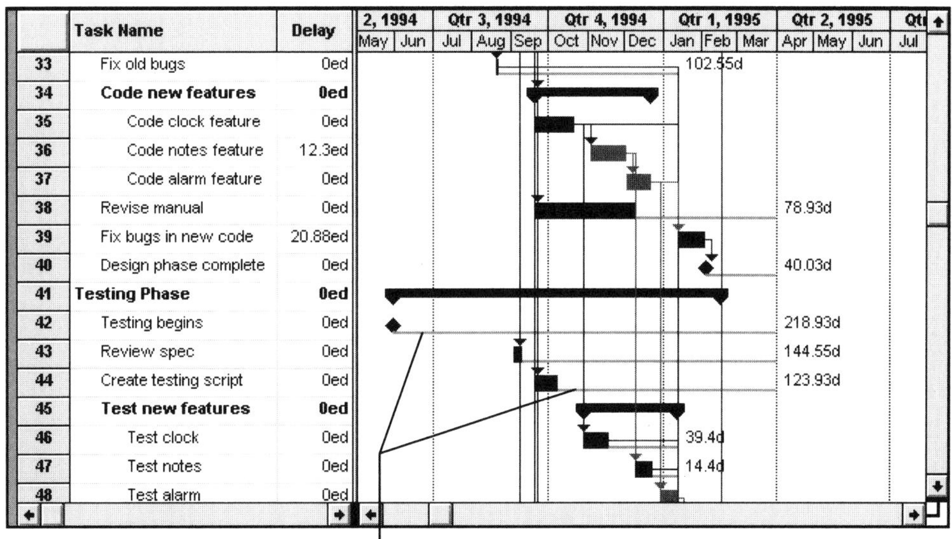

These bars show the amount of slack time for each task.

CHECKING RELATIONSHIPS AND CONSTRAINTS

The purpose of checking relationships and constraints is to make sure you haven't imposed a relationship or constraint that isn't absolutely necessary. For example, see if you can accelerate the schedule by changing the relationship between tasks so the tasks overlap, or try adding lag between tasks to use overallocated resources better. Resources are overallocated when they are assigned to more tasks than they can do at one time.

Check for constraints that force a task to start or finish on a certain date. Such constraints may be causing scheduling problems. Replacing Must Start On constraint, for example, with As Soon As Possible, or even changing it to Start No Earlier Than or Start No Later Than as appropriate, may give you more flexibility in solving scheduling problems. Remember that Must Start On and Must Finish On constraints always make a task critical, so use them sparingly.

Checking Relationships

To review the relationships between tasks, use the Gantt Chart to see graphically how tasks are related now. Look at sequential tasks to see if they can be overlapped. Place the Task PERT Chart below the Gantt Chart to see the immediate predecessors and successors to the task selected on the Gantt Chart and the relationships between the tasks. This will help you find tasks that could be performed in a different order to either save time or free resources.

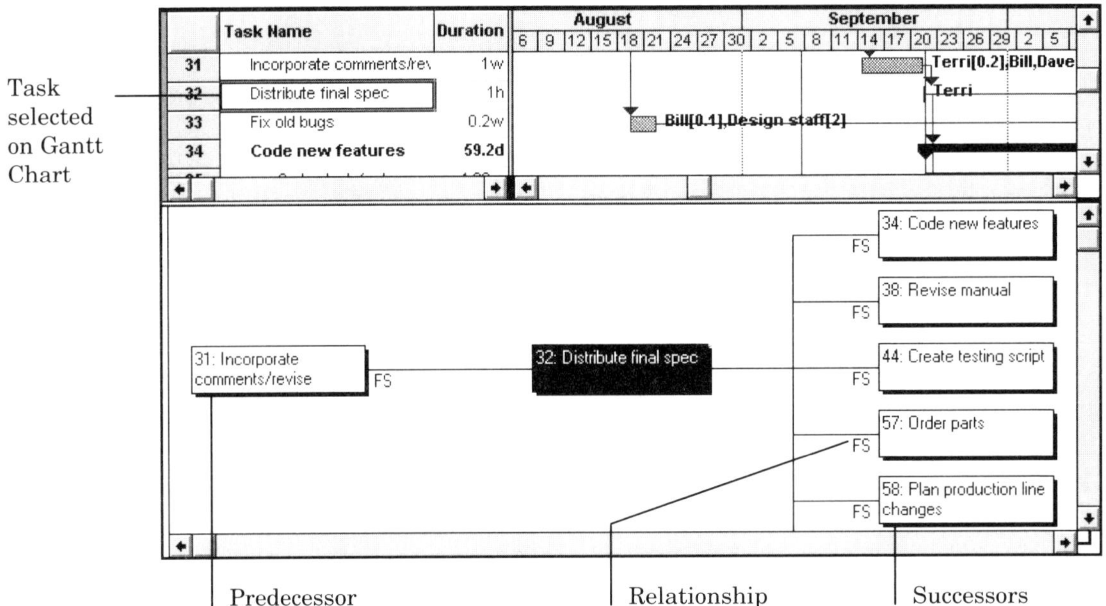

Look at predecessors and successors on the Task PERT Chart to make sure relationships reflect how you plan to perform the tasks. The relationship and lead or lag time between each pair of tasks is shown between the tasks.

Checking Constraints

Check the constraints to make sure all constraints other than As Soon As Possible are necessary. To check constraints on all tasks, apply the Constraint Dates table to the Task Sheet. To see a list of tasks that have a constraint other than As Soon As Possible, apply the Tasks With Fixed Dates filter to the Task Sheet.

Choose View More Views. In the Views box, select Task Sheet, and then choose the Apply button. To apply the Constraint Dates table, choose View Table/More Tables. In the Tables box, select Constraint Dates, and then choose the Apply button.

	Task Name	Duration	Constraint Type	Constraint Date
24	Present results	4h	As Soon As Possible	
25	Investigation phase complete	0d	Finish No Later Than	8/19/94 10:00AM
26	**Design Phase**	**98.85d**	**As Soon As Possible**	
27	Design begins	0d	As Soon As Possible	
28	Prepare initial spec	2.5w	As Soon As Possible	
29	Distribute for review	1h	As Soon As Possible	
30	Meet with reviewers	4h	As Soon As Possible	
31	Incorporate comments/revise	1w	As Soon As Possible	

Make sure that constraints other than As Soon As Possible are necessary.

If you want to see only those tasks that have a constraint other than As Soon As Possible, apply the Tasks With Fixed Dates filter. To do this, select Tasks With Fixed Dates from the Filter box on the Formatting toolbar. The Tasks With Fixed Dates filter also shows all tasks with an actual start date. To display all the tasks again, select All Tasks in the Filter box or choose Tools Filtered For/All Tasks.

When you check constraints, you may find constraints that you don't remember entering. Any time you enter a scheduled start date for a task, for example on the Task Form in the Start box, Microsoft Project enters a constraint of Start No Earlier Than. When you change the start date with the mouse or create a new task by dragging on the Gantt Chart or Calendar, Microsoft Project also enters a Start No Earlier Than constraint. Change any constraint that is unnecessary or is not appropriate.

Checking Resources

Use the resource views to check the resource pool, see which resources are overallocated (assigned too many tasks), check when resources are scheduled to work on tasks, and look for highs and lows in resource use. Checking for overallocated and underallocated resources is important because it shows problem areas in your project. For example, it might be warning you that the same person is assigned to two full-time tasks on the same day. Obviously, one person can't do both tasks, so you'll either need to move the tasks around or assign someone else to one of the tasks. In Chapter 9, you'll see various ways to take care of overallocated resources.

Reviewing a List of Resources

To see a list of all resources in the resource pool, plus information about peak usage, apply the Summary table to the Resource Sheet.

Choose View Resource Sheet. Then choose View Table/Summary.

	Resource Name	Group	Max. Units	Peak	Std. Rate	Ovt. Rate	Cost	Work
1	**Marcia**	**Marketing**	**1**	**2.1**	**$50,000.00/y**	**$0.00/h**	**$13,701.92**	**566.8h**
2	Marketing staff	Marketing	3	3	$32,000.00/y	$0.00/h	$17,969.23	1168h
3	Jim	Marketing	1	0	$32,500.00/y	$0.00/h	$0.00	0h
4	**Cheryl**	**Marketing**	**1**	**1.25**	**$16,000.00/y**	**$11.50/h**	**$1,630.76**	**212h**
5	**Janet**	**Marketing**	**1**	**1.1**	**$47,500.00/y**	**$0.00/h**	**$9,043.27**	**396h**
6	Roberto	Marketing	1	1	$30,000.00/y	$0.00/h	$115.38	8h
7	Carmen	Marketing	1	1	$60,000.00/y	$0.00/h	$230.77	8h
8	Research Inc	Vendor	1	1	$500.00/d	$0.00/h	$5,000.00	80h
9	Dave	Design	1	1	$60,000.00/y	$0.00/h	$10,311.06	357.45h
10	Bill	Design	1	1	$25,000.00/y	$0.00/h	$3,771.83	313.82h
11	Terri	Design	1	1	$6.50/h	$9.75/h	$284.70	43.8h
12	Design staff	Design	3	3	$25,000.00/y	$0.00/h	$8,230.77	684.8h
13	Sales engineers	Sales	3	3	$32,000.00/y	$0.00/h	$10,455.38	679.6h
14	Testing staff	Testing	3	2	$25,000.00/y	$0.00/h	$7,211.55	600h
15	Marilynn	Testing	1	1	$32,500.00/y	$0.00/h	$7,391.15	473.03h
16	**Production engineers**	**Production**	**2**	**4**	**$32,500.00/y**	**$0.00/h**	**$5,125.00**	**328h**
17	Production team	Production	10	3	$25,000.00/y	$0.00/h	$2,644.23	220h
18	**Nancy**	**Production**	**1**	**1.5**	**$32,500.00/y**	**$0.00/h**	**$2,062.50**	**132h**
19	Shop crew	Production	5	3	$15.00/h	$22.50/h	$1,800.00	120h

Ready | Level: Marcia | NUM

Overallocated resources are bold or red.

Peak column shows highest number allocated at any time.

Level message indicates Marcia is overallocated.

When the number in the Peak column is greater than the number in the Max. Units column, it means the resource is overallocated because more units are assigned to tasks than there are units available.

When a resource is overallocated, Microsoft Project tells you by displaying “Level” at the bottom of the screen. If more than one resource is overallocated, the name of the first overallocated resource in the list is displayed.

If you want to see only those resources that are overallocated, apply the Overallocated Resources filter. To do this, select the filter from the Filter box on the Formatting toolbar, or choose Tools Filtered For/Overallocated Resources. To display all the resources again, select All Resources from the Filter box, or choose Tools Filter For/All Resources.

You can also sort this list according to the cost of using a resource on the project. If you must cut costs, you may want to look at the high end and decide how to decrease your use of the most expensive resources.

To sort by cost, choose Tools Sort/Sort By. In the Sort By box, select Cost. Select the Descending option. Choose Sort.

The most costly resource will now be on top and least costly on the bottom.

To return to ID number order, choose Tools Sort/By ID.

If you create a combination view with the Task Sheet over the Resource Form showing the schedule fields, you can see the tasks to which the selected resource is assigned, and then decide how you can reduce this resource's participation on tasks.

Checking Resource Usage

The Resource Usage view shows you all resources in a spreadsheet format and their usage during each time period. Use the Resource Usage view to check work allocation for all resources in your project. This information will help you decide which resources have too much work (overallocated) and which need more work (underallocated). In Chapter 9, as you are refining your schedule, this information will help you decide which resources you can shift to accelerate tasks or to solve overallocation.

The Resource Usage view can display several types of information:

- Peak units used during each period for each resource
- Work during each period for each resource
- Cumulative work to date for each period
- Overallocated work for each resource during each period
- Percentage of allocation for each resource during each period
- Remaining availability of each resource during each period
- Cost of using each resource during each period
- Cumulative cost to date for each period

To see the amount of work assigned to each resource during each period, choose View Resource Usage.

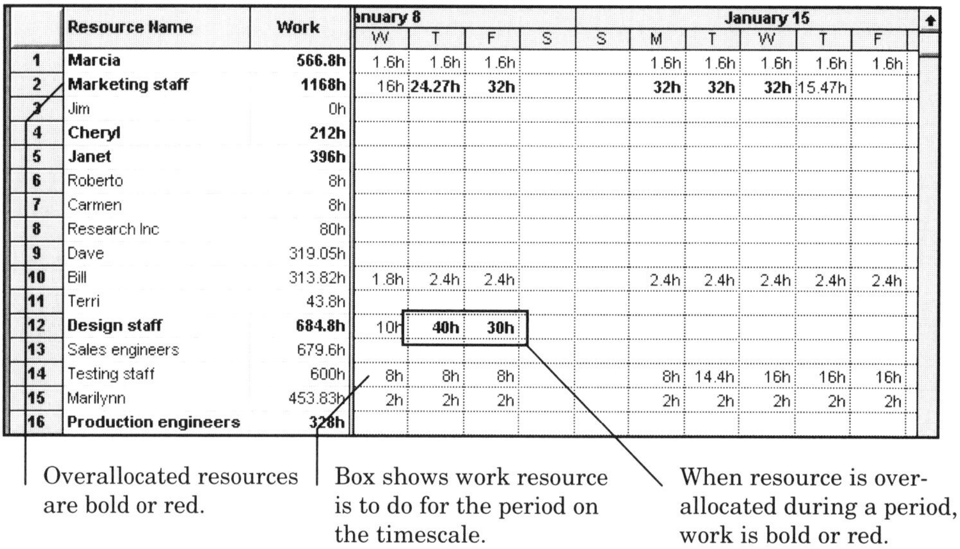

	Resource Name	Work	anuary 8 W	T	F	S	January 15 S	M	T	W	T	F
1	**Marcia**	**566.8h**	1.6h	1.6h	1.6h			1.6h	1.6h	1.6h	1.6h	1.6h
2	**Marketing staff**	**1168h**	16h	**24.27h**	**32h**			**32h**	**32h**	**32h**	15.47h	
3	Jim	0h										
4	**Cheryl**	**212h**										
5	**Janet**	**396h**										
6	Roberto	8h										
7	Carmen	8h										
8	Research Inc	80h										
9	Dave	319.05h										
10	Bill	313.82h	1.8h	2.4h	2.4h			2.4h	2.4h	2.4h	2.4h	2.4h
11	Terri	43.8h										
12	**Design staff**	**684.8h**	10h	**40h**	**30h**							
13	Sales engineers	679.6h										
14	Testing staff	600h	8h	8h	8h			8h	14.4h	16h	16h	16h
15	Marilynn	453.83h	2h	2h	2h			2h	2h	2h	2h	2h
16	**Production engineers**	**328h**										

Overallocated resources are bold or red.

Box shows work resource is to do for the period on the timescale.

When resource is overallocated during a period, work is bold or red.

To change the type of information in the boxes, use the Format Details commands. For example, to see the percentage of total capacity that each resource is allocated during the period, choose Format Details/Percent Allocation.

If you place the Resource Usage view below a task view, such as the Gantt Chart, you can use the Format Details/Selected Tasks Only command to view resource information for only those tasks selected in the task view.

In the following illustration, Marketing staff is scheduled to work at 200 percent on the two tasks selected on the Gantt Chart. Prior to that, the Marketing staff is underallocated. You can identify this by their percentages being less than 100.

	Task Name	Duration	January 1 / January 8
72	Set up sales meetings	1d	
73	Contact major dealers	1d	
74	Prepare marketing materia	4w	keting staff[2],Documentation dept.
75	Prepare packaging	2w	Marcia[0.2],Marketing
76	Prepare for major announ	2w	
77	Make announcement	1d	

	Resource Name	Work	M	T	W	T	F	S	S	M	T	W	T	F	S	S	M
			January 1							**January 8**							
1	Marcia	566.8h	20	20	20	20	20			20	40	40	29	20			20
2	Marketing staff	1168h	66	66	66	66	66			68	200	200	165	133			131
21	Documentation dept.	720h	100	100	100	100	100			100	100	100	48				

Tasks for which resource information is displayed on the Resource Usage view. To specify information for selected tasks only, choose Format Details/Selected Tasks Only.

Marketing staff is underallocated.

Marketing staff is overallocated.

A percentage less than 100 indicates the resource is underallocated on the selected tasks during the period on the timescale; a percentage greater than 100 indicates the resource is overallocated on the selected tasks during the period on the timescale.

To resolve overallocated resources, try shifting one of the tasks such that it occurs earlier or later, or assign other resources to the task to reduce the number of units required of the overallocated resource.

Changing the Timescale You can change the timescale so the usage boxes cover as much or as little time as you want. Double-click the timescale or choose the Format Timescale to change the major timescale (the upper dates) or the minor timescale (the lower units).

To quickly show more detail in the schedule, click the Zoom In button on the Standard toolbar or press Ctrl+/ (on the keypad) in Windows or Command+/ (on the keypad) on the Macintosh.

To quickly show less detail in the schedule, click the Zoom Out button on the Standard toolbar or press Ctrl+* (on the keypad) in Windows or Command+* (on the keypad) on the Macintosh.

Changing Work Units Initially, the units on the Resource Usage view are hours. You can change these units to minutes, days, or weeks. Choose Tools Options, and then select the Schedule tab. In the Show Work In box, select the units you want, and choose OK.

Checking Resource Task Assignments

On the Resource Form, you can see the list of tasks to which each resource is assigned. This will help you decide how to change assignments for tasks with overallocated resources and where you might find additional resources to work on tasks you want to accelerate.

Choose View More Views. In the Views box, select Resource Form, and then choose the Apply button. To show the schedule fields, choose Format Details/Schedule.

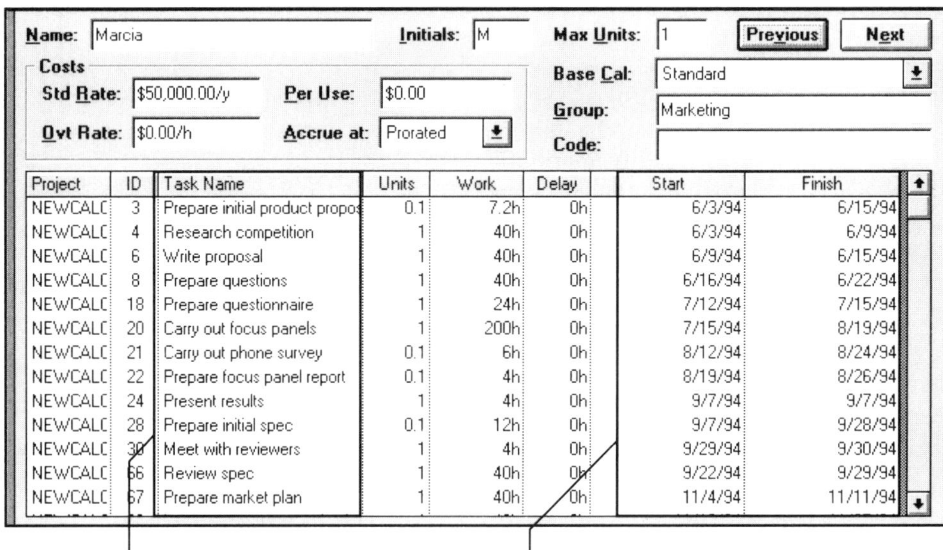

Project	ID	Task Name	Units	Work	Delay	Start	Finish
NEWCALC	3	Prepare initial product propos	0.1	7.2h	0h	6/3/94	6/15/94
NEWCALC	4	Research competition	1	40h	0h	6/3/94	6/9/94
NEWCALC	6	Write proposal	1	40h	0h	6/9/94	6/15/94
NEWCALC	8	Prepare questions	1	40h	0h	6/16/94	6/22/94
NEWCALC	18	Prepare questionnaire	1	24h	0h	7/12/94	7/15/94
NEWCALC	20	Carry out focus panels	1	200h	0h	7/15/94	8/19/94
NEWCALC	21	Carry out phone survey	0.1	6h	0h	8/12/94	8/24/94
NEWCALC	22	Prepare focus panel report	0.1	4h	0h	8/19/94	8/26/94
NEWCALC	24	Present results	1	4h	0h	9/7/94	9/7/94
NEWCALC	28	Prepare initial spec	0.1	12h	0h	9/7/94	9/28/94
NEWCALC	30	Meet with reviewers	1	4h	0h	9/29/94	9/30/94
NEWCALC	66	Review spec	1	40h	0h	9/22/94	9/29/94
NEWCALC	67	Prepare market plan	1	40h	0h	11/4/94	11/11/94

Tasks to which this resource is assigned.

Check the dates resource is scheduled to start and finish work on each task.

Checking the Usage Graph for Resources

On the Resource Graph, you can see the same types of information as is available on the Resource Usage view, such as peak units, work, cumulative work, percent allocation, cost, and cumulative cost. Initially, the view shows a graph of the peak use of one resource at a time. This is the peak use that occurs at one moment during the period indicated on the timescale. For example, in the following illustration, three units of Design staff are assigned to work from Tuesday through Tuesday. They may not all be assigned to full-day tasks each day, but during some part of those six days, three Design staff are needed.

To see the Resource Graph, choose View Resource Graph.

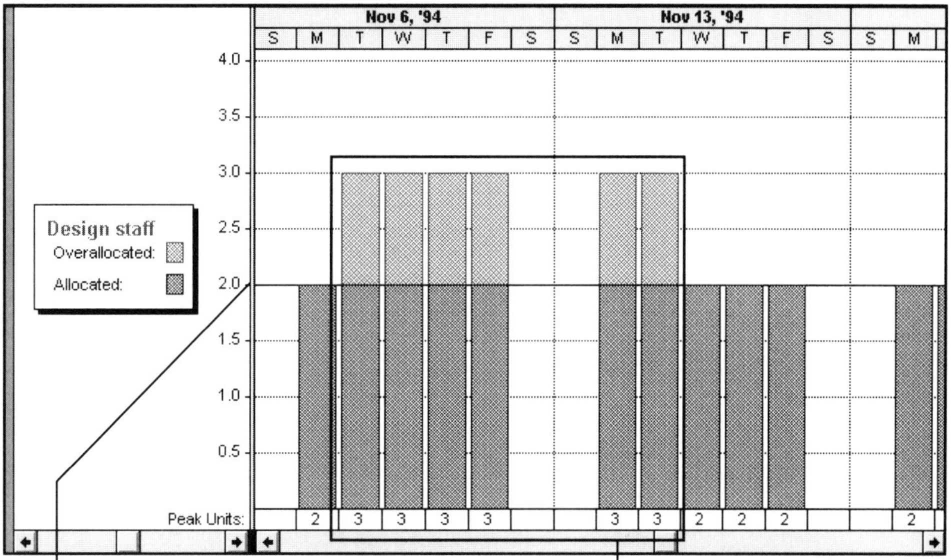

Availability line at two units shows that a maximum of two Design staff are available at one time.

Design staff is overallocated during these six days.

To see more or less detail, change the timescale.

To change the type of information displayed on the graph, use the Format Details commands. For example, to see work or availability, choose Format Details/Work or Format Details/Availability.

You can also view information for a group of resources or view a group and an individual resource at the same time. To change this, you use the Format Bar Styles command. You also use this command to change the type of graph displayed—area or bar or line, for example. For more information about customizing this view, see Chapter 16, "Using Microsoft Project Tools."

Use the Resource Graph to help decide how to move tasks around so resources are not overallocated. By combining this view with another view, such as the Gantt Chart, you see the tasks causing the overallocation as well as the period during which a resource is overallocated.

CHECKING COSTS

There are several ways you can check costs in Microsoft Project. You can check cumulative cost over the life of the project, check the total cost for each task, and check the individual resource costs on each task.

Checking Cumulative Cost

To check cumulative resource costs for the project and compare them to new costs as they occur, use the Resource Graph. Choose Format Details/Cumulative Cost. Then choose Format Bar Styles to control what is displayed on the graph.

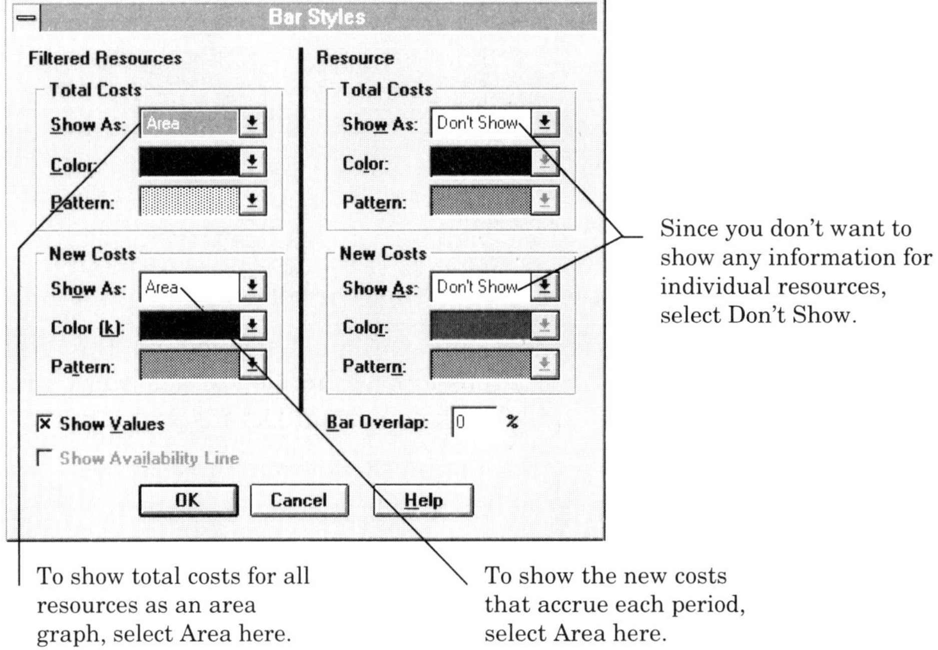

The following illustration shows the cumulative cost and new cost for each period as an area graph.

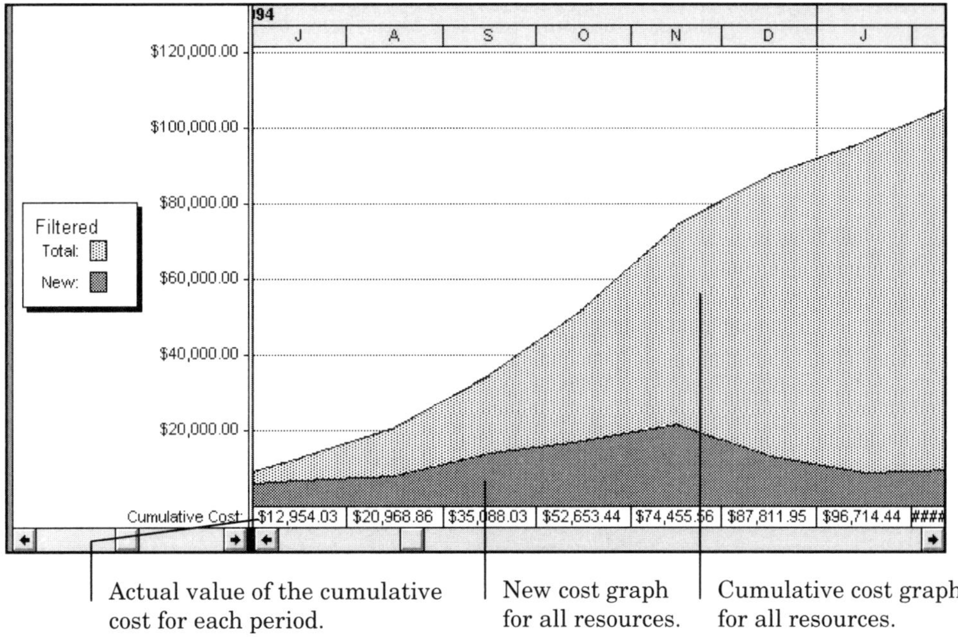

Checking Cost for Each Task

To look at costs for each task, apply the Cost table to the Task Sheet. Choose View More Views, select Task Sheet and choose the Apply button. To display the Cost table, choose View Table/Cost.

	Task Name	Fixed Cost	Total Cost	Baseline	Variance	Actual	Remaining
1	**Investigation Phase**	**$0.00**	**$17,906.41**	**$0.00**	**$17,906.41**	**$0.00**	**$17,906.41**
2	Investigation begins	$0.00	$0.00	$0.00	$0.00	$0.00	$0.00
3	**Prepare initial product pro**	**$0.00**	**$3,325.25**	**$0.00**	**$3,325.25**	**$0.00**	**$3,325.25**
4	Research competition	$0.00	$1,308.65	$0.00	$1,308.65	$0.00	$1,308.65
5	Review customer comment	$0.00	$1,101.93	$0.00	$1,101.93	$0.00	$1,101.93
6	Write proposal	$0.00	$914.42	$0.00	$914.42	$0.00	$914.42
7	**Plan focus panel**	**$0.00**	**$1,249.52**	**$0.00**	**$1,249.52**	**$0.00**	**$1,249.52**
8	Prepare questions	$0.00	$914.42	$0.00	$914.42	$0.00	$914.42
9	**Arrange sites**	**$0.00**	**$132.21**	**$0.00**	**$132.21**	**$0.00**	**$132.21**
10	Contact hotels	$0.00	$61.54	$0.00	$61.54	$0.00	$61.54
11	**Arrange for equipm**	**$0.00**	**$70.67**	**$0.00**	**$70.67**	**$0.00**	**$70.67**
12	Determine needed e	$0.00	$39.90	$0.00	$39.90	$0.00	$39.90
13	Contact local office	$0.00	$30.77	$0.00	$30.77	$0.00	$30.77
14	**Get panel members**	**$0.00**	**$202.89**	**$0.00**	**$202.89**	**$0.00**	**$202.89**
15	Contact local reps for r	$0.00	$79.81	$0.00	$79.81	$0.00	$79.81
16	Contact suggested pan	$0.00	$123.08	$0.00	$123.08	$0.00	$123.08
17	**Plan phone questionnaire**	**$0.00**	**$385.19**	**$0.00**	**$385.19**	**$0.00**	**$385.19**
18	Prepare questionnaire	$0.00	$369.81	$0.00	$369.81	$0.00	$369.81
19	Get list of users to call	$0.00	$15.38	$0.00	$15.38	$0.00	$15.38
20	Carry out focus panels	$0.00	$6,119.24	$0.00	$6,119.24	$0.00	$6,119.24

The Cost table shows the cost of each task.

There are no values in the Baseline fields yet because you have not saved the baseline schedule. When you save the baseline schedule, the values in the Total Cost fields are copied into the Baseline fields. There are no values in the Actual fields yet because you have not incurred any costs. When you enter information about progress on tasks, Microsoft Project calculates actual costs based on the work performed on each task.

Checking Individual Resource Costs

To look at the individual resource costs that make up the task cost, use a combination view with the Task Sheet on top and, on the bottom, the Task Form showing resource cost fields (choose Format Details/Resource Cost).

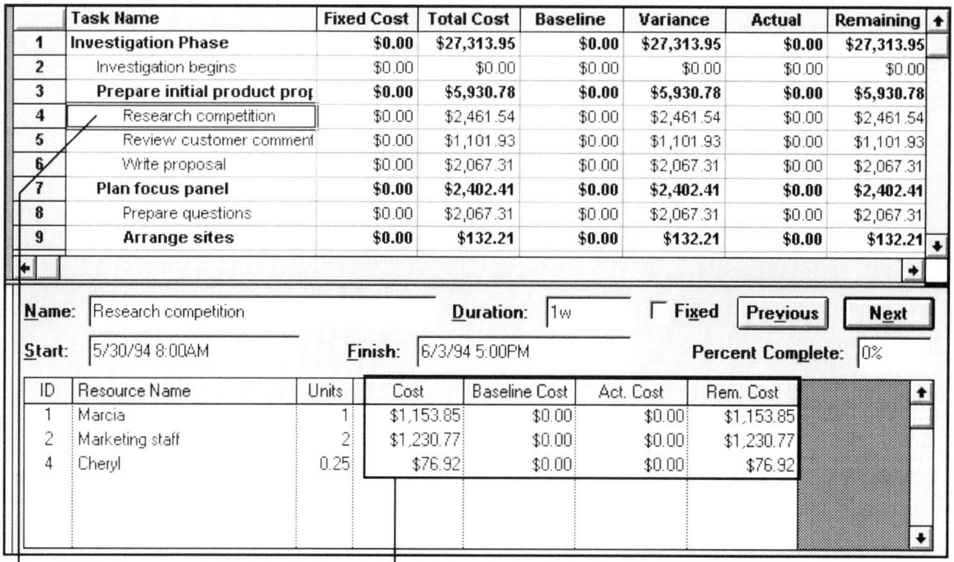

	Task Name	Fixed Cost	Total Cost	Baseline	Variance	Actual	Remaining
1	**Investigation Phase**	**$0.00**	**$27,313.95**	**$0.00**	**$27,313.95**	**$0.00**	**$27,313.95**
2	Investigation begins	$0.00	$0.00	$0.00	$0.00	$0.00	$0.00
3	**Prepare initial product pro**	**$0.00**	**$5,930.78**	**$0.00**	**$5,930.78**	**$0.00**	**$5,930.78**
4	Research competition	$0.00	$2,461.54	$0.00	$2,461.54	$0.00	$2,461.54
5	Review customer comment	$0.00	$1,101.93	$0.00	$1,101.93	$0.00	$1,101.93
6	Write proposal	$0.00	$2,067.31	$0.00	$2,067.31	$0.00	$2,067.31
7	**Plan focus panel**	**$0.00**	**$2,402.41**	**$0.00**	**$2,402.41**	**$0.00**	**$2,402.41**
8	Prepare questions	$0.00	$2,067.31	$0.00	$2,067.31	$0.00	$2,067.31
9	**Arrange sites**	**$0.00**	**$132.21**	**$0.00**	**$132.21**	**$0.00**	**$132.21**

Name: Research competition Duration: 1w Fixed Previous Next

Start: 5/30/94 8:00AM Finish: 6/3/94 5:00PM Percent Complete: 0%

ID	Resource Name	Units	Cost	Baseline Cost	Act. Cost	Rem. Cost
1	Marcia	1	$1,153.85	$0.00	$0.00	$1,153.85
2	Marketing staff	2	$1,230.77	$0.00	$0.00	$1,230.77
4	Cheryl	0.25	$76.92	$0.00	$0.00	$76.92

Select the task whose costs you are interested in.

The resource cost fields at the bottom of the Task Form show the cost of using each resource on the selected task.

The next chapter shows you how to take what you learned as you evaluated your schedule and use it to refine the schedule until it fits your needs.

9

Refining the Schedule and Freezing the Baseline

In the last chapter, you identified areas in the schedule that need adjusting—critical tasks that need to be shortened, resources that are overallocated, and so on. Your goal now is to adjust the schedule until it is satisfactory.

This step may take some time and several passes until you determine the best schedule for the situation. This exercise will help you understand your project and the schedule, and be conscious of the compromises you are making to meet your goals.

When the schedule meets your needs, you save or "freeze" this schedule as your plan, or baseline. By freezing the baseline, you have a record of your original schedule information. Later, when the project is underway, you can compare progress to this baseline.

REFINING THE SCHEDULE

When you evaluated your schedule, you probably found areas that could be improved. Now, you need to try out possible solutions to the scheduling problems. One of the major advantages of using project management software is that you can try a solution—for example, add resources to a critical task—and then look at the impact on the project in terms of time, cost, and resource usage. If the first solution you try does not work, you can continue experimenting until you come up with the best solution for this project. This is often called "what-if" analysis. For instance, what if you added resources to a task on the critical path. How would this shorten the critical path and how would it change the project and task costs?

The following lists offer some ideas for shortening the project, reducing cost, and resolving resource conflicts.

If the project finish date is too late, look for ways to shorten the critical path. You could:

- Add resources to critical tasks to shorten their duration, either by hiring new resources or by shifting resources from tasks with slack to critical tasks.
- Work overtime on critical tasks or add another shift.
- Change task sequence, add lead or lag time, or remove unnecessary constraints.
- Change the scope of tasks in the project if the finish date is a higher priority than the scope. For example, if a manual must be ready to ship by the time the software is ready, and writing the manual is a critical task causing the manual to be ready after the software, you could reduce the pages in the manual to a number you can write in the shorter time allowed.
- Reduce the scope of the project so you can delete some of the tasks. For example, suppose you have a list of features you want to add to a new calculator product, and your goal is to introduce the new product in time for the biggest sales period of the year. Lacking time to implement all the new features and make the target date, you could reduce the scope by cutting features until you feel confident you can introduce the new product on time.

If the costs are too high, you could:

- Assign the most costly resources to fewer tasks and replace them with less costly resources.
- Get additional bids for tasks performed for a contracted rate by an outside contractor.
- For resources that have a per-use charge, move tasks around so you can perform all tasks using that resource at once. For example, if you need a crane to do work on a building and also to hang a sign, consider installing the sign when you have the crane on site to do the

other work, even though the "Hang sign" task doesn't have to be done until later in the project.

- Reduce task or project scope so you need fewer resources to complete the tasks in the project. For example, if your budget for designing the new calculator is less than the cost indicated in the current schedule, you can cut features so the design phase will take less time and therefore fewer resources and less money to complete.

If there are conflicts for the resources, you could:

- Shift tasks to level out resource usage.
- Shift underallocated resources to tasks whose resources are overallocated.
- Hire additional resources.
- Work longer hours or additional shifts.
- Break tasks into smaller tasks to give you more flexibility in scheduling resources.

Be sure you involve the project team in any major changes you propose to the schedule. You want everyone to know about, be involved in deciding on, and approve of any change that affects their area.

FREEZING THE SCHEDULE

When you are satisfied with the schedule, you save, or freeze, this schedule so you can use it for tracking progress after the project is under way. This original schedule is called the baseline. The baseline schedule is a record of the original task dates and resource and cost information. You can track and control your project only if you have the original schedule to compare what actually happens against what you planned for the project.

USING MICROSOFT PROJECT

At this stage of the planning process, you use Microsoft Project to experiment with adjustments to the schedule. You add resources, change work, adjust calendars, and so on, entering the new information in the same way you entered the original information into Microsoft Project.

Each time you change the schedule, check the File Summary Info dialog box to see how the changes affect the project finish date. Choose the Statistic button to check project costs. Check the schedule as you did in Chapter 8 to review the critical path, slack time, dependencies, constraints, resources, and costs. If you don't like the change, you can undo it and try something else.

If you are not making the final decisions, but are providing information to others, you can keep track of the most likely alternatives and then share these options. This gives management the data to make an informed decision about how the project should be carried out. For example, if your project is over budget, you can present two options: one showing the cost and schedule for implementing the full scope, and a second showing what would have to be cut to meet the original budget.

When you finish adjusting the schedule, use the Tools Tracking/Save Baseline command to save the baseline. If you are waiting for a decision from management or a client about which schedule alternative is acceptable, save the baseline after you have that decision and have made the schedule match it. Just make sure to save the baseline before the project gets under way and before you begin entering progress information.

Experimenting with the Schedule

As you experiment with your schedule, Microsoft Project helps you decide which changes best fit your needs. Microsoft Project calculates the new schedule and costs; you decide if the change is for the better. For example, if you add resources to a task to speed it up, you can compare the shorter time with the higher cost and decide if this is a compromise you want to make. By trying different solutions, you can see how the schedule is affected by each solution and how the costs change, until you find the best compromise between time and cost.

The following tables list ideas for experimenting with the schedule, how you do it in Microsoft Project, and the possible effects on the schedule.

TO DECREASE PROJECT DURATION

When your goal is to decrease project duration, you want to find ways to reduce the duration of the tasks on the critical path. Shortening other tasks won't change the overall duration of the project.

Option	In Microsoft Project, use	Effect on schedule
Add resources to critical tasks to shorten their duration or shift resources from noncritical tasks to critical tasks	Task Form, resources fields; Task Sheet or Gantt Chart, Resource Names field	May decrease task duration if task uses resource-driven scheduling; may increase duration of tasks that lose resources
Add overtime work for resources with the latest finish date on critical tasks	Task Form, Ovt. Work field (Format Details/Resource Work); Resource Form, Ovt. Work field (Format Details/Work)	Decreases task duration if task uses resource-driven scheduling
Change project calendar or resource calendars to increase working hours or add additional shifts	Tools Change Working Time	Decreases duration of project because scheduled finish dates for tasks will be sooner
Change order of tasks, add lead or lag time, or remove unnecessary constraints	Task Form, predecessors fields; Task Sheet or Gantt Chart, Predecessors field	Lead and lag time can decrease project duration by overlapping tasks; constraints can reduce scheduling flexibility
Reduce scope of critical tasks	Gantt Chart, Duration field	Decreases duration of tasks to reflect the decrease in scope
Reduce scope of the project	Task Sheet; Gantt Chart	Decreases project duration by deleting tasks no longer included in the scope

TO REDUCE COSTS

When costs are an important factor on your project, there are methods for reducing cost that will affect duration and resource usage. You have to juggle the options to determine which solution is best for this project.

Option	In Microsoft Project, use	Lower costs if
Replace costly resources with less costly ones	Task Form, resources fields	Less costly resources do not cause work to increase such that task cost is not decreased
Get additional bids for flat-rate tasks	Task Sheet with Cost table applied	New bids are lower
Reduce per-use charge by changing task sequence such that tasks using certain resources can be completed simultaneously	Task Form, predecessors fields; Resource Form to change per-use rate	You have fewer per-use charges
Reduce task or project scope	Gantt Chart to delete tasks; Task Form to change resources on tasks with reduced scope	You need fewer resources for the reduced scope
Reduce task fixed costs	Task Sheet with Cost table applied	New fixed costs are lower

TO RESOLVE RESOURCE CONFLICTS

Resolving resource conflicts will most likely affect either costs or project duration or both. Again, you have to choose your solutions to overallocations based on the other requirements (time versus cost) of the project.

Option	In Microsoft Project, use	Effect on schedule
Shift underallocated resources to tasks whose resources are over-allocated	Gantt Chart or Task Sheet over Resource Usage view showing percentages	On resource-driven tasks, may decrease duration of tasks that get additional resources; may increase duration of tasks that lose resources
Hire additional resources	Task Form, resources fields; Task Sheet or Gantt Chart, Resource Names field; Resource Information dialog box to change Max Units	On resource-driven tasks, may decrease duration of tasks that get additional resources; will increase cost
Add overtime work for overallocated resources	Task Form, Ovt. Work field (Format Details/Resource Work); Resource Form, Ovt. Work field (Format Details/Work)	Decreases task duration if the task uses resource-driven scheduling
Work longer hours or additional shifts	Tools Change Working Time	On resource-driven tasks, may make tasks that get additional resources finish sooner
Break tasks into smaller tasks or reorder tasks to use resources better	Task Sheet; Gantt Chart	May resolve overallocations by shifting parts of tasks to times when resources are available
Shift tasks to level out resource usage	Resource Allocation view	May change project duration

To help you decide which schedule changes are best, look at the Project Statistics dialog box to check the effect of the change on the project finish date and project cost. Click the Project Statistics button on the Tracking toolbar, or choose File Summary Info and then choose the Statistics button.

Project Statistics for NEWCALC.MPP

File Name: NEWCALC.MPP
Directory: C:\PROJ40\
Template:
Title: New calculator
Created: 5/21/94 Revision Number: 1
Last Saved: 5/21/94 Last Saved By: gwenl
Last Printed: Last Saved Size: 77 kBytes

Close | Help

Statistics:

Percent Complete: Duration: 0% Work: 0%

	Start	Finish
Current	5/30/94	4/3/95
Baseline	NA	NA
Actual	NA	NA
Variance	0d	0d

Check for changes in the finish date here.

	Duration	Work	Cost
Current	220.33d	7165.55h	$111,083.30
Baseline	0d	0h	$0.00
Actual	0d	0h	$0.00
Remaining	220.33d	7165.55h	$111,083.30

Check for changes in the cost here.

DECREASING PROJECT DURATION

There are several approaches you can use to shorten a project and change the project finish date, from adding resources to changing the scope of the project or individual tasks. Naturally, when you are trying to finish a project sooner, the tasks of interest to you are those on the critical path. Adding resources to noncritical tasks or changing the scope of noncritical tasks won't decrease the project duration. Use one or several of the approaches, depending on how radical a change you need to make and what other constraints you have, such as the budget and limited resources.

The time you save on a critical task may not be reflected in the project duration. For example, suppose you add resources to accelerate a critical task, which changes its duration from three weeks to two and makes it noncritical; another task that was previously noncritical may now become critical, resulting in, perhaps, a savings of only two days in the project duration. Or if your project has more than one critical path, you'll need to shorten critical tasks on all critical paths, not on just one.

Assigning More Resources

One way to complete critical tasks faster is to assign more resources—if the tasks use resource-driven scheduling. You can move the resources from other projects, from other tasks—tasks with slack, for example—or hire additional resources. Adding resources to a task that uses fixed-duration scheduling won't change task duration.

For task duration to decrease, you must increase resource units for the resource whose scheduled finish date is the latest on the task. For example, in the following illustration, the Marketing staff is scheduled to finish the "Prepare market plan" task last, on September 30.

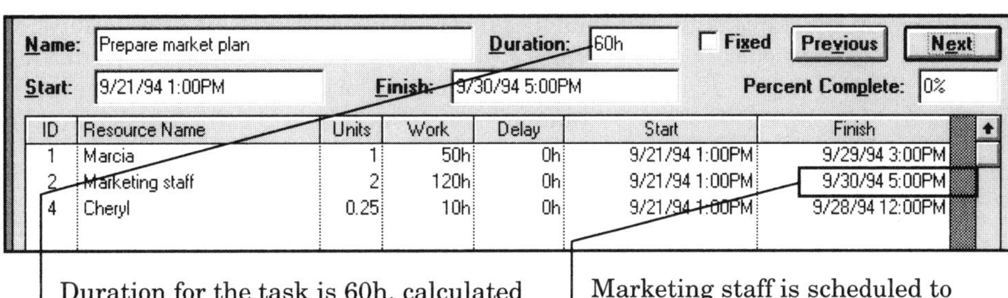

Duration for the task is 60h, calculated by dividing the work for the Marketing staff (120h) by 2 Marketing staff units.

Marketing staff is scheduled to finish last on the task so this is the resource to which you add units.

To decrease task duration, you must add additional Marketing staff units. If you add one unit, for a total of three, the finish date for the resource changes to September 28. The duration for the task changes to 50 hours, however, because Marcia's finish date is now the latest on the task, driving the task duration.

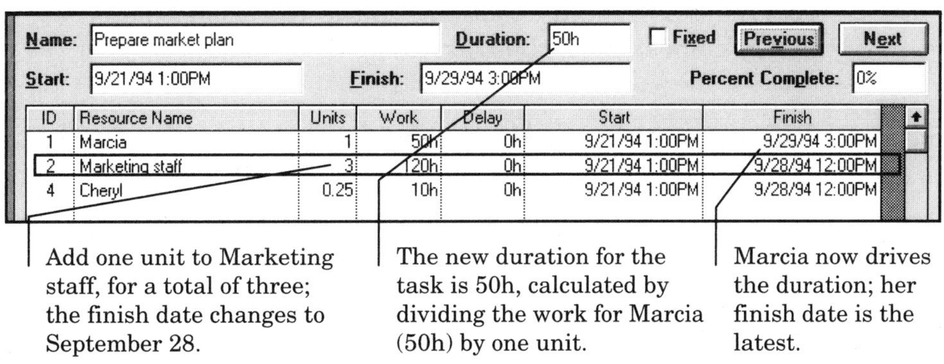

Add one unit to Marketing staff, for a total of three; the finish date changes to September 28.

The new duration for the task is 50h, calculated by dividing the work for Marcia (50h) by one unit.

Marcia now drives the duration; her finish date is the latest.

If you add new resource names instead of changing units, however, you must change the work for the existing resources to make the task duration decrease. For example, suppose you add a new resource, Jane, to help Marcia. Jane will do 20 hours of Marcia's work. But Microsoft Project has no way of knowing that Jane is doing Marcia's work, so you must change Marcia's work to 30 hours.

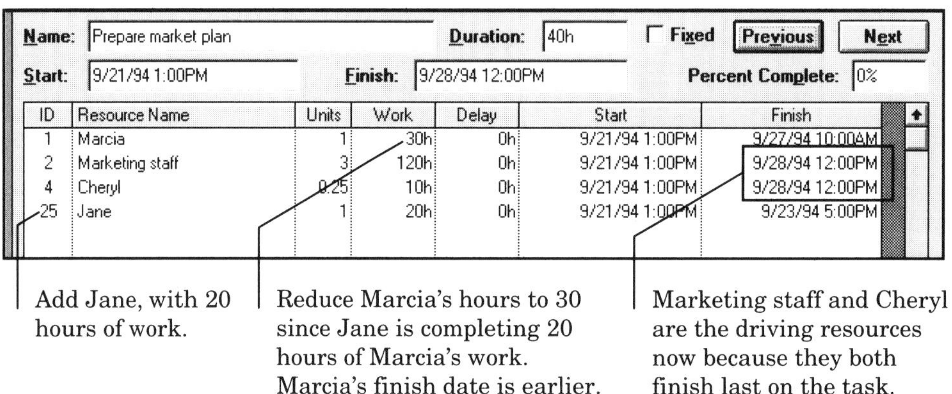

You can also have Microsoft Project split the work for you. Use a combination view with the Task Sheet above the Task Form. Apply the Work table to the Task Sheet. After you have entered the new resources, enter the total work again in the Work field on the Task Sheet. Microsoft Project will recalculate the work for each resource. For an example, see "Adding Another Shift" on page 178.

If you have not used Microsoft Project to enter and assign resources to the tasks in your project, you have to determine how the task will be shortened if you add additional resources. It's up to you to make assumptions about the working speed of the resources, and then estimate a new duration for the task. Enter the new duration just as you entered the original duration—in the Duration field on the Gantt Chart or Task Sheet, or in the Duration box on the Task Form.

Working Longer Hours on Resource-driven Tasks

If certain resources are in short supply, you can specify longer work hours for a resource. Longer hours can be specified in one of the following two ways.

- If you want a resource to work extra time on a specific task at an overtime rate, you indicate overtime work for the task in the Ovt. Work field on the Task Form or Resource Form.
- If you want a resource to work longer hours on all tasks during a certain period at a standard rate, you extend the working hours on its resource calendar.

If you are using resource-driven scheduling, Microsoft Project recalculates the finish date for a resource when you add overtime work or lengthen the working hours.

The resource with the latest scheduled finish date on the task is the one that must work longer. Otherwise, task duration does not decrease.

Name: Prepare initial spec Duration: 2.25w Fixed Previous Next
Start: 8/19/94 10:00AM Finish: 9/5/94 12:00PM Percent Complete: 0%

ID	Resource Name	Units	Work	Delay	Start	Finish
1	Marcia	0.1	8h	0h	8/19/94 10:00AM	9/2/94 10:00AM
9	Dave	1	80h	0h	8/19/94 10:00AM	9/2/94 10:00AM
10	Bill	1	80h	0h	8/19/94 10:00AM	9/2/94 10:00AM
11	Terri	0.2	18h	0h	8/19/94 10:00AM	9/5/94 12:00PM

Change these working hours because this resource is scheduled to finish last on the task.

Adding longer hours for Marcia, Dave, or Bill will not decrease task duration nor change the scheduled finish date for the task.

ADDING OVERTIME WORK

If you want to add overtime work on a specific task or tasks, and you want this overtime work to be paid for at the overtime rate, enter the additional hours in the Ovt. Work field on the Task Form or Resource Form. You enter an overtime rate of pay on the Resource Form or Resource Sheet, or in the Resource Information dialog box.

When you enter overtime work, Microsoft Project subtracts the value in the Ovt. Work field from the value in the Work field, before calculating duration:

$$\text{duration} = (\text{work} - \text{ovt. work}) / \text{units}$$

If this resource is scheduled to finish last on the task and is thus the resource driving the task duration, adding overtime work reduces the amount of work, and thus the duration. Do not change the calendar for this resource to reflect the extra time.

To enter overtime work on the Task Form, choose Format Details/Resource Work.

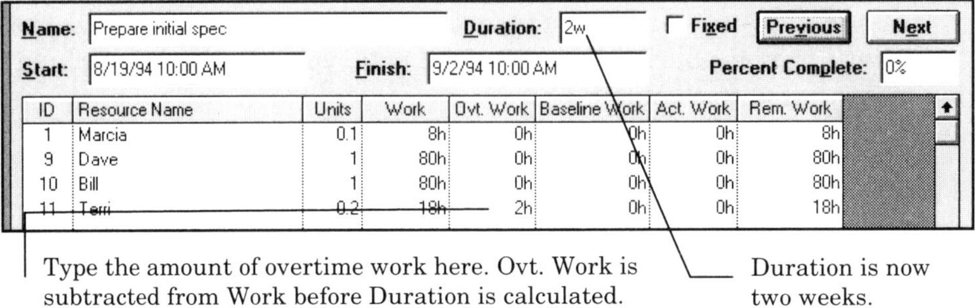
Name: Prepare initial spec Duration: 2w Fixed Previous Next
Start: 8/19/94 10:00 AM Finish: 9/2/94 10:00 AM Percent Complete: 0%

ID	Resource Name	Units	Work	Ovt. Work	Baseline Work	Act. Work	Rem. Work
1	Marcia	0.1	8h	0h	0h	0h	8h
9	Dave	1	80h	0h	0h	0h	80h
10	Bill	1	80h	0h	0h	0h	80h
11	Terri	0.2	18h	2h	0h	0h	18h

Type the amount of overtime work here. Ovt. Work is subtracted from Work before Duration is calculated.

Duration is now two weeks.

To add a rate for overtime work, double-click the resource, or select the resource, and then click the Information button on the Standard toolbar or choose Insert Resource Information.

Resource Information
Name: Terri Initials: T Max Units: 1 OK
Costs
Std Rate: $6.50/h Per Use: $0.00 Base Cal: Standard Cancel
Ovt Rate: $9.75/h Accrue at: Prorated Group: Design Help
Code:

Type the overtime rate here.

To enter overtime work and the overtime pay rate on the Resource Form, choose Format Details/Work.

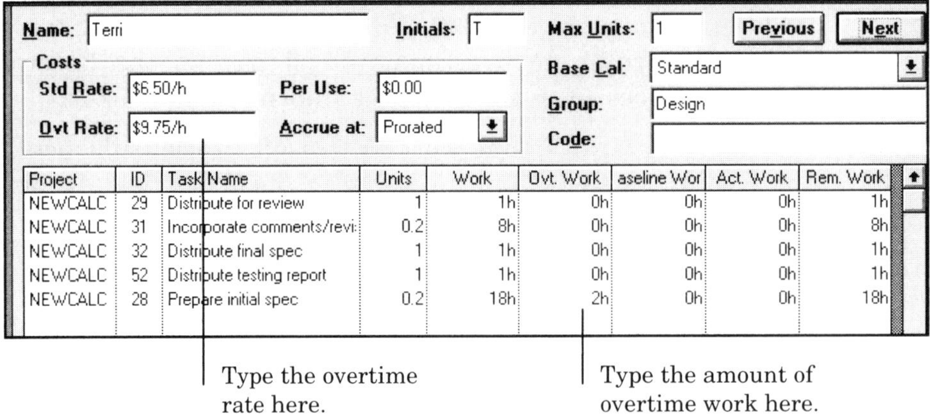
Name: Terri Initials: T Max Units: 1 Previous Next
Costs
Std Rate: $6.50/h Per Use: $0.00 Base Cal: Standard
Ovt Rate: $9.75/h Accrue at: Prorated Group: Design
Code:

Project	ID	Task Name	Units	Work	Ovt. Work	aseline Wor	Act. Work	Rem. Work
NEWCALC	29	Distribute for review	1	1h	0h	0h	0h	1h
NEWCALC	31	Incorporate comments/revi	0.2	8h	0h	0h	0h	8h
NEWCALC	32	Distribute final spec	1	1h	0h	0h	0h	1h
NEWCALC	52	Distribute testing report	1	1h	0h	0h	0h	1h
NEWCALC	28	Prepare initial spec	0.2	18h	2h	0h	0h	18h

Type the overtime rate here.

Type the amount of overtime work here.

CHANGING THE CALENDAR

If you want to add longer hours for one or more resources for certain periods during a project, or for the whole project, you can change the working hours and days for those resources on their resource calendars. You can also change the working hours and days on the project calendar to increase working time for all resources. If this is a feasible solution for your resources and you are using resource-driven scheduling, the tasks will be completed in a shorter time.

When you lengthen working hours, these additional hours are paid at the standard rate, not the overtime rate. If you want the hours billed at the overtime rate, you must enter the time as overtime work on individual tasks.

To change a resource calendar, choose Tools Change Working Time.

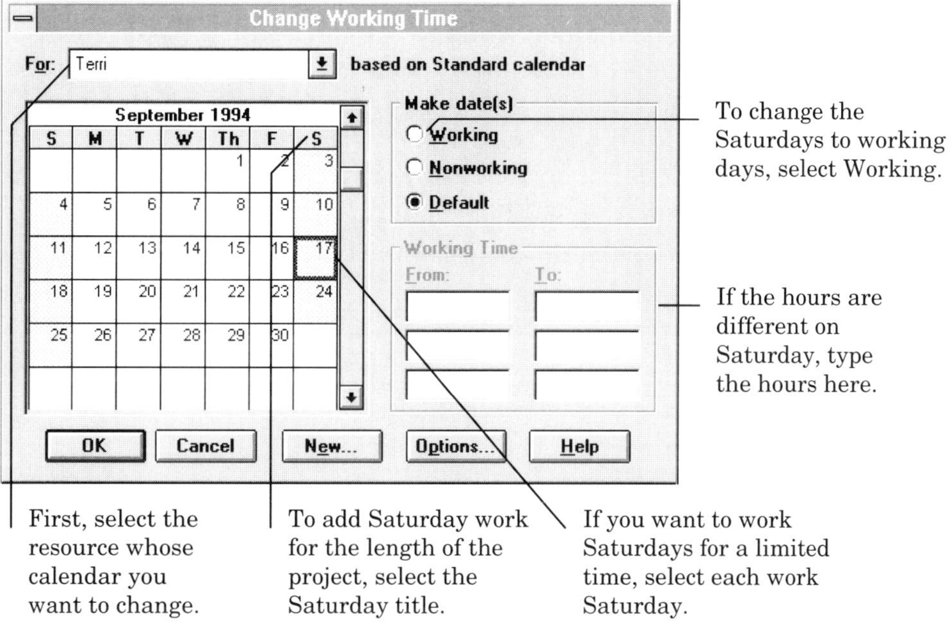

If you want to lengthen the working hours for weekdays, select the day titles and then type the new working hours under Working Time. To lengthen working hours for certain days, just select the days. Tasks that this resource is assigned to during the period with longer working hours will finish sooner, if the resource was the driving resource scheduled to finish last on the task.

Check the task finish date on the Task Form to see the change. Even though the finish dates for tasks using this resource may be earlier than the original finish date, the duration shown in the Duration box won't change because of how duration is calculated. Duration is always calculated by dividing the work by the units, and work hasn't changed.

Adding Another Shift

Another way to decrease project duration is to add another shift of resources to critical tasks. For example, if you have additional resources you can assign to tasks, but don't have the equipment for all resources to use at once, you can add another shift. To add another shift, you do three things:

1. Place the Task Sheet on top and the Task Form on the bottom in a combination view. On the Task Sheet, choose View Table/Work.
2. Assign this new shift to the task on the Task Form. For example, on the "Set up production test" task, you might have assigned "Production team." Now you want to finish this task faster, so you decide to add the Production team swing shift. In the Resource Name field on the Task Form, type **Production team-swing**.

   The new assignment will be assigned work equal to the duration of the task and the total work for the task will be doubled.

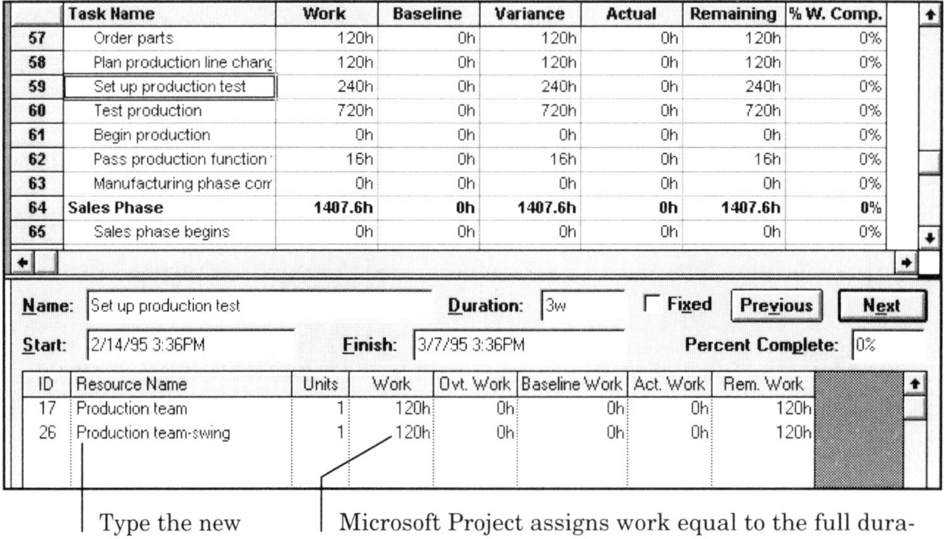

	Task Name	Work	Baseline	Variance	Actual	Remaining	% W. Comp.
57	Order parts	120h	0h	120h	0h	120h	0%
58	Plan production line chang	120h	0h	120h	0h	120h	0%
59	Set up production test	240h	0h	240h	0h	240h	0%
60	Test production	720h	0h	720h	0h	720h	0%
61	Begin production	0h	0h	0h	0h	0h	0%
62	Pass production function	16h	0h	16h	0h	16h	0%
63	Manufacturing phase com	0h	0h	0h	0h	0h	0%
64	**Sales Phase**	**1407.6h**	**0h**	**1407.6h**	**0h**	**1407.6h**	**0%**
65	Sales phase begins	0h	0h	0h	0h	0h	0%

ID	Resource Name	Units	Work	Ovt. Work	Baseline Work	Act. Work	Rem. Work
17	Production team	1	120h	0h	0h	0h	120h
26	Production team-swing	1	120h	0h	0h	0h	120h

Type the new resource name.

Microsoft Project assigns work equal to the full duration of the task and doubles the total work on the task.

But what you want is for the new resource to take half the burden of the task. On the Task Sheet, type the original total work in the Work field for the task. The total work will then be split between the two resources.

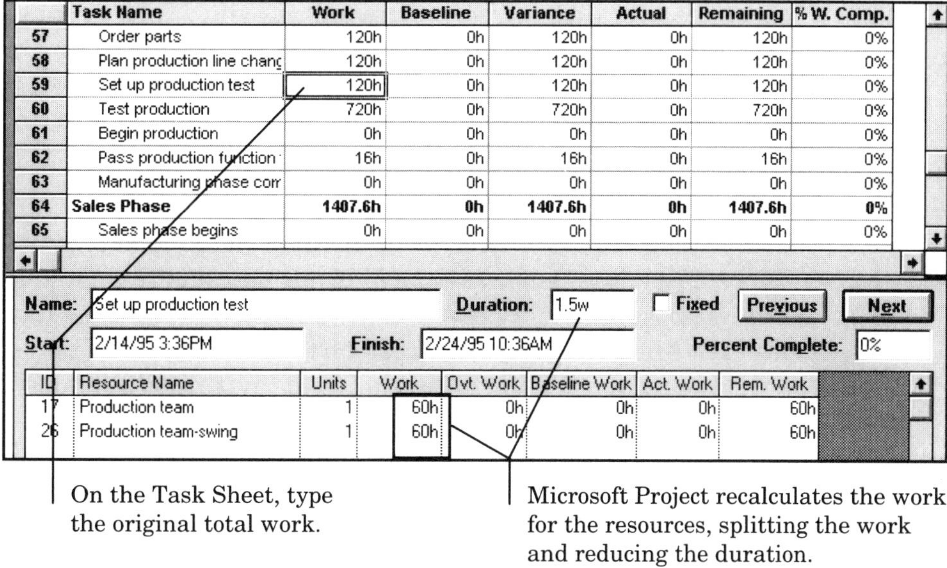

On the Task Sheet, type the original total work.

Microsoft Project recalculates the work for the resources, splitting the work and reducing the duration.

3. Change the resource calendar for Production team-swing to reflect the night hours. Choose Tools Change Working Time.

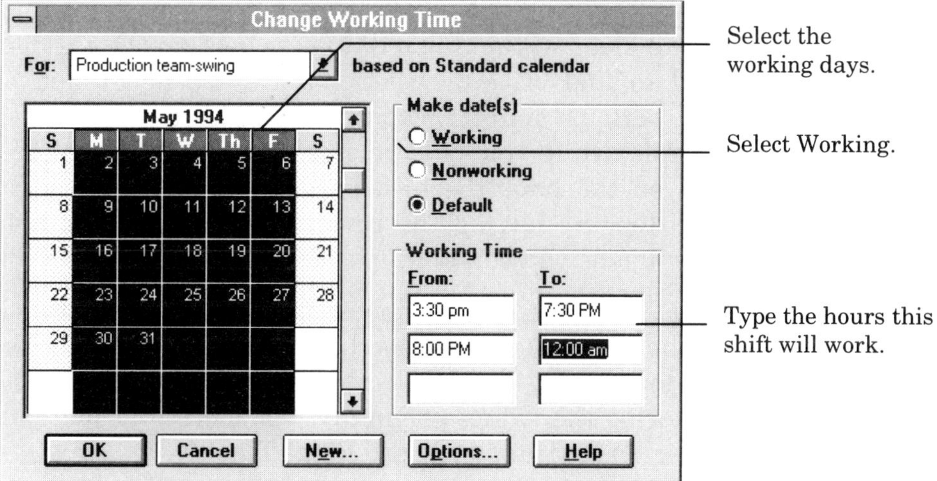

Select the working days.

Select Working.

Type the hours this shift will work.

If you have many resources that work shifts, create a base calendar for each shift. Then select the appropriate base calendar for each resource as you add new resources to the resource pool or assign new resources to tasks. You can specify a base calendar on the Resource Form or in the Resource Information dialog box. For example, suppose you have resources working three shifts—day, swing, and graveyard—and you have created a base calendar for each shift reflecting their working hours. Make sure you select the appropriate base calendar for each new resource so it will have the correct working hours in its resource calendar. For more information, see Chapter 16, "Using Microsoft Project Tools."

Indicating Hours When Your Shift Works Overnight When a shift works day hours, such as 8 to 5, every day has the same hours. When a shift works overnight, however, the hours on the first day and the last day are different from the rest of the work days. For example, if the work hours are 6 p.m. to 6 a.m., Sunday through Thursday, you enter the information as follows:

- Select Sundays. Under Working Time, type **6 pm** to **12 am**.
- Select Monday, Tuesday, and Wednesday. Under Working Time, type **12 am** to **6 am**, and **6 pm** to **12 am**.
- Select Thursdays. Under Working Time, type **12 am** to **6 am**.

Changing Task Dependencies

One way to bring in the finish date is to overlap the tasks on the critical path and to find critical tasks that can be performed earlier in the schedule, perhaps simultaneously with other critical tasks. Be creative. For example, while you can't review a market plan before it is written, perhaps you can have the first part reviewed while the second part is being written. By having the review cycle start after half the writing task is complete, you can perhaps cut time off the project duration.

To change the task dependencies, use the Task Entry view. You can change the task predecessors, change the relationship between tasks, and add lead or lag time. Use the same procedures as those you used when entering the values originally. For more information, see Chapter 6, "Making Tasks Happen at the Right Time."

Think carefully about all constraints and look for Must Start On or Must Finish On constraints to eliminate. When you use a "must" date, it limits the flexibility of the schedule since Microsoft Project must use these dates instead of the dates it calculates.

Make sure you mean to have the constraints that are there. It's easy to accidentally enter a Start No Earlier Than constraint by changing the start date of a task on the Gantt Chart with the mouse or by creating tasks with the mouse on the Gantt Chart or Calendar. If you discover a constraint you don't need, change the constraint in the Type box on the Advanced tab in the Task Information dialog box.

Decreasing Task Scope

By decreasing the scope of a critical task, you can shorten its duration and reduce the duration of the project by at least a portion of the reduction on the task. For example, suppose in your investigation phase for a new product, you planned to spend five weeks studying five competitors' products. When you see the schedule, however, you realize that this task is on the critical path; since the schedule needs to be shortened, perhaps you can be less thorough than originally planned. You may decide not to study two of the products at all because their market share is so small, thus saving up to two weeks on the task. Or you may decide to do an abbreviated study on these two products, perhaps half a week each, thus saving up to one week on the task. Whatever you decide about changing the scope of the task, be sure every one involved understands the new scope and its effect on the project overall.

Once you have decided the new scope, determine the new duration with help from the project team. Enter the new duration on the Gantt Chart.

Changing Project Scope

If a project must be finished by a certain date, no matter what, you may have to reduce the scope of the project as a whole to make this date. This decision must be made with the support of the project team, your client, and management. You can generate a series of options and their finish dates to help others decide the best compromise.

For example, on the new calculator project, if you cut features A, B, and C, you may save three weeks; if you cut four other features, you may save two weeks. How do you decide which group of features to cut and what the time savings will be? You can put together a list of all the features in order of importance, along with the durations of the tasks to implement each feature. Use a custom field to enter an "importance" ranking for each feature, and then sort on this custom field so the most important features are at the top of the list. If you know how much time you need to save, you can use this list to determine which features to cut.

Be sure you get agreement from the project team and management that decreasing scope is an acceptable solution. You can prepare a presentation showing the schedule with the full scope—too long and too costly, based on the original goals—and the schedule with the new scope, to show management or a client the effect of changing scope. This will give them the data they need to choose between the greater scope, later date, and higher cost, or the more limited scope, earlier date, and lower cost.

In Microsoft Project, you indicate a change in project scope by deleting tasks that will no longer be performed. You can do this on the Gantt Chart or Task Sheet. After you delete tasks, review the dependencies on the remaining tasks to make sure they are correct.

Reducing Costs

You can use several approaches to reduce costs, from changing the resources assigned to tasks to decreasing the scope of the project or tasks. Use one or a combination of approaches, depending on how much you need to cut and how critical the budget is. If the budget is more important on this project than other factors, you may decide to cut the scope or allow the project to finish later than originally planned, to keep costs in line.

Changing Resource Assignments

While resources may not be interchangeable, there may be ways to use a less costly resource on a task. For example, perhaps you can assign apprentice-level workers to certain tasks currently assigned to more skilled workers. Be sure to reconsider duration, however, because the less skilled resources may take longer to perform the tasks.

To change resources, select the tasks using the resources you want to replace, and then click the Resource Assignment button on the Standard toolbar or choose Insert Resource Assignment.

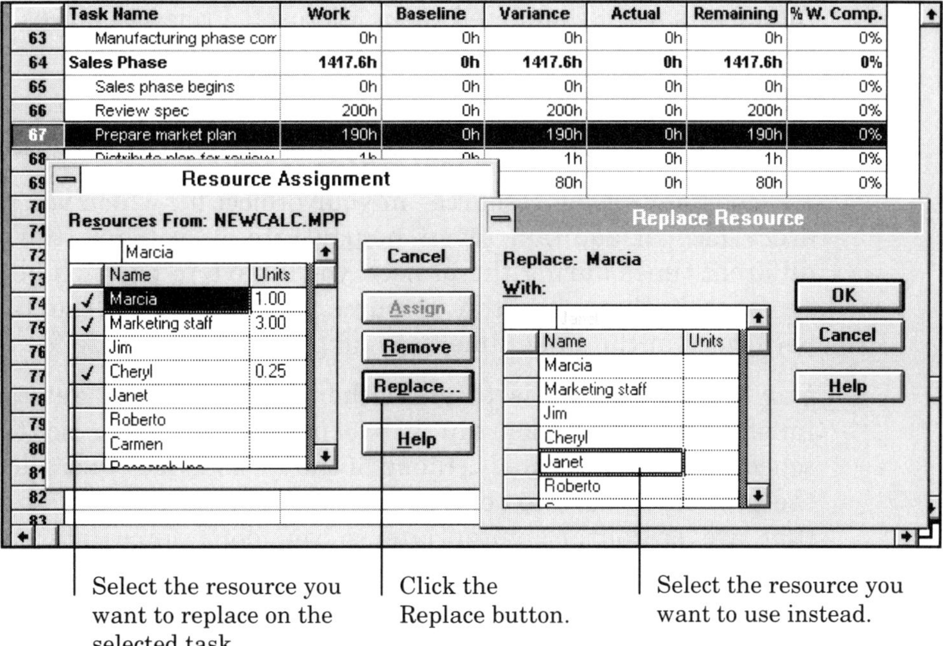

Select the resource you want to replace on the selected task.

Click the Replace button.

Select the resource you want to use instead.

If the task uses resource-driven scheduling, be sure to change the work for the resource if you expect it to differ from the original plan.

Changing Task Cost

Usually Microsoft Project calculates task costs for you, based on the fixed task costs and the cost of the resources assigned. Until a task is complete, you can enter the cost for a task only when you have assigned no resources to the task.

To change cost for an unfinished task that has resources assigned, use the other methods in this section; to change cost for a task that has no resources assigned—perhaps because the task is being performed by an outside contractor—try getting additional bids for the task. For example, if you are planning to hire an outside research firm to conduct a phone survey of your customers, you can request bids from other companies to find a lower bid.

You change a cost for a task on the Task Sheet, with the Cost table applied. Choose View More Views. In the Views box, select Task Sheet, and then choose the Apply button. Then choose View Table/Cost. Remember, if you change the cost of a task with assigned resources and the task is not a completed task, Microsoft Project replaces the cost you entered with the cost it calculates.

Changing Task Relationships to Reduce Per-use Cost

You may have some resources in your project for which you pay a fee for every use, in addition to an hourly rate. If you use the resource at different times during the project, you'll have to pay this per-use fee for every task that uses the resource. See if any of the tasks can be performed at the same time to avoid paying this per-use fee repeatedly.

One way to do this is to put either a start-to-start relationship or a finish-to-finish relationship between the two tasks so they will be scheduled simultaneously. If one of the tasks is moved earlier or later in the project, be sure to remove the original predecessors and successors that are no longer appropriate so you don't force later parts of the schedule to occur out of order.

For example, suppose the "Hang sign" task requires a crane and was scheduled at the end of the project, with the "Final site cleanup" task as its successor. When you move the sign task to be concurrent with the building tasks that also use the crane, you do not want the cleanup task to be moved up in the schedule too. Delete the relationship between the two tasks, and link the cleanup task to the original predecessor of the sign task.

To prevent Microsoft Project from charging the per-use fee every time it finds the resource assigned to a task, do one of the following:

- Divide the per-use fee by the number of tasks using the resource, and enter this value as the per-use fee. For example, if you plan to use a resource, such as a crane, on three tasks during the project, but have arranged the schedule such that all three tasks occur at the same time, you will, actually, incur only one per-use fee rather than three. The per-use fee you enter into Microsoft Project for the resource would be one-third of the actual per-use cost because the cost is divided among the three tasks. Use this method when you are able to complete at the same time all tasks to which the resource is assigned.

- Name the resource in two ways and include a per-use fee on one and not on the other. For each group of tasks that use the resource and will be performed simultaneously, assign the resource with the per-use fee to one of the tasks and the resource without the per-use fee to the rest of the tasks. For example, you could have Crane1 with the per-use fee and Crane2 without. If you have three tasks using the crane at the same time, assign Crane1 to one of the tasks and Crane2 to the other two. If, later in the schedule, you have four tasks occurring simultaneously and using the crane, assign Crane1 to one task, and Crane2 to the other three. Use this method when you cannot complete at the same time all tasks that use the resource.

Enter the per-use fee in the Per Use box on the Resource Form or in the Resource Information dialog box.

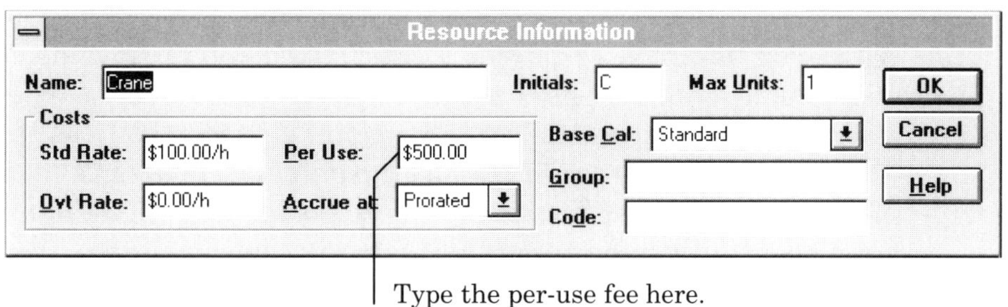

Type the per-use fee here.

Decreasing Scope to Lower Cost

Just as you can reduce scope to shorten project duration, you can reduce scope to lower costs. If cost is the most important factor on this project, use what-if analysis to decide how much of the project you must cut to meet the cost limits.

Since cost is almost always reduced when work is reduced, you know you can lower costs by reducing work. You can either cut the scope of the project by deleting tasks or cut the scope of some tasks in the project. For example, if you are preparing a marketing brochure, you may decide to lower costs by reducing the size of the brochure and using two colors instead of four. When you cut tasks, delete them on the Gantt Chart or Task Sheet. When you change the scope of tasks, change the work and duration for the tasks to reflect their new scope.

Resolving Resource Conflicts

There are several ways to resolve resource conflicts, such as leveling resources by moving tasks, moving underallocated resources to tasks needing additional resources, or working longer hours. Again, use the approach or approaches that fit your needs for this project. For example, if the project finish date is more important than cost, you may be able to hire many additional resources to complete the tasks with overallocated resources. Or perhaps you have no need for additional resources after this project; in this case, it would be more appropriate for resources to work longer hours. The best solution depends on the time and budget parameters for the project.

Leveling Resources

When you assigned resources to tasks, you might have seen a message at the bottom of the screen that a resource needed to be leveled. And when you checked for tasks with overallocated resources in Chapter 8, you probably found several. One resource may be assigned to several tasks that occur at the same time (overallocated); this same resource may be working at only 20 percent capacity later in the project (underallocated). In the best interests of the project and the resources, you want to use all resources as evenly as possible, with no one overworked and no one idle.

Microsoft Project shows you how your resources are used—where the peaks and valleys are—and helps you even out resource use. Once you have established that a resource is overallocated or underallocated, you can move tasks or resources around, or Microsoft Project can move tasks around for you. This is called *resource leveling*. The goal of leveling resources is to have resources available as needed for critical tasks.

HAVING MICROSOFT PROJECT LEVEL RESOURCES

Microsoft Project levels resources by moving tasks such that tasks requiring the same resources are no longer scheduled at the same time. Microsoft Project chooses the task to delay based on information you have entered such as relationships, dates, priority, and task constraints and on information calculated by Microsoft Project, such as slack time and dates. You can control which tasks are delayed by using a priority and requiring that Microsoft Project consider priority before the other criteria.

While leveling is a very powerful feature, it may not always result in the best solution from your standpoint because it cannot take into account subtle information only you know about your project. Leveling is just a set of rules that use fixed criteria to decide which task among a set of tasks to delay to solve the conflict. This process is repeated for all existing conflicts. You should always review the changes made by Microsoft Project to make sure the schedule is what you have in mind.

Keep the following guidelines in mind as you work with leveling:

- Use leveling only after entering everything you know about each task. If tasks have a sequence, enter the relationships to create that sequence before leveling.
- If the sequence of tasks is not important, you can use leveling to spread tasks out over time. For example, if one resource has several tasks assigned, but none of the tasks depends on the other tasks, the resource can work on the tasks in any order. If you level this resource, the resource is no longer overallocated because the tasks are now spread over time, but there is no relationship between the tasks.
- Use constraints and priorities sparingly, as the exception rather than the rule. Use a constraint when an external force, such as a requirement by a client or contract, specifies a task be finished by a certain date. Use a priority when a task absolutely cannot be delayed or when you prefer certain tasks be delayed if leveling is necessary.
- Don't use leveling when you are scheduling from a finish date. When you schedule from a finish date, Microsoft Project schedules each task to begin as late as possible to finish by the date you entered as the finish date. There is no slack, so there is no room to delay tasks.

Leveling is not the answer to every scheduling problem. The following list will help you understand what Microsoft Project leveling will and won't do for you:

- There are many solutions to scheduling problems; Microsoft Project finds one of these in most cases. But because all Microsoft Project can do is delay tasks, it will not make those other types of decisions you might make, such as adding a resource or changing duration instead of delaying a task.
- Gaps may appear in the schedule after you level. Gaps occur when your schedule is complex and includes constraints, actual start dates, complicated relationships, and priorities other than Medium. These factors limit the flexibility Microsoft Project has when leveling.

- Microsoft Project does not try every solution and then compare them all. It resolves one set of conflicts at a time. Because your view of the project is much broader, you may see a more appropriate solution than one Microsoft Project suggests.

Initially, Microsoft Project levels resources only when you choose the Level Now button in the Tools Resource Leveling dialog box. In this dialog box, you also control how tasks are delayed, how tasks are selected to be delayed, and whether leveling should occur automatically instead of manually.

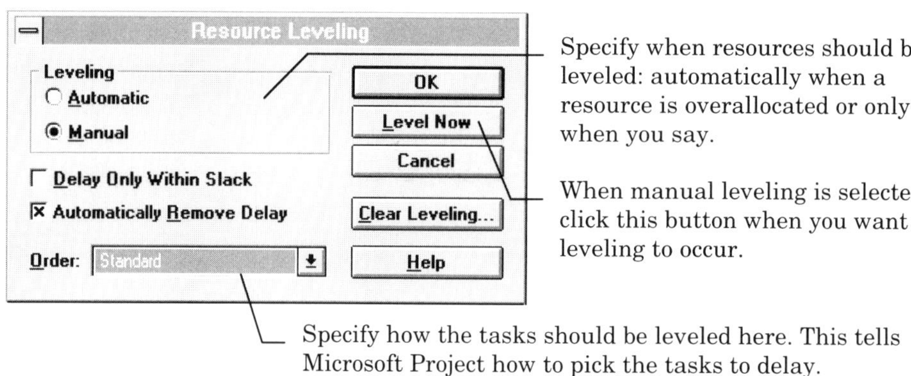

The Delay Only Within Slack option tells Microsoft Project whether it can slip the end date to level resources. Select this check box only when the finish date must not be changed; clear the check box when it is acceptable for the finish date to move out.

The Automatically Remove Delay option tells Microsoft Project whether it should first remove all existing values in the task Delay field before leveling. Select this check box if you want to start over with no delay on any tasks; clear the check box if you want to keep task delay you have already added.

In the Order box, you select what Microsoft Project should look at when it picks a task to delay: ID Only (task with highest ID is delayed); Standard (Microsoft Project determines a task to delay based on predecessors, slack time, dates, priority, and constraints); or Priority, Standard (Microsoft Project determines a task to delay by checking priority first, and then predecessors, slack time, dates, and constraints).

Priority is a task ranking you assign on the Task Details Form or on the General tab in the Task Information dialog box. There are 10 choices, from Lowest to Do Not Level. Until you change the priority, Microsoft Project assigns Medium priority. Tasks with the priority of Do Not Level will not be delayed. Use priority to control leveling—if certain tasks must not be leveled, assign Do Not Level to these tasks. To assign a certain priority to several tasks at once, select the tasks, click the Information button on the Standard toolbar or choose Insert Task Information, select the priority you want in the Priority box, and then choose OK.

When Microsoft Project levels, it adds delay to tasks so that resources are available as needed on other tasks. You can see the delay by displaying the Delay Gantt view.

The Delay Gantt includes bars for task delay and for slack. In the following illustration, delay bars are narrow lighter bars to the left; slack bars are narrow darker bars to the right. On a color monitor, delay bars are mustard and slack bars are teal. The Delay table is used with the Delay Gantt and includes the Delay column and the Successors column (scroll right to see the successors) so you can determine what tasks will be affected if you add delay to a task. Use the slack bar to see which tasks have room to be delayed without affecting the project end date.

To display the Delay Gantt, choose View More Views. In the Views box, select Delay Gantt, and then choose the Apply button.

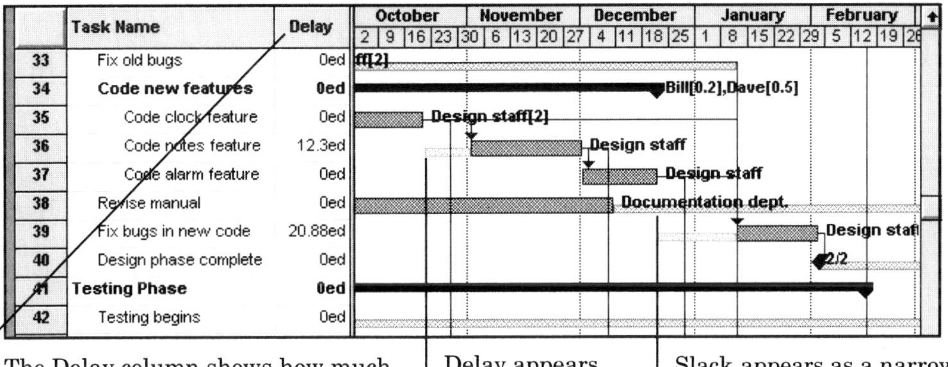

The Delay column shows how much the task has been delayed. "ed" means elapsed days. Elapsed time includes nonworking time, such as weekends, as well as working time.

Delay appears as a narrow bar to the left.

Slack appears as a narrow bar to the right.

To remove the delay Microsoft Project added, choose the Clear Leveling button in the Tools Resource Leveling dialog box. If you like some of the changes Microsoft Project made, but not others, select those tasks from which you want to remove delay before you choose the command.

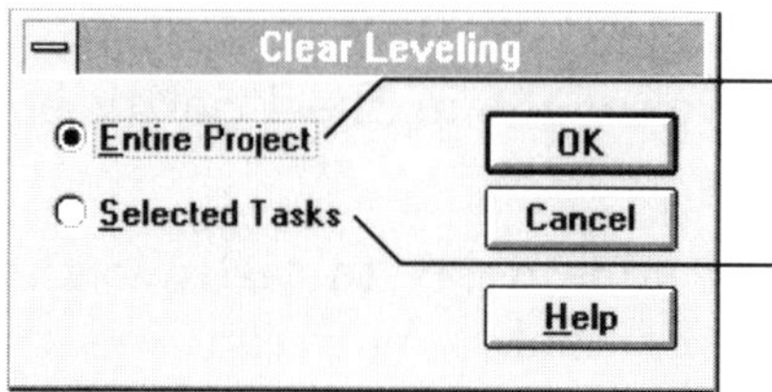

To remove all the delay added by you or Microsoft Project, select Entire Project.

To remove delay from certain tasks, select the tasks before you choose the command, and then select Selected Tasks.

LEVELING RESOURCES YOURSELF

To level an overallocated resource yourself, you can:

- Move a task to which the overallocated resource is assigned elsewhere in the project. To move a task, change the predecessors and successors or add lead or lag time to the task so the task occurs at a different time in the schedule.
- Use the Leveling Cue Cards. To start them, click the Leveling CueCards button on the Resource Management toolbar and then follow the directions on the screen.
- Use the Resource Allocation view to find overallocated resources and the tasks causing the overallocation. To display this view, click the Resource Allocation View button on the Resource Management toolbar or choose View More Views, select Resource Allocation in the Views box, and then choose Apply. The Resource Allocation view has the Resource Usage view on top and the Delay Gantt on the bottom. Click the Goto Overallocation button on the Resource Management toolbar to move to the next overallocation, and then check the Delay Gantt for the tasks causing the overallocation. In the Delay field on the Delay Gantt, add delay to one of the tasks. Scroll the table right to check the successors to the task to see which tasks may be affected by the delay. Continue stepping through the overallocations.
- Increase the duration of resource-driven tasks to which the overallocated resource is assigned by decreasing the percentage of time the resource spends on each task, leaving time for the resource to work on other tasks. To change the percentage of time a resource spends on a task, change the value in the Units field for the resource in the Resource Assignment dialog box. For example, if you want an

individual resource to work half-time on a task, change the value in the Units field from 1 to 0.5. On a resource-driven task that has one resource, the duration will double.

Remember, it is not necessary to resolve all overallocations. For example, if a resource is only overallocated by 0.1 hour, you can probably ignore it. Since most work estimates are not that accurate, chances are this amount of overallocation won't cause a problem in completing your project on time.

Assigning Additional Resources

If a task has overallocated resources assigned, you can hire additional resources, shift resources from other tasks, or add another shift. For more information, see "Assigning More Resources" on page 173 and "Adding Another Shift" on page 178 earlier in this chapter.

Working Longer Hours

Another way to take care of overallocated resources is to have the resource work longer hours or work overtime. This is the same approach discussed earlier in this chapter. For more information, see "Working Longer Hours on Resource-driven Tasks" on page 174.

Breaking Tasks into Smaller Tasks to Shift Resources

If a task uses several different resources, you may find some resources are not available when the task is scheduled. One way around this is to break the task into smaller tasks such that resources are needed at different times instead of being scheduled all at once.

For example, if Cheryl, who is to type the market plan for the "Prepare Market Plan" task, is not available at the scheduled time, you could break the task into "Write market plan" and "Type market plan." The typing task could be scheduled when Cheryl is available, but the rest of the task, now "Write market plan," can occur as originally scheduled.

Another approach to this, instead of actually breaking the task into smaller tasks, is controlling when the resources work on the task by using the resource Delay field on the Task Form or Resource Form. For more information, see Chapter 7, "Assigning People, Equipment, and Costs to Tasks."

FREEZING THE BASELINE SCHEDULE

Once the schedule is acceptable, you want to save it so you'll have a baseline against which to compare progress as the project unfolds. To freeze the baseline schedule, you use the Tools Tracking/Save Baseline command. This command copies the start and finish dates, work, cost, and durations into the Baseline fields. The only way you can track your project is by saving this record of your original schedule.

Choose Tools Tracking/Save Baseline.

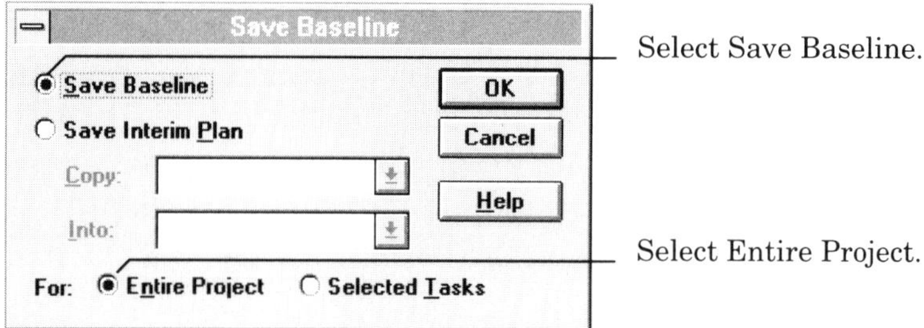

Saving Other Sets of Start and Finish Dates In the Save Baseline dialog box, you have a choice of the information you copy and a choice of the fields into which you copy the information. If you want to save another set of dates, such as at a milestone along the way, you can copy dates that you have entered into the Start1/Finish1, Start2/Finish2, Start3/Finish3, Start4/Finish4, or Start5/Finish5 custom fields. When you copy these other dates, only the start and finish dates are saved, not the cost and work information.

Once you have set the baseline, you can review all baseline information by applying the Baseline table to the Task Sheet. Choose View More Views. In the Views box, select Task Sheet, and then choose the Apply button. Then choose View Table/More Tables. In the Tables box, select Baseline and then choose the Apply button.

	Task Name	Baseline Dur.	Baseline Start	Baseline Finish	Baseline Work	Baseline Cost
1	**Investigation Phase**	**59.25d**	**5/30/94 8:00AM**	**8/19/94 10:00AM**	**1255.6h**	**$17,906.41**
2	Investigation begins	0d	5/30/94 8:00AM	5/30/94 8:00AM	0h	$0.00
3	**Prepare initial product p**	**13d**	**5/30/94 8:00AM**	**6/15/94 5:00PM**	**292.4h**	**$3,325.25**
4	Research competition	1w	5/30/94 8:00AM	6/3/94 5:00PM	130h	$1,308.65
5	Review customer comr	3d	6/6/94 8:00AM	6/8/94 5:00PM	72h	$1,101.93
6	Write proposal	1w	6/9/94 8:00AM	6/15/94 5:00PM	80h	$914.42
7	**Plan focus panel**	**5d**	**6/16/94 8:00AM**	**6/22/94 5:00PM**	**121.2h**	**$1,249.52**
8	Prepare questions	1w	6/16/94 8:00AM	6/22/94 5:00PM	80h	$914.42
9	**Arrange sites**	**2d**	**6/16/94 8:00AM**	**6/17/94 5:00PM**	**16.4h**	**$132.21**
10	Contact hotels	1d	6/16/94 8:00AM	6/16/94 5:00PM	8h	$61.54
11	**Arrange for equi**	**1d**	**6/17/94 8:00AM**	**6/17/94 5:00PM**	**8.4h**	**$70.67**
12	Determine need	4h	6/17/94 8:00AM	6/17/94 12:00PM	4.4h	$39.90
13	Contact local of	4h	6/17/94 1:00PM	6/17/94 5:00PM	4h	$30.77
14	**Get panel members**	**3d**	**6/20/94 8:00AM**	**6/22/94 5:00PM**	**24.8h**	**$202.89**
15	Contact local reps f	1d	6/20/94 8:00AM	6/20/94 5:00PM	8.8h	$79.81
16	Contact suggested	2d	6/21/94 8:00AM	6/22/94 5:00PM	16h	$123.08
17	**Plan phone questionnai**	**3.25d**	**6/23/94 8:00AM**	**6/28/94 10:00AM**	**50h**	**$385.19**
18	Prepare questionnaire	3d	6/23/94 8:00AM	6/27/94 5:00PM	48h	$369.81
19	Get list of users to call	2h	6/28/94 8:00AM	6/28/94 10:00AM	2h	$15.38
20	Carry out focus panels	4w	6/28/94 10:00AM	7/26/94 10:00AM	480h	$6,119.24
21	Carry out phone survey	1w	7/26/94 10:00AM	8/2/94 10:00AM	40h	$2,500.00

The Baseline table shows the baseline duration, the baseline start and finish dates for each task, the baseline work, and the baseline cost.

In the next chapter, you'll learn how to produce reports to present the project. Using Microsoft Project, you can create a variety of reports that show the schedule now, and how it can be changed, with costs and benefits of each possible schedule.

10

Communicating the Plan

You and your planning team have spent a lot of time creating the perfect plan and schedule for this project. Now you are ready to share that plan. You want to show management or a client exactly how you will make this project happen. Or perhaps you want to get support from management for the project goals, timing, and expenditures. And you want everyone involved in executing the project tasks to know what is planned and what their involvement is.

At this stage, you report on the schedule, the planned resource use, and the projected costs. By sharing this information with all members of the team, you gain support for the project. Everyone feels a part of the team, sees the big picture, and knows at the outset what they are trying to accomplish and for whom and why.

DIFFERENT REPORTS FOR DIFFERENT PEOPLE

One big advantage of using project management software is that once you have entered all the project information, you can create many reports, each including only the information and detail appropriate for the recipients. For example, you can create summary level reports for management, projected cost reports for the accounting department, and individual task-level reports for each supervisor. Since all reports are based on the same core set of information, it is easy and quick to give others what they need. You can be selective about the data in each report. Do not send all information to everyone. They may end up reading none of it, thus missing what is relevant to them.

At one extreme, you have the reports you prepare for top management in which you include more summary information than details. It is unnecessary, for example, to send top management the breakdown of every single task; they do not have time to review the plan at that level of detail. Send them a summary of major milestones, dates, and costs, plus the project goals.

At the other extreme are the reports you put together for the task supervisors, which contain maximum detail. Supervisors can use these to manage the actual work because all the tasks in which they are involved are listed, with schedule information, resources used, and notes about each task.

USING MICROSOFT PROJECT

Since Microsoft Project now contains all your project information, you can generate any report appropriate for your audience. For example, if you have outlined your project, you can collapse the outline to show only top-level summary tasks, and then print the Gantt Chart to show graphically when these major phases will occur. Or print the Overview/Top-Level Tasks report to show not only the top-level summary tasks and their durations, but also the percent complete and cost for each phase.

Either of these reports, along with the Overview/Project report showing project dates, costs, and other project-wide statistics, is a good report for top management and others who do not want details. Or you can collapse the Gantt Chart, and then expand only those summary tasks relevant for each supervisor. All supervisors then have a picture of the whole, plus the details for their groups.

There are two ways to print information in Microsoft Project. You can print:

- Basic views that come with Microsoft Project, plus views you create based on these views. These views are the Gantt Chart, PERT Chart, Calendar, Task Sheet, Resource Sheet, Resource Graph, and Resource Usage view. You print these views using the File Print command.

- Basic reports that come with Microsoft Project, plus reports you create based on these reports. You print these reports using the View Reports command.

You use tables, filtering, and sorting to change the information in the views; you use the Format commands to change the way the information looks in the views. You have similar control over the information and the way the information looks in reports.

The following tables list common types of reports, and what you use to generate the report in Microsoft Project.

SUMMARY REPORTS

Summary reports can show everything from a statistical summary of the project (number of tasks, resources, cost, duration, and so on) to a summary of major phases and milestones in the project. The following table lists several summary reports available in Microsoft Project.

To show	In Microsoft Project, print
Summary of the project, including number of tasks and resources, cost, work, duration, start and finish dates, and project notes	Overview/Project report
Summary of major phases, with bar chart showing the start and finish dates	Gantt Chart, with outline collapsed
Summary of major phases, showing duration, start and finish dates, cost, and percent complete	Overview/Top-Level Tasks report
Milestones in the project and top-level summary tasks	Overview/Milestones report

TASKS, CRITICAL PATH, AND RESOURCES ASSIGNED

When you want to get down to more detail about the tasks in the project, you can print a report showing details about individual tasks instead of details for the project as a whole or major phases in the project. The following table lists several ways to report on tasks in the project and when they are scheduled to occur.

To show	In Microsoft Project, print
List of tasks and durations, plus bar chart of tasks and critical path	Gantt Chart, with pattern changed for critical task bars
List of critical tasks and their successors	Overview/Critical Tasks report
Which tasks will be performed and in what sequence	PERT Chart
Tasks and notes about the tasks	Task report, with Notes check box selected
List of tasks and their work and costs	Task Sheet with Summary table applied
List of tasks, start and finish dates, and assigned resources	Task Sheet with Entry table applied
Task schedule—list of tasks scheduled during a time period	Custom periodic Task report or Current Activities/Tasks Starting Soon report
Schedule of tasks printed on a calendar	Calendar view

RESOURCE REPORTS

Resource reports generally show two types of information: statistics about the resources, such as pay rate or personal information you have entered; and tasks they are scheduled to work on. The following table lists several ways you can get both types of information from your project.

To show	In Microsoft Project, print
List of all resources assigned to work on the project	Resource Sheet or Resource report
Level of resource use during each period (day, week, month, quarter, or year)	Resource Usage view
Resource work and cost	Resource Sheet with Summary table applied or Resource Usage view showing work
List of resources and the tasks to which each is assigned	Assignments/Who Does What report
List of resources, the tasks to which each is assigned, and the hours worked on each task during each week	Assignments/Who Does What When report
Individual task list—list of tasks a resource is assigned to work on during the next period	Assignments/Weekly To-Do List report
Resource schedule—list of resources scheduled to work on tasks during a time period	Workload/Resource report

COST REPORTS

Microsoft Project provides several ways to print cost information. You can print resource costs, task costs, cumulative costs, or a table showing cash flow over time. Using the Resource Graph, you can also print graphs of most cost information.

To show	In Microsoft Project, print
Task costs and totals	Costs/Budget report
Expected task costs	Costs/Budget report
Forecast of task costs—how much money and when	Costs/Weekly Cash Flow report
Forecast of resource costs—how much money and when	Resource Usage view, showing costs
Cumulative resource cost over the life of the project	Resource Graph displaying cumulative cost for all resources

To change the information in a view and adjust the width and titles of table columns, apply a different table using the View Table commands. To filter information so that only certain related information appears, such as critical tasks only, apply a filter using the Filter box on the Formatting toolbar. To sort the tasks or resources so they appear in the order of your choosing instead of ID number order, use the Tools Sort commands.

To change the information in a report, choose the View Reports command and then double-click Custom. Select the type of report you want to change, and then edit the report to change the table or filter applied and sort the information however you like. The tables and filters available when you customize a report are the same as those used with the views. By creating custom tables and filters, you can print a report that shows exactly what you want.

In views that contain a table, such as the Gantt Chart, Task Sheet, Resource Sheet, and Resource Usage view, you can control where pages break using the Insert Page Break command. These manual page breaks are tied to the task or resource selected when you choose Insert

Page Break, and control where pages break in both printed views and reports. When you print, you can choose to have manual page breaks ignored if they are not appropriate in what you are printing.

When you create a new view or report by changing the table, filter, sort order, text, and so on, you name it so that you can use it over and over. Views and reports are automatically saved with your project, as are the tables and filters you create. Microsoft Project saves them for you when you save the project. The next time you want to use the same report format with new data, just select that report or view. You can, of course, use the Organizer to share these views and reports with other projects or put them in your global template. For more information about the Organizer, about sharing views and reports, and about creating tables and filters, see Chapter 16, "Using Microsoft Project Tools."

In the next sections, you'll see how to set up the page and print a view and a report. This information is followed by several examples of printed views and reports, plus the instructions for creating each one.

Before You Print If you want to check your printer setup before printing, in Microsoft Project for Windows, choose File Print and then choose the Printer button in the Print dialog box. In Microsoft Project for the Macintosh, you select a printer in the Chooser.

SETTING UP THE PAGE

Before you print anything, you need to make sure the page is set up the way you want. To do this, you use the File Page Setup command. Each view and report has its own page setup. Not all options are available with all views or reports.

The Page Setup dialog box has several tabs, each controlling one aspect of the page layout, including margins, headers, footers, legends, and the direction you want to print on the paper.

Margins are set in the units your country uses: either inches or centimeters. In the United States, the margin is measured in inches from the edge of the paper.

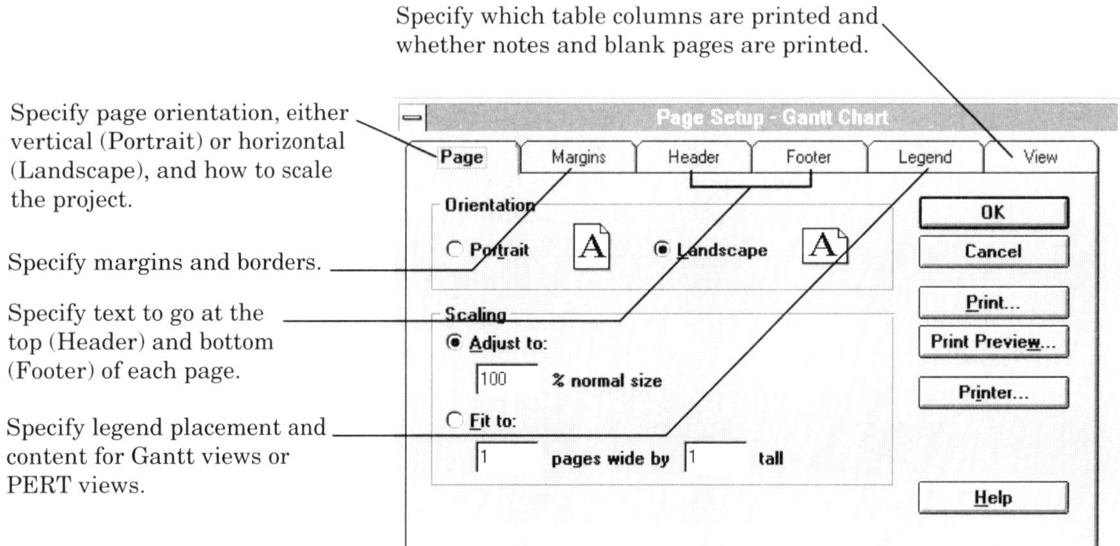

To enter a header or footer, first click the Header or Footer tab. To control the position of text in the header or footer, click the Left, Center, or Right tab. Then type or select the information to go in that position.

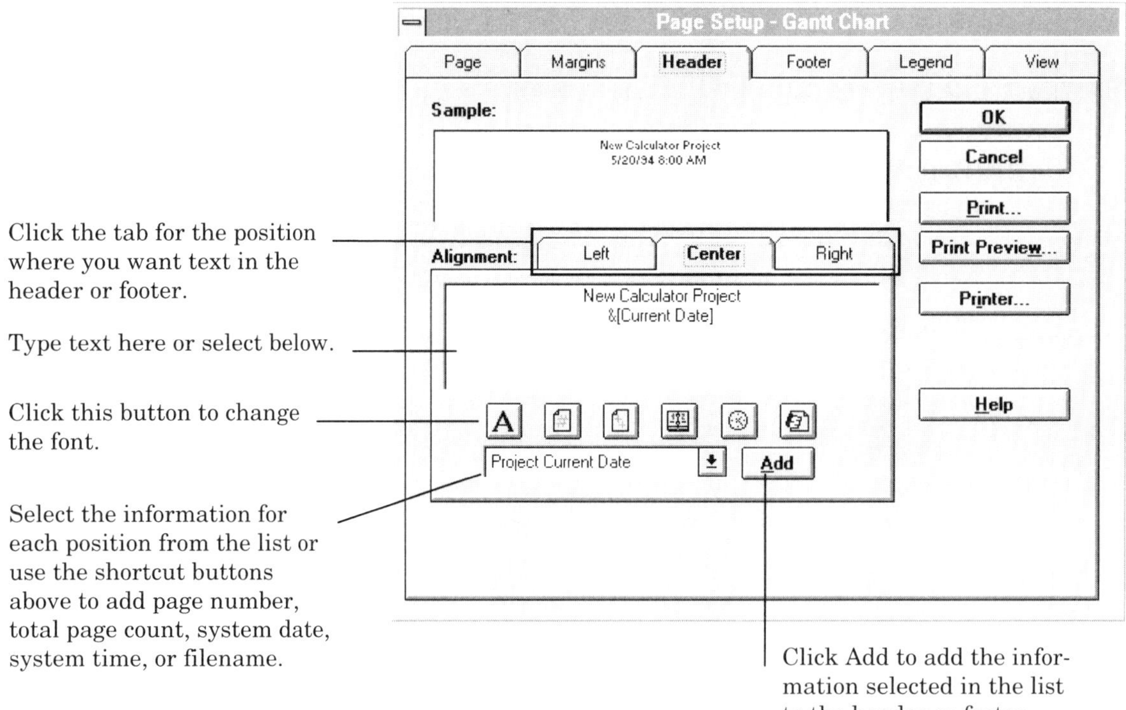

PRINTING

The instructions in this section show how to print views and reports using the File Print and View Reports commands. This section also covers previewing the pages before you print.

Printing a View

To print a view, first make the view look the way you want and display the information you want. For example, apply a different table or filter, sort the tasks or resources, or format the text or gridlines. Then preview the pages, to make sure they look the way you want.

To preview a view, click the Print Preview button on the Standard toolbar or choose the File Print Preview command. The following illustration shows the first page of the Gantt Chart.

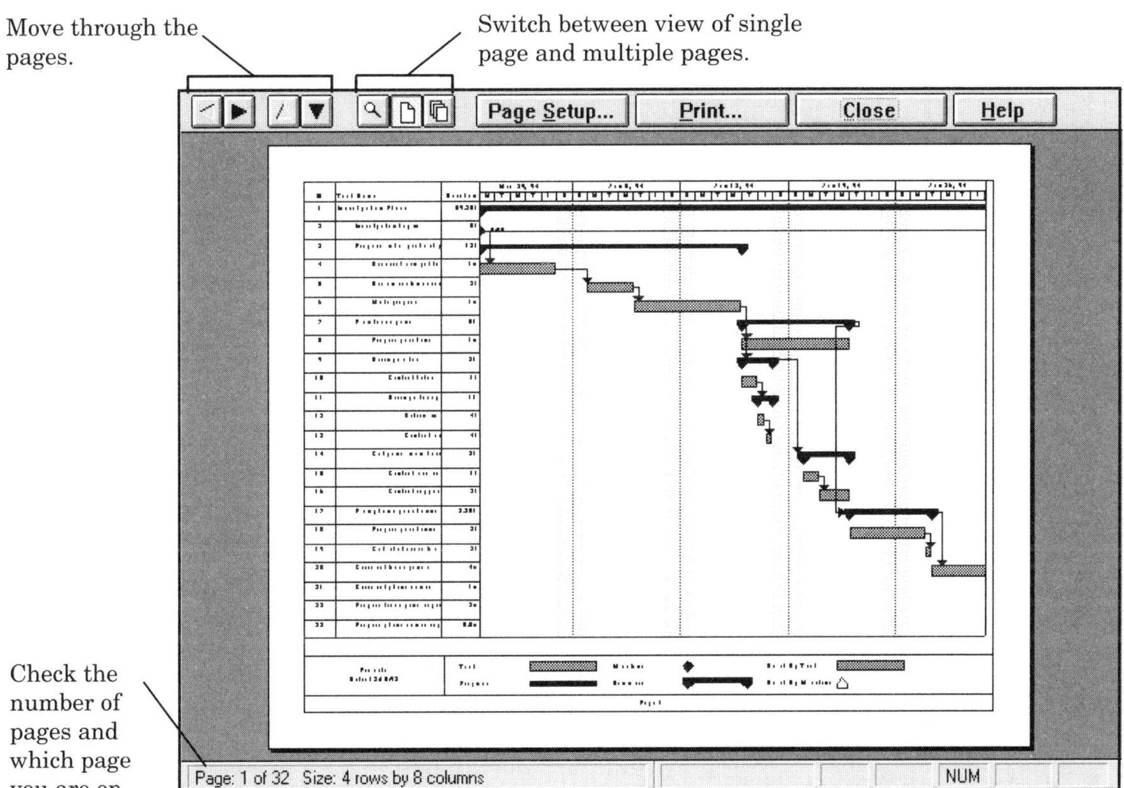

To change the margins, header, footer, orientation of the page, and so on, choose the Page Setup button.

To switch between views of the pages, you can use the buttons at the top of the screen (the magnifying glass, the single page, and the multiple page buttons) or you can use the mouse. Click a page to go from multiple page view to single page view to magnified page view. Click outside the page to go the opposite direction.

When you are ready to print, choose the Print button. In the Print dialog box, you can specify the pages you want to print or the period on the timescale, if the view uses the timescale.

The following illustration shows the Print dialog box in Microsoft Project for Windows. In Microsoft Project for the Macintosh, the Microsoft Project options are the same, but there are additional standard Macintosh options that aren't discussed here.

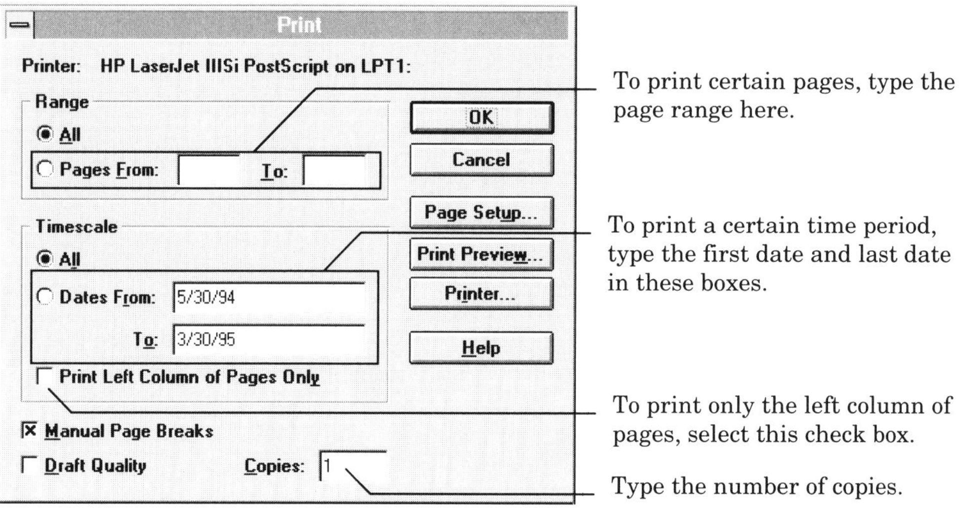

If you added manual page breaks in your view, and want the page breaks you added to be used when the view or report is printed, select the Manual Page Breaks check box.

When you are ready to print, choose the OK button.

If you want to go back to previewing the pages in the view, perhaps to check the effect of using the manual page breaks or to see how the limited time period will fall on the pages, choose the Print Preview button.

To print without previewing the pages, just click the Print button on the Standard toolbar or choose File Print. When you click the Print button on the Standard toolbar, printing starts immediately using the current settings in the Print dialog box. If you want to check or change the settings in the Print dialog box, choose File Print.

Printing a Report

To print a report, choose View Reports. The reports provided with Microsoft Project are grouped by category.

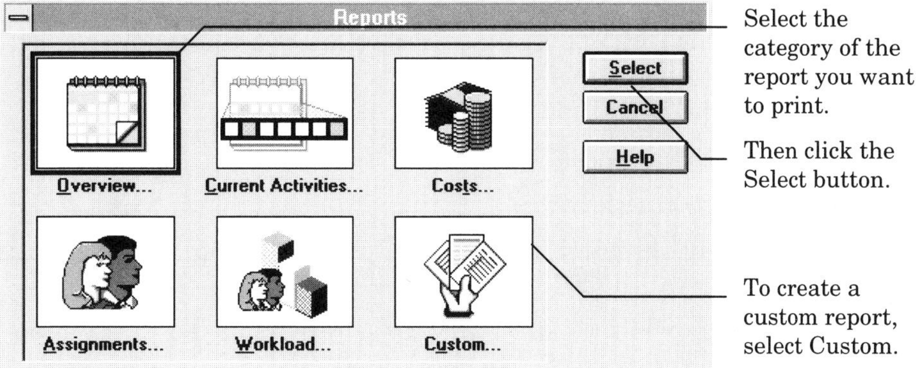

You can also double-click the category.

Once you've selected a category, repeat the process to select a specific report to print. When you select a report from any area except Custom, the report is automatically displayed so you can preview the pages. While previewing, choose the Page Setup button to change the margins, header, footer, orientation of the page, and so on. When all is as you want it, choose the Print button.

To create a report that is different from those provided with Microsoft Project, select Custom and then choose the New, Copy, or Edit button. You can type a new report name, change the table and filter used for the report, sort the information, format the text, and specify that other types of information, such as totals or notes, be included.

The following illustration shows the dialog box for creating a custom task report. The dialog boxes for creating other custom reports are similar.

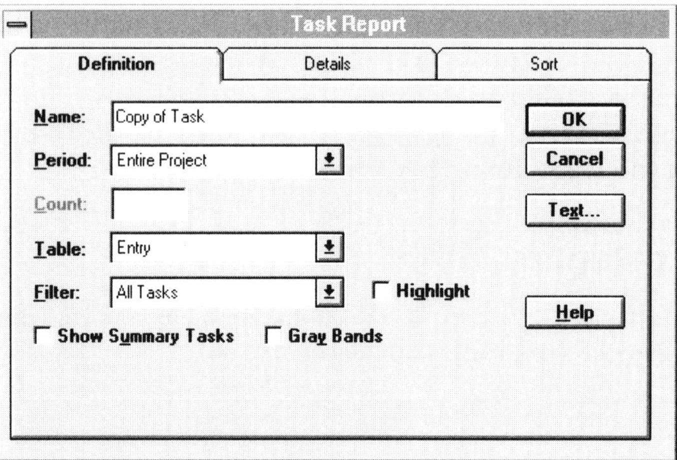

Select the Definition tab to:

- Name the report.
- Specify the table used.
- Specify the filter used and whether it should be a highlighting filter (select the Highlight check box).
- Specify whether summary tasks are displayed in the report (select the Show Summary Tasks check box).
- Control the fonts used (choose the Text button).

Select the Details tab to:

- Specify whether to include schedule, cost, or work information. This is the same information you see in the fields at the bottom of the Task Form or Resource Form (select the Schedule, Cost, or Work check box).
- Show totals for the categories you selected above (select the Show Totals check box).
- Include boxes around the details you included in the report (select the Border Around Detail check box).
- Specify whether to include notes, objects, predecessors, or successors (select the Notes, Objects, Predecessors, or Successors check box).
- Control the fonts used for the details (choose the Text button).

Choose the Sort tab to change the order of the tasks.

Reports you create are added to the list in the Custom Reports dialog box. The next time you want to use the same report, just select the report and choose the Print button.

To preview the pages in your new report, select the Preview button in the Custom Reports dialog box.

When Do You Use New? When Copy? When Edit? When you create a new report, you can choose between three buttons. How do you decide which to use? Use New to create a new report that is not based on an existing one. Use Copy to create a new report that is similar to an existing one. The initial settings in the report definition dialog box will be those from the report you copied. The copied report remains unchanged. Use Edit to change an existing report if you no longer want the original one.

Sample Reports

This section shows several printed views and reports with specific instructions for creating each one. Following each procedure is a list explaining how to customize the view or report to show exactly what you want and to look the way you prefer.

The reports in this section are the simplest reports, to give you an idea of the reporting capability in Microsoft Project if you do practically nothing but print what is already available.

Hints when printing reports:

- If you are using outlining and your outline is collapsed, your printed view will contain only those tasks visible on the screen.
- If your columns are too wide to fit across one page, try printing in landscape mode. To change between portrait mode (page is printed vertically) and landscape mode (page is printed horizontally), use the Page Setup dialog box and select either the Landscape option or the Portrait option under Orientation on the Page tab. To see the Page Setup dialog box, you can choose File Page Setup or, if you are previewing the pages, choose the Page Setup button.

Project Summary

The project summary report includes totals for the number of tasks, cost, duration, work amounts, and number of resources, as well as project start and finish dates, and project notes from the File Summary Info dialog box.

Compusystems
Marcia Cryer
as of 5/10/94

Dates			
Start:	5/30/94	Finish:	3/30/95
Baseline Start:	NA	Baseline Finish:	NA
Actual Start:	NA	Actual Finish:	NA
Start Variance:	0d	Finish Variance:	0d

Duration			
Scheduled:	218.93d	Remaining:	218.93d
Baseline:	0d	Actual:	0d
Variance:	218.93d	Percent Complete:	0%

Work			
Scheduled:	7083.15h	Remaining:	7083.15h
Baseline:	0h	Actual:	0h
Variance:	7083.15h	Percent Complete:	0%

Costs			
Scheduled:	$121,897.29	Remaining:	$121,897.29
Baseline:	$0.00	Actual:	$0.00
Variance:	$121,897.29		

Task Status		Resource Status	
Tasks not yet started:	80	Resources:	22
Tasks in progress:	0	Overallocated Resources:	5
Tasks completed:	0		
Total Tasks:	80	Total Resources:	27

Notes

Goal: New, improved calculator ready for next back-to-school campaign.
Scope: Do add the most requested features, fix bugs in existing code, and update manual to include new features. Do not redo all code, change packaging, or rewrite entire manual.
Assumptions: Technoloty is available to implement features; programmers will be available to do the work; existing packaging will work.

TO PRINT A PROJECT SUMMARY REPORT

1. Choose View Reports.
2. In the Reports dialog box, double-click Overview.
3. Double-click Project.
4. When you are ready to print, choose the Print button.
5. Choose OK.

All you can change on this report is the font type, color, and size.

Summary of Tasks and Dates

If you have outlined your project, you can collapse the outline to show only the major phases and when they occur. If you print the Gantt Chart with the outline collapsed, you have a good presentation piece for a meeting or for an executive summary for management.

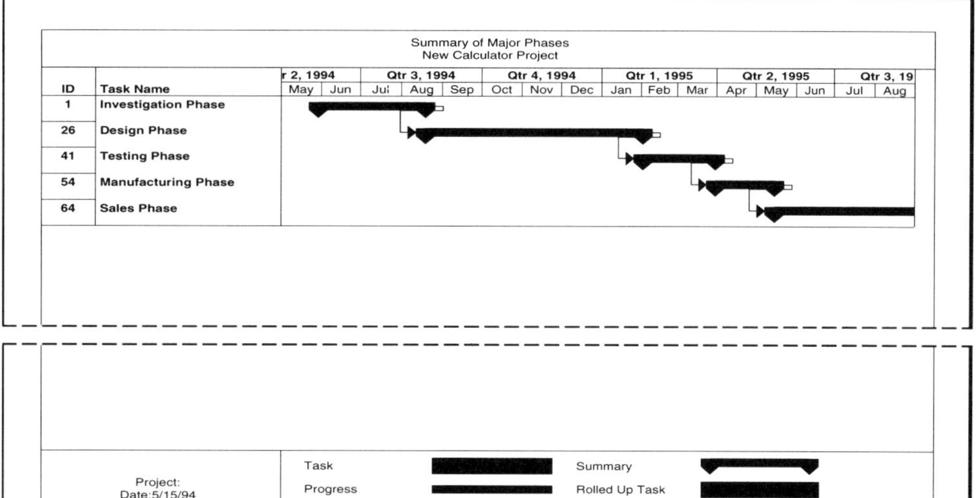

TO CREATE A SUMMARY GANTT CHART

1. Choose View Gantt Chart.
2. To select all the tasks, click the Task Name column title.
3. Collapse the outline by clicking the Hide Subtasks button on the Formatting toolbar or by choosing Tools Outlining/Hide Subtasks.
4. Click the Zoom Out button on the Standard toolbar until you see quarters over months, or the time period you want.

   You can also use the View Zoom command or the Format Timescale command to change the timescale.

5. To preview the view and then print, click the Print Preview button on the Standard toolbar or choose File Print Preview.
6. When you are ready to print, choose the Print button.

   To print without previewing, choose File Print.

7. Choose OK.

To show all tasks again, click the Show All Tasks button on the Formatting toolbar or choose Tools Outlining/Show All Tasks.

To make the Gantt Chart show just what you want, you can change the following:

You can change	Use this command
Bars shown for each task, by adding bars or removing bars	Format Bar Styles
Appearance of one bar	Format Bar
How the text looks for a category of tasks or for one task	Format Text Styles or Format Font
Which text appears on the chart for a type of task or for one task	Format Bar Styles, Text tab or Format Bar, Bar Text tab
Order of the tasks	Tools Sort
Color and pattern of the gridlines	Format Gridlines
Amount of time showing on the chart and the units for the major and minor timescales	Format Timescale or View Zoom
Information in the legend	File Page Setup
Columns of information	View Table
Which tasks are included or highlighted in the view	Tools Filtered For

Tasks and the Critical Path

If you want a graphic representation of the project showing tasks and the critical path, change the critical task bars so they stand out, and then print the Gantt Chart. You can see the durations and the start and finish dates of tasks on the bar chart, plus the critical tasks.

TO CHANGE THE CRITICAL TASK BARS AND PRINT THE GANTT CHART

1. Choose View Gantt Chart.
2. To change the critical task bars: Click the GanttChartWizard button on the Standard toolbar or choose Format GanttChart-Wizard. On the second screen, select Critical Path. Click the Finish button, then Format It, and then Exit Wizard.

3. Double-click the timescale or choose Format Timescale.
4. In the Units boxes under Major Scale and Minor Scale, select the timescale units you want, and choose OK.

   For example, to duplicate the example showing months over weeks: In the Units box under Major Scale, select Months; in the Units box under Minor Scale, select Weeks.
5. Choose File Print.
6. Choose OK.

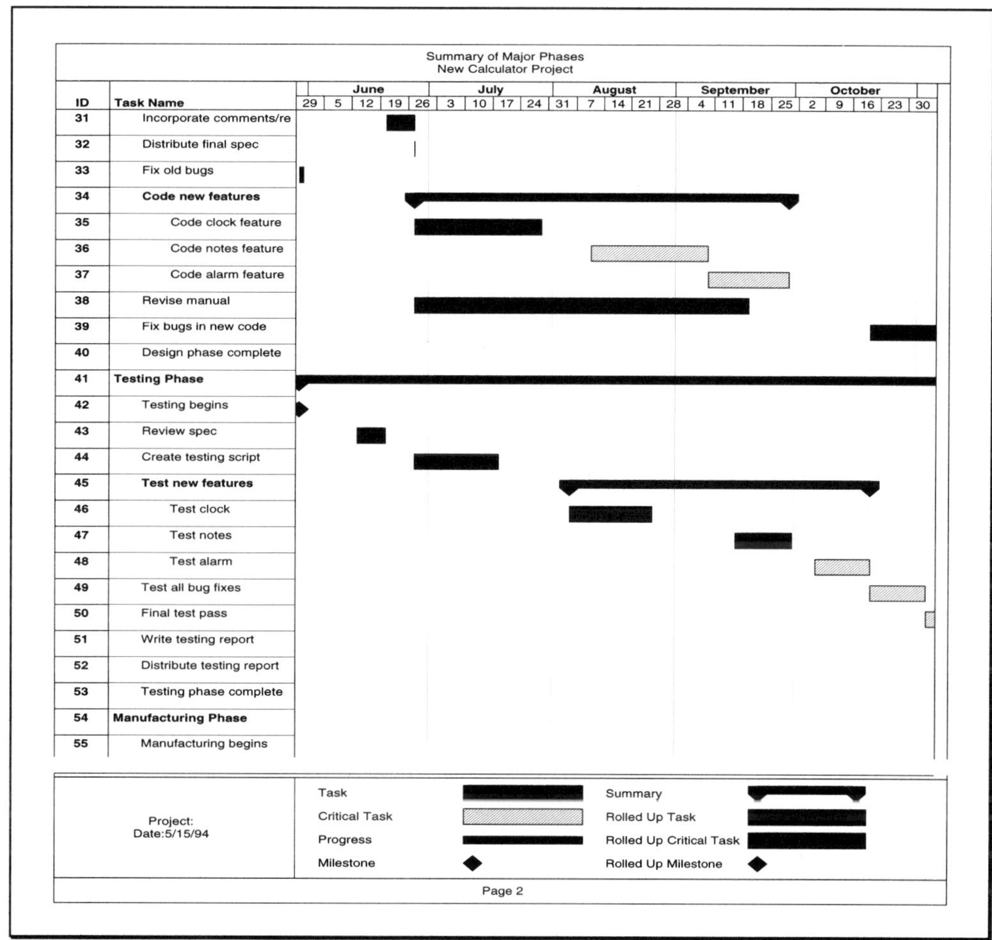

For a list of all the thing you can change on the Gantt Chart, see the table on page 210.

All Tasks and Their Sequence

To show the tasks included in the plan and in what order they will be performed, print the PERT Chart—either with full-size nodes or with small nodes containing ID number only.

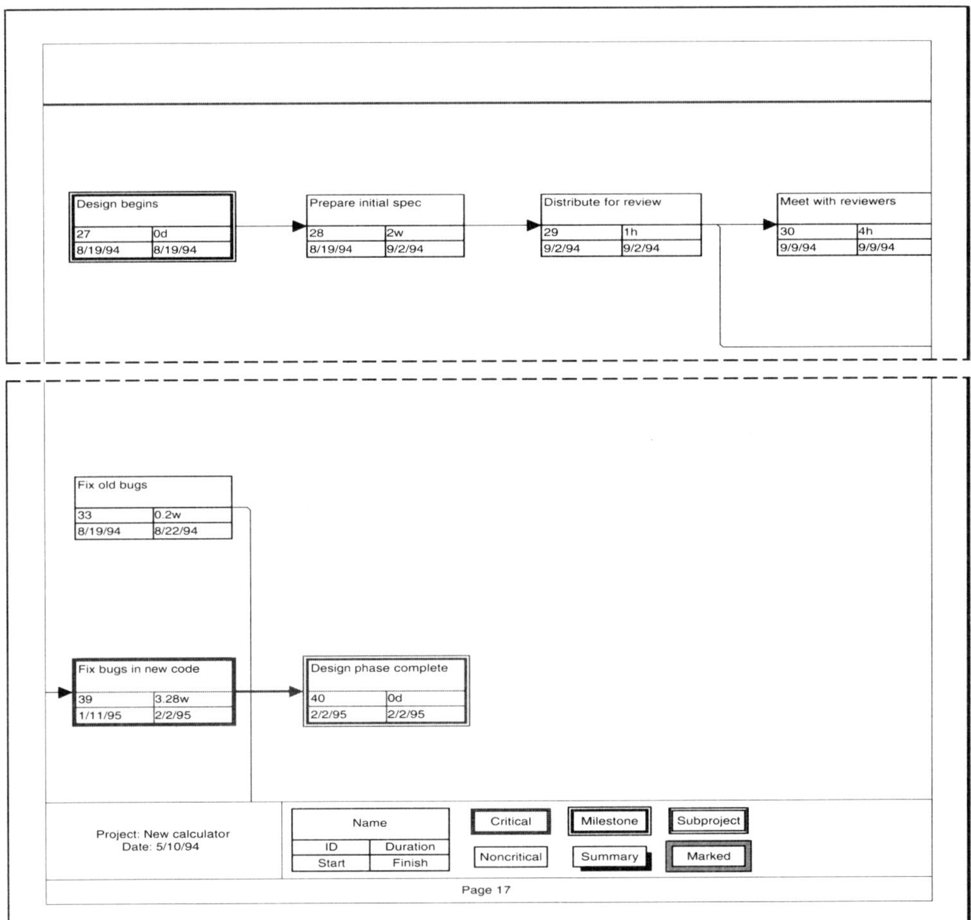

TO PRINT THE PERT CHART

1. Choose View PERT Chart.
2. To include a legend on every page, choose File Page Setup.
3. On the Legend tab, select Legend On Every Page, and choose OK.
4. Choose File Print.
5. Choose OK.

You can, of course, preview the PERT Chart before you print. While previewing, choose the Page Setup button to set up the legend.

If nodes on the PERT Chart are breaking across pages, use the Adjust For Page Breaks check box in the Layout dialog box to keep nodes together. Choose Format Layout and select the check box. Then choose Format Layout Now, and the nodes will be adjusted so they do not fall on two pages.

To print the PERT Chart with small nodes, choose Format Box Styles. On the Contents tab, select Smallest (ID Only) in the Size box. Then print the PERT Chart.

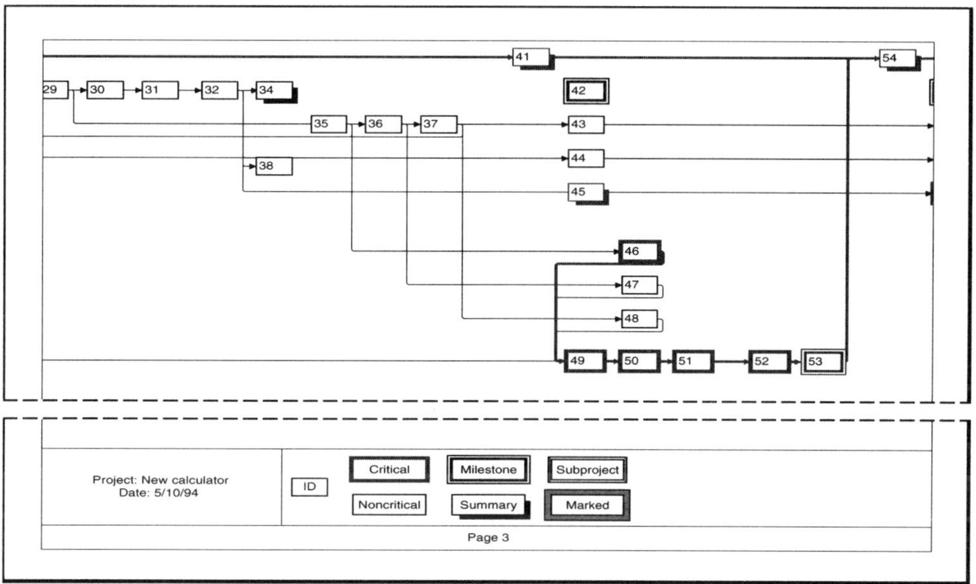

To make the PERT Chart show just what you want, you can change the following:

You can change	Use this command
Information in each node	Format Box Styles, Contents tab
How the text looks	Format Text Styles
How the borders look	Format Box Styles, Borders tab
Lines and arrows	Format Layout
Information in the legend	File Page Setup

List of Tasks, Dates, and Resources

You can print a list of the tasks, their start and finish dates, and the resources assigned to the tasks by printing the Task Sheet with the Entry table applied.

New calculator

ID	Task Name	Duration	Start	Finish	Predecess	Resource Names
1	**Investigation Phase**	**59.25d**	**5/30/94**	**8/19/94**		
2	Investigation begins	0d	5/30/94	5/30/94		
3	**Prepare initial product proposal**	**13d**	**5/30/94**	**6/15/94**	**2**	**Marcia[0.1]**
4	Research competition	1w	5/30/94	6/3/94	2	Marcia,Marketing staff[2],Cheryl[0.25]
5	Review customer comment cards	3d	6/6/94	6/8/94	4	Janet,Marketing staff,Cheryl
6	Write proposal	1w	6/9/94	6/15/94	5	Marcia,Janet
7	**Plan focus panel**	**5d**	**6/16/94**	**6/22/94**		
8	Prepare questions	1w	6/16/94	6/22/94	6	Marcia,Janet
9	**Arrange sites**	**2d**	**6/16/94**	**6/17/94**	**6**	
10	Contact hotels	1d	6/16/94	6/16/94		Cheryl
11	**Arrange for equipment**	**1d**	**6/17/94**	**6/17/94**	**10**	
12	Determine needed equipn	4h	6/17/94	6/17/94		Cheryl,Janet[0.1]
13	Contact local offices	4h	6/17/94	6/17/94	12	Cheryl
14	**Get panel members**	**3d**	**6/20/94**	**6/22/94**	**9**	
15	Contact local reps for names	1d	6/20/94	6/20/94		Cheryl,Janet[0.1]
16	Contact suggested panel mem	2d	6/21/94	6/22/94	15	Cheryl
17	**Plan phone questionnaire**	**3.25d**	**6/23/94**	**6/28/94**	**7**	
18	Prepare questionnaire	3d	6/23/94	6/27/94		Marcia,Marketing staff
19	Get list of users to call	2h	6/28/94	6/28/94	18	Cheryl
20	Carry out focus panels	4w	6/28/94	7/26/94	17	Marcia,Marketing staff,Janet
21	Carry out phone survey	1w	7/26/94	8/2/94	20	Research Inc
22	Prepare focus panel report	2w	8/2/94	8/16/94	21	Marcia[0.1],Marketing staff[2],Cheryl
23	Prepare phone survey report	0.5w	8/16/94	8/18/94	22	Research Inc
24	Present results	4h	8/18/94	8/19/94	23,22	Marcia
25	Investigation phase complete	0d	8/19/94	8/19/94	24	
26	**Design Phase**	**119.65d**	**8/19/94**	**2/2/95**	**1**	

TO PRINT A TASK SHEET

1. Choose View More Views.
2. In the Views box, select Task Sheet and choose the Apply button.
3. If the Entry table is not applied, choose View Table/Entry.
4. Choose File Print.
5. Choose OK.

If you have outlined the project, you can collapse and expand the project as appropriate for the level of detail in your report. For example, if you collapse the project to show summary tasks only, then expand one summary task at a time, you can create an individualized report for the manager of each major phase, showing the project as a whole, plus task details for each manager's phase.

TO PRINT A CUSTOMIZED TASK SHEET

1. Display the Task Sheet.
2. To select all the tasks, click the Task Name column title.
3. Collapse the outline by clicking the Hide Subtasks button on the Formatting toolbar or by choosing Tools Outlining/Hide Subtasks.

4. Select the summary task you want to expand and then click the Show Subtasks button on the Formatting toolbar or choose Tools Outlining/Show Subtasks.
5. To preview the view and then print, click the Print Preview button on the Standard toolbar or choose File Print Preview.
6. When you are ready to print, choose the Print button.

   To print without previewing, choose File Print.
7. Choose OK.

New calculator

ID	Task Name	Duration	Start	Finish	Predecess	Resource Names
1	**Investigation Phase**	**59.25d**	**5/30/94**	**8/19/94**		
2	Investigation begins	0d	5/30/94	5/30/94		
3	**Prepare initial product proposal**	**13d**	**5/30/94**	**6/15/94**	**2**	**Marcia[0.1]**
4	Research competition	1w	5/30/94	6/3/94	2	Marcia,Marketing staff[2],Cheryl[0.25]
5	Review customer comment cards	3d	6/6/94	6/8/94	4	Janet,Marketing staff,Cheryl
6	Write proposal	1w	6/9/94	6/15/94	5	Marcia,Janet
7	**Plan focus panel**	**5d**	**6/16/94**	**6/22/94**		
8	Prepare questions	1w	6/16/94	6/22/94	6	Marcia,Janet
9	**Arrange sites**	**2d**	**6/16/94**	**6/17/94**	**6**	
10	Contact hotels	1d	6/16/94	6/16/94		Cheryl
11	**Arrange for equipment**	**1d**	**6/17/94**	**6/17/94**	**10**	
12	Determine needed equipn	4h	6/17/94	6/17/94		Cheryl,Janet[0.1]
13	Contact local offices	4h	6/17/94	6/17/94	12	Cheryl
14	**Get panel members**	**3d**	**6/20/94**	**6/22/94**	**9**	
15	Contact local reps for names	1d	6/20/94	6/20/94		Cheryl,Janet[0.1]
16	Contact suggested panel mem	2d	6/21/94	6/22/94	15	Cheryl
17	**Plan phone questionnaire**	**3.25d**	**6/23/94**	**6/28/94**	**7**	
18	Prepare questionnaire	3d	6/23/94	6/27/94		Marcia,Marketing staff
19	Get list of users to call	2h	6/28/94	6/28/94	18	Cheryl
20	Carry out focus panels	4w	6/28/94	7/26/94	17	Marcia,Marketing staff,Janet
21	Carry out phone survey	1w	7/26/94	8/2/94	20	Research Inc
22	Prepare focus panel report	2w	8/2/94	8/16/94	21	Marcia[0.1],Marketing staff[2],Cheryl
23	Prepare phone survey report	0.5w	8/16/94	8/18/94	22	Research Inc
24	Present results	4h	8/18/94	8/19/94	23,22	Marcia
25	Investigation phase complete	0d	8/19/94	8/19/94	24	
26	**Design Phase**	**119.65d**	**8/19/94**	**2/2/95**	**1**	
41	**Testing Phase**	**40.13d**	**2/2/95**	**3/31/95**	**26**	
54	**Manufacturing Phase**	**31d**	**3/31/95**	**5/15/95**	**53,41**	
64	**Sales Phase**	**79.92d**	**5/15/95**	**9/1/95**	**54**	

To make the Task Sheet show just what you want, you can change the following:

You can change	Use this command
How the text looks for one task	Format Font
How the text looks for a category of tasks	Format Text Styles
Order of the tasks	Tools Sort
Color and pattern of the gridlines	Format Gridlines
Columns of information	View Table
Which tasks are included or highlighted in the view	Tools Filtered For

Tasks and Notes

To print a list of all the tasks, plus any notes you have entered about the tasks, print the Task report and select the Notes check box. You may want to print task notes if you have included information such as task scope or assumptions about duration in a note with each task. Choose Insert Task Notes to see and enter notes. Many of the supplied reports, such as those in the Overview category, also include notes.

TO PRINT A TASK REPORT SHOWING NOTES

1. Choose View Reports.
2. In the Reports dialog box, double-click Custom.
3. In the Reports box, select Task.
4. Choose the Copy button.
5. In the Name box, type **Tasks and Notes**.
6. To print notes, select the Details tab and then select the Notes check box.
7. Choose OK.
8. To preview the report and then print, choose the Preview button. When you are ready to print, choose the Print button.

   To print the report without previewing, choose the Print button.
9. Choose OK.

New calculator

ID	Task Name	Duration	Start	Finish	Predecessors
2	Investigation begins	0d	5/30/94	5/30/94	
4	Research competition	1w	5/30/94	6/3/94	2
	Assumptions: Competition report from Research, Inc. will be here by 5/25.				
5	Review customer comment cards	3d	6/6/94	6/8/94	4
	Make sure the mail room has forwarded all comment cards to marketing by 6/5/94.				
6	Write proposal	1w	6/9/94	6/15/94	5
	Assumptions: Marcia and Janet willl have finished marketing tour and be available to start on the proposal.				
8	Prepare questions	1w	6/16/94	6/22/94	6
10	Contact hotels	1d	6/16/94	6/16/94	
12	Determine needed equipment	4h	6/17/94	6/17/94	
13	Contact local offices	4h	6/17/94	6/17/94	12
	Contingency plan: If local offices don't have equipment, get name of local rental company.				
15	Contact local reps for names	1d	6/20/94	6/20/94	
16	Contact suggested panel members	2d	6/21/94	6/22/94	15
18	Prepare questionnaire	3d	6/23/94	6/27/94	
19	Get list of users to call	2h	6/28/94	6/28/94	18
20	Carry out focus panels	4w	6/28/94	7/26/94	17
21	Carry out phone survey	1w	7/26/94	8/2/94	20
22	Prepare focus panel report	2w	8/2/94	8/16/94	21
23	Prepare phone survey report	0.5w	8/16/94	8/18/94	22
24	Present results	4h	8/18/94	8/19/94	23,22
25	Investigation phase complete	0d	8/19/94	8/19/94	24
27	Design begins	0d	8/19/94	8/19/94	
28	Prepare initial spec	2w	8/19/94	9/2/94	27
29	Distribute for review	1h	9/2/94	9/2/94	28
30	Meet with reviewers	4h	9/9/94	9/9/94	29FS+1w
31	Incorporate comments/revise	1w	9/9/94	9/16/94	30
32	Distribute final spec	1h	9/16/94	9/16/94	31
33	Fix old bugs	0.2w	8/19/94	8/22/94	2
35	Code clock feature	4.68w	9/19/94	10/20/94	
36	Code notes feature	4.28w	11/2/94	12/1/94	35

To make the Task report show just what you want, you can change the following:

You can change	Use this option in the Task Report dialog box
Columns of information	Definition tab, Table box
Which tasks are printed	Definition tab, Filter box
Whether summary tasks are printed	Definition tab, Show Summary Tasks check box
Order of the tasks	Sort tab
Whether schedule, cost, and work information are printed	Details tab, Schedule, Cost, and Work check boxes
Whether totals, predecessors, and successors are printed	Details tab, Show Totals, Predecessors, and Successors check boxes
How the text looks	Text button

Task Work and Cost, Including Totals

To see the work and cost for each task, print the Task Sheet with the Summary table applied.

New calculator

ID	Task Name	Duration	Start	Finish	% Comp.	Cost	Work
1	**Investigation Phase**	**59.25d**	**5/30/94**	**8/19/94**	**0%**	**$25,744.71**	**1255.6h**
2	Investigation begins	0d	5/30/94	5/30/94	0%	$0.00	0h
3	**Prepare initial product proposal**	**13d**	**5/30/94**	**6/15/94**	**0%**	**$5,496.16**	**292.4h**
4	Research competition	1w	5/30/94	6/3/94	0%	$2,269.23	130h
5	Review customer comment cards	3d	6/6/94	6/8/94	0%	$1,101.93	72h
6	Write proposal	1w	6/9/94	6/15/94	0%	$1,875.00	80h
7	**Plan focus panel**	**5d**	**6/16/94**	**6/22/94**	**0%**	**$2,210.10**	**121.2h**
8	Prepare questions	1w	6/16/94	6/22/94	0%	$1,875.00	80h
9	**Arrange sites**	**2d**	**6/16/94**	**6/17/94**	**0%**	**$132.21**	**16.4h**
10	Contact hotels	1d	6/16/94	6/16/94	0%	$61.54	8h
11	**Arrange for equipment**	**1d**	**6/17/94**	**6/17/94**	**0%**	**$70.67**	**8.4h**
12	Determine needed equipment	4h	6/17/94	6/17/94	0%	$39.90	4.4h
13	Contact local offices	4h	6/17/94	6/17/94	0%	$30.77	4h
14	**Get panel members**	**3d**	**6/20/94**	**6/22/94**	**0%**	**$202.89**	**24.8h**
15	Contact local reps for names	1d	6/20/94	6/20/94	0%	$79.81	8.8h
16	Contact suggested panel members	2d	6/21/94	6/22/94	0%	$123.08	16h
17	**Plan phone questionnaire**	**3.25d**	**6/23/94**	**6/28/94**	**0%**	**$961.53**	**50h**
18	Prepare questionnaire	3d	6/23/94	6/27/94	0%	$946.15	48h
19	Get list of users to call	2h	6/28/94	6/28/94	0%	$15.38	2h
20	Carry out focus panels	4w	6/28/94	7/26/94	0%	$9,961.54	480h
21	Carry out phone survey	1w	7/26/94	8/2/94	0%	$2,500.00	40h
22	Prepare focus panel report	2w	8/2/94	8/16/94	0%	$3,269.23	248h
23	Prepare phone survey report	0.5w	8/16/94	8/18/94	0%	$1,250.00	20h
24	Present results	4h	8/18/94	8/19/94	0%	$96.15	4h
25	Investigation phase complete	0d	8/19/94	8/19/94	0%	$0.00	0h
26	**Design Phase**	**119.65d**	**8/19/94**	**2/2/95**	**0%**	**$43,044.16**	**2108.15h**
27	Design begins	0d	8/19/94	8/19/94	0%	$0.00	0h
28	Prepare initial spec	2w	8/19/94	9/2/94	0%	$3,585.04	186h
29	Distribute for review	1h	9/2/94	9/2/94	0%	$6.50	1h
30	Meet with reviewers	4h	9/9/94	9/9/94	0%	$384.61	20h
31	Incorporate comments/revise	1w	9/9/94	9/16/94	0%	$1,686.62	88h
32	Distribute final spec	1h	9/16/94	9/16/94	0%	$6.50	1h
33	Fix old bugs	0.2w	8/19/94	8/22/94	0%	$201.93	16.8h
34	**Code new features**	**67.8d**	**9/19/94**	**12/21/94**	**0%**	**$16,903.81**	**1026.72h**
35	Code clock feature	4.68w	9/19/94	10/20/94	0%	$4,500.00	374.4h
36	Code notes feature	4.28w	11/2/94	12/1/94	0%	$2,057.69	171.2h
37	Code alarm feature	2.88w	12/1/94	12/21/94	0%	$1,384.62	115.2h

TO PRINT A TASK SHEET SHOWING WORK AND COST

1. Choose View More Views.
2. In the Views box, select Task Sheet, and choose the Apply button.
3. Choose View Table/Summary.
4. To preview the view, click the Print Preview button on the Standard toolbar or choose File Print Preview.
5. When you are ready to print, choose the Print button.
6. Choose OK.

To customize the Task Sheet, see the table on page 215.

To see task work and cost, including totals, print the Task report with the Summary table applied. The outline was collapsed and then partially expanded to include the totals in the following illustration.

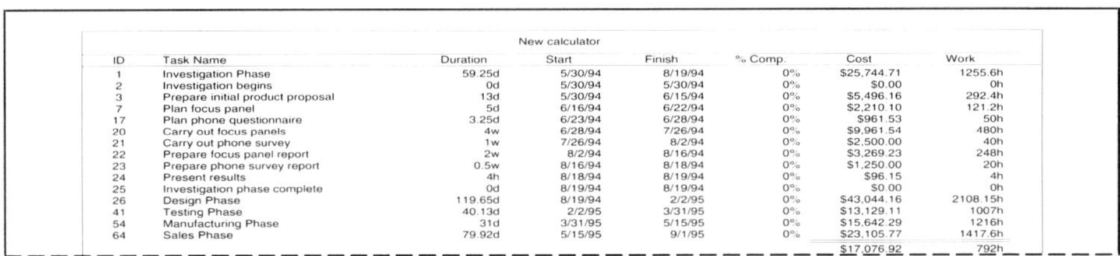

New calculator

ID	Task Name	Duration	Start	Finish	% Comp.	Cost	Work
1	Investigation Phase	59.25d	5/30/94	8/19/94	0%	$25,744.71	1255.6h
2	Investigation begins	0d	5/30/94	5/30/94	0%	$0.00	0h
3	Prepare initial product proposal	13d	5/30/94	6/15/94	0%	$5,496.16	292.4h
7	Plan focus panel	5d	6/16/94	6/22/94	0%	$2,210.10	121.2h
17	Plan phone questionnaire	3.25d	6/23/94	6/28/94	0%	$961.53	50h
20	Carry out focus panels	4w	6/28/94	7/26/94	0%	$9,961.54	480h
21	Carry out phone survey	1w	7/26/94	8/2/94	0%	$2,500.00	40h
22	Prepare focus panel report	2w	8/2/94	8/16/94	0%	$3,269.23	248h
23	Prepare phone survey report	0.5w	8/16/94	8/18/94	0%	$1,250.00	20h
24	Present results	4h	8/18/94	8/19/94	0%	$96.15	4h
25	Investigation phase complete	0d	8/19/94	8/19/94	0%	$0.00	0h
26	Design Phase	119.65d	8/19/94	2/2/95	0%	$43,044.16	2108.15h
41	Testing Phase	40.13d	2/2/95	3/31/95	0%	$13,129.11	1007h
54	Manufacturing Phase	31d	3/31/95	5/15/95	0%	$15,642.29	1216h
64	Sales Phase	79.92d	5/15/95	9/1/95	0%	$23,105.77	1417.6h
						$17,076.92	792h

TO PRINT A TASK REPORT SHOWING WORK AND COST, PLUS TOTALS

1. Choose View Reports.
2. In the Reports dialog box, double-click Custom.
3. In the Reports box, select Task.
4. Choose the Copy button.
5. In the Name box, type **Task Work and Cost**.
6. In the Table box, select Summary.
7. To show summary tasks, select the Show Summary Tasks check box.
8. To print totals, select the Details tab, select the Show Totals check box, and then choose OK.
9. To preview the report and then print, choose the Preview button.
10. When you are ready to print, choose the Print button.
11. Choose OK.

To make the this report show what you want, see the table on page 217.

Task Schedule

To get started with the actual work on the project tasks, you'll want to print a list of tasks to be performed, when they have to be performed, and who will work on them. These are your actual working documents to let people know exactly what to do and when to do it, like a "to do" list.

To generate this schedule, print a Task report showing a list of tasks by the period you specify. You can print either the whole thing from project start to finish or just a portion. Periodically as you track the project, print a new list of tasks reflecting the latest status of the project, so everyone is always working with the latest schedule.

New calculator
Task Schedule

ID	Task Name	Duration	Start	Finish	Predecessors
Week of May 29					
2	Investigation begins	0d	5/30/94	5/30/94	
4	Research competition	1w	5/30/94	6/3/94	2

ID	Resource Name	Units	Work	Delay	Start	Finish
1	Marcia	1	40h	0h	5/30/94	6/3/94
2	Marketing staff	2	80h	0h	5/30/94	6/3/94
4	Cheryl	0.25	10h	0h	5/30/94	6/3/94

ID	Task Name	Duration	Start	Finish	Predecessors
Week of June 5					
5	Review customer comment cards	3d	6/6/94	6/8/94	4

ID	Resource Name	Units	Work	Delay	Start	Finish
2	Marketing staff	1	24h	0h	6/6/94	6/8/94
4	Cheryl	1	24h	0h	6/6/94	6/8/94
5	Janet	1	24h	0h	6/6/94	6/8/94

ID	Task Name	Duration	Start	Finish	Predecessors
6	Write proposal	1w	6/9/94	6/15/94	5

ID	Resource Name	Units	Work	Delay	Start	Finish
1	Marcia	1	40h	0h	6/9/94	6/15/94
5	Janet	1	40h	0h	6/9/94	6/15/94

ID	Task Name	Duration	Start	Finish	Predecessors
Week of June 12					
6	Write proposal	1w	6/9/94	6/15/94	5

ID	Resource Name	Units	Work	Delay	Start	Finish
1	Marcia	1	40h	0h	6/9/94	6/15/94
5	Janet	1	40h	0h	6/9/94	6/15/94

ID	Task Name	Duration	Start	Finish	Predecessors
8	Prepare questions	1w	6/16/94	6/22/94	6

ID	Resource Name	Units	Work	Delay	Start	Finish
1	Marcia	1	40h	0h	6/16/94	6/22/94
5	Janet	1	40h	0h	6/16/94	6/22/94

ID	Task Name	Duration	Start	Finish	Predecessors
10	Contact hotels	1d	6/16/94	6/16/94	

ID	Resource Name	Units	Work	Delay	Start	Finish
4	Cheryl	1	8h	0h	6/16/94	6/16/94

ID	Task Name	Duration	Start	Finish	Predecessors
12	Determine needed equipment	4h	6/17/94	6/17/94	

ID	Resource Name	Units	Work	Delay	Start	Finish
4	Cheryl	1	4h	0h	6/17/94	6/17/94
5	Janet	0.1	0.4h	0h	6/17/94	6/17/94

ID	Task Name	Duration	Start	Finish	Predecessors
13	Contact local offices	4h	6/17/94	6/17/94	12

ID	Resource Name	Units	Work	Delay	Start	Finish
4	Cheryl	1	4h	0h	6/17/94	6/17/94

ID	Task Name	Duration	Start	Finish	Predecessors
Week of June 19					
8	Prepare questions	1w	6/16/94	6/22/94	6

ID	Resource Name	Units	Work	Delay	Start	Finish
1	Marcia	1	40h	0h	6/16/94	6/22/94
5	Janet	1	40h	0h	6/16/94	6/22/94

ID	Task Name	Duration	Start	Finish	Predecessors
15	Contact local reps for names	1d	6/20/94	6/20/94	

ID	Resource Name	Units	Work	Delay	Start	Finish
4	Cheryl	1	8h	0h	6/20/94	6/20/94
5	Janet	0.1	0.8h	0h	6/20/94	6/20/94

ID	Task Name	Duration	Start	Finish	Predecessors
16	Contact suggested panel members	2d	6/21/94	6/22/94	15

ID	Resource Name	Units	Work	Delay	Start	Finish
4	Cheryl	1	16h	0h	6/21/94	6/22/94

ID	Task Name	Duration	Start	Finish	Predecessors
18	Prepare questionnaire	3d	6/23/94	6/27/94	

ID	Resource Name	Units	Work	Delay	Start	Finish
1	Marcia	1	24h	0h	6/23/94	6/27/94
2	Marketing staff	1	24h	0h	6/23/94	6/27/94

Week of June 26

TO PRINT A TASK SCHEDULE

1. Choose View Reports.
2. In the Reports dialog box, double-click Custom.
3. In the Reports box, select Task.
4. Choose the Copy button.
5. In the Name box, type **Task Schedule**.
6. In the Period box, select Weeks.
7. To print gray bands between the weeks for a visual separator, select the Gray Bands check box.
8. To include assigned resources, select the Details tab and then select the Schedule check box.
9. To remove the border around the resources, clear the Border Around Details check box.
10. Choose OK.
11. To preview the report and then print, choose the Preview button.
12. When you are ready to print, choose the Print button.

    To print the report without previewing, choose the Print button.
13. Choose OK.

To make the Task Schedule show just what you want, you can change the following:

You can change	Use this option in the Task Report dialog box
Columns of information	Definition tab, Table box
Which tasks are printed	Definition tab, Filter box
Order of the tasks	Sort tab
Period for which information is printed: days, weeks, months, quarters, or years	Definition tab, Period box
How many periods	Definition tab, Count box
Whether resource assignments are printed	Details tab, Schedule check box
How the text looks	Text button

Monthly Calendar of Tasks

To print a calendar showing the tasks scheduled to occur each day, print the Calendar view.

TO PRINT THE MONTHLY CALENDAR

1. Choose View Calendar.
2. To preview the view and then print, click the Print Preview button on the Standard toolbar or choose File Print Preview.
3. When you are ready to print, choose the Print button.

To print without previewing, choose File Print.

4. In the Dates From and To boxes under Timescale, type the first date and last date for the period you want to print.
5. Choose OK.

To make the Calendar show just what you want, you can change the following:

You can change	**Use this command**
Which tasks are printed	Tools Filtered For
How calendar looks, including headings, boxes, shading, and calendar that controls the non-working days displayed on the calendar	Format Timescale
How tasks are represented—bar or line, color and pattern, and text on bars	Format Bar Styles
How the text looks	Format Text Styles

List of Resources

To print a list of all the resources working on the project, print the Resource Sheet.

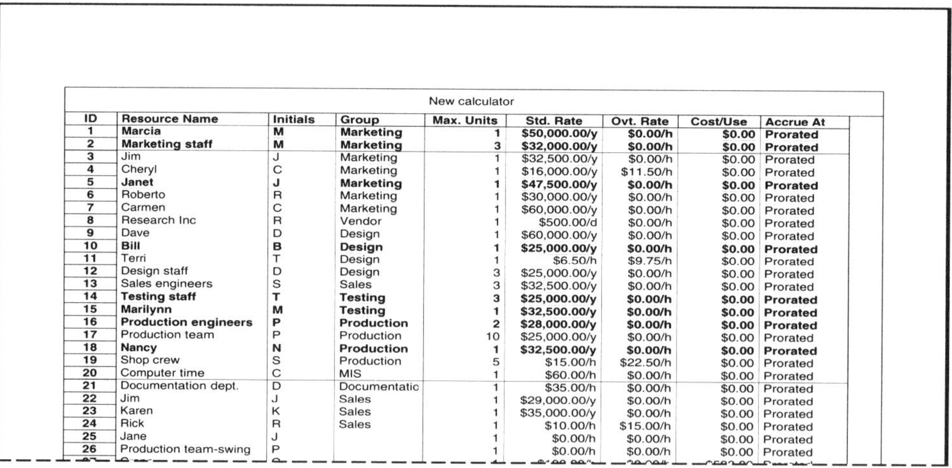

New calculator

ID	Resource Name	Initials	Group	Max. Units	Std. Rate	Ovt. Rate	Cost/Use	Accrue At
1	**Marcia**	**M**	**Marketing**	**1**	**$50,000.00/y**	**$0.00/h**	**$0.00**	**Prorated**
2	**Marketing staff**	**M**	**Marketing**	**3**	**$32,000.00/y**	**$0.00/h**	**$0.00**	**Prorated**
3	Jim	J	Marketing	1	$32,500.00/y	$0.00/h	$0.00	Prorated
4	Cheryl	C	Marketing	1	$16,000.00/y	$11.50/h	$0.00	Prorated
5	**Janet**	**J**	**Marketing**	**1**	**$47,500.00/y**	**$0.00/h**	**$0.00**	**Prorated**
6	Roberto	R	Marketing	1	$30,000.00/y	$0.00/h	$0.00	Prorated
7	Carmen	C	Marketing	1	$60,000.00/y	$0.00/h	$0.00	Prorated
8	Research Inc	R	Vendor	1	$500.00/d	$0.00/h	$0.00	Prorated
9	Dave	D	Design	1	$60,000.00/y	$0.00/h	$0.00	Prorated
10	**Bill**	**B**	**Design**	**1**	**$25,000.00/y**	**$0.00/h**	**$0.00**	**Prorated**
11	Terri	T	Design	1	$6.50/h	$9.75/h	$0.00	Prorated
12	Design staff	D	Design	3	$25,000.00/y	$0.00/h	$0.00	Prorated
13	Sales engineers	S	Sales	3	$32,500.00/y	$0.00/h	$0.00	Prorated
14	**Testing staff**	**T**	**Testing**	**3**	**$25,000.00/y**	**$0.00/h**	**$0.00**	**Prorated**
15	**Marilynn**	**M**	**Testing**	**1**	**$32,500.00/y**	**$0.00/h**	**$0.00**	**Prorated**
16	**Production engineers**	**P**	**Production**	**2**	**$28,000.00/y**	**$0.00/h**	**$0.00**	**Prorated**
17	Production team	P	Production	10	$25,000.00/y	$0.00/h	$0.00	Prorated
18	**Nancy**	**N**	**Production**	**1**	**$32,500.00/y**	**$0.00/h**	**$0.00**	**Prorated**
19	Shop crew	S	Production	5	$15.00/h	$22.50/h	$0.00	Prorated
20	Computer time	C	MIS	1	$60.00/h	$0.00/h	$0.00	Prorated
21	Documentation dept.	D	Documentatic	1	$35.00/h	$0.00/h	$0.00	Prorated
22	Jim	J	Sales	1	$29,000.00/y	$0.00/h	$0.00	Prorated
23	Karen	K	Sales	1	$35,000.00/y	$0.00/h	$0.00	Prorated
24	Rick	R	Sales	1	$10.00/h	$15.00/h	$0.00	Prorated
25	Jane	J		1	$0.00/h	$0.00/h	$0.00	Prorated
26	Production team-swing	P		1	$0.00/h	$0.00/h	$0.00	Prorated

TO PRINT A LIST OF RESOURCES

1. Choose View Resource Sheet.
2. To preview the view and then print, choose the Print Preview button on the Standard toolbar or choose File Print Preview.
3. When you are ready to print, choose the Print button.

   To print the view without previewing, choose File Print.
4. Choose OK.

To make the Resource Sheet show just what you want, you can change the following:

You can change	Use this command
How the text looks for one resource	Format Font
How the text looks for a category of resources	Format Text Styles
Order of the resources	Tools Sort
Color and pattern of the gridlines	Format Gridlines
Columns of information	View Table
Which resources are included or highlighted in the view	Tools Filtered For

Resource Use During the Project

Print the Resource Usage view to show the percentage each resource is used during each period. To specify the period, use the Format Timescale command.

TO PRINT A LIST OF RESOURCES AND THEIR USE DURING THE PROJECT

1. Choose View Resource Usage.
2. Choose Format Details/Percent Allocation.
3. Choose Format Timescale.
4. In the Units boxes under Major Scale and Minor Scale, select the timescale units you want, and choose OK.

   For example, to duplicate the example showing months and weeks: In the Units box under Major Scale, select Months; in the Units box under Minor Scale, select Weeks.

5. To print the ID and Resource Name columns on every page, choose File Page Setup. On the View tab, select the Print First x Columns On All Pages check box, and then type **2** in the box.
6. To preview the view and then print, click the Print Preview button on the Standard toolbar or choose File Print Preview.
7. When you are ready to print, choose the Print button.

   To print without previewing, choose File Print.
8. Choose OK.

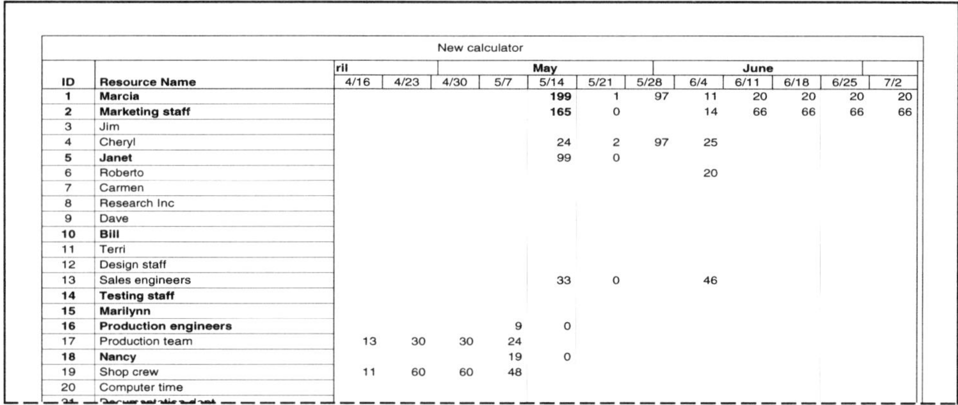

New calculator

ID	Resource Name	4/16	4/23	4/30	5/7	5/14	5/21	5/28	6/4	6/11	6/18	6/25	7/2
		ril				May				June			
1	**Marcia**					**199**	1	97	11	20	20	20	20
2	**Marketing staff**					**165**	0		14	66	66	66	66
3	Jim												
4	Cheryl					24	2	97	25				
5	**Janet**					99	0						
6	Roberto								20				
7	Carmen												
8	Research Inc												
9	Dave												
10	**Bill**												
11	Terri												
12	Design staff												
13	Sales engineers					33	0		46				
14	**Testing staff**												
15	**Marilynn**												
16	**Production engineers**				9	0							
17	Production team	13	30	30	24								
18	**Nancy**				19	0							
19	Shop crew	11	60	60	48								
20	Computer time												

To make the Resource Usage view show just what you want, you can change the following:

You can change	Use this command
Information displayed in each box	Format Details
How the text looks for one resource	Format Font
How the text looks for a category of resources	Format Text Styles
Order of the resources	Tools Sort
Color and pattern of the gridlines	Format Gridlines
Amount of time covered by each usage box and the heading for the major and minor scales	Format Timescale
Columns of information	View Table
Which resources are included or highlighted in the view	Tools Filtered For

Expected Resource Work and Cost

The Resource Sheet with the Summary table applied shows the total work and the cost of each resource assigned to work on the project; the Resource Usage view shows the cost by period so you can predict your expenditures. Resources that are overallocated are bold.

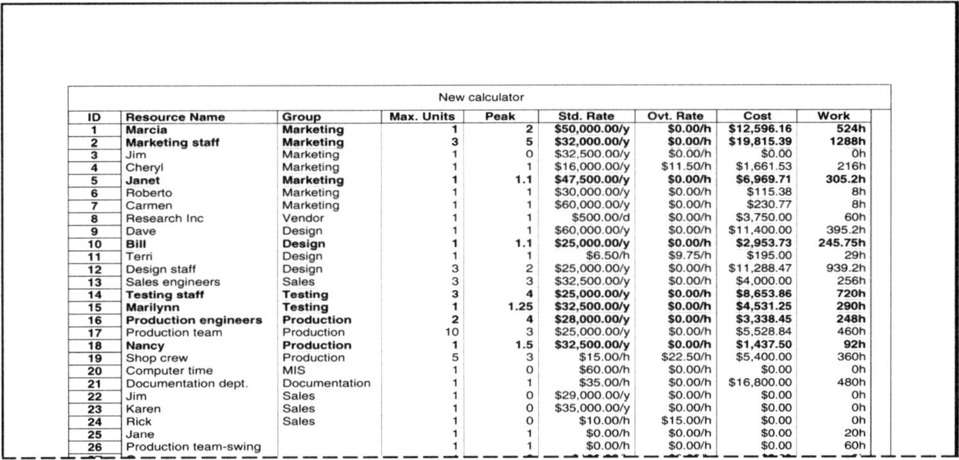

New calculator

ID	Resource Name	Group	Max. Units	Peak	Std. Rate	Ovt. Rate	Cost	Work
1	**Marcia**	**Marketing**	**1**	**2**	**$50,000.00/y**	**$0.00/h**	**$12,596.16**	**524h**
2	**Marketing staff**	**Marketing**	**3**	**5**	**$32,000.00/y**	**$0.00/h**	**$19,815.39**	**1288h**
3	Jim	Marketing	1	0	$32,500.00/y	$0.00/h	$0.00	0h
4	Cheryl	Marketing	1	1	$16,000.00/y	$11.50/h	$1,661.53	216h
5	**Janet**	**Marketing**	**1**	**1.1**	**$47,500.00/y**	**$0.00/h**	**$6,969.71**	**305.2h**
6	Roberto	Marketing	1	1	$30,000.00/y	$0.00/h	$115.38	8h
7	Carmen	Marketing	1	1	$60,000.00/y	$0.00/h	$230.77	8h
8	Research Inc	Vendor	1	1	$500.00/d	$0.00/h	$3,750.00	60h
9	Dave	Design	1	1	$60,000.00/y	$0.00/h	$11,400.00	395.2h
10	**Bill**	**Design**	**1**	**1.1**	**$25,000.00/y**	**$0.00/h**	**$2,953.73**	**245.75h**
11	Terri	Design	1	1	$6.50/h	$9.75/h	$195.00	29h
12	Design staff	Design	3	2	$25,000.00/y	$0.00/h	$11,288.47	939.2h
13	Sales engineers	Sales	3	3	$32,500.00/y	$0.00/h	$4,000.00	256h
14	**Testing staff**	**Testing**	**3**	**4**	**$25,000.00/y**	**$0.00/h**	**$8,653.86**	**720h**
15	**Marilynn**	**Testing**	**1**	**1.25**	**$32,500.00/y**	**$0.00/h**	**$4,531.25**	**290h**
16	**Production engineers**	**Production**	**2**	**4**	**$28,000.00/y**	**$0.00/h**	**$3,338.45**	**248h**
17	Production team	Production	10	3	$25,000.00/y	$0.00/h	$5,528.84	460h
18	**Nancy**	**Production**	**1**	**1.5**	**$32,500.00/y**	**$0.00/h**	**$1,437.50**	**92h**
19	Shop crew	Production	5	3	$15.00/h	$22.50/h	$5,400.00	360h
20	Computer time	MIS	1	0	$60.00/h	$0.00/h	$0.00	0h
21	Documentation dept.	Documentation	1	1	$35.00/h	$0.00/h	$16,800.00	480h
22	Jim	Sales	1	0	$29,000.00/y	$0.00/h	$0.00	0h
23	Karen	Sales	1	0	$35,000.00/y	$0.00/h	$0.00	0h
24	Rick	Sales	1	0	$10.00/h	$15.00/h	$0.00	0h
25	Jane		1	1	$0.00/h	$0.00/h	$0.00	20h
26	Production team-swing		1	1	$0.00/h	$0.00/h	$0.00	60h

TO PRINT A RESOURCE SHEET SHOWING WORK AND COST INFORMATION

1. Choose View Resource Sheet.
2. Choose View Table/Summary.
3. To preview the view and then print, click the Print Preview button on the Standard toolbar or choose File Print Preview.
4. When you are ready to print, choose the Print button.

   To print the view without previewing, choose File Print.
5. Choose OK.

To make the Resource Sheet show just what you want, see the table on page 223.

On the Resource Usage view, you can show the cost of each resource during the period you select. For example, you can check weekly costs, or monthly costs, depending on how you change the timescale.

TO PRINT A LIST OF ALL RESOURCES AND THEIR COST DURING THE PROJECT

1. Choose View Resource Usage.
2. Choose Format Details/Cost.
3. Choose Format Timescale.
4. In the Units boxes and Label boxes under Major Scale and Minor Scale, select the timescale units you want, and choose OK. If the boxes in the Resource Usage view contain ### instead of a number, change the value in the Enlarge box until numbers show.
5. To preview the view and then print, click the Print Preview button on the Standard toolbar or choose File Print Preview.
6. When you are ready to print, choose the Print button.

   To print the view without previewing, choose File Print.
7. Choose OK.

To make the Resource Usage view show just what you want, see the table on page 224.

Resource Schedules

Three reports included with Microsoft Project show resources and the tasks to which they are assigned. These three reports are in the Assignments category and are illustrated on the following pages.

TO PRINT A RESOURCE ASSIGNMENT REPORT

1. Choose View Reports.
2. In the Reports dialog box, double-click Assignments.
3. In the Assignment Reports dialog box, double-click the report you want to print.
4. For the Weekly To-Do List, type the name of the resource whose tasks you want to print.
5. When you are ready to print, choose the Print button.
6. Choose OK.

To customize any of these reports, choose View Reports. In the Reports dialog box, double-click Custom. In the Reports box, select the report name, and choose the Copy button. Then change or add to the report as suits your needs.

The three Assignments reports are:

- The Who Does What report lists each resource, with the tasks to which it is assigned listed below the resource name. The start, finish, and delay for each task are included.

Who Does What
New calculator

5/15/94

ID	Resource Name						Work
14	Marilynn						290h
	ID	Task Name	Units	Work	Delay	Start	Finish
	30	Meet with reviewers	1	4h	0h	9/9/94	9/9/94
	44	Create testing script	1	120h	0h	2/2/95	2/23/95
	45	Test new features	0.25	30h	0h	2/2/95	2/23/95
	49	Test all bug fixes	0.2	16h	0h	2/23/95	3/9/95
	50	Final test pass	1	80h	0h	3/9/95	3/23/95
	51	Write testing report	1	40h	0h	3/23/95	3/30/95
4	Janet						305.2h
	ID	Task Name	Units	Work	Delay	Start	Finish
	5	Review customer comment cards	1	24h	0h	6/6/94	6/8/94
	6	Write proposal	1	40h	0h	6/9/94	6/15/94
	8	Prepare questions	1	40h	0h	6/16/94	6/22/94
	12	Determine needed equipment	0.1	0.4h	0h	6/17/94	6/17/94
	15	Contact local reps for names	0.1	0.8h	0h	6/20/94	6/20/94
	20	Carry out focus panels	1	160h	0h	6/28/94	7/26/94
	66	Review spec	1	40h	0h	5/15/95	5/22/95
18	Shop crew						360h
	ID	Task Name	Units	Work	Delay	Start	Finish
	60	Test production	3	360h	0h	4/21/95	5/12/95
8	Dave						395.2h
	ID	Task Name	Units	Work	Delay	Start	Finish
	28	Prepare initial spec	1	80h	0h	8/19/94	9/2/94
	30	Meet with reviewers	1	4h	0h	9/9/94	9/9/94
	31	Incorporate comments/revise	1	40h	0h	9/9/94	9/16/94
	34	Code new features	0.5	271.2h	0h	9/19/94	12/21/94
16	Production team						460h
	ID	Task Name	Units	Work	Delay	Start	Finish
	56	Review spec	1	40h	0h	3/31/95	4/7/95
	59	Set up production test	1	60h	0h	4/11/95	4/21/95
	60	Test production	3	360h	0h	4/21/95	5/12/95
	61	Begin production	5	0h	0h	5/12/95	5/12/95

- The Who Does What When report also lists each resource and the tasks assigned to the resource. But instead of showing the start and finish dates for the resource's work on each task, this report shows the hours to be worked on the task during each period.

Who Does What When
New calculator

5/15/94

	6/9	6/10	6/11	6/12	6/13	6/14	6/15	6/16	6/17	6/18
Janet	8h	8h			8h	8h	8h	8h	8.4h	
Review customer comment cards										
Write proposal	8h	8h			8h	8h	8h			
Prepare questions								8h	8h	
Determine needed equipment									0.4h	
Contact local reps for names										
Carry out focus panels										
Review spec										
Shop crew										
Test production										
Dave										
Prepare initial spec										
Meet with reviewers										
Incorporate comments/revise										
Code new features										
Production team										
Review spec										
Set up production test										
Test production										
Begin production										
Documentation dept.										
Revise manual										
Marcia	8.8h	8.8h			8.8h	8.8h	8.8h	8h	8h	
Prepare initial product proposal	0.8h	0.8h			0.8h	0.8h	0.8h			
Research competition										
Write proposal	8h	8h			8h	8h	8h			
Prepare questions								8h	8h	

- The Weekly To-Do List prints all the tasks to which one resource is assigned. You specify the resource when you print the report. Print a report for each resource so everyone assigned to the project knows what they need to do and when they need to do it.

Weekly To Do List
New calculator
5/15/94

ID	Task Name	Duration	Start	Finish	Predecessors	Resource Names
Week of May 29						
4	Research competition	1w	5/30/94	6/3/94	2	Marcia,Marketing staff[2],Ch
Week of June 5						
6	Write proposal	1w	6/9/94	6/15/94	5	Marcia,Janet
Week of June 12						
6	Write proposal	1w	6/9/94	6/15/94	5	Marcia,Janet
8	Prepare questions	1w	6/16/94	6/22/94	6	Marcia,Janet
Week of June 19						
8	Prepare questions	1w	6/16/94	6/22/94	6	Marcia,Janet
18	Prepare questionnaire	3d	6/23/94	6/27/94		Marcia,Marketing staff
Week of June 26						
18	Prepare questionnaire	3d	6/23/94	6/27/94		Marcia,Marketing staff
20	Carry out focus panels	4w	6/28/94	7/26/94	17	Marcia,Marketing staff,Janet
Week of July 3						
20	Carry out focus panels	4w	6/28/94	7/26/94	17	Marcia,Marketing staff,Janet
Week of July 10						
20	Carry out focus panels	4w	6/28/94	7/26/94	17	Marcia,Marketing staff,Janet
Week of July 17						
20	Carry out focus panels	4w	6/28/94	7/26/94	17	Marcia,Marketing staff,Janet
Week of July 24						
20	Carry out focus panels	4w	6/28/94	7/26/94	17	Marcia,Marketing staff,Janet
Week of August 14						
24	Present results	4h	8/18/94	8/19/94	23,22	Marcia
Week of September 4						
30	Meet with reviewers	4h	9/9/94	9/9/94	29FS+1w	Dave,Bill,Marcia,Nancy,Mari
Week of May 14						
66	Review spec	1w	5/15/95	5/22/95	29	Marcia,Janet,Marketing staff
67	Prepare market plan	40h	5/15/95	5/22/95	32,24	Marketing staff[3],Cheryl[0.2
Week of May 21						
66	Review spec	1w	5/15/95	5/22/95	29	Marcia,Janet,Marketing staff
67	Prepare market plan	40h	5/15/95	5/22/95	32,24	Marketing staff[3],Cheryl[0.2
Week of May 28						
69	Incorporate comments	1w	5/29/95	6/5/95	68FS+1w	Marcia,Cheryl
Week of June 4						
69	Incorporate comments	1w	5/29/95	6/5/95	68FS+1w	Marcia,Cheryl

Expected Task Cost

To print a list of all tasks and their fixed cost and total cost, print the Budget report.

TO PRINT A BUDGET REPORT

1. Choose View Reports.
2. In the Reports dialog box, double-click Costs.
3. Double-click Budget.
4. When you are ready to print, choose the Print button.
5. Choose OK.

Budget Report
New calculator

12/13/93

ID	Task Name	Fixed Cost	Total Cost	Baseline	Variance
38	Revise manual	$0.00	$16,800.00	$16,800.00	$0.00
20	Carry out focus panels	$0.00	$9,961.54	$6,119.24	$3,842.30
60	Test production	$0.00	$9,726.92	$9,726.92	$0.00
74	Prepare marketing materials	$0.00	$5,692.31	$4,923.85	$768.46
35	Code clock feature	$0.00	$4,500.00	$4,500.00	$0.00
66	Review spec	$0.00	$3,730.77	$2,770.19	$960.58
28	Prepare initial spec	$0.00	$3,585.04	$3,392.92	$192.12
39	Fix bugs in new code	$0.00	$3,469.15	$3,469.15	$0.00
44	Create testing script	$0.00	$3,317.31	$3,317.31	$0.00
22	Prepare focus panel report	$0.00	$3,269.23	$3,077.11	$192.12
50	Final test pass	$0.00	$3,173.08	$3,173.08	$0.00
67	Prepare market plan	$0.00	$2,884.61	$1,924.03	$960.58
75	Prepare packaging	$0.00	$2,846.16	$2,461.92	$384.24
76	Prepare for major announcement	$0.00	$2,846.16	$2,461.92	$384.24
21	Carry out phone survey	$0.00	$2,500.00	$2,500.00	$0.00
78	Support sales force	$0.00	$2,500.00	$2,500.00	$0.00
4	Research competition	$0.00	$2,269.23	$1,308.65	$960.58
49	Test all bug fixes	$0.00	$2,173.08	$2,173.08	$0.00
36	Code notes feature	$0.00	$2,057.69	$2,057.69	$0.00
6	Write proposal	$0.00	$1,875.00	$914.42	$960.58
8	Prepare questions	$0.00	$1,875.00	$914.42	$960.58
57	Order parts	$0.00	$1,701.92	$1,701.92	$0.00
31	Incorporate comments/revise	$0.00	$1,686.62	$1,686.62	$0.00
56	Review spec	$0.00	$1,644.23	$1,644.23	$0.00
58	Plan production line changes	$0.00	$1,615.38	$1,615.38	$0.00
46	Test clock	$0.00	$1,442.31	$1,442.31	$0.00
37	Code alarm feature	$0.00	$1,384.62	$1,384.62	$0.00
69	Incorporate comments/revise plai	$0.00	$1,269.23	$308.65	$960.58
23	Prepare phone survey report	$0.00	$1,250.00	$1,250.00	$0.00
5	Review customer comment cards	$0.00	$1,101.93	$1,101.93	$0.00
47	Test notes	$0.00	$961.54	$961.54	$0.00
48	Test alarm	$0.00	$961.54	$961.54	$0.00
18	Prepare questionnaire	$0.00	$946.15	$369.81	$576.34
59	Set up production test	$0.00	$721.15	$721.15	$0.00
51	Write testing report	$0.00	$625.00	$625.00	$0.00
71	Contact sales force	$0.00	$625.00	$625.00	$0.00
30	Meet with reviewers	$0.00	$384.61	$288.56	$96.05
73	Contact major dealers	$0.00	$240.38	$240.38	$0.00
62	Pass production function to Si	$0.00	$232.69	$232.69	$0.00
77	Make announcement	$0.00	$230.77	$230.77	$0.00
72	Set up sales meetings	$0.00	$225.00	$186.58	$38.42
33	Fix old bugs	$0.00	$201.93	$201.93	$0.00
16	Contact suggested panel membe	$0.00	$123.08	$123.08	$0.00
24	Present results	$0.00	$96.15	$0.10	$96.05
80	Project complete	$0.00	$0.00	$0.00	$0.00
		$0.00	$110,985.79	$98,651.97	$12,333.82

Page 1

To show the weekly cash flow for tasks, print the Weekly Cash Flow report.

Weekly Cash Flow
New Calculator
Marcia Cryer

5/15/94

	5/29/94	6/5/94	6/12/94	6/19/94	6/26/94	7/3/94
Investigation Phase						
Investigation begins						
Prepare initial product proposal	$96.15	$96.15	$57.69			
Research competition	$2,269.21					
Review customer comment cards		$1,101.91				
Write proposal		$749.99	$1,124.99			
Plan focus panel						
Prepare questions			$749.99	$1,124.99		
Arrange sites						
Contact hotels			$61.53			
Arrange for equipment						
Determine needed equipment			$39.89			
Contact local offices			$30.76			
Get panel members						
Contact local reps for names				$79.79		
Contact suggested panel members				$123.07		
Plan phone questionnaire						
Prepare questionnaire				$630.76	$315.37	
Get list of users to call					$15.38	
Carry out focus panels					$1,867.77	$2,490.37
Carry out phone survey						
Prepare focus panel report						
Prepare phone survey report						
Present results						
Investigation phase complete						
Design Phase						

TO PRINT A WEEKLY CASH FLOW REPORT

1. Choose View Reports.
2. In the Reports dialog box, double-click Costs.
3. Double-click Weekly Cash Flow.
4. When you are ready to print, choose the Print button.
5. Choose OK.

Cumulative Costs for a Project

To print a graph showing the cumulative costs for a project, print the Resource Graph.

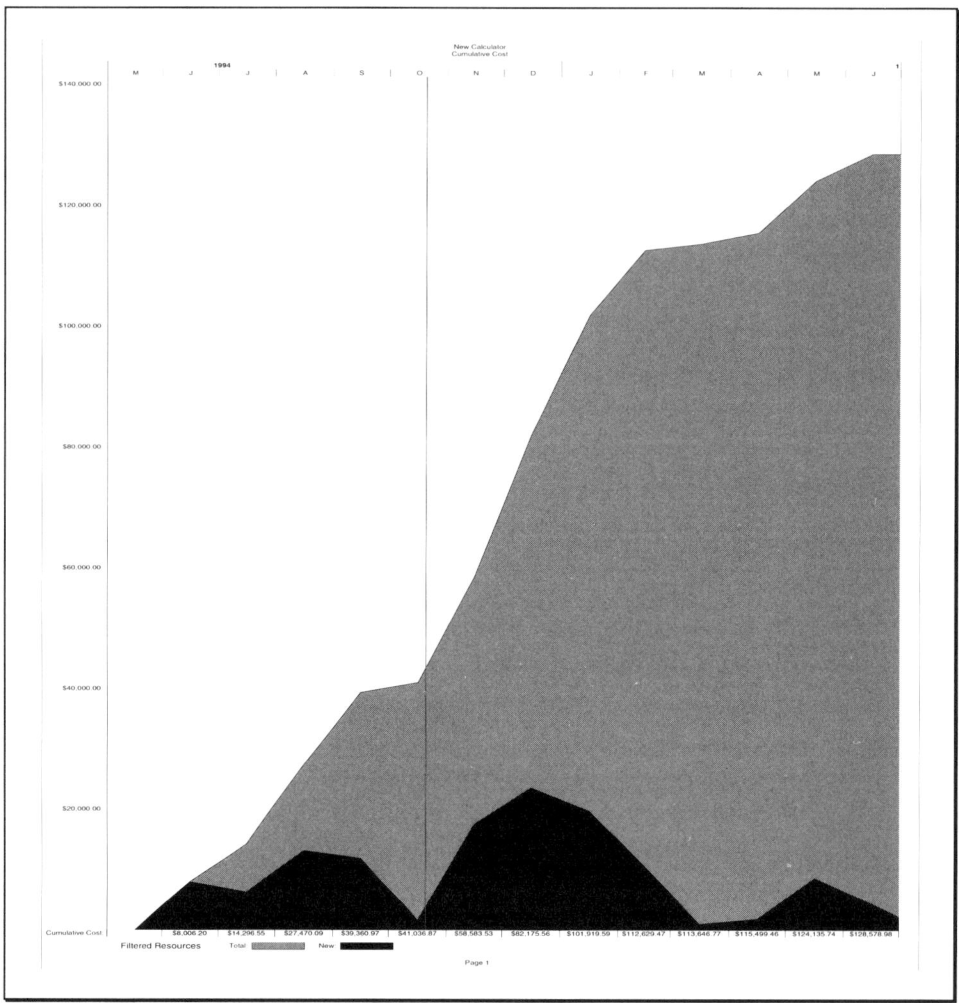

The previous illustration also includes the new costs that accrue each period.

TO PRINT A CUMULATIVE COST REPORT

1. Choose View Resource Graph.
2. Choose Format Details/Cumulative Cost.
3. Choose Format Bar Styles. Under Filtered Resources, in the Show As boxes for Total Costs and New Costs, select Area. In the Show As boxes under Resource, select Don't Show. Choose OK.
4. Click the Zoom Out button on the Standard toolbar until you see quarters over months, or the time period you want.

   You can also use the Timescale dialog box to change the timescale.
5. To preview the view and then print, click the Print Preview button on the Standard toolbar or choose File Print Preview.
6. When you are ready to print, choose the Print button.

   To print the view without previewing, choose File Print.
7. Choose OK.

To make the Resource Graph show just what you want, you can change the following:

You can change	Use this command
Information displayed on the graph	Format Details commands
Type of graph and what it is displayed for	Format Bar Styles
How the text looks	Format Text Styles
Color and pattern of gridlines	Format Gridlines
Amount of time showing on the graph and the units for the major and minor timescales	Format Timescale

PART IV

TRACKING PROGRESS AND MANAGING THE PROJECT

Managing a project is an ongoing process that begins once you create the project and ends when the project is complete. It's the continual process of adjusting task and resource information to reflect what has actually occurred, and monitoring the changes in the schedule so that you are aware of situations that could affect the outcome of your project.

Once the project gets going, your job changes from project planning to project tracking and managing. This involves the following steps:

- Collecting information about progress on the tasks (Chapter 11).
- Entering this "actual" data into Microsoft Project (Chapter 11).
- Comparing actual progress with the baseline schedule (Chapter 12).
- Analyzing the comparison to find problems areas, the causes of the problems, and solutions to these problems to get the project back on track (Chapter 12).
- Communicating progress, problems, and solutions to the project team and management (Chapter 13).

You repeat these steps over and over throughout the life of the project.

11

Tracking Progress and Updating the Schedule

Your job, now that the project is under way, is to keep track of what is actually happening on the project. When are the tasks actually starting and finishing? At any point in time, how much work has been done on tasks in progress? How much remains to be done? What tasks are ahead of schedule? Behind schedule? What tasks are taking less or more time than planned? Just how much slack time is left in the schedule? And how are costs and work tracking with the baseline schedule?

To answer these questions, you periodically collect actual start and finish dates and other data about how tasks are progressing, such as what percentage of the work has been completed on a task, or how much longer a task will take.

After you collect this information, update the schedule and then compare the current schedule with your baseline schedule. This comparison shows where each task stands—whether it is on track, or behind or ahead of schedule—and helps you identify problem areas. You can then use this information to change the schedule as necessary to keep the project on track.

Tracking the progress of your tasks is the only way you can stay informed about project status and is the basis for controlling and reporting on the project. By tracking and updating, you get an up-to-date schedule that shows when the project will finish and what it will cost as currently scheduled. Tracking also tells you when you have reached milestones. Celebrating these milestones can boost team morale and give recognition to those working on the project.

By keeping track of progress on tasks, you also develop a history for use in future project planning. If you know how long tasks actually took, you can use this information the next time you schedule a similar project.

COLLECTING PROJECT DATA

When you collect project data, where do you start? What data do you want? How do you collect it? Who does it? How often? And then what do you do with it?

WHAT DO YOU COLLECT?

When you collect data, you are, first of all, interested in the tasks on which there is or should be activity. Collect some combination of the following for each task.

For tasks that should have started or are in progress:

- Actual start date (or expected start date if the task still has not started)
- Percent complete for duration
- Actual duration so far
- Remaining duration
- Percent work complete
- Actual work completed
- Expected finish date
- Expected duration, if progress to date indicates that scheduled duration is wrong

For tasks that have finished or should have finished:

- Actual finish date (or expected finish date if the task is not yet finished)
- Actual duration
- Actual work completed
- Actual cost after a task is complete if you are tracking actual cost

For tasks that have not started yet:

- Change in duration estimate
- Change in work estimate

You also want to collect other information, such as notes about deviation from the schedule on the tasks in progress, or information about tasks not yet in progress. For example, if resources were not available as expected, note this fact along with why; if some problem has occurred in executing a task, note any information you can gather about the problem. If you are now able to better define a task duration, note the new duration so you can update the schedule to see how the change will affect project completion. You will use this information in Chapter 12 when you are analyzing the updated schedule.

WHERE DO YOU GET THE DATA?

There are several ways you can collect data on task progress:

- You can collect all the data yourself. This might be feasible on a small project where you are keeping track of everything.
- Have the supervisor or manager report on the tasks in their area.
- Have the individual responsible for each task provide a status report.
- Verify progress through inspection, quality control, or test data.

The data collected should be based on some measurable physical progress, not just the time that has passed since that task started. Time from the start date to the present may not reflect the actual working time spent on the task nor progress made on the task: resources may not be actually working on the task as scheduled or actual progress may be faster or slower than planned. Measuring progress for physical tasks, such as laying pipe or erecting a building, is easier because you can measure the physical results; it is more difficult for "thinking" tasks, such as writing, designing, or programming. However, even in these areas, there is an end product that can be broken into measurable tasks.

Try to use objective data where possible. For what has happened, use sources such as time sheets, bills for materials and services from vendors, purchase orders, and other direct charges to projects. If a task involves using a certain quantity of a material, such as laying pipe or stringing wire, you can base progress on the quantity used to date versus expected total use, such as feet of pipe used versus the quantity needed for the completed task.

It is hard to be objective when estimating percent complete and remaining work or duration, but by using information from all your sources, you should be able to come up with data in which you have some confidence. Here, the judgment or experience of those responsible for the tasks will help when deciding just how far along a task is.

Agree on how you will measure progress, and how often, before you start the project. This should be discussed and settled in the planning stages. Those who will be collecting progress data should be involved in deciding how it will be measured.

How Often?

How frequently you collect data depends on the length of the project and on how closely you want to track progress. The shorter the project and the more closely you need to track, the more often you should collect data and update the schedule. The frequency also depends on the requirements of management or your client. When determining frequency, think about how critical it is that the schedule reflect reality at any point in time. For example, if you report biweekly, your schedule could be as much as two weeks off. This could be perfectly acceptable on some projects, but not on other projects.

You may decide to collect data and generate status reports at different intervals. For example, you may want task supervisors to collect data frequently and track progress daily, but report to you weekly; you may pass on summary information to management or a client monthly.

Decide the frequency before you start the project so everyone knows what is expected. If you later find you need to collect data more frequently, be sure to inform everyone so they can respond as requested.

USING MICROSOFT PROJECT

When you saved your baseline schedule in Chapter 9, either with the Tools Tracking/Save Baseline command, or when prompted by the PlanningWizard, Microsoft Project saved the original schedule, costs, and work information in the Baseline fields. The baseline schedule is kept separately from the current schedule so you can compare the two. Now you need to enter the information you have collected about task progress in the Actual fields. This information shows what has actually occurred on the project. You continually update the schedule with progress information so you always know the current status of the project. Microsoft Project replaces the dates in the current schedule so they match the actual dates you enter.

There are two ways you can enter actual information:

- For tasks whose actual start or finish date matches that in the current schedule, you can use the Tools Tracking/Update Project command to have Microsoft Project copy the scheduled start or finish date into the Actual Start or Actual Finish field.
- For tasks that have deviated from the schedule, you can type the actual values into Microsoft Project.

To show a task has started, you can enter any of the following:

- Actual start date
- Percent complete
- Actual duration
- Remaining duration

To show a task has finished, you can enter any of the following:

- Actual finish date
- Percent complete of 100
- Actual duration greater than or equal to the scheduled duration
- Remaining duration of zero

To show progress on a task, you can enter any of the following:

- Percent complete
- Actual duration
- Remaining duration

To indicate the scheduled duration has changed:

- If the task uses resource-driven scheduling, change one of the following:
  - Work for the resources assigned to the task

- Duration
- Remaining Duration—if it is greater than that calculated by Microsoft Project, the duration is changed

- If the task uses fixed-duration scheduling, change the duration.

The following table shows where you can enter progress information in Microsoft Project.

To enter	You can use
Actual start and finish dates	Update Tasks dialog box; Task Details Form; Task Sheet with Tracking table applied; mouse on the Gantt Chart
Percent complete	Update Tasks dialog box; mouse on the Gantt Chart; Task Sheet with Tracking table applied; Task Form
Actual and remaining duration	Update Tasks dialog box; Task Sheet with Tracking table applied
Scheduled duration	Update Tasks dialog box; Task Form, Work fields or Duration box; mouse on the Gantt Chart

To display the Update Tasks dialog box, click the Update Tasks button on the Tracking toolbar, or choose Tools Tracking/Update Tasks.

USING THE TRACKING TOOLBAR

The Tracking toolbar contains shortcut buttons to help you enter tracking information.

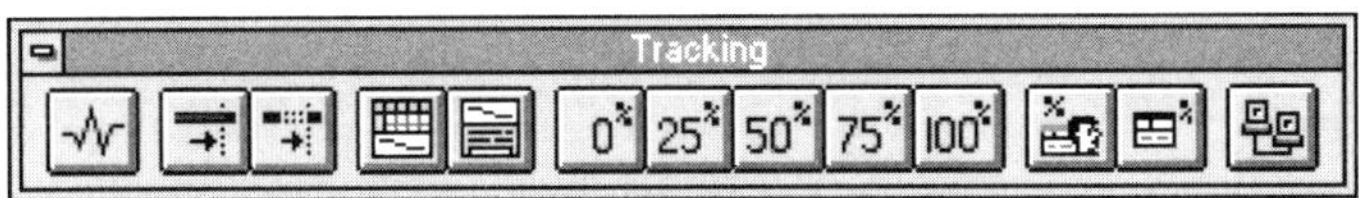

TO DISPLAY THE TRACKING TOOLBAR

1. Choose View Toolbars.
2. In the Toolbars box, select Tracking.
3. Choose the Show button.

To see what any button is for, place the mouse pointer over the button. After a moment, a ToolTip will appear, telling you what the button does. If you want more information, hold down the mouse button as you point to the button. In the status bar, a more detailed description will appear. When you are finished reading about the button, drag the pointer off the toolbar button before releasing the mouse button. The action won't be carried out.

Several of the buttons are described in more detail in this chapter when they are used.

Choosing the Tracking Method

Before you start tracking, you need to decide how Microsoft Project should track work. Initially, Microsoft Project automatically ties work to percent complete. When you update percent complete for tasks, Microsoft Project updates the actual work and cost fields accordingly. To calculate these values, Microsoft Project assumes work and cost to date are proportional to the percent complete for the task and multiplies the total work or cost by the percent complete.

If you want work tied to percent complete and do not want to track work yourself, you do not have to do anything.

If you do not want work tied to percent complete and want to track work yourself, you need to break this connection. To do so, choose Tools Options. On the Schedule tab, clear the Updating Task Status Updates Resource Status check box. Do this only when you need to track work very closely and want to enter actual work information yourself to keep track of exactly how much work has been performed on each task.

Collecting the Data

Using Microsoft Project, you can print a list of those tasks for which you need to collect data. Naturally, you do not need to collect data on all tasks if only a few are in progress. You can filter the Task Sheet to show only those tasks for which you want progress information, and create a new table to apply to the Task Sheet that includes blanks for writing information about progress.

For example, if you collect data on start and finish dates, percent complete, and remaining duration, you can create a new table containing columns for the scheduled information you want to track, plus blank columns where you write the corresponding actual information. Use custom fields, such as Text5 or Number1, for the blank columns. Apply this table to the Task Sheet and print the Task Sheet.

Data Collection Sheet
June 30, 1994

ID	Name	Sched. Start	Start	% Comp.	Rem. Dur.	Sched. Fin.	Finish
1	**Investigation Phase**	**5/30/94**				**8/19/94**	
2	Investigation begins	5/30/94				5/30/94	
3	**Prepare initial product proposal**	**5/30/94**				**6/15/94**	
4	Research competition	5/30/94				6/3/94	
5	Review customer comment cards	6/6/94				6/8/94	
6	Write proposal	6/9/94				6/15/94	
7	**Plan focus panel**	**6/16/94**				**6/22/94**	
8	Prepare questions	6/16/94				6/22/94	
9	**Arrange sites**	**6/16/94**				**6/17/94**	
10	Contact hotels	6/16/94				6/16/94	
11	**Arrange for equipment**	**6/17/94**				**6/17/94**	
12	Determine needed equipment	6/17/94				6/17/94	
13	Contact local offices	6/17/94				6/17/94	
14	**Get panel members**	**6/20/94**				**6/22/94**	
15	Contact local reps for names	6/20/94				6/20/94	
16	Contact suggested panel member:	6/21/94				6/22/94	
17	**Plan phone questionnaire**	**6/23/94**				**6/28/94**	
18	Prepare questionnaire	6/23/94				6/27/94	
19	Get list of users to call	6/28/94				6/28/94	
20	Carry out focus panels	6/28/94				7/26/94	
21	Carry out phone survey	7/26/94				8/2/94	
22	Prepare focus panel report	8/2/94				8/16/94	
23	Prepare phone survey report	8/16/94				8/18/94	
24	Present results	8/18/94				8/19/94	

After you print the view, write the appropriate information in the blank fields as you collect the data.

TO CREATE A DATA COLLECTION SHEET

1. Choose View Table/More Tables, and create a table containing the columns you want. For instructions on creating a table, see Chapter 16, "Using Microsoft Project Tools."
2. Choose View More Views, select Task Sheet in the Views box, and choose the Apply button.
3. To apply the table you just created, choose View Table/More Tables, select the new table in the Tables box, and choose the Apply button.
4. Select the Date Range filter from the Filter box on the Formatting toolbar.
5. Type the dates as prompted and choose OK. The filter will find all tasks that are scheduled to start or finish between the two dates.
6. Click the Print button on the Standard toolbar, or choose File Print and then choose OK.

By applying the Date Range filter, only tasks scheduled to start or finish during the dates you specify are listed on the Task Sheet. As you collect the data, you write the information in the blanks. Then enter the information into Microsoft Project.

In addition to the Date Range filter, Microsoft Project includes other filters that limit the list of tasks to those in progress or not yet started.

To see tasks that	Use this filter
Have started (an actual start date has been entered) but have not finished (no finish date has been entered)	In Progress Tasks
Are incomplete (percent complete is less than 100)	Incomplete Tasks
Have a scheduled start date earlier than a date you enter when you apply the filter	Should Start By
Have not started (no actual start date)	Unstarted Tasks

You can also create a filter that looks for any subset of tasks that is appropriate for you. Then you can create a custom view for collecting your data that includes the table and the filter you created. Each time you need to collect progress data, you display this view. If the filter is an interactive filter that requires dates, you'll be prompted for the dates. For more information about creating a table, filter, and custom view, see Chapter 16, "Using Microsoft Project Tools."

If you are using Microsoft Mail, you can gather data from team members by using the Workgroup commands. Use the Tools Workgroup/ Request Task Update command to gather data from assigned resources about progress on tasks. Microsoft Project sends an electronic mail message to the resources assigned to the tasks you want to update. The assigned resources then reply to the message, indicating the actual start and finish dates, work to date, and remaining work, as well as including comments about the progress to date. When you receive their reply, you can click the Update Project button in the reply to automatically move the new information into Microsoft Project. Any comments are added to the Notes field. This feature reduces your data input time and simplifies the task of collecting progress information.

COPYING SCHEDULED DATES INTO ACTUAL FIELDS

For tasks whose start or finish date matches the current schedule, use the Tools Tracking/Update Project command and select the Update Work As Complete Through option to copy their scheduled dates into the Actual fields. When you do this, here's what happens:

- If a task should have started, the scheduled start date is copied into the Actual Start field.
- If a task should have finished, the scheduled finish date is copied into the Actual Finish field.
- The percent complete is either calculated to match the amount of time that has passed to date on the task (select Set 0%–100% Complete) or left at 0% until the task is complete (select Set 0% Or 100% Complete Only).

You can use the Update As Scheduled button on the Tracking toolbar if you are happy with the following settings in the Update Project dialog box:

- The date used to update work is the current date.
- The percent complete is calculated to match the amount of time that has passed to date on the task.
- Only the selected tasks are updated. If you want all tasks to be updated, select the entire project before clicking the button.

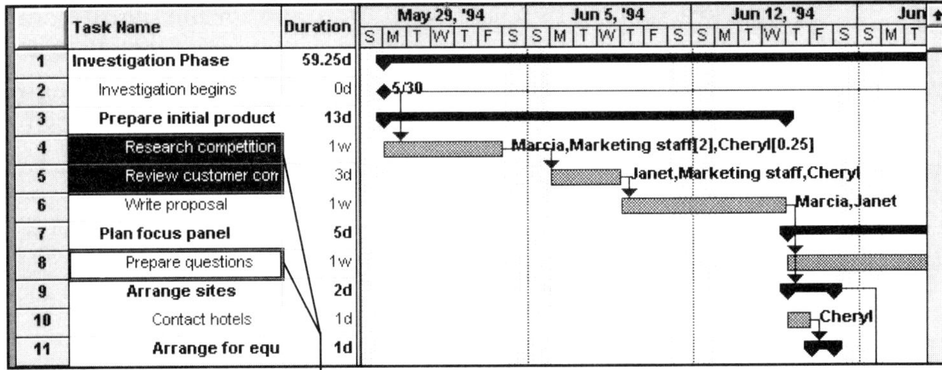

Select the tasks that started or finished as scheduled.

To select nonadjacent tasks with the mouse, hold down Ctrl in Windows or Command on the Macintosh as you select additional tasks. With the keys, press F8, select the first group of tasks, press Shift+F8, move to the next group of tasks, and repeat the sequence.

Choose Tools Tracking/Update Project.

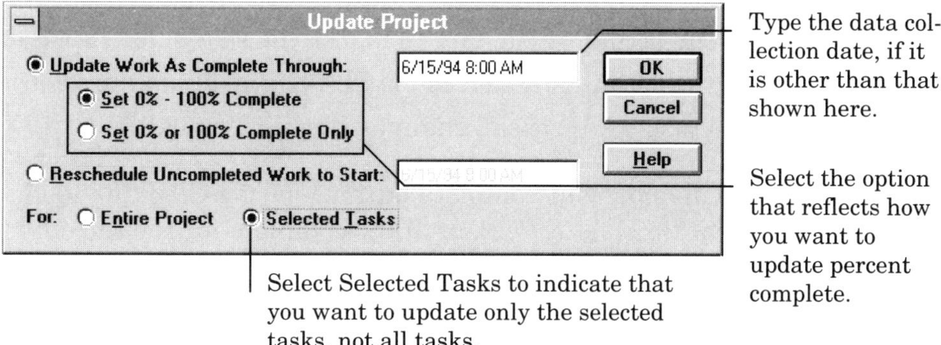

If all tasks are on schedule, you do not have to select all the tasks before you choose Tools Tracking/Update Project. Just select the Entire Project option in the Update Project dialog box.

ENTERING PERCENT COMPLETE

To update percent complete for tasks in progress, you can use one of the following methods.

- On the Gantt Chart, drag on the task bar with the mouse or click a percent complete button on the Tracking toolbar.
- In the Update Tasks dialog box, enter percent complete in the % Complete box.
- On the Task Sheet, click a percent complete button on the Tracking toolbar or apply the Tracking table and type a number.

For tasks that are progressing on schedule, you can use the Tools Tracking/Update Project command to have percent complete calculated for you as described in the previous section. The percent complete is calculated based on the update date and where the task should be on this date.

When you enter percent complete, Microsoft Project does the following:

- Sets the actual start date to match the scheduled start date.
- Calculates the actual duration and remaining duration.

If you enter 100 as the percent complete, Microsoft Project does the following:

- Sets the actual finish date to match the scheduled finish date.
- Sets the actual duration to match the scheduled duration.
- If the task was critical, changes it to noncritical.

Use the five percent complete buttons on the Tracking toolbar to quickly enter 0%, 25%, 50%, 75%, or 100% complete for the selected tasks.

Changing Percent Complete with the Mouse

On the Gantt Chart, percent complete is shown as a narrow black progress bar superimposed on the task bar.

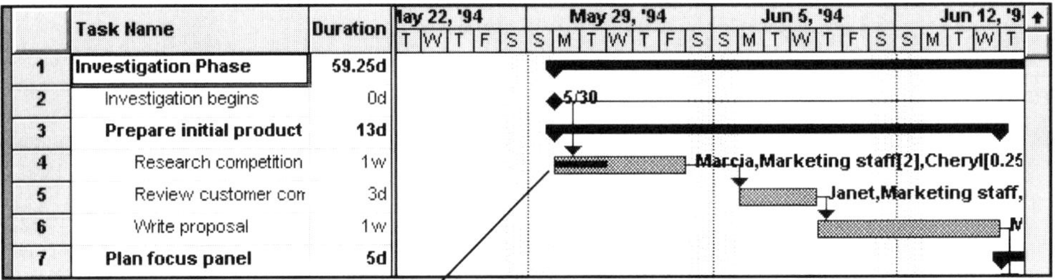

The thin black bar shows percent complete.

You can drag the percent complete bar to indicate progress. The mouse pointer changes to a percent sign when positioned to change percent complete.

Changing Percent Complete in the Update Tasks Dialog Box

To use the Update Tasks dialog box, first select the task you want to update. Then click the Update Tasks button on the Tracking toolbar or choose Tools Tracking/Update Tasks. Type the percent complete in the % Complete box.

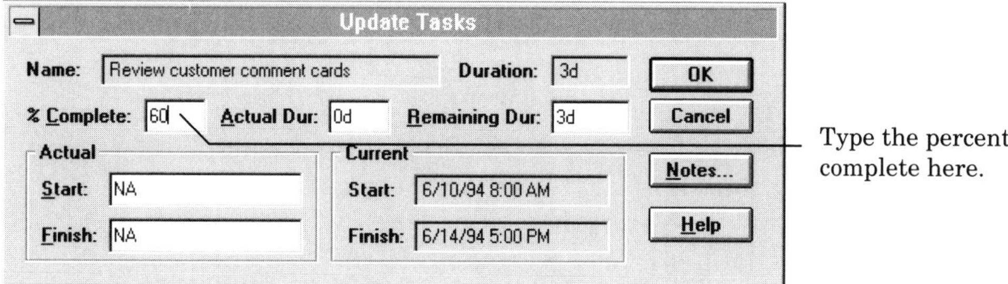

Type the percent complete here.

You can also enter a percent complete in the Task Information dialog box or on the Task Form. To enter percent complete in the Task Information dialog box, just double-click the task on the Gantt Chart, Task Sheet, or PERT Chart, and then type the percent complete in the Percent Complete box.

Changing Percent Complete on the Task Sheet

On the Task Sheet, you can enter percent complete in the % Comp. column on the Tracking table. Choose View More Views, select the Task Sheet in the Views box, and then choose the Apply button. To display the Tracking table, choose View Table/Tracking.

	Task Name	Act. Start	Act. Finish	% Comp.	Act. Dur.	Rem. Dur.	Act. Cost	Act. Work
1	**Investigation Phase**	**5/30/94 8:00 AM**	**NA**	**3%**	**2d**	**57.25d**	**$523.50**	**53.6h**
2	Investigation begins	NA	NA	0%	0d	0d	$0.00	0h
3	**Prepare initial produ**	**5/30/94 8:00 AM**	**NA**	**15%**	**2d**	**11d**	**$523.50**	**53.6h**
4	Research competiti	5/30/94 8:00 AM	NA	40%	0.4w	0.6w	$523.46	52h
5	Review customer c	NA	NA	0%	0d	3d	$0.00	0h
6	Write proposal	NA	NA	0%	0w	1w	$0.00	0h
7	**Plan focus panel**	**NA**	**NA**	**0%**	**0d**	**5d**	**$0.00**	**0h**
8	Prepare questions	NA	NA	0%	0w	1w	$0.00	0h
9	**Arrange sites**	**NA**	**NA**	**0%**	**0d**	**2d**	**$0.00**	**0h**
10	Contact hotels	NA	NA	0%	0d	1d	$0.00	0h

Type the percent complete in this column.

If you have several tasks with the same percent complete, you can use the Edit Fill Down command to enter the percent complete for all tasks at once. Just type the percent complete in the topmost task. Select that field and the percent complete field for all other tasks with the same percent complete. Then choose Edit Fill Down. The fields you select must be in the same column but do not have to be adjacent.

ENTERING ACTUAL START AND FINISH DATES

To enter actual start and finish dates, use the Update Tasks dialog box or the Task Sheet with the Tracking table applied. You can also use the mouse on the Gantt Chart to indicate a start date if the task has a percent complete other than zero. When you enter an actual start or finish date, it replaces the date in the schedule.

You do not have to enter a start date if the task started as scheduled. When you enter a percent complete, Microsoft Project assumes the task started as scheduled and puts this date in the Actual Start field.

You do not have to enter a finish date if the task finished as scheduled. When you enter 100 as the percent complete, Microsoft Project assumes the task finished as scheduled and puts that date in the Actual Finish field. When you finish a critical task, it changes to noncritical.

Until you enter actual information, the Actual date fields contain NA.

When you enter actual start dates, you may get a message from the PlanningWizard that there is a scheduling problem or, if the Planning-Wizard is turned off, a message that a task cannot be completed in the time available. You will see this message when the actual start date is later than the late start date and there is no longer time for the task to be completed in the time allowed by successor tasks. This is called negative slack. Negative slack tells you there is a problem in the schedule—that you no longer have time to complete the task or a later task that depends on this task. Chapter 12 includes a discussion about negative slack that will help you determine what corrective action to take.

Entering Actual Dates in the Update Tasks Dialog Box

To use the Update Tasks dialog box, select the task and click the Update Tasks button on the Tracking toolbar or choose Tools Tracking/Update Tasks.

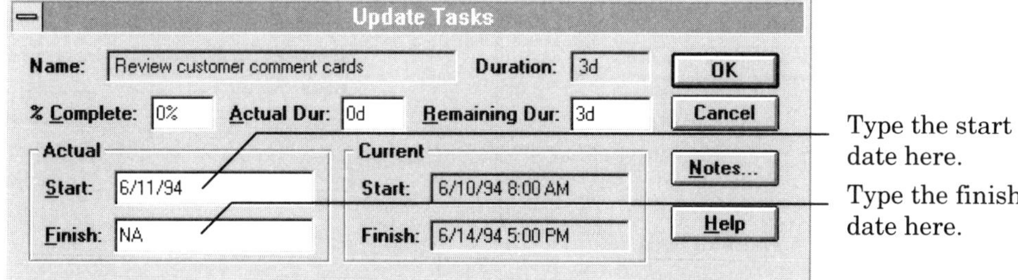

Entering Actual Dates on the Task Sheet

To enter actual dates on the Task Sheet, apply the Tracking table. The Tracking table includes columns for actual start and finish dates.

Choose View More Views. In the Views box, select Task Sheet, and then choose the Apply button. To display the Tracking table, choose View Table/Tracking.

	Task Name	Act. Start	Act. Finish	% Comp.	Act. Dur.	Rem. Dur.	Act. Cost	Act. Work
1	**Investigation Phase**	**5/30/94 8:00 AM**	**NA**	**3%**	**2d**	**57.25d**	**$523.50**	**53.6h**
2	Investigation begins	NA	NA	0%	0d	0d	$0.00	0h
3	**Prepare initial produ**	**5/30/94 8:00 AM**	**NA**	**15%**	**2d**	**11d**	**$523.50**	**53.6h**
4	Research competiti	5/30/94 8:00 AM	6/15	40%	0.4w	0.6w	$523.46	52h
5	Review customer c	NA	NA	0%	0d	3d	$0.00	0h
6	Write proposal	NA	NA	0%	0w	1w	$0.00	0h
7	**Plan focus panel**	**NA**	**NA**	**0%**	**0d**	**5d**	**$0.00**	**0h**
8	Prepare questions	NA	NA	0%	0w	1w	$0.00	0h
9	**Arrange sites**	**NA**	**NA**	**0%**	**0d**	**2d**	**$0.00**	**0h**
10	Contact hotels	NA	NA	0%	0d	1d	$0.00	0h
11	**Arrange for e**	**NA**	**NA**	**0%**	**0d**	**1d**	**$0.00**	**0h**
12	Determine n	NA	NA	0%	0h	4h	$0.00	0h
13	Contact loca	NA	NA	0%	0h	4h	$0.00	0h
14	**Get panel memb**	**NA**	**NA**	**0%**	**0d**	**3d**	**$0.00**	**0h**

In the Actual Start field, type the start date for the task.

In the Actual Finish field, type the finish date for the task.

Setting Actual Start Dates with the Mouse

On the Gantt Chart, you can drag the left end of a task bar to set the start date, if the task has a percent complete other than zero. When you point to the left end of the progress bar (thin black bar), the mouse pointer changes to a left-pointing arrow.

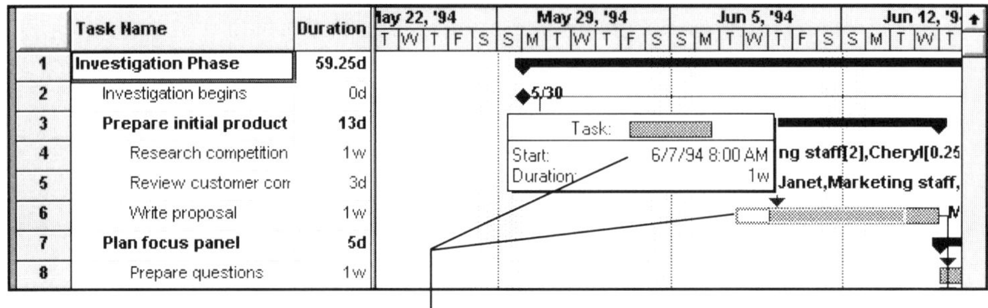

Drag the left end of the bar until the correct actual start date is displayed in the box.

Entering Duration Information

There are three duration values you can enter: actual duration to date, remaining duration on the task, and scheduled duration if this has changed from your original estimate.

Entering Actual or Remaining Duration

When you enter the actual duration to date or the remaining duration, Microsoft Project calculates percent complete and the other duration value. If you enter a percent complete, both the actual duration and remaining duration are calculated. If you enter a remaining duration that is greater than that calculated by Microsoft Project, Microsoft Project recalculates the scheduled duration, as follows:

Scheduled duration = Actual duration + Remaining duration

To enter duration, use the Update Tasks dialog box. Select the task and then click the Update Tasks button on the Tracking toolbar or choose Tools Tracking/Update Tasks.

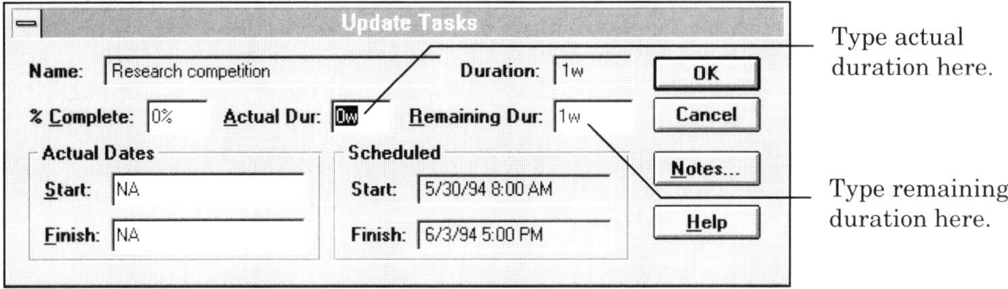

Type actual duration here.

Type remaining duration here.

You can also enter duration on the Task Sheet with the Tracking table applied. The Tracking table includes columns for actual duration and remaining duration.

Entering Scheduled Duration

There are two ways to change scheduled duration. One is to type a new value for duration anywhere you can enter a duration, such as the Duration field on the Task Sheet or Gantt Chart, or in the Duration box on the Task Form, just as you entered the original duration estimates.

The second way to change scheduled duration is to enter a value for remaining duration that is larger than that calculated by Microsoft Project. The scheduled duration is then recalculated by adding the actual duration and the remaining duration, as discussed in the previous section.

If you increase duration for a task that uses resource-driven scheduling, Microsoft Project assigns the additional work to the resource driving the task duration. If this is not what you want, change the work scheduled for the resources on the Task Form, using the resource work fields at the bottom of the form (choose Format Details/Resource Work).

You can also change the scheduled duration on the Gantt Chart with the mouse. When you point to the right end of a task bar, the mouse pointer changes to a right-pointing arrow. Drag this to increase or decrease task duration.

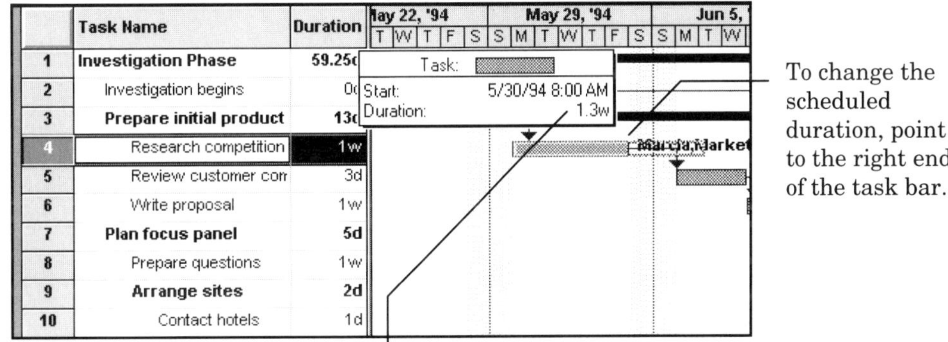

When the pointer changes, drag the bar until the duration in the box is what you want.

Rescheduling the Remaining Duration

When you are tracking tasks, you may find that progress on some tasks is occurring before other tasks are completed. Or you may find that work started on a task but then the resources were diverted to another task, causing work to stop on the original task.

In Microsoft Project, you can show progress on a task and then have the remaining duration be rescheduled to begin on the date you specify or to reflect the status of its predecessors. To do this, you select the Reschedule Uncompleted Work To Start option in the Update Project dialog box and then type the date on which you want work resumed. You can also use the Reschedule Work button on the Tracking toolbar to reschedule the remaining duration for the selected tasks, if the current date is the appropriate date for the work to resume.

When you use this feature, Microsoft Project enters a stop date in the Stop field for the task, based on the progress you indicated, and a resume date in the Resume field, based on the update date. You can add these fields to a table to review the changes to the dates for these tasks. If you want to control when the task resumes, use the Resume No Earlier Than field to enter a date before which the task will not be resumed. Again, you can add the Resume No Earlier Than field to any table. For more information about creating tables, see Chapter 16, "Using Microsoft Project Tools."

Entering Actual Work and Cost Information

If you left the Updating Task Status Updates Resource Status option selected on the Schedule tab in the Tools Options dialog box and you are entering progress information for tasks, such as percent complete, duration information, and so on, you can enter actual work and cost only after a task is complete. If you enter an actual work amount while a task is in progress and have entered progress information for the task, Microsoft Project will replace the work you enter with the value it calculates based on percent complete.

If you are tracking work yourself, and you turned off the Updating Task Status Updates Resource Status option, enter the actual work information on the Task Form, using the resource work fields at the bottom. Enter the actual work for each resource assigned to the task, not for the task as a whole.

Choose View More Views. In the Views box, select Task Form, and then choose the Apply button. Choose Format Details/Resource Work.

Name: Research competition Duration: 1w Fixed Previous Next

Start: 5/30/94 8:00 AM Finish: 6/3/94 5:00 PM Percent Complete: 40%

ID	Resource Name	Units	Work	Ovt. Work	Baseline Work	Act. Work	Rem. Work
1	Marcia	1	40h	0h	40h	16h	24h
2	Marketing staff	2	80h	0h	80h	32h	48h
4	Cheryl	0.25	10h	0h	10h	4h	6h

Type the actual work in the Act. Work field for each resource on the Task Form.

You can also enter work in the Actual Work field on the Task Sheet with the Work table applied. The actual work is divided among the resources assigned to the task.

After a task is complete, you can enter an actual work amount for each resource or for the task. Regardless of how you have set the Updating Task Status Updates Resource Status option, Microsoft Project will not recalculate actual work or cost after remaining work is zero. You can also enter work information if you are not entering other progress information. Microsoft Project will not recalculate work if it has no other information about progress on the task.

Microsoft Project tracks costs automatically by calculating them based on the amount of actual work completed. When a task is complete, however, you can enter the actual cost if it is different from that calculated by Microsoft Project. Do not enter actual costs before a task is complete. If you do, Microsoft Project will recalculate the cost based on work progress.

To enter an actual cost after the task is complete, choose View More Views. In the Views box, select Task Form, and then choose the Apply button. Choose Format Details/Resource Cost. If a task has resources assigned, you cannot enter a cost for the task as a whole, but must enter actual cost for each resource assigned to the task.

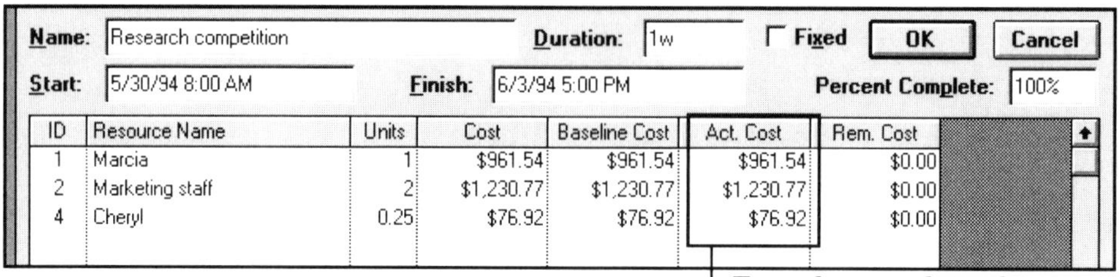

Name: Research competition **Duration:** 1w ☐ Fixed **OK** **Cancel**

Start: 5/30/94 8:00 AM **Finish:** 6/3/94 5:00 PM **Percent Complete:** 100%

ID	Resource Name	Units	Cost	Baseline Cost	Act. Cost	Rem. Cost
1	Marcia	1	$961.54	$961.54	$961.54	$0.00
2	Marketing staff	2	$1,230.77	$1,230.77	$1,230.77	$0.00
4	Cheryl	0.25	$76.92	$76.92	$76.92	$0.00

Type the actual cost here for each resource after the task is complete.

Your schedule now reflects the actual progress made on tasks in the project. In the next chapter, you will compare the actual information just entered with the baseline schedule saved in Chapter 9.

12

Controlling the Project to Stay on Track

No matter how diligent you are with your planning, the implementation of the project probably will not match your baseline schedule. There are several reasons: your assumptions may be inaccurate, the scope of a task or the project may change, resources may not be available as scheduled, materials may be late, or tasks may simply require an amount of work different from your estimate. You prepared for this when you created the plan by thinking through and stating your plans as clearly as possible. Now you are ready to deal with the unexpected and recognize change and its causes when it occurs. The essential thing to remember is that things do change, and it is all right—as long as you are aware how the changes will affect your schedule, and you take the appropriate action.

Controlling or managing a project involves not only spotting problem areas, but also finding solutions for these problems. That is what this chapter is about—seeing how progress on tasks compares with the baseline, understanding the differences, and then reaching the appropriate solution.

To control or manage a project, you follow these basic steps:

- Evaluate progress by comparing the current schedule, which reflects the actual information you entered in Chapter 11, to the baseline schedule you saved in Chapter 9.

- Analyze the differences between the two schedules and determine what is causing the variance.
- Based on your analysis, decide what to do about the variances. Change the schedule? Add resources? Decrease the project scope? Or perhaps do nothing because the projected dates and costs are acceptable.

EVALUATING PROGRESS TO DATE

To evaluate progress to date, compare the current schedule to the baseline schedule. The difference between the two is called variance.

First, check when the project will finish and what it will cost, now that you have updated the schedule with progress information. The finish date and costs indicate how the project will finish if you change nothing more.

Then check variance in each task and resource. Check:

- Start and finish dates—did the task start or finish early, on time, or late?
- Percent complete—is the task ahead, on schedule, or behind?
- Scheduled finish date—is the task scheduled to finish early, on time, or late?
- Work—is work low, as scheduled, or high?
- Cost—is cost low, as scheduled, or high?

For finished tasks, check the variance between the actual duration, work, and cost, and the baseline numbers. You may need to adjust the schedule to compensate for the completed tasks.

ANALYZING VARIANCE

The next step is to determine causes of a variance. Variance highlights places in the schedule that need investigating. When you investigate a variance, decide if it was a one-time occurrence, such as a predecessor finishing late and forcing a late start on a successor task, or a continuing problem, such as work progressing more slowly than planned.

You may already know why progress on tasks does not match the baseline from information you gathered as you collected progress statistics. For example, you may know that a task start was delayed because materials needed for the task arrived late, or that a strike has halted work on some tasks.

But the answer may not be that straightforward. One tool to help you decide if tasks are progressing as planned is earned value. Earned value tells you whether you are spending more or less than you planned for the actual work that has been completed up to this point, and shows you how much tasks will cost at completion if the trend continues. For example, if you have completed 50 percent of work on a task, but have spent 75 percent of the planned budget, you know you need to find out what is costing more than expected.

The following table will help you analyze a variance in your schedule.

Problem	Investigate
Task started late	Predecessor tasks for late finish Resource availability
Resources not working hours as scheduled	Conflicting assignments Insufficient staff Absence or vacation Materials not available
Progress slower than planned	Start date of task Speed at which resources are working Materials not available

Collecting this information helps you decide what to do about the rest of the schedule. When you are deciding how to deal with tasks that are behind schedule, you need to predict the remaining duration on each task. If a task is going more slowly than scheduled, and progress continues at the same rate, how long will the task take if nothing is done to change the current rate of progress? For example, the resources may be working fewer hours than expected or they may be working slower than expected. How do you decide what applies for each task?

Remaining duration on a task can be predicted in one of three ways. You can:

- Decide that, based on the data you collected, the problems that caused the past schedule delays, such as a late start, or slow work, are taken care of, and the remaining duration does not need to be adjusted for the task. For example, if the delay was caused by late arrival of material, but performance of the resource is on schedule, you do not want to assume that past slippage in a task will continue and so you leave the duration as scheduled.

- Assume that progress up to the present is representative of the future and adjust remaining duration as necessary to see when the task will finish and how that affects the rest of the schedule.
- Ask those involved in the task how they expect the task to progress and to estimate remaining duration.

You also want to consider how the rest of the project is likely to progress. Are past delays indicative of future delays? If the remainder of the project is unrelated to the part that was late, you may be more confident in the rest of the project proceeding as scheduled. If the remainder of the project includes work on tasks that are already behind schedule, you have to analyze why these tasks were delayed and whether the delay is likely to continue. If work is just proceeding more slowly than planned in one area, or many areas, consider re-analyzing duration estimates on future tasks to reflect the actual working speed on current tasks.

For example, suppose productivity for a resource is lower than expected because the original estimates were overly optimistic. You not only need to calculate new durations for tasks in progress based on observed performance, but also to look at other tasks to which this resource is assigned, to decide if the durations on those tasks need to be revised. If you find that all your estimates are off by 50 percent after one month of progress and the problem seems to be that estimates are overly optimistic, you might want to consider revising all duration estimates to reflect progress so far.

DETERMINING CORRECTIVE ACTION

Once you have analyzed a variance in the schedule, you need to decide what to do about it. Do you reschedule the project? If you still want to meet the original finish date, you need to decide how to change the schedule to achieve that date. Whether you determine that a delay was a one-time occurrence or a continuing problem, what do you do about it?

If a task in progress is behind schedule, or if the finish date for the project is now too late, use the same methods discussed in Chapter 9 for refining the schedule to speed up ongoing or future tasks. The following lists are not comprehensive—they are just a way to help you get started.

Speed up critical tasks by:

- Assigning overtime work
- Hiring additional staff
- Adding shifts
- Using subcontractors
- Training existing resources to do other tasks
- Shifting resources from other projects or from noncritical tasks

Reschedule tasks by:

- Making tasks concurrent if possible, instead of sequential
- Changing the project's scope by eliminating or simplifying tasks
- Changing scope of critical tasks to shorten them

If you find it necessary to make a change, or if change is being imposed by management or a client, be sure to think it through as thoroughly as you did the initial tasks in the plan. Use the original planning team to determine the best course of action so you have everyone's input about solutions. Reconsider the original assumptions. Do they still apply? If so, be sure to take them into account. If they have changed, be sure to consider your latest set of assumptions.

Once you determine the best solution, communicate changes in the schedule to all interested parties. And if you are adding new tasks, add them to your baseline schedule.

USING MICROSOFT PROJECT

You have already entered all the progress information to date into Microsoft Project. Now you are ready to look at the updated schedule and compare it to the baseline schedule. In this section, you will see how to:

- Evaluate progress to date by comparing actual progress on tasks to the baseline schedule.

- Analyze variances to focus on problem areas.
- Test proposed changes to the schedule and decide which alternatives are best.
- Add new tasks to the baseline schedule.

EVALUATING PROGRESS TO DATE

Use Microsoft Project views, tables, filters, and sorting to locate variance between the baseline schedule and the current schedule. The following table shows where to go in Microsoft Project to find the information you want about the latest schedule and where the variances are.

To see	Use
Current project finish date and costs, plus variance in project dates, duration, cost, and work	File Summary Info command, Statistics button
Summary of percent complete for major phases	Task Sheet with outline collapsed and Summary table applied
Graphically whether tasks are on schedule	Gantt Chart
Tasks that were supposed to start but have not	Task Sheet with Should Start By or Unstarted Tasks filter applied
A comparison of baseline and scheduled durations	Tracking Gantt
Variance in task start and finish dates, task cost, or task work	Task Sheet with Variance, Cost, or Work table applied and Work or Cost Overbudget filter applied
Amount of slack time remaining in the schedule	Task Sheet with Schedule table applied; Detail Gantt; Delay Gantt
Tasks that are behind schedule	Task Sheet with Slipping Tasks filter applied
Graphically the amount tasks have slipped	Detail Gantt

Checking the Project Finish Date and Total Cost

Click the Project Statistics button on the Tracking toolbar, or choose the File Summary Info command and then the Statistics button, to check the current finish date and what the total duration, work, and cost will be if no additional changes are made to the schedule.

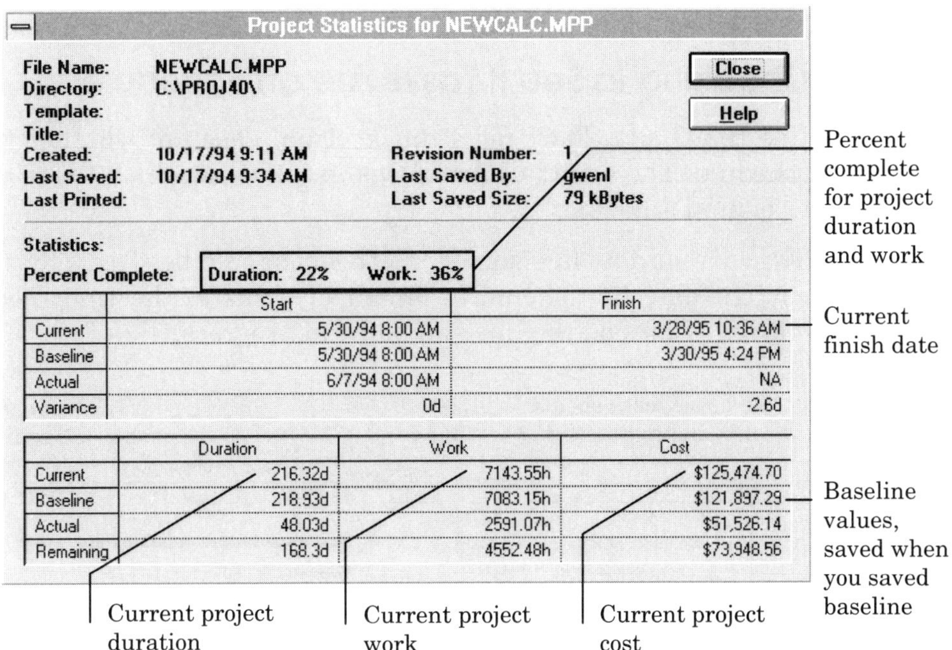
Project Statistics for NEWCALC.MPP

File Name: NEWCALC.MPP
Directory: C:\PROJ40\
Template:
Title:
Created: 10/17/94 9:11 AM
Last Saved: 10/17/94 9:34 AM
Last Printed:
Revision Number: 1
Last Saved By: gwenl
Last Saved Size: 79 kBytes

Close
Help

Statistics:
Percent Complete: Duration: 22% Work: 36%

	Start	Finish
Current	5/30/94 8:00 AM	3/28/95 10:36 AM
Baseline	5/30/94 8:00 AM	3/30/95 4:24 PM
Actual	6/7/94 8:00 AM	NA
Variance	0d	-2.6d

	Duration	Work	Cost
Current	216.32d	7143.55h	$125,474.70
Baseline	218.93d	7083.15h	$121,897.29
Actual	48.03d	2591.07h	$51,526.14
Remaining	168.3d	4552.48h	$73,948.56

Reviewing Percent Complete of Major Phases

If you have outlined your project, you can collapse the outline to see the percent complete of the major phases. Percent complete for subtasks is summarized by the summary tasks.

Choose View More Views. In the Views box, select Task Sheet, and then choose the Apply button. Choose View Table/Summary.

To collapse the outline, select all the tasks (click the Task Name title), and then click the Hide Subtasks button on the Formatting toolbar or choose Tools Outlining/Hide Subtasks.

	Task Name	Duration	Start	Finish	% Comp.	Cost	Work
1	Investigation Phase	59.25d	6/7/94 8:00 AM	8/29/94 10:00 AM	100%	$30,583.18	1367.6h
26	Design Phase	111.15d	8/29/94 10:00 AM	1/31/95 11:12 AM	26%	$42,051.85	2073.75h
41	Testing Phase	185.33d	5/30/94 8:00 AM	2/13/95 10:36 AM	5%	$14,091.61	1068.6h
54	Manufacturing Phase	31d	2/13/95 10:36 AM	3/28/95 10:36 AM	11%	$15,642.29	1216h
64	Sales Phase	165.92d	5/30/94 8:00 AM	1/16/95 4:20 PM	13%	$23,105.77	1417.6h
81							

The percent complete reflects the percent complete of all tasks subordinate to each summary task.

Checking to See If Tasks Are on Schedule

Use the Gantt Chart for a quick visual check of whether tasks are on schedule. The Gantt Chart shows graphically which tasks are ahead of or behind schedule.

The current date line shows where you should be. Tasks to the left of the current date line should be finished; tasks to the right need not have started. Tasks on the line should be in progress.

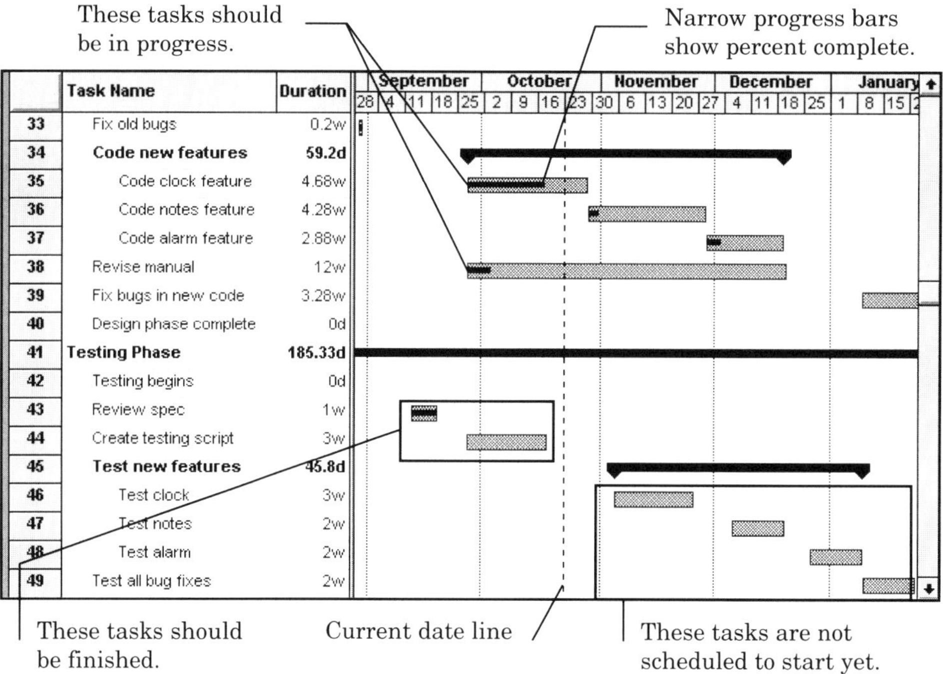

Changing the Current Date Line The location of the current date line should match the date when data was collected rather than today's date. To change the current date line, choose File Summary Info. Type the appropriate date in the Current Date box, and then choose OK.

Listing Tasks That Should Have Started

By filtering the Task Sheet or Gantt Chart, you can list all tasks that should have started but have not. The Should Start By filter finds tasks with a scheduled start date prior to the date you enter when you apply the filter, but that do not yet have an actual start date entered.

Select Should Start By from the Filter box on the Formatting toolbar. Type the data collection date in the dialog box. All tasks that do not have an actual start date but were scheduled to start before the date you typed are displayed on the Gantt Chart.

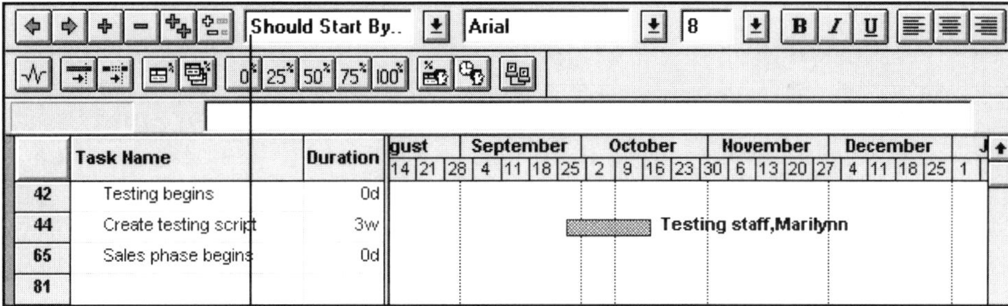

Filter box shows the filter applied. All the tasks now showing should have started, but no actual start date has been entered for them.

Comparing Baseline and Scheduled Duration

The Tracking Gantt is a special Gantt Chart that comes with Microsoft Project. It has one set of bars for baseline duration and another for scheduled duration. Use the Tracking Gantt to check for changing task durations as well as to visually check and compare start and finish dates.

Using the GanttChartWizard, you can also add baseline bars to any Gantt Chart.

To display the Tracking Gantt, choose View More Views. In the Views box, select Tracking Gantt, and then choose the Apply button.

On the Tracking Gantt chart, the top bars showing the scheduled duration are filled in as the percent complete changes.

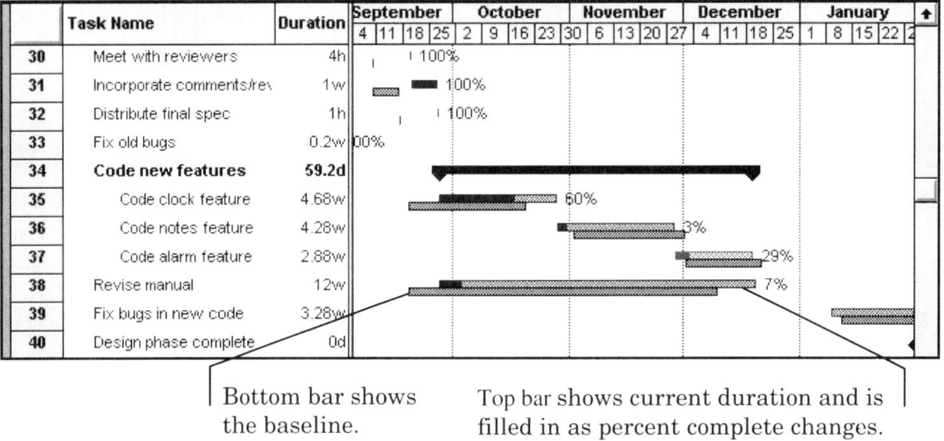

Checking for Variance in Dates, Work, and Cost

Use the Task Sheet to check for variance in start and finish dates, task work, and task cost. Variance is the difference between the baseline dates, work, or cost and the currently scheduled dates, work, or cost.

DATE VARIANCE

To check for variance in start and finish dates, apply the Variance table to the Task Sheet. Choose View More Views. In the Views box, select Task Sheet, and then choose the Apply button. To display the Variance table, choose View Table/Variance.

	Task Name	Start	Finish	Baseline Start	Baseline Finish	Start Var.	Finish Var.
1	**Investigation Phas**	**6/7/94 8:00 AM**	**8/29/94 10:00 AM**	**5/30/94 8:00 AM**	**8/19/94 10:00 AM**	**6d**	**6d**
2	Investigation beg	6/7/94 8:00 AM	6/7/94 8:00 AM	5/30/94 8:00 AM	5/30/94 8:00 AM	6d	6d
3	**Prepare initial**	**6/7/94 8:00 AM**	**6/23/94 5:00 PM**	**5/30/94 8:00 AM**	**6/15/94 5:00 PM**	**6d**	**6d**
4	Research co	6/7/94 8:00 AM	6/15/94 5:00 PM	5/30/94 8:00 AM	6/3/94 5:00 PM	6d	8d
5	Review cust	6/14/94 8:00 AM	6/15/94 12:00 PM	6/6/94 8:00 AM	6/8/94 5:00 PM	6d	4.5d
6	Write propos	6/17/94 8:00 AM	6/23/94 5:00 PM	6/9/94 8:00 AM	6/15/94 5:00 PM	6d	6d
7	**Plan focus pan**	**6/24/94 8:00 AM**	**6/30/94 5:00 PM**	**6/16/94 8:00 AM**	**6/22/94 5:00 PM**	**6d**	**6d**
8	Prepare ques	6/24/94 8:00 AM	6/28/94 5:00 PM	6/16/94 8:00 AM	6/22/94 5:00 PM	6d	4d
9	**Arrange sit**	**6/24/94 8:00 AM**	**6/27/94 5:00 PM**	**6/16/94 8:00 AM**	**6/17/94 5:00 PM**	**6d**	**6d**
10	Contact h	6/24/94 8:00 AM	6/24/94 5:00 PM	6/16/94 8:00 AM	6/16/94 5:00 PM	6d	6d

Scheduled dates — Baseline dates — Variance in start dates — Variance in finish dates

You may need to scroll right to see the Finish Var. column.

To limit the tasks displayed, apply a filter such as In Progress Tasks. The In Progress Tasks filter displays only those tasks for which there is an actual start date, but no actual finish date. Use this filter to review date variance for tasks in progress. To apply the In Progress Tasks filter, select In Progress Tasks from the Filter box on the Formatting toolbar.

To review the start and finish variance for completed tasks, apply the Completed Tasks filter. Only those tasks with a percent complete of 100 are displayed. Use this filter to review completed tasks whose variance from the schedule may be causing problems now. To apply the Completed Tasks filter, select Completed Tasks from the Filter box on the Formatting toolbar.

WORK VARIANCE

To check for variance in task work, apply the Work table to the Task Sheet. Choose View Table/Work.

	Task Name	Work	Baseline	Variance	Actual	Remaining	% W. Comp.
1	**Investigation Phase**	**1367.6h**	**1255.6h**	**112h**	**1367.6h**	**0h**	**100%**
2	Investigation begins	0h	0h	0h	0h	0h	0%
3	**Prepare initial product prc**	**308.4h**	**292.4h**	**16h**	**308.4h**	**0h**	**100%**
4	Research competition	182h	130h	52h	182h	0h	100%
5	Review customer commei	36h	72h	-36h	36h	0h	100%
6	Write proposal	80h	80h	0h	80h	0h	100%
7	**Plan focus panel**	**89.2h**	**121.2h**	**-32h**	**89.2h**	**0h**	**100%**
8	Prepare questions	48h	80h	-32h	48h	0h	100%
9	**Arrange sites**	**16.4h**	**16.4h**	**0h**	**16.4h**	**0h**	**100%**
10	Contact hotels	8h	8h	0h	8h	0h	100%
11	**Arrange for equipn**	**8.4h**	**8.4h**	**0h**	**8.4h**	**0h**	**100%**

Actual work for this task was higher than planned.

Actual work for this task was lower than planned.

Again, use the In Progress Tasks filter or Completed Tasks filter to limit the list of tasks displayed. Use the In Progress Tasks filter to check for variance in work on tasks in progress; if you find a task that is out of line, check the resources assigned to the task to determine the cause. Use the Completed Tasks filter to check for completed tasks that may have caused the schedule of current or future tasks to slip.

COST VARIANCE

To check for variance in task cost, apply the Cost table to the Task Sheet. Choose View Table/Cost.

	Task Name	Fixed Cost	Total Cost	Baseline	Variance	Actual	Remaining
1	**Investigation Phase**	**$0.00**	**$30,583.18**	**$25,744.71**	**$4,838.47**	**$30,583.18**	**$0.00**
2	Investigation begins	$0.00	$0.00	$0.00	$0.00	$0.00	$0.00
3	**Prepare initial product pro**	**$0.00**	**$5,852.90**	**$5,496.16**	**$356.74**	**$5,852.90**	**$0.00**
4	Research competition	$0.00	$3,176.93	$2,269.23	$907.70	$3,176.93	$0.00
5	Review customer comment	$0.00	$550.97	$1,101.93	($550.96)	$550.97	$0.00
6	Write proposal	$0.00	$1,875.00	$1,875.00	$0.00	$1,875.00	$0.00
7	**Plan focus panel**	**$0.00**	**$1,460.10**	**$2,210.10**	**($750.00)**	**$1,460.10**	**$0.00**
8	Prepare questions	$0.00	$1,125.00	$1,875.00	($750.00)	$1,125.00	$0.00
9	**Arrange sites**	**$0.00**	**$132.21**	**$132.21**	**$0.00**	**$132.21**	**$0.00**
10	Contact hotels	$0.00	$61.54	$61.54	$0.00	$61.54	$0.00
11	**Arrange for equipm**	**$0.00**	**$70.67**	**$70.67**	**$0.00**	**$70.67**	**$0.00**

Because actual work for this task was higher than planned, cost is also higher.

Because actual work for this task was lower than planned, cost is also lower.

Apply the Cost Overbudget filter to display only those tasks whose actual cost is greater than planned cost. To apply the Cost Overbudget filter, select Cost Overbudget from the Filter box on the Formatting toolbar. Again, use the In Progress Tasks filter or Completed Tasks filter to look at current and past tasks.

Checking for Slack in the Schedule

Slack tells you how much flexibility you have in your schedule. If you find a negative value in the Total Slack column, it means that, as currently scheduled, you do not have enough time in the schedule to complete that task.

To check slack, apply the Schedule table to the Task Sheet. Choose View Table/Schedule.

	Task Name	Start	Finish	Late Start	Late Finish	Free Slack	Total Slack
32	Distribute final spec	9/26/94	9/26/94	9/26/94	9/26/94	0d	0d
33	Fix old bugs	8/29/94	8/30/94	8/29/94	8/30/94	0d	0d
34	**Code new features**	**9/27/94**	**12/19/94**	**9/27/94**	**12/19/94**	**0d**	**0d**
35	Code clock feature	9/27/94	10/28/94	9/27/94	10/28/94	0d	0.6d
36	Code notes feature	10/28/94	11/28/94	10/28/94	12/2/94	0d	4.2d
37	Code alarm feature	11/28/94	12/19/94	11/28/94	12/19/94	0d	0d
38	Revise manual	9/27/94	12/19/94	9/27/94	3/28/95	70.33d	70.33d
39	Fix bugs in new code	1/9/95	1/31/95	3/3/95	3/28/95	0d	39.93d
40	Design phase complete	1/31/95	1/31/95	3/28/95	3/28/95	39.93d	39.93d

Free Slack and Total Slack columns tell you how much slack time remains in your schedule.

Slack time is also displayed on the Detail Gantt and the Delay Gantt. To apply either of these views, choose View More Views, select the view name in the Views box, and choose the Apply button. The following illustration shows slack on the Detail Gantt.

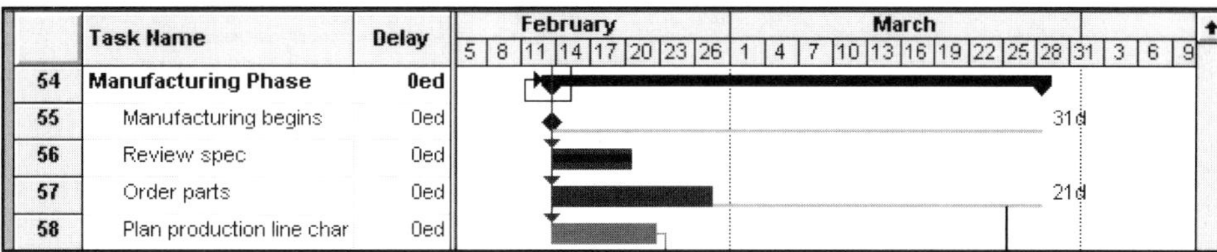

Slack time is displayed as a narrow bar on the right of the task bar (teal on a color monitor or printer). The actual amount of slack time appears to the right of the bar.

Listing Tasks That Are Behind Schedule

To see all the tasks that are behind schedule, you can apply the Slipping Tasks filter to the Task Sheet. Microsoft Project displays only those tasks scheduled to finish later than planned. This helps you focus on problem areas in your project. Select Slipping Tasks from the Filter box on the Formatting toolbar.

	Task Name	Duration	Start	Finish	Predecessors	Resource Names
35	Code clock feature	4.68w	9/27/94 8:00 AM	10/28/94 11:12 AM		Design staff[2]
38	Revise manual	12w	9/27/94 8:00 AM	12/19/94 5:00 PM	32	Documentation dept.
44	Create testing script	3w	9/27/94 8:00 AM	10/17/94 5:00 PM	32	Testing staff,Marilyn
46	Test clock	3w	11/4/94 11:12 AM	11/25/94 11:12 AM	35FS+1w	Testing staff
64	**Sales Phase**	**165.92d**	**5/30/94 8:00 AM**	**1/16/95 4:20 PM**		
69	Incorporate comments/re	1w	10/11/94 9:00 AM	10/18/94 9:00 AM	68FS+1w	Marcia,Cheryl
70	Distribute final market plar	1h	10/18/94 9:00 AM	10/18/94 10:00 AM	69	Cheryl
71	Contact sales force	0.33w	10/18/94 10:00 AM	10/19/94 4:20 PM	70	Sales engineers[3]
72	Set up sales meetings	1d	10/19/94 4:20 PM	10/20/94 4:20 PM	71	Marcia[0.2],Cheryl,Sa
73	Contact major dealers	1d	10/20/94 4:20 PM	10/21/94 4:20 PM	72	Roberto,Sales engine
74	Prepare marketing materia	4w	10/21/94 4:20 PM	11/18/94 4:20 PM	73	Marcia[0.2],Marketing
75	Prepare packaging	2w	11/18/94 4:20 PM	12/2/94 4:20 PM	74	Marcia[0.2],Marketing
76	Prepare for major announ	2w	12/2/94 4:20 PM	12/16/94 4:20 PM	75	Marcia[0.2],Marketing
77	Make announcement	1d	12/16/94 4:20 PM	12/19/94 4:20 PM	76	Carmen
78	Support sales force	4w	12/19/94 4:20 PM	1/16/95 4:20 PM	77	Sales engineers
79	Sales phase complete	0d	1/16/95 4:20 PM	1/16/95 4:20 PM	78	
80	Project complete	0d	1/16/95 4:20 PM	1/16/95 4:20 PM	79	

All the tasks now showing on the Task Sheet are scheduled to finish later than planned.

To see all tasks again, select All Tasks from the Filter box.

Slippage is also displayed on the Detail Gantt. To apply this view, choose View More Views. In the Views box, select Detail Gantt, and then choose the Apply button.

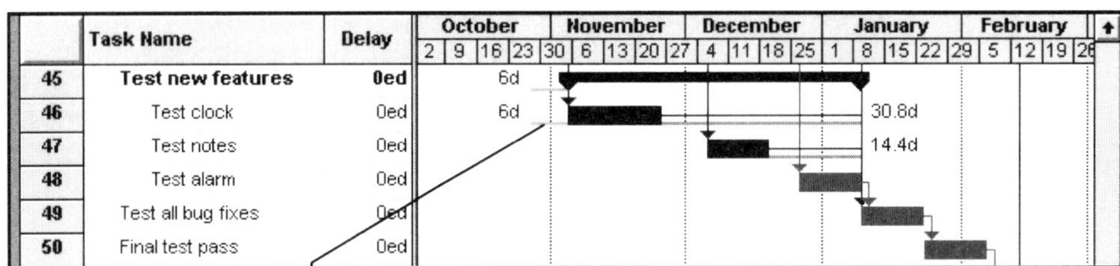

Slippage is displayed as a narrow bar on the left of the task bar (mustard on a color monitor or printer). The actual amount of slippage appears to the left of the bar.

ANALYZING VARIANCE

Having located the variances in the schedule, now determine the causes. To do this, you may need more data. Talk to those involved in any task not on schedule. Find answers to the questions suggested earlier in this chapter. Use the following tools to help in this analysis:

To see	Use
Tasks that caused the project cost or work to increase	Task Sheet, with Cost or Work table applied and Cost Overbudget or Work Overbudget filter applied
Resources that caused project cost or work to increase	Resource Sheet, with Cost or Work table applied and Cost Overbudget or Work Overbudget filter applied
A list of tasks in progress, to check whether any of these are interfering with other tasks	Task Sheet, with In Progress Tasks filter applied
Variance between baseline duration and actual duration to date, expressed as costs	Task Sheet, with Earned Value table applied

Task Cost or Work Variance

Identifying tasks costing more than planned can help you decide how to control costs on the rest of the schedule. For example, if the resources on a task are costing more per hour than originally budgeted, you may want to check for those resources in later tasks to decide how to handle the potential cost overrun on those tasks. By placing the Task Form below the Task Sheet, you can compare the actual cost of each resource on an over budget task with the baseline cost.

In the following illustration, the Task Sheet in the top view has the Cost table applied so you can see the cost information for each task. (Choose View Table/Cost to apply the table.) With the Cost Overbudget filter applied, the Task Sheet shows only those tasks that are over budget. (Select Cost Overbudget from the Filter box on the Formatting toolbar.)

On the Task Form, choose Format Details/Resource Cost to display the list of resources working on the task and their costs.

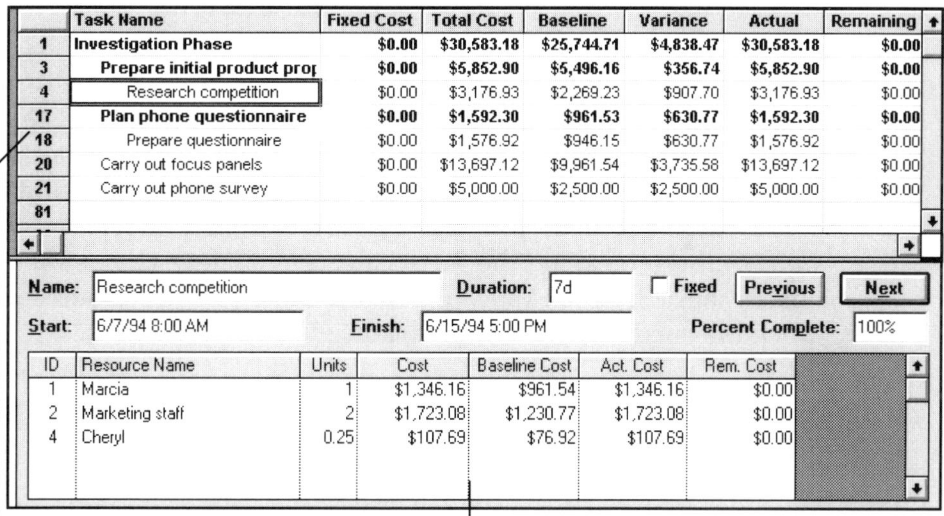

	Task Name	Fixed Cost	Total Cost	Baseline	Variance	Actual	Remaining
1	**Investigation Phase**	**$0.00**	**$30,583.18**	**$25,744.71**	**$4,838.47**	**$30,583.18**	**$0.00**
3	**Prepare initial product pro**	**$0.00**	**$5,852.90**	**$5,496.16**	**$356.74**	**$5,852.90**	**$0.00**
4	Research competition	$0.00	$3,176.93	$2,269.23	$907.70	$3,176.93	$0.00
17	**Plan phone questionnaire**	**$0.00**	**$1,592.30**	**$961.53**	**$630.77**	**$1,592.30**	**$0.00**
18	Prepare questionnaire	$0.00	$1,576.92	$946.15	$630.77	$1,576.92	$0.00
20	Carry out focus panels	$0.00	$13,697.12	$9,961.54	$3,735.58	$13,697.12	$0.00
21	Carry out phone survey	$0.00	$5,000.00	$2,500.00	$2,500.00	$5,000.00	$0.00
81							

Name: Research competition Duration: 7d Fixed Previous Next

Start: 6/7/94 8:00 AM Finish: 6/15/94 5:00 PM Percent Complete: 100%

ID	Resource Name	Units	Cost	Baseline Cost	Act. Cost	Rem. Cost
1	Marcia	1	$1,346.16	$961.54	$1,346.16	$0.00
2	Marketing staff	2	$1,723.08	$1,230.77	$1,723.08	$0.00
4	Cheryl	0.25	$107.69	$76.92	$107.69	$0.00

Task Sheet has Cost Overbudget filter and Cost table applied, so it shows only over budget tasks and cost information.

Task Form lists the resources assigned to the selected task, along with their cost information.

In this example, all resources contributed to the variance in costs since the actual costs for all three resources were higher than the baseline costs.

To see all tasks again, select All Tasks from the Filter box on the Formatting toolbar.

To see if the same resource or subcontractor is always over budget, put the Resource Sheet under the Task Sheet. Check the list of resources on the Resource Sheet assigned to each task on the Task Sheet. Apply the Cost table to the Resource Sheet to see cost information, including variance, for each resource.

	Task Name	Fixed Cost	Total Cost	Baseline	Variance	Actual	Remaining
14	**Get panel members**	**$0.00**	**$202.89**	**$202.89**	**$0.00**	**$202.89**	**$0.00**
15	Contact local reps for r	$0.00	$79.81	$79.81	$0.00	$79.81	$0.00
16	Contact suggested pan	$0.00	$123.08	$123.08	$0.00	$123.08	$0.00
17	**Plan phone questionnaire**	**$0.00**	**$1,592.30**	**$961.53**	**$630.77**	**$1,592.30**	**$0.00**
18	Prepare questionnaire	$0.00	$1,576.92	$946.15	$630.77	$1,576.92	$0.00
19	Get list of users to call	$0.00	$15.38	$15.38	$0.00	$15.38	$0.00
20	Carry out focus panels	$0.00	$13,697.12	$9,961.54	$3,735.58	$13,697.12	$0.00
21	Carry out phone survey	$0.00	$5,000.00	$2,500.00	$2,500.00	$5,000.00	$0.00

	Resource Name	Cost	Baseline Cost	Variance	Actual Cost	Remaining
1	Marcia	$14,326.93	$12,596.16	$1,730.77	$11,788.46	$2,538.47
2	Marketing staff	$20,061.55	$19,815.39	$246.16	$10,215.39	$9,846.16
5	Janet	$7,700.48	$6,969.71	$730.77	$7,700.48	$0.00

This task is over budget.

Resources assigned to the task. All resources on the task are over budget because the value in the Variance field is positive.

You can get similar information for work variance. Apply the Work table and Work Overbudget filter to the Task Sheet in the top view, and choose Format Details/Resource Work on the Task Form in the bottom view. To see if the same resource or subcontractor is always working more than planned, put the Resource Sheet under the Task Sheet. Select all the tasks on the Task Sheet, and check the list of resources on the Resource Sheet. Apply the Work table to the Resource Sheet to see work information, including variance, for each resource.

Resource Cost or Work Variance

By checking for resources that worked more or less than planned on completed tasks, you get information on what might be causing a task now in progress to be behind schedule. This will tell you specifically where you need more data about what is causing the variance.

Choose View Resource Sheet. Choose View Table/Work. Select Work Overbudget from the Filter box on the Formatting toolbar.

	Resource Name	% Comp.	Work	Overtime	Baseline	Variance	Actual	Remaining
1	Marcia	82%	596h	0h	524h	72h	490.4h	105.6h
2	Marketing staff	51%	1304h	0h	1288h	16h	664h	640h
5	Janet	100%	337.2h	0h	305.2h	32h	337.2h	0h
8	Research Inc	100%	100h	0h	60h	40h	100h	0h
28								
29								

All resources now showing on the Resource Sheet have scheduled work greater than the baseline.

Check the Variance column for the difference between scheduled work and the baseline.

To see all resources again, choose All Resources from the Filter box.

You can see similar information for cost variance. On the Resource Sheet, apply the Cost table and the Cost Overbudget filter.

Another way to view information about individual resources and if they are varying from the baseline plan is to use the Work Tracking or Cost Tracking custom form. For example, to see how much Marcia has varied from baseline on her work, select Marcia on the Resource Sheet. Choose Tools Customize/Forms. In the Forms box, select Work Tracking, and then choose the Apply button.

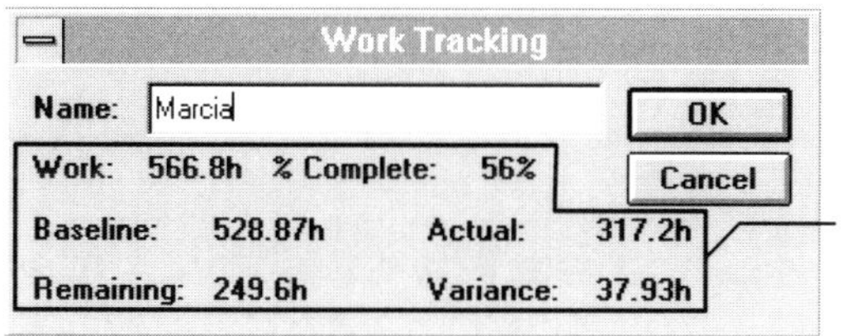

View details about work for the selected resource.

Earned Value

The Earned Value table compares where you expect to be (the baseline percent complete) with where you are (the actual percent complete). The Earned Value table does not show percent complete, however; instead, it shows everything in terms of costs. It shows the dollars you planned to spend (baseline percent complete times baseline cost) compared to the dollars you have actually spent (actual percent complete times baseline cost).

The column titles on the Earned Value table have the following meanings:

Title	Means	Description
BCWS	Budgeted Cost of Work Scheduled	Baseline percent complete times the baseline cost
BCWP	Budgeted Cost of Work Performed	Actual percent complete times the baseline cost to date
ACWP	Actual Cost of Work Performed	Actual cost to date
SV	Earned Value Schedule Variance	BCWP minus BCWS
CV	Earned Value Cost Variance	BCWP minus ACWP
BAC	Budgeted At Completion	Baseline cost
FAC	Forecast At Completion	Scheduled cost
Variance	Variance	BAC minus FAC

To apply the Earned Value table, choose View Table/More Tables. In the Tables box, select Earned Value, and then choose the Apply button.

Task Name	BCWS	BCWP	ACWP	SV	CV	BAC	FAC	Variance
Investigation Phase	**$25,744.71**	**$25,744.71**	**$30,583.18**	**$0.00**	**$4,838.47**	**$25,744.71**	**$30,583.18**	**$4,838.47**
Investigation begins	$0.00	$0.00	$0.00	$0.00	$0.00	$0.00	$0.00	$0.00
Prepare initial product	**$5,496.16**	**$5,496.16**	**$5,852.90**	**$0.00**	**$356.74**	**$5,496.16**	**$5,852.90**	**$356.74**
Research competition	$2,269.23	$2,269.23	$3,176.93	$0.00	$907.70	$2,269.23	$3,176.93	$907.70
Review customer com	$1,101.93	$1,101.93	$550.97	$0.00	($550.96)	$1,101.93	$550.97	($550.96)
Write proposal	$1,875.00	$1,875.00	$1,875.00	$0.00	$0.00	$1,875.00	$1,875.00	$0.00
Plan focus panel	**$2,210.10**	**$2,210.10**	**$1,460.10**	**$0.00**	**($750.00)**	**$2,210.10**	**$1,460.10**	**($750.00)**
Prepare questions	$1,875.00	$1,875.00	$1,125.00	$0.00	($750.00)	$1,875.00	$1,125.00	($750.00)
Arrange sites	**$132.21**	**$132.21**	**$132.21**	**$0.00**	**$0.00**	**$132.21**	**$132.21**	**$0.00**
Contact hotels	$61.54	$61.54	$61.54	$0.00	$0.00	$61.54	$61.54	$0.00
Arrange for equ	**$70.67**	**$70.67**	**$70.67**	**$0.00**	**$0.00**	**$70.67**	**$70.67**	**$0.00**
Determine nee	$39.90	$39.90	$39.90	$0.00	$0.00	$39.90	$39.90	$0.00
Contact local c	$30.77	$30.77	$30.77	$0.00	$0.00	$30.77	$30.77	$0.00
Get panel member:	**$202.89**	**$202.89**	**$202.89**	**$0.00**	**$0.00**	**$202.89**	**$202.89**	**$0.00**
Contact local reps	$79.81	$79.81	$79.81	$0.00	$0.00	$79.81	$79.81	$0.00
Contact suggeste	$123.08	$123.08	$123.08	$0.00	$0.00	$123.08	$123.08	$0.00
Plan phone questionn	**$961.53**	**$961.53**	**$1,592.30**	**$0.00**	**$630.77**	**$961.53**	**$1,592.30**	**$630.77**
Prepare questionnaire	$946.15	$946.15	$1,576.92	$0.00	$630.77	$946.15	$1,576.92	$630.77
Get list of users to cal	$15.38	$15.38	$15.38	$0.00	$0.00	$15.38	$15.38	$0.00

To see earned value for one task at a time, use the custom form called Earned Value. First select the task of interest. Then choose Tools

Customize/Forms. In the Forms box, select Earned Value, and then choose the Apply button.

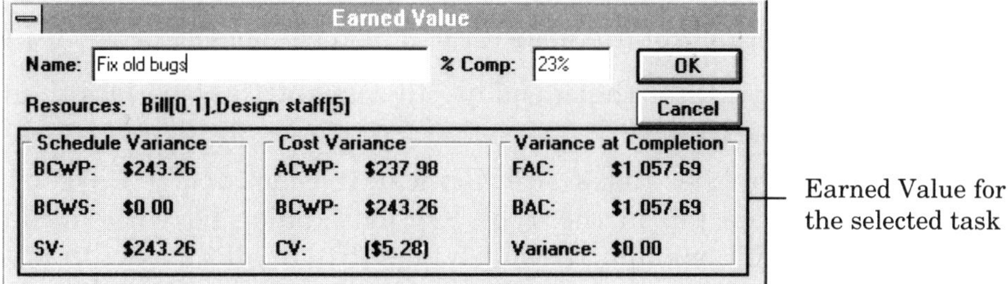

Earned Value for the selected task

Determining Corrective Action

You should now have enough information to have formed some ideas about how to correct tasks with problems. You could add new resources. Or would shifting resources from another task be better? Or maybe you are considering changing the scope of the project by deleting some tasks or changing the scope of future tasks.

List possible solutions and then use Microsoft Project to try the solutions and see the effect on the schedule, resources, and project cost. Repeat the steps in Chapters 8 and 9 to refine the schedule. For example, try shifting resources from one task to another, and see how it affects the future tasks and the finish date of the project. Or if you add resources, check the project finish date and project cost to see how they changed. Use the Gantt Chart, Task Sheet, and Task Form to change durations, change resources, and add or delete tasks.

Remember also to consider reviewing possible changes you may need to make on future tasks. For example, you may want to review all future tasks that use a resource that is behind schedule on a task now in progress. Apply the Using Resource filter to the Task Sheet to display all tasks using the resource of interest. Then decide what to do about the task durations. Get the project team together to decide. For example, you may want to increase all durations. Or add resources to all the tasks using this resource to maintain the original duration estimates. Or cut scope on this set of tasks.

Another thing to check as you look for solutions is tasks that are now near critical. Knowing that a task is almost critical may help you determine how to handle another problem. For example, suppose you need to shift resources from one task to another. If a task will become critical if you remove its resources, you may not want to borrow these resources for another task.

To see tasks that are near critical, you can do one of two things:

- Create a filter that displays all tasks with slack less than an amount you specify.
- Change the Tasks Are Critical If Slack <= x Days option on the Schedule tab in the Tools Options dialog box to a value other than zero. For example, if you change it to 3, all tasks with less than three days of slack time are displayed when you apply the Critical filter to the Task Sheet. To distinguish critical tasks with zero slack from those with a little slack, apply the Schedule table to the Task Sheet. Check the Total Slack field for how much slack time is available for the task. Or display the Detail Gantt or Delay Gantt to check the amount of slack time for each task.

You may also want to check for overallocated resources as you work on solutions. If a resource is already overallocated during a certain period, you know that it is part of your problem, and not part of your solution. To view overallocated resources, apply the Overallocated Resources filter to the Resource Sheet. Place the Resource Sheet over the Resource Usage view to see when each resource is overallocated. This will help you decide how to move tasks around to take advantage of open times for resources, and eliminate those times when resources are overallocated.

Use the Gantt Chart to see how the changes affect the project as a whole; use the Project Statistics dialog box to check the new finish date and total work and cost for the project. Repeat the steps in Chapter 9, as needed, to optimize the schedule again.

Adding New Tasks to the Baseline Schedule

If it is necessary to add tasks to the schedule, either because you needed to break up tasks so resources would be available or because changes imposed by a client or management require new tasks, add these new tasks to the baseline schedule so you can track their progress.

To do this, you select the new tasks, and then choose Tools Tracking/Save Baseline.

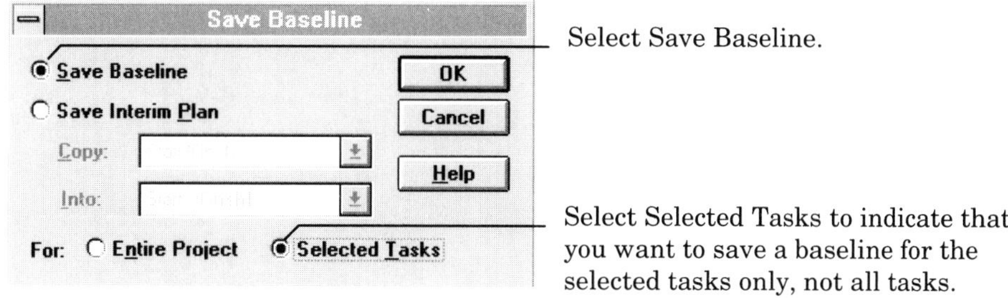

When you are ready to track progress on these new tasks, their baseline values will be available along with all the other baseline values.

The next chapter has more information about communicating with those on the project team, management, or a client. More sample reports are included to help you convey the appropriate information at this stage in the project.

13

Communicating Progress

Keeping everyone informed about an ongoing project is an important part of your job. Once a project is under way, you periodically share information about progress. Management or a client will want to know how things are progressing, and project team members need to have the latest schedule information.

You communicate four types of information:

- Summary reports show information about progress on tasks.
- "Exception" reports show schedule variance.
- "Solution" reports show possible resolutions to problems and how the schedule looks with each possible solution. These reports give management the data to make decisions about the exceptions.
- "Direction" reports for task supervisors let them know the tasks to be performed and the resources needed during the next period.

When preparing a report for management or a client, include a summary report plus reports on problem areas—exception reports—and either the solution or proposals for them—solution reports—for which you may need support, such as money or resources. These reports show both the project's progress and a list of exceptions so management can see what to concentrate on. If tasks are proceeding as planned, you have nothing to report other than a general status, noting that all is as planned. If there is variance in the progress, show these areas, along with a summary of the information you gathered on the causes and solutions.

To control a project effectively, management needs to get reports that contain the right amount of information, no more—they don't need reams of paper about every detail—and no less—they do need sufficient detail to make an informed decision. This information should be distributed quickly so that decisions can be made about how to get the project back on track as soon as possible.

Just as in the reports you created earlier, you might want to create several reports, each appropriate for the recipient, either summary or detail. Don't try to generate one huge report that fits everyone.

If possible, generate reports that show the problems and solutions graphically. Those receiving the reports can get the information they need much more quickly from a chart or graph than from words. If you make the information easily accessible, you are more likely to get a timely response when you need a decision quickly.

The frequency of progress reports depends on the requirements of management, a client, or contract. It also depends on the recipient. You may, for example, print direction reports often for work supervisors, giving them detailed task and resource lists for the next period, but not so often for management who may just want periodic reassurance that there is progress. You know best the reporting requirements of your organization. Set up a reporting cycle that satisfies these requirements.

USING MICROSOFT PROJECT

When you generate reports to communicate progress information, you use the same tools used in Chapter 10 to print the original schedule reports. You can print views and reports, using any combination of a table and filter that shows what you want and is appropriate for the view or report.

When preparing exception reports, filter the tasks or resources to pinpoint the area of concern and avoid excessive detail. For example, you could filter the resource pool so only the resources whose scheduled work is greater than planned appear or are highlighted in the report. That way, the recipient of the report does not have to look through all the resources in the resource pool to find those few resources with problems.

Sorting can also highlight problem areas. For example, you could sort the resource pool so that resources with the greatest variance in work head the list. These are the resources that require your readers' attention.

Another way to highlight tasks of interest is to select the tasks you want to stand out and then change the font, style, or color of the text for the selected tasks. In the Format Font dialog box, select the font, style, and color (if you have a color printer) to make the selected tasks stand out from the rest of the tasks. You can also use the items on the Formatting toolbar to change font and font size of the selected tasks and to make them bold, italic, or underlined.

If you used a certain combination of view, table, and filter in Chapter 12 to locate variance, and then find a solution to the variance, you might want to print that view, or use that table and filter in a report.

Before printing, be sure the appropriate printer is selected and set up properly, and the page is set up as you want in the Page Setup dialog box. For more information, see Chapter 10, "Communicating the Plan."

PRINTING SUMMARY REPORTS

To show a summary of progress on tasks and to show generally where the project stands, you can print any of the following views or reports.

To show	Print
Progress on tasks	Gantt Chart; PERT Chart; Task Sheet with Tracking table applied
Percent complete and baseline versus actual duration	Tracking Gantt
Summary of progress	Overview/Project report
Summary of progress on major phases including cost and work	Overview/Top-Level Tasks report
Completed tasks, including duration, start and finish dates, and cost and work numbers	Current Activities/Completed Tasks report

Showing Task Progress

There are several ways you can show progress on tasks. To show progress graphically, print the Gantt Chart or the PERT Chart.

Since the Gantt Chart includes progress bars and shows the date on which you collected the data, print the Gantt Chart to show the amount of progress on tasks and how progress compares to where you expected to be by the data collection date.

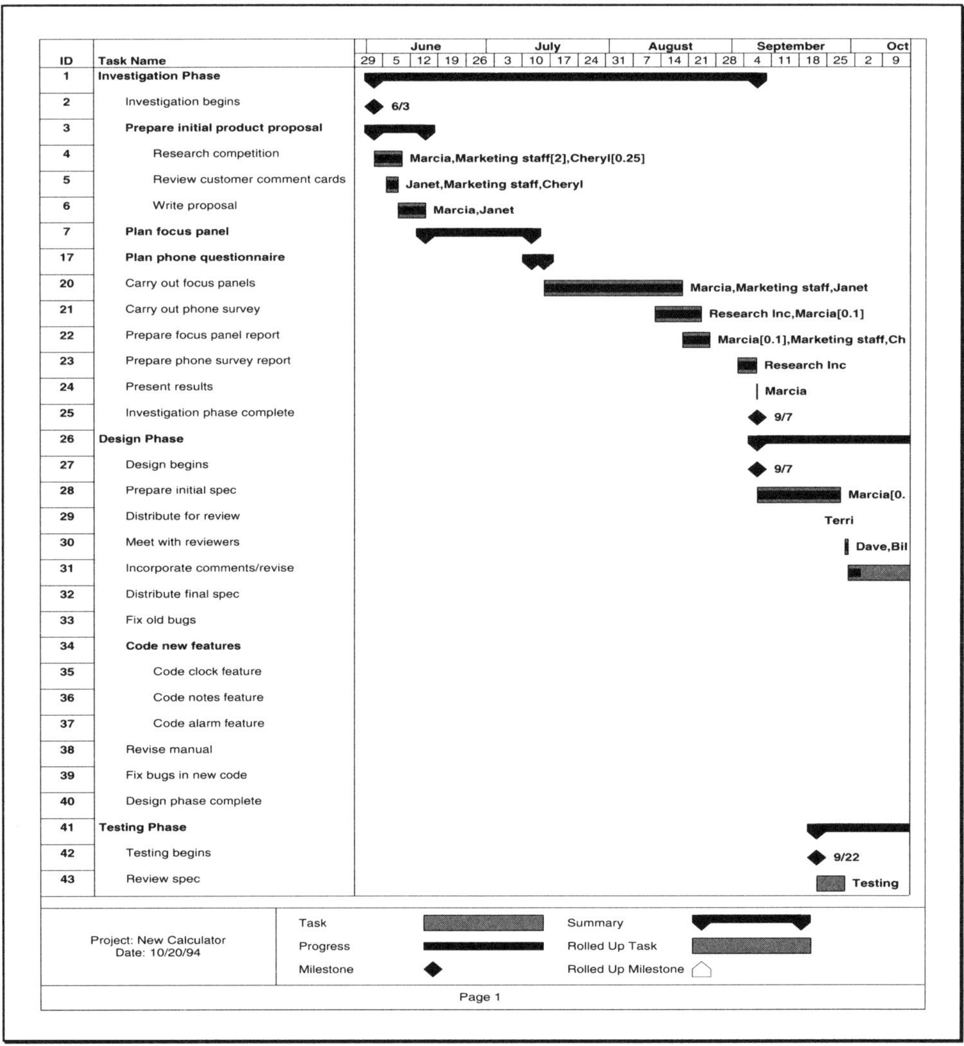

The current date line should match the date on which you collected data. You change this date in the Summary Info dialog box.

The progress bars reflect the progress information entered about each task. Just as on screen, by comparing progress to the current date line, you see at a glance which tasks are on schedule, and which are ahead or behind.

TO PRINT THE GANTT CHART

1. Choose View Gantt Chart.
2. Choose Format Timescale.
3. In the Units boxes under Major Scale and Minor Scale, select the timescale units you want, and choose OK.

   For example, to duplicate the example showing months and every seventh day: In the Units box under Major Scale, select Months; under Minor Scale, select Days and type **7** in the Count box.
4. To change the current date line so it matches the data collection date, choose File Summary Info.
5. In the Current Date box, type the data collection date, and choose OK.
6. To have the data collection date printed in the legend, instead of today's date, choose File Page Setup, and select the Legend tab.
7. To replace &[Date] with &[Current Date]: On the Center tab, select &[Date]. In the list below, select Project Current Date, and choose the Add button.
8. To preview the view and then print, choose the Print Preview button.
9. When you are ready to print, choose the Print button.

   To print without previewing, choose the Print button in the Page Setup dialog box.
10. Choose OK.

Print the PERT Chart to show graphically tasks that have not started, tasks that are in progress (percent complete greater than 0 but less than 100), and tasks that are finished. For tasks that have started but not finished, the PERT node has one diagonal line. For tasks that are finished, the PERT node has two diagonal lines. In the next illustration, the finish date in each PERT node has been replaced with the percent complete.

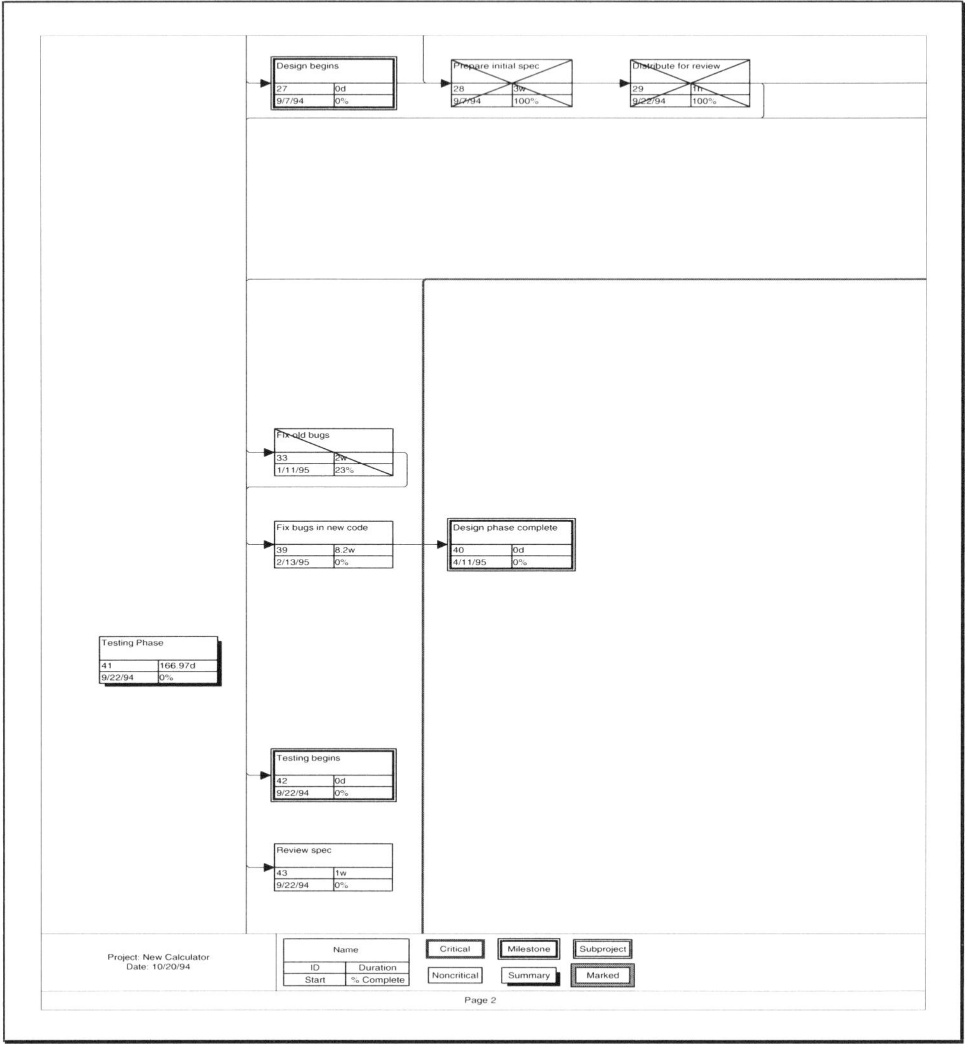

TO PRINT THE PERT CHART

1. Choose View PERT Chart.
2. To replace the scheduled finish date with the percent complete in each node, double-click outside a node or choose Format Box Styles.
3. In the box containing Finish, select % Complete, and choose OK.
4. To preview the view and then print, click the Print Preview button on the Standard toolbar or choose File Print Preview.
5. When you are ready to print, choose the Print button.

To print without previewing, choose File Print.

6. Type the number of copies and the page range you want to print.
7. Choose OK.

You can also print a list of tasks showing information about progress. For example, you can print the Task Sheet with the Tracking table applied to show the actual start and finish dates for tasks, the percent complete, and actual and remaining duration. If an actual start or finish date has not been entered, the field contains NA.

TO PRINT THE TASK SHEET SHOWING PROGRESS

1. Choose View More Views.
2. In the Views box, select Task Sheet, and choose Apply.
3. Choose View Table/Tracking.
4. To preview the view and then print, click the Print Preview button on the Standard toolbar or choose File Print Preview.
5. When you are ready to print, choose the Print button.

   To print without previewing, choose File Print.
6. Choose OK.

Showing Percent Complete and Changing Durations

Print the Tracking Gantt chart to show how schedules are changing as tasks progress, and also to show the percent complete for each task.

TO PRINT THE TRACKING GANTT CHART

1. Choose View More Views.
2. In the Views box, select Tracking Gantt and choose the Apply button.
3. Choose Format Timescale.
4. In the Units boxes under Major Scale and Minor Scale, select the timescale units you want, and choose OK.

   For example, to duplicate the example showing months and weeks: In the Units box under Major Scale, select Months; under Minor Scale, select Days and type **7** in the Count box.
5. To preview the view and then print, click the Print Preview button on the Standard toolbar or choose File Print Preview.

6. When you are ready to print, choose the Print button.

   To print without previewing, choose File Print.

7. Choose OK.

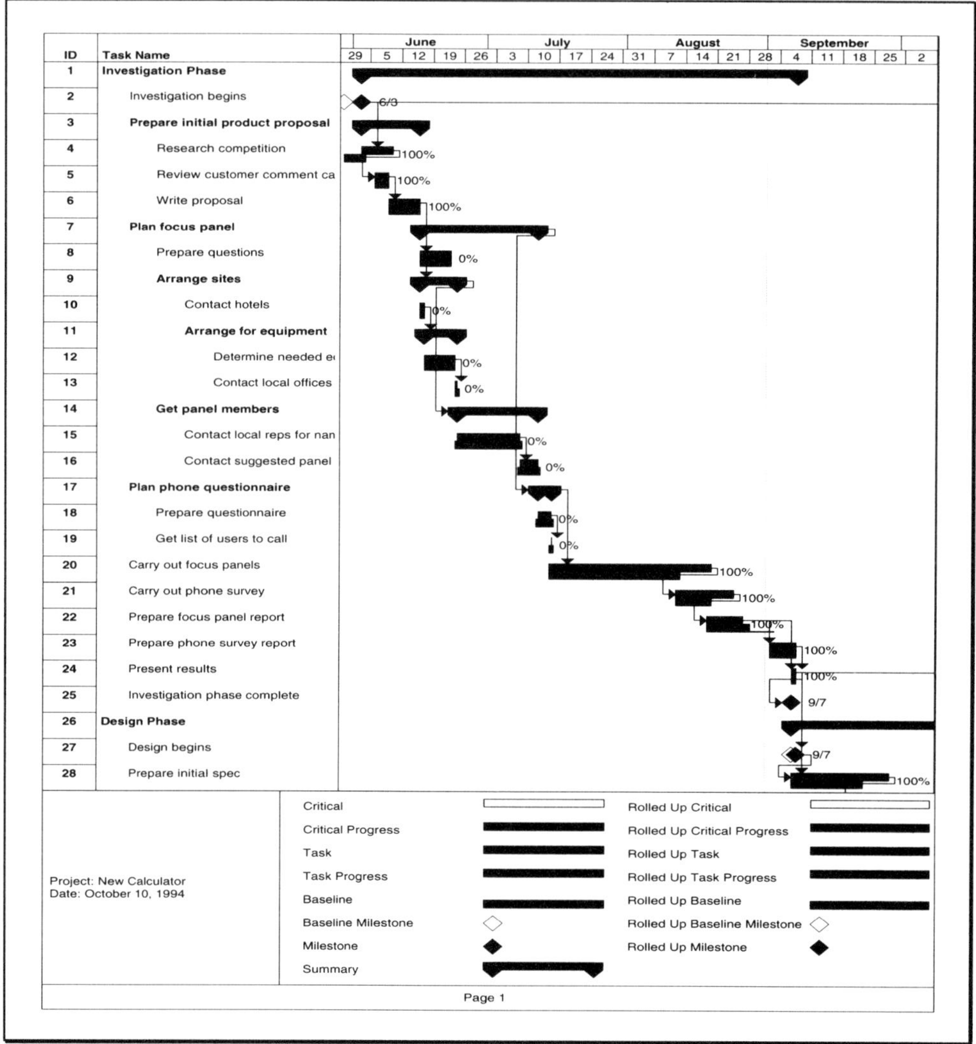

You specify legend information in the Page Setup dialog box.

Printing a Project Summary Report

To give management or a client a quick review of where the project stands, print the Overview/Project report. This report includes information about task duration, cost, work, and progress for the project as a whole, including statistics on tasks in progress and completed.

New Calculator
compusystems
Marcia Cryer
as of 10/20/94

Dates			
Start:	5/30/94	Finish:	6/12/95
Baseline Start:	5/30/94	Baseline Finish:	6/12/95
Actual Start:	6/3/94	Actual Finish:	NA
Start Variance:	4d	Finish Variance:	0d

Duration			
Scheduled:	266.92d	Remaining:	233.52d
Baseline:	270.93d	Actual:	33.41d
Variance:	-4d	Percent Complete:	13%

Work			
Scheduled:	7111.3h	Remaining:	5750.72h
Baseline:	7093.37h	Actual:	1360.58h
Variance:	17.93h	Percent Complete:	19%

Costs			
Scheduled:	$128,579.50	Remaining:	$98,495.26
Baseline:	$126,648.42	Actual:	$30,084.24
Variance:	$1,931.08		

Task Status		Resource Status	
Tasks not yet started:	62	Resources:	24
Tasks in progress:	4	Overallocated Resources:	6
Tasks completed:	14		
Total Tasks:	80	Total Resources:	30

Notes

Goal: New, improved calculator ready for next back-to-school promotion.
Scope: Do add the most-requested features, fix bugs in existing code, and update the manual to include new features. Do not redo all code, change packaging, or rewrite entire manual.
Assumptions: Technology is available to implement features; programmers will be available to do the work; existing packaging will work.

TO PRINT A PROJECT SUMMARY REPORT

1. Choose View Reports.
2. In the Reports dialog box, double-click Overview.
3. Double-click Project.
4. While previewing, choose Page Setup to change the page orientation or margins.

If any of the information at the top of the page is incorrect, close preview and then choose File Summary Info to change it.

5. When you are ready to print, choose the Print button.
6. Choose OK.

Printing a Summary of Progress on Major Phases

If you included an outline in your project, you can print the Overview/Top-Level Tasks report to show progress information on major phases of the project. The percent complete for each top-level task is a summary of progress on the tasks subordinate to each summary task.

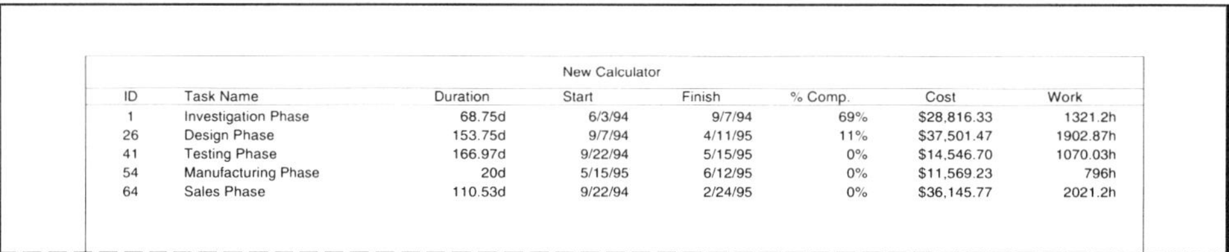

New Calculator

ID	Task Name	Duration	Start	Finish	% Comp.	Cost	Work
1	Investigation Phase	68.75d	6/3/94	9/7/94	69%	$28,816.33	1321.2h
26	Design Phase	153.75d	9/7/94	4/11/95	11%	$37,501.47	1902.87h
41	Testing Phase	166.97d	9/22/94	5/15/95	0%	$14,546.70	1070.03h
54	Manufacturing Phase	20d	5/15/95	6/12/95	0%	$11,569.23	796h
64	Sales Phase	110.53d	9/22/94	2/24/95	0%	$36,145.77	2021.2h

TO PRINT A SUMMARY OF PROGRESS ON MAJOR PHASES

1. Choose View Reports.
2. In the Reports dialog box, double-click Overview.
3. Double-click Top-Level Tasks.
4. To change the setup of the pages, choose Page Setup.
5. When you are ready to print, choose the Print button.
6. Choose OK.

Printing a Summary of Costs

To print a summary of costs to date, print the Costs/Budget report. The report includes total cost, baseline cost, variance, actual, and remaining costs. Tasks are sorted from most costly to least costly.

Budget Report
New Calculator
Marcia Cryer
10/20/94

ID	Task Name	Fixed Cost	Total Cost	Baseline	Variance	Actual	Remaining
38	Revise manual	$0.00	$14,400.00	$14,400.00	$0.00	$0.00	$14,400.00
20	Carry out focus panels	$0.00	$12,451.92	$9,961.54	$2,490.38	$12,451.92	$0.00
74	Prepare marketing materials	$0.00	$10,492.31	$10,492.31	$0.00	$0.00	$10,492.31
78	Support sales force	$0.00	$7,384.62	$7,384.62	$0.00	$0.00	$7,384.62
75	Prepare packaging	$0.00	$5,246.16	$5,246.16	$0.00	$0.00	$5,246.16
66	Review spec	$0.00	$4,951.92	$4,951.92	$0.00	$0.00	$4,951.92
28	Prepare initial spec	$0.00	$3,908.05	$3,832.73	$75.32	$3,908.05	$0.00
21	Carry out phone survey	$0.00	$3,894.23	$2,596.15	$1,298.08	$3,894.23	$0.00
57	Order parts	$0.00	$3,750.00	$3,750.00	$0.00	$0.00	$3,750.00
44	Create testing script	$0.00	$3,317.31	$3,317.31	$0.00	$0.00	$3,317.31
60	Test production	$0.00	$3,242.31	$3,242.31	$0.00	$0.00	$3,242.31
76	Prepare for major announcement	$0.00	$2,846.16	$2,846.16	$0.00	$0.00	$2,846.16
39	Fix bugs in new code	$0.00	$2,365.38	$2,365.38	$0.00	$0.00	$2,365.38
4	Research competition	$0.00	$2,269.23	$2,269.23	$0.00	$2,269.23	$0.00
67	Prepare market plan	$0.00	$2,269.23	$2,269.23	$0.00	$0.00	$2,269.23
35	Code clock feature	$0.00	$2,250.00	$2,250.00	$0.00	$0.00	$2,250.00
49	Test all bug fixes	$0.00	$2,211.54	$2,211.54	$0.00	$0.00	$2,211.54
50	Final test pass	$0.00	$2,211.54	$2,211.54	$0.00	$0.00	$2,211.54
36	Code notes feature	$0.00	$2,057.69	$2,057.69	$0.00	$0.00	$2,057.69
22	Prepare focus panel report	$0.00	$1,932.68	$3,865.38	($1,932.70)	$1,932.68	$0.00
31	Incorporate comments/revise	$0.00	$1,894.62	$1,894.62	$0.00	$420.76	$1,473.86
6	Write proposal	$0.00	$1,875.00	$1,875.00	$0.00	$1,875.00	$0.00
56	Review spec	$0.00	$1,730.77	$1,730.77	$0.00	$0.00	$1,730.77
59	Set up production test	$0.00	$1,658.65	$1,658.65	$0.00	$0.00	$1,658.65
37	Code alarm feature	$0.00	$1,384.62	$1,384.62	$0.00	$0.00	$1,384.62
69	Incorporate comments/revise pla	$0.00	$1,269.23	$1,269.23	$0.00	$0.00	$1,269.23
23	Prepare phone survey report	$0.00	$1,250.00	$1,250.00	$0.00	$1,250.00	$0.00
43	Review spec	$0.00	$1,105.77	$1,105.77	$0.00	$0.00	$1,105.77
5	Review customer comment card:	$0.00	$1,101.93	$1,101.93	$0.00	$1,101.93	$0.00
33	Fix old bugs	$0.00	$1,057.69	$1,057.69	$0.00	$237.98	$819.71
58	Plan production line changes	$0.00	$937.50	$937.50	$0.00	$0.00	$937.50
51	Write testing report	$0.00	$625.00	$625.00	$0.00	$0.00	$625.00
71	Contact sales force	$0.00	$609.23	$609.23	$0.00	$0.00	$609.23
72	Set up sales meetings	$0.00	$469.23	$469.23	$0.00	$0.00	$469.23
30	Meet with reviewers	$0.00	$389.81	$389.81	$0.00	$389.81	$0.00
73	Contact major dealers	$0.00	$361.53	$361.53	$0.00	$0.00	$361.53
62	Pass production function to Si	$0.00	$250.00	$250.00	$0.00	$0.00	$250.00
77	Make announcement	$0.00	$230.77	$230.77	$0.00	$0.00	$230.77
24	Present results	$0.00	$96.15	$96.15	$0.00	$96.15	$0.00
68	Distribute plan for review	$0.00	$7.69	$7.69	$0.00	$0.00	$7.69
70	Distribute final market plan	$0.00	$7.69	$7.69	$0.00	$0.00	$7.69
29	Distribute for review	$0.00	$6.50	$6.50	$0.00	$6.50	$0.00
32	Distribute final spec	$0.00	$6.50	$6.50	$0.00	$0.00	$6.50
52	Distribute testing report	$0.00	$6.50	$6.50	$0.00	$0.00	$6.50
2	Investigation begins	$0.00	$0.00	$0.00	$0.00	$0.00	$0.00
25	Investigation phase complete	$0.00	$0.00	$0.00	$0.00	$0.00	$0.00
27	Design begins	$0.00	$0.00	$0.00	$0.00	$0.00	$0.00
40	Design phase complete	$0.00	$0.00	$0.00	$0.00	$0.00	$0.00
42	Testing begins	$0.00	$0.00	$0.00	$0.00	$0.00	$0.00
53	Testing phase complete	$0.00	$0.00	$0.00	$0.00	$0.00	$0.00
55	Manufacturing begins	$0.00	$0.00	$0.00	$0.00	$0.00	$0.00
61	Begin production	$0.00	$0.00	$0.00	$0.00	$0.00	$0.00
63	Manufacturing phase complete	$0.00	$0.00	$0.00	$0.00	$0.00	$0.00
65	Sales phase begins	$0.00	$0.00	$0.00	$0.00	$0.00	$0.00
79	Sales phase complete	$0.00	$0.00	$0.00	$0.00	$0.00	$0.00
80	Project complete	$0.00	$0.00	$0.00	$0.00	$0.00	$0.00
		$0.00	$111,784.66	$109,853.58	$1,931.08	$29,834.24	$81,950.42

TO PRINT A SUMMARY OF COSTS TO DATE

1. Choose View Reports.
2. In the Reports dialog box, double-click Costs.
3. Double-click Budget.
4. To change the setup of the pages, choose Page Setup.
5. When you are ready to print, choose the Print button.
6. Choose OK.

Printing a List of Completed Tasks

To show all the tasks that have been completed, print the Current Activities/Completed Tasks report. This report includes the tasks completed each month, along with work and cost totals for each.

Completed Tasks
New Calculator
Marcia Cryer

10/20/94

ID	Task Name	Duration	Start	Finish	% Comp.	Cost	Work
June 1994							
2	Investigation begins	0d	6/3/94	6/3/94	100%	$0.00	0h
4	Research competition	1w	6/3/94	6/9/94	100%	$2,269.23	130h
5	Review customer comment cards	3d	6/6/94	6/8/94	100%	$1,101.93	72h
6	Write proposal	1w	6/9/94	6/15/94	100%	$1,875.00	80h
July 1994							
20	Carry out focus panels	5w	7/15/94	8/19/94	100%	$12,451.92	600h
August 1994							
20	Carry out focus panels	5w	7/15/94	8/19/94	100%	$12,451.92	600h
21	Carry out phone survey	1.5w	8/12/94	8/24/94	100%	$3,894.23	66h
22	Prepare focus panel report	1w	8/19/94	8/26/94	100%	$1,932.68	124h
September 1994							
23	Prepare phone survey report	0.5w	9/2/94	9/7/94	100%	$1,250.00	20h
24	Present results	4h	9/7/94	9/7/94	100%	$96.15	4h
25	Investigation phase complete	0d	9/7/94	9/7/94	100%	$0.00	0h
28	Prepare initial spec	3w	9/7/94	9/28/94	100%	$3,908.05	189.13h
29	Distribute for review	1h	9/22/94	9/22/94	100%	$6.50	1h
30	Meet with reviewers	4h	9/29/94	9/30/94	100%	$389.81	20.8h

TO PRINT A LIST OF COMPLETED TASKS

1. Choose View Reports.
2. In the Reports dialog box, double-click Current Activities.
3. Double-click Completed Tasks.
4. To change the setup of the pages, choose Page Setup.
5. When you are ready to print, choose the Print button.
6. Choose OK.

PRINTING EXCEPTION REPORTS

There are many ways you can generate a report showing exceptions to the scheduled project.

To show	Print
Tasks that should have started	Current Activities/Should Have Started Tasks report
Tasks whose finish dates have slipped	Current Activities/Slipping Tasks report
Tasks that have a work amount different from baseline	Task Sheet or Task report with Work table applied and Work Overbudget filter applied
Tasks costing more than baseline	Costs/Overbudget Tasks report
Resources working more than baseline	Resource Sheet or Resource report with Work table applied and Work Overbudget filter applied
Resources costing more than baseline	Costs/Overbudget Resources report

To show	Print
Resources now overallocated due to changes in the schedule	Assignments/Overallocated Resources report
Earned value	Costs/Earned Value report

Showing Tasks That Should Have Started

To see a list of all tasks that were scheduled to start, but for which you have not entered a start date, print the Current Activities/Should Have Started Tasks report.

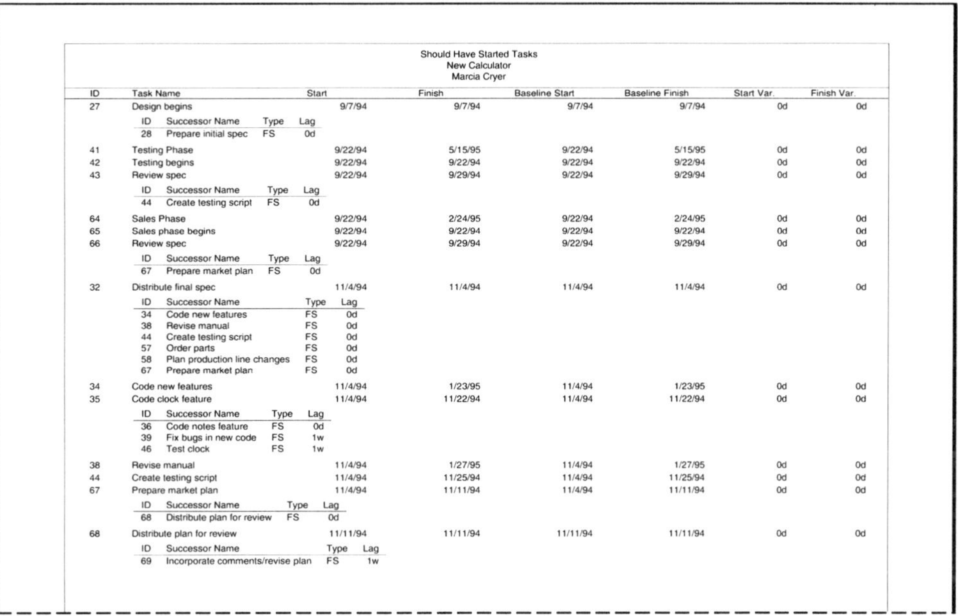

Should Have Started Tasks
New Calculator
Marcia Cryer

ID	Task Name	Start	Finish	Baseline Start	Baseline Finish	Start Var.	Finish Var.
27	Design begins	9/7/94	9/7/94	9/7/94	9/7/94	0d	0d

ID	Successor Name	Type	Lag
28	Prepare initial spec	FS	0d

ID	Task Name	Start	Finish	Baseline Start	Baseline Finish	Start Var.	Finish Var.
41	Testing Phase	9/22/94	5/15/95	9/22/94	5/15/95	0d	0d
42	Testing begins	9/22/94	9/22/94	9/22/94	9/22/94	0d	0d
43	Review spec	9/22/94	9/29/94	9/22/94	9/29/94	0d	0d

ID	Successor Name	Type	Lag
44	Create testing script	FS	0d

ID	Task Name	Start	Finish	Baseline Start	Baseline Finish	Start Var.	Finish Var.
64	Sales Phase	9/22/94	2/24/95	9/22/94	2/24/95	0d	0d
65	Sales phase begins	9/22/94	9/22/94	9/22/94	9/22/94	0d	0d
66	Review spec	9/22/94	9/29/94	9/22/94	9/29/94	0d	0d

ID	Successor Name	Type	Lag
67	Prepare market plan	FS	0d

ID	Task Name	Start	Finish	Baseline Start	Baseline Finish	Start Var.	Finish Var.
32	Distribute final spec	11/4/94	11/4/94	11/4/94	11/4/94	0d	0d

ID	Successor Name	Type	Lag
34	Code new features	FS	0d
38	Revise manual	FS	0d
44	Create testing script	FS	0d
57	Order parts	FS	0d
58	Plan production line changes	FS	0d
67	Prepare market plan	FS	0d

ID	Task Name	Start	Finish	Baseline Start	Baseline Finish	Start Var.	Finish Var.
34	Code new features	11/4/94	1/23/95	11/4/94	1/23/95	0d	0d
35	Code clock feature	11/4/94	11/22/94	11/4/94	11/22/94	0d	0d

ID	Successor Name	Type	Lag
36	Code notes feature	FS	0d
39	Fix bugs in new code	FS	1w
46	Test clock	FS	1w

ID	Task Name	Start	Finish	Baseline Start	Baseline Finish	Start Var.	Finish Var.
38	Revise manual	11/4/94	1/27/95	11/4/94	1/27/95	0d	0d
44	Create testing script	11/4/94	11/25/94	11/4/94	11/25/94	0d	0d
67	Prepare market plan	11/4/94	11/11/94	11/4/94	11/11/94	0d	0d

ID	Successor Name	Type	Lag
68	Distribute plan for review	FS	0d

ID	Task Name	Start	Finish	Baseline Start	Baseline Finish	Start Var.	Finish Var.
68	Distribute plan for review	11/11/94	11/11/94	11/11/94	11/11/94	0d	0d

ID	Successor Name	Type	Lag
69	Incorporate comments/revise plan	FS	1w

TO PRINT TASKS THAT SHOULD HAVE STARTED BUT HAVE NOT

1. Choose View Reports.
2. In the Reports dialog box, double-click Current Activities.
3. Double-click Should Have Started Tasks.
4. In the Start By box, type the data collection date.
5. To change the setup of the pages, choose Page Setup.
6. When you are ready to print, choose the Print button.
7. Choose OK.

If you have included notes with your tasks about the causes of late starts, the notes automatically are included in the report.

You can also print tasks that have started late by printing the Task Sheet with the Variance table applied and a filter that looks for tasks with a positive number in the Start Variance field. The filter criterion would be "Start Variance Greater 0." For more information about creating this filter, see Chapter 16, "Using Microsoft Project Tools."

Showing Tasks That Are Slipping

To see all tasks that are scheduled to finish late, print the Current Activities/Slipping Tasks report. This report shows the variance between current dates and baseline dates.

Slipping Tasks
New Calculator
Marcia Cryer

10/20/94

<table>
<tr><th>ID</th><th>Task Name</th><th>Start</th><th>Finish</th><th>Baseline Start</th><th>Baseline Finish</th><th>Start Var.</th><th>Finish Var.</th></tr>
<tr><td>26</td><td>Design Phase</td><td>9/7/94</td><td>5/3/95</td><td>9/7/94</td><td>4/11/95</td><td>0d</td><td>15.54d</td></tr>
<tr><td>41</td><td>Testing Phase</td><td>9/22/94</td><td>6/6/95</td><td>9/22/94</td><td>5/15/95</td><td>0d</td><td>15.6d</td></tr>
<tr><td>64</td><td>Sales Phase</td><td>9/22/94</td><td>3/6/95</td><td>9/22/94</td><td>2/24/95</td><td>0d</td><td>5.54d</td></tr>
<tr><td>31</td><td>Incorporate comments/revis</td><td>9/30/94</td><td>11/11/94</td><td>9/30/94</td><td>11/4/94</td><td>0d</td><td>5.54d</td></tr>
<tr><td></td><td colspan="7"><table><tr><th>ID</th><th>Successor Name</th><th>Type</th><th>Lag</th></tr><tr><td>32</td><td>Distribute final spec</td><td>FS</td><td>0d</td></tr></table></td></tr>
<tr><td>32</td><td>Distribute final spec</td><td>11/14/94</td><td>11/14/94</td><td>11/4/94</td><td>11/4/94</td><td>5.54d</td><td>5.54d</td></tr>
<tr><td></td><td colspan="7"><table><tr><th>ID</th><th>Successor Name</th><th>Type</th><th>Lag</th></tr><tr><td>34</td><td>Code new features</td><td>FS</td><td>0d</td></tr><tr><td>38</td><td>Revise manual</td><td>FS</td><td>0d</td></tr><tr><td>44</td><td>Create testing script</td><td>FS</td><td>0d</td></tr><tr><td>57</td><td>Order parts</td><td>FS</td><td>0d</td></tr><tr><td>58</td><td>Plan production line changes</td><td>FS</td><td>0d</td></tr><tr><td>67</td><td>Prepare market plan</td><td>FS</td><td>0d</td></tr></table></td></tr>
<tr><td>34</td><td>Code new features</td><td>11/14/94</td><td>2/14/95</td><td>11/4/94</td><td>1/23/95</td><td>5.54d</td><td>15.6d</td></tr>
<tr><td>35</td><td>Code clock feature</td><td>11/14/94</td><td>12/5/94</td><td>11/4/94</td><td>11/22/94</td><td>5.54d</td><td>8.84d</td></tr>
<tr><td></td><td colspan="7"><table><tr><th>ID</th><th>Successor Name</th><th>Type</th><th>Lag</th></tr><tr><td>36</td><td>Code notes feature</td><td>FS</td><td>0d</td></tr><tr><td>39</td><td>Fix bugs in new code</td><td>FS</td><td>1w</td></tr><tr><td>46</td><td>Test clock</td><td>FS</td><td>1w</td></tr></table></td></tr>
<tr><td>38</td><td>Revise manual</td><td>11/14/94</td><td>2/6/95</td><td>11/4/94</td><td>1/27/95</td><td>5.54d</td><td>5.54d</td></tr>
<tr><td>44</td><td>Create testing script</td><td>11/14/94</td><td>12/5/94</td><td>11/4/94</td><td>11/25/94</td><td>5.54d</td><td>5.54d</td></tr>
<tr><td>67</td><td>Prepare market plan</td><td>11/14/94</td><td>11/21/94</td><td>11/4/94</td><td>11/11/94</td><td>5.54d</td><td>5.54d</td></tr>
<tr><td></td><td colspan="7"><table><tr><th>ID</th><th>Successor Name</th><th>Type</th><th>Lag</th></tr><tr><td>68</td><td>Distribute plan for review</td><td>FS</td><td>0d</td></tr></table></td></tr>
<tr><td>68</td><td>Distribute plan for review</td><td>11/21/94</td><td>11/21/94</td><td>11/11/94</td><td>11/11/94</td><td>5.54d</td><td>5.54d</td></tr>
<tr><td></td><td colspan="7"><table><tr><th>ID</th><th>Successor Name</th><th>Type</th><th>Lag</th></tr><tr><td>69</td><td>Incorporate comments/revise plan</td><td>FS</td><td>1w</td></tr></table></td></tr>
<tr><td>69</td><td>Incorporate comments/revis</td><td>11/28/94</td><td>12/5/94</td><td>11/18/94</td><td>11/25/94</td><td>5.54d</td><td>5.54d</td></tr>
<tr><td></td><td colspan="7"><table><tr><th>ID</th><th>Successor Name</th><th>Type</th><th>Lag</th></tr><tr><td>70</td><td>Distribute final market plan</td><td>FS</td><td>0d</td></tr></table></td></tr>
<tr><td>70</td><td>Distribute final market plan</td><td>12/5/94</td><td>12/5/94</td><td>11/25/94</td><td>11/25/94</td><td>5.54d</td><td>5.54d</td></tr>
<tr><td></td><td colspan="7"><table><tr><th>ID</th><th>Successor Name</th><th>Type</th><th>Lag</th></tr><tr><td>71</td><td>Contact sales force</td><td>FS</td><td>0d</td></tr></table></td></tr>
<tr><td>71</td><td>Contact sales force</td><td>12/5/94</td><td>12/7/94</td><td>11/25/94</td><td>11/29/94</td><td>5.54d</td><td>5.54d</td></tr>
<tr><td></td><td colspan="7"><table><tr><th>ID</th><th>Successor Name</th><th>Type</th><th>Lag</th></tr><tr><td>72</td><td>Set up sales meetings</td><td>FS</td><td>0d</td></tr></table></td></tr>
<tr><td>72</td><td>Set up sales meetings</td><td>12/7/94</td><td>12/8/94</td><td>11/29/94</td><td>11/30/94</td><td>5.54d</td><td>5.54d</td></tr>
<tr><td></td><td colspan="7"><table><tr><th>ID</th><th>Successor Name</th><th>Type</th><th>Lag</th></tr><tr><td>73</td><td>Contact major dealers</td><td>FS</td><td>0d</td></tr></table></td></tr>
<tr><td>73</td><td>Contact major dealers</td><td>12/8/94</td><td>12/9/94</td><td>11/30/94</td><td>12/1/94</td><td>5.54d</td><td>5.54d</td></tr>
<tr><td></td><td colspan="7"><table><tr><th>ID</th><th>Successor Name</th><th>Type</th><th>Lag</th></tr><tr><td>74</td><td>Prepare marketing materials</td><td>FS</td><td>0d</td></tr></table></td></tr>
<tr><td>74</td><td>Prepare marketing materials</td><td>12/9/94</td><td>1/6/95</td><td>12/1/94</td><td>12/29/94</td><td>5.54d</td><td>5.54d</td></tr>
<tr><td></td><td colspan="7"><table><tr><th>ID</th><th>Successor Name</th><th>Type</th><th>Lag</th></tr><tr><td>75</td><td>Prepare packaging</td><td>FS</td><td>0d</td></tr></table></td></tr>
<tr><td>45</td><td>Test new features</td><td>12/12/94</td><td>3/7/95</td><td>11/29/94</td><td>2/13/95</td><td>8.84d</td><td>15.6d</td></tr>
<tr><td>36</td><td>Code notes feature</td><td>12/19/94</td><td>1/17/95</td><td>12/5/94</td><td>1/3/95</td><td>10d</td><td>10d</td></tr>
<tr><td></td><td colspan="7"><table><tr><th>ID</th><th>Successor Name</th><th>Type</th><th>Lag</th></tr><tr><td>37</td><td>Code alarm feature</td><td>FS</td><td>0d</td></tr><tr><td>47</td><td>Test notes</td><td>FS</td><td>1w</td></tr></table></td></tr>
<tr><td>75</td><td>Prepare packaging</td><td>1/6/95</td><td>1/20/95</td><td>12/29/94</td><td>1/12/95</td><td>5.54d</td><td>5.54d</td></tr>
<tr><td></td><td colspan="7"><table><tr><th>ID</th><th>Successor Name</th><th>Type</th><th>Lag</th></tr><tr><td>76</td><td>Prepare for major announcement</td><td>FS</td><td>0d</td></tr></table></td></tr>
<tr><td>37</td><td>Code alarm feature</td><td>1/17/95</td><td>2/14/95</td><td>1/3/95</td><td>1/23/95</td><td>10d</td><td>15.6d</td></tr>
<tr><td></td><td colspan="7"><table><tr><th>ID</th><th>Successor Name</th><th>Type</th><th>Lag</th></tr><tr><td>39</td><td>Fix bugs in new code</td><td>FS</td><td>0d</td></tr><tr><td>48</td><td>Test alarm</td><td>FS</td><td>1w</td></tr></table></td></tr>
<tr><td>76</td><td>Prepare for major announce</td><td>1/20/95</td><td>2/3/95</td><td>1/12/95</td><td>1/26/95</td><td>5.54d</td><td>5.54d</td></tr>
<tr><td></td><td colspan="7"><table><tr><th>ID</th><th>Successor Name</th><th>Type</th><th>Lag</th></tr><tr><td>77</td><td>Make announcement</td><td>FS</td><td>0d</td></tr></table></td></tr>
<tr><td>77</td><td>Make announcement</td><td>2/3/95</td><td>2/6/95</td><td>1/26/95</td><td>1/27/95</td><td>5.54d</td><td>5.54d</td></tr>
<tr><td></td><td colspan="7"><table><tr><th>ID</th><th>Successor Name</th><th>Type</th><th>Lag</th></tr><tr><td>78</td><td>Support sales force</td><td>FS</td><td>0d</td></tr></table></td></tr>
<tr><td>78</td><td>Support sales force</td><td>2/6/95</td><td>3/6/95</td><td>1/27/95</td><td>2/24/95</td><td>5.54d</td><td>5.54d</td></tr>
</table>

TO PRINT TASKS SCHEDULED TO FINISH LATE

1. Choose View Reports.
2. In the Reports dialog box, double-click Current Activities.
3. Double-click Slipping Tasks.
4. To change the setup of the pages, choose Page Setup.
5. When you are ready to print, choose the Print button.
6. Choose OK.

You can also print the Detail Gantt to display tasks that are slipping. Choose View More Views, select Detail Gantt in the Views box, and choose the Apply button. Then print the view just as you print any view.

To see a list of all tasks that actually finished late, display the Task Sheet and apply the Variance table and a filter that looks for tasks with a positive number in the Finish Variance field. For more information about creating this filter, see Chapter 16, "Using Microsoft Project Tools."

You can, of course, print the Task report instead of the Task Sheet, using the same tables and filters. One advantage of printing the Task report is that you can include notes in the report. If you have included notes with your tasks about the causes of late finishes, print the notes to share this information with those receiving the report.

Showing Tasks That Have a Different Work Amount

Print the Task Sheet or Task report with the Work table and the Work Overbudget filter applied to show the work for all tasks that are over budget.

New Calculator
Work Overbudget Report

ID	Task Name	Work	Baseline	Variance	Actual	Remaining	% W. Comp.
1	**Investigation Phase**	**1321.2h**	**1306.4h**	**14.8h**	**1321.2h**	**0h**	**100%**
20	Carry out focus panels	600h	480h	120h	600h	0h	100%
21	Carry out phone survey	66h	44h	22h	66h	0h	100%
26	**Design Phase**	**2049.57h**	**1899.73h**	**149.83h**	**254.15h**	**1795.42h**	**12%**
28	Prepare initial spec	189.13h	186h	3.13h	189.13h	0h	100%
31	Incorporate comments/re	128.87h	120h	8.87h	23.42h	105.45h	18%
34	**Code new features**	**943.97h**	**806.13h**	**137.83h**	**0h**	**943.97h**	**0%**
35	Code clock feature	240h	187.2h	52.8h	0h	240h	0%
37	Code alarm feature	160h	115.2h	44.8h	0h	160h	0%
41	**Testing Phase**	**1083.55h**	**1070.03h**	**13.52h**	**0h**	**1083.55h**	**0%**
45	**Test new features**	**402.55h**	**389.03h**	**13.52h**	**0h**	**402.55h**	**0%**

TO PRINT TASKS WITH WORK GREATER THAN SCHEDULED

1. Choose View More Views. In the Views box, select Task Sheet and choose the Apply button.
2. Choose View Table/Work.
3. From the Filter box on the Formatting toolbar, choose Work Overbudget.
4. To preview the view and then print, click the Print Preview button on the Standard toolbar or choose File Print Preview.
5. When you are ready to print, choose the Print button. To print without previewing, choose File Print.
6. Choose OK.

Again, you can print the Task report instead of the Task Sheet and include notes in the report about the causes of work variances.

Showing Tasks That Have a Different Cost Amount

Print the Costs/Overbudget Tasks report to show all tasks with costs higher than planned.

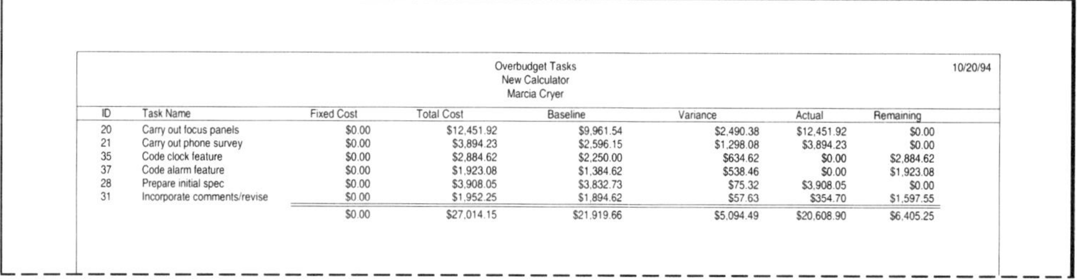

Overbudget Tasks
New Calculator
Marcia Cryer

10/20/94

ID	Task Name	Fixed Cost	Total Cost	Baseline	Variance	Actual	Remaining
20	Carry out focus panels	$0.00	$12,451.92	$9,961.54	$2,490.38	$12,451.92	$0.00
21	Carry out phone survey	$0.00	$3,894.23	$2,596.15	$1,298.08	$3,894.23	$0.00
35	Code clock feature	$0.00	$2,884.62	$2,250.00	$634.62	$0.00	$2,884.62
37	Code alarm feature	$0.00	$1,923.08	$1,384.62	$538.46	$0.00	$1,923.08
28	Prepare initial spec	$0.00	$3,908.05	$3,832.73	$75.32	$3,908.05	$0.00
31	Incorporate comments/revise	$0.00	$1,952.25	$1,894.62	$57.63	$354.70	$1,597.55
		$0.00	$27,014.15	$21,919.66	$5,094.49	$20,608.90	$6,405.25

TO PRINT TASKS WITH COST GREATER THAN SCHEDULED

1. Choose View Reports.
2. In the Reports dialog box, double-click Costs.
3. Double-click Overbudget Tasks.
4. To change the setup of the pages, choose Page Setup.
5. When you are ready to print, choose the Print button.
6. Choose OK.

If you include notes (choose Insert Task Notes) about the cause of the variance, you can change the Overbudget Tasks report to include these notes. Choose View Reports, double-click Custom, and then select Overbudget Tasks. Choose the Copy button. On the Details tab, select the Notes check box and choose OK. Now print the copy of the report instead of the original.

Showing Resources That Have a Different Work Amount

Print the Resource Sheet or Resource report with the Work table and the Work Overbudget filter applied to show the work for all resources that are over budget.

New Calculator
Resources Working More than Scheduled
as of 10/20/94

ID	Resource Name	% Comp.	Work	Overtime	Baseline	Variance	Actual	Remaining
1	**Marcia**	**67%**	**566.8h**	**0h**	**528.87h**	**37.93h**	**381.2h**	**185.6h**
8	Research Inc	100%	80h	0h	60h	20h	80h	0h
9	Dave	25%	397.68h	0h	357.45h	40.23h	99.85h	297.83h
11	Terri	20%	52.67h	0h	43.8h	8.87h	10.68h	41.98h
12	Design staff	2%	782.4h	0h	684.8h	97.6h	18h	764.4h
15	Marilynn	1%	486.55h	0h	473.03h	13.52h	4h	482.55h

TO PRINT RESOURCES WITH WORK GREATER THAN SCHEDULED

1. Choose View Resource Sheet.
2. Choose View Table/Work.
3. From the Filter box on the Formatting toolbar, select Work Overbudget.
4. To preview the view and then print, click the Print Preview button on the Standard toolbar or choose File Print Preview.
5. When you are ready to print, choose the Print button. To print without previewing, choose File Print.
6. Choose OK.

You can also print a Resource report using the same table and filter and include notes about the causes of work variances. To enter notes about resources, choose Insert Resource Notes.

Showing Resources That Have a Different Cost Amount

Print the Costs/Overbudget Resources report to show the cost for all over budget resources.

Overbudget Resources
New Calculator
Marcia Cryer

10/20/94

ID	Resource Name	Cost	Baseline Cost	Variance	Actual Cost	Remaining
1	Marcia	$13,701.92	$12,713.14	$988.78	$9,240.37	$4,461.55
8	Research Inc	$5,000.00	$3,750.00	$1,250.00	$5,000.00	$0.00
9	Dave	$11,471.64	$10,311.06	$1,160.58	$2,880.29	$8,591.35
11	Terri	$342.33	$284.70	$57.63	$69.44	$272.89
12	Design staff	$9,403.85	$8,230.77	$1,173.08	$216.35	$9,187.50
15	Marilynn	$7,602.34	$7,391.15	$211.19	$62.50	$7,539.84
		$47,522.08	$42,680.82	$4,841.26	$17,468.95	$30,053.13

TO PRINT RESOURCES WITH COST GREATER THAN SCHEDULED

1. Choose View Reports.
2. In the Reports dialog box, double-click Costs.
3. Double-click Overbudget Resources.
4. To change the setup of the pages, choose Page Setup.
5. When you are ready to print, choose the Print button.
6. Choose OK.

You can also print the Resource Sheet with the Cost table and the Cost Overbudget filter applied to show the cost for all over budget resources.

Or you could create a Resource report using the Cost table and Cost Overbudget filter and including the tasks to which each resource is assigned. This report would show you which assignments caused the resource to be over budget.

TO PRINT OVER BUDGET RESOURCES AND TASK COSTS

1. Choose View Reports.
2. In the Reports dialog box, double-click Custom.
3. In the Reports box, select Overbudget Resources and choose the Copy button.
4. In the Name box, type **Resources Overbudget and Tasks**.
5. On the Details tab, select the Cost check box under Task.
6. Choose OK.
7. To preview the report, choose the Preview button.
8. When you are ready to print, choose the Print button.
9. Choose OK.

Resources Overbudget and Tasks
New Calculator
Marcia Cryer

10/20/94

ID	Resource Name	Cost	Baseline Cost	Variance	Actual Cost	Remaining
1	Marcia	$13,701.92	$12,713.14	$988.78	$9,240.37	$4,461.55

ID	Task Name	Units	Cost	Baseline Cost	Act. Cost	Rem. Cost
3	Prepare initial product proposal	0.1	$250.00	$250.00	$250.00	$0.00
4	Research competition	1	$961.54	$961.54	$961.54	$0.00
6	Write proposal	1	$961.54	$961.54	$961.54	$0.00
8	Prepare questions	1	$961.54	$961.54	$961.54	$0.00
18	Prepare questionnaire	1	$576.92	$576.92	$576.92	$0.00
20	Carry out focus panels	1	$4,807.69	$3,846.15	$4,807.69	$0.00
21	Carry out phone survey	0.1	$144.23	$96.15	$144.23	$0.00
22	Prepare focus panel report	0.1	$96.15	$192.31	$96.15	$0.00
24	Present results	1	$96.15	$96.15	$96.15	$0.00
28	Prepare initial spec	0.1	$288.46	$213.14	$288.46	$0.00
30	Meet with reviewers	1	$96.15	$96.15	$96.15	$0.00
66	Review spec	1	$961.54	$961.54	$0.00	$961.54
67	Prepare market plan	1	$961.54	$961.54	$0.00	$961.54
69	Incorporate comments/revise plan	1	$961.54	$961.54	$0.00	$961.54
72	Set up sales meetings	0.2	$38.46	$38.46	$0.00	$38.46
74	Prepare marketing materials	0.2	$769.23	$769.23	$0.00	$769.23
75	Prepare packaging	0.2	$384.62	$384.62	$0.00	$384.62
76	Prepare for major announcement	0.2	$384.62	$384.62	$0.00	$384.62

ID	Resource Name	Cost	Baseline Cost	Variance	Actual Cost	Remaining
8	Research Inc	$5,000.00	$3,750.00	$1,250.00	$5,000.00	$0.00

ID	Task Name	Units	Cost	Baseline Cost	Act. Cost	Rem. Cost
21	Carry out phone survey	1	$3,750.00	$2,500.00	$3,750.00	$0.00
23	Prepare phone survey report	1	$1,250.00	$1,250.00	$1,250.00	$0.00

ID	Resource Name	Cost	Baseline Cost	Variance	Actual Cost	Remaining
9	Dave	$11,471.64	$10,311.06	$1,160.58	$2,880.29	$8,591.35

ID	Task Name	Units	Cost	Baseline Cost	Act. Cost	Rem. Cost
28	Prepare initial spec	1	$2,555.29	$2,555.29	$2,555.29	$0.00
30	Meet with reviewers	1	$115.38	$115.38	$115.38	$0.00
31	Incorporate comments/revise	1	$1,153.85	$1,153.85	$209.62	$944.23
34	Code new features	0.5	$7,647.12	$6,486.54	$0.00	$7,647.12

ID	Resource Name	Cost	Baseline Cost	Variance	Actual Cost	Remaining
11	Terri	$342.33	$284.70	$57.63	$69.44	$272.89

ID	Task Name	Units	Cost	Baseline Cost	Act. Cost	Rem. Cost
29	Distribute for review	1	$6.50	$6.50	$6.50	$0.00
30	Meet with reviewers	0.2	$5.20	$5.20	$5.20	$0.00
31	Incorporate comments/revise	0.2	$317.63	$260.00	$57.74	$259.89
32	Distribute final spec	1	$6.50	$6.50	$0.00	$6.50
52	Distribute testing report	1	$6.50	$6.50	$0.00	$6.50

ID	Resource Name	Cost	Baseline Cost	Variance	Actual Cost	Remaining
12	Design staff	$9,403.85	$8,230.77	$1,173.08	$216.35	$9,187.50

ID	Task Name	Units	Cost	Baseline Cost	Act. Cost	Rem. Cost
33	Fix old bugs	2	$961.54	$961.54	$216.35	$745.19
35	Code clock feature	2	$2,884.62	$2,250.00	$0.00	$2,884.62
36	Code notes feature	1	$2,057.69	$2,057.69	$0.00	$2,057.69
37	Code alarm feature	1	$1,923.08	$1,384.62	$0.00	$1,923.08
39	Fix bugs in new code	2	$1,576.92	$1,576.92	$0.00	$1,576.92

ID	Resource Name	Cost	Baseline Cost	Variance	Actual Cost	Remaining
15	Marilynn	$7,602.34	$7,391.15	$211.19	$62.50	$7,539.84

ID	Task Name	Units	Cost	Baseline Cost	Act. Cost	Rem. Cost
30	Meet with reviewers	1	$62.50	$62.50	$62.50	$0.00
43	Review spec	1	$625.00	$625.00	$0.00	$625.00
44	Create testing script	1	$1,875.00	$1,875.00	$0.00	$1,875.00
45	Test new features	0.25	$1,914.84	$1,703.65	$0.00	$1,914.84
49	Test all bug fixes	0.2	$1,250.00	$1,250.00	$0.00	$1,250.00
50	Final test pass	1	$1,250.00	$1,250.00	$0.00	$1,250.00
51	Write testing report	1	$625.00	$625.00	$0.00	$625.00

		Cost	Baseline Cost	Variance	Actual Cost	Remaining
		$47,522.08	$42,680.82	$4,841.26	$17,468.95	$30,053.13

Showing Resources That Are Overallocated

To print a list of all resources that are currently assigned more work than you have units available, print the Assignments/Overallocated Resources report.

TO PRINT OVERALLOCATED RESOURCES

1. Choose View Reports.
2. In the Reports dialog box, double-click Assignments.
3. Double-click Overallocated Resources.
4. To change the setup of the pages, choose Page Setup.
5. When you are ready to print, choose the Print button.
6. Choose OK.

Overallocated Resources
New Calculator
Marcia Cryer

10/20/94

ID	Resource Name	Work
16	Production engineers	328h

ID	Task Name	Units	Work	Delay	Start	Finish
56	Review spec	1	40h	0h	6/6/95	6/13/95
57	Order parts	1	160h	0h	6/6/95	7/4/95
58	Plan production line changes	2	60h	0h	6/6/95	6/12/95
59	Set up production test	1	60h	0h	6/12/95	6/21/95
61	Begin production	2	0h	0h	6/28/95	6/28/95
62	Pass production function to Si	1	8h	0h	6/28/95	6/29/95

ID	Resource Name	Work
21	Documentation dept.	720h

ID	Task Name	Units	Work	Delay	Start	Finish
38	Revise manual	1	480h	0h	11/14/94	2/6/95
74	Prepare marketing materials	1	160h	0h	12/9/94	1/6/95
75	Prepare packaging	1	80h	0h	1/6/95	1/20/95

ID	Resource Name	Work
18	Nancy	132h

ID	Task Name	Units	Work	Delay	Start	Finish
30	Meet with reviewers	1	4h	0h	9/29/94	9/30/94
56	Review spec	1	40h	0h	6/6/95	6/13/95
57	Order parts	0.5	80h	0h	6/6/95	7/4/95
62	Pass production function to Si	1	8h	0h	6/28/95	6/29/95

ID	Resource Name	Work
4	Cheryl	212h

ID	Task Name	Units	Work	Delay	Start	Finish
4	Research competition	0.25	10h	0h	6/3/94	6/9/94
5	Review customer comment cards	1	24h	0h	6/6/94	6/8/94
10	Contact hotels	1	8h	0h	6/16/94	6/16/94
12	Determine needed equipment	1	40h	0h	6/17/94	6/23/94
13	Contact local offices	1	4h	0h	6/24/94	6/24/94
15	Contact local reps for names	1	8h	0h	6/24/94	6/27/94
16	Contact suggested panel members	1	16h	0h	7/8/94	7/12/94
19	Get list of users to call	1	2h	0h	7/15/94	7/15/94
22	Prepare focus panel report	1	40h	0h	8/19/94	8/26/94
67	Prepare market plan	0.25	10h	0h	11/14/94	11/21/94
68	Distribute plan for review	1	1h	0h	11/21/94	11/21/94
69	Incorporate comments/revise plan	1	40h	0h	11/28/94	12/5/94
70	Distribute final market plan	1	1h	0h	12/5/94	12/5/94
72	Set up sales meetings	1	8h	0h	12/7/94	12/8/94

ID	Resource Name	Work
5	Janet	396h

ID	Task Name	Units	Work	Delay	Start	Finish
5	Review customer comment cards	1	24h	0h	6/6/94	6/8/94
6	Write proposal	1	40h	0h	6/9/94	6/15/94
8	Prepare questions	1	40h	0h	6/16/94	6/22/94
12	Determine needed equipment	0.1	4h	0h	6/17/94	6/23/94
15	Contact local reps for names	0.1	8h	0h	6/24/94	7/8/94
20	Carry out focus panels	1	200h	0h	7/15/94	8/19/94
22	Prepare focus panel report	1	40h	0h	8/19/94	8/26/94
66	Review spec	1	40h	0h	9/22/94	9/29/94

ID	Resource Name	Work
1	Marcia	566.8h

ID	Task Name	Units	Work	Delay	Start	Finish
3	Prepare initial product proposal	0.1	7.2h	0h	6/3/94	6/15/94
4	Research competition	1	40h	0h	6/3/94	6/9/94
6	Write proposal	1	40h	0h	6/9/94	6/15/94
8	Prepare questions	1	40h	0h	6/16/94	6/22/94
18	Prepare questionnaire	1	24h	0h	7/12/94	7/15/94
20	Carry out focus panels	1	200h	0h	7/15/94	8/19/94
21	Carry out phone survey	0.1	6h	0h	8/12/94	8/24/94
22	Prepare focus panel report	0.1	4h	0h	8/19/94	8/26/94

Earned Value Report

To generate an earned value report, print the Costs/Earned Value report. For more information about earned value, see pages 271–273 in Chapter 12.

TO PRINT EARNED VALUE

1. Choose View Reports.
2. In the Reports dialog box, double-click Costs.
3. Double-click Earned Value.
4. To change the setup of the pages, choose Page Setup.
5. When you are ready to print, choose the Print button.
6. Choose OK.

Earned Value
New Calculator
Marcia Cryer

10/20/94

Task Name	BCWS	BCWP	ACWP	SV	CV	BAC	FAC	Variance
Investigation begins	$0.00	$0.00	$0.00	$0.00	$0.00	$0.00	$0.00	$0.00
Research competition	$2,269.23	$2,269.23	$2,269.23	$0.00	$0.00	$2,269.23	$2,269.23	$0.00
Review customer comment cards	$1,101.93	$1,101.93	$1,101.93	$0.00	$0.00	$1,101.93	$1,101.93	$0.00
Write proposal	$1,875.00	$1,875.00	$1,875.00	$0.00	$0.00	$1,875.00	$1,875.00	$0.00
Prepare questions	$1,875.00	$1,875.00	$1,875.00	$0.00	$0.00	$1,875.00	$1,875.00	$0.00
Contact hotels	$61.54	$61.54	$61.54	$0.00	$0.00	$61.54	$61.54	$0.00
Determine needed equipment	$399.04	$399.04	$399.04	$0.00	$0.00	$399.04	$399.04	$0.00
Contact local offices	$30.77	$30.77	$30.77	$0.00	$0.00	$30.77	$30.77	$0.00
Contact local reps for names	$244.23	$244.23	$244.23	$0.00	$0.00	$244.23	$244.23	$0.00
Contact suggested panel membe	$123.08	$123.08	$123.08	$0.00	$0.00	$123.08	$123.08	$0.00
Prepare questionnaire	$946.15	$946.15	$946.15	$0.00	$0.00	$946.15	$946.15	$0.00
Get list of users to call	$15.38	$15.38	$15.38	$0.00	$0.00	$15.38	$15.38	$0.00
Carry out focus panels	$9,961.54	$9,961.54	$12,451.92	$0.00	$2,490.38	$9,961.54	$12,451.92	$2,490.38
Carry out phone survey	$2,596.15	$2,596.15	$3,894.23	$0.00	$1,298.08	$2,596.15	$3,894.23	$1,298.08
Prepare focus panel report	$3,865.38	$3,865.38	$1,932.68	$0.00	($1,932.70)	$3,865.38	$1,932.68	($1,932.70)
Prepare phone survey report	$1,250.00	$1,250.00	$1,250.00	$0.00	$0.00	$1,250.00	$1,250.00	$0.00
Present results	$96.15	$96.15	$96.15	$0.00	$0.00	$96.15	$96.15	$0.00
Investigation phase complete	$0.00	$0.00	$0.00	$0.00	$0.00	$0.00	$0.00	$0.00
Design begins	$0.00	$0.00	$0.00	$0.00	$0.00	$0.00	$0.00	$0.00
Prepare initial spec	$3,832.73	$3,832.73	$3,908.05	$0.00	$75.32	$3,832.73	$3,908.05	$75.32
Distribute for review	$6.50	$6.50	$6.50	$0.00	$0.00	$6.50	$6.50	$0.00
Meet with reviewers	$389.81	$389.81	$389.81	$0.00	$0.00	$389.81	$389.81	$0.00
Incorporate comments/revise	$1,060.98	$341.03	$354.70	($719.95)	$13.67	$1,894.62	$1,952.25	$57.63
Distribute final spec	$0.00	$0.00	$0.00	$0.00	$0.00	$6.50	$6.50	$0.00
Fix old bugs	$0.00	$243.26	$237.98	$243.26	($5.28)	$1,057.69	$1,057.69	$0.00
Code clock feature	$0.00	$0.00	$0.00	$0.00	$0.00	$2,250.00	$2,884.62	$634.62
Code notes feature	$0.00	$0.00	$0.00	$0.00	$0.00	$2,057.69	$2,057.69	$0.00
Code alarm feature	$0.00	$0.00	$0.00	$0.00	$0.00	$1,384.62	$1,923.08	$538.46
Revise manual	$0.00	$0.00	$0.00	$0.00	$0.00	$14,400.00	$14,400.00	$0.00
Fix bugs in new code	$0.00	$0.00	$0.00	$0.00	$0.00	$2,365.38	$2,365.38	$0.00
Design phase complete	$0.00	$0.00	$0.00	$0.00	$0.00	$0.00	$0.00	$0.00
Testing begins	$0.00	$0.00	$0.00	$0.00	$0.00	$0.00	$0.00	$0.00
Review spec	$1,105.77	$0.00	$0.00	($1,105.77)	$0.00	$1,105.77	$1,105.77	$0.00
Create testing script	$0.00	$0.00	$0.00	$0.00	$0.00	$3,317.31	$3,317.31	$0.00
Test clock	$0.00	$0.00	$0.00	$0.00	$0.00	$1,442.31	$1,442.31	$0.00
Test notes	$0.00	$0.00	$0.00	$0.00	$0.00	$961.54	$961.54	$0.00
Test alarm	$0.00	$0.00	$0.00	$0.00	$0.00	$961.54	$961.54	$0.00
Test all bug fixes	$0.00	$0.00	$0.00	$0.00	$0.00	$2,211.54	$2,211.54	$0.00
Final test pass	$0.00	$0.00	$0.00	$0.00	$0.00	$2,211.54	$2,211.54	$0.00
Write testing report	$0.00	$0.00	$0.00	$0.00	$0.00	$625.00	$625.00	$0.00
Distribute testing report	$0.00	$0.00	$0.00	$0.00	$0.00	$6.50	$6.50	$0.00
Testing phase complete	$0.00	$0.00	$0.00	$0.00	$0.00	$0.00	$0.00	$0.00
Manufacturing begins	$0.00	$0.00	$0.00	$0.00	$0.00	$0.00	$0.00	$0.00
Review spec	$0.00	$0.00	$0.00	$0.00	$0.00	$1,730.77	$1,730.77	$0.00
Order parts	$0.00	$0.00	$0.00	$0.00	$0.00	$3,750.00	$3,750.00	$0.00
Plan production line changes	$0.00	$0.00	$0.00	$0.00	$0.00	$937.50	$937.50	$0.00
Set up production test	$0.00	$0.00	$0.00	$0.00	$0.00	$1,658.65	$1,658.65	$0.00
Test production	$0.00	$0.00	$0.00	$0.00	$0.00	$3,242.31	$3,242.31	$0.00
Begin production	$0.00	$0.00	$0.00	$0.00	$0.00	$0.00	$0.00	$0.00
Pass production function to Si	$0.00	$0.00	$0.00	$0.00	$0.00	$250.00	$250.00	$0.00
Manufacturing phase complete	$0.00	$0.00	$0.00	$0.00	$0.00	$0.00	$0.00	$0.00
Sales phase begins	$0.00	$0.00	$0.00	$0.00	$0.00	$0.00	$0.00	$0.00
Review spec	$4,951.92	$0.00	$0.00	($4,951.92)	$0.00	$4,951.92	$4,951.92	$0.00
Prepare market plan	$0.00	$0.00	$0.00	$0.00	$0.00	$2,269.23	$2,269.23	$0.00
Distribute plan for review	$0.00	$0.00	$0.00	$0.00	$0.00	$7.69	$7.69	$0.00
Incorporate comments/revise plai	$0.00	$0.00	$0.00	$0.00	$0.00	$1,269.23	$1,269.23	$0.00
Distribute final market plan	$0.00	$0.00	$0.00	$0.00	$0.00	$7.69	$7.69	$0.00
Contact sales force	$0.00	$0.00	$0.00	$0.00	$0.00	$609.23	$609.23	$0.00
Set up sales meetings	$0.00	$0.00	$0.00	$0.00	$0.00	$469.23	$469.23	$0.00
Contact major dealers	$0.00	$0.00	$0.00	$0.00	$0.00	$361.53	$361.53	$0.00
Prepare marketing materials	$0.00	$0.00	$0.00	$0.00	$0.00	$10,492.31	$10,492.31	$0.00
Prepare packaging	$0.00	$0.00	$0.00	$0.00	$0.00	$5,246.16	$5,246.16	$0.00
Prepare for major announcement	$0.00	$0.00	$0.00	$0.00	$0.00	$2,846.16	$2,846.16	$0.00
Make announcement	$0.00	$0.00	$0.00	$0.00	$0.00	$230.77	$230.77	$0.00
Support sales force	$0.00	$0.00	$0.00	$0.00	$0.00	$7,384.62	$7,384.62	$0.00
Sales phase complete	$0.00	$0.00	$0.00	$0.00	$0.00	$0.00	$0.00	$0.00
Project complete	$0.00	$0.00	$0.00	$0.00	$0.00	$0.00	$0.00	$0.00
	$38,058.28	$31,523.90	$33,463.37	($6,534.38)	$1,939.47	$116,914.16	$120,075.95	$3,161.79

SHOWING POSSIBLE SOLUTIONS

When you find a problem and then use "what-if" analysis to come up with proposed solutions, share these solutions with management, a client, or the project team. Print the same views and reports for the proposals so the recipients can compare the schedule now with how it will be if you change it. For example, if you move tasks to ease resource overallocation, change task dependencies to shorten the critical path, and add resources to a group of tasks to accelerate them, you will want to show how the schedule, work, and cost will change for the project.

To show	Print
New schedule	Gantt Chart; Tracking Gantt
New project finish date, cost, and work	Overview/Project report
Change in costs for individual tasks	Costs/Budget report
Change in costs for individual resources	Costs/Overbudget Resources report
Change in earned value	Costs/Earned Value report

You print these reports as described earlier in this chapter, and then highlight those sections you want the recipient to concentrate on. One way to highlight the information is to select the tasks or resources, and then change the font, style, and color of the text, as described earlier in this chapter. The tasks or resources you select don't have to be sequential. For example, to show how adding resources to certain tasks will change the schedule, select these tasks and make the text bold. Point out the change in the critical path on the Gantt Chart and the finish date in the Overview/Project report.

Printing Direction Reports

Just as you printed work schedules for the work supervisors before the project started, continue to print these reports as needed throughout the project. It is especially important to print these reports any time you make a change to the schedule that will affect the way a task is carried out or the timing for a task.

To show	Print
Tasks to be performed during the next period	Current Activities/Tasks Starting Soon report
Resources used during the next period	Assignments/Who Does What When report

Print these reports as often as necessary. For more information about printing these reports, see Chapter 10, "Communicating the Plan."

PART V

MULTIPLE PROJECTS, SHARING INFORMATION, AND USING THE TOOLS

Part V describes several features included in Microsoft Project that will make your project management job easier. While these tools are not directly related to the project management process, they are related to the everyday mechanics of getting your job done.

- Chapter 14 shows how to use subprojects and work with multiple projects, a very real occurrence in today's busy world.
- Chapter 15 shows how to share information between Microsoft Project and Microsoft Excel, Lotus 1-2-3, or Microsoft Word. Using Microsoft Excel, you can create graphs of your cost information, and share resource information that might already be in a Microsoft Excel file. Using Word, you can write a report, and then place selected information from Microsoft Project directly into the report. Chapter 15 also shows how you can share task information and get status reports from resources if you have Microsoft Mail.
- Chapter 16 gives explicit procedures for using, customizing, and creating Microsoft Project tables, filters, views, menus, toolbars, and forms.

14

Managing Multiple Projects

For many project managers, the biggest challenge in their day is juggling several projects, all starting and finishing at different times, and using the same set of resources. Microsoft Project can help you keep track of all your projects and avoid resource conflicts, making sure resources are not needed at the same time on different projects.

You can work with multiple projects in many ways. For example:

- Use a template containing all tasks normally done in a project. If many of your projects are similar—for example, developing marketing brochures, or designing buildings—create a project template to use as the basis for future projects. Each time you get a new project, just open the template, and then customize it to match the current project.
- Create projects for groups of tasks you do over and over; use these projects as subprojects within other projects. For example, if one part of every new product is creating documentation, you might have a project containing all the steps to produce the manual, from the manual design document to printing. You would use this project as a subproject in each new project for a product that required a manual.
- Link tasks between projects such that the dates in one project can control the dates in another.
- Store all resource information in one project, and then link all other projects to the project containing the resources.
- Open the projects of interest and view resource use for all projects.
- Combine all projects in one window to see how the schedules overlap, check resource use, or create one report summarizing all projects.

USING A PROJECT TEMPLATE

A project template is a good shortcut for quickly creating projects having the same basic tasks. First, create the project template—it contains the basic tasks. Save the project as a template file. Then, each time you have a new project similar to the template you created, open the template file. When you save the template, you are automatically prompted for a new filename, so you don't have to worry about changing the template accidentally. Change the copy of the template to match your current project.

For example, if you manage a documentation group, your projects often may be preparing manuals for your products. All manuals require the same basic phases: Plan, Write, Edit, Format, QA, Print; within these phases, the tasks are similar for each manual. What may change from project to project is the duration of each task, depending on the size of the piece you are preparing and the resources involved. Each time you are faced with a new project, start with the template and then customize the tasks to match the specifics of the new project.

TO CREATE A TEMPLATE

1. Create a project containing all the basic tasks.
2. Click the Save button on the Standard toolbar or choose File Save As.
3. If PlanningWizards are on, the Save A Baseline? dialog box will appear. Select Save Without a Baseline, and choose OK.
4. In the File Name box, type a name for the template.
5. In the Save File As Type box, select Template. The extension MPT is automatically added to your filename so you can identify the file as a template.
6. Choose OK.

TO USE A TEMPLATE

1. Click the Open button on the Standard toolbar or choose File Open.
2. To limit the list of files to templates, select Templates (*.mpt) in the List Files Of Type box.
3. Select the file you want to open, and choose OK.
4. Change the details in the project.

5. Click the Save button on the Standard toolbar or choose File Save.
6. If PlanningWizards are on, the Save A Baseline? dialog box will appear. Select Save Without a Baseline and choose OK.
7. In the File Name box, type the name for the project and choose OK. The file is saved as a project file, not a template.

USING SUBPROJECTS

A subproject is a group of tasks that has its own project file, but is represented as a single task in another project, called a master project.

Use subprojects:

- To keep the most detailed tasks in a project separate from the master project. This makes it easy for each subproject manager to keep track of their tasks, and allows the manager of the whole project to see a project summary without dealing with the detail tasks included in the subprojects.
- When you have similar sets of tasks to perform in many projects. Rather than re-entering the same set of tasks each time they occur in a project, you can specify sets of tasks as subprojects. From then on, you enter and manage the subproject as one task.
- To conserve memory in your computer. If you don't open subprojects, the amount of computer memory needed to calculate project information is reduced.

Work with the master project when you are interested in the broadest view; work with individual subprojects when you want to concentrate on more detailed tasks.

Subprojects have the following advantages:

- You avoid entering the same set of tasks over and over, for each new project.
- If some step changes in the subproject, you change it once—in the subproject—instead of over and over in each project that contains the subproject.
- If you are working with very large projects, using subprojects can help you conserve memory. You can leave the subprojects closed except when you need to work with the tasks in the subproject.

You may think of your projects modularly, with each module being a separate subproject. These subprojects are then combined to make your master project. You can use a subproject over and over in one project or in many projects. It is similar to outlining in that it is another way to organize your tasks into a hierarchy—instead of subtasks, however, the detail tasks are in a subproject. Use subprojects when you want to use a set of tasks over and over; use an outline when you don't.

Each subproject is summarized by a subproject task instead of a summary task. A subproject task summarizes the tasks in the subproject, just as a summary task does. The duration for a subproject task is the number of working days in the subproject, from the earliest start date to the latest finish date, using the project calendar. The percent complete, cost, and work are the totals for the tasks in the subproject.

For example, if you are scheduling all new products for the next two years, you could have a subproject for a new business calculator, one for a new high-end scientific calculator, and another for a calculator upgrade. These subprojects would be included in a master project, and each subproject could contain additional subprojects for the planning, design, manual, and so on.

Master Project: Two-year Product Plan

- New business calculator (subproject)
- New scientific calculator (subproject)
- Calculator upgrade (subproject)
- and so on

The individual projects would each contain the following tasks:

- Planning (subproject)
- Design (subproject)
- Manual (subproject)
- and so on

If the subproject is always the same—same resources, same duration for each task within the subproject, and so on—you can use the same subproject name over and over, as needed, in any master projects. If you use this method, however, you can't track resource usage across projects, nor can you track progress. A better way is to rename the file each time you use it so you can track resource usage across projects and track progress. Choose File Save As to duplicate the file and save it with a new name, and then change any details within the subproject as appropriate. For example, you may have a subproject called Manual that includes all the basic steps for creating a manual; each time you use the subproject, rename it and change the duration for tasks in the subproject depending on the manual size and style.

CREATING A SUBPROJECT

What makes a project a subproject is not how you create it, but how you later use it. When you create a project that you plan to use as a subproject, follow the same steps as creating any project.

TO CREATE A SUBPROJECT

1. Choose File New.
2. In the Summary Info dialog box, enter information about the subproject.

   The Summary Info dialog box appears only if the Prompt For Summary Info For New Projects check box is selected on the General tab in the Tools Options dialog box.
3. Type the tasks in this project.
4. Enter durations and dependencies.
5. Assign resources. If you want to use the resources from another project, choose Tools Multiple Projects/Share Resources, and select the project containing the resources you want to share.
6. To save the project, choose File Save As.
7. If PlanningWizards are on, the Save A Baseline? dialog box will appear. Select Save Without a Baseline and choose OK.
8. Type a name for the file and choose OK.

   Don't save the file as a template—to use the file as a subproject, it must be a project file, not a template file.

If you want to track resource usage across projects, do use resource pools with subprojects because you can manage your resources better. Since a subproject is used in another project, use either the resources from the master project, or from the project in which all the resource information is stored. For more information, see "Sharing Resources Among Projects" later in this chapter.

You can also change a group of existing tasks into a subproject.

TO CREATE A SUBPROJECT FROM EXISTING TASKS

1. Open the project containing the tasks you want in a subproject.
2. Select the rows containing the tasks. To select a row, either click the left-most column (ID in most tables included with Microsoft Project) or move to the row and press Shift+Spacebar.
3. If you want to remove the tasks from the project, click the Cut button on the Standard toolbar or choose Edit Cut (Task); to copy them, click the Copy button on the toolbar or choose Edit Copy (Task).

   If the Cut or Copy command says Cell instead of Task, repeat step 2 to select rows instead of cells.
4. To create a new project, choose File New.
5. In the Summary Info dialog box, enter information about the subproject.

   The Summary Info dialog box appears only if the Prompt For Summary Info For New Projects check box is selected on the General tab in the Tools Options dialog box.
6. To insert the tasks into the new project, click the Paste button on the Standard toolbar or choose Edit Paste.
7. To save the project, choose File Save As.
8. If PlanningWizards are on, the Save A Baseline? dialog box will appear. Select Save Without a Baseline and choose OK.

USING A SUBPROJECT

To use a subproject, enter one task in the master project to represent the subproject. For example, one of the tasks in the new calculator project is "Revise manual." This task can be a subproject task that represents the Manual subproject.

The new calculator project contains the following tasks:

36. Code alarm feature
37. Revise manual
38. Fix bugs in new code
and so on

The subproject task, "Revise manual," represents all the tasks in the Manual subproject, which contains the following tasks:

1. Write manual design document
2. Distribute design document for review
3. Revise design document
4. Write manual

and so on

To enter a subproject task, use the Advanced tab in the Task Information dialog box.

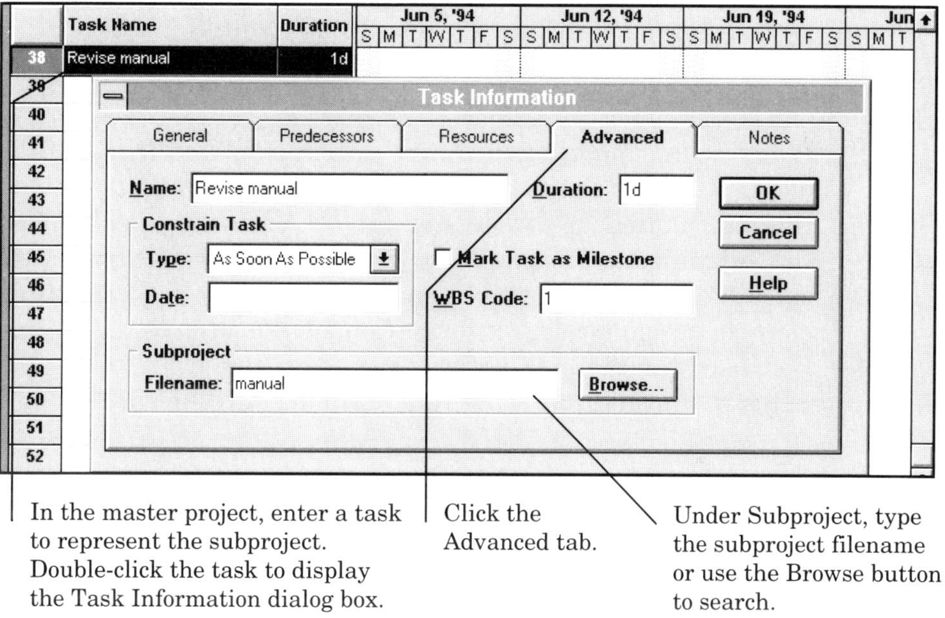

After you choose OK, Microsoft Project changes the duration for the task to match that of the subproject. The duration for a subproject task is the number of working days in the subproject, from the earliest start date to the latest finish date, using the project calendar. Microsoft Project calculates this value; you can't type a duration for a subproject task.

	Task Name	Duration	Jun 5, '94	Jun 12, '94	Jun 19, '94	Jun
			S M T W T F S	S M T W T F S	S M T W T F S	S M T
38	Revise manual	12w				
39	Fix bugs in new code	3.28w				
40	Design phase complete	0d				

Microsoft Project calculates the duration of the subproject and enters it as the duration for the subproject task.

When you type the name of the subproject file, you don't have to include the path or, in Microsoft Project for Windows, the MPP extension unless the file uses a different extension. Microsoft Project searches for a file by that name and replaces what you typed with the full path to the subproject file. If it can't find the subproject, Microsoft Project displays a dialog box similar to the File Open dialog box in which you specify the drive and directory or folder containing the file.

While you can use a template file to create your subproject, you can't use a template file as the subproject name you enter in the Task Information dialog box.

When you assign a resource to a subproject task, the resource is assigned for the full duration of the subproject. If the tasks in the subproject change, causing the duration of the subproject task to change, the work assigned to the resource changes to match.

If you open a project containing subprojects and the subprojects are not open, Microsoft Project displays a message asking if you want to update the information in the master project with the latest information from the subprojects. Choose Yes if you want Microsoft Project to get the latest information from the subproject file; choose No if you don't want to change the subproject information in the project file you are opening. Because you can use subprojects over and over, the start and finish dates in the subproject file reflect the most recent use of the subproject.

Reporting Project Information Using Subprojects

Just as with an outline, you can use subprojects to control the amount of detail included in a report. By placing the detail tasks in subprojects instead of in the master project, you can create reports with the level of detail you want. For example, if you just print the master project, you'll see all the tasks that represent the subprojects, but none of the detail tasks in the subprojects. For those who need the details, create reports by opening the subprojects and printing them. For more information about viewing information for both the master project and subprojects, see "Viewing Multiple Projects" later in this chapter.

LINKING TASKS BETWEEN PROJECTS

When you use a subproject, the dates in the master project always control the dates in the subproject. The subproject task in the master project is linked to the tasks around it, and the start date for the subproject task is used by the subproject as its start date.

You may have occasions, however, when you want the dates in a project to control the dates in a master project. Or you may want to link a task in one project with a task in another. To do this, you use the Edit Copy command to copy information from a task in one project and then the Edit Paste Special command to paste it into a task in the other project.

Using Edit Paste Special with the Paste Link option selected instead of Edit Paste creates a link between the information you copied and the information you pasted. Any time the original information changes, the information you pasted changes too. Suppose, for example, you copy a finish date from a task in one project and paste it as the start date for a task in another project. Now the original task slips, causing the finish date to change. The start date in the other project also changes.

When you paste a date into the Start field, Microsoft Project responds as if you had typed the date, and assigns a Start No Earlier Than constraint to the task. As this may cause problems later in your schedule, you may want to copy and paste the entire task instead of just the date.

To check for these types of links between projects or within a project, choose Edit Links. All relevant links are listed in the dialog box.

SHARING RESOURCES AMONG PROJECTS

If your resources work on more than one project at the same time, you can use one shared resource pool—all resources in one project—to manage resource use. In Microsoft Project, you can open all the projects using the resource pool, and then use the Resource Usage view and Resource Graph to see how resources are allocated. Or use the fields at the bottom of the Resource Form to check the tasks in all open projects to which a resource is assigned. For more information about checking resource usage, see "Viewing Multiple Projects" next in this chapter.

To share resources, open the project containing the resources and then open the project that will use them. You tell Microsoft Project that you want to share a resource pool by using the Tools Multiple Projects/Share Resources command.

Choose Tools Multiple Projects and then choose Share Resources.

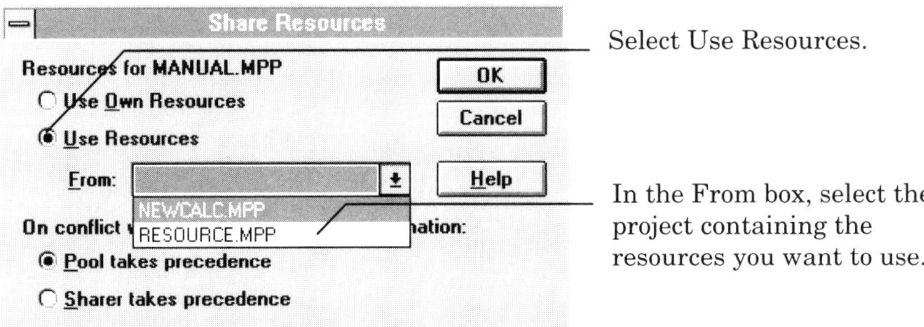

All resources in the resource pool are now available for you to use in your project. If you add resources to the project containing the resources or to any project sharing them, these new resources are added to the resource pool and are available to all projects sharing this resource pool.

If you later want to disconnect, or unlink, a project from a resource pool—for example, if you are finished with the project—use the Tools Multiple Projects/Share Resources command and select the Use Own Resources option. The resource information for the project you disconnect is removed from the resource pool and placed in the project you disconnected.

You can create a "resource" project containing resources and no tasks. This is a good approach if you have one set of resources and many projects. When you update resource information, such as changing the rate of pay, the cost and schedule automatically change as appropriate in each project. When you finish a project, you can unlink it from the resource pool and delete the project file, leaving the resource pool intact.

If you already have resources in your projects and you decide a separate resource pool would be better, you can create a resource project from existing projects. All resource information in each project is moved to the resource pool.

TO CREATE A RESOURCE PROJECT FROM EXISTING PROJECTS

1. Choose File New and enter the summary information.
2. Choose File Save As; don't save the baseline in the PlanningWizard.

3. Type a name for the resource project and choose OK.
4. For each project that is to use the resource pool, open the project, and then choose Tools Multiple Projects/Share Resources.
5. Select the Use Resources option.
6. In the From box, select the name of the resource project you just created, and choose OK.

You can also create a resource project from scratch. Just create a new project and enter all the resources, either by typing them or importing a list from another application. For example, if you have a list of resources in another application, such as Microsoft Excel or Lotus 1-2-3, you can import this information into an existing project or a new resource project. For more information about importing information from another application, see Chapter 15, “Sharing Information.”

TO CREATE A RESOURCE PROJECT

1. Choose File New and enter the summary information.
2. Choose View Resource Sheet.
3. Enter all resource information.
4. Choose File Save As; don’t save the baseline in the PlanningWizard.

Use the Tools Multiple Projects/Share Resources command to attach all existing projects to this resource project.

VIEWING MULTIPLE PROJECTS

If you are managing multiple projects, there are probably times when you want one big report summarizing them all. Or, if your projects share a resource pool, you want to look at resource usage across all projects.

There are several ways you can open and view multiple project files.

- To open multiple projects and combine them in a new project, use the Tools Multiple Projects/Consolidate Projects command. You select all projects you want to open; they are combined into one new project, which is linked to the original projects. You can save this new combined project as a project file. For more information, see “Consolidating Projects” next in this chapter.

- To temporarily combine projects that are already open into one window, use the Window New Window command. You can select which open projects you want in the combined project as well as the view for the combined project. For more information, see "Combining Open Projects" later in this chapter.
- If you want several related files opened each time you use Microsoft Project, save the files together as a workspace file. The actual files are not saved in the workspace; the workspace file contains the names of the open files instead. For more information, see "Saving A Workspace" later in this chapter.

CONSOLIDATING PROJECTS

Consolidated projects are useful when you want to combine projects into a new project and save them in their consolidated state. Since each project is linked to its separate file, any changes you make to a task in a project, either in its separate version or in the consolidated version, appear in the other file as well. To open multiple projects and combine them in a new project, use the Tools Multiple Projects/Consolidate Projects command.

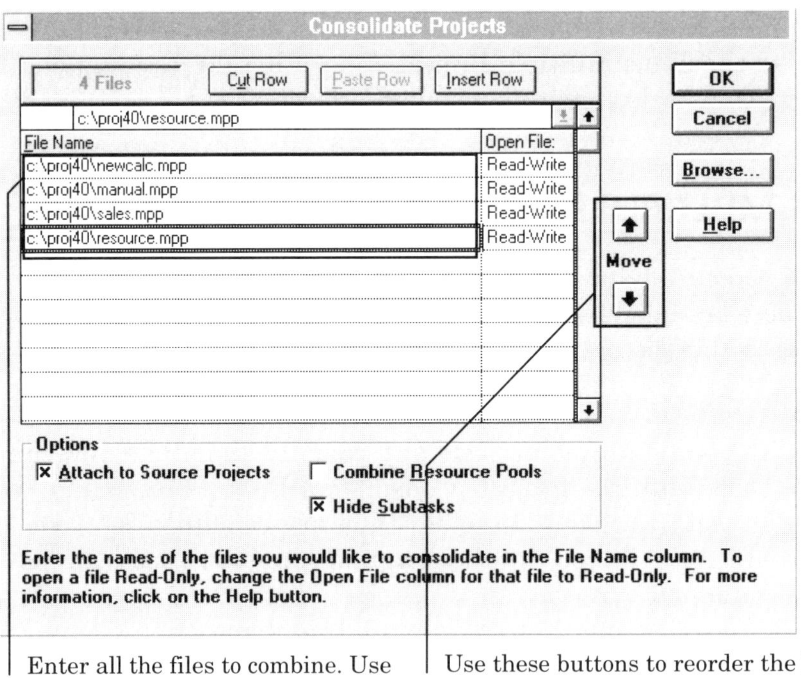

Enter all the files to combine. Use the Browse button to select files.

Use these buttons to reorder the list so projects appear in the order you want.

After you've selected all the files and checked the order, choose OK. All projects are opened and displayed in a new project. If the Hide Subtasks check box was selected in the Consolidate Projects dialog box, the new project looks as follows, with a project summary task summarizing each individual project.

Task Name	Duration
NEWCALC.MPP	450.93d
MANUAL.MPP	60d
SALES.MPP	248.8d

Summary task for each project opened. Double-click a summary task to expand the outline or click the Show All Tasks button on the Formatting toolbar to display all tasks in each project.

With all the files open, you can check the tasks or resource usage across all projects. For example, you can check all tasks to which a resource is assigned in all open projects. Or create one report showing information for all tasks in all projects.

When you look at resource usage in a combined project, the resource views show information for all projects. For example, use the Resource Form over the Task Form to see all the tasks to which a resource is assigned, plus details about each task.

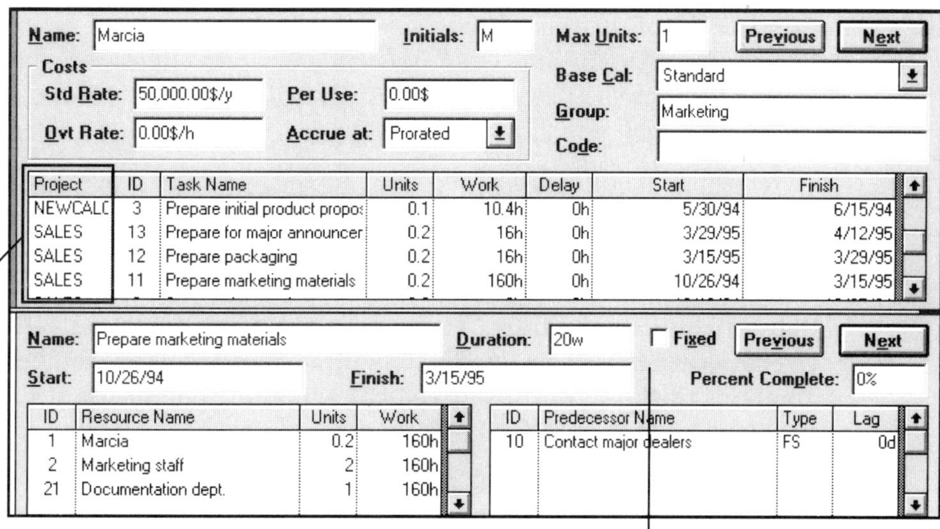

Resource Form shows all tasks to which resource is assigned in all open projects. The project name is listed so you can identify each task.

Task Form shows details about each task to which resource is assigned.

By checking task details, including the other resources assigned to the task, you can decide whether and how to change resource assignments.

Use the Resource Form over the Resource Graph to see details about a resource's assignments, plus a graph of the resource's allocation.

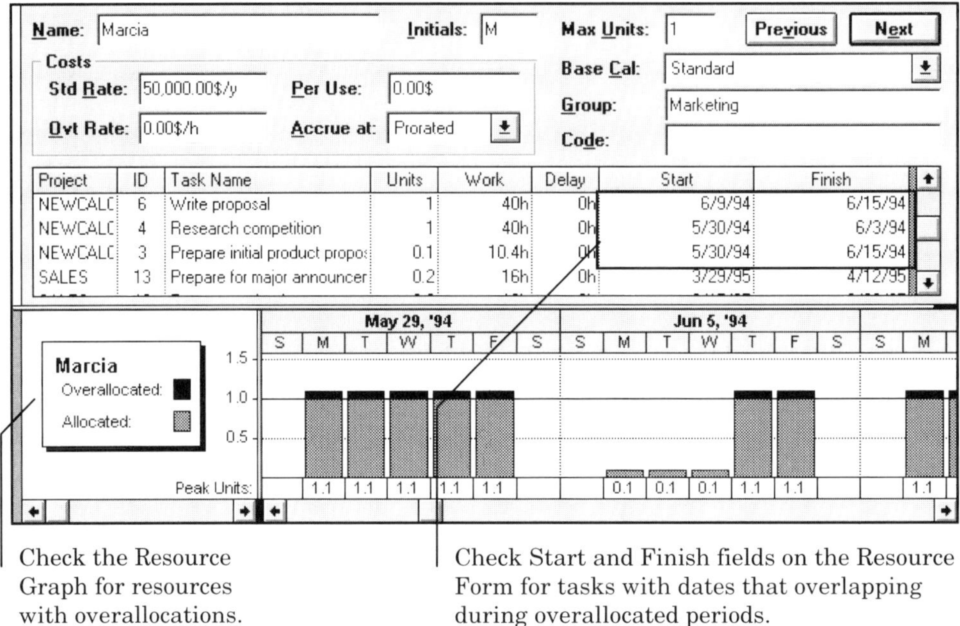

Check the Resource Graph for resources with overallocations.

Check Start and Finish fields on the Resource Form for tasks with dates that overlapping during overallocated periods.

Another helpful combination view is the Resource Usage view over the Resource Form. In the Resource Usage view, check for overallocations for all resources (choose Format Details/Percent Allocation). In the Resource Form, you can see which tasks are causing the overallocations.

Two other useful views are the Resource Allocation view (Resource Usage view over the Delay Gantt) and the Resource Graph over the Gantt Chart. Use these combination views to locate overallocated resources in the top view, and then check the tasks causing the overallocation on the Gantt Chart. To help locate overallocations, click the Goto Overallocation button on the Resource Management toolbar (use View Toolbars to show the Resource Management toolbar) or press Alt+F5 in Windows or Option+F5 on the Macintosh.

The following illustration shows the Resource Allocation view. To display the Resource Allocation view, choose View More Views, select Resource Allocation in the Views box, and then choose the Apply button.

Or if the Resource Management toolbar is displayed, click the Resource Allocation View button on the toolbar.

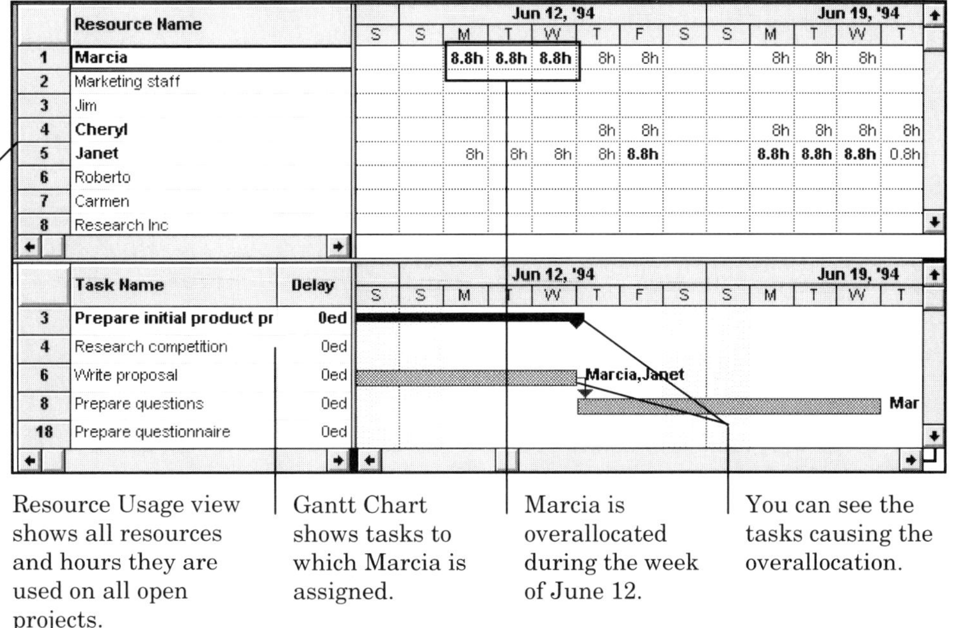

Resource Usage view shows all resources and hours they are used on all open projects.

Gantt Chart shows tasks to which Marcia is assigned.

Marcia is overallocated during the week of June 12.

You can see the tasks causing the overallocation.

COMBINING OPEN PROJECTS

When you have a set of projects open but don't want a consolidated project, you can combine them in one window using the Window New Window command. For example, you may want to temporarily combine projects to create a summary report of all the projects you are managing.

Choose Window New Window.

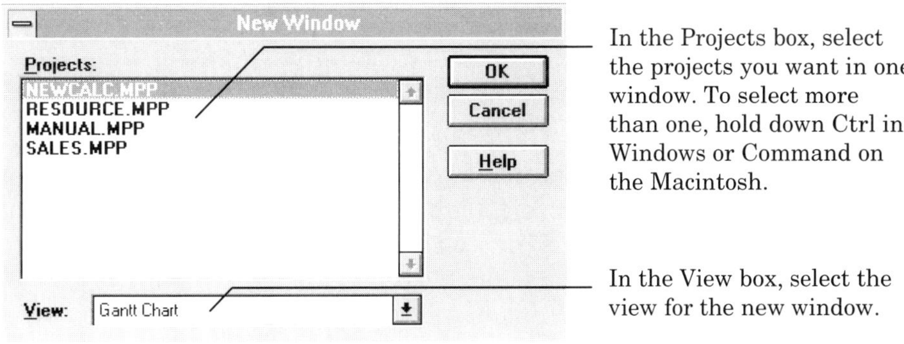

In the Projects box, select the projects you want in one window. To select more than one, hold down Ctrl in Windows or Command on the Macintosh.

In the View box, select the view for the new window.

The new window will contain all the tasks from the projects you select. Each project will retain its task ID numbers, so task ID numbers will be repeated. Initially the tasks will be grouped by project. By collapsing the outlines and using Rollup and Flag fields, you can create a summary report with one bar, or a few bars, for each project, with all important milestones rolled up to the summary bars. You can also create a summary bar for the entire project by selecting the Project Summary Task check box on the Views tab in the Tools Options dialog box.

You can organize the information in any way that suits the type of report you need to generate. For example, you can sort the tasks by department to show all the tasks in all the projects assigned to each department. You may want to add the Project field to the Task Sheet so that the project for each task can be identified after you sort the projects.

Saving a Workspace

When you often work with multiple projects and especially subprojects and a resource project, you may want these projects open so the information in the subprojects and resource pool is available. If there is a certain set of projects you often use together, such as a master project, its subprojects, and the resource project, you can open these projects, and then save them as a workspace. The workspace file contains only a list of the open files; the project information remains in the project files. When you open a workspace file, all files that were open when you saved a workspace file are opened at once.

To save a workspace file, choose File Save Workspace. In Microsoft Project for Windows, workspace files are saved with the extension MPW so you can identify them when you are opening files. Use the File Open command to open a workspace.

Hiding a Window Sometimes you might want a project open, such as the project containing the resources, such that its information is available to the project on which you are working, but you don't want to actually work with the project. You can hide a project by choosing the Window Hide command. The information in the project is available but you don't see the project on the screen. If you later want to use the project, you choose Window Unhide to show the project again.

15

Sharing Information

Departments in an organization don't operate in a vacuum, although many often act as if they do. The information used or created by one department would often be useful to another if it was easy to share the information. With Microsoft Project, it is easy.

There are many kinds of information you can share, such as:

- Views, reports, tables, filters, forms, toolbars, menu bars, and macros—all the tools in Microsoft Project—so everyone in the company has the same set at their fingertips.
- Calendars so everyone has the latest information about working days and hours for the company.
- Resource pool file containing all resources available for projects, plus their individual calendars and other resource information. For more information about creating a resource pool, see Chapter 14, "Managing Multiple Projects."

You can also exchange information with other applications to do things that Microsoft Project doesn't do. For example, with a spreadsheet application, such as Microsoft Excel or Lotus 1-2-3, you can:

- Move resource cost information from the spreadsheet application to Microsoft Project to calculate task and project costs, and then move task costs back to the spreadsheet application to draw cost curves. Since many companies already have a database containing resources or cost information, you can move information between the spreadsheet or database application and Microsoft Project instead of entering the information again.

- If you are using the PERT method of determining durations, as discussed in Chapter 5, “Estimating Time to Perform Tasks,” use a spreadsheet application to calculate the duration estimates, and then move these estimates to Microsoft Project.

Microsoft Project can read files created by other software applications, including Microsoft Excel, FoxPro, Lotus 1-2-3, dBase III and IV, CSV files, and other text files, so that if you have information in another application, you will not need to retype it in Microsoft Project.

Microsoft Project can also dynamically exchange information with other applications that have this feature, such as Microsoft Excel and Microsoft Word. So instead of opening files from other applications, you can use the Edit Copy and Edit Paste Special commands to copy information, such as costs from Microsoft Excel, and then paste it into Microsoft Project. If the data changes in Microsoft Excel, it will also change in Microsoft Project.

Other ways you can use project information in another application include:

- Illustrating a report or other document about the project using a word processing application, such as Microsoft Word. You can insert project information, such as a Gantt Chart or Task Sheet, in a document.
- Attaching a Microsoft Excel chart to your Gantt Chart. Start Microsoft Excel and Microsoft Project, and arrange the windows so that you can see both applications. Drag a Microsoft Excel chart onto your Gantt Chart.
- Including a copy of the project Gantt Chart in a mail message or Microsoft Word document. While viewing the Gantt Chart, click the Copy Picture button on the Standard toolbar. Paste the picture in the mail message or document.

Not only can you send a copy of your project in an electronic mail message, you can use the Microsoft Project workgroup features to share information about the project with the resources on the project, and to update the progress on the tasks. To use these features, you must have Microsoft Mail or some other MAPI-compliant electronic mail program.

Using workgroup features, you can:

- Route projects to reviewers from Microsoft Project using the File Add Routing Slip command.

- Send a message to the people responsible for a set of tasks. Select the tasks you want. Choose Tools Workgroup/Send Schedule Note.
- Send task requests to resources. Choose Tools Workgroup/Send Task Request.
- Request task updates from resources. Choose Tools Workgroup/Request Task Update.
- If you have Microsoft Schedule+, you can set reminders for tasks in your project. Choose Tools Workgroup/Set Reminder or click the Set Reminder button on the Workgroup toolbar.

SHARING TOOLS

In Microsoft Project, each project file contain all the tools—the views, tables, filters, reports, forms, macros, toolbars and calendars—in the project. When you create a new project, the project is based on GLOBAL.MPT in Windows, or Global Template on the Macintosh, so all views and other tools in the global template are included in the new project. You can move any tool from any open project file or template into any other open project file using the Organizer.

You can create other template files, containing whatever set of tools you want. Because you can add or delete commands on the menus, as well as change the menu bar, you can create a totally customized version of Microsoft Project. For example, you can create a company template, with a customized menu bar, toolbar, custom reports and views, and calendar, to be used by everyone in the company for all projects, so that all reports will look alike, no matter who creates them, and working hours will be consistent for all projects. For information about customizing Microsoft Project, see Chapter 16, "Using Microsoft Project Tools."

To use any tool created in another project or in another template, including a view, report, macro, form, table, filter, calendar, toolbar, or menu bar, use the Organizer to copy it from the file that contains it to the open project.

You can get to the Organizer in several ways, including: View More Views; View Table/More Tables; View Toolbars; Tools Filtered For/More Filters; Tools Customize/Menu Bars; and Tools Customize/Forms. Each of these dialog boxes contains an Organizer button; the Organizer dialog box includes a tab for each area, to help you locate the items you want to copy.

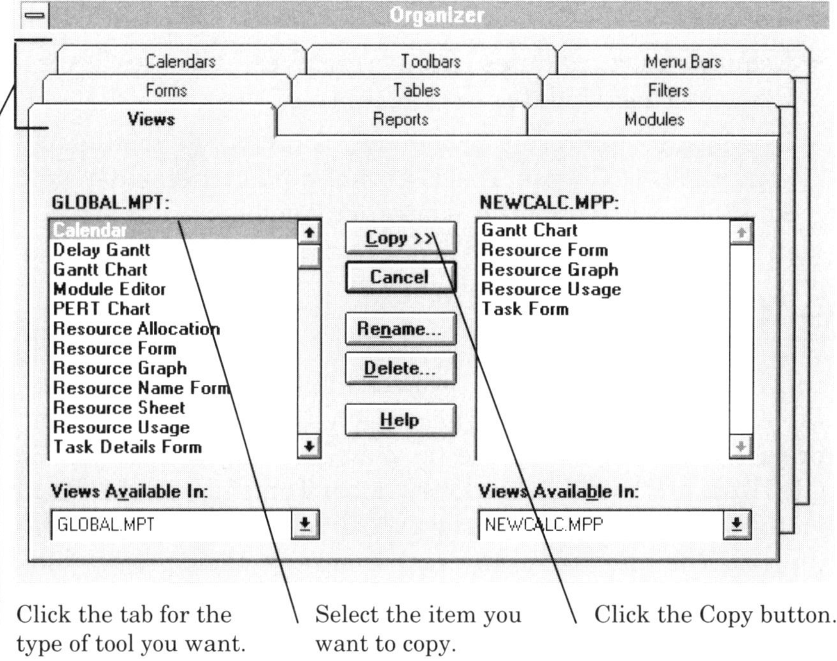

Click the tab for the type of tool you want.

Select the item you want to copy.

Click the Copy button.

The selected tool will be copied from one file to the other. In the boxes at the bottom of the dialog box (Views Available In on the Views tab), you can change the files from or to which you are coping, so you can move any tool from or to any file.

To create a company-wide template, change the global template to contain exactly what you want, and share the file with everyone in your company. When anyone opens an existing file or creates a new file, all items in their system will be consistent.

EXCHANGING INFORMATION WITH A SPREADSHEET OR DATABASE APPLICATION

How you exchange data between applications depends partly on the version of the applications you are using. You can exchange information by opening a file of another type, or you can use Edit Copy and Edit Paste if the other application supports them. If you are using applications that include Object Linking and Embedding (OLE) version 2.0, you can drag-and-drop information between the two applications. For example, if you are using Microsoft Project version 4.0 and Microsoft Excel version 5.0, you can drag information from one to the other.

Regardless of how you exchange information, there are two basic steps:

- Create a table, if one doesn't already exist, containing the fields you want to import (bring into Microsoft Project) or export (take out of Microsoft Project).
- Choose File Save or File Copy to export the information; choose File Open, Edit Paste, or Edit Paste Special to import the information. Or use drag-and-drop, if this is available to you.

When you are exporting information, the table tells Microsoft Project which fields to export. For example, if you want to export task names and durations, you'd create a table with the Name and Duration fields. When you are importing information, the table tells Microsoft Project where to put the information. For example, if you are importing resource names and pay rates from Microsoft Excel, you'd create a table containing those two fields (resource Name and Standard Rate).

If there is a column of information in another application that you want to import into Microsoft Project, but Microsoft Project doesn't have a matching field—such as manager or skill level—you can use a custom field. Custom fields in Microsoft Project can be used for anything you want. There are 10 custom text fields for tasks, 5 custom number fields for tasks, and 5 custom text fields for resources.

After you have the table, there are two ways to import information and two ways to export information.

TO IMPORT INFORMATION

- Use the File Open command and select the file created in the other application. Microsoft Project will detect that this file is not in Microsoft Project format, and ask for the name of the table you want to use. The table tells Microsoft Project what the information is—resource names and costs, for example—so it is entered into the project in the correct fields.
- Use the Edit Paste or Edit Paste Special command to import information cut or copied from another application. Before choosing Paste or Paste Special, you must first apply the table to the view as Microsoft Project does not prompt you for a table as it does when you

use File Open. Information is pasted into the table starting from the left-most column. If you are using an application with OLE version 2.0, you can also drag information between the two applications.

When do you use Paste; when do you use Paste Special? Use Edit Paste when you want the copied information to stay as it is right now. Even if the original information changes, the copied information stays as you pasted it. Use Edit Paste Special and select the Paste Link option when you want to create a link between the information you copied and the pasted information. If the original information changes, the pasted information also changes. To review the links in and out of a project, use the Edit Links command.

TO EXPORT INFORMATION

- Use the File Save As command to save the information in a format the other application recognizes. Microsoft Project will ask for the name of the table you want to use. The fields in the table tell Microsoft Project which information to copy to the file.
- Use the Edit Copy command to export information to another application that uses the Clipboard. Before choosing Edit Copy, you must apply the table to the view, and select the information you want to copy. If you are using an application with OLE version 2.0, you can also drag information between the two applications.

The following two examples can be used as examples for exchanging information with any application, not just Microsoft Excel. Follow the steps in "Importing Resources and Costs from Microsoft Excel" to import from any spreadsheet or database application; follow the steps in "Calculating Durations in Microsoft Excel" for exporting information from Microsoft Project to another application and for importing information back into Microsoft Project. The only difference when using an application other than Microsoft Excel is that, when exporting from Microsoft Project, you select a different file format—one that matches the application to which you are exporting the information. In either case, if you are importing or exporting different fields, be sure the fields in the table match the information you want to import or export.

IMPORTING RESOURCES AND COSTS FROM MICROSOFT EXCEL

Both ways of importing are included in this section. First, the example explains how to import using the File Open command. Importing using Edit Copy in Microsoft Excel and Edit Paste in Microsoft Project follows.

Importing Using the File Open Command

Suppose you have the following information in Microsoft Excel and you want to import into Microsoft Project the information in the first three columns: the resource name, salary, and overtime rate.

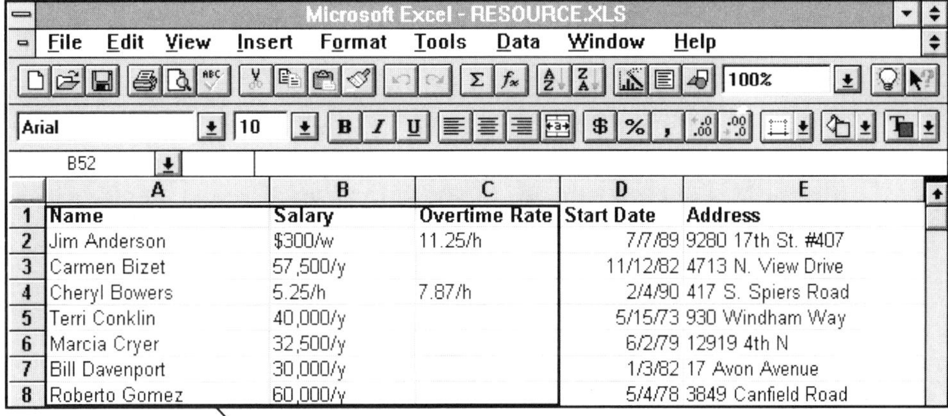

	A	B	C	D	E
1	Name	Salary	Overtime Rate	Start Date	Address
2	Jim Anderson	$300/w	11.25/h	7/7/89	9280 17th St. #407
3	Carmen Bizet	57,500/y		11/12/82	4713 N. View Drive
4	Cheryl Bowers	5.25/h	7.87/h	2/4/90	417 S. Spiers Road
5	Terri Conklin	40,000/y		5/15/73	930 Windham Way
6	Marcia Cryer	32,500/y		6/2/79	12919 4th N
7	Bill Davenport	30,000/y		1/3/82	17 Avon Avenue
8	Roberto Gomez	60,000/y		5/4/78	3849 Canfield Road

You want to import the information in columns A, B, and C.

In Microsoft Excel: Save the worksheet as you normally do.

In Microsoft Project: Create a resource table with the three columns—Name, Standard Rate, and Overtime Rate—if one doesn't already exist. While these fields are included in the Entry table for resources, the order is not the same as for the information you are importing, so you must create a separate table. Choose View Table/More Tables, select the Resource option, and then choose the New button.

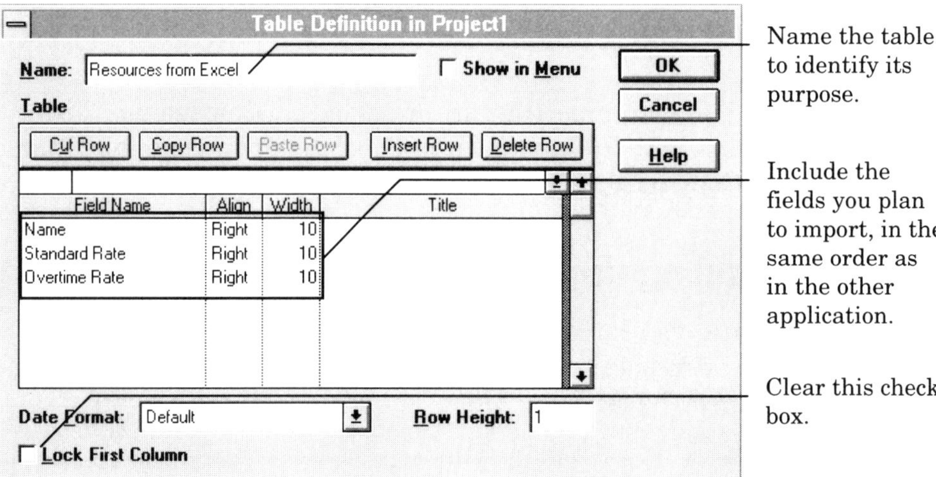

In the Align and Width columns, use the default values Microsoft Project enters after you select the field names. All information will be imported regardless of the settings. For more information about creating a table, see Chapter 16, "Using Microsoft Project Tools."

When applied to the Resource Sheet, the table looks like this:

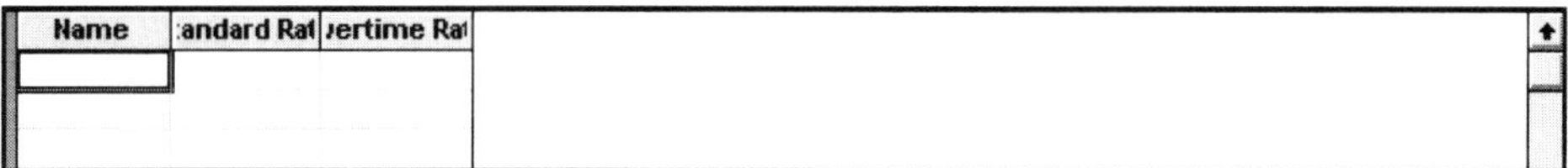

To import the information from Microsoft Excel, choose File Open in Microsoft Project.

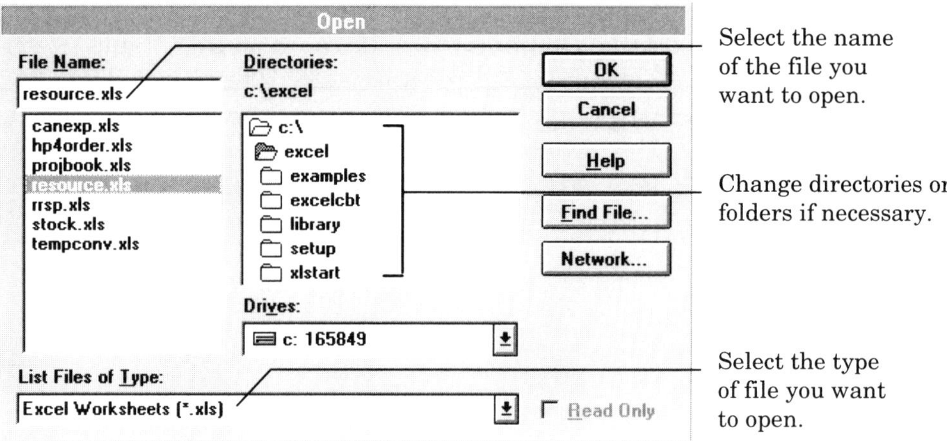

Microsoft Project will detect that this is not a Microsoft Project file, and display the Import dialog box, where you specify whether tasks or resources are being imported, and the table to use to import the information.

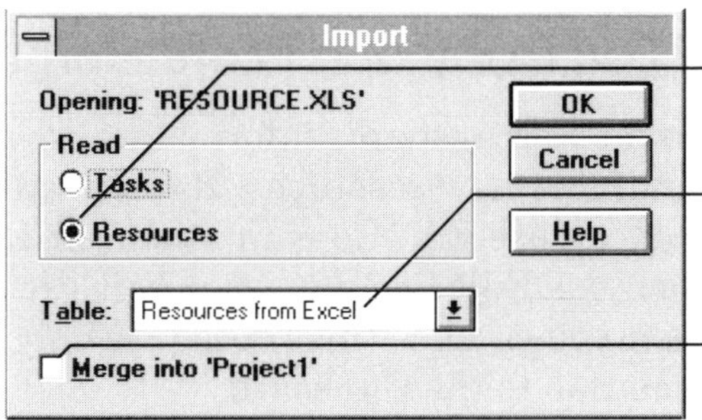

Select the Resources option to indicate you are importing resources.

Select the table containing the columns for the information you are importing from Microsoft Excel.

The Merge Into check box controls where the information is placed—in the current project or in a new file.

When you import information, it can either replace information already in the project or be placed in a new project. This is controlled with the Merge Into check box. If you don't want to replace the existing information, clear this check box; the information is placed in its own file and temporarily named the same as the file you imported. You can then copy the new information into the current project, as appropriate.

If the Merge Into check box is selected, the information replaces existing information in the current project. For example, if you already have a list of resources in your project, and you import information that includes a list of resources, these resources will replace the existing resources. This may be what you want—for example, if this is the full list of resources in your company, and you periodically get a file from personnel containing an updated list of all resources and salaries.

Import Errors If you put titles on your columns in Microsoft Excel, you may get error messages when you import the information into Microsoft Project. For example, the Salary and Overtime Rate titles in cells B1 and C1 in the illustration on page 323 will cause error messages because Microsoft Project is expecting a number in the Rate fields, not text. The error message identifies the location (row and column) of the field causing the error and tells you what's wrong (for example, "Rate not valid"). The messages warn you of problems, but don't prevent Microsoft Project from importing the information in the file. If you want to keep the titles in Microsoft Excel because the database is used for other purposes and needs the headings, just ignore the messages when you import the information. In Microsoft Project, delete the row containing the headings.

You will also get error messages if the columns do not match the kind of information you are importing, such as if you select the wrong table. In this case, you will get lots of error messages, one for every field you import; you'll probably want to stop importing and check your table.

Importing Using the Edit Copy and Paste Commands

Suppose you already have all your resource information in your project, but you want to add a handful of new resources. Rather than importing all the resources again, you can use Edit Copy in Microsoft Excel to copy the new resources, and then use Edit Paste in Microsoft Project to paste the information. Remember, you can use this procedure only if the other application can save information to the Clipboard.

In Microsoft Project: You must have a table that matches the columns and order of the information you are importing. Apply the table containing the appropriate columns to the Task Sheet, if you are importing tasks, or the Resource Sheet if you are importing resources. For example, to copy resource names, salaries, and overtime rates, apply the Resources From Excel table, used in the previous example, to the Resource Sheet.

In Microsoft Excel: Select the information you want to copy, and then choose Edit Copy.

In Microsoft Project: Select the field after the last resource. Choose Edit Paste. The information will be pasted into Microsoft Project, starting at the left-most field.

Using Drag-and-Drop instead of Edit Copy and Paste If you are using applications with OLE version 2.0, such as Microsoft Excel version 5.0 and Microsoft Project version 4.0, you can copy and paste using drag-and-drop. Open both applications and position them so you can see them both. After selecting the information in Microsoft Excel that you want copy, drag it to the appropriate position in Microsoft Project.

Calculating Durations in Microsoft Excel

This section includes an example using the File Save As and File Open commands, and then a description of how to do the same thing using Edit Copy and Edit Paste.

Exchanging Data Using the File Save As and File Open Commands

If you are using the PERT method to determine task duration, you can use Microsoft Excel to calculate the durations for you.

In Microsoft Project: Export your list of tasks to Microsoft Excel, as follows.

Create a table containing fields for the task name and, if you want to use the same table when you import the information back into Microsoft Excel, duration.

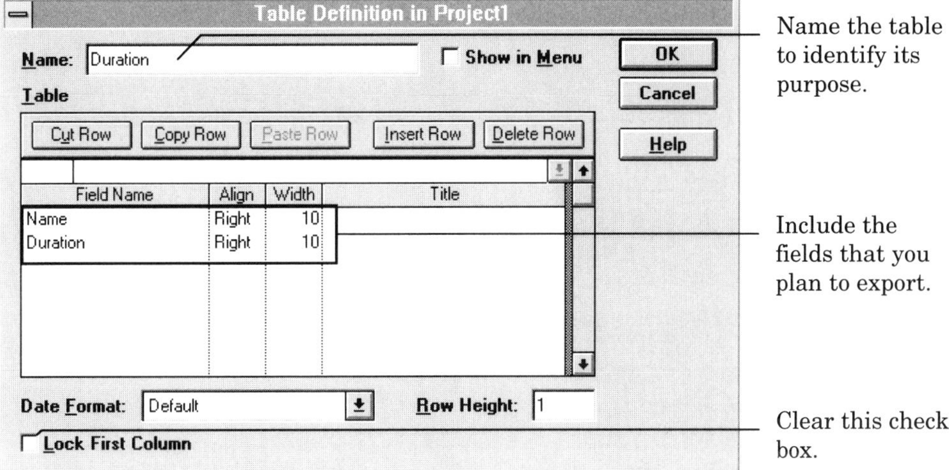

For more information about creating a table, see Chapter 16, "Using Microsoft Project Tools."

Choose File Save As. The following illustration shows the File Save As dialog box in Microsoft Project for Windows. In the Macintosh version, you select a file format in the Formats box.

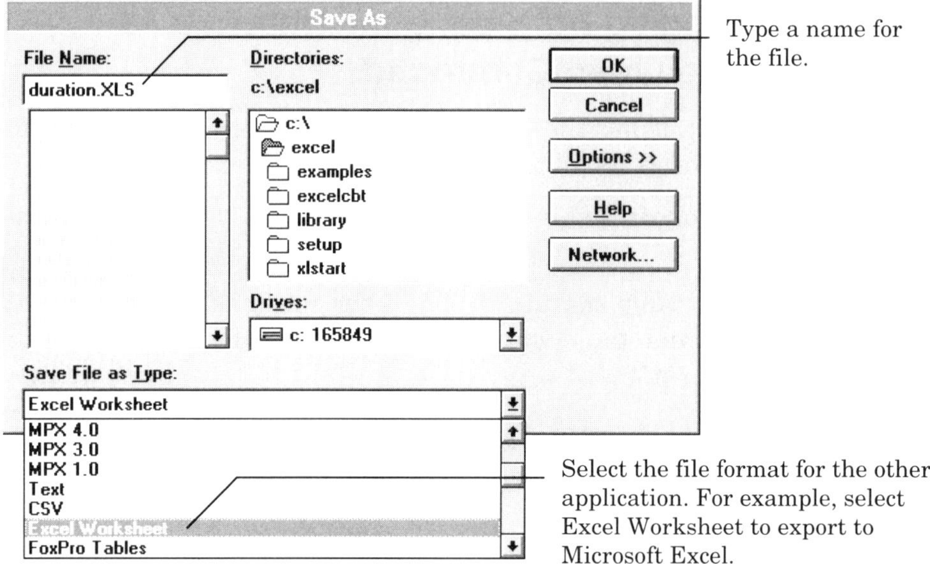

After you choose OK, Microsoft Project displays the Export dialog box where you specify which information to save in the file and the table to use.

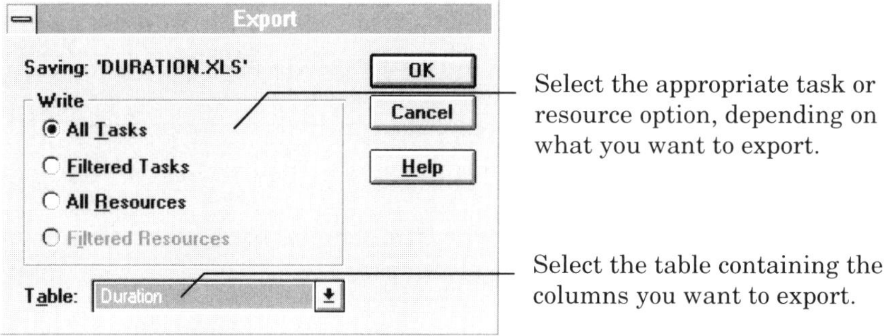

You could also filter the list of tasks or resources before you export so only those that meet the requirements in the filter are exported. For example, if you want to use the PERT method to determine durations for the tasks performed by the Design group only, and you have a column in which you enter the department, you could filter the tasks such that only those tasks assigned to Design will appear in the view. Then in the Export dialog box, select the Filtered Tasks option. The partial list of tasks is exported instead of the complete list.

If you are using outlining, you might want to hide the summary tasks before saving the file because summary task durations are always calculated by Microsoft Project. To hide summary tasks, choose Tools Options. On the View tab, clear the Summary Tasks check box and choose OK. In the Export dialog box, select the Filtered Tasks option.

In Microsoft Excel: To open the file you just created, choose File Open. Double-click the file you want to open.

The file contains all tasks you exported and their initial durations.

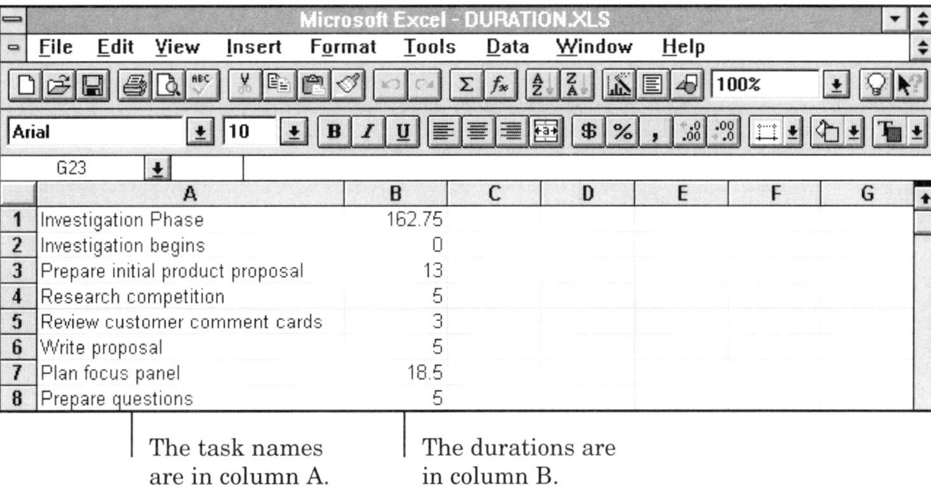

The task names are in column A.

The durations are in column B.

Add columns for the three duration estimates and standard deviation.

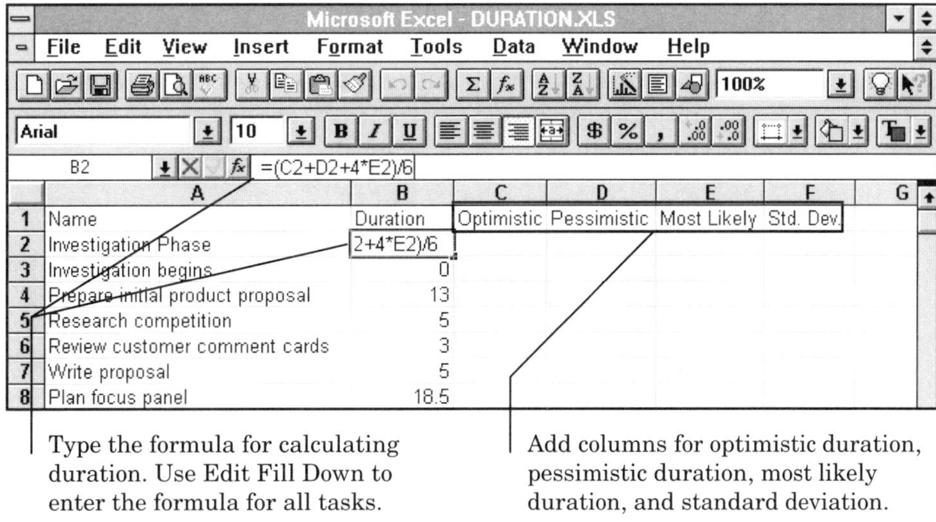

Type the formula for calculating duration. Use Edit Fill Down to enter the formula for all tasks.

Add columns for optimistic duration, pessimistic duration, most likely duration, and standard deviation.

To have Microsoft Excel calculate the value in the Duration column for each task, you need to enter the equation. The duration is the weighted average of the three duration estimates. Type **=(c2+d2+4*e2)/6** in B2. Select B2 and the cells below B2 and then choose Edit Fill Down.

To calculate the standard deviation, type **=stdev(c2:e2)** in cell F2. Select F2 and the cells below F2 and then choose Edit Fill Down.

Gather your duration estimates from those involved in the tasks and enter them for each task. Microsoft Excel will calculate the duration and standard deviation for you.

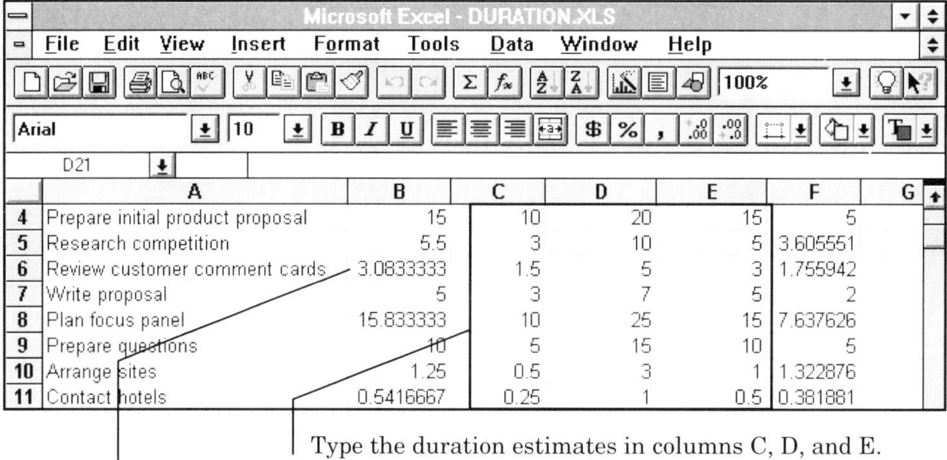

	A	B	C	D	E	F	G
4	Prepare initial product proposal	15	10	20	15	5	
5	Research competition	5.5	3	10	5	3.605551	
6	Review customer comment cards	3.0833333	1.5	5	3	1.755942	
7	Write proposal	5	3	7	5	2	
8	Plan focus panel	15.833333	10	25	15	7.637626	
9	Prepare questions	10	5	15	10	5	
10	Arrange sites	1.25	0.5	3	1	1.322876	
11	Contact hotels	0.5416667	0.25	1	0.5	0.381881	

Type the duration estimates in columns C, D, and E.

Microsoft Excel calculates duration (and standard deviation) based on the three estimates.

Until you enter data in columns C, D, and E, column F, the column containing the standard deviation, will show the #DIV/0 error. As soon as you enter the duration estimates, the error will be replaced by the standard deviation.

Save the file as a normal Microsoft Excel file.

In Microsoft Project: To open the Microsoft Excel file you just created, choose File Open. Select the filename. Microsoft Project detects that it is not a Microsoft Project file and displays the Import dialog box.

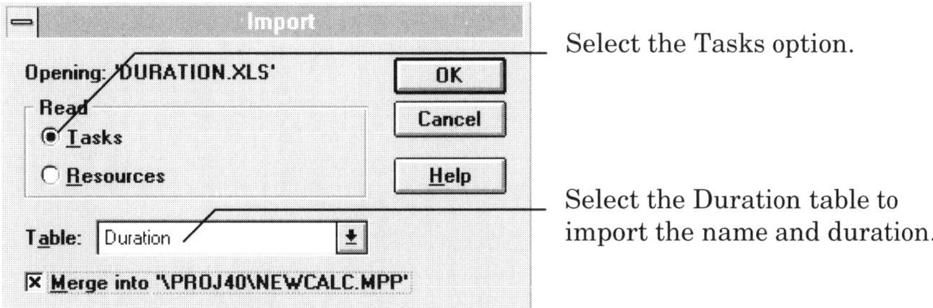

All tasks and their durations are imported into Microsoft Project. Because Name and Duration are the only fields in your table, the other columns—Optimistic, Pessimistic, Most Likely, and Std. Dev.—in the Microsoft Excel file are ignored.

Exchanging Data Using the Edit Copy and Edit Paste Commands

To calculate durations for just a few tasks, you can use the Clipboard to export the list of tasks and then import the estimated durations. Remember, to use this method, the application receiving the information must be able to use the Clipboard.

In Microsoft Project: Filter the tasks such that only those tasks for which you need durations calculated are displayed in the view. For example, if the tasks are all those handled by one department, you could filter on "Department," if you have included such a field in your task list. Or you could mark all the tasks for which you need durations calculated by adding the Marked field to any table. Type Yes in the field to mark a task. Now filter the tasks so that only the Marked tasks are displayed.

Apply the table containing only those columns you want to export. For example, apply the Duration table created in the previous example to export the name and duration for the tasks. Select all the tasks. Choose Edit Copy or click the Copy button on the Standard toolbar.

In Microsoft Excel: Choose Edit Paste. Add columns for the three duration estimates and standard deviation. Add the equations for weighted average and standard deviation as described earlier in this example. Gather the three estimates for each task and enter them on the spreadsheet. When you are finished, select the tasks and durations (columns A and B), and choose Edit Copy.

In Microsoft Project: Select the area where you want the tasks to be pasted. Choose Edit Paste. The tasks will be pasted starting from the left-most field of the selected row.

Using Drag-and-Drop instead of Edit Copy and Paste If you are using applications with OLE version 2.0, such as Microsoft Excel version 5.0 and Microsoft Project version 4.0, you can copy and paste using drag-and-drop. Open both applications and position them so you can see them both. After selecting the information you want to copy, drag it to the other application.

EXCHANGING INFORMATION WITH LOTUS 1-2-3 OR DBASE

Exchanging information with Lotus 1-2-3 or dBase is similar to exchanging information with Microsoft Excel. You create a table containing columns for the information you want to import or export. To import, you open a WKS, WK1, or WK3 file for Lotus 1-2-3, or a DBF file for dBase. Microsoft Project asks for the table, and places the information in either the open project or a new project, as you specify. To export, you save the file in the WKS, WK1, or WK3 format for Lotus 1-2-3, or DBase III or dBase IV format for dBase.

USING PROJECT INFORMATION IN MICROSOFT WORD

You can also share information from Microsoft Project with a word processing application, such as Microsoft Word. Using the Clipboard, you can copy a view from Microsoft Project, and place it in a document you are creating in Microsoft Word. For example, if you are preparing a report on various alternatives to solve a schedule conflict, you could place a Microsoft Project Gantt Chart in the report to support your conclusions.

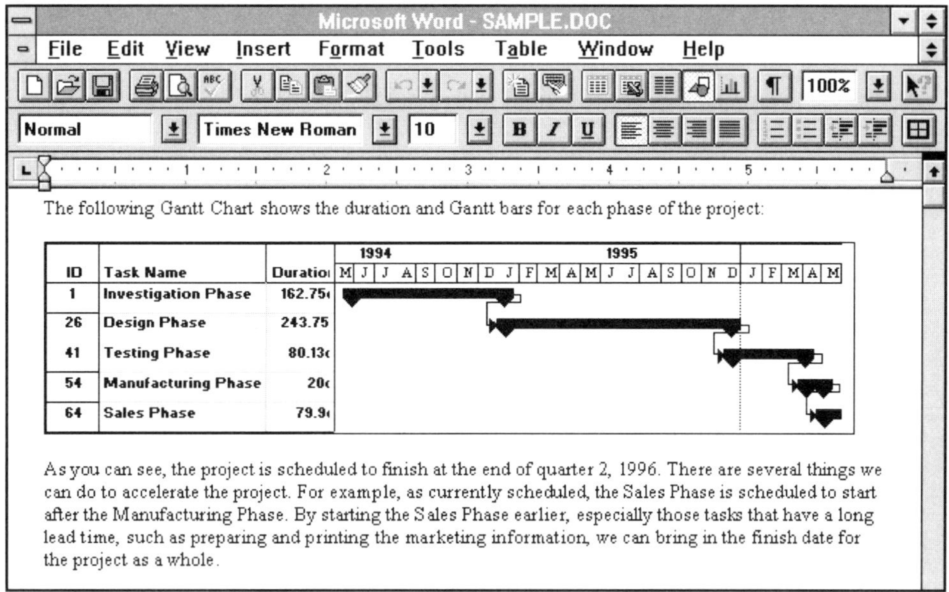

To do this, select the tasks you want to include in the picture, and click the Copy Picture button on the Standard toolbar. The copied picture is static—that is, it is not linked to the data in Microsoft Project.

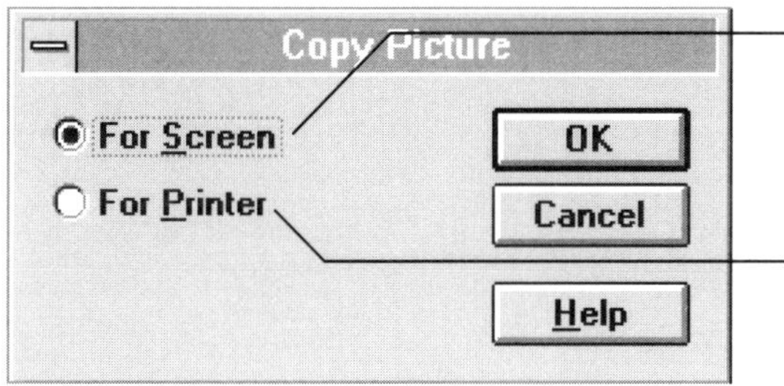

Select For Screen when you want the copied object to look good on screen—for example, if you plan to distribute it in Microsoft Mail.

Select For Printer when you plan to print the document and want the information from Microsoft Project to appear correctly when printed.

Use Copy Picture when you want a snapshot in time of a project. When you double-click the picture in Microsoft Word, you can edit it as a drawing but it is not recognized as a project.

To copy a project so it remains linked to Microsoft Project, use Edit Copy. After you paste the project into Word, you can double-click it to edit it in Microsoft Project.

After copying the picture in Microsoft Project, open the other application. Go to where you want to paste the picture and choose Edit Paste.

16

Using Microsoft Project Tools

The tools in Microsoft Project are the keys to making the software do just what you want—to see what you want and print what you want. Once you have edited or created one table, filter, view, toolbar, report, or custom form, you'll see that the others are edited or created in a similar manner.

Use this chapter to create the tables, filters, views, and calendars you found useful as you read the chapters. Once you have followed an example or two here, you'll be able to create whatever you need.

This chapter includes the steps for:

- Changing or creating a table
- Changing or creating a filter
- Changing or creating a view
- Customizing the menus to include only those commands you use most often
- Changing or creating a calendar
- Sorting to control the order of information in a view
- Changing the Gantt Chart to make it look just as you want
- Changing the Resource Graph to show the information you want, presented in the format you want
- Customizing the toolbars
- Creating a custom form

Also in this chapter is a brief introduction to Microsoft Project macros.

TABLES

Tables specify the fields you see in the view. Because you control which fields appear in a table, you can customize tables to show exactly the information of interest to you. You can change the fields in a table in two ways. You can change a column in the table that is displayed or you can create, edit, or copy a table using the View Table/More Tables command.

CHANGING A COLUMN IN THE DISPLAYED TABLE

If all you want to do is change the width of a column in the displayed table, you can do a couple of things:

- To make the column as wide as the longest information in the column, just double-click the column border to the right of the column title.
- To make the column any width you want, just drag the column border to the right of the column title.

The mouse pointer changes to a bar with arrows pointing left and right when it is over a column border, indicating that you can double-click or drag the border.

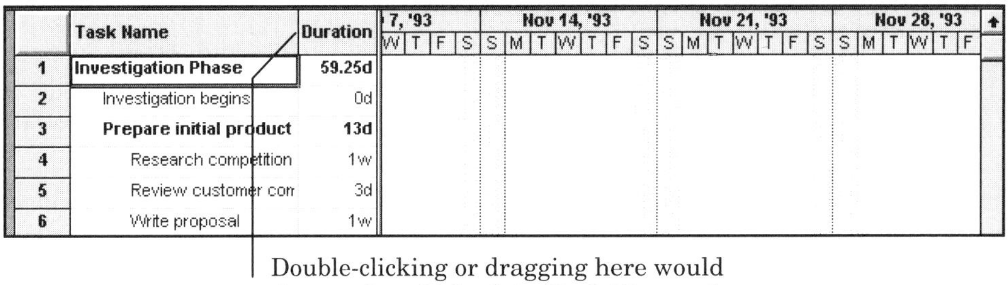

	Task Name	Duration	7, '93	Nov 14, '93	Nov 21, '93	Nov 28, '93
			W T F S	S M T W T F S	S M T W T F S	S M T W T F
1	**Investigation Phase**	**59.25d**				
2	Investigation begins	0d				
3	**Prepare initial product**	**13d**				
4	Research competition	1w				
5	Review customer com	3d				
6	Write proposal	1w				

Double-clicking or dragging here would change the width of the Task Name column.

To change the type of information a column contains, the column title, or the alignment of the information in the column, double-click the title of the column you want to change. In Windows, you can also select the column and press Alt+F3; on the Macintosh, you can press Option+Shift+F3 after selecting the column.

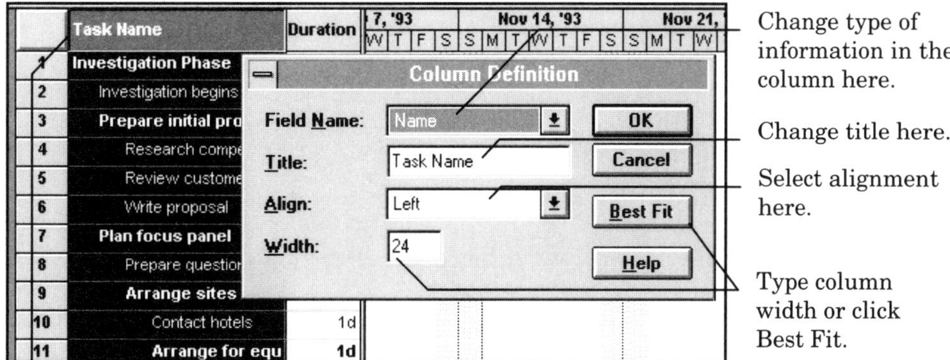

First, double-click the column whose definition you want to change.

To change the type of information in the column, select a different field name in the Field Name box. To change the title of the column, type a title in the Title box. You can name a column anything you want.

You can type the number of characters you want in the column or click the Best Fit button to change the width of the column.

Tables are saved with the project, so the next time you apply this table in this project, the change will still be there. If you don't want to make a permanent change to the displayed table, use the View Table/More Tables command to copy the table, then change the copy.

Changing an Existing Table

To change an existing table, use one of the following methods:

- If you want to retain the original table, make a copy of the table by choosing the Copy button in the More Tables dialog box.
- If you want to change the original table permanently, choose the Edit button in the More Tables dialog box.

The example in this section shows how to add the WBS field and the Manager field to the Entry table. You follow the same procedure to add any field to any existing table.

When you want to add a field that doesn't exist in Microsoft Project, use a custom field. Microsoft Project provides 10 custom text fields for tasks and 5 custom text fields for resources. Microsoft Project also provides 10 custom date fields and 5 custom number fields for tasks.

The following example shows how to make the following changes to a copy of the Entry table:

- Delete a field
- Change the width of a field
- Add the WBS field and the Manager field

Choose View Table/More Tables.

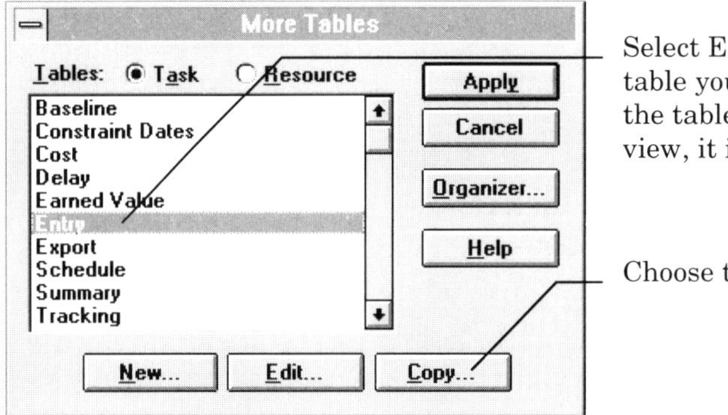

Select Entry, the name of the table you want to change. If the table is displayed in the view, it is already selected.

Choose the Copy button.

If you want to change the table permanently and don't want to keep the original, choose the Edit button instead.

The Table Definition dialog box shows all the columns in the Entry table, the alignment of information in each column, the column width, and column title. If the Title column is blank, the field name is used.

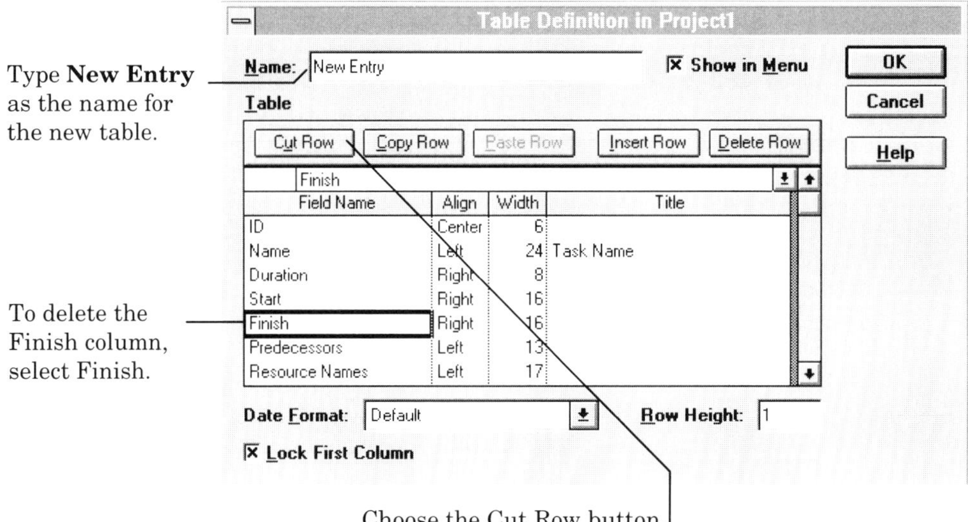

Type **New Entry** as the name for the new table.

To delete the Finish column, select Finish.

Choose the Cut Row button.

Now insert the WBS field between the Duration field and the Start field.

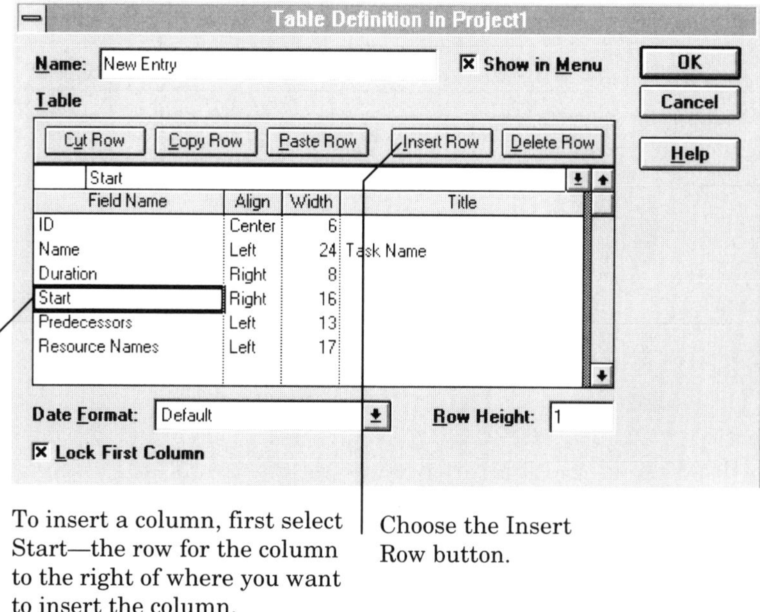

To insert a column, first select Start—the row for the column to the right of where you want to insert the column.

Choose the Insert Row button.

You'll see a blank line inserted in the table definition.

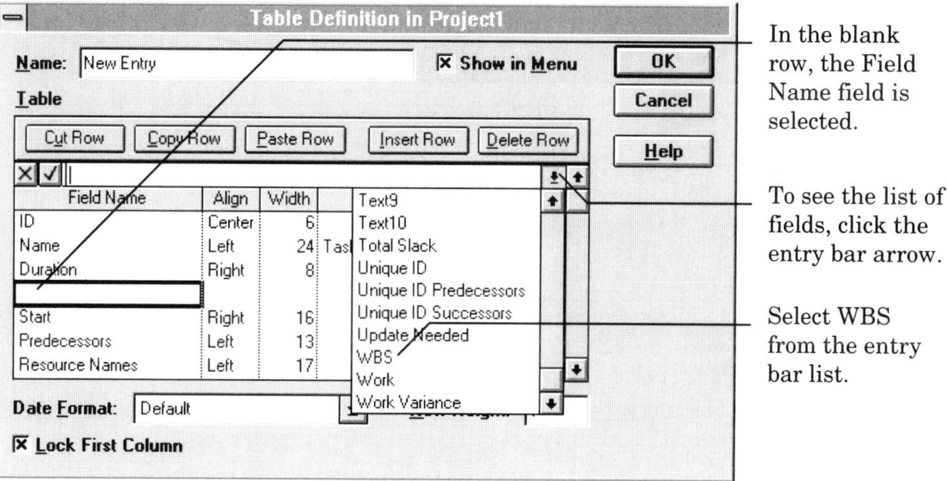

Reduce the size of the Predecessors column so you have more room for the new columns.

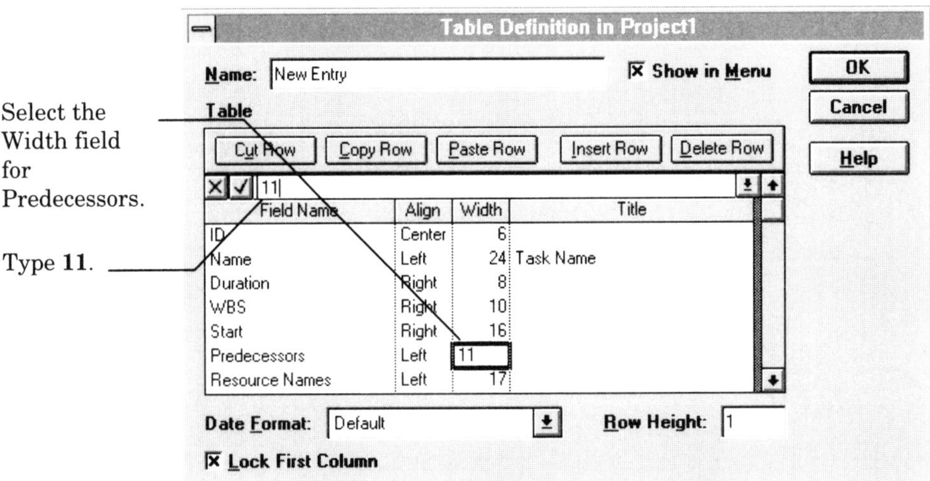

Add the Manager column before Resource Names. Since Microsoft Project doesn't include a manager field, use a custom field.

Select Resource Names, the row for the column to the right of where you want to insert the new column. Choose the Insert Row button.

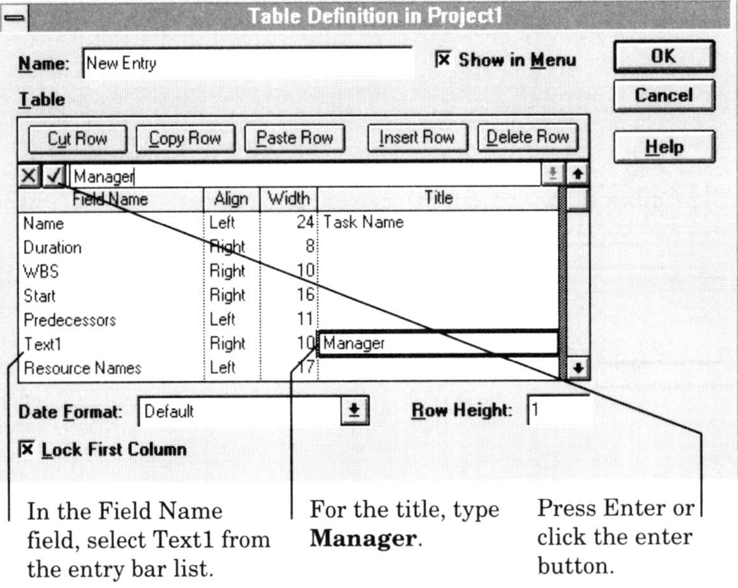

Choose OK.

To apply this table, choose the Apply button. When you apply this table to the Task Sheet, it looks like this:

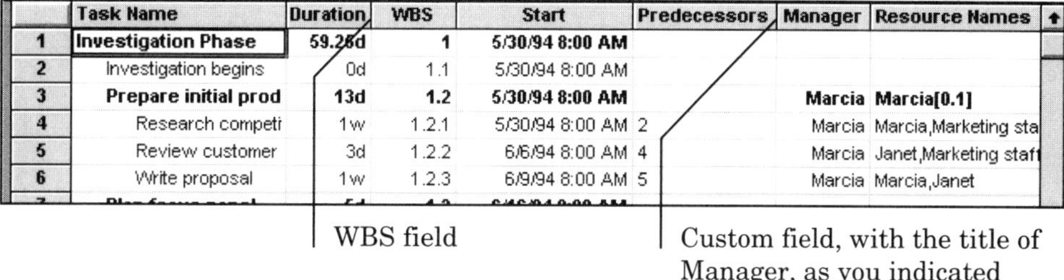

	Task Name	Duration	WBS	Start	Predecessors	Manager	Resource Names
1	**Investigation Phase**	**59.25d**	**1**	**5/30/94 8:00 AM**			
2	Investigation begins	0d	1.1	5/30/94 8:00 AM			
3	**Prepare initial prod**	**13d**	**1.2**	**5/30/94 8:00 AM**		**Marcia**	**Marcia[0.1]**
4	Research competi	1w	1.2.1	5/30/94 8:00 AM	2	Marcia	Marcia,Marketing sta
5	Review customer	3d	1.2.2	6/6/94 8:00 AM	4	Marcia	Janet,Marketing staf
6	Write proposal	1w	1.2.3	6/9/94 8:00 AM	5	Marcia	Marcia,Janet

CREATING A NEW TABLE

You can create any table you want, with whatever fields you need for any purpose. Follow the steps in this section for creating the following tables:

- Data collection table in Chapter 11, "Tracking Progress and Updating the Schedule"
- Table for importing resource information (name, standard pay rate, overtime rate) in Chapter 15, "Sharing Information"
- Table for exporting task name and duration in Chapter 15, "Sharing Information"

The following example shows how to create the data collection table. Choose View Table/More Tables.

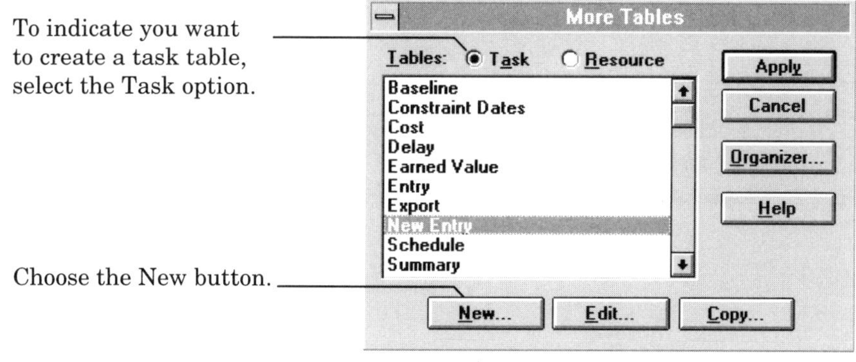

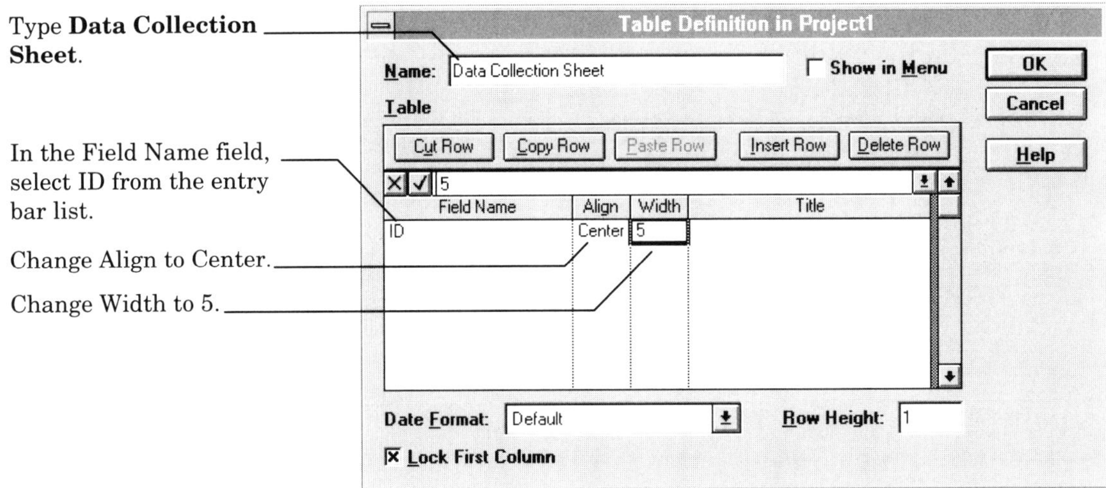

When you enter a field name, Microsoft Project enters default values of "Right" in the Align field and "10" in the Width field. You can change these by selecting a different value from the entry bar list. If the width you want isn't an increment of five, which are your choices in the entry bar list, you can type any value.

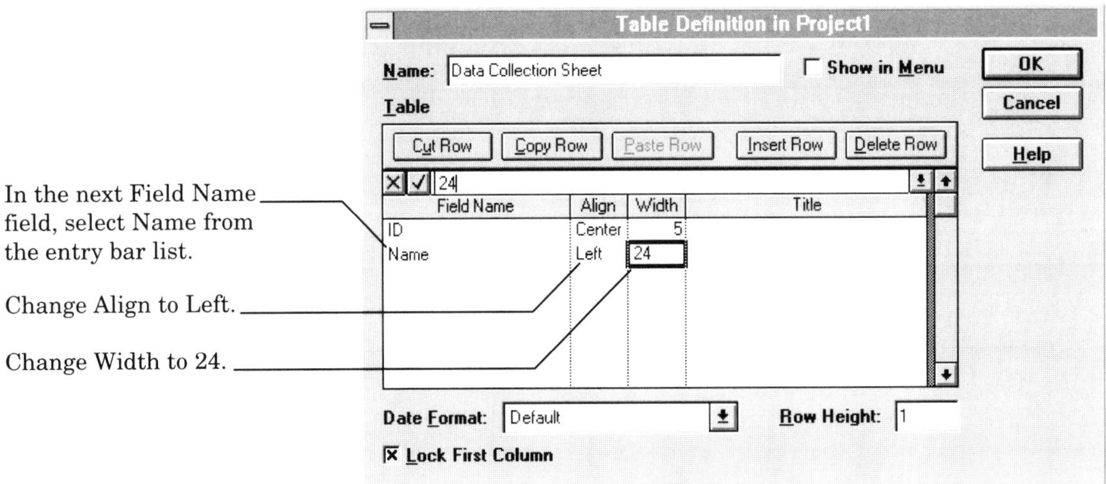

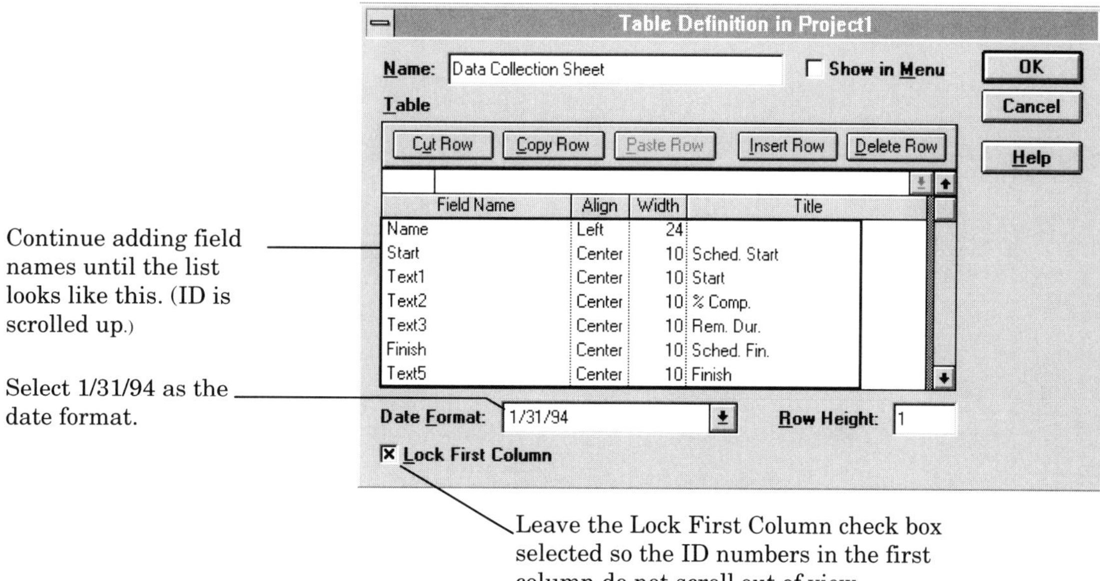

Choose OK.

To apply the table, choose the Apply button. When you apply the table to the Task Sheet, the columns look like this:

	Name	Sched. Start	Start	% Comp.	Rem. Dur.	Sched. Fin.	Finish
1	**Investigation Phase**	**5/30/94**				**1/11/95**	
2	Investigation begins	5/30/94				5/30/94	
3	**Prepare initial product**	**5/30/94**				**6/15/94**	
4	Research competition	5/30/94				6/3/94	
5	Review customer com	6/6/94				6/8/94	
6	Write proposal	6/9/94				6/15/94	
7	**Plan focus panel**	**6/16/94**				**7/12/94**	
8	Prepare questions	6/16/94				6/22/94	
9	**Arrange sites**	**6/16/94**				**6/24/94**	
10	Contact hotels	6/16/94				6/16/94	

Creating a table may take a bit of trial and error. Once you create a table and apply it to a view, you'll probably discover titles you forgot to change, or columns that are too narrow or wide, or perhaps that the order of fields is not what you want, and so on. Just edit the table—either by double-clicking the title of the column you want to change and using the Column Definition dialog box, or by choosing the Edit button in the More Tables dialog box—until it is as you want it.

FILTERS

Filters control which tasks or resources are displayed or highlighted: all, or a subset based on the filter you apply. For example, if you apply the Milestones filter, only the tasks that are milestones are displayed or highlighted. Microsoft Project checks the Milestone field to determine which tasks to display or highlight. If the Milestone field contains Yes, the task is displayed or highlighted; if the Milestone field contains No, the task is not displayed or highlighted.

You can create any type of filter you want. When you create a filter, all you are doing is telling Microsoft Project which field to look at and what you want the field to contain. A filter can do one of three things:

- Always look for the same thing, as the Milestones filter does.
- Look for a value you specify each time you apply the filter, such as finding all tasks that use the resource you enter when you apply the filter. This is called an interactive filter.
- Compare the values in two fields, such as comparing the baseline start date and the actual start date for a task. This is called a calculated filter.

The easiest way to understand how to create and change filters is to look at some of the filters that come with Microsoft Project.

The following illustration shows the Milestones filter in the Filter Definition dialog box.

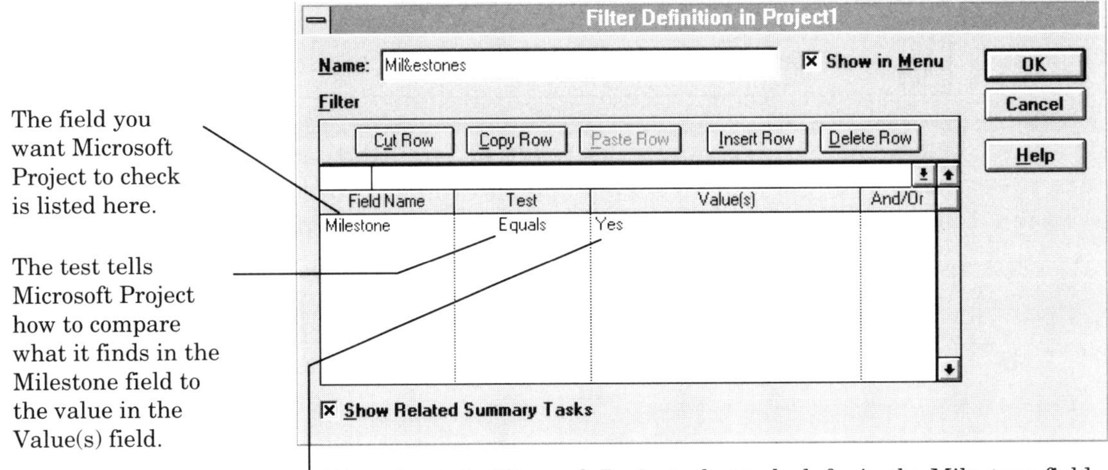

For the Milestones filter, Microsoft Project checks the Milestone field for each task. If the value in the field is (equals) Yes, the task is displayed or highlighted. If the field contains No, the task is not displayed or highlighted.

The next illustration shows the Task Range filter, an interactive filter that prompts you to enter the first task ID and last task ID of the range you want to see every time you use the filter.

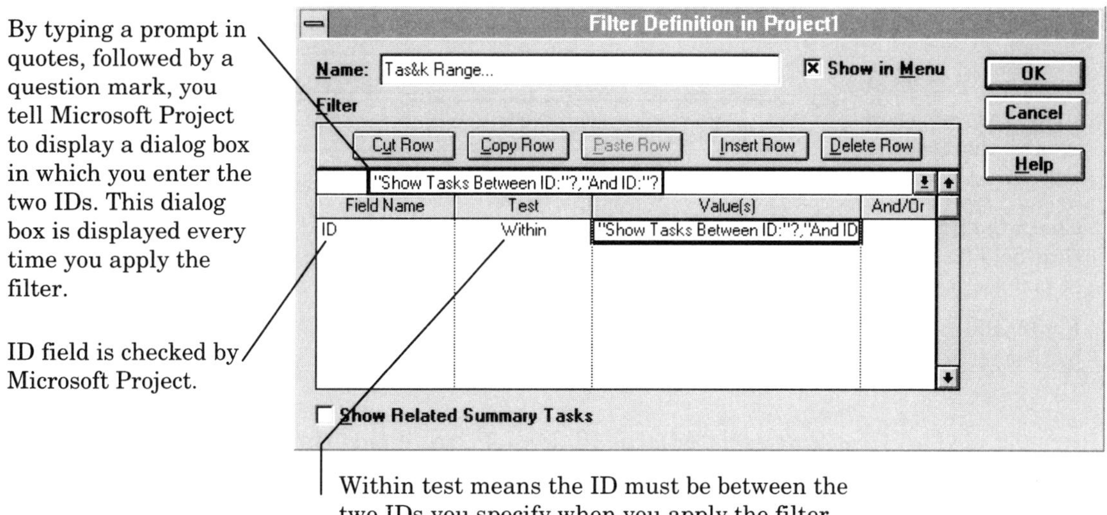

By typing a prompt in quotes, followed by a question mark, you tell Microsoft Project to display a dialog box in which you enter the two IDs. This dialog box is displayed every time you apply the filter.

ID field is checked by Microsoft Project.

Within test means the ID must be between the two IDs you specify when you apply the filter.

When you apply the filter, you see the following dialog box. Note how the text between the quotes in the Value(s) field matches the text in the dialog box.

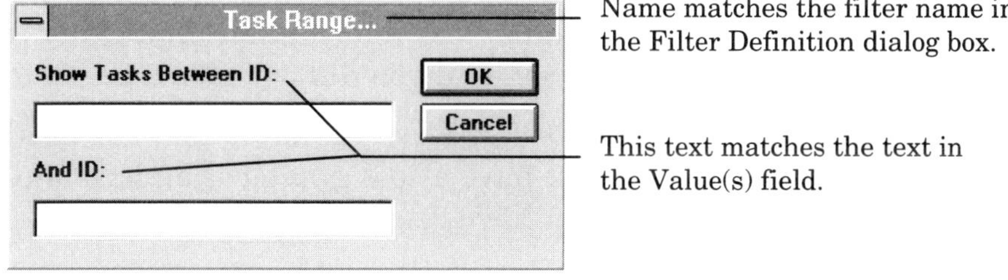

Name matches the filter name in the Filter Definition dialog box.

This text matches the text in the Value(s) field.

To use the dialog box: In the first box, type the ID for the lowest task number you want Microsoft Project to display; in the second box, type the ID for the highest task number you want Microsoft Project to display. Choose OK. Microsoft Project displays or highlights all tasks with an ID between the two.

The next illustration shows two things: a calculated filter that compares the values in two fields and how to use one filter to check more than one field.

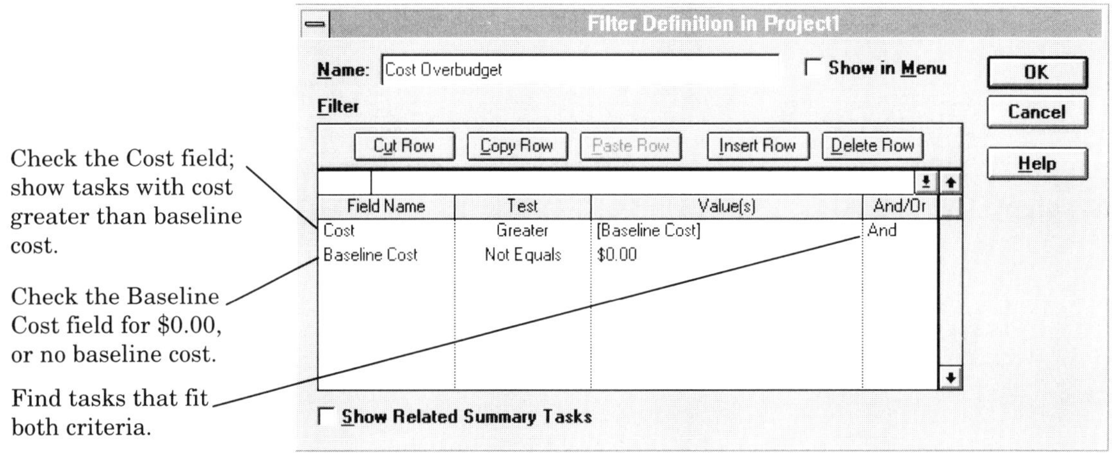

The first row tells Microsoft Project to check the Cost field and display the task if the cost is greater than the value in the Baseline Cost field. By entering a field name in square brackets in the Value(s) field, you tell Microsoft Project to compare the values in the two fields.

The second row tells Microsoft Project to check the Baseline Cost field for $0.00—the value it contains if you have not chosen Tools Tracking/Save Baseline to copy the scheduled costs into the baseline cost fields. If the field contains $0.00, you do not want the filter to display the task because it is meaningless information—naturally the cost field will be higher than the baseline if you did not save a baseline schedule.

The "And" tells Microsoft Project that for a task to be displayed or highlighted, the task must have a cost greater than baseline cost (line 1) *and* the baseline cost must have been saved (line 2).

Microsoft Project will display or highlight only those tasks for which a baseline cost exists and scheduled cost is greater than the baseline cost. When you create a calculated filter, use the entry bar list to select the field name for the Value(s) field. All the names in the list include the square brackets so you don't have to type them.

CHANGING AN EXISTING FILTER

To change an existing filter, choose Tools Filtered For/More Filters. Suppose you want to find all tasks scheduled to start before a date you specify. You could change the Date Range filter as follows.

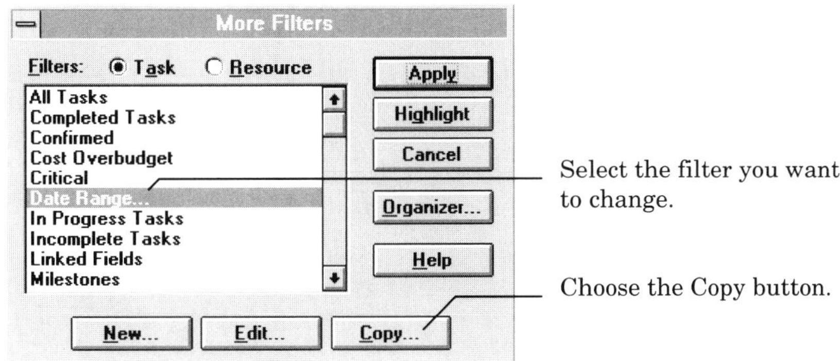

Select the filter you want to change.

Choose the Copy button.

If you don't want to keep the original filter, choose the Edit button instead.

Change the name to **Start Before**.

You are not interested in the Finish field so select Finish and choose the Cut Row button.

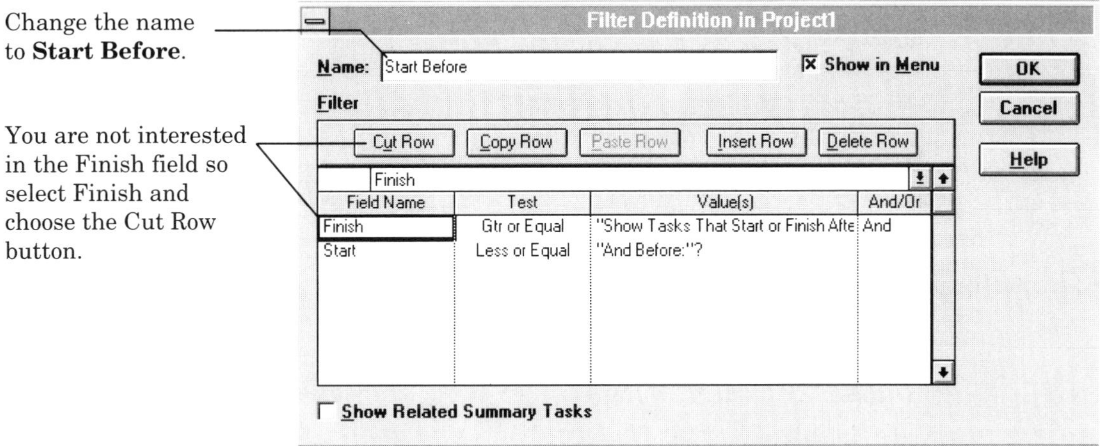

You are still interested in searching the Start field, so you want to keep that row, but change the test and value used.

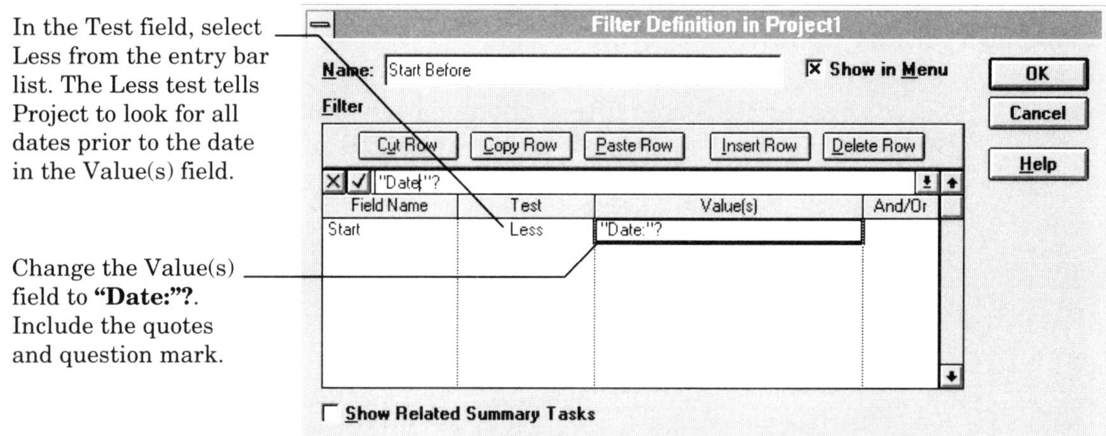

The text in the Value(s) field tells Project to display a dialog box when you apply the filter in which you enter a date. Press Enter or click the enter button. Choose OK.

To apply the filter, choose the Apply button. When you apply this filter, you'll see the following dialog box.

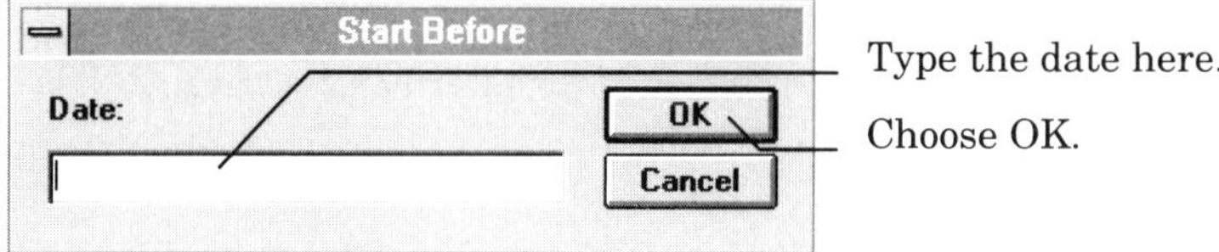

All tasks scheduled to start before the date you type will be displayed.

Creating a New Filter

You can create a filter to look for any information in any field. You can, of course, also filter using custom fields. For example, if you use custom resource field Text1 as the Manager field, you can filter to see all resources reporting to a certain person. Or if you use custom task field Text3 as the Department field, you can filter to see all tasks performed by one department.

The following example shows how to create a resource filter using a custom text field.

Choose Tools Filtered For/More Filters.

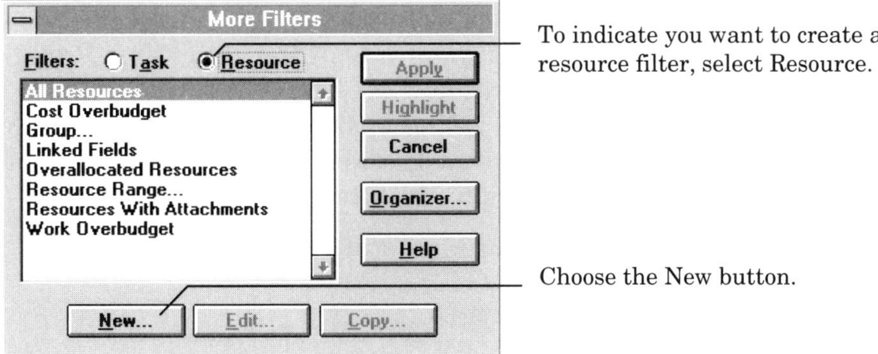

Enter information as shown below. In the Field Name and Test fields, you can select the entry from the entry bar list.

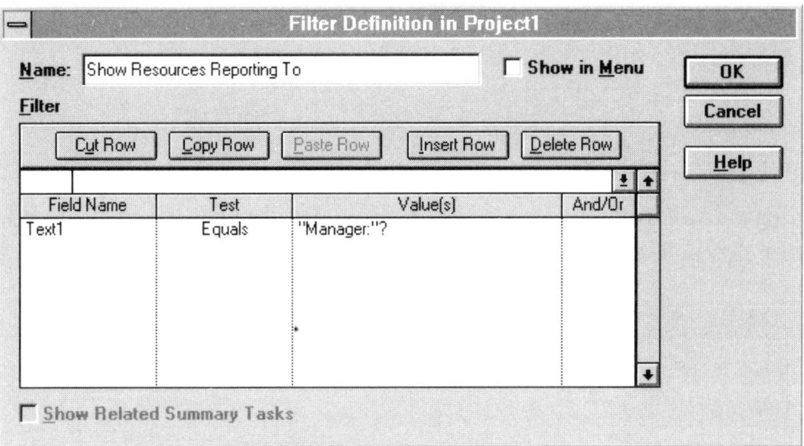

When you are finished entering the information, choose OK.

The test looks for a matching value in the Text1 field for each resource. The value "Manager:"? makes this an interactive filter so that each time you use the filter, you can specify the name of the manager you want to find.

When you apply the filter, you see the following:

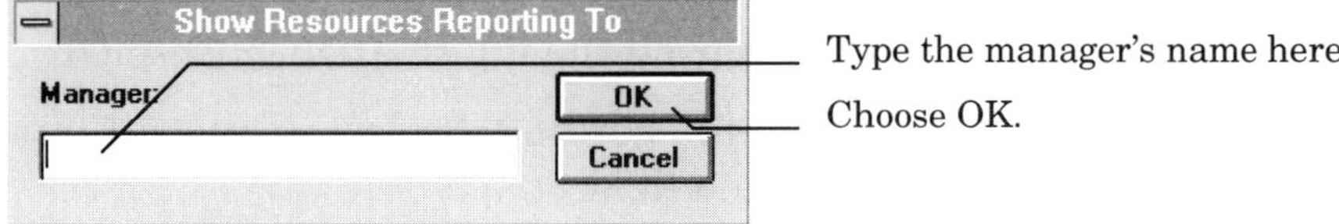

The next example shows how to create a filter to display or highlight all marked tasks. When you apply this filter, Microsoft Project checks the Marked field for the value Yes. Those tasks you have marked—by adding the Marked field to the Task Sheet and typing Yes for those you want to mark—have Yes in the Marked field and will be displayed or highlighted when you apply the filter.

Choose Tools Filtered For/More Filters.

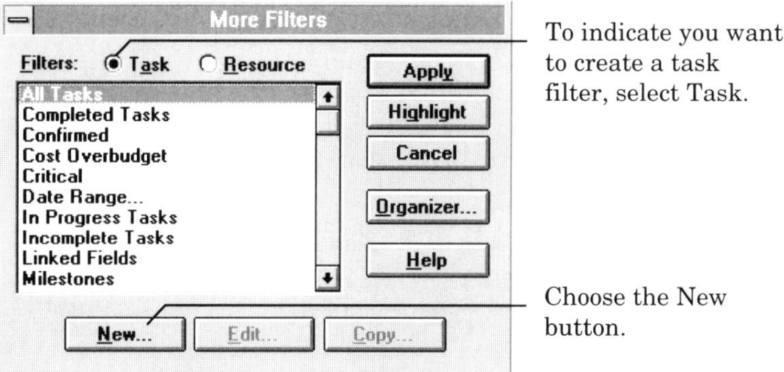

Enter information as shown below. In the Field Name and Test fields, you can select the entry from the entry bar list.

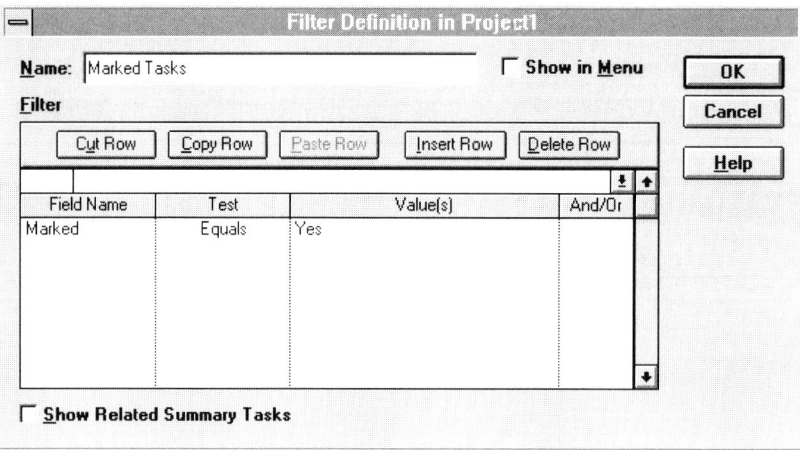

When you are finished entering the information, choose OK.

When you apply this filter, Microsoft Project displays those tasks with the value Yes in the Marked field.

VIEWS

When you discover the perfect combination of view, table, and filter to create reports for your company or analyze your schedule, you can save the combination as a new named view that you or anyone can display. This is a simple way to standardize reports in your company, and an easy way for anyone to generate reports.

All views are saved with the project, as are the tables, filters, macros, custom forms, and toolbars. For more information about sharing views with others, see Chapter 15, "Sharing Information."

As with tables and filters, you have three ways to customize a view. You can change an existing view by editing it, copy an existing view and change the copy, or create a new view.

Want Your Original Views, Tables, Filters, and Reports Back? All the original tools and settings are in the template file called BACKUP.MPT in Windows or Backup Template on the Macintosh. You can copy one tool out of the backup template using the Organizer, or you can copy the backup template and rename it to match the name of the template you are using. If you are using the global template, rename BACKUP.MPT to GLOBAL.MPT in Windows or Global Template on the Macintosh. For more information about the Organizer, see Chapter 15, "Sharing Information."

CHANGING AN EXISTING VIEW

When you change an existing single view, the View Definition dialog box shows the table and filter currently used for the view. When you choose the Edit or Copy button, you can change one part and leave the other parts as they are. For example, you can start with the Task Sheet, which has the Entry table and the All Tasks filter applied, change the name to Tracking Task Sheet, and change the Entry table to the Tracking table. Then any time you display the Tracking Task Sheet, you'll see the Task Sheet with the Tracking table applied. You can, of course, use any tables and filters you have created in a view. The procedures are different for single views and combination views.

Single View

The following example shows how to start with the Task Sheet and create the Tracking Task Sheet. Choose View More Views.

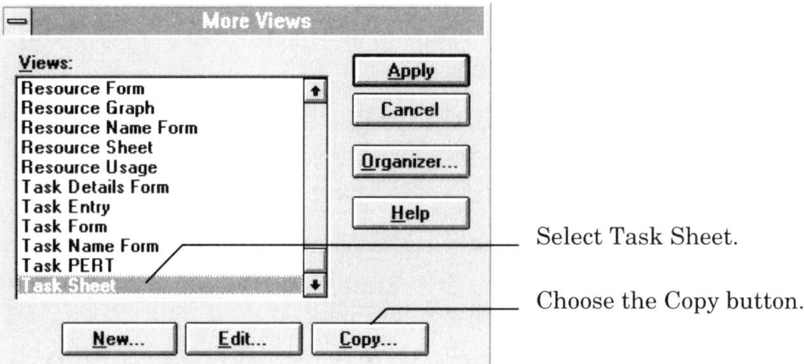

If you don't want the original Task Sheet any more, choose the Edit button instead.

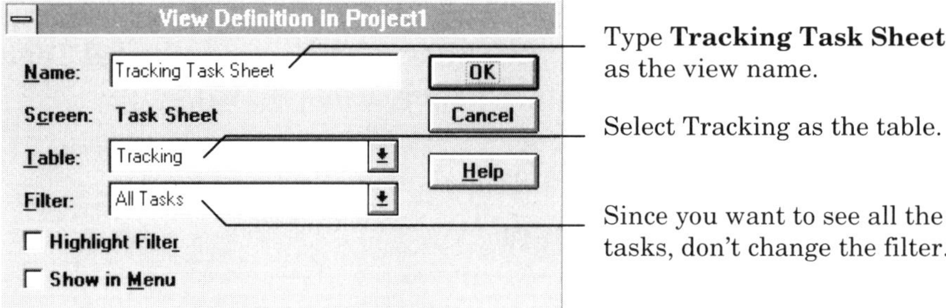

Choose OK.

When you apply the Tracking Task Sheet, you'll automatically have the Tracking table applied to the Task Sheet.

Combination View

When you change a combination view, you change the top and bottom views, not the table and filter used in them. If you want to change the table or filter, create a new single view with the appropriate table and filter and use it as part of the new combination view.

Suppose you've found that you use the Gantt Chart over the Task PERT Chart quite often to check relationships as you look at the schedule. Instead of creating the combination view on screen every time you want to use it, you can create a named view to apply any time you want to use the combination. You can copy and change the Task Entry view so that it contains the Gantt Chart over the Task PERT chart.

Choose View More Views.

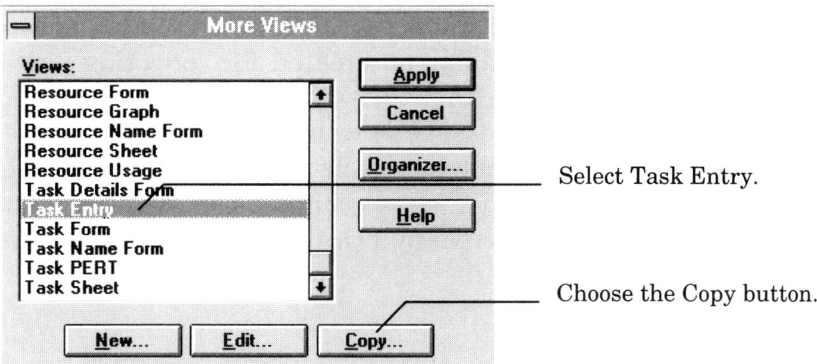

If you don't want the original Task Entry view any more, choose the Edit button instead.

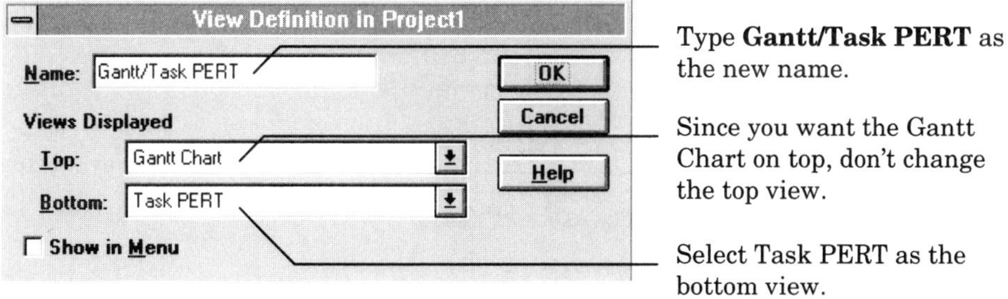

Choose OK.

Each time you apply this view, you'll see the Gantt Chart over the Task PERT Chart.

CREATING A NEW VIEW

Creating a new view is just as easy as changing an existing view, except you may have to select more information. The procedures are different for single views and combination views.

New Single View

Suppose when you collect progress data, you apply to the Task Sheet the Data Collection Sheet table you created for collecting actual data, and the Start Before filter to limit the tasks displayed. Rather than applying the table and filter each time you want to collect data, create a new view composed of the parts. When you display this view, you'll be prompted for the date to use, and then see only those tasks scheduled to start before the date you specify. By printing this view, you have your form for collecting progress data.

Choose View More Views.

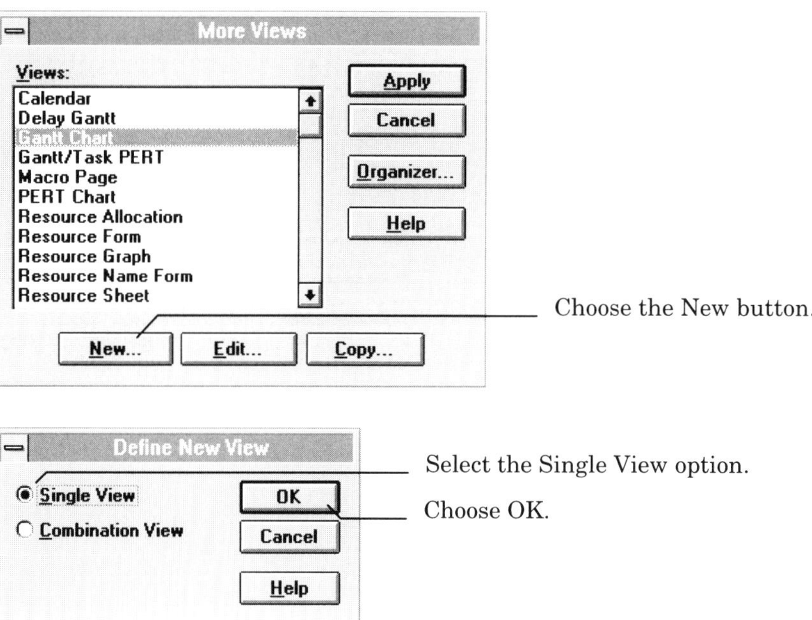

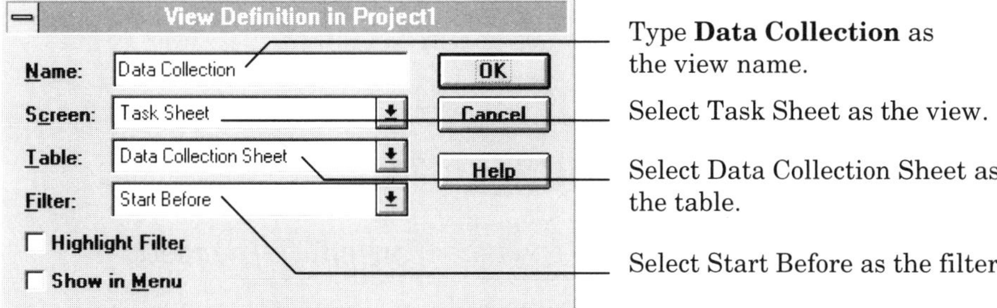

Choose OK.

When you display this view, the Start Before filter will prompt for the date, and then only those tasks scheduled to start before that date will be displayed. If you want the filter to highlight the tasks instead of displaying only those tasks, select the Highlight Filter check box when you create the filter in the View Definition dialog box.

New Combination View

Suppose you find that you are often combining two views—for example, the Resource Usage view and the Task Sheet. It would be easier and quicker for you to create a named combination view so that in the future you can display this view instead of combining the two on screen.

Choose View More Views. Choose the New button.

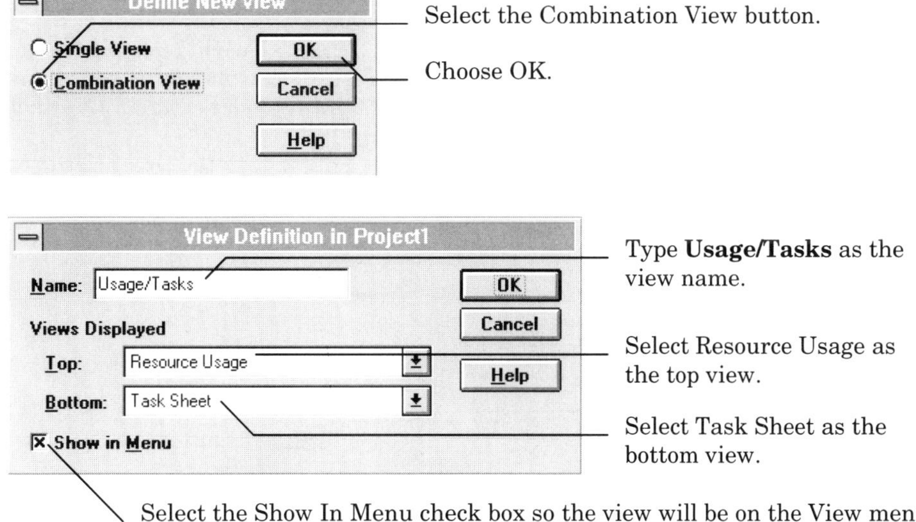

Now any time you want to display this view, you can choose it from the View menu.

CUSTOMIZING THE MENUS

There are a couple ways you can customize the menus.

- Using the Tools Customize/Menu Bars command, you can change the menus any way you want. You can change the names on the menu bar, add a new menu, and change the commands on each menu and submenu. This powerful feature lets you show only what you want to show in Microsoft Project, making it easier for novice users in your company to use Project.
- You can also change the View menu and the Table and Filtered For submenus whenever you create or change a view, table, or filter.

CUSTOMIZING THE MENUS AND MENU BAR

As with other customizable features, you can copy or edit an existing menu bar or create a new one. Initially, there are two menu bars: one that you see when there is a file open, called Standard; and one you see when no file is open, called Standard (no file).

Choose Tools Customize/Menu Bars.

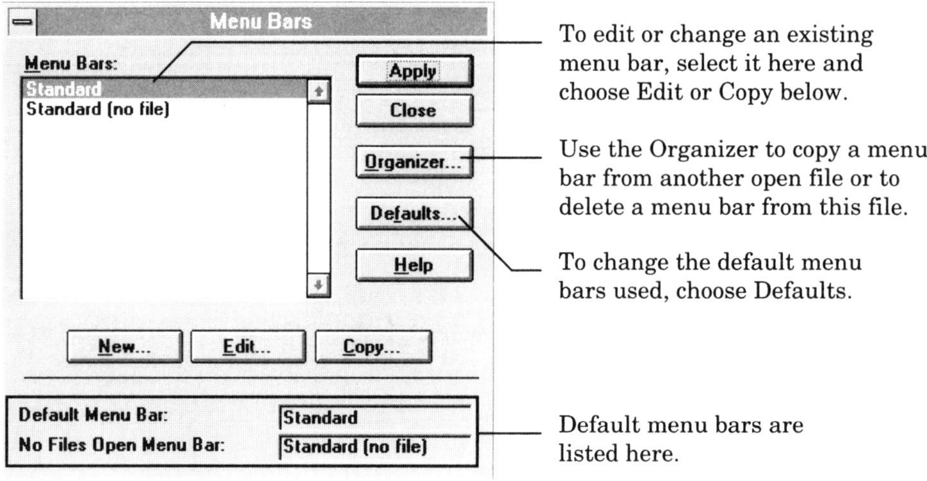

When you edit, copy, or create a new menu bar, the Menu Bar Definition dialog box is displayed. When you choose the Edit or Copy button, this dialog box contains the definition for the menu bar you selected.

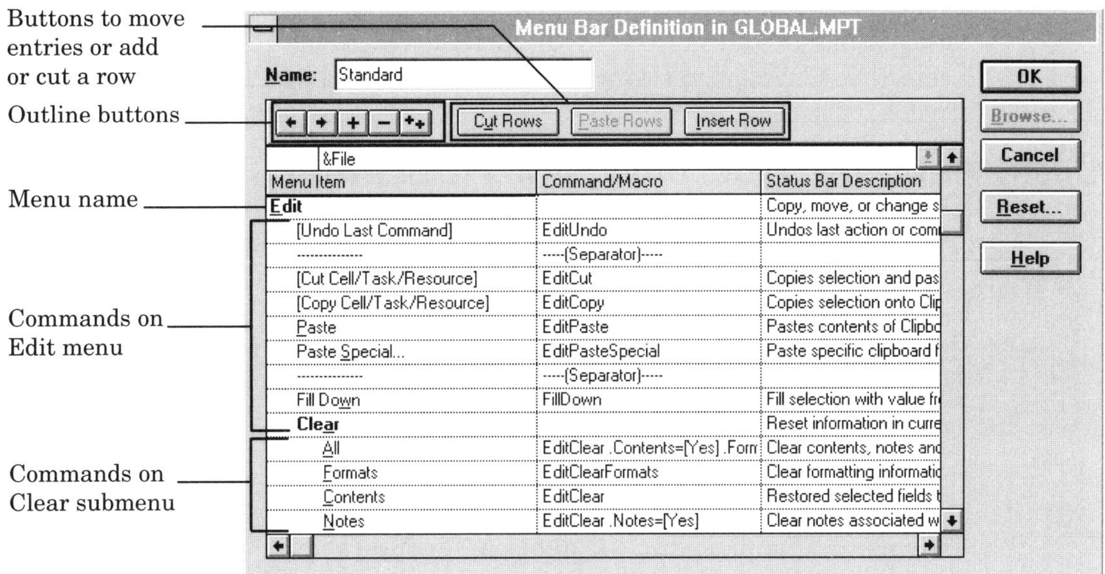

The outline level controls where an entry appears. Entries at the far left in the Menu Item column are listed on the menu bar. Entries at the next level are the commands on the menu; entries at the third level are commands on a submenu, as shown above for the Clear submenu. Look at the Edit Clear command in Microsoft Project to see how it works.

Entries in brackets, such as Edit [Cut Cell/Task/Resource], indicate that the wording on the menu changes depending on the state of Microsoft Project, in this case, depending on what is selected.

In Windows, if you want to be able to choose a menu or command using the keys, you can specify the letter in the name you want to be used. This letter will be underlined in the name on the menu, just as in the other names on the menus. For example, see &File in the entry bar in the previous illustration. The F is underlined in File on the menu bar. Any letter in the name can be the one. All you have to do is put an ampersand (&) before the letter in the name.

The Command/Macro column contains what Microsoft Project should do when the command is selected. The commands you can enter in this column are listed in the entry bar list. The commands are fairly self-explanatory, and include the menu and command name used in Microsoft Project. Scroll through this list and you'll recognize the commands.

The Status Bar Description column contains text that appears in the status bar at the bottom of the screen when the menu or command is selected. You can type any text here, up to 51 characters.

CUSTOMIZING THE VIEW, TABLE, AND FILTER MENUS

You can also change the View menu and the Table and Filtered For submenus whenever you create or change a view, table, or filter. You control the views, tables, and filters that appear on their respective menus using the Show In Menu check box in the definition dialog box. When the Show In Menu check box is selected, the name appears on the menu or submenu; when the check box is cleared, the name does not appear on the menu.

The following illustration shows how to add a table to the Table submenu. The procedure is identical for filters and views.

Choose View Table/More Tables. In the Tables box, select the table you want on the menu, and choose the Edit button. In Windows, to allow users to select the table using the keys, include an ampersand (&) in front of the letter you want to use to select the table.

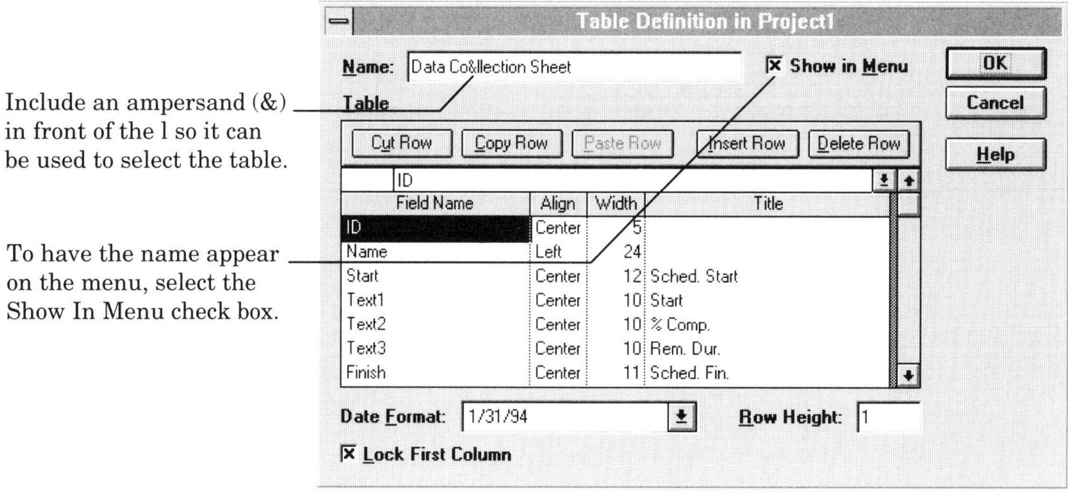

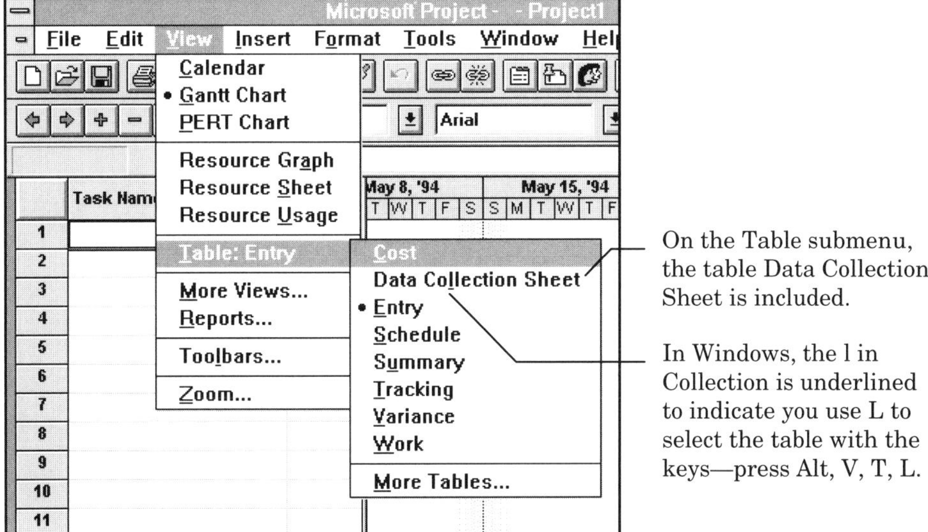

To create a custom View menu, or Table or Filtered For submenu, clear the Show In Menu check box for every view, table, or filter you do not want on the menu. Be sure the check box is selected for every view, table, or filter you want on the menu. This information is saved with the project and can be saved in the global template.

To customize the Filtered For submenu, use the Tools Filtered For/More Filters command. All filters are automatically added to the Filter box on the Formatting toolbar.

To customize the View menu, use the View More Views command.

CALENDARS

If you want to create several base calendars, perhaps because you need three shifts each day, this section will help you do it.

First, create a calendar for one of the shifts, say the day shift, which includes all holidays and the normal working days for the company or project as a whole. Then copy this calendar, rename it, and change it to reflect the work hours for the different shifts.

Creating a New Calendar

Suppose the normal working days for your company are Monday through Friday, and working hours are 7 a.m. to 11 a.m. and 11:30 a.m. to 3:30 p.m. To create a base calendar with these settings, plus one day off for the founder's birthday (April 1), choose Tools Change Working Time.

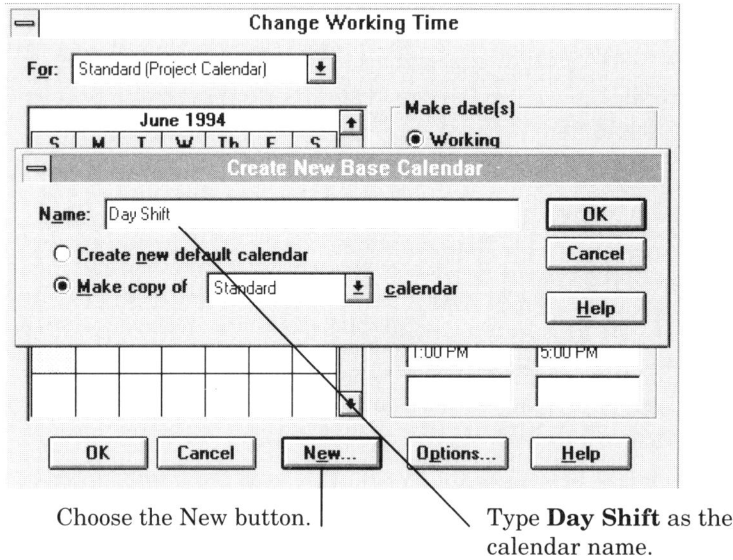

Choose the New button.

Type **Day Shift** as the calendar name.

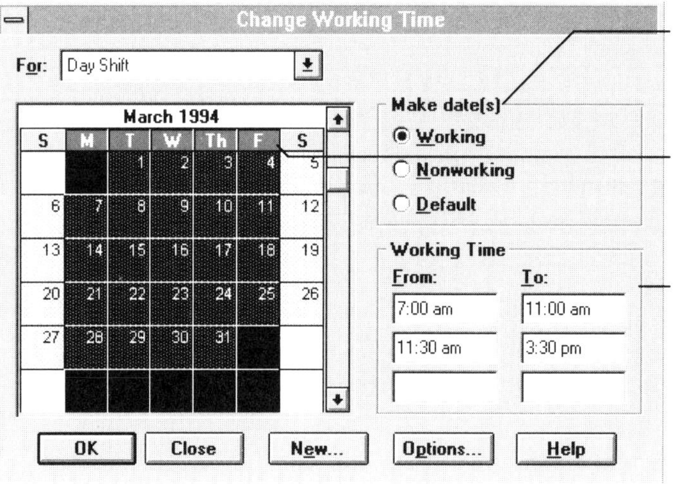

Working days already are Monday through Friday; no need to change anything here.

To change working hours, first select the day titles M, T, W, Th, and F.

Type the hours shown here.

Next, add the founder's birthday as a holiday.

Select April 1.

Select the Nonworking option.

Choose OK.

The Day Shift calendar is created. To make this the base calendar for the project, select this calendar in the Calendar box on the Project tab the Summary Info dialog box.

CHANGING AN EXISTING CALENDAR

Now that you have created one calendar with the basics in it, you can copy this calendar for the other two shifts.

Suppose the swing shift works 3 p.m. to 11:30 p.m., with half an hour for dinner from 7 to 7:30. Make a copy of the Day Shift calendar, and then change the hours to match the swing shift.

Choose Tools Change Working Time. Choose the New button.

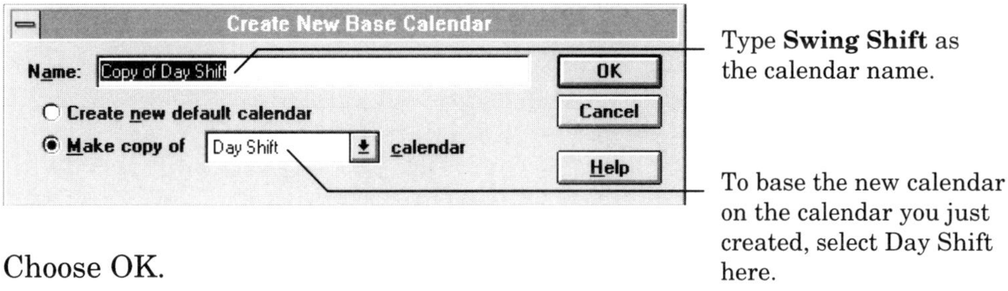

Choose OK.

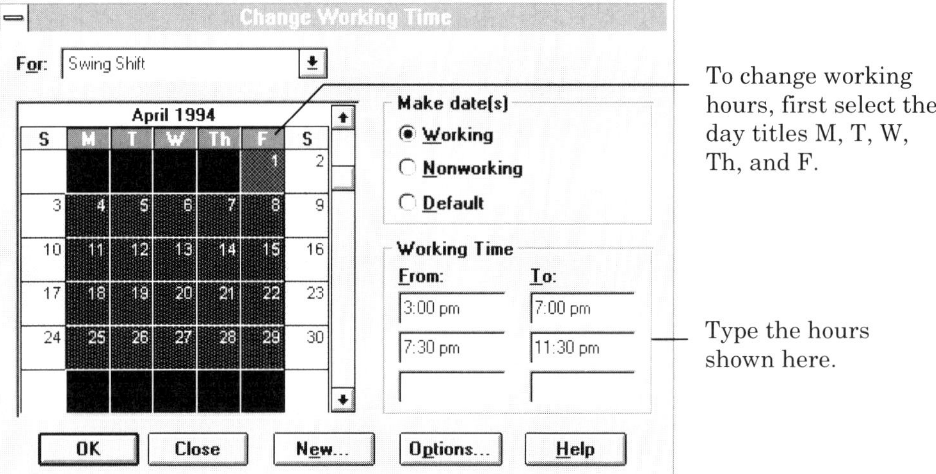

Choose OK.

The holiday for the founder is already in the calendar because you copied the Day Shift calendar.

Last, create the graveyard shift calendar—11 p.m. to 3 a.m. and 3:30 a.m. to 7:30 a.m. They start on Sunday nights, so you change the working days. Because their hours cross midnight, setting them is different.

Choose Tools Change Working Time. Choose the New button.

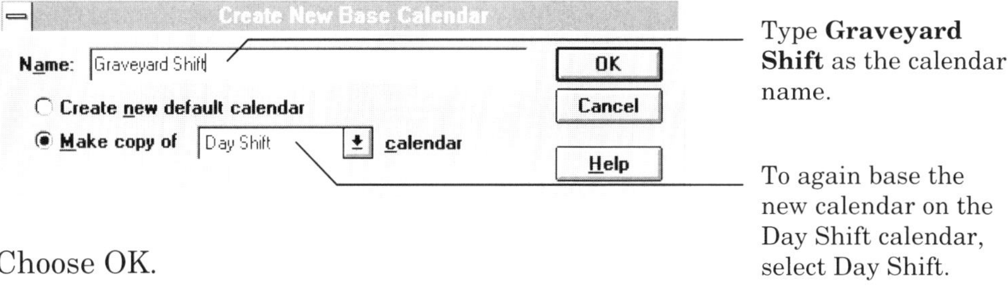

Choose OK.

First, enter the working hours for Sunday.

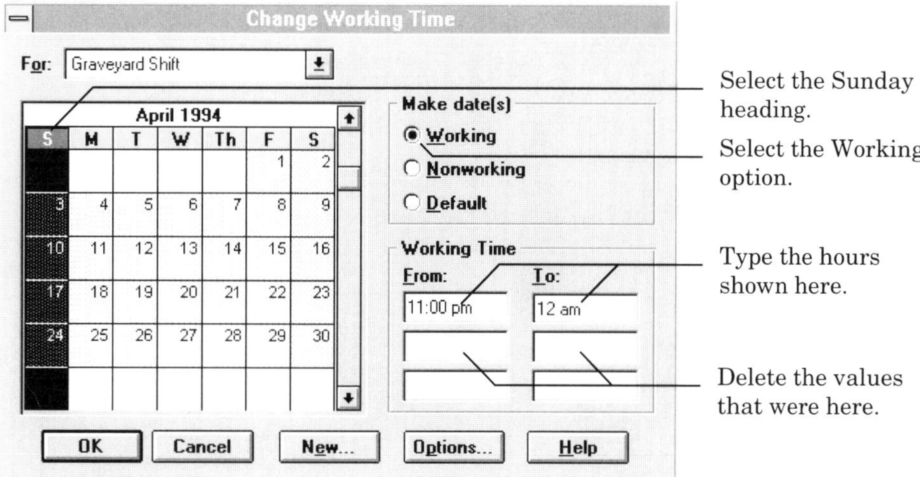

Next, enter the working hours for Monday through Thursday.

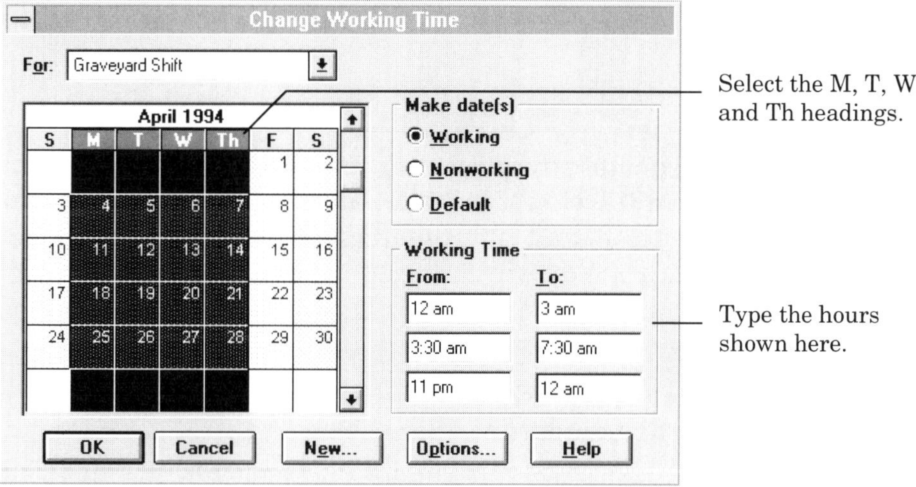

Finally, enter the working hours for Friday, as shown on the next page.

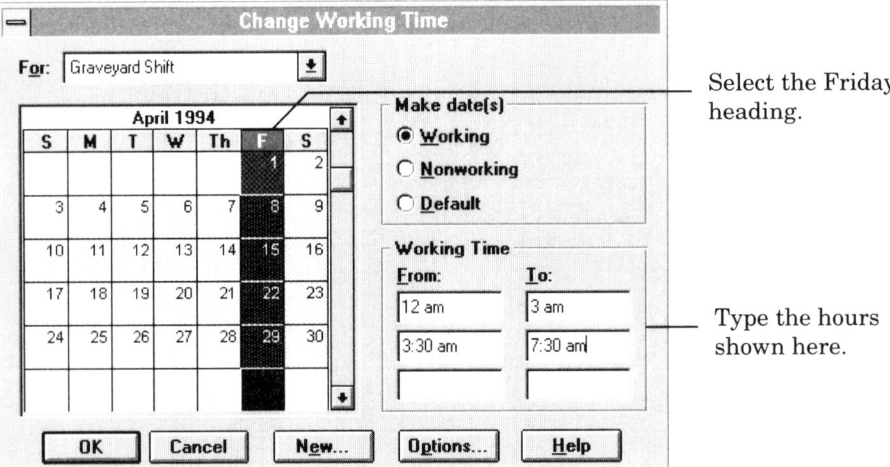

Choose OK.

As you assign resources, if the resource works a shift other than day, be sure to assign the correct base calendar to each resource or resource group, depending on their working schedule.

SORTING

Sorting is another tool you can use to control the way information is presented in the views. Initially, all tasks are in task ID number order, starting with 1, and all resources are in resource ID number order, starting with 1. You can change the order by sorting on any field, even a custom field. You can sort in ascending order (from low to high) or in descending order (from high to low).

If you want to quickly sort by date, you can click the Sort By Date button on the Standard toolbar.

If you are using outlining, you can choose whether to maintain the outline order when you sort. If you choose to maintain the outline order, all tasks at the highest level are sorted first according to the field you specify; then the second level tasks are sorted within their summary tasks; then the third level within their summary tasks, and so on.

To sort, choose the Tools Sort command. The Sort submenu displays common ways you might sort—by start date, finish date, priority, cost, and ID. Select one of these commands if this is what you want to do. Or choose Sort By to specify a different order. For example, if you want to sort the list of resources so they are in alphabetical order, select the Resource Name field. Or if you want to sort by duration, with the longest task at the top of the list, and by baseline start date, do the following:

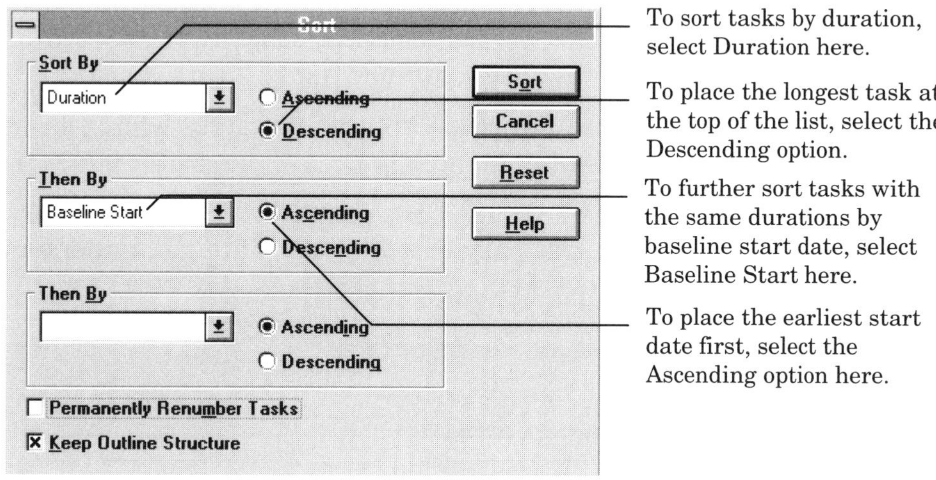

Choose the Sort button.

The tasks in the displayed view will be rearranged such that the longest task is at the top of the list; any time two or more tasks have the same duration, the task with the earlier baseline start date comes first.

You can also renumber when you sort. For example, if you entered your resources in random order, but now want them permanently in alphabetical order with ID numbers to match, you would set up the Sort dialog box to sort by Name, and select the Permanently Renumber Tasks check box. The resources will be sorted alphabetically and then their ID numbers changed to be sequential once again. On task views, renumbering is available only when the Keep Outline Structure check box is selected.

Because it wouldn't be useful to do so, you can't sort the PERT Chart.

FORMATTING THE GANTT CHART

Using the commands on the Format menu, you can change the appearance of the Gantt Chart. You can create a chart to meet virtually anyone's reporting requirements, from adding special symbols, to defining new bars, rolling up dates, and adding text to the bars.

The GanttChartWizard includes a wide variety of looks already prepared for you. Run it first and check the options available in Step 2 of the Wizard. Continue through the wizard to customize other options, such as the type of bars displayed and the text on the Gantt Chart. To run the GanttChartWizard, click the GanttChartWizard button on the Standard toolbar or choose Format GanttChartWizard.

If the GanttChartWizard doesn't offer exactly what you need, use the Format Bar Styles command.

The Bar Styles dialog box contains a considerable amount of information, but it is easy to work with, once you understand what it is telling you.

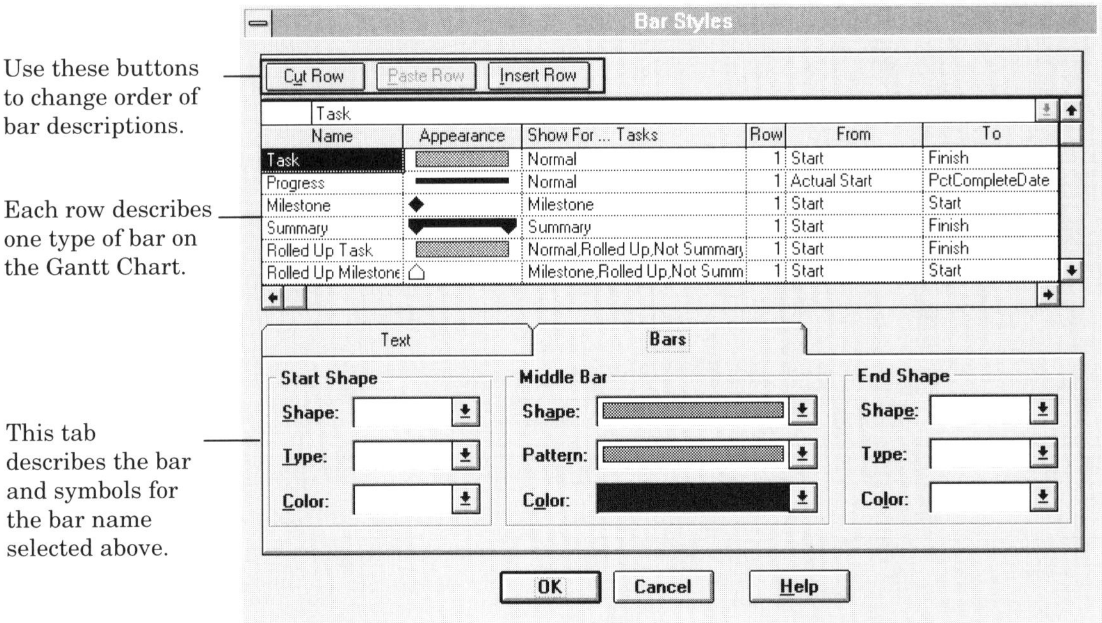

The Start Shape box describes the shape, type, and color for the symbol at the start of each bar; the Middle Bar box describes the bar width, pattern, and color; and the End Shape box describes the shape, type, and color for the symbol at the finish of each bar.

Select the Text tab to add text to the bar. You can include the contents of any field at the left, top, right, bottom, or inside a bar.

In the Bar Styles dialog box, the information in each row tells you the following:

Column	Specifies
Name	Purpose of the bar. You can type anything you want; the name is printed in the legend to identify the bar.
Appearance	Sample bar; you change it by changing the options in the Start Shape, Middle Bar, and End Shape boxes.
Show For ... Tasks	Kind of tasks for which the bar is displayed. "Normal" means a task that is neither a summary task nor a milestone.
Row	Vertical placement of the bar; each task can have up to four rows of bars.
From	Where in time to begin the bar. You select a field for the beginning of the bar, such as Start; the date in the Start field is then used as the starting point for the bar.
To	Where in time to end the bar. You select a field for the end of the bar, such as Finish; the date in the Finish field is then used as the ending point for the bar.

Bars are drawn in the order they appear in the Bar Styles dialog box, with the top bar being drawn first. If you have two bars drawn in the same row, one narrow and the other wide, the wide bar should be listed first in the dialog box so the narrow bar will be superimposed on the wide one, instead of being obscured by it.

FORMATTING THE RESOURCE GRAPH

The Format Bar Styles command allows you to change the appearance of the Resource Graph and control the information displayed. You can create a graph to meet many needs. For example, you can show peak usage for one resource. Or, you can show work for one resource and all resources to compare the two; show cumulative cost for all resources assigned to tasks in the project; or percent allocation for a resource on a set of tasks.

The Bar Styles dialog box for the Resource Graph changes depending on the type of information displayed on the graph and the position of the view in a combination view.

When the Resource Graph is the only view, is the top view in a combination view, or is below another resource view, the dialog box looks similar to the following illustration. The names for each group of options change depending on the type of information displayed on the Resource Graph. The following illustration shows the Bar Styles dialog box when Format Details/Work is selected.

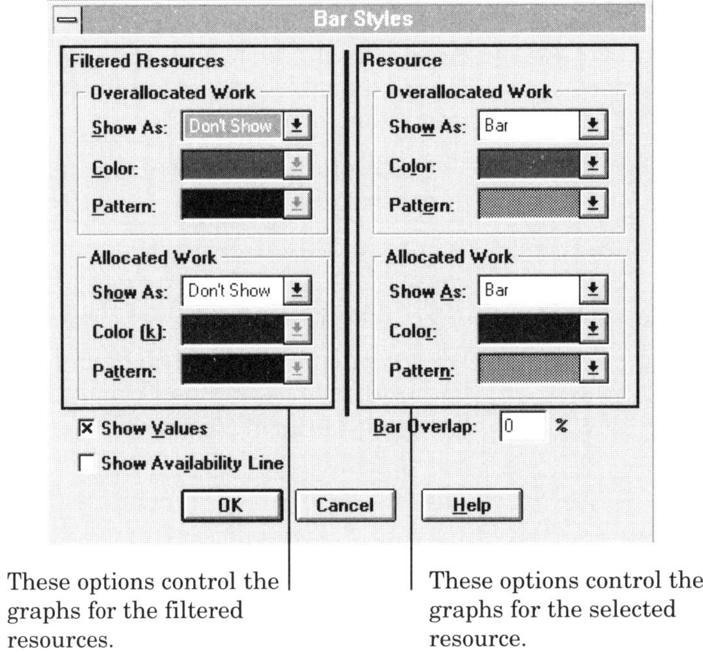

The Resource Graph can include up to four graphs. For each graph you don't want to appear, select Don't Show instead of a graph type.

The resources included for the filtered resource group depend on the filter applied. When the All Resources filter is applied, the graph for Filtered Resources shows information for all the resources in the project. If the Cost Overbudget filter is applied, the filtered resources graph shows information for the resources that fit this filter.

When the Resource Graph is below a task view, the graph shows information about one resource only. For this resource, you can see information for all tasks to which the resource is assigned during each time period, or information for selected tasks only. The Bar Styles dialog box options are similar, but the heads on the left and right are All Tasks and Selected Tasks instead of Filtered Resources and Resource.

There is an endless number of ways you can change the Resource Graph to show exactly the information you want. The following example shows how to change the Resource Graph to display percent allocation, both allocated and overallocated, for the filtered resources and for a single resource.

On the Resource Graph, choose Format Details/Percent Allocation. Double-click the graph or choose Format Bar Styles.

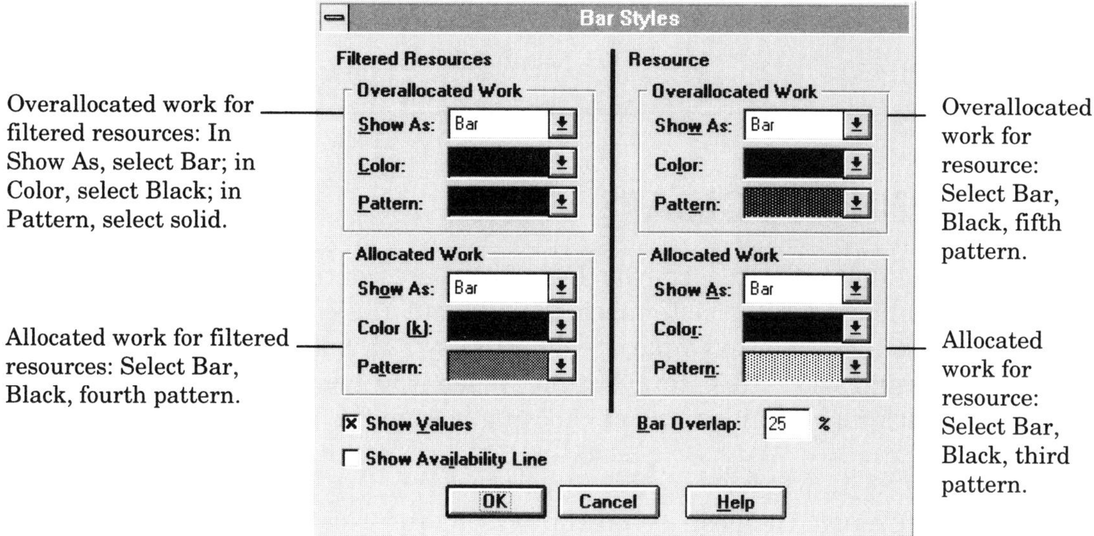

Choose OK. In the following illustration, the bars on the Resource Graph show percent allocation for one resource, Production engineers, and also for filtered resources. If you filter the resources to include all resources in the Production department, this can help you see if others in the Production department might be available to take on some of the work the Production engineers are doing. Click the Goto Overallocation button on the Resource Management toolbar to move through time to locate the next overallocated resource.

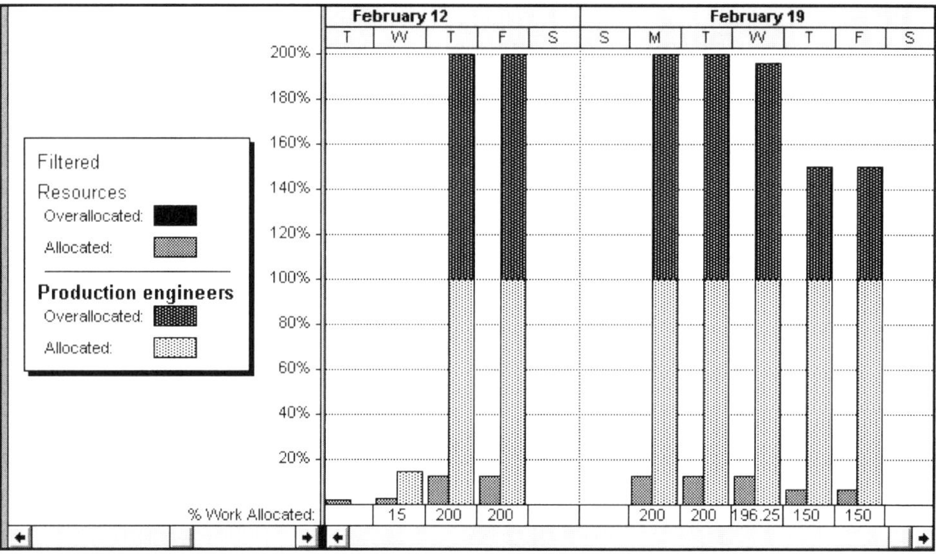

CUSTOMIZING TOOLBARS

In Microsoft Project, you have complete control over the toolbars. The toolbars can be customized to carry out the commands and actions you use most. For example, if you often switch between two tables, you can assign each table to a button. When you want to use the other table, click its button instead of choosing it from the View Table submenu.

For toolbars, you can:

- Change the position on the screen. Just hold down Shift and drag the toolbar anywhere in the window.
- Change the order of the buttons. Just hold down Shift and drag the button to the new location.
- Remove buttons. Just hold down Shift and drag the button off the toolbar.
- Change the toolbars displayed.
- Change the buttons on each toolbar.

For toolbar buttons, you can:

- Change the look of the buttons.
- Change the command carried out when you click a button.

- Change the ToolTip and status bar text displayed for the button.
- Insert a blank button, create a pattern for the button, and assign a command to it.

You can, of course, create new toolbars or copy toolbars from other open files or templates using the Organizer. To delete a toolbar from your file, use the Delete button in the Organizer dialog box.

CHANGING THE TOOLBARS

The quickest way to change the displayed toolbars is to point to any toolbar and click the right mouse button or Ctrl+click if your mouse has one button. In the shortcut menu, click the name of the toolbar to show or hide. Those toolbars currently displayed have a check mark next to their names on the shortcut menu.

You can also use the View Toolbars command to show and hide toolbars. In the Toolbars dialog box, you can also reset a toolbar you have changed, change the buttons on a toolbar, create new toolbars, and go to the Organizer to copy toolbars from other open files.

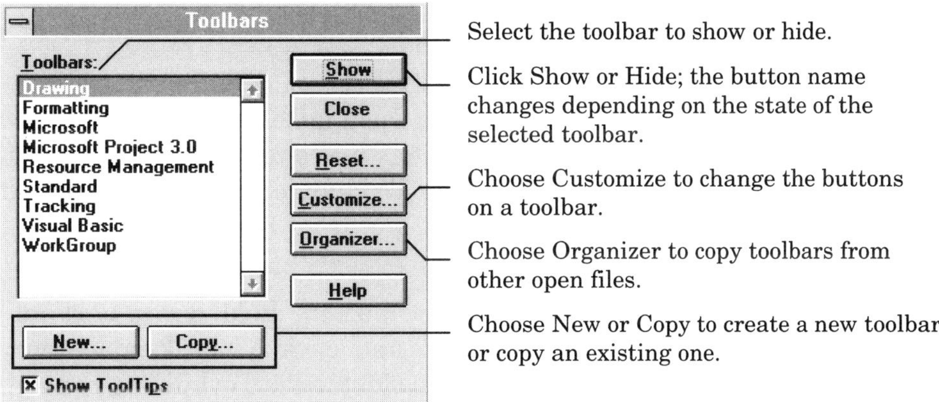

When you want to add a button to a toolbar, choose the Customize button or choose Tools Customize/Toolbars. Find the button you want and drag it into place on the toolbar. The buttons are grouped into categories to make it easier to find the one you want.

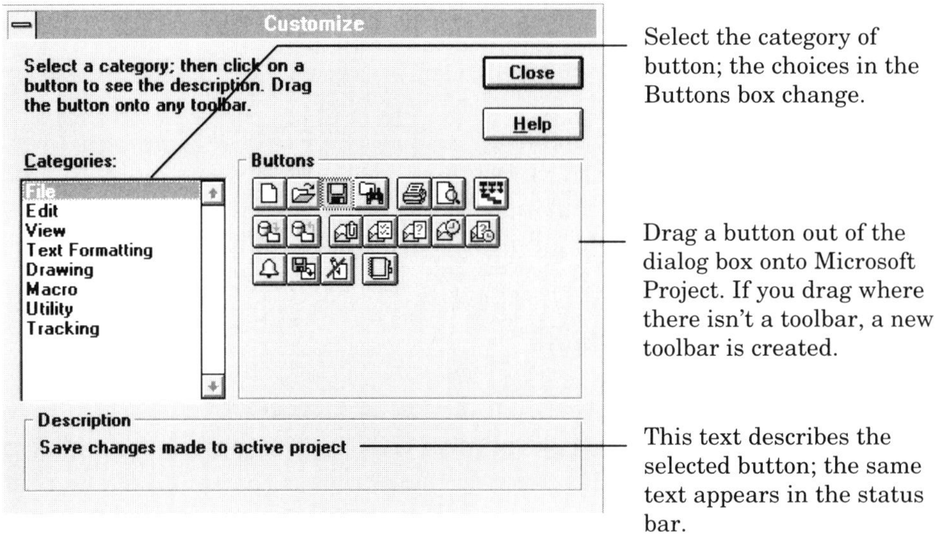

Select the category of button; the choices in the Buttons box change.

Drag a button out of the dialog box onto Microsoft Project. If you drag where there isn't a toolbar, a new toolbar is created.

This text describes the selected button; the same text appears in the status bar.

CHANGING THE TOOLBAR BUTTONS

To change the look of a toolbar button or the command assigned to the button, hold down Ctrl in Windows or Command on the Macintosh and click the button. Or point to the button and click the right mouse button or Ctrl+click if your mouse has one button; on the shortcut menu, select Customize Tool.

Any changes you make in the Customize Tool dialog box—from changing the button picture to changing the command assigned to the button—affect the button you clicked. To change the picture, you can either edit the existing picture or select one from the Picture box, which has over 160 pictures in it.

If you want to create a new button, hold down Ctrl in Windows or Command on the Macintosh and click a blank space on a toolbar. A blank button is added and the Customize Tool dialog box appears.

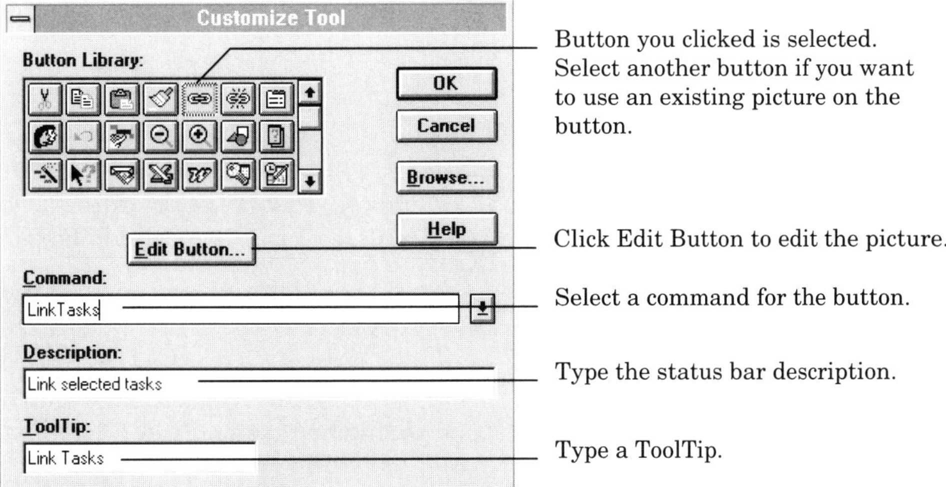

When you select the command or action you want associated with the button, you can type an argument in square brackets after the command. An argument tells the command what to do, such as which view to display. For example, to have a button display the Resource Allocation view, you would select the ViewApply command from the list and then type **[Resource Allocation]** following the command name.

When you choose the Edit Button button, you can change the pixels in the picture, change the colors, and preview the button.

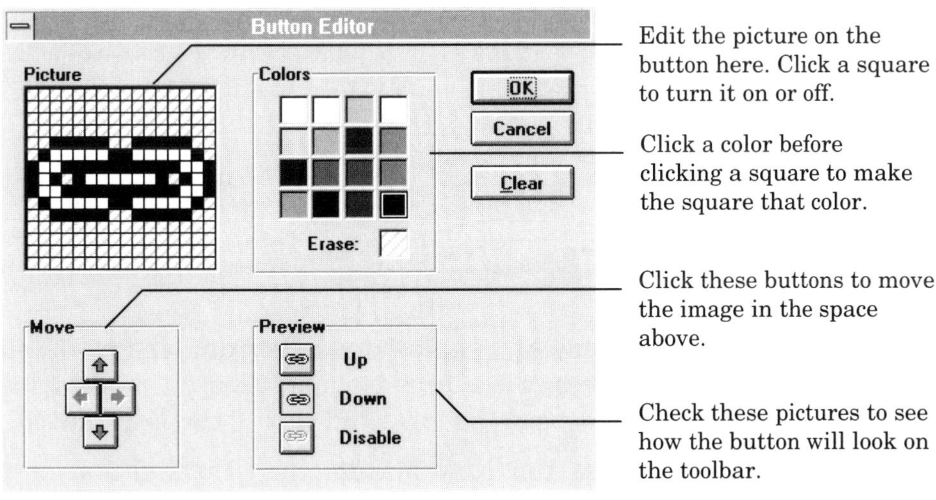

When you are finished, choose OK.

CUSTOM EDIT FORMS

Edit forms are dialog boxes you use to enter information about selected tasks or resources. The Task Information and Resource Information dialog boxes that are displayed when you click the Information button on the Standard toolbar or choose Insert Task Information or Insert Resource Information are examples of edit form dialog boxes.

You can create your own dialog boxes to enter the information that is common in your company. For example, if you are interested only in the percent work complete and the date a task started, you can create a custom edit form containing these fields. The information you enter in this dialog box will be added to all the tasks selected when you displayed the form.

To create a custom edit form, you choose Tools Customize/Forms. As is the case with other tools, you can choose to edit an existing form, copy an existing form and change it, or create a new form. The following example shows how to create a new form so you can enter percent work complete and the actual start date for tasks.

Choose Tools Customize/Forms.

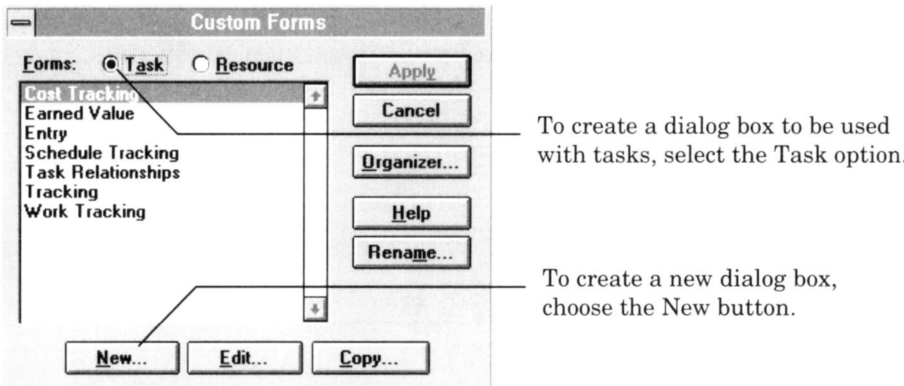

If you want to copy an existing dialog box and change it, select the one you want to copy in the Forms box and choose the Copy button; to edit an existing form, select the form and choose the Edit button.

When you choose the New button, the Copy button, or the Rename button, you see the following dialog box in which you name the form.

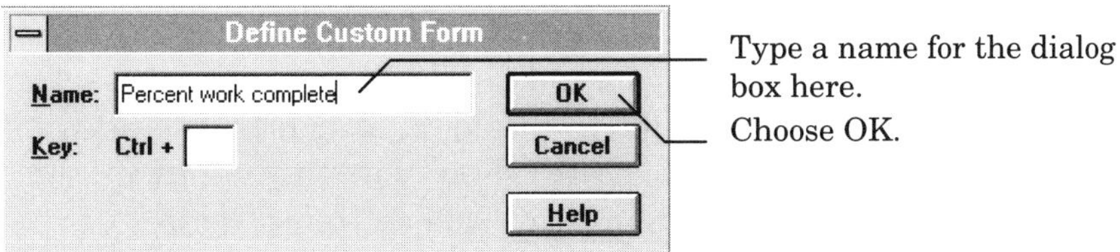

The Dialog Editor starts. The Dialog Editor is a separate application included with Microsoft Project, and used to specify the fields you want in your dialog box and their arrangement. To create the example form, add fields for the task name, the start date, the actual start date, and the percent work complete. First add the text to label each field. Choose Item Text.

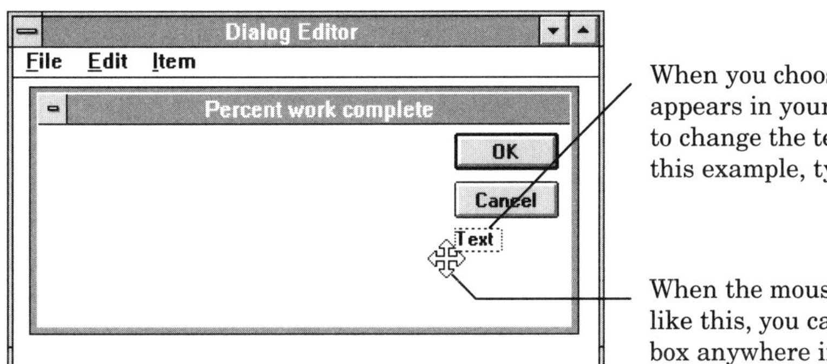

When you choose Item Text, this appears in your dialog box. Type to change the text in the box. For this example, type Task Name.

When the mouse pointer looks like this, you can drag the text box anywhere in the dialog box.

Drag the text box to the left side of the screen. Each time you press Enter, another text item appears so you can continue adding the items you want in the form. Add three more items, as indicated in the following illustration.

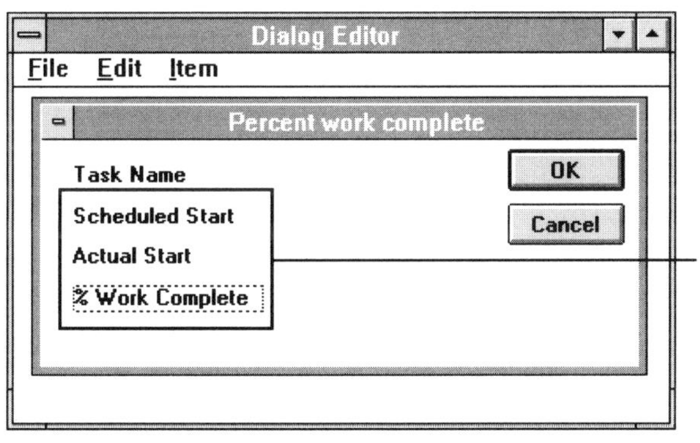

Press Enter and type the name to label each field you plan to add.

Next you enter the fields to go with each label. To do this, use the Item Fields command. When you add a field, it can either be set up so you can change the information for the field, or it can be included as static text. Static text means that it will show you the value in the field at the moment, but you can't change it. Choose Item Fields.

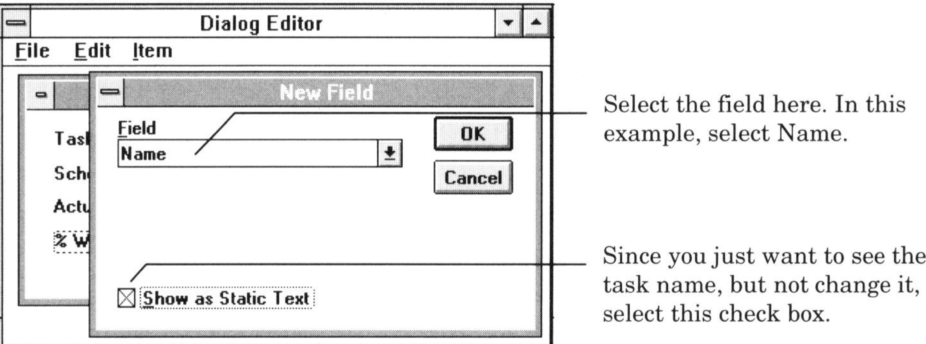

Choose OK.

The field is added below the four text fields. Drag the field to the right of the Task Name label.

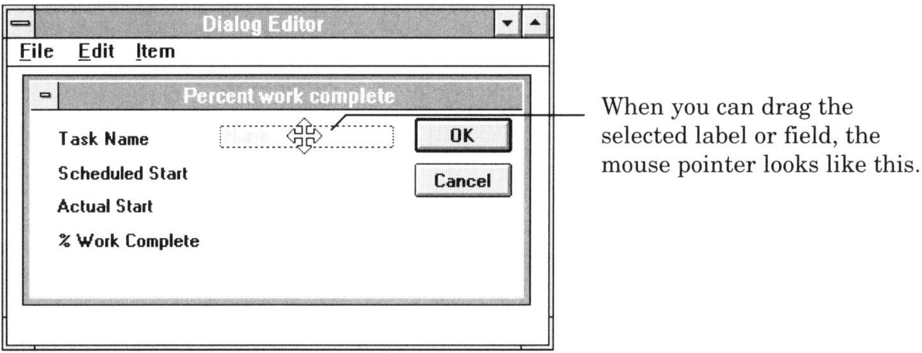

You can also use the commands on the Edit menu to move items around.

Add the Start field as static text, and add the Actual Start field and % Work Complete fields as text you can change (clear the Show As Static Text check box in the New Field dialog box). Fields for which you'll be able to enter values in the dialog box have a solid border; those that are static have no border unless they are selected.

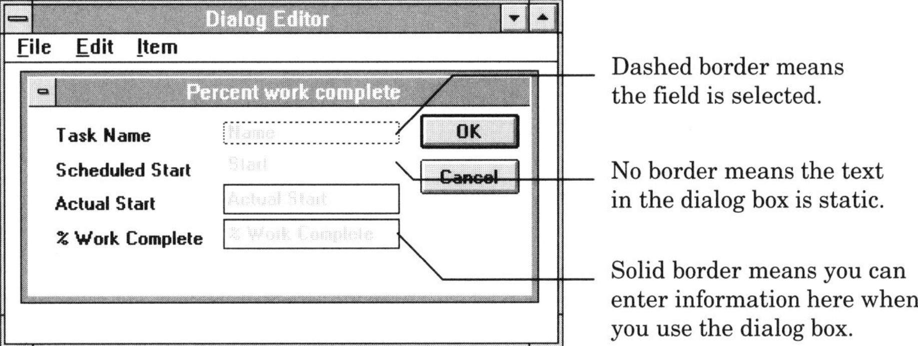

You can move the fields around and change the size of the dialog box until everything is arranged and sized just as you want it. To move and size fields and the dialog box, use the mouse or the commands on the Edit menu.

When you are finished with your dialog box, you choose File Exit in Windows or File Quit on the Macintosh to return to Microsoft Project. To display your new dialog box, choose the Apply button in the Custom Forms dialog box. When you are tracking your project, you can use the new dialog box to enter the actual start date and the percent work complete for each task.

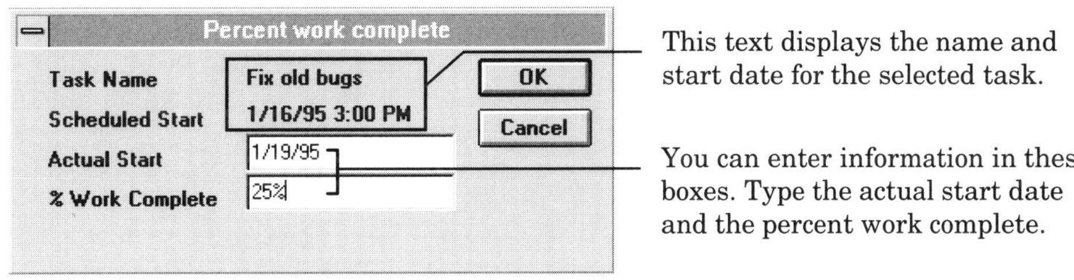

You can also display a custom form by assigning it to a button on a toolbar or adding the form to any menu.

MACROS

In Microsoft Project, you can create macros to do repetitive tasks, such as print a set of monthly reports, search the Notes box for certain text, or format text in a specific way. The quickest way to create a macro is to record the keystrokes using the Tools Record Macro command. You can also use Visual Basic for applications (VBA) to create or edit macros.

After you record a macro, you run it by choosing Tools Macros. Select the macro you want to run and choose the Run button. You can also click the Run Macro button on the Visual Basic toolbar to run a macro.

To edit a macro, choose Tools Macros. In the Macro Name box, select the name of the macro you want to edit or view. Choose the Edit button. The view changes to the Module Editor view, which contains the lines in your macro.

For help using VBA , use Microsoft Project Help. Choose Help Contents and select Visual Basic Reference. The reference section includes areas on using Visual Basic, a programming language summary, and reference information. The language summary lists and explains all commands, along with the arguments for each. While working on a macro, you can get help with a keyword in your macro by selecting the keyword and pressing F1 in Windows or Command+/ or the Help key on the Macintosh. The Help topic will explain the syntax and use of the keyword and, if it includes sample code, you can cut the sample and paste it into your macro.

Information about writing macros with Microsoft VBA is beyond the scope of this book. But there are books available about this programming language, which is also used with other Microsoft applications, including Microsoft Excel version 5.0. Check with your local computer book seller for more information.

INDEX

-1-

12-hour clock, 116

-A-

abbreviations
  duration, 91
  lead or lag time, 107
  rate of pay, 124
  task relationships, 110
accelerating schedule, 153
accrual methods, 125
active view bar, 105
activities. *See* task
actual cost, 236
  entering, 252–54
    after task complete, 252, 253
    on Task Form illustrated, 254
  printing to date, 286
Actual date fields containing NA, 248
actual dates replace scheduled dates, 248
actual duration, 236, 239
  calculated when enter percent complete, 250
  entering, 240, 250–51
  percent complete and, 246
Actual fields, 164, 239
actual finish date, 236, 239
  how to enter, 240
  matches current schedule, 239
  percent complete and, 246
  when to enter, 248
Actual Finish field, 244
actual information, entering, 239
actual start date, 236, 239, 263
  how to enter, 240
  matches current schedule, 239
  percent complete and, 246, 248
  setting with mouse, 249–50
  when to enter, 248
Actual Start field, 244
actual work completed, 236, 252–54
ACWP field, 272
adding
  buttons to toolbar, 372
  commands to menu, 357
  custom field to a table illustrated, 340
  holiday illustrated, 361
  lag to resolve overallocations, 153
  notes to resources, 293
  notes to tasks, 92, 216, 292
  overtime work, 175–76
adding *(continued)*
  shifts, 259
  table to Table submenu illustrated, 358
  task reminders, 319
  tasks to baseline schedule, 274–75
adjusting the schedule, 165–93
alignment, changing column, 342
All Resources filter, applying, 156, 271
All Tasks filter, 150, 155, 267, 269
analyzing differences between baseline and current schedules, 256
analyzing variance, 256–58
  table for investigating, 257
  using Microsoft Project, 268–73
applying
  filter, 17–18
  table, 15–16
  view, 18
arranging tasks, 70–73
arrows on PERT Chart, controlling, 213
As Late As Possible constraint, 101
As Soon As Possible constraint, 101, 154
assigning resources, 117–36
  adding new resource to resource pool, 130
  adding resources to shorten duration, 173–74
  advantages of, 117
  changing work assignment, 129
  Task Form, 132
  task views, 128–30
  to several tasks at once, 130
  to summary tasks and subproject tasks, 129
  to tasks, 127–32
  typing in Resource Names field, 129
  typing several resources for one task, 129
  why do so, 117
Assignments reports
  Overallocated Resources report, 289, 295
  Weekly To-Do List report, 199
  Who Does What report, 199
  Who Does What When report, 199, 298
assumptions, 140
  defined, 55
  defining for project, 57–59
  for durations, 92
  guidelines for listing, 58
  project, 55
Attach Note button on Standard toolbar, 92
attaching project to resource pool, 311
automatic calculation, turning off, 151
Automatically Add New Resources check box, 132
availability, showing resource
  Resource Graph, 161
  Resource Usage view, 157

–B–

BAC field, 272
Backup Template, 351
BACKUP.MPT, 351
backward pass to calculate schedule, 141
backward scheduling, 60
Bar Styles dialog box
  Gantt Chart illustrated and explained, 366
  Resource Graph
    allocated and overallocated work illustrated, 369
    cumulative and new cost illustrated, 162
    illustrated and explained, 368
bars on Calendar, changing appearance of, 222
bars on Gantt Chart, changing appearance of, 210, 365–67
base calendar, 133, 134
  changing base calendar for resource, 133–34
  customizing, 359–64
  defined, 61
  for each shift, 180
  link to resource calendar, 133
  multiple, 62, 63, 133
  specifying for a resource, 133
baseline
  comparing with updated schedule, 235
  freezing, 165, 167
  PlanningWizard prompt to save, 75
Baseline fields, 164, 238
baseline schedule, 164, 238
  adding tasks to, 274–75
  and evaluating progress, 255, 256
  comparing with current, 260–68
  contents of, 192
  creating, 167
  freezing in Microsoft Project, 192–93
  viewing on Task Sheet, 193
Baseline table
  applying, 193
  illustrated, 193
  viewing baseline schedule, 193
BCWP field, 272
BCWS field, 272
borders, changing on PERT nodes, 213
bottom-up method, 70
  creating outline using, 81
brainstorming task list, 69
Budget report, 200, 286, 298
  illustrated, 229, 287
  procedure for printing, 228, 287
Button Editor dialog box illustrated, 373
button on toolbar
  adding new button to toolbar, 372
  customizing toolbar buttons, 372–73
  identifying purpose of, 241

–C–

Calculate Project button, 151
calculated filter, 344
  illustrated, 346
calculating
  automatic, turning off, 151
  duration for resource, 122
  durations in Microsoft Excel, 326–32
  schedule, 7
    example, 140
    when manual calculation is on, 151
  work, 121–23
calendars
  about project, 61–63
  adding longer hours, 177–78
  base, 61
  changing base, 361–64
  changing resource, 133–34
  creating, 360–61
  customizing, 359–64
  default settings, 62
  defined, 61
  extending working hours, 175
  for fixed-duration scheduling, 133
  for scheduling, 133
  from another project, 319
  how Microsoft Project uses, 56, 61
  indicating overnight hours, 180
  link between base and resource, 133
  multiple base, 63
  project, 177, 361
  resource, 61, 120
  saving, 64
  setting base, 61–63
  sharing, 64, 317
  shifts, 62
  Standard, 62
Calendar view, 26–27
  appearance of bars and text, 222
  changing
    height or width, 27
    look, 222
    tasks included on, 222
  combination view, 27
  constraint entered when drag task, 155
  creating task, 27
  customizing, 27, 222
  displaying, 221
  previewing, 221
  printing, 136, 198, 221–22
    procedure, 221–22
  printed, illustrated, 221
  text on calendar, 222
Cancel button, 46
cash flow, 119

Change Working Time dialog box
  adding holiday illustrated, 361
  creating new calendar illustrated, 360
  entering hours spanning two days illustrated, 363
  illustrated, 362
changing
  alignment of information in column, 336–37
  appearance of Gantt Chart, 365–67
  appearance of Resource Graph, 367–78
  base calendar used by resource, 133–34
  calendar, 361–64
    adding longer hours, 177–78
  column, 16
    content, 336–37
    in displayed table, 337–41
    width illustrated, 339
  combination view, 352–353
  commands on the menus, 356–59
  cost, 184
  current date, 281
  days that make task critical, 147, 274
  direction of printing on paper, 207
  displayed table, 337–41
  existing view, 351–53
  filters, 18, 344–50
  font or color of task or resource, 279
  information in a view, 200
  menu bar, 356–59
  order of tasks or resources, 364–65
    before printing, 200
  percent complete
    Task Sheet, 247
    Tracking table, 247
    Update Tasks dialog box, 246–47
  resource assignments
    illustrated, 183
    in Microsoft Project, 182–83
    to reduce costs, 182–83
  resource calendar, 133–34
  resource information for several resources at once, 126
  scope
    to decrease duration, 181–82
    to lower costs, 185
  single view, 352
  status bar text, 358
  tables, 16, 336–43
  task cost, 183–84
  task dependencies, 25
    to decrease duration, 180–81
  tasks displayed, 200
  tasks to milestones, 75
  timescale, 159
  title of column, 336–37
  toolbar button order, 370
  toolbars, 370–73
changing *(continued)*
  views, 19, 351–56
  width of column, 336
  work
    for a resource, 130–32
    illustrated on Task Entry view, 131
  working days or hours, 62
    for resource, 134
check box in dialog box, 47
checking
  constraints, 153–55
  cost variance, 265–66
  costs, 162–64
  if tasks on schedule, 262–63
  list of resources, 38
  more than one field in a filter, 346
  over or under allocated resources, 274
  project finish date and cost, 171–72, 261
  proposed changes to schedule, 274
  relationships, 153–55
  resources, 155–61
    allocation, 36, 40
    allocation across projects, 309
    cost, 36, 40, 164
    cost or work variance, 270–71
    usage, 157–59
    work, 36, 40
  task assignments, 160
    across projects, 309
  task cost, 163–64
  work variance, 265
checking for
  links between projects, 309
  slack in the schedule, 266
  tasks that should have started, 260
  tasks that started late, 290
  variance in dates, work, and cost, 264–66
choosing a command, 44–45
choosing menu or command with keys
  specifying key to be used, 357
click with mouse defined, 12
Clipboard, 331, 332
Close button, 46
closing a combination view, 43
collapsing an outline, 214, 261
collecting progress data, 236–38
  how often, 238
  using Microsoft Mail, 243
  using Microsoft Project, 241–43
  what to collect, 236–37
  where to get it, 237–38
column
  adding custom field illustrated, 340
  alignment, changing, 336–37
    Table Definition dialog box, 342
  changing, 16, 337–41

column *(continued)*
  changing width, 336
    illustrated, 339
    Table Definition dialog box, 342
  content, changing, 336–37
  making same width as information, 336
  title, changing, 336–37
  width, changing, 39, 336–37
Column Definition dialog box illustrated, 337
columns printed, controlling, 224
combination view, 42–43
  and Calendar view, 27
  and Resource Graph, 37
  and Resource Usage view, 41
  creating, 43
    Gantt/Task PERT illustrated, 353
    new, 355–56
combined projects, working with, 316
combining open projects, 315–16
combining projects to view together, 301
combining projects visually, 312
comma as list separator character, 111
commands
  changing on View menu, Table or Filtered For submenu, 356, 358
  choosing, 44–45
  customizing menus, 356–59
  followed by ..., 45
  naming convention, 12
  submenu, 12
  using, 44
command on menu, changing command associated with, 357
comments about project
  entering, 61
  printing, 208
common reports, 197–201
communicating
  plan, 195–231
  progress, 277–98
  why important to, 195
company name, entering, 60
comparing
  baseline and current schedule, 235
  baseline and current start and finish dates on Tracking Gantt, 263
  baseline and scheduled duration, 260, 263–64
  current schedule to baseline on Tracking Gantt, 23
  group data to individual resource on Resource Graph, 161
  values in two fields, 344
  where you are with where you planned to be, 271
Completed Tasks filter, 265, 266
  applying, 265
Completed Tasks report, 279, 287–88
  illustrated, 287
  procedure for printing, 288
computer and project management, 5–7
conserving computer memory, 303
Consolidate Projects dialog box, 313
  illustrated, 312
constraint dates
  caution about using, 100
  default if don't type one, 114
  defined, 100
  entering, 114
  overriding calculated schedule dates, 113
  using effectively, 113
Constraint Dates table, 115, 145, 154
  applying, 154
  illustrated, 155
constraints, 97, 100–102, 140, 144, 180, 181
  checking, 145, 153–55
    to resolve scheduling problems, 153
    to shorten critical path, 143
  default, 113
  effect of on schedule, 169
  entering, 112–16
  examples of using, 102
  finding those you didn't enter, 155
  time used by default, 115
  types, 101
    changing, 114
  using in Microsoft Project, 112–16
contingency plan, 58
controlling
  costs, 269
  detail in reports using subprojects and master projects, 308
  look of Resource Graph, 161
  periods printed in reports, 220
  project to stay on track, 255–75
  when tasks scheduled using calendars, 61
  when work occurs on task, 131–32
conventions used in book, 12
Copy button on Standard toolbar, 306
Copy Picture button on Standard toolbar, 318, 333
Copy Picture dialog box illustrated, 333
copying
  combination view, 352–353
  Fill Down command, 126, 247
  filter, 347–48
  information so it changes when original changes, 322
  scheduled dates into actual fields, 243–45
  single view, 352
  table, 337–41
  tasks, 306
  views, 351–56

corrective action, determining, 258–59, 273–74
cost, 140, 144
  accrual method, 124
  as calculated by Microsoft Project, 183
  benefits of planning, 119
  changing for tasks, 183–84
  changing for unfinished task, 183
  checking, 162–64
    in Microsoft Project, 146
    resource, 164
    resource variance, 270–71
    task, 163–64
  creating custom report showing, 294
  cumulative vs. new, 162–63
  data to enter for resources, 119, 124
  default, 124
  entering
    actual cost values, 252–54
    fixed cost for a task, 135
    for task with no resources assigned, 183
    per-use fees, 185
  estimating, 119–20
  evaluating progress, 256
  format for typing, 124
  how calculated, 120
  how Microsoft Project tracks, 253
  ideas to lower, 166–67
  lowering by decreasing scope, 185
  on Task report, 217
  options for reducing, 170
  printing
    by period, 225
      procedure, 226
    cumulative costs graph, 200, 230–31
    resources costing more than planned, 288
    summary of costs to date, 286–87
    task cost, 226–30
    tasks costing more than planned, 288
  recalculated until task complete, 253
  reducing, 182–85
    by reducing scope, 167
    per-use fees, 184–85
    work to reduce cost, 185
  Resource Graph, 160
  reviewing, 144
  sorting resources by, 157
  subproject task, 304
  value you enter replaced by Project, 184
  what to do if too high, 146
  why include, 118
  within budget, 145
cost account numbers, adding field for, 76
cost curves, creating with spreadsheet application, 317
cost details, including in report, 206
cost for resources over project life, 145
cost for tasks over project life, 145
cost information, exchanging with spreadsheet application, 317
cost of resource on each task, 162
cost of using resource
  displaying on Resource Usage view, 157
Cost Overbudget filter, 260, 266, 294
  applying, 266, 269
  illustrated, 346
  locating resources that increased cost, 268
  locating tasks that increased cost, 268
  resource variance, 271
  viewing tasks over budget, 269
Cost table, 15, 145, 260, 269
  applying, 184, 266, 269
  displaying, 135, 163
  entering a fixed cost on, 135
  for resources, 270
  for tasks, 266
  illustrated, 163, 266
  locating resources that increased cost, 268
  locating tasks that increased cost, 268
  printing over budget resources, 294
  resource cost variance, 271
  reviewing task costs, 163
  to change costs, 184
  to view variance for resources on Resource Sheet, 270
cost totals, showing in report, 218
Cost Tracking custom form, displaying, 271
cost variance
  checking, 265–66
  for resources, 271
  locating tasks with, 269–70
  printing tasks with cost variance, 292–93
  printing to date, 286
Costs reports
  Budget report, 200, 286, 298
  Earned Value report, 289, 296, 298
  Overbudget Resources report, 288, 293, 298
  Overbudget Tasks report, 288, 292
  Weekly Cash Flow report, 200
CPM, 7
Create New Base Calendar dialog box
  based on existing calendar illustrated, 361
  illustrated, 360
creating
  combination view, 43, 355–56
  custom edit forms, 374–77
  data collection table, 341
  Data Collection view illustrated, 354–55
  filters, 18, 344–50
  graph of cumulative cost, 162
  list to decide importance of tasks, 181
  macros, 377–78
  new calendar, 360–61
  new custom form, 374–77, 374
  new single view, 354–55

creating (continued)
report, 205–7
resource pool from existing project, 310–11
resource pool from scratch, 311
Resource Usage view over Task Sheet, 355
schedule alternatives, 168
schedule, basic steps, 4
subproject, 305–6
procedure, creating from existing project, 306
procedure, creating new project, 305
summary bar for entire project, 316
table, 16, 341–43
table to import resources, standard rate, overtime rate, 323
task
Calendar view, 27
Gantt Chart, 74
PERT Chart, 25, 74
template procedure, 302
view, 19, 354
to collect data, 241
criteria for filters, 16
Critical column, 150
Critical filter, 17, 145, 149
applying, 149
displaying as highlighting filter, 150–51
illustrated on Task Sheet, 149
viewing near-critical tasks, 274
critical path, 7, 140–42, 141, 142, 143, 144, 146, 172
changing, 142
changing with GanttChartWizard, 210
checking in Microsoft Project, 145, 147–51
checking task order, relationships, constraints on, 143
defined, 140
multiple, 141
on Gantt Chart, 147
on PERT Chart, 24, 148
printing, 198, 210–11
shortening, 140, 172–82
by changing dependencies, 180–81
by changing project scope, 181–82
by working longer hours, 174–78
ideas for decreasing, 166, 169
when have multiple, 173
time saved on task not reflected in project finish date, 142
why important to identify, 147
Critical Path Method of scheduling, 7, 140
critical tasks, 7, 140–42, 186
accelerating, 259
becoming noncritical when finished, 246
changing time that makes task critical, 147
checking in Microsoft Project, 147–51
completing faster, 173
finishing makes task noncritical, 248
identifying those near critical, 273, 274
critical tasks (continued)
making text stand out, 148
on Gantt Chart, 147
on PERT Chart, 24
on Task Sheet, 148–51
reducing scope to shorten duration, 181
resources available for, 186
shortened duration not reflected in project finish date, 172
specifying how much slack, 51
using Critical filter to view on Task Sheet, 149
why important to identify, 147
Critical Tasks report, 198
CSV file format, 318
cumulative cost
checking, 162–63
over life of project, 162
printing graph of, 230–31
report, procedure for printing, 231
Resource Graph, 160, 231
Resource Usage view, 157
cumulative work
Resource Graph, 160
Resource Usage view, 157
currency
appearance of, 52
changing symbol and placement, 124
Current Activities reports
Completed Tasks report, 279, 287
Should Have Started Tasks report, 288, 289–90
Slipping Tasks report, 288
illustrated, 290
Tasks Starting Soon report, 198, 298
current date, changing, 281
current date line, 262, 281
changing, 263, 281
current schedule and evaluating progress, 255, 256
custom edit forms, 374–77
custom fields, 126, 337
in a filter, 348
number fields for tasks, 321, 337
resource fields, 321
sorting or filtering on, 126
text fields, 126, 321, 337
when importing information, 321
Custom Forms dialog box illustrated, 374
Customize (toolbar) dialog box illustrated, 372
Customize Tool dialog box, 372
illustrated, 373
customizing
Calendar view, 27, 222
calendars, 359–64
Filtered For submenu, 359
filters, 344–50
Gantt Chart, 21, 210, 365–67
menus, 356–59
Microsoft Project, 49–52, 319, 335–78

customizing *(continued)*
PERT Chart, 25, 213
reports, 200
Resource Form, 35
Resource Graph, 37, 231, 367–78
Resource Sheet, 39, 223
Resource Usage view, 41, 224
supplied reports, 226
tables, 336–43
Task Form, 29
Task report, 217
Task Sheet, 33
toolbar buttons, 372–73
toolbars, 48, 370–73
views, 351–56
Cut button on Standard toolbar, 306
cutting tasks, 306
CV field, 272

–D–

data collection date, 263, 280
data collection sheet, creating, 242, 354
data collection table, 341
Data Collection view, creating, 354–55
date
changing current, 281
controlling from task in another project, 309
entering, 115–16
master project controls dates in subproject, 309
new task starts on, controlling, 51
printed in legend, changing, 281
separator characters, 116
sorting by, 364
Date Range filter, 17, 243
applying, 242
changing, 347
date variance, checking, 264–65
dates resources work on tasks, 160
dates, reviewing project, 140
day shift calendar, creating, 360–61
day week starts on, changing, 51
dBase, 332
file formats, 318
decreasing
column width, 336
duration, 172–82
adding shift, 178–80
decreasing task scope, 181
working longer hours, 174–78
default
constraint, 113
constraint date, 114
cost rate unit, 124
date new task starts on, 51
overtime rate, changing, 126
relationship, 106
default *(continued)*
resume work date, 252
scheduling method, 93, 95
standard rate, changing, 126
time, changing, 116
unit for duration, 91
view, changing, 76
Define Custom Form dialog box illustrated, 375
Define New View dialog box
creating new combination view illustrated, 355
creating new single view illustrated, 354
Del key, 109
delay bar on Delay Gantt, 22
delay between tasks, 97, 99–100
Delay field for resources, 131
resolving overallocations by shifting when work occurs on task, 191
Delay field for tasks, 43
delaying tasks to level resources, 188
Delay Gantt, 22, 43
displaying, 189, 267
in Resource Allocation view, 42, 190, 315
slack time on, 145, 152, 274, 260, 267
viewing delay added by leveling, 189
delay, removing delay added by leveling, 190
Delay table, 22
delaying work for a resource, 130–32
deleting
column in a table illustrated, 338
relationship on PERT Chart, 112
relationship on Task Form, 109
summary task, 81
dependencies, 97
between tasks, 24
changing to shorten duration, 180–81
checking to shorten critical path, 143
entering
Gantt Chart, 103–104
PERT Chart, 111–112
Task Entry view, 105–109
Task Sheet, 109–11
Detail Gantt, 22, 145
displaying, 152, 267, 268
printing slipping tasks, 291
slack time on, 152, 260, 267, 274
illustrated, 153, 267
slippage illustrated, 260, 268
detail in reports
controlling using master projects and subprojects, 308
controlling using outlining 286
determining corrective action, 258–59, 273–74
determining when resources assigned to tasks, 160
diagonal lines on PERT Chart, 281
dialog boxes
creating custom. *See* forms
using, 44, 45–47

Dialog Editor, 375
  creating custom form illustrated, 375–77
direction reports, 277
  printing, 298
disconnecting from resource pool, 310
displaying
  all resources, 156
  all tasks, 155
  Calendar view, 221
  Delay Gantt, 189, 267
  Detail Gantt, 152, 268, 291
  list in dialog box, 46
  Organizer, 319
  Resource Sheet, 225
  toolbars, 48, 371–72
  Task Sheet, 32
  Tracking Gantt, 263
  views, 18
divider bar, 20
Don't Tell Me About This Again check box, 151
double-clicking with mouse
  defined, 12
  on PERT Chart, 25
  on Resource Sheet, 39
  on Task Sheet or Gantt Chart, 33
  subproject task, 33
  summary task, 33
  task, 33
drag-and-drop, 321, 332
  defined, 12
  moving tasks, 76
dragging start or finish and creating constraint, 155
dragging task on Gantt or Calendar and creating constraint, 113
Drawing toolbar, 48
driving resource, shortening duration by working longer hours, 177
duration
  abbreviations table, 91
  calculating in Microsoft Excel, 92, 326–32
  calculation when have overtime work, 175
  changes when add resources. *See* resource-driven scheduling
  changing
    by entering larger remaining duration, 250
    for task using resource-driven scheduling, 251
    to indicate schedule change for resource-driven task, 240
    working hours per day or week, 95
  comparing baseline and current, 263–64
  decreasing, 172–82
    adding new resource names, 174
    adding shift, 178–80
    assigning more resources, 173–74
    changing dependencies, 180–81
    changing task scope, 181
decreasing *(continued)*
    changing project scope, 181–82
    increasing resource units, 173
    when not assigning resources, 174
    working longer hours, 174–78
  default, 74
  default unit used, 51, 91
  defined, 87
  doesn't change when work longer hours, 178
  entering
    actual or remaining, 250–51
    in Microsoft Project, 90, 91–92
  estimates
    change in, 237
    importance of recognizing that are estimates, 87
    units to use, 88
  estimating, 87–96
    based on history, 89
    using experience, 90
    using PERT method, 90
  for resource, 122
  formula
    calculating duration when change remaining duration, 250
    PERT method of calculating, 330
  guidelines for determining, 88–89
  how Microsoft Project calculates, 95
  ideas for decreasing in Microsoft Project, 169
  including assumptions, 88
  increasing to resolve overallocations, 190
  indicating if changed, 236
  methods for determining, 89–90
  noting assumptions, 92
  of subproject task, 304, 307
  predicting remaining duration, 257–58
  printing report showing baseline and actual, 279
  project duration defined, 140
  rescheduling remaining, 252
  summary tasks, 81
  unchanged by number of resources. *See* fixed-duration scheduling
  units used to calculate, 95
  updating
    scheduled duration, 251
    typing new value for duration, 251
    typing value for remaining duration, 251
  who determines, 88
dynamically exchanging information, 318

–E–

early finish date defined, 141
early start date defined, 141
earned value, 257, 271–73
  for one task, 272
  printing, 289

Earned Value custom form, 272
  displaying, 273
  illustrated, 273
Earned Value report, 289, 298
  illustrated, 296
  printing procedure, 296–97
Earned Value table, 268, 271
  applying, 272
  columns defined, 272
  illustrated, 272
Edit Clear/Contents command, 111
Edit Copy (Task) command, 306
Edit Copy command
  and exchanging information with other applications, 318
  and exporting information, 322, 331
  linking tasks between projects, 309
Edit Cut (Task) command, 306
Edit Delete Task command, 109
Edit Fill Down command, 126
  entering same percent complete for multiple tasks, 247
edit forms, creating, 374–77
Edit Link Tasks command, 103
Edit Links command, 322
  checking for links between projects, 309
Edit Paste command, 306
  importing information, 321, 332
Edit Paste Special command
  and exchanging information with other applications, 318
  importing information, 321
  linking tasks between projects, 309
Edit Paste vs. Edit Paste Special, 321
Edit Unlink Tasks command, 104
editing
  calendars, 359–64
  filters, 18, 347–48
  single view, 352
  table, 16, 337–41
  views, 19, 351–56
elapsed lead or lag time, entering as percentage, 108
elapsed time
  defined, 91
  entering lead or lag time in, 108
electronic mail
  routing project schedule,86
  using to update task status, 243
entering
  actual dates in Update Tasks dialog box, 248–49
  actual or remaining duration illustrated in Update Tasks dialog box, 250
  actual work
    after task complete, 253
    and cost, 252–54
    illustrated on Task Form, 253
entering *(continued)*
  constraint date, 114
  dates, 115–16
  dependencies
    on PERT Chart, 111–12
    on Task Sheet, 109–11
  duration, 91–92
    on tasks in progress, 250–51
  finish dates, 247–50
  fixed cost for task or resource, 135
  general project information, 59–61
  information into Microsoft Project, 48–49
  lead or lag time on Task Entry view, 107–9
  milestones, 74–77
  percent complete, 245–47
    fields changed based on, 246
  predecessors
    Gantt Chart, 103–04
    PERT Chart, 111–12
    Task Entry view, 105
    Task Sheet, 109–11
  progress, 240
  relationship on Task Entry view, 106–7
  resources, 123–27
    basic approaches, 120
    data you need to know, 123, 127
    on Resource Form, 127
    on Resource Sheet, 125–26
  start dates, 247–50
  tasks, 74–77
  time, 115–16
entry bar
  defined, 44
  turning on and off, 52
  using, 44, 48–49
entry bar list, 48–49
  assigning resources on Task Form, 132
  assigning resources using, 129
  resources in, 127
Entry table, 15
  applying, 214
errors when importing information, 325–26
estimating
  costs, 119–20
  duration
    based on average, 90
    based on history, 89
    using experience, 90
    using PERT method, 90
  resource needs, 118–19
  time for tasks, 87–96
evaluating
  progress to date, 255, 256, 260–68
  schedule, 139–64
    what to check, 139–40
    what to check in Microsoft Project, 144
examples of using constraints, 102

exception reports, 277
  printing, 288–97
  using filters to limit information, 278
  using sorting to put problems on top, 279
exchanging information, 32
  basic steps, 321
  Resource Sheet, 38
  spreadsheet or database application, 320
  Task Sheet, 33
  using a table to identify information, 321
  using Edit Copy and Edit Paste, 331
  using File Save As and File Open, 327–31
  with Lotus 1-2-3 or dBase, 332
  with Microsoft Excel, 326–32
  with other applicationfs, 317
expanding outline, 215
expected duration, 236
expected finish date, 236
expenditures printed by period, 225
experience to estimate duration, 90
experimenting with schedule, 7 ADD CH8?
Export dialog box illustrated, 328
exporting tasks, 322
  and outlining, 329
  to Microsoft Excel, 327–29
  using filters, 328

–F–

FAC field, 272
features of project management software, 8
FF relationship. *See* finish-to-finish
fields
  resource, 14
  resource assignment, 14
  task, 13
fields displayed, changing on PERT Chart, 213
File Add Routing Slip command, 86, 318
File Find File command, 61
file formats read by Microsoft Project, 318
File New command
  appearance of Summary Info dialog box, 59, 305
File Open command, 321
File Page Setup command, 201, 210
  changing columns printed on each page, 224
  dialog box illustrated, 202
  PERT Chart legend, 213
File Print command, 86, 116, 203, 205
File Print Preview command, 203
File Save As command, 85
  exporting information, 322
  saving a file in Excel format, 327
File Save Workspace command, 316
File Send command, 86, 116, 136
File Summary Info command, 59
  changing current date, 263
  checking costs, 145
File Summary Info command *(continued)*
  checking project finish date, 145, 146
  checking project finish date, duration, work, costs
    illustrated, 261
File Summary Info dialog box, 208
File Summary Info, Statistics dialog box
  checking project finish date and costs, 168, 171–72
Filter box on Formatting toolbar, 17, 149, 150, 200
  applying All Tasks filter, 155, 156
  applying Overallocated Resources filter, 156
  applying Tasks With Fixed Dates filter, 155
Filter Definition dialog box
  Cost Overbudget filter illustrated, 346
  creating a new filter illustrated, 349
  interactive filter illustrated, 345
  Milestones filter illustrated, 344
  Task Range filter illustrated, 345
Filtered For submenu, changing commands on, 356, 358
filtered resource, 368
filtering, 200
  on custom field, 126
  using WBS code, 84
filters, 14
  about, 16–18
  All Resources, 156
  All Tasks, 150
  applying, 17–18
  calculated, 344
  changing, 18
    existing, 347–48
    in a report, 200
    test used, illustrated, 347
    value used, illustrated, 347
  checking for tasks that started late, 290
  checking more than one field illustrated, 346
  comparing values in two fields, 17, 344
  copying, 347–48
  creating, 18, 243, 344–50
    filter for marked tasks, 350
    filter to find task scheduled to start before a
      date, 347
    Marked Tasks filter illustrated, 350
    new, 348–50
    Show Resources Reporting To illustrated, 349
    Start Before filter illustrated, 347
  criteria, 16, 344–46
  Critical, 17
  custom fields and, 348
  customizing, 344–50
  customizing the Filtered For submenu, 359
  Date Range, 17
  deleting a criterion, 347
  displaying all resources, 156
  displaying all tasks, 150
  displaying as highlighting filter, 150–51
  editing, 347–48

filters *(continued)*
  explained, 17
  highlighting, 16
  In Progress Tasks, 243
  Incomplete Tasks, 243
  interactive, 17, 344
  list of, 17
  resetting to original set, 351
  sharing, 317
  Should Start By, 243
  Slipping Tasks, 17
  specifying values when applying, 17, 344
  three types described, 344
  Unstarted Tasks, 243
  using from another project, 319
  using highlighting filter in a view, 355
  Using Resource, 27
  using when exporting, 328
finding solutions, 255
finish accrual method defined, 125
finish date
  changing dependencies to bring in, 180–81
  checking, 140, 145, 146, 261
  entering actual dates, 247–50
  evaluating progress, 256
  ideas for bringing in, 166
  matches current schedule, 239
  moving when leveling resources, 188
  setting for task, 100–102
  typing or dragging and entering constraint, 155
  what to do if too late, 146
Finish No Earlier Than constraint
  defined, 101
  entered by dragging or typing a date, 113
Finish No Later Than constraint
  defined, 101
  using to warn of slipping tasks, 113
Finish Var. column, 265
finish-to-finish defined, 99
finish-to-start
  creating link, 103–4
  defined, 98
  disadvantages, 99
fiscal year, changing starting month for, 51
fixed cost, 120
  defined, 135
  entering, illustrated, 135
Fixed Cost field, 135
fixed-duration scheduling
  adding resources to tasks with, 173
  and duration, work, units calculations, 123
  and work calculation, 121
  calendar used, 133
  changing duration for task, 240
  defined, 93
  examples, 93
fixed-duration scheduling *(continued)*
  making it default method, 95
  specifying, 94
Fixed field, 94
float time, 7. *See also* slack time
fonts, changing in report, 206
footer, 201
form
  assigning to toolbar or menu, 377
  creating new, 374–77
  using Dialog Editor to create, illustrated, 375–77
  using from another project, 319
Format Bar command, 21, 210
Format Bar Styles command
  adding bars for slack, 152
  Calendar view, 27, 222
  Gantt Chart, 21, 210, 366
  Resource Graph, 37, 161, 162, 231, 367
    illustrated, 369
    showing cumulative costs, 231
Format Box Styles command, 24, 25, 213
Format Details commands
  Resource Form, 34
  Resource Graph, 37, 161, 231
  Resource Usage view, 41, 158, 224
  Task Form, 28
Format Details/Cost command, 226
Format Details/Cumulative Cost command, 162, 231
Format Details/Percent Allocation command, 158, 223
Format Details/Predecessors & Successors command, 109
Format Details/Resource Cost command
  entering actual costs on Task Form, 253
  entering fixed cost for resource, 135
  Task Form, 164, 269
Format Details/Resource Schedule command, 122
  delaying resource work, 131
Format Details/Resource Work command
  adding overtime work, 176
  Task Form, 253, 270
Format Details/Resources & Successors command, 109
Format Details/Schedule command
  Resource Form, 160
  delaying resource work, 131
Format Details/Selected Tasks Only command
  Resource Usage view, 158
Format Details/Work command, 176
Format Font command
  dialog box, 279
  Gantt Chart, 21, 210
  Resource Sheet, 223
  Resource Usage view, 224
  Task Sheet, 32, 215
Format GanttChartWizard command, 366
  changing critical task bars, 147

Format Gridlines command
  Calendar view, 27
  Gantt Chart, 21, 210
  Resource Graph, 37, 231
  Resource Sheet, 39, 223
  Resource Usage view, 41, 224
  Task Sheet, 32, 215
Format Layout command
  Gantt Chart, 104
  PERT Chart lines and arrows, 213
Format Layout Now command, 25
Format Text Styles command
  Calendar view, 27, 222
  changing critical tasks on Task Sheet, 148
  changing look of text on PERT Chart, 213
  Gantt Chart, 21, 210
  PERT Chart, 25
  Resource Graph, 37, 231
  Resource Sheet, 38, 39, 223
  Resource Usage view, 41, 224
  Task Sheet, 32, 215
Format Timescale command
  Calendar view, 27, 222
  Gantt Chart, 21, 210
  Resource Graph, 37, 231
  Resource Usage view, 41, 223, 224, 226
formatting
  Gantt Chart, 365–67
  Resource Graph, 367–78
Formatting toolbar, 47, 146, 150
  applying filter, 18
  make task or resource stand out, 279
forms
  creating custom, 374–77
  resetting to original set, 351
  sharing, 317
formula
  PERT scheduling method, 90
  work calculation, 121
forward pass to calculate schedule, 140
forward scheduling, 60
free slack time
  defined, 143
  viewing on Task Sheet, 152
freezing baseline schedule, 165, 167, 192–93
frequency of data collection, 238
FS relationship. *See* finish-to-start

–G–

Gantt bar chart, 20
Gantt bars
  examples showing lead and lag time, 99–100
  formatting, 210
  order in which drawn, 367
Gantt Chart, 20–23
  adding baseline bars, 263
  adding Microsoft Excel chart to, 318
  assigning resources, 128–30
  changing
    actual start date with mouse illustrated, 250
    bars and look of bars, 210
    columns on Gantt table, 210
    default view, 76
    duration with mouse illustrated, 251
    font, 210
    gridlines, 210
    information in legend, 210
    order of tasks, 210
    percent complete with mouse illustrated, 246
    tasks displayed, 210
    timescale, 210
  checking
    critical path, 145
    if tasks on schedule, 260, 262–63
      illustrated, 262
    proposed changes to schedule, 274
    relationships, 153–54
  constraint entered when drag task, 155
  controlling where pages break, 200
  critical path illustrated, 147
  customizing, 20–21, 210
  double-clicking on, 33
  entering
    milestone, 74
    percent complete, 245
    progress information with mouse, 240
    task, 74
  formatting, 365–67
  including in an electronic mail message, 318
  link lines between tasks, removing, 104
  linking tasks, 103–4
  making one bar stand out, 210
  moving, 21
  narrow black progress bar, 246
  percent complete bar illustrated, 246
  print preview, 203–4
  printing, 136
    critical path, 198, 210–11
    major phases, 196, 197
    new schedule, 298
    outline collapsed to summarize schedule, 209
    progress compared to expected, 280
      procedure, 281
    progress on tasks, 279
    summary report of major phases procedure, 209
  setting actual start date with mouse, 249–50
  showing
    durations, 95
    linked tasks, 103
    tasks that should have started, 263

Gantt Chart *(continued)*
summary report with outline collapsed, illustrated, 209
text on, 210
viewing slack time, 152
Gantt Chart over Resource Usage view
illustrated, 159
to see resource usage for selected tasks, 158
Gantt Chart over Task PERT
checking predecessors and successors, 154
checking relationships, 145
creating named combination view, 353
illustrated, 154
Gantt Chart showing progress, illustrated, printed, 280
Gantt Chart under Resource Graph, 161, 314
Gantt table, 20
Gantt/Task PERT combination view, 353
GanttChartWizard, 20, 366
adding bars for slack, 152
adding baseline bars, 263
changing critical task bars, 147
changing critical tasks, 210
GanttChartWizard button on Standard toolbar, 366
getting project back on track, 257
global template, 64, 319
Global Template, 64, 319, 351
GLOBAL.MPT, 64, 319, 351
goal-setting process, 56–59
goals
setting
advantages, 55
for project, 51–64
guidelines, 56–57
testing validity of, 56
who sets, 55–56
Goto Overallocation button on Resource Management toolbar, 190, 314, 369
graveyard shift calendar, creating, 362
gridlines
Resource Sheet, 223
Resource Usage view, 224
Task Sheet, 215
guidelines
estimating durations, 88–89
estimating resources, 118
goals, 56–57
leveling resources, 187
milestones, 67–68
task sequence, 98
tasks, 66–67

-H-

headers, 201, 202
Hide Subtasks button on Formatting toolbar, 82, 214, 261
hiding
project, 316
tasks in outline, 81–82
toolbars, 48, 371–72
hierarchy, creating
outline, 78–81
subprojects, 304
WBS, 83–85
highlighting filters, 16, 150–51
using in a view, 355
highlighting task or resource in report, 279, 298
hiring additional resources, 173
history
developing by tracking progress, 236
to estimate duration, 89
holiday, adding to calendar, 61
illustrated, 361
resource calendar, 134
hours
entering hours that span two days illustrated, 363
hours per day or week
changing hours worked, 51
changing units used in duration calculations, 95

-I-

identifying problem areas, 235
identifying template files, 302
Import dialog box illustrated, 325
importing
dragging information from another application into Project, 326
errors, 325–26
list of tasks, 75
replacing information vs. creating new project, 325
resources and costs from Microsoft Excel, 323–26
using Edit Copy and Edit Paste, 326
using File Open, 323–26
ways to, 321
In Progress Tasks filter, 265, 266
applying, 265
checking tasks in progress, 268
described, 243
Incomplete Tasks filter described, 243

increasing column width, 336
increasing resource units to decrease duration, 173
Indent button on Formatting toolbar, 80
indending task in outline, 80
indicating key to use to choose menu or command, 357
indicating schedule has changed, 239
information
  exporting, 322
  importing, 321
Information button on Standard toolbar, 94, 114, 126, 134
Insert Page Break command, 200
Insert Resource Assignment command, 130
  changing resource assignments, 183
Insert Resource Information command, 134
  adding overtime rate, 176
  entering information for several resources, 126
Insert Resource Notes command, 293
Insert Task Information command
  Advanced tab, 114
  entering constraint, 114
  Resources tab, 94
Insert Task Notes command, 92
  adding notes to tasks, 292
  entering and reviewing notes, 216
inserting
  column in table illustrated, 339
  cut or copied tasks, 306
  tasks, 79
interactive filter, 17, 344
  dialog box illustrated, 345
  illustrated, 345

–J–

judging future progress based on past performance, 258

–K–

keeping detailed tasks in separate project, 303
keeping repetitive tasks in subprojects, 303
key combinations, 12
keys
  changing timescale to show less or more detail in schedule, 159
keywords, using to find files, 60, 61

–L–

lag time. *See* lead or lag time
landscape mode, 207
late finish date defined, 141
late start date defined, 141
latest date to start project, 60
lead or lag time, 97, 99–100
  adding on PERT Chart, 112
  adding to decrease duration, 180
  adding to resolve overallocations, 153
  entering as a percentage, 108
  entering on Task Entry view, 107–9
  examples, 99–100, 108
  how indicate, 107
  shown on Task PERT, 154
  table of unit abbreviations, 107
left-pointing arrow mouse pointer, 249
legend, 201
  changing current date printed, 281
  setting up in PERT Chart, 213
level message in status bar, 129, 186
  illustrated, 156
Leveling Cue Cards, 190
leveling resources, 22, 186–91
  guidelines for, 187, 190–91
  how Microsoft Project levels, 189
  how Microsoft Project selects tasks to delay, 188
  moving project end date, 188
  removing delay, 190
  using Microsoft Project to, 186–90
lines on Gantt Chart, removing or adding link lines between tasks, 104
lines on PERT Chart, controlling look of, 213
Link Tasks button on Standard toolbar, 103
linking tasks, 103
  automatically, 51
  between projects, 309
  Calendar view, 27
  creating finish-to-start relationship, 103–4
  Gantt Chart, 103–4
  PERT Chart, 111–112
linking dates between projects, 301
links between applications, 322
list separator character, 129
listing tasks
  and milestones, 69–70
  behind schedule, 267–68
  that should have started, 263
locating overallocations, 314
longer work hours
  and resource-driven scheduling, 177
  paid at standard rate, 177
  specifying in Microsoft Project, 174–75
Lotus 1-2-3, 317, 332
  file formats, 318

–M–

macros, 377–78
  help creating, 378
  sharing, 317
  using from another project, 319
magnifying glass in print preview, 204

major phases, 70, 78
  printing summary of, 197
  printing summary of progress on, 286
  report showing summary of progress on, 279
  reviewing percent complete for, 262
major timescale, 159
making information stand out in reports, 298
making task or resource stand out, 279
manager
  entering project manager name, 59, 60
  including field for, 126, 337
Manager field, adding to a table, 337
managing a project, 255
  defined, 1
  steps, 255–56
managing multiple projects, 301–16
man-hours, 128
manual page breaks, 200, 204
MAPI-compliant electronic mail program, 318
margins, 201
Marked field, 350
marked tasks, creating filter to find, 350
master project, 129, 306, 316
  and subprojects, 303
  controlling detail in reports, 308
  dates control dates in subproject, 309
  opening when subprojects aren't open, 308
  when to work with master vs. subprojects, 303
Max. Units column, 156
measuring progress, agreeing on how, 238
menu bar, 44
  customizing, 356–59
  defined, 44
  resetting to originals, 351
  sharing, 317
  using from another project, 319
Menu Bar Definition dialog box illustrated, 357
Menu Bars dialog box illustrated, 356
menus
  customizing, 356–59
  Standard, 356
  Standard (no file), 356
  using, 44
methods, scheduling, 93–95
Microsoft Excel, 317
  estimating durations, 92
  exporting tasks to, 327–29
  file formats, 318
  importing information from illustrated, 324
  importing resources and costs from, 323–26
  opening file exported from Project, 329
  salary information in, 120
Microsoft FoxPro file formats, 318
Microsoft Mail, 86, 116, 136
  collecting status information, 243
  using workgroup features, 318
Microsoft Project
  advantages of, 7–9
  basics, 11–52, 44–49
  customizing, 49–52, 319, 335–78
  preferences, 50
  scheduling methods, 93–95
  views, 19
Microsoft Project 3.0 toolbar, 48
Microsoft Schedule+, 319
Microsoft toolbar, 48
Microsoft Word, 318
  Gantt Chart in Word document, 332–33
milestones
  changing several tasks to, 75
  creating list of, 69–70
  defined, 65
  entering, 74–77
  guidelines, 67–68
  identifying when reached, 236
  naming, 68
  placement of, 67
  printing, 197
Milestones filter, illustrated, 344
Milestones report, 197
minor timescale, 159
minus sign in outline, 82–83
Module Editor view, 19, 378
months, ways to enter, 116
More Filters dialog box illustrated, 347
More Views dialog box
  copying combination view illustrated, 353
  copying single view illustrated, 352
  creating new single view illustrated, 354
mouse
  changing
    actual start date illustrated, 250
    column width, 336
    duration on Gantt Chart illustrated, 251
    pages shown in print preview, 204
    percent complete, 246
  constraint added when drag date, 155
  creating task on PERT Chart, 74, 112
  dragging to assign resources, 128
  entering
    predecessor on Task Sheet, 109
    predecessor, 105–6
    progress information on Gantt Chart, 240
    relationships on PERT Chart, 111–12
    task on Calendar view, 27
    task on PERT Chart, 112
  identifying purpose of toolbar buttons, 241
  PERT Chart, 25
  setting actual start date, 249–50
  terms, 12

mouse pointer
bar with left-and-right arrows, 336
left-pointing arrow, 249
percent sign mouse pointer, 246
right-pointing arrow, 251
moving
calendar to global file, procedure, 64
end date when leveling, 188
on Gantt Chart, 21
tasks, 76
tasks in an outline, 81
to overallocated tasks and resources, 190
toolbar, 370
MPT, 302
MPW, 316
multiple base calendars, 133
creating, 63
using, 63
multiple critical paths, 173
multiple page button in print preview, 204
multiple projects
combining, 311, 312
managing, 301–16
opening, 311, 312
sharing resources, 309–11
viewing, 311–15
assignments and graph of allocation, 314
overallocated resources and tasks causing, 314
ways to view, 311
workspace file, 312
Multiple Resource Information dialog box, 126
multiple selection, 13
Multiple Task Information dialog box, 94
Must Finish On constraint, 153, 180
and critical path, 147
defined, 101
Must Start On constraint, 153, 180
and critical path, 147
defined, 101
replacing, 153

–N–

NA
in Actual date fields, 248
in Actual Start or Actual Finish field, 283
naming
milestones, 68
tasks, 67
naming a table, illustrated, 338
narrow black bar on Gantt Chart, 246
negative slack
defined, 143
explained, 248
turning off message about, 151
negative total slack defined, 151
New Window dialog box, illustrated, 315
nodes on PERT Chart, 25
nonadjacent tasks or resources, selecting, 245
noncritical path on PERT Chart, 24
noncritical tasks, 7, 143, 144
PERT Chart, 24
nonworking time, adding to calendar illustrated, 361
normal task bars, 20
normal working days, changing, 360–61
notes
collecting with progress information, 237
entering and reviewing
for resources, 293
for tasks, 92, 216, 292
on Resource Form, 35
on Task Form, 29
in Current Activities/Should Have Started Tasks report, 290
including in reports, 206
printing, 198, 216–17
project notes, 208
numbers on outline, 82–83

–O–

Object Linking and Embedding (OLE), 321
objective data for measuring progress, 237
objects
editing or inserting, 28, 34
entering or viewing on Resource Form, 35
entering or viewing on Task Form, 29
including in reports, 206
OK button, 46
OLE version 2.0-enabled applications, 326, 332
opening
last file when starting, 50
Microsoft Excel file in Microsoft Project, 330
illustrated, 324
multiple projects, 311, 312
template files, 302
optimistic estimates, effect on schedule, 87
optimistic time, 90
option button in dialog box, 46
order of tasks, 97, 98
Organizer, 319, 351
displaying, 319
illustrated, 320
sharing calendars, 64
sharing reports or views, 201
sharing toolbars, 371
organizing tasks, 70–73
outlining, 78–81
subprojects, 304
WBS, 83–85
original schedule, 165, 167

outline, 71
  and exporting tasks, 329
  and reports, 207
  and sorting, 364
  bottom-up method, 81
  collapsing, 81–82, 214, 261
    to review percent complete of major phases, 261
    to show summary of project, 209
  creating, 77, 78
    bottom-up method, 81
    top-down method, 78–81
  described, 71–72
  expanding, 81–82, 215
    to show all tasks, 210
  illustration in Microsoft Project, 78
  no indentation, solution to, 81
  numbers on, 82–83
    and WBS coding system, 84
    viewing, 83
  options, 21, 33
  printing to show major phases, 196
  reorganizing, 81
  symbols on, 82–83
  to create WBS, 83
  using mouse to indent/outdent tasks, 80
  using to print summary of progress, 286
  vs. subprojects, 304
outline buttons on Formatting toolbar, 78
  don't show, solution, 81
Outline Symbols button on Formatting toolbar, 83
overallocated resources, 129, 160
  checking for, 155
  defined, 186
  finding on Resource Usage view, 157
  level message, 156
  printing, 295–96
  resolving, 159, 186–91
    adding lag to tasks, 153
    don't have to resolve all, 191
    ideas for resolving, 167
    increasing duration, 190
    working longer hours, 191
  tasks causing, 161
  viewing on Resource Sheet, 156
  why important to locate, 155
Overallocated Resources filter
  applying, 156
  viewing overallocated resources, 156, 274
Overallocated Resources report, 289
  illustrated, 295
  procedure for printing, 295
overallocated work, displaying, 157
Overbudget Resources report, 288, 293, 298
  illustrated, 294
  procedure for printing, 294
overbudget tasks, determining cause of, 269
Overbudget Tasks report, 288, 292
  adding notes to, 292
  illustrated, 292
  procedure for printing, 292
overlapping tasks, 97, 99–100
overtime, specifying, 174–75
overtime rate, 175, 177
  adding, illustrated, 176
  default value for, 50
    changing default, 126
  entering, 176
overtime work, 177, 259
  adding in Microsoft Project, 175–76
  adding longer hours to calendar, 177–78
  assigning to driving resource, 175
  calculation of duration with, 175
  resource-driven scheduling and, 175
Overview reports, 208
  Critical Tasks report, 198
  Milestones report, 197
  Project report, 196, 197, 279, 284, 298
  Top-Level Tasks report, 196, 197, 279, 286

–P–

page breaks, controlling when printing, 200
page setup
  changing columns printed on each page, 224
  changing for report, 205
  changing while previewing, 204
  for printing, 201–2
Page Setup dialog box illustrated, 202
pages printed, specifying, 204
parts of a window, 44
part-time hours, 133
part-time work, indicating in Resource Assignment dialog box, 191
Paste button on Standard toolbar, 306
pasting tasks, 306
pay rates, default values for, 50
Peak column, 156
peak units
  Resource Graph, 160
  Resource Usage view, 157
peak use, defined, 160
percent allocation
  Resource Graph, 160
  Resource Usage view, 223
percent complete, 239
  and actual start date, 248
  breaking link to work, 252–54
  calculated vs. 0 or 100%, 244
  calculated when enter actual or remaining duration, 250

percent complete *(continued)*
- changing
  - Task Sheet, 247
  - Tracking table, 247
  - Update Tasks dialog box, 246–47
- duration calculated, 250
- entering, 240
  - same value for multiple tasks, 247
  - when tracking progress, 245–47
- evaluating progress, 256
- fields changed based on, 246
- not updating work, 241
- of subproject task, 304
- printing on Tracking Gantt, 283–84
- printing report showing, 279
- reviewing for major phases, 262
- showing on PERT Chart, 282
- updating also updates work and cost, 241

percent complete and work, tied vs. independent, 241

percent complete buttons on Tracking toolbar, 245, 246

percent complete for duration, 236

percent complete of 100%
- and actual finish date, 248
- fields changed based on, 246

percent sign mouse pointer, 246

percent work complete, 236

percentage of allocation on Resource Usage view, 157

periods printed in reports, changing, 220

PERT Chart, 24–25
- adding lead or lag time, 112
- and sorting, 365
- arranging nodes, 25
- changing
  - borders, 213
  - fields in node, 282
  - information in node, 213
  - look of text, 213
- combination view with Task Form, 112
- controlling how nodes break across pages, 213
- creating task, 74, 112
- critical path, 147, 148
  - checking, 145
  - illustrated, 148
- customizing, 25, 213
- deleting relationship, 112
- diagonal lines on PERT nodes, 281
- entering relationships, 111–12
- entering tasks and milestones, 74
- legend, 213
- lines and arrows, controlling look of, 213
- moving, 25
- moving tasks, 75

PERT Chart *(continued)*
- printing, 198, 212–13
  - illustrated, 212
  - procedure, 212
  - small nodes illustrated, 213
  - to show progress, 279, 281
    - procedure, 282
- setting up legend, 213

PERT method to estimate duration, 90
- calculating durations in Microsoft Excel, 318, 326–32
- formula, 90

per-use cost
- entering, 185
- reducing, 166, 184–85

pessimistic estimates, effect on schedule, 87

pessimistic time, 90

phases, major, 70, 78

physical tasks, measuring progress for, 237

plan
- communicating, 195–231
- evaluating, 139–64
- setting a baseline, 192–93
- uses for, 4–5

planning, advantages of, 4–5

PlanningWizard, 85
- advice from, 77
- and schedule problems, 113
- explaining scheduling problems, 248
- Save A Baseline? dialog box, 302, 305
- saving baseline, 238
- turning on and off, 50, 77, 151
- when saving, 75

plus sign on outline, 82–83

point with mouse defined, 12

portrait mode, 207

predecessor tasks, 154
- and successors, entering both, 109
- changing to decrease duration, 180
- defined, 98
- deleting on Task Form, 109
- determining, 98
- entering multiple predecessors on Task Sheet, 111
- entering on Task Entry view, 105–6
- including in reports, 206
- including on Task report, 217

Predecessors field on Gantt Chart or Task Sheet, 109

predecessors fields on Task Form, 28

preferences, 50

preliminary budget, 118

previewing pages, 203–4
- Calendar view, 221
- change view of page, 204
- custom report, 207

previewing pages *(continued)*
Gantt Chart, 203
report, 205
Resource Graph, 231
Resource Usage view, 224
Task Sheet, 215
Print button on Standard toolbar, 86, 116, 205
Print dialog box, illustrated, 204
print preview. *See* previewing pages
Print Preview button on Standard toolbar, 203
printer, specifying, 86
printer setup, checking before printing, 201
printing, 85–86, 203–7
Calendar view, 221–22
columns that print on each page, 224
completed tasks, 287–88
controlling where pages break, 200
cost by period, 225
cumulative costs graph, 230–31
Detail Gantt to show slipping tasks, 291
direction reports, 298
durations on Task Sheet, 96
durations, predecessors, relationships, 116
earned value, 289
after changing schedule, 298
expected task cost, 200
forecast of task cost cash flow, 200
Gantt Chart showing progress vs. baseline, 280
procedure, 281
graph of cumulative cost, 200
gray bands to separate sections in reports, 220
limited time period, specifying in Print dialog box, 204
list of
resources, 222–23
resources and tasks to which each is assigned, 199
tasks and durations on Gantt Chart, 198
tasks scheduled during a time period, 198
tasks showing progress, 283
major phases, 209
new finish date, work, and cost after changing schedule, 298
new schedule showing suggested changes, 298
notes, 206
over budget resources, 293–95
overallocated resources, 289, 295–96
percent complete and changing durations, 283–84
PERT Chart, 212–13
procedure, 212
show progress, procedure, 282
previewing before, 203–4
procedure for Task Sheet, 214
project statistics, 196
project summary report, 279–88
reports, 205–7, 197
Resource Graph showing cumulative costs, 230

printing *(continued)*
Resource Sheet, procedure, 223
resources
cost after changing schedule, 298
costing more than planned, 288
costs and when occur, 200
in resource pool, 199
schedule, 226–28
use during
each period, 199
next period, 298
project, 223–24
with work variance, 293
work and cost, 199, 225–26
working more than planned, 288
resources, tasks, and hours, 199
setting up the page, 201–2
starting immediately when click Print button on toolbar, 205
summary
costs to date, 286–87
major phases and statistics, 197
major phases on Gantt Chart, 197
progress, 279
progress on major phases, 286
project statistics, 197
reports, 279–88
Task Sheet with collapsed outline to show summary, procedure, 214
tasks
and constraints, 116
and notes, 198
and notes report, 216–17
and sequence, 212–13
cost, 226–30
after changing schedule, 298
cost and totals, 200
cost and work, 198
costing more than planned, 288
dates and resources, 214–15
finishing late, 290–91
on a monthly calendar, 116, 198
relationships, 116
scheduled for next period, 298
should have started, 288, 289–90
started late, 290
to be done and sequence, 198
whose finish date has slipped, 288
with cost variance, 292–93
with work different from planned, 288
with work variance, 291–92
work and cost totals, 217–18
to show entire schedule, 136
views, 196, 203–5
Weekly Cash Flow report, procedure, 230
weekly to-do list for each resource, 199
work and cost totals, 218

priority, controlling task leveled, 188
problem areas, identifying in schedule, 235
problems causing past delays
  continuing and effect on remaining duration, 258
  solved and effect on remaining duration, 257
progress
  bars, 281
  communicating, 277–98
  data
    based on measurable progress, not time, 237
    entering in Microsoft Project, 240
    entering when not match schedule, 239
    where to get it, 237–38
  entering actual information, 239
  evaluating, 255, 256, 260–68
  reports showing task progress, 279, 280–83
    frequency, 278
  showing on tasks report, 279
  slower than planned, what to investigate, 257
  tracking, 235–54
project
  assumptions, 55
    defining, 57–59
    guidelines for listing, 58
    recording, 61
  bringing back on track, 273–74
  calendar, 361
    increasing work hours, 177
  containing resources only, 310
  costs, 260
    checking in Microsoft Project, 146
    how calculated, 120
    illustrated in Project Statistics dialog box, 172
    reviewing, 144
    ways to lower, 144
  creating summary bar for, 316
  data
    collecting, 236–38
    how Microsoft Project tracks, 13–14
  dates, reviewing, 140
  defined, 3
  duration
    decreasing, 140, 172–82
      by assigning more resources, 173–74
      ideas for decreasing, 166, 169
    defined, 140
  entering general information, 59–61
  evaluating progress on the final dates and cost, 256
  finish date, 140, 144, 260
    bringing in by using more resources, 173–74
    checking, 140, 145, 146, 261
    illustrated in Project Statistics dialog box, 172
    what to do if too late, 146
project *(continued)*
  goals
    guidelines for setting, 56–57
    setting, 51–64, 56
    testing validity of, 56
  hiding open project, 316
  manager, 3
  managing, defined, 1
  name, entering, 59
  notes
    entering, 60, 61
    printing, 208
  objectives, 140
  reports showing progress on, 279
  routing to group electronically, 86
  saving, 75, 85
  scope, 55
    changing to
      decrease duration, 181–82
      lower cost, 167
    creating options for changing, 182
    decreasing by prioritizing tasks, 181
    defining, 57
  sending electronically, 86
  shortening, 172–82
  start date, entering, 59–60
  statistics, 146
    printing, 197
  team, 4
  template, 76
  title, entering, 60
  tracking progress, 1, 235–54
  unhiding, 316
  variance in dates, duration, cost, work, 260
  view, pasting into word processing application, 318
Project field, 316
project management defined, 3
project management software, 3–4, 5–7
  advantages, 195
  features, 8
Project report, 197, 279, 284, 298
  changing information on, 285
Project Statistics button on Tracking toolbar
  checking project finish date and cost, 145, 146, 171–72
  checking project finish date, duration, work, costs illustrated, 261
Project Statistics dialog box
  checking proposed changes to schedule, 274
  finish date and cost illustrated, 172
  illustrated, 146
  viewing effects of change on project finish and cost, 171–72

project summary report, 207–8
  illustrated, 208, 285
  printing, 284–86
  procedure for printing, 208, 285
projected cost reports, 195
projects
  combining in one window, 315–16
  combining to view all schedules at once, 301
  linking tasks between, 309
  managing multiple, 301–16
  viewing multiple, 311–15
proposals, costs needed to generate, 119
prorated accrual method defined, 125

-R-

rate abbreviations table, 124
recovering original views, 351
reducing costs, 182–85
  ideas, 166–67
  options in Microsoft Project, 170
refining the schedule, 165–93
  methods, 165–67
  using Microsoft Project, 167–93
relationship abbreviations table 110
relationship types, 98–99
  table of, 106
relationships, 140, 144
  accelerating tasks, 145
  between tasks, 98–99
    changing to decrease duration, 180
  changing on PERT Chart, 112
  checking, 153–54
    Gantt Chart, 153
    Microsoft Project, 145, 153–55
  default assigned automatically, 106
  deleting
    PERT Chart, 112
    Task Sheet, 111
  entering
    PERT Chart, 111–12
    Task Entry view, 106–7
  finish-to-finish, 99
  finish-to-start, 98
  reducing resource overallocation, 145
  removing, 104
  shorten critical path, 143
  shown on Task PERT, 154
  start-to-finish, 99
  start-to-start, 99
remaining availability on Resource Usage view, 157
remaining duration, 236, 239
  and percent complete, 246
  calculated when enter percent complete, 250
remaining duration *(continued)*
  changing to indicate schedule change for resource-driven task, 240
  entering, 240, 250–51
  greater than scheduled duration, 250
  predicting, 257–58
  rescheduling, 252
removing
  buttons from toolbar, 370
  relationships between tasks, 104
  table from Table submenu, 358
  tasks from project, 306
renumbering tasks or resources, 365
reorganizing an outline, 81
Replace Assignment dialog box illustrated, 183
reporting cycle, 278
reports
  and outlining, 207
  border around details, 220
  Budget, 228
  Calendar, 221–22
  changing, 205–7
    filter, 206
    fonts, 206
    page setup, 205
    periods printed in, 220
    table, 206
  common, 197–201
  communicating progress, 277–98
  completed tasks, 287–88
  controlling content for the audience, 278
  controlling how pages break, 200
  creating, 205–7
    new vs. editing vs. copying, 207
  critical path on Gantt Chart illustrated, 210–11
  cumulative costs graph, 230–31
  customizing, 200
  customizing supplied reports, 226
  different depending on audience, 195–96
  drawing boxes around details, 206
  exception reports, 288–97
  font, 206
  for management, 196
  for task supervisors, 196
  frequency of progress reports, 278
  from another project, 319
  Gantt Chart showing summary of major phases, procedure, 209
  hints for printing, 207
  including
    notes, 206
    objects, 206
    predecessors or successors, 206
    resources in Task report, 220
    schedule, cost, work information, 206
    totals for cost or work, 206

reports *(continued)*
list of resources, 222–23
milestones, 197
previewing, 205
printing, 197, 205–7
gray bands to separate sections, 220
summary reports, 279–88
task schedule, 219–20
tasks and notes, 198
procedure
cumulative cost, 231
resource assignment report, 226
resource usage report, 223–24
Weekly To-Do List report, 226
Who Does What report, 226
Who Does What When report, 226
work and cost, 218
progress on tasks, 279
project summary, 207–8, 284–86
resetting to original reports, 351
resources
schedule, 226–28
use during project, 223–24
work and cost, 225–26
samples for communicating initial plan, 207–31
saving, 201
setting up the page, 201–2
sharing, 201, 317
showing
summary tasks, 206
task progress, 280–83
solution, 297–98
sorting information in, 206
summary
costs to date, 286–87
major phases and statistics, 197
multiple projects, 311–15
progress on major phases, 286
Task Sheet with collapsed outline, 214
tasks and dates, 209–10
whole, plus details on part, 214
tasks
cost, 226–30
dates, resources on Task Sheet, 214–15
notes, 216–17
sequence, 212–13
work and cost totals, 217–18
using subprojects and master projects, 308
Weekly Cash Flow, 229
Weekly To-Do List illustrated, 228
Who Does What illustrated, 227
Who Does What When illustrated, 227
requesting task updates electronically, 319
Reschedule Uncompleted Work To Start option, 252
Reschedule Work button on Tracking toolbar, 252
rescheduling remaining duration, 252
default date used, 252
rescheduling tasks to address variance, 259
resolving overallocated resources, 159
assigning additional resources, 191
breaking up tasks to shift resources, 191
resolving resource conflicts, 186–91
Resource Allocation view, 42, 43, 314
displaying, 190, 314
finding overallocations and delaying tasks, 190
illustrated, 315
Resource Allocation View button on Resource Management toolbar, 190, 315
Resource Assignment button on Standard toolbar, 130
to change resource assignments, 183
Resource Assignment dialog box, 127
adding new resource and cost information, 130
assigning multiple resources using, 128
changing units to decrease involvement on task, 190
dragging to assign resources, 128
illustrated, 128
illustrated for changing assignments, 183
resource assignment fields, 14
resource assignment information
Resource Form, 34
Task Sheet, 28
resource assignments
changing in Microsoft Project, 182–83
changing to reduce costs, 182–83
resource calendars, 120, 133, 177
changing, 133–34
changing work hours, 177, 179
defined, 61, 133
extending working hours, 175
link to base calendar, 133
returning to default values, 134
resource conflicts
resolving, 186–91
ideas, 167
options in Microsoft Project, 171
resource controlling finish date, 122
resource cost
checking, 164
data you need, 119, 124
fields on Task Form, 145, 164
how calculated, 120
over project life, 145
printing, 225–26
printing forecast of cost and when occurs, 200
sorting by, 157
resource duration, 122
resource estimates based on history, 118
resource fields, 14

resource filters, 17
Resource Form, 34–35
 adding overtime work and rate illustrated, 175–76
 changing
  base calendar, 133
  resources schedules, 145
  task assignments, 160
   across projects, 309
 customizing, 35
 displaying, 34, 127, 160
 entering per-use fee, 185
 entering resources, 123, 127
 illustrated with schedule fields, 160
 including information in report, 206
 overtime rate of pay, 175
 specifying base calendar on, 180
 specifying overtime work, 175
 using, 35
 with Task Sheet to see tasks resource is assigned to, 157
Resource Form fields, moving to with keys, 35
Resource Form over Resource Graph illustrated, 314
Resource Form over Task Form illustrated, 313
Resource Form under Resource Usage view, 314
Resource Graph, 36–37
 changing
  font, 231
  information displayed on, 231
  timescale, 231
  type of graph, 231
  type of information, 161
 checking
  allocation across projects, 309
  cumulative cost for resources, 145
  peak resource usage on, 145
  resource usage, 160–61
 cumulative and new cost, 162–63
  illustrated, 163
  printed, 230
 customizing, 37, 231, 367–78
 displaying, 161, 231
 gridlines, 231
 in combination view, 37
 initial data shown, 160
 peak units illustrated, 161
 previewing, 231
 printing, 231
  cumulative costs, 200, 230
   procedure, 231
 turning off a graph, 368
 types of information available, 160
Resource Graph Bar Styles dialog box, 367
Resource Graph over Gantt Chart
 viewing overallocated resources and tasks
  causing, 161
  in multiple projects, 314
 resource graphs, viewing for a group, 161
Resource Graph under Resource Form, 314
resource information, entering for several resources at once, 126
Resource Information dialog box, 35
 changing base calendar on, 133
 displaying, 133
 entering per-use fee, 185
 overtime rate of pay, 175
 specifying base calendar, 133, 180
resource leveling
 defined, 186
 using Microsoft Project, 186–90
Resource Leveling dialog box illustrated, 188
resource list, sorting by ID, 157
Resource Management toolbar, 48, 190
 displaying, 314
 Leveling CueCards button, 190
Resource Name Form, 35
Resource Names field, assign resources, 129, 132
resource notes, entering, 293
resource overallocations resolving, 171, 186–91
resource pool, 14, 120, 127, 180, 309, 316
 adding resources automatically, controlling, 50
 adding resources to from any project, 310
 assigning resources not in, 127
 attaching project to, 311
 checking, 155
 creating
  from existing project, procedure, 310–11
  from scratch, procedure, 311
 disconnecting from, 310
 printing, 199
 reviewing, 156–57
 sharing, 120, 317
 storing resource information in one project, 301
 using with subprojects, 305
resource project, 310
resource rates in Microsoft Excel, 120
Resource report, 199
 overbudget resources and task assignments, 294
  illustrated, 295
 overbudget resources and task costs report
  procedure, 294
 resource pool, 199
 resources with work variance, 288, 293
 work variance and notes, 293
resource schedule, printing, 199, 226–28

resource schedule fields
  changing work amount, 129
  illustrated, 131
resource schedules on tasks, checking, 145
Resource Sheet, 38–39
  changing
    column width, 39
    columns of information, 223
    font to make one resource stand out, 223
    fonts, 223
    gridlines, 223
  checking resources on, 144
  controlling resources displayed, 223
  controlling where pages break, 200
  customizing, 39, 223
  displaying, 125, 156, 223, 225, 270, 293
  double-clicking, 39
  entering resources, 123, 125–26
  locating resources that increased cost or work, 268
  printing, 136, 222–23
    illustrated, 222
    overbudget resources, 294
    procedure, 223
    resource pool, 199
    resources with work variance, 288, 293
    work and cost, 199, 225
      procedure, 225
    work variance illustrated, 293
      procedure, 293
  reviewing resources on, 156
  showing work and cost printed, illustrated, 225
  showing work variance, illustrated, 271
  sorting on, 223
Resource Sheet over Resource Usage view
  checking when resources are under and
    overallocated, 274
resource tables, 15
resource usage
  checking, 157–59
    graph of, 160–61
    in Microsoft Project, 145
  for selected tasks, 158
  reviewing across multiple projects, 311–15
  variation over project, 145
Resource Usage view, 40–41, 160
  changing
    columns, 224
    look of text, 224
    time period covered, 159
    timescale, 223, 224
    type of information displayed, 224
  checking
    allocation across projects, 309
    resource use over project, 145
    work allocation on, 157
  controlling resources displayed, 224
  controlling where pages break, 200
Resource Usage view *(continued)*
  customizing, 41, 224
  displaying, 158
    percent allocation, 223
  gridlines on, 224
  in combination view, 41
  information that can be displayed, 157
  making one resource stand out, 224
  previewing, 224
  printing, 199, 223–24
    cost per time period, 225
      procedure, 226
    costs, 200
    illustrated, 224
    procedure for printing, 223–24
    work, 199
  sorting resources, 224
Resource Usage view over Delay Gantt, 190. *See*
  Resource Allocation view
Resource Usage view over Resource Form
  checking overallocations and tasks for multiple
    projects, 314
Resource Usage view over Task Sheet
  creating combination view, 355
Resource Usage view under Gantt Chart, 158, 159
resource use during each period, printed, 199
resource use over project, 145
resource work
  changing, illustrated on Task Entry view, 131
  controlling when occurs on task, 131–32
  delaying, 131–32
  how calculated, 130
  illustrated on Task Entry view, 130
  printing, 225–26
resource work and cost, printing, 199
resource work fields
  entering actual work on Task Form, 252
resource work variance
  illustrated on Resource Sheet, 271
resource-driven scheduling, 173
  changing
    duration for a task using, 251
    work for new resource assignment, 183
  defined, 93
  effect of changing duration, work, or units, 121–23
  examples, 93
  indicating schedule change for task, 239
  longer working hours, 175, 177
  overtime work, 175
resource-driven tasks
  increasing duration by changing resources to part-
    time, 190
resources, 144
  adding custom field, 126
  advantages of assigning, 117
  approaches for entering, 120

resources *(continued)*
assigning
correct base calendar, 364
in Resource Names field, 129
more to resolve overallocations, 191
more to shorten duration, 173–74
on any task view, 128–30
on Task Form, 132
to several tasks at once, 130
to subproject task, 308
to summary tasks and subproject tasks, 129
to tasks, 127–32
changing base calendar used by, 133–34
changing or delaying work, 130–32
changing order of, 364–65
checking
assignments to tasks, 160
cost variance, 270–71
for over and under allocations, 144
in Microsoft Project, 155–61
task assignments across projects, 309
usage, 157–59
variance, 270
when scheduled to work, 155
work variance, 270–71
code, 124
data you need to know when entering, 123
driving task duration and overtime work, 175
entering, 123–27
fixed cost for, 135
manager, 126
Resource Form, 127
Resource Sheet, 125–26
skill level code, 126
estimating, 118–19
fields, 28
finding under and overallocations on Resource Usage view, 157
groups, 124
guidelines
estimating, 118
leveling, 190–91
hiring more, 173
how Microsoft Project schedules, 121–23
ideas for resolving overallocations, 167
importing from another application, 311
including in Task report, 220
individuals, 124
leveling to solve overallocations, 186–91
managing across projects, 309
moving from spreadsheet application to Microsoft Project, 317
not working hours as scheduled, what to investigate, 257
overallocated, 129
resources *(continued)*
printing
list of, 222–23
overallocated resources, 295–96
overbudget resources, 293–95
resources
costing more than planned, 288
overallocated, 289
used during next period, 298
working more than planned, 288, 293
schedule, 226–28
tasks and hours, 199
Weekly To-Do List, 228
with assigned tasks, 199
work and cost, 225–26
renumbering, 365
reviewing
in Microsoft Project, 145
list of, 156–57
task assignments in multiple projects, 313
selecting nonadjacent, 245
sharing among projects, 309–11
showing highest usage, 156
specifying overtime, 174–75
those that caused cost or work to increase, 268
using evenly over project, 144
viewing all, 271
viewing usage across multiple projects, 301
viewing variance for individual resources, 271
why important to locate under and over allocations, 155
working longer hours, 177
working on multiple projects, 309–11
Resources Overbudget and Tasks report
creating and printing, 294
Resume field, 252
Resume No Earlier Than field, 252
reviewing
future tasks based on progress to date, 273
links between projects or applications, 322
resource details, 34
schedule for errors, 139
schedule, what to check, 139–40
task assignments in multiple projects, 313
right-pointing arrow mouse pointer, 251
routing projects to reviewers electronically, 318
row, selecting, 306
Run Macro button on Visual Basic toolbar, 378

–S–

sample reports
communicating initial plan, 207–31
communicating progress, 277–98

Save A Baseline? dialog box, 302
PlanningWizard, 305
Save As dialog box
saving a file in Excel Worksheet format
illustrated, 328
Save button on Standard toolbar, 85
saving
baseline, 192–93
prompt by PlanningWizard, 85
calendar, 64
file in Microsoft Excel format, illustrated, 327
project, 75
start and finish date history, 192
tasks, 85
workspace, 316
schedule
accelerating by overlapping tasks, 153
adjustments, experimenting in Microsoft Project, 168–72
bringing back on track, 273–74
calculation, 7
checking for errors, 140
communicating, 195–231
comparing with baseline, 260–68
creating alternatives, 168
details, including in report, 206
determining corrective action, 258–59
duration
and percent complete, 246
changing, 251
by entering larger remaining duration, 250
entering in Microsoft Project, 240
evaluating, 139–64
experimenting with, 7
freezing, 167, 192–93
ideas for shortening, 166
including on Task report, 217
indicating change in, 239
making efficient with lead or lag time, 100
methods for refining, 165–67
printing task list, 219–20
refining, 165–93
shortening, 140
updating to reflect progress, 235–54
what to check when reviewing, 139–40
schedule fields, Resource Form, 34, 145
displaying, 160
to see tasks resource assigned to, 157
Schedule table, 145, 151, 260
applying, 152, 266
checking slack time, 151, 152, 266
slack time illustrated, 266
viewing near critical tasks, 274
scheduled start and finish dates and percent complete, 246
scheduling
backward from finish date, 60
calendar used by Microsoft Project, 133
forward from start date, 60
how resources are scheduled, 121–23
scheduling messages, 113, 248
turning on and off, 51, 151
scheduling methods, 93–95
changing
default method, 95
for several tasks, 94
to fixed duration, 94
default, 93, 94
specifying, 94–95
using Fixed field to see method, 94
when no resources assigned, 93
scheduling tasks, 97–116
using calendars, 62
scheduling tight, 89
scope
changing to shorten project, 166, 181
defined, 55
defining for outside contractor, 57
effect of reducing on duration, 169
guidelines for defining, 57
project, 55, 57
task, 67
scroll bar
defined, 44
turning on and off, 52
selecting, 13
from list in dialog box, 46
nonadjacent tasks or resources, 245
row, 306
tasks, 103, 104
semi-colon as list separator character, 111
sending task requests electronically, 319
separating numbers in dates, 116
sequence of tasks, 98
Set 0% Or 100% Complete Only option, 244
Set 0%–100% Complete option, 244
Set Reminder button on Workgroup toolbar, 319
setting finish date for task, 100–102
setting project goals, 51–64
setting start date for task, 100–102
setting up the page for printing, 201–2
changing while previewing, 204
SF relationship. *See* start-to-finish
Share Resources dialog box, illustrated, 310
sharing
calendars, 64
information, 317–33
reports or views, 201
resources among projects, 309–11
schedule, 136

sharing *(continued)*
task list through email, 86
tools, 319–20
shift workers, calendars for, 62
shifting tasks to resolve overallocations, 159
shifts
adding to decrease duration, 178–80
base calendars for, 180
calendars for, 63
creating calendars for, 359–64
shortcut menu for toolbars, 371
shortening critical path
by overlapping tasks, 153
ideas for, 166
when no resources assigned to tasks, 174
with lead or lag time, 100
shortening duration when no resources assigned to tasks, 174
Should Have Started Tasks report, 288, 289–90
illustrated, 289
procedure for printing, 289
Should Start By filter, 243, 260
applying, 263
showing tasks that should have started, 263
Show All Tasks button on Formatting toolbar, 82, 210
Show Resources Reporting To filter
creating, 349
dialog box illustrated, 349
Show Scheduling Messages check box, 151
Show Subtasks button on Formatting toolbar, 82, 215
showing
all resources, 271
all tasks, 155
finished tasks, 239
highest usage of resource, 156
more or less detail in schedule, 159
started tasks, 239
task progress, 239, 277, 280–83
tasks in outline, 81–82
toolbars, 48, 371–72
single view, creating new, 354–55
skill level, including field for, 126
slack bar, 22
slack time, 7, 140, 141, 143, 144
checking in Microsoft Project, 145, 151–53, 266
checking time remaining in schedule, 260
defined, 141
Delay Gantt, 267, 274
Detail Gantt, 267, 274
illustrated, 153
free, defined, 143
Gantt Chart, 152
slack time *(continued)*
negative, defined, 143
Task Sheet, 152
illustrated, 152
total, defined, 143
why minimize, 151
slippage on Detail Gantt, 22, 268
slipping tasks
printing, 288, 290–91
using Finish No Later Than to warn you, 113
Slipping Tasks filter, 17, 260, 267
applying, 267
Slipping Tasks report, 288
illustrated, 290
procedure for printing, 291
solution reports, 277, 297–98
Sort By Date button on Standard toolbar, 364
Sort dialog box, 150, 365
Sort submenu, 364
sorting, 364–65
and outlining, 364
before printing, 200
by
date, 364
duration, 149
and start date illustrated, 365
descending, illustrated, 150
ID number, 150
combined projects, 316
on custom field, 126
report, 206
resources by cost, 157
using in progress reports, 279
using WBS code, 84
specifying base calendar for a resource, 133
speeding up tasks, 259
splitting work
between resources, 178–79
on task, 131–32
when add new resource, 174
square brackets, 129
SS relationship. *See* start-to-start
Standard calendar, 62
standard deviation, formula, 330
Standard menu, 356
Standard (no file) menu, 356
standard rate
changing default, 126
default value for, 50
used for longer work hours, 177
Standard toolbar, 47, 146
start accrual method defined, 125
Start Before filter, 354
creating, 347
dialog box illustrated, 348

start date
entering, 60
entering actual dates, 247–50
evaluating progress, 256
matches current schedule, 239
setting for task, 100–102
typing or dragging and entering constraint, 155
when to enter actual start date, 248
start date for project, entering, 59–60
Start No Earlier Than constraint, 153
defined, 101
entered when type or drag date, 113, 155, 181
Start No Later Than constraint, 153
defined, 101
Start1/Finish1 through Start5/Finish5
for saving sets of dates, 192
starting and stopping work on a task, 252
start-to-finish defined, 99
start-to-start defined, 99
Statistics dialog box
checking finish date and costs, 168
displaying, 146
viewing variance in overall project statistics, 260
status bar
changing text associated with command, 358
defined, 44
displaying information about toolbar buttons, 241
level message, 129, 156, 186
text, changing
for commands, 364
for toolbar buttons, 371
turning on and off, 52
Stop field, 252
storing resource information in a separate project, 301
submenu, 12
choosing commands from, 45
subordinate tasks, 261
defined, 77–78
subproject name, typing in Subproject box, 308
subproject task in master project
assigning resource, 129, 308
defined, 304
duration, 307
entering, 307
work for resource assigned, 308
subprojects, 316
advantages, 303
conserving computer memory, 303
creating, 305–6
from existing project, procedure, 306
new project, procedure, 305
dates controlled by master project, 309
dates in when use multiple times, 308
defined, 76, 303
don't save file as template, 305
keeping repetitive tasks in, 303
subprojects *(continued)*
tracking progress and resources using, 304
using, 303–8
resource pools to track resources across projects, 305
same over and over vs. copying and renaming, 304
to do repetitive processes in multiple projects, 301
vs. outlining, 304
when not open when open master project, 308
when to work with master project vs. subprojects, 303
why use, 303
subtasks
and sorting, 364
defined, 77–78
hiding, 81–82
showing, 81–82
successor tasks, 154
defined, 98
entering, 109
including in reports, 206
including on Task report, 217
Successors field, 22
adding to Task Sheet, 111
summary bar for entire project, 316
Summary Info dialog box, 59
appearing when use File New, 305
changing current date, 281
Document tab, 60
Project tab, 59
summary of tasks and dates report, 209–10
summary reports, 195, 197, 277
printing, 279–88
Summary table, 136, 145, 260
applying, 156, 218
applying for resources, 225
displaying, 261
illustrated, 156
percent complete for major phases illustrated, 262
printed, 217
printing
Task report illustrated, 218
resource cost and work, 199, 225
task cost and work, 198
reviewing resources using, 156
summary task bars, 20
summary tasks
and sorting, 364
assigning resources to, 129
collapsing, 81–82
defined, 77–78
deleting, 81
duration, 81
expanding, 81–82

summary tasks *(continued)*
  Gantt Chart, 20
  hiding, 329
  moving, 81
  PERT Chart, 24
  showing in report, 206, 218
  summarizes percent complete of subtasks, 261
SV field, 272
swing shift calendar, creating, 361–64
symbols on outline, 82–83

–T–

Table Definition dialog box
  adding table to submenu illustrated, 358
  changing Entry table illustrated, 338
  creating table to export name and duration, 327
  illustrated, creating resource table, 324
  specifying key to use to choose table illustrated, 358
Table submenu, changing commands on, 356, 358
tables, 14, 15–16
  adding custom field illustrated, 340
  adding to Table submenu illustrated, 358
  applying, 15–16, 242
  changing, 16
    alignment of information in Table Definition dialog box, 342
    column width illustrated, 339
      Table Definition dialog box, 342
    displayed table, 337–41
    existing table, 337–41
    in a report, 200
  column
    adding, 339, 340
    changing, 336–37
    deleting, 338
  copying, 337–41
  Cost, 15
  creating, 16, 341–43
    data collection table, 341–43
    to export tasks and durations to Excel, 327
    to import resources, standard rate, overtime rate, 323
  customizing, 336–43
  deleting a column illustrated, 338
  editing, 337–41
  Entry, 15
  importing or exporting information, 321
  inserting a column illustrated, 339
  list of, 15
  naming illustrated, 338
  resetting to originals, 351
tables *(continued)*
  resource, 15
  sharing, 317
  specifying table in report, 206
  task, 15
  Tracking, 15
  using from another project, 319
tabs in dialog boxes, 47
task and date summary report, 209–10
task assignments, checking, 160
task constraints, 100–102
task costs
  changing, 183–84
  how calculated, 120
  over project, 145
  printing, 217, 226–30
    forecast of cash flow, 200
task delay, removing, 190
task dependencies, 97, 180
  changing
    PERT Chart, 25
    to shorten duration, 180–81
  checking
    PERT Chart, 25
    checking to shorten critical path, 143
Task Dependency dialog box
  Gantt Chart, 104
  PERT Chart, 112
Task Details Form, 29–30
  entering progress information, 240
  setting task priority for leveling, 188
task duration
  decreasing by adding resources to driving resource, 173–74
  defined, 87
  estimating, 87–96
Task Entry view, 42, 130
  changing dependencies, 180
  displaying, 105
task fields, 13
  specifying fields to use, 15
task filters, 17
Task Form, 28–29
  adding overtime work, 175
  assigning resources, 132
  changing percent complete, 247
  changing work, 130–32
  checking task finish date, 178
  customizing, 29
  delaying work, 130–32
    resource work, 131–32
  deleting a relationship, 109
  displaying, 28, 253
    costs for resources, 269

Task Form *(continued)*
  entering
    actual costs illustrated, 254
    actual work illustrated, 253
    actual work yourself, 252
    fixed cost for resource on, 135
    overtime work illustrated, 176
    progress information, 240
    start date on, 155
  illustration showing resource finish dates, 173
  including information in report, 206
  specifying overtime work, 175
  using, 29
Task Form fields, moving to with keys, 29
Task Form, resources fields
  adding resources to shorten duration, 169
Task Form under Resource Form, 313
Task Form under Task Sheet, 145, 164, 178–79, 269
Task Information dialog box
  changing constraints, 181
  changing percent complete, 247
  displaying, 247
Task Information dialog box, Advanced tab
  entering a subproject task illustrated, 307
Task Information dialog box, General tab
  setting task priority for leveling, 188
task list
  ways to create, 69
  who creates, 69
Task Name Form, 29–30
task notes
  entering, 92, 216
  printing, 216–17
task order, 97, 98
  checking to shorten critical path, 143
Task PERT Chart, 31, 154
  under Gantt Chart to check relationships, 154
Task Range dialog box illustrated, 345
Task Range filter, illustrated, 345
task relationships, 97, 98–99
  deleting on Task Sheet, 111
  finish-to-finish, 99
  finish-to-start, 98
  removing, 104
  start-to-finish, 99
  start-to-start, 99
Task report
  customizing, 217
  including
    notes, 198
      procedure, 216
    tasks by period, 219–20
    variance and notes, 291
    work variance, 288, 291

Task report *(continued)*
  printing cost, work, totals procedure, 218
  sorting on, 217
  tasks and notes, 216–17
  tasks scheduled during a time period, 198
Task Report dialog box
  customizing report, 217
  illustrated, 205–6
task schedule
  customizing, 220
  illustrated, 219
  printing, 198, 219–20
  procedure for creating, 220
  procedure for printing, 220
task scope
  decreasing to shorten project, 181
  reducing to lower cost, 167
task sequence, 97, 140
  guidelines for determining, 98
Task Sheet, 32–33
  and Summary table printed, illustrated, 217
  applying, 152
  assigning resources, 128–30
    to several tasks, 130
  changing
    column width, 33
    columns, 215
    cost, 184
    font for one task, 215
    font used, 215
    gridlines, 215
    order of tasks, 215
    percent complete, 247
    tasks displayed by filtering, 215
  checking
    constraints, 145, 154
    critical path, 145
    slack time, 145, 260, 266
    slipping tasks, 260
    tasks in progress, 268
    tasks that should have started, 260
    variance, 260, 264
      date, work, cost, 264–66
      work, 270
  collapsed/expanded outline illustrated, 215
  collapsing outline to print summary report, 214
  controlling where pages break, 200
  critical tasks on, 147, 148–51
  customizing, 32–33, 215
  deleting relationship, 111
  displaying, 32
  displaying tasks behind schedule, 267
  double-clicking, 33

Task Sheet *(continued)*
entering
actual and remaining duration, 251
actual dates, 248, 249
illustrated, 249
actual work, 253
constraints, 115
dependencies, 109–11
fixed cost, 135
milestone, 74
percent complete illustrated, 247
task, 74
tracking information, 240
illustrated showing task costs, 163
linking tasks with finish-to-start relationship, 104
locating tasks that increased cost or work, 268
outlining, 21, 33
percent complete for major phases illustrated, 262
previewing, 215
printing, 85–86, 96, 136
collapsed/expanded outline, procedure, 214
procedure, 214
cost and work, 198
progress on tasks, 279, 283
procedure, 283
tasks, dates, resources, 214–15
tasks starting or finishing late, 290, 291
work, cost, totals, 217–18
procedure, 218
work variance, 288
illustrated, 291–92
procedure, 292
reviewing costs, 163
slack time illustrated, 152, 266
sorting, 215
viewing
baseline schedule, 193
costs, 269
earned value, 268
percent complete, 260
slack time, 152
tasks that should have started, 263
variance illustrated, 264
Task Sheet over Resource Form, 157
Task Sheet over Resource Sheet
checking if same resource always working more than planned, 270
illustrated, 270
resources assigned to each task, 270
Task Sheet over Task Form
checking actual cost with baseline cost, 269
checking task cost, 145
Task Sheet over Task Form *(continued)*
showing costs for tasks illustrated, 269
splitting work between resources illustrated, 178–79
task and resource costs illustrated, 164
to review costs, 164
Task Work and Cost report, procedure for creating, 218
task-level reports, 195
tasks
about, 65–86
accelerating, 259
actual cost greater than planned, 266
adding on PERT Chart, 25, 112
assigning resources, 127–32
assumptions, 67
automatically linking, 51
bars, 20
breaking up to shift resources, 191
causing cost or work to increase, 268
changing
cost for unfinished task, 183
duration when using fixed-duration scheduling, 240
order of, 364–65
priority so can't be leveled, 188
schedule when using resource-driven scheduling, 239
time that makes task critical, 147
to milestones, 75
checking
tasks behind schedule, 260
tasks that should have started, 260
if on schedule, 262–63
Gantt Chart, 260
resource assignments across projects, 309
controlling date starts on, 51
cost variance, 269–70
cost, checking, 163–64
creating
Calendar view, 27
PERT Chart, 74
creating list of, 69–70
critical, 140–42
data needed to assign resources, 127
data to collect for
finished tasks, 236
tasks in progress, 236
tasks not started, 237
defined, 65, 66
delay between, 97, 99–100
demoting, 80

- tasks *(continued)*
  - displaying
    - all tasks, 267
    - those behind schedule, 267–68
    - those in progress, 265
    - those that are complete, 265
  - duration of summary task, 81
  - earned value for, 272
  - entering, 74–77
    - fixed cost, 135
    - Gantt Chart, 74
    - PERT Chart, 74
    - successor tasks, 109
    - Task Sheet, 74
  - evaluating progress on, 256
  - finishing simultaneously, 98, 99
  - fixed cost for, 120
  - guidelines for determining, 66–67
  - highlighting in report, 279
  - identifying those that should have started, 263
  - importance of listing, 66
  - importing list from other program, 75
  - indicating actual start or finish date, 239
  - indicating change in, 239
  - inserting, 79
  - keeping detailed tasks in separate project, 303
  - lead or lag time between, 99–100
  - linking
    - Calendar view, 27
    - dates between projects, 301
    - with one command, 103
  - measuring progress, 237
  - moving, 76
    - PERT Chart, 75
    - to resolve overallocation, 190
  - naming, 67
  - near critical, 273
  - organizing, 70–73
  - outlining, 77
  - overlapping, 97, 99–100
  - predecessor, 98
  - printing
    - cost and totals, 200
    - cost variance, 292–93
    - costing more than planned, 288
    - finish date has slipped, 288
    - finished late, 291
    - list of completed, 287–88
    - monthly calendar, 198
    - scheduled for next period, 298
    - scheduled to finish late, 290–91
    - should have started, 288, 289–90
    - slipping, 290–91
    - started late, 290
    - work different from planned, 288
    - work variance, 291–92
- tasks *(continued)*
  - questions to check validity of, 69
  - renumbering, 365
  - report
    - showing completed plus statistics, 279
    - showing progress on, 279
  - rescheduling to address variance, 259
  - reviewing possible solutions based on progress to date, 273
  - saving, 85
  - scheduling, 97–116
  - scope, 67
  - selecting, 103, 104
    - nonadjacent, 104, 245
  - setting start or finish date, 100–102
  - shifting to resolve overallocations, 159
  - showing progress on, 239
  - started late, what to investigate, 257
  - starting and stopping work, 252
  - starting simultaneously, 98, 99
  - successor, 98
  - tables, 15
  - viewing
    - haven't started, 243
    - incomplete, 243
    - should start by a date you specify, 243
    - started but not finished, 243
  - work, printed, 217
  - work variance, 269–70
  - working on simultaneously, 98, 99
- Tasks and Notes report, 216–17
- Tasks Are Critical If Slack <= *x* Days option, 147, 274
- tasks in progress, locating those interfering with other tasks, 268
- Tasks Starting Soon report, 198, 298
- Tasks With Fixed Dates filter, 145
  - applying, 155
  - checking for constraint dates, 154
- template, 302–3
  - can't use as subproject, 305
  - defined, 302
  - file extension for, 302
  - global, 319, 351
  - opening template files, 302
  - procedure for creating, 302
  - saving, 76
  - using, 302–3
  - using as starting point for projects, 301
- template file, using to create subproject, 308
- Templates (*.mpt), 302
- text
  - changing on PERT Chart, 213
  - changing on Resource Graph, 231
- text box in dialog box, 46

text files, using in Microsoft Project, 318
text in report, changing, 217
Text Styles dialog box
  changing critical task font illustrated, 149
Text1—Text5, 126
thinking tasks, measuring progress for, 237
time
  default used, 116
  entering, 115–16
  estimating for tasks, 87–96
time period printed, specifying, 204
time units for duration estimates, 88
timescale
  changing on Resource Graph, 231
  changing on Resource Usage view, 159, 223
tips when start Microsoft Project, turning on and off, 50
to-do list
  printing, 219
  printing for each resource, 199
toolbar buttons
  changing
    command assigned to, 370
    look of, 370
  customizing, 372–73
  displaying a view, 372–73
  displaying information in status bar, 241
  identifying purpose of, 48, 241
  moving to a toolbar, 371
toolbars
  changing, 370–73
    displayed toolbars, 371–72
    order of buttons, 370
  customizing, 370–73
  defined, 44
  deleting, 371
  displaying Resource Management toolbar, 314
  displaying Tracking toolbar, 240
  hiding, 371–72
  moving, 370
  removing buttons, 370
  resetting to originals, 351, 371
  sharing, 317
  showing, 371–72
  using, 47–48
  using from another project, 319
Toolbars dialog box illustrated, 371
tools, sharing, 319–20
Tools Change Working Time command, 62, 134
  changing
    existing calendar, 361
    resource work hours, 179
      illustrated, 177
  creating new calendar illustrated, 360
  Default option explained, 134
Tools Customize/Forms command, 374
  applying
    Cost Tracking custom form, 271
    Earned Value custom form, 273
    Work Tracking custom form, 271
  creating new form illustrated, 374–77
  displaying the Organizer, 319
Tools Customize commands
  Menu Bars command, 356
    displaying the Organizer, 319
    illustrated, 356
  Toolbars command
    changing buttons on a toolbar, 371
Tools Filtered For commands, 17, 210
  All Resources command, 156
  All Tasks command, 150, 155
  More Filters command
    changing existing filter, 347
    customizing the Filtered For submenu, 359
    displaying the Organizer, 319
  More Filters dialog box
    creating a new resource filter illustrated, 348
    creating new task filter illustrated, 350
  Overallocated Resources command, 156
Tools Macros command
  editing a macro, 378
  running a macro, 378
Tools Multiple Projects commands
  Consolidate Projects command, 311, 312
  Share Resources command, 305, 310, 311
Tools Options command, 95
  Calculation tab
    turning off automatic calculation, 151
  changing time that makes task critical, 147
  General tab
    turning off PlanningWizard, 151
  preferences in, 50
  Schedule tab
    breaking tie between work and percent complete, 241
    turning off scheduling messages, 151
Tools Outlining commands
  Hide Subtasks command, 82, 214, 261
  Show All Tasks command, 82, 210
  Show Subtasks command, 82, 215
Tools Outlining submenu, 78
Tools Record Macro command, 377
Tools Resource Leveling dialog box
  choosing Level Now to level resources, 188
  removing delay, 190
Tools Sort command, 200, 210, 215, 364
  By ID command, 150, 157
  Sort By command, 365
    cost, 157
    critical tasks, 150

Tools Tracking commands
 Save Baseline command, 168, 238
  adding new tasks to baseline illustrated, 275
  saving baseline, 192
 Update Project command
  calculating percent complete, 245
  dialog box illustrated, 245
  entering actual information when matches scheduled, 239
  updating tasks that started or finished on time, 243–45
 Update Tasks command, 240
  changing percent complete, 246
  entering actual dates, 248
  entering duration, 250
Tools Workgroup commands
 Request Task Update command, 243, 319
 Send Schedule Note command, 319
 Send Task Request command, 319
 Set Reminder command, 319
ToolTip, 48, 241
 changing for toolbar button, 371, 373
top-down method, 69, 70
 creating outline using, 78–81
Top-Level Tasks report, 196, 197, 279, 286
 illustrated, 286
 procedure for printing, 286
total cost
 checking, 261
 for each task, 162
 printing to date, 286
Total Cost field, 164
Total Slack field, 274
total slack time, 147
 defined, 143
 viewing on Task Sheet, 152
totals in reports, 206, 217, 218
Tracking Gantt, 23, 260
 baseline and scheduled duration bars illustrated, 264
 comparing baseline and scheduled duration, 263
 displaying, 263
 printing
  baseline and percent complete, procedure, 283–84
  progress, 279
  new schedule, 298
tracking information
 collecting, 236–38
 entering in Microsoft Project, 240
tracking method, choosing, 241
tracking progress, 235–54
 collecting actual dates to reflect, 235
 to get historical data for future projects, 89
 using Microsoft Project, 238–54
 why do it, 235
tracking project using baseline schedule, 167
Tracking table, 15
 changing percent complete, 247
 displaying, 247, 249
 entering
  actual and remaining duration on, 251
  actual dates, 248, 249
   illustrated, 249
  percent complete, 245
   illustrated, 247
 printing progress on tasks, 279, 283
  procedure, 283
Tracking Task Sheet, creating illustrated, 352
Tracking toolbar, 48, 146
 displaying, 146, 240
 illustrated, 240
 using, 240–41
tracking work, tied to percent complete, 241
turning off
 automatic calculation, 151
 PlanningWizard, 151
 scheduling messages, 151
 tip of the day, 50
typing
 finish date and creating constraint, 113, 155
 relationships on Task Sheet or Gantt Chart, 110
 start date and creating constraint, 113, 155
 subproject name in Subproject box, 308

-U-

underallocated resources
 defined, 186
 finding on Resource Usage view, 157
 why important to locate, 155
underlined letter in menu or command name
 specifying, 357
unhiding a window, 316
units of time for duration estimates, 88
Unlink Tasks button on Standard toolbar, 104
unlinking from resource pool, 310
Unstarted Tasks filter, 243, 260
Update As Scheduled button on Tracking toolbar, 244
Update Project dialog box
 illustrated, 245
 setting used when use Update As Scheduled button, 244
 stopping and starting work on a task, 252
Update Tasks button on the Tracking toolbar, 240
 changing percent complete, 246
 entering actual dates, 248
 entering duration, 250
Update Tasks dialog box
 changing percent complete, 246–47
 changing percent complete illustrated, 247
 displaying, 240

Update Tasks dialog box *(continued)*
  entering
    actual dates illustrated, 248–49
    actual or remaining duration illustrated, 250
    progress information, 240
Update Work As Complete Through option
  updating on-schedule tasks, 244
updating
  entire project when on schedule, 245
  on-schedule tasks, 244
  percent complete, methods, 245
  schedule, why do it, 235
  task status using electronic mail, 243
Updating Task Status Updates Resource Status
  check box, 241
  and link between percent complete and work, 252–54
updating the schedule using Microsoft Project, 238–54
usage boxes on Resource Usage view
  changing time period covered, 159
Usage/Tasks view, creating, 355
using
  dialog box, 45–47
  entry bar, procedure, 49
  project template, 302–3
  subproject, 306–8
  template, 302–3
using Microsoft Project
  adding overtime work, 175–76
  analyzing variance, 268–73
  assigning resources to tasks, 127–32
  changing resource calendar, 133–34
  checking
    critical tasks, 147–51
    project finish date and costs, 146
    relationships and constraints, 153–55
    resources, 155–61
    slack time, 151–53
  collecting progress data, 241
  communicating plan, 196–231
  communicating progress, 278–98
  controlling project to stay on track, 259–75
  copying scheduled dates into actual fields, 243–45
  creating templates, 302–3
  decreasing project duration, 172–82
  entering
    actual or remaining duration, 250–51
    actual start and finish dates, 247–50
    constraints, 112–16
    durations, 91–92
    fixed cost, 135
    general project information, 59
    lead or lag time, 107–9
    percent complete, 245–47
    predecessor, 105–6
    predecessor, relationship, lead, or lag, 104–12
using Microsoft Project *(continued)*
  entering *(continued)*
    relationship, 106–7
    resources, 123–27
    resources and costs, 120–36
    task dependencies, 102–16
    tasks and milestones, 74–77
  evaluating schedule, 144–64
  freezing baseline schedule, 192–93
  linking tasks in finish-to-start relationship, 103–4
  managing multiple projects, 301–16
  organizing tasks, 83–85
  printing, 85–86, 96
    exception reports, 288–97
    summary reports, 279–88
  refining schedule, 167–93
  saving calendars, 64
  saving project, 85
  setting the project calendar, 61–63
  sharing tools, 319–20
  sorting, 364–65
  specifying scheduling method, 94–95
  subprojects, 303–8
  tools, 335–78
  tracking progress, 238–54
  updating the schedule, 238–54
  using multiple base calendars, 63
  viewing multiple projects, 311–15
using Microsoft Project tools, 335–78
Using Resource filter, 27
  checking all tasks assigned to resource behind schedule, 273
using subprojects, 303–8

–V–

vacation, 133
  adding to resource calendar, 134
  entering in calendar, 61
variance
  analyzing, 256–58
    using Microsoft Project, 268–73
  between baseline and actual duration, 268
  checking, 260, 264–66
  defined, 256, 264
  determining corrective action, 258–59
  in Earned Value table, 272
  in overall project statistics, 260
  locating tasks with cost or work variance, 269–70
  printing
    cost variance to date, 286
    exception reports, 288–97
    resources with work variance, 293
    tasks with cost variance, 292–93
    tasks with work variance, 291–92
    variance between baseline and scheduled dates, 290–91

variance *(continued)*
  reports about, 277
  table, using Microsoft Project to locate, 260
  viewing for individual resources, 271
Variance table, 260, 264
  applying, 264
  illustrated, 264
  printing tasks that started or finished late, 290–91
variation in resource usage, 145
View Calendar command, 221
View Definition dialog box
  Gantt/Task PERT combination view illustrated, 353
  new combination view illustrated, 355
  new single view illustrated, 355
  Tracking Task Sheet illustrated, 352
  Usage/Tasks view, 355
View menu
  changing commands on, 356, 358
  customizing, 359
View More Views command, 19
  copying and changing
    view, 352
    combination view illustrated, 353
  creating
    Data Collection view illustrated, 354
    new combination view, 355
    Tracking Task Sheet, 352
  customizing the View menu, 359
  displaying
    Detail Gantt, 152, 291
    Organizer, 319
    Resource Form, 160
    Task Sheet, 163
    Tracking Gantt, 263
View Reports command, 197, 203, 205
  Assignments reports, 226
  Budget report, 228
  creating
    Task report showing cost, work, totals, 218
    Task report with notes, 216
    task schedule or to-do list, 220
  customizing reports, 200
  printing Assignment reports, 226
  Weekly Cash Flow report, 230
View Resource Graph command, 161, 231
View Resource Sheet command, 156, 223, 225, 270
View Resource Usage command, 158, 223, 226
View Table commands, 210, 215
  changing information in a view, 200
  Cost command, 163, 184, 266, 269
View Table commands *(continued)*
  More Tables command, 15, 337
    adding or removing a table from the Table submenu, 358
    applying Constraint Dates table, 154
    copying or editing a table illustrated, 338
    creating a new table illustrated, 341
    creating resource table illustrated, 323
    displaying the Organizer, 319
  Schedule command, 152, 266
  Summary command, 156, 218
    resources, 225
    to view percent complete, 261
  Tracking command, 247
  Variance command, 264
  Work command, 178, 265, 270
View Toolbars command, 48, 371
  displaying
    Organizer, 319
    Resource Management toolbar, 314
    Tracking toolbar, 146, 240
View Zoom command, 210
viewing
  delay added by leveling on Delay Gantt, 189
  multiple projects, 311–15
  overbudget tasks, 269
  resource data for multiple projects, 40
views, 14
  about, 18–43
  changing, 19, 351–56
    combination view, 352–53
    default, 52, 76
    existing view, 351–53
    single view, 352
  combination PERT over Task Form, 112
  creating, 19
    new, 354
      combination view, 355–56
      single view, 354–55
    Tracking Task Sheet illustrated, 352
  custom, 19
  customizing, 351–56
  customizing Views menu, 359
  displaying, 18
  Module Editor, 19
  previewing before printing, 203–4
  printing, 196, 203–5
  resetting to originals, 351
  saved with project, 351
  sharing, 201, 317
  supplied with Microsoft Project, 19
  using from another project, 319

views you can print, 196
Visual Basic, 48
  editing a macro, 19
  help using, 378
Visual Basic for applications (VBA), 377

-W-

waiting to begin work, 131–32
WBS, 71, 72–73, 77
  defined, 72
  in Microsoft Project, 83–85
WBS Code box, 83
WBS code, filtering or sorting on, 84
WBS coding system
  and outline numbers in Microsoft Project, 84
  using your own, 83
WBS field
  adding to a table, 337
    illustrated, 339
  adding to Task Sheet, 84
  printing, 86
Weekly Cash Flow report, 200
  illustrated, 229
  procedure for printing, 230
Weekly To-Do List report, 199
  illustrated, 228
what-if analysis defined, 166
Who Does What report, 199
  illustrated, 227
Who Does What When report, 199, 298
  illustrated, 227
why plan doesn't match actual, 255
width, changing column width, 342, 343, 346
window, hiding and unhiding, 316
Window Hide command, 316
Window New Window command, 312, 315
Window Unhide command, 316
work
  adding overtime, 175–76
  breaking connection to percent complete, 241
  calculation for each resource, 130
  changing
    for resource assignment, 129, 130–32
    illustrated on Task Entry view, 131
    to indicate schedule change for resource-driven task, 239
  checking resource variance, 270–71
  default unit used, 51
  defined, 121
  delaying for a resource, 130–32
  disconnecting from percent complete, 252–54
work *(continued)*
  entering actual, 252–54
    on Task Form, 253
    yourself, controlling, 51
  evaluating progress, 256
  for resource assigned to subproject task, 308
  including in Task report, 217
  longer hours in calendar, 177–78
  reducing to lower costs, 185
  Resource Graph, 160
  Resource Usage view, 157–58
  splitting between resources, 179
  stopping and starting on a task, 252
  subproject task, 304
  tracking yourself, 252
  viewing on Task Form, 130
work breakdown structure. *See* WBS
work calculation formula, 121
work details, including in report, 206
work estimate, changing, 237
Work Overbudget filter, 260, 270, 288, 291, 293
  applying, 292, 293
  resources that increased work, 268
  tasks that increased work, 268
work package, 73
Work table, 260, 265, 288
  applying, 265, 292
  applying to Resource Sheet, 270, 293
  checking resource work variance, 270
  checking task work variance, 270
  entering actual work, 253
  illustrated, 265
  locating resources that increased work, 268
  locating tasks that increased work, 268
  printing resources with work variance, 293
  printing showing work variance, 291
work totals, showing in report, 218
Work Tracking custom form, 271
work units, changing default, 159
work variance, 270
  checking, 265
  illustrated, 265
  locating tasks with, 269–70
  printing, 291–92
  printing resources with work variance, 293
workgroup features, 318
WorkGroup toolbar, 48
working days, changing, 62
  normal working time for your company, 360–61
  resource calendar, 134
working hours. changing, 62
  extending, 175
  resource calendar, 134

working longer hours to resolve overallocations, 191
working on tasks simultaneously, 98
Workload/Resource report, 199
workspace
  file extension, 316
  identifying workspace files, 316
  opening, 316
  saving, 316
  viewing multiple projects, 312
  what is saved in, 316

–Z–

Zoom In button on Standard toolbar, 159
Zoom Out button on Standard toolbar, 159
  changing timescale on Resource Graph, 231